Tom McNally's
Fishermen's Bible

Tom McNally's Fishermen's Bible

3rd Edition

by Tom McNally

Editorial Assistance
by Bob McNally

JOLEX, INC.
Paramus, New Jersey

Published by Jolex, Inc., Paramus, New Jersey, in cooperation
with the John Olson Company. Published simultaneously in
Canada by Plainsman Publications Ltd., Vancouver, B.C.

First printing: July, 1976

LC Number 74-6538

ISBN: 0-89149-021 3 Casebound

ISBN: 0-89149-016-7 Paper

Distributed by:

        THE JOHN OLSON COMPANY
        299 Forest Ave., Box 767
        Paramus, New Jersey 07652

Manufactured in the United States of America

Contents

Figure 1. E. L. "Buck" Perry, Spoonplugging and structure fishing expert.

BUCK PERRY REVEALS HIS BASS FISHING SECRETS!

One of the best-known and most-revered bass fishermen in America is a former college engineering professor, E.L. "Buck" Perry, of Hickory, N.C. Perry is the "father of structure fishing," and creator of the famed "Spoonplug" lure and the spoonplug system of fishing.

Although thousands of fishermen now know about spoonplugging, few actually are familiar with spoonplugging techniques. The majority do not know how to spoonplug, and therefore continue to catch few bass.

All that may change, though, because at last Perry has put everything he knows about bass fishing and spoonplugging into a new book called, simply, "SPOONPLUGGING."

Buck's book is readable, done in simple terms, a book by a master bass fisherman for other bass fishermen. Starting with an explanation of spoonplugging, Perry's book covers such things

as: the basic movements of fish, structure types, breaks and break lines, contact points, good structure requirements, delta, weather, water color, controls, tools (lures, etc.), presentation of lures, live bait vs. artificial, working typical structure, fishing situations, mapping and interpretation, presentation of spoonplugs, and, finally, mental aspects.

The following material, excerpted from Perry's book in chapter form—and presented word-for-word precisely as Perry wrote it—is but a small portion of what will be recorded in history as the most authentic, most practical book on black bass fishing ever produced.

Perry's 275-page book, "SPOONPLUGGING," is profusely illustrated and sells for $9.90. It is available from E.L. Perry, P.O. Box 66, Hickory, N.C., 28601, and from Fishing Facts, P.O. Box 4169, Milwaukee, Wis., 53210.

CHAPTER 1

Fishing Situations

Buck Perry Reveals His Bass Fishing Secrets!

A great many fishermen live in a very small fishing world. That is, the waters they fish are restricted to a small area, the different types of water they fish are limited, and they fish for only one or two species.

In some cases, the fisherman is not able to change this situation. Although, he may wish to travel extensively and fish strange waters, he just never gets the chance to do so.

But, in the majority of cases, the fisherman does have access to several species of fish, as well as a choice of different waters. Yet, he continues to fish the same waters for the same species season after season; refusing to expand his horizons by venturing into strange waters. He may take his vacation at a distant lake, where he has heard there is great fishing. Then, spends a great deal of his time, and money, trying to find a guide who can show him **where** to fish. Most likely the weather will be bad, and the guide will tell him, he should have taken his vacation last month.

Why is this so?

Basically, this reluctance is based on the fact that the fisherman does not 'know' strange water. Through experience, or through some friend he has come to know some of the fishable areas in certain waters; and, through trial and error, has found a way to be successful on occasions. This knowledge may have taken years to come

by, so he is reluctant to take his fishing time and fish waters about which nothing is known.

At first glance this reasoning may make good sense. But, to a Spoonplugger, there is no such thing as 'strange waters'. All are fished in a routine manner. There will be a short period of time when new water may be **unfamiliar** —but his fishing procedures are the same regardlesss of what water he is fishing. A Spoonplugger looks forward to the challenge of fishing new waters, and for different species. There is an added satisfaction and knowledge, to his fishing new water and working it out. The thrill of catching fish can become secondary to the thrill of putting a particular water 'in his hip pocket'.

The Spoonplugger can work out strange waters because he has learned the basic facts concerning fish. He is aware that deep water is the home of fish; that periodically they move from this deep water, not in a haphazard manner, but on well defined migration routes, and how far they move and how long they stay is dependent upon weather and water conditions.

Natural lakes come in all sizes and shapes. Some have masses of weeds, some have less. Some have hard clean bottoms, others have dirty ones. Some have several deep holes, others have one or none. Some have clear water, others have cloudy.

Artificial reservoirs also come in a variety of sizes and

Figure 2.   Perry's new book, "SPOONPLUGGING," and an assortment of Spoonplugs.

shapes. They contain many different types of structures and water colors. Some are built in highlands, some in lowlands and flatlands.

There are certain fishing waters, both natural and artificial, that are not normally classified as lakes or reservoirs, all of which play a part in fishing.

In a book of this size and style, it would be impossible to classify all the lakes and reservoirs, and discuss the why's and wherefores. Furthermore, it would be a mistake to do so, at this period of your study. But, I will discuss some fishing situations that **are important at this time.**

Figure 3 is a top view of a large shallow lake. It is several miles across. The areas near the shorelines are covered **solid** with grass, weeds, and pads. This extends out to a dept of 4–5 feet. Beyond the solid weeds, exist scattered weed patches. These are located in water 6–7 feet in depth. All the rest of the water, the greater part, is free of any vegetation. **But, the bottom is covered with a thick layer of muck.** The area free of weeds runs for a mile or more, and only increases in depth of 8–9 feet. Then suddenly at nine (9) feet it breaks to 11 feet. Upon investigation, here in the center of the lake, exists a long narrow slot. The width is only 50–100 feet, but it runs for over a mile in length. The deepest water in the slot, is a small section, 14 feet deep.

A lake of this type can whip the average fisherman. Even those who call this 'HIS lake,' will have quite a few fishless days. The reason it creates problems, is primarily due to the fact the fisherman does not know where the 'home' of the fish is; and, to his not knowing what 'deep water' is. He may have read or heard at some time, that the deep water was the home of the fish. But, this did not apply in his case, as he did not have any deep water. And, HE caught fish and HE didn't catch them in deep water. He says; "I catch them up in the solid weeds and around the scattered weed patches. In the spring I murder the fish there."—Then you come back at him with; "Where do you catch them after that?" He says; Oh I don't fish much after that, it gets too hot, and the fish don't bite."

This fisherman didn't want any answers to begin with, for if he had wanted some, this situation presented no problems he couldn't handle.

If he had looked closer he would have noted that when he found fish, it was in the spring near the spawning season. Further observations would have shown him he didn't catch them EVERY day. Also, if he did

catch them for a few days running, he did not catch them IN THE SAME PLACE every day. They might have been close, but not in the same spot. In fact, he never found them in the EXACT spot on any two occasions. This should have told him this area wasn't the HOME of the fish.

If he had extended his observations for a period of time, he would have found; the SEASONAL migrations of the fish, due primarily to the spawning urge, would have put the fish in, or close, to the solid weeds. The weather and water conditions were good, so the fish drifted around in the area for a spell. After the spawning, he would probably have found them, not at the solid weeds, but in, or around, the weed patches. Shortly there-after they would seem to disappear.

It was at this time the fisherman decided to go home, and not go fishing much. **The fish did the same thing. They went 'home'—the slot.** They now spend most of their time here, and won't go very far, until about the time the fisherman decides to go fishing again—next spring.

These types of shallow lakes are a welcome sight to a Spoonplugger. The fish are all balled up in a small area, and ready for the plucking. The depth is so little they can't get away, and the best part is, he's way out there all by himself.

Due to the **depths** and **flats** involved, the daily movements of the fish are limited to the slot, or the edges of the slot. It would appear that you have the fish hemmed in. This is true, but the **problem** facing you, in making a good catch, would be in **presentation of lures.**

When working areas such as this in warmer weather, you may find you can't 'buy a bite'—CASTING. The warm water, plus the dirty bottom will limit your Depth and Speed control so much, you just can't make them 'take'. TROLLING the breaklines and the slot is the way to go. No areas are so deep they can't be reached with lures. Speed control, however fast, presents no problem, and Depth control can be maintained 'right on the money'.

Line length (and lure selection) becomes critical in trolling the breaklines, and the slot. The lures must not dig into the muck, nor should they be too far above it. The best way to find the correct line length is let out the line until the lure strikes the muck, then quickly retrieve until the lure is running free. If the lure continues to foul, wind in until it doesn't. Once the lure is running clear of the muck, drop line back very slowly until the

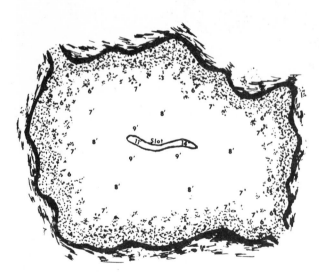

Figure 3

lure is just skipping over the higher parts of the muck. The bumping of the muck will cause the lures to foul. Vigorous jerks of the rod will clear the lure in most cases, without a loss of depth control—if Spoonplugger equipment is being used. It is best to check the breaklines thoroughly before moving into the slot.

I get a chuckle every time I run into a situation such as this. I recall the first time Terry O'Malley ran into it in Florida. He and Vic Sanders were fishing a lake, similar to the one in our discussion, and it was hilarious the way they told it.

They had worked the breaklines without success, and had moved into the slot. When they caught the first fish, they immediately threw a marker. They reversed the trolling pass, and when the fish took, they threw another marker. This gave them a marker to the north, and one to the south.

They anchored and began casting the area between the markers. After failing on the cast, they went back to trolling. This time they made a trolling pass from the east toward the west—at right angles to the north-south line. This pass produced a double—both got a fish. They threw a marker on the west side.

The trolling pass toward the east, got another double. They threw the fourth marker. Now, they had the fish completely surrounded by markers. These, plus their observations of the fish caught, gave them the exact spot where the fish were.

"Now, by cracky, we're going to load the boat."

They threw everything they had at them, they moved the boat to several positions—not a fish. They went back to trolling, it was as easy as picking cherries. The fish were there, but **Depth and Speed control made the catch.**

There are many fishing waters where the same procedure must be used for **exact** Depth and Speed control. There are lakes where the bottom is covered with weeds, moss or brush. Though pressed for space, something should be said about those with brush.

Figure 4 is a cross section, or a side view of a 'Delta' situation, or a view of a channel with the breaklines running along the edges.

The amount of bushes along the edges of a stream channel in a reservoir, is normally greater than in any other part. The availability of moisture created heavy growth before the area was flooded. Once this growth is cut, the saplings and bushes spring up rapidly. By the time the area gets covered with water, we have a situation such as Figure 4.

The ridge or the breaklines along the edge of the channel, can run for long distances without a break in uniformity. And, if you limit your presentation to CASTING, you will have trouble finding the fish. The fish will use the bushes ('breaks') in their movements and migrations. But, **the bushes do not tell you where the fish will be.** The bottom structure will determine what brush or bush might be productive. If you cast this situation, it is possible to work over and around this brush, but you will be limited on Depth and Speed control. It also isn't likely you will be at the right place at the right time, especially if weather and water conditions produce only a short movement.

Here again, TROLLING is the way to go. The purpose is to find the fish, and trolling is the easiest and best way to accomplish this. AFTER the fish are located, then you can see how CASTING works.

Lure size and line length must allow you to hit or tip the bushes with the lures. If you stay hung up all the time, you are either running too large a lure, or letting out too much line. If you **never** hit a bush, you are still wrong, and must change lures, or run more line.

Correct depth does not mean every little twig or bush has to be hit, or tipped. But it does mean all the 'peaks' should be hit. A few minutes is normally all the time it takes to get the right combination of lure size and line length.

At times it takes vigorous rod action to keep the lures ripping through the twigs and branches. Correct trolling

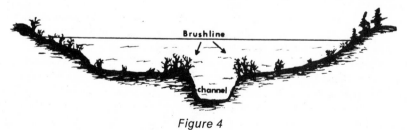

Figure 4

gear will allow this to be done without the loss of lures or being continually hung. A free running lure that sinks will be better than one that floats. A sinking lure will be much easier to release from a hang, than a floating type. I designed the Spoonplug, so that when the lip comes in contact with an object, a heavy steady pressure will cause it to whirl up and over the possible hang; then immediately go back to the desired depth. If a Spoonplugger is staying hung up too much, he is either running too large a lure, too much line, or not applying enough pressure.

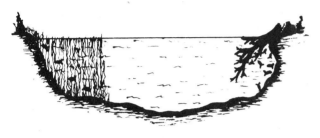

Figure 5

Figure 5 is a cross section, or a side view of a Canal, Slough, or Stream. In various parts of the country, you will find shallow lakes that look just like this.

In water of this type, the over-all depth, is just about the same. In some cases, the center section might be slightly deeper, but normally, no great change in depth is found. In some, the weeds will be on both sides, in others brush, or a combination of brush and weeds. In some, the shoreline will be 'under-cut' by the movements of the water.

The 'home', or the area, where the fish spend the greater part of their time is under the weeds, brush, or 'under-cut' in the bank.

In the past, I have seen fishermen try to use this situation, to disprove the fact that the deep water is the home of the fish. But close observations will show that there doesn't exist any deep water to speak of. **The whole thing is shallow.** It would be a natural thing for the fish to take up housekeeping under the weeds, brush, or bank. This gives them the needed protection from the light. If you ever fish an area such as this, and you find no deep water, and no cover, you'll not likely find any fish. But if you fish an area such as Figure 5, your best bet is to find the deepest water available under the cover (weeds, pads, hyacinths, brush, under-cut, etc.). In

a situation such as Figure 5, you will find the fish in the weeds or under the brush most of the time. At movement periods they may venture out along the outside of the weedline and brushline, and if conditions are excellent out into the open water. During certain parts of the season, fish could be found out in the open area for quite a period of time. But this does not mean that on every movement period they migrate out into the open water. A majority of the time they move in or under the weeds and brush. A good way to check where they are is to troll the weedline and brushline. If you don't find the fish, it indicates they are under the cover.

To get to the fish back under the weeds and brush, can be difficult at times, but with a little thought and effort it can be done. A surface or weedless lure could be used to check their respective areas. But getting the lure rather deep in these weeds and brush would be better most of the time. You can maneuver the boat slowly along the weedline, dropping your lures, or bait, down through the weeds. More than likely the fish are rather dormant and not moving around very much, and you will have to find them. Often a certain spot, or spots, will be more productive than others. But in many cases, and especially in the case of weeds, the spot with the greatest action may change from day to day. As discussed under "Artificials vs. Live Bait", in situations like this, live bait will often give better Depth and Speed control than artificials.

In some shallow LAKES of this nature, the **mass** of the water is covered with weeds. Only a few narrow slots, or small areas, are free of weeds. In these cases it is difficult to find the fish in the weeds. I have found, the best bet is to concentrate all efforts at the clear areas. Often I have to wait for quite a period of time for the fish to appear, but when they move good—here they come.

You should, in all cases, look at your fishing waters in respect to the light conditions, and especially to the presence or absence of "Breaks."

Figure 6 is a top view of a portion of a river. This could be a section of a **flowing** river, or it could be an old river channel (cut-off) that was formed by the river changing course.

All rivers contain breaks and breaklines. Some are created by the raising and lowering of the water levels, while others are produced by erosion, or by deposits of silt and sand. Water currents tend to flow in a straight line, thus cutting into any shore in their path, with increased velocity. At the same time this occurs, the water currents have moved away from the inside of the bend, slowing the water and allowing silt, mud, or sand to settle out. On the 'inside' of the bend, where the silt settles, a more shallow flat area is created. The cutting, which occurs on the 'outside' of the bend, produces many breaks, and deep water. The deepest water is always on the "outside" of the bend, as indicated.

Other breaks and breaklines are created by erosion, which occurs when there is a difference in hardness of shoreline strata, and by cave-ins. Others are created by the 'cuts' of feeder streams. All of these breaks and breaklines are "markers" which fish can see and locate themselves by, when they move or migrate.

you find a good break, or good sharp breakline on the "inside"—work it.

It is always wise to look at an area, not only from a daily standpoint but from a yearly standpoint as well. In fishing an area such as this, the shallow side and the backwater areas must be checked during the spawning and near spawning season (which is usually a high water condition). When fish are in this area, you have a scatter zone condition and it should be fished as such.

Note on the drawing the break which is shown on the sloping side. This break is a small channel or gully which was produced by a small stream flowing into the main river, or by drainage of the flats after a high water condition.

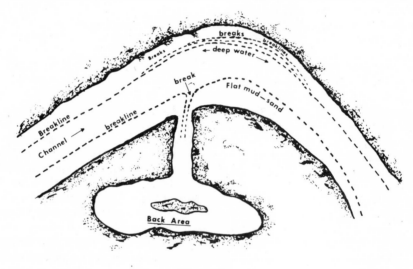

Figure 6

Migrations, or movements, during the warmer part of the season will be toward the deep, steep side, rather than toward the flat areas—which appears opposite of what occurs in lakes and reservoirs. The deeper channel is the home, and although the shore appears steep, the overriding factor in this case is the deep water and breaks that exist. The area on the outside of the bend, with its steeper banks; the breaks and breaklines; and the deepest water, is where you should spend your time.

The flat sloping sides, which the settling silt and sand created, have a very smooth surface—almost as smooth as an old bald head. Fish will not use areas which are completely void of breaks and guide posts. However, if

The cutting of this small channel or gully formed a perfect break in this large flat area. It also created a visual path from the deep water toward the backwater areas. During the spawning period this path would be used, since the waters on the steeper side would be less suitable for spawning. It would be wise to note any cuts, or eroded channels during a low water period, as this would be useful information to have when fishing during spawning and high water periods.

During most of the season, stick to the steeper sides—especially, after the water level falls and temperatures become warmer. If a cut or break is found on the shallow side, such as the one shown, work and test it, but limit this testing to the points where entrance is made into the main channel.

Methods of presentation will vary in a river area such as this. When working the backwater areas under a high water condition, casting is easier and more thorough. When water levels are lower and the deeper breaklines and breaks are worked, trolling is far superior in every respect for locating fish and catching them.

⁘ ⁘ ⁘ ⁘ ⁘ ⁘

Early season can be tough for many fishermen. Most rush the season and forget that water does not warm up as fast as "fishing fever." Under the colder, or early season fishing conditions, we often forget also, that fishing can be quite different from that experienced last summer.

In our study of structure, weather and water conditions, we normally think in terms of a DAILY observation. After all, we are interested in the condition that exists the day we go fishing.

This is good, and necessary—even essential. But when we consider the many weather and water conditions that exist from one part of the season to another, and the many different types of structure found in reservoirs, we are faced with the fact that if we want to be fishing the most productive structures, at all times, in reservoirs (man-made lakes) we better look at structure from a SEASONAL standpoint. In other words—are we on the best structure for this time of year?

The makeup of most natural lakes, and especially those of small acreage, do not have as many **types** of structure as do reservoirs. Normally, in natural lakes, the deep water is in the form of a hole rather than a channel. This hole, or deep water, may be limited in area and may be located in only one small area of the lake.

The contours of the bottom, in natural lakes, are more uniform without the abruptness and changes of a reservoir.

Most natural lakes are also quite predictable in regards to what is present. The deep water consists of a hole or holes, most structure is in the form of 'bars' which run out from the shoreline, and some lakes may have humps or underwater islands. If you go from one side of the lake to the other, or from one end to the other, there is, in most cases, not a great deal of change in structure types. The depths may vary to some degree, but in the overall picture the fisherman would not be concerned too much with which good structure he should fish— regardles of what time of year it is.

This is not the case when we consider reservoirs (man-made lakes). Here we must consider structure from the SEASONAL point of view if we want to be on the most productive ones. In reservoirs we have a multitude of different type structures. We have steep shores, flats, long bars, river and feeder stream channels, coves, bays, deltas, underwater islands, humps, etc. We have many man-made structures such as; submerged roadbeds, causeways, dams, borrow pits, etc. All of which means that in most parts of a reservoir the structure may, or will be completely different from those in another part of the reservoir. AND that this need not only be true from the lower end, up to the upper end, but could be true in just a short hop across the channel. It is for this reason we have to look at structure from a SEASONAL standpoint if we want to be on the best ones at all times.

In this study we will concern ourselves primarily with largemouth bass rather than other species. However, **it would be well to view all species in the light of the following.** Largemouth bass, as a rule, do not venture any

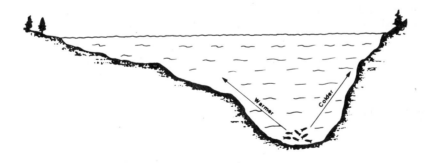

Figure 7

great distance from a particular home area. We will **view our study as his growing up in a particular area, then dying of old age in this one, home area.**

In order for us to arrive at the best structure, from a seasonal point of view, let us review or recall some of the basic movements or migrations habits of the fish.

In Figure 7 is a cross section of a typical reservoir. There will be areas with long, sloping bottoms—with long structures. A channel of some description, and areas that have steep, short structure with a quick drop off into deep water.

mind we can now proceed to the question of staying on the best structure from a SEASONAL point of view.

In Figure 8 you are looking at a top view of a section of a reservoir. This particular section shows where the original river channel made a swing or a bend. The flow of water was from left to right. In studying this sketch you will note three sections; (1)—The 'inside' of the curve has produced a wide, flat area with long, flatter, structures. (2)—The 'outside' of the bend in the channel has produced a steeper, deeper section close to shore, with short, deep structure. (3)—The feeder

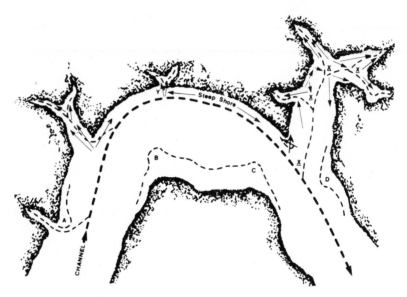

Figure 8

I have placed the fish in the channel in a typical winter or colder season position. During these colder parts of the season (late fall, winter, and early spring), there will be short, scattered migrations from the deep channel towards the steep shoreline and short structures. This, as you should see, would provide the shortest route to the shallows for a limited, scattered migration. This area would provide immediate access back to deep water. The fish would never be very far from home.

In the warmer part of the season (late spring, summer, or early fall) the movements of the fish will be toward the longer routes and flatter structures.

Figure 7 is the mental picture you should have in mind for the SEASONAL migration of fish. With this in

stream has produced a 'cove', or bays with varied bottom conditions and short structure.

Let's assume that in fishing the longer, flatter structures (A, B, C and D) during the past summer they were found to be productive. BUT, when they were checked in the colder part of the season, little success was had. What gives? What do we do?

During the colder period, structures A, B, C and D should be checked because at times they may yield a fish or two. In some areas fishermen use high speed boats to run from one end of the lake to another, checking and rechecking these longer, warmer season structures without giving any thought to other areas that might be more productive. This procedure produces a lot of action (boat that is) with questionable results. Weather and water conditions would have to be very cooperative to produce a nice string of fish on these structures during the early or colder parts of the season. Short, scattered movements, which these areas might produce, would easily be missed by a constant rider.

The above procedure is not recommended. After a short check of structures A, B, C, and D the fisherman should move to the other types of structure in the area.

With Figure 8 still in mind, the first section a fisherman should check would be that found along the deep, steep shoreline. The first casting or trolling pass might not produce a single fish, or it could produce a 'lone' fish. This would be quite normal for this part of the season. Several additional passes could be made before another fish is caught. Then a subsequent pass could produce a limit catch. The fisherman should consider himself very lucky if he finds a large number of fish moving at any one time.

The next area to check would be the feeder streams and coves found off the deeper sections. When weather and water conditions are good, the fish will move at times into the channel of feeder streams. From there they will migrate into the shallows. This is especially true if the water color is different from that in the main body of water. The short bars, found in the coves, can at times be highly productive in the colder part of the season.

The migration of fish from the main channel into the feeder stream channels is the reason why many fishermen score in bays and coves early in the season. These areas must be checked. They can be checked by trolling or casting. Casting, however would allow this area to be checked more thoroughly. The troller could check some of the breaks (marked X) without too much trouble. He would, however have trouble keeping the lures in position in the small bays and congested areas. Casting, as indicated by the small arrows, would be better and would give better coverage.

An important thing to remember in working these colder season areas, is Speed control. You may find you are unable to troll slow enough in some areas to be successful. This means you will have to cast and use lures that give a slower speed.

At times you may find the fish in the shallow coves. Your casts are made up close to the shoreline, and a slow retrieve used, but you do not get any 'takers'. Then you find that you cannot make a straight retrieve, but you have to let the lure slowly sink before moving it toward the boat. The fish are taking the lure as it sinks. Sometimes they take on the first 'sink'. At other places and times, it's after you stop the retrieve and let it sink several times before completing the retrieve. There is nothing unusual about this—it's pure Depth and Speed control for the time. However, you better not get in a rut, less than a week later this speed could be out of date, and the straight retrieve becomes the one that produces.

There are several things that should be kept in mind when fishing these areas in colder or early seasons. (1)—Migration is mostly spotty. (2)—When a productive area has been found, considerable time should be spent working it over thoroughly. (3)—If a particular area such as a small bay off a steep shoreline (as in 'Y') has proven productive, other spots of similar nature should be looked for and tested. This would hold true for ANY area found to be productive at this particular time. (4)—The 'speed' will be slow.

Early season success in these areas can be bad for the average fisherman. He will spend too much time in these areas later on in the season. He will never realize what has happened to his good fishing, and will have to wait until the season rolls around again to once again have any appreciable success.

An important notation that should be made on Figure 8 is that when working coves and bays in the cooler season a good hand rule to follow would be; (1)—pick coves and bays that are close to the deepest water in the area (channel.) (2)—DO NOT SPEND TIME IN BAYS AND COVES WHICH DO NOT CONTAIN SOME SORT OF CHANNEL OR FEEDER STREAMS. In other words, if a cove or bay is a wide flat area, with no sign of a channel—stay out.

A good rule of thumb, to apply to seasonal movements of bass and the fishing in a reservoir, would be to start with the first part of the year. In the colder weather the first consideration would be to the steeper shorelines with the steep, short structures. As the season moves toward the prespawning season, check the steeper shores less and increase attention toward coves, bays, and short bars in these areas. These coves or bays, with their shorter structures, would be worked heavy during the spawning season. After the spawning season; leave the steep shoreline, most of the coves and bays, and direct attention to the longer, flatter structures in the main body of the reservoir. In other words, the spawning season would be the dividing line between the steeper, shorter (cold weather) structures and the flatter, longer (warm weather) structures. In the late fall, head back toward the colder weather side.

I might point out at this time, that when the fish drop back to deeper water after spawning, there can be a delay, or "spotty" movements and migrations before they start moving good toward the warm weather structures. The movements do not become good **until the water warms to greater depths.** Just how hot the weather is, will determine how long this "slow" period exists. This slow period will often cause many fishermen to hang up their tackle for the season, thinking the fishing is over due to the hot weather—little realizing in a short while the fish are moving better, feeding better, growing better, striking better. The **best** being on the hottest muggiest days.

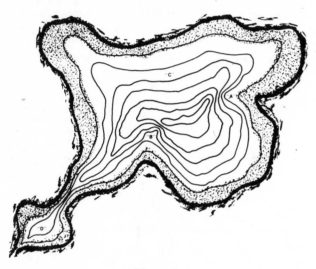

Figure 9

In Figure 9 we have a top view of a natural lake. When viewing the migration of fish from a SEASONAL point of view it is somewhat different from that found in reservoirs. This does not imply that the habits and instincts of fish are different, but that in most natural lakes the STRUCTURES USED DO NOT CHANGE, BUT WILL REMAIN THE SAME THROUGHOUT THE SEASON. However, if by chance your natural lake has the same features as discussed in the reservoir—short structure—steep shoreline, etc., then the same principle would apply. Those natural lakes; with a stream flowing through, such as a lake chain, and some wider sections

of streams, at times called lakes, often have features as found in reservoirs. Figure 9 is adequate for our study at this time.

Figure 9 shows the contour and structure available in a natural lake. Added to this, is a shallow channel or slough leading off to a small expanse of water. This could be a small, shallow lake connected to the main lake by a narrow channel.

The deepest water in the lake is a large section in the center of the larger body of water. This would be the home of the fish (winter or summer). In studying the structure available, there are two main structures in the form of a bar (A & B). The section marked "C" has no well defined structure, breakline, nor breaks. It is a flat, sloping bottom. The **breaklines** that occur on structures A and B are the only "steep" bottoms available. Thus they would be the **shortest** route to shallower water for limited or scattered migrations—just like the steeper sections of a reservoir. These would give the fish an immediate drop-back or access to the **deepest** water. So, in early season, and pre-spawn season, these steeper sections of the structure would be used.

As the pre-spawn season approaches, it is highly probable that in certain weather and water conditions, some fish may migrate, for short periods, into the feeder channel leading to the back-waters of the slough or small, shallow lake. The possibility of this would increase as the spawning season neared.

In the overall picture, the two main structures (A & B) would be considered as the main migration routes for both cold and warm seasons. In the colder pre-spawn period, the deeper breaks and breaklines would receive the SHORT, SCATTERED, UNPREDICTABLE migrations. As the season progresses the movements should become better and better and be more to the shallow portions of the structures. During the spawning season the most productive, shallow places in the lake, should be in the near shallows of those two, main structures. If the lake has a slough or a small channel leading off into a bay, or a small section such as 'D', then this too should be checked. After the spawning season the same, main structures (A & B) would receive the migration as per weather and water conditions that exist.

One further thought might be in order at this time in regards to considering fishing from a SEASONABLE standpoint. Too often, during the pre-spawn and the spawning season, fishermen rush to the water expecting to find the fish in the shallows. They become puzzled when they don't find them there. They tend to forget that how far a fish moves on migration, and how long they stay is dependent upon weather and water conditions that exist at that particular time. They neglect weather and water, and if the deeper parts of the structures are checked at all—it's a short check—done in a half hearted manner. They return to the shallows **with no regard to where it is** because "the fish just gotta be there—it's that time of the year."

The pre-spawn and spawning season is a period of changing weather and water conditions. Fish react to these changes just as they do in any part of the season. Weather and water condition can wreck a spawning season. This is one of the reasons why there are missing age groups in most waters. A good rule to follow during this period is; the closer the spawning season the more fish can be **expected** in the shallows. Be happy when this occurs. One trip may be good and the next bad. One year might be good and the next bad.

Regardless how many times I say the speed control will vary during the season—reaching a maximum in hot weather, and a minimum in the colder—I find the average fisherman encounters a great deal of difficulty in adapting his speed control to the season. He has a tendency to forget how much this control can change during the season. He will tend to stick with one speed too long

after a reduction, or an increase in speed is called for. Maybe he hasn't fished for a couple months, and doesn't realize the speed factor may have changed. You must remember that speed control can change from a trolling speed with the motor practically full throttle (5–10 H.P.) in the hottest weather, to a speed in the cold part, to a jump type lure that is moving so slowly it seems an eternity between each new cast.

My experience through the years has proven to me that few fishermen absorb anything but the operation and controls that were present when contact was made with the fish—a specific lure produced at a particular place, and in a certain way. They failed at a later date because they assumed where the fish would be, and what it took to catch him. This kind of thinking results in failure. You must never believe that a particular presentation, depth, speed, or color is best. Being neutral in every respect on every trip is a must. Only after fish have been located is it safe to say that something appears best, but certainly not before, nor on future trips.

Whatever the time of year it might be, or whatever the weather and water conditions may be, regardless of how short and slow the movement might be, your best chance of catching fish is by fishing the most potentially productive water. You will never catch fish by fishing where they ain't.

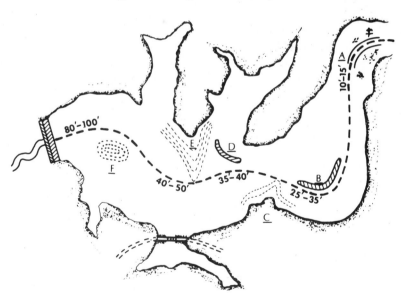

Figure 10

Unlike bass, who may die of old age in a particular area, certain species of fish such as walleye, northern, white bass, etc., may travel considerable distances in a lake or body of water. But regardless of the species, **when fish are in a particular area, they use the structure that exists in that area.**

Two things have occurred in the last few years that require some thought when speaking of walleyes. First: his habitat has been extended. Planting is done in areas where he did not previously exist. Millions of fishermen are now exposed to this species, whereas, not too long ago he was confined primarily to lakes and streams in the northern, or colder parts, of the country. Second: In areas where he was formerly a prime fish, new dams have created waters slightly different from the natural lakes of former times.

Figure 10 is a top view of a lake created by a dam on a stream in an area where the walleye reigns, or a lake where he has been introduced.

When thinking about walleye in such a reservoir, you must think in terms of a yearly migration as well as a daily one. I am by no means decreasing the importance of a daily migration. The success on the day you go fishing is your primary goal. Yet, you will do well not to forget a very important factor, the yearly movement of this fish. It could well be the determining factor for success on that particular day you are on the water. You should already know that this species travels, for it is common knowledge that walleyes appear in the streams at the headwaters of the lake shortly after 'ice out' for spawning activities.

First;—place these fish at the headwaters of the lake shortly after 'ice out', **or after spawning activities.** You would fish with good success in the areas marked "A". Fish may be found along the drop-off, or around the stumps, brush and rocks in the more shallow water. The channel may not be more than 10 or 15 feet deep in this area.

For a time, fishing is pretty good in area "A". Then you find you are having better luck a short distance downstream toward the dam. Many fish are caught along the channel and on the slightly deeper 'break' areas, such as bar "B" (a delta condition)—which is 20–25 feet deep. You quickly note they are on the channel side —not on the backside.

A little later in the season, you find you have better success still further down stream, toward the dam; on the deeper breaks and structures which are not too far from the deepest water; such as bar "C", which reaches the 25–30 foot channel—or where the channel swings in close to the end. Or; on the deeper **breaklines** of a flat section that extends out quite a distance from shore, where the water in the channel is 35–40 feet in depth —such as "D".

As the hotter part of the season rolls around (July– August), you may find you have to move still further toward the dam and deeper water. The structures and breaks in this deepest section of the lake will be productive, provided you can reach them; such as the under- water island or hump "F". However, in most cases, if the channel has a depth of 35 feet or better, you can still get walleyes from the structure near the channel such as "D" and "E".

The next season, start all over again—beginning at the shallower headwaters.

As stated before, the walleye is considered rather a slow fish. But, he does speed up as the water warms. In the first part of the season, you may find when working a lure such as a jig, you have to work it (on the bottom) with only a slight twitch of the rod tip. Then later in the season, you would have to go to a larger jig, and give a full swing of the rod to get enough speed control.

Normally, a jump-type lure, or even live bait would have the best speed control in colder water, but as the waters warm, a free-swimming bottom bumping lure is best.*

During our study on movements of fish and in basic presentation of lures, the statement was made that when lures are presented below the 8 to 10 foot level (deep water) they must be presented ON THE BOTTOM. I also pointed out that some species of fish may have some slightly different characteristics. This reference pri- marily concerned fish that may suspend themselves at structure **after migration.** We are not concerned with suspension problems in shallow water, as all sections of this water would be checked, regardless of species.

In this discussion, I will be concerned with species such as walleye, northern, muskie, and white bass. These fish, when suspended, will take a free running lure in deep water (below 8 to 10 feet).

Figures 11 and 12 show a group of walleyes (or northerns) that have migrated up to a breakline on structure. These fish have not as yet moved up on struc- ture, but are suspended slightly off the breakline. These species do not suspend themselves very far away— mostly just a few feet—and hardly ever exceeding 10 to 15 feet horizontally. The suspension is usually in relationship to the depth of the breakline, and in most instances the **depth** of the breakline will mark the **depth** of the suspended fish.

Depth control is very important when these fish are suspended; and you must be aware that these fish will at times take a free running lure as well as a walking lure, when in this position.

Just as a walking lure is correct when these fish are up on structure, a walking lure is also correct when they are suspended off the breakline. A walking lure as it comes off the breakline has the correct depth. A trolling pass made toward the break from the deep water side may not produce, as the depth is not likely to be correct—but this would not be so when the pass is made that allows the lure **to walk OFF the breakline.**

If you try to run your lures free-running without any regard to depth control, you're not likely to score very often. But by directing all efforts toward walking the structure, the lure is running free (when it comes off the structure) at the proper depth, and any suspended fish would be aware of it. This way you have depth control either bumping or free-running.

You should note at all times whether fish took the lure just before hitting the breakline, on the breakline, or directly after leaving the breakline. This tells if the fish are suspended. You then could select lure size and line length

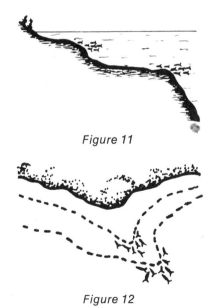

Figure 11

Figure 12

to secure proper depth (breakline) and work out from the breakline to determine what degree of suspension is present. Spend very little time doing this if fish are not located, get back to a walking lure.

Other species of fish such as trout, pan fish, crappie, etc., will suspend themselves off structure. Depth control for these can be maintained by the breakline, both horizontally and vertically. In this situation you should see that trolling would probably be the best way to become aware of this situation, and also to provide the best way to maintain depth and speed control. Casting would present no problems when the fish have moved up on structure, but when they are suspended off the structure it could present problems for speed and depth control.

To carry the suspension situation further, I will only mention salmon, and not go into other deep sea, or saltwater species, (they would be the same). Since salmon have been introduced into freshwater lakes and reservoirs this species has gained popularity. Depth control for salmon in the shallows would present no problems, as your approach would be the same as for bass, walleye, northern, etc. It is when these fish move into deeper water that you may run into a depth control problem.

There should be no problem presenting lures at different depths over visible structure in deep water; such as a hump or underwater island. Where you may have trouble is when you are a long distance from shore, very deep, and with no visible structure to speak of.

The following covers an area in Lake Michigan, where the salmon is so popular. The controls necessary to locate and catch salmon in this area, is a guide to use in finding fish in other areas of the lake, or other salmon waters.

The newcomer to Lake Michigan, fishing for the different trout, and especially for Coho Salmon, can become quite confused as to what equipment is needed, and utterly perplexed as to the best way to go about catching fish. He is often misled into thinking that a lot of sophisticated equipment is needed; equipment that requires only a little less than a college professor's knowledge to properly use and operate.

Lake Michigan fishing is somewhat different from other types of fishing, in that the largeness of this body of water and the deep breaklines, miles from shore, normally will require bigger boats and motors than for the small lakes or reservoirs. However, there are shallow breaklines and weather conditions which will allow smaller boats and motors to be used with perfect safety. But, regardless of whether the deep or shallow breaklines are worked, the basic needs and controls used in this particular lake are no different from that of any other. Fish in this body of water react to weather and water conditions, and his instincts for survival, do not differ from that of other species in other waters.

There are two basic controls necessary to catch fish in this lake, as well as other waters. These being DEPTH and SPEED control. Size of lures, colors of lures, actions of lures, depth sounders, thermometers, down riggers, etc., are AIDS that assist in catching fish. But, at the same time, every aid in the book could be used and if the lure or bait is not put where the fish are, and moved at the right speed to make him 'take', you might as well be home mowing the lawn.

No one can control weather and water conditions; but, DEPTH and SPEED can be controlled in such a way as to offset the effects of these, at least to the extent that you do not have to worry about finding the fish and making a satisfactory catch. With proper control, you do not concern yourself with haphazard presentation of lures, or running around trying to find where 'suitable temperatures may be found. Even if it were remotely possible to locate fish by those methods, proper controls will arrive at the same place, in the shortest time, with the least effort and maximum success. One thing for sure, a fish doesn't have a thermometer in his head; and being a cold blooded animal doesn't have the remotest idea about water temperatures, or preference for any. Temperature controls body functions—not desires, or comfort.

Speed control in these waters isn't too extreme. But 100 RPM on the motor can make all the difference in the world. Speed is slow in colder water, increasing as the weather and water warms. Varying the speed to find the most effective one is important.

Depth control is much more than fishing shallow, medium and deep. Depth control means, WHERE, WHEN, WHAT, WHY, and HOW.

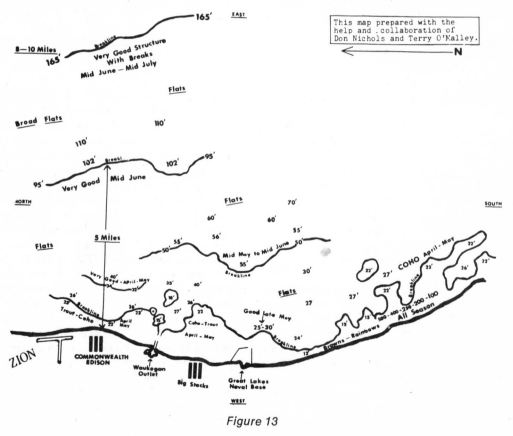

Figure 13

Figure 13 is a top view of 'structure' off Waukegan, Illinois. This is quite a large structure, as is most all of the structures in Lake Michigan.

I have not drawn in the total structure, nor in complete detail, but have placed on the structures those areas where fish are likely to be located. There are two important things to remember when seeking fish. First, you can have structure and no fish, but you won't have fish without structure. Second, when fish move on structure, they either pause or stop at a 'break' in the structure.

'Breaks' come in all shapes and sizes in the overall picture of fishing, but in the case of this body of water, the breaks come mainly in the form of a 'breakline'. That is, a place on structure where there is a sudden or gradual change in depth.

Breaklines in Lake Michigan are fairly constant in depth in a given area, and normally extend the total width of the structure (not shown in drawing). In fact, in many instances the same breakline may exist throughout the entire west side of the lake. Thus the fisherman should check for the same depth breaklines when fishing other areas. They may vary slightly in depth, but should be located close. These breaklines were, in all probability, formed by former lake levels, water currents and movements of glaciers. Good areas and their location on the different breaklines have been marked with approximate depths.

On the west side of the lake, the breaklines can be quite far apart on a structure, and between these breaklines are large flat non-productive areas. These large flat areas are usually void of breaks in any form. The break in the structure is not a rapid increase in depth, but is a gradual slope—and, in most cases, the increase in depth will not be too great. The shallower breaklines will quite often not increase in depth more than ten feet.

The best spots along any of the breaklines would be on the northeast corners of all turns or curves; caused by the direction and flow of the glaciers in the formation of the lake. Here the sharpest breaklines are found and they contain additional 'breaks'—such as rocks, dips, humps, etc.

Since the Coho is a migratory fish, I have shown month dates that should be most productive for this particular area, as well as breaklines. Exactly which breakline, and at what depth the fish will actually be on any given date will be determined by the weather and water conditions that exist at the time. Your job is to check each breakline as the season, or weather and water conditions,

call for. A shift in the wind could change the productive breakline. Study Figure 13 very carefully and thoroughly.

Figure 14 is a cross-section view of breaklines in the lake. In this drawing, depth control is shown in terms of feet. How deep do we fish or test?

When viewing the basic suspension of fish in most waters, I only consider the 'horizontal' in relationship to the breakline. But when considering certain varieties of saltwater fish, and the greater depths found in the ocean waters, I consider the 'vertical' in relationship to the breakline or breaks, as I move toward deep water.

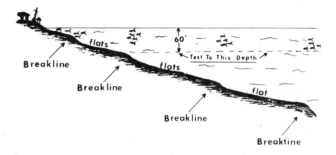

Figure 14

With my depth control, I am not complicating the subject, nor am I placing the lures at depths where much time would be wasted. I am not stating that fish may not exist below these depths at certain weather and water conditions; but, I am saying that you will have the desired results if you follow this type of depth control. Instead of moving to greater depths in feet on a particular breakline, it would be better to move to a deeper breakline; if, after thorough testing, no fish are found.

I will suggest the sizes of Spoonplugs that could be used to control Depth, in feet. These lures were specifically designed for DEPTH and SPEED, **both at the same time.** When a certain size is used with a certain amount of line, there is no fear that correct depth is obtained for that lure; then if the lure passes the fish at the correct speed he will take it. When using a No-Bo Trolling Line, with all of the stretch removed, and with color markings every 30 feet, additional control of depth is had. This line, used on the Spoonpluggers T-45 rod, and the #101 trolling reel, is adequate for fishing this lake.

The seven sizes of Spoonplugs (500, 400, 250, 200, 100, 700, 800 Series) will normally check all breaklines which may exist down to a depth of 50 feet. When break-lines are located at 100 feet, or better, then additional depths shoud be checked. This will call for some aid in getting the lures deeper, and this can be accomplished by using a wire line or a down-rigger. **The deeper the breakline, the deeper the mass of fish will be located.** In working the deep breaklines, the two smallest lures (500 and 400 Series) may very well be dispensed with.

Let me suggest a procedure that I have found quite satisfactory. The shallow structures and breaklines (near shore) can be checked for fish by running all sizes of Spoonplugs, bumping all bottoms as far as they allow. These same lures can be used 'free-swimming' out to, and beyond, the 50 foot depth.

Then I approach the 95 to 100 foot breakline. The upper water would be checked with a 250, 200, and 100 series lure. I could run them simultaneously or individually. While doing this, I would use a 200 series on a wire line or on a down-rigger set at 25 feet.

I would work along the breakline for quite a distance. If no action is had, I would re-adjust my down-rigger or run more wire line to the 35 foot depth. (All the while checking the upper water with the 250, 200 and 100 series). Normally, regardless of weather and water conditions, this control will suffice for a breakline of this depth.

If no success is had, I proceed DIRECTLY to the next breakline using the same depth control. The only change that will be made is to check below the 35 foot depth before moving on to a deeper breakline. After checking at the 35 foot depth, check the 45, then the 55–60 foot level before proceeding to a deeper breakline. Subsequent breaklines would be checked in the same way.

You should remember that Coho (like other fish) become more active at different periods of the day. If you feel that you might have missed the fish on a particular breakline, check it again.

As with other fish, light conditions have an important influence on the depth at which salmon will be found. Early in the day and again in late afternoon, you will generally find the fish shallower than during mid-day. For this reason, if you are catching salmon over a break-line and lose them, be sure to check deeper before moving to another breakline. Conversely, if you lose them late in the day, check shallower before leaving that breakline.

One rule of thumb to keep in mind is that when fishing breaklines shallower than 60 feet, fish will generally be found closer to the surface than they will be when over deeper breaklines. Check all depths, but concentrate on the 5 to 25 foot depths when fishing the shallow breaks.

In mid-summer, 20 to 40 feet will usually be the most productive depths unless water and weather conditions are ideal. If conditions are ideal, **many salmon may be found suspended 10 to 15 feet from the surface over a breakline that is 100 feet or more in depth.**

When using a down-rigger, and too many 'break-offs', tangles, premature releases, etc., are experienced, remove the release mechanism and replace it with a light monofilament line (4 to 6 lb. test is usually sufficient). This will cure the release problems and produce more fish.

Figure 15 shows a trolling pattern for checking break-lines. The trolling pass should be along, or parallel to, the direction of the breakline. The path of the boat can swing in and out along the breakline, thus showing you the actual breakline and, at the same time, allow you to determine the area where the fish are located. Most of the time, the fish will be located somewhere on the **down-slope of the breakline.**

It takes little imagination to see that if the trolling pass is made **across** the breakline, that only a small area is checked, and there is little likelihood that fish would be found at this particular spot.

As I finish up this particular section, there is probably one thing bugging you—"How do I find or follow the Breaklines if I have no Depth Sounder?"

As I have stated before, the Depth Meter is an aid, and in this instance would serve that purpose very well. Fortunately, or otherwise, you may be in the same boat as I have been in the past—you do not have one.

There are several ways that I have overcome the problems when fishing areas such as this. When possible, I check contour maps, to see the approximate depths and possible structure or breaks in deeper water. Shore-line sightings can give me the approximate directions, etc. I also have 'markers' handy in case I can use them. Lots of times in a situation such as this, I am unable to use either for finding or following deep breaklines.

I always look for a group of boats working an area. This normally tells me that there is structure of some nature in the area. Provided, of course, the FIRST boat didn't stop there due to his motor conking out. This happens quite often, especially in smaller lakes.

The thing that I have depended upon the most in the past, is just what I used to find, Crappie schools as a youngster. **I SEE where they are.** The forage fish, shad,

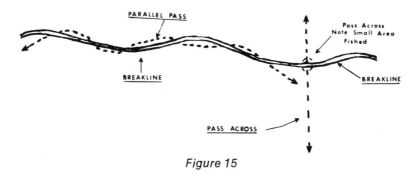

Figure 15

alewives, etc., use structure also, and will stack themselves along a breakline. The oil slick that this produces is not only visible, but produces a strong fish odor when the boat moves through it. At times you have to make allowances for the wind drift of this slick, but this presents no problem. How do you think the birds find the areas where the fish are? Where these bait fish are stacked, is normally the area on the breakline where the fish you are after are located.

٭ ٭ ٭ ٭ ٭ ٭

GET THE HECK OUT OF THE TREES:

I am still discussing Fishing Situations, but the subject matter to follow, contains so much fishing information, relating to all sections of this book, I am giving it a title—"Get the heck out of the trees." Two very important fishing situations—the Causeway, and the Rip-Rap along the dam—are discussed here only. Don't just READ this section, STUDY it. By this time you should know why each statement is made.

In the late 1940's and early 1950's, I was covering most of the south "preachin" fish behavior, the importance of structure, how weather and water played an important part in successful fishing and what was necessary to catch big fish consistently. During this period, I ran into many 'Yankees' from the north who were in the south for the winter. Many of them were shown what SPOONPLUGGING would do.

It took several years for me to find out why I never heard from any of them when they returned north and fished their local waters. It seems that some of them had reasoned that bass in the south were different from those of the north, so the same techniques would not apply. But the main reason given for not applying Spoonplugging to their local fishing was because their natural lakes were full of weeds, and it simply "would not go over in their type of lakes."

I asked many if they had tried it. Most of them admitted that they hadn't bothered. Those that had made an attempt reported that all they could catch was weeds.

My reply was, "Why didn't you get the heck out of the weeds?"

It took quite a few years, and a great number of eye-opening lunker catches from their waters, to show them that Spoonplugging WAS the answer to fishing their natural lakes, even with weeds.

For a number of years I have pointed out to the shoreline fisherman and the dyed-in-the-wool weed caster, that the day would come when they would be forced to leave the shorelines and weeds in many of the natural lakes, whether they wanted to or not. Since many of the lakes are completely ringed with vacation homes and fishing piers, the waters so full of vacationers and joy-riders that unless drastic changes were forthcoming, they could even be forced from the lake completely, as far as fishing was concerned.

Unfortunately, this situation has come to pass in too many areas where natural lakes are the predominant fishing waters. It is for this reason that I stress the importance of reservoirs. For the foreseeable future, reservoirs (man-made lakes) will be the fishing waters for this country. If you have done most of your fishing in the smaller natural lakes, you will find it tough sledding when faced with huge impoundments. Just looking out across that large expanse of water will give you the shakes. Your first reaction will be, "Where in the heck do I start?"

In recent years, many reservoirs have been built where huge areas of trees were left standing, and these trees were practically covered, by the rising water. Just facing a reservoir covered with trees presents a formidable problem. It brings to mind the old adage, "You can't see the forest for the trees."

I recall vividly the first time I took Mama (my Good Wife) fishing in a reservoir where the trees had been left standing. We were fishing the trees and forest areas in South Carolina's Lake Marion, in the Santee-Cooper complex. I refer to it as a complex due to the fact that this large body of water is made up of two reservoirs. One is Lake Marion, the so-called upper reservoir built on the Santee River, and the lower Lake Moultrie located on the Cooper River. The two bodies of water are joined by a large man-made canal. The water flows from Lake Marion through the canal to Lake Moultrie. When the reservoirs were built most of the lower lake was cleared of trees, but in Lake Marion, large forest areas were left standing and subsequently flooded.

Santee-Cooper has long been renowned, not only for black bass fishing, but for the land-locked salt water stripers which it contains. The thought of catching some lunker fish, however, was not uppermost in Mama's mind as we fished the tree areas many years ago.

Her constant complaint was, "Dern it, I've got a dang hang again" or, "For heaven's sake, can't we get out of these trees?", and, "Why are we beating our brains out blind casting. We know so little about this reservoir, and with the present weather we should be trolling to locate some fish instead of playing snag-and-seek among the trees."

I tried to explain to her that in many instances the trees were standing on good structure and, regardless of the trees, the fish still used the structure for basic movements and migrations. Also, the trees themselves served as breaks for the fish to pause or stop at—and, in turn, the fisherman could see these breaks, so here the fisherman and the fish could come together.

A Good Wife doesn't always accept fishing facts. Her comment was, "Let's get out of these dang trees, or you can take me home."

It just so happened that this reservoir was typical of most where many trees were left standing, we COULD get out of the trees quite easily. We got out of the trees and shortly after were in a group of lunker fish where we both had one coming at the same time. "I told you so", she remarked, "And don't you ever take me back into another blind jungle again."

I haven't.

I later had to admit to her that in most cases, the best structure and most productive water is in those areas where you would **not** be bothered with trees.

Today, many fishermen have the same reaction as did my wife, when faced with the problem of standing trees.

Please note that I said "standing trees", not brush or bushes. These are an entirely different subject.

Much has been said and written about the new reservoirs which are being built throughout the country where masses of trees were left standing. Much of it lauding the successful catches made, with much emphasis being placed on fishing in the trees. Many fine pictures have been made which show the fishermen out among the trees. As a consequence, many fishermen have flocked to these new reservoirs with great expectations, but often with less spectacular results.

In talking about reservoirs of this particular type, let us consider them in a similar light such as I faced when fishing natural lakes which contained a heavy growth of weeds. The problem is not only where to start, but is also **where not to start.** A common denominator prevails in all fishing waters which gives to each a sameness, and you must know exactly what to do in order to arrive at productive structure and then make a decent catch. You must have an understanding of structure and the ability to put this understanding to work successfully, regardless of the water or the problem encountered.

In any new reservoir the water is very rich in food content. This condition produces very fast growing fish. **A growing** fish strikes, or grabs, most anything that looks like food. In this yearling stage, the fish are many in numbers, widely distributed and eager to take most anything thrown at them. Large schools of these yearling fish can be found throughout most areas of the reservoir. Thus, most any fisherman able to see and dunk a bait catches at least some yearling fish.

Some of the areas in a newly formed reservoir produce better than others, as is natural; but, as the reservoir gets older and the fish get bigger, the most productive areas become increasingly less in number. This is the time when you face quite a few problems. You have no idea where to fish, are limited to blind casting, and in most cases are limited to certain types of lures that may not give good depth or speed control. You have been so "brainwashed" with trees that you go straight to them, blundering around among them like a lost dog as far as structure and fish are concerned.

As the reservoir gets older, structure becomes all the more important as it is the key to fish movement. This same rule holds true whether fishing in or out of trees. So if you fish the forest areas, you must be able to locate the most productive areas; and the tree areas that will produce fish are located on structure.

At this time, two things stand out in my mind. First,

as these reservoirs get older, less will be said and written about them, and fewer and fewer fishermen will be flocking to them. Second, now is the time to start stressing the importance of structure, and to put trees in their right perspective. If this is not done, then the time will come when truly you—as a fisherman—will find that you really "can't see the forest for the trees". In other words, now is the time to start getting you OUT OF THE TREES. In doing this, I am not saying that areas with trees do not produce. What I am saying is that the day comes in the life of any reservoir when it gets some age and the fish get "sot" in their ways. The bonanza is over for those who could not see the "**reservoir for the trees.**" And now, instead of telling you to get the heck out of the weeds, I am now going to say, "Get the heck out of the trees."

When thinking about reservoirs where trees were left standing, I put them in three categories:

(1) Those COMPLETELY covered with trees and vegetation.

(2) Those where areas were cleared of trees except in the upper shallower-end areas, or in coves, bays, or feeder streams.

(3) Those where the major portions are covered with exposed standing trees, but do contain some clear areas.

To clarify these somewhat, a little more detail may be in order.

When thinking about No. 1, where the lakes or reservoirs are COMPLETELY covered with trees, I put little emphasis on these, as they are usually shallow and the total area covered with water is small. These should be put more into the category of a pond. They are usually found in flat, swampy areas and cannot be classified as a major source of fishing water.

In this type of water, you would have to follow the old stream bed to locate any appreciable structure or water depths. In some, you will not find any indication of a channel or deeper water. In this case, it would be necessary to move back into the growth and observe the shoreline. There may be times when the shallow shoreline is difficult to reach, but most of the time enough can be seen so that any extrusion or other features of the shoreline would indicate structure.

In category No. 2 you will find many large reservoirs, which are major sources of fishing water. As stated, the major portion of the reservoir has been cleared. Only the upper shallower areas, coves, feeder streams, etc., have standing trees.

In most instances, the area with trees should **not** be considered as the major area to fish. If you have knowledge of the seasonal migration and movements of fish, you are aware that you would use these areas for short periods during the season. These periods being during the colder and earlier parts of the season. These areas are "off" season; and, for all practical purposes are of less importance as fishing water when viewed in the light of the rest of the reservoir.

Category No. 3 is the (major) reservoir for our discussion. A number of these have been built over the country during the past years. This type is usually built in rather flat country, and should be classified more as a Flatland Reservoir, rather than a Lowland or a Highland type.

These reservoirs, and the subsequent lake, covers a large acreage of flat or semi-flat country. In most instances, the overall depth is not great and many large **flat** areas exist which are completely covered with exposed standing trees.

At first glance, it appears that the whole dang lake is covered with trees; and, if you are not in the frame of mind to cope with trees or do not know how to go about fishing them. It would appear that this is a body of water that should be passed up.

But, if you will take a closer look at the whole reservoir, then you begin to see that you CAN get out of the trees. AND, a still closer observation will show that better structure and good fishing can be found in the cleared areas, more so than in the areas completely covered with trees. One look out across that dense growth of trees can show just how flat and void of structure the area is. You may not see a single indication that a ridge or any other type of structure exists. It appears that all of the trees are standing on a great big solid flat. Your observation may not be far wrong, as in most cases this is absolutely true.

I prefer to think of reservoirs, where standing trees are present, as having (3) main areas where productive structure is located, and where any type of lures or bait can be presented in any desired manner. AND these areas are free of trees.

(1) Former farming lands.

(2) River and feeder stream channels.

(3) Man-made structures.

In the case of former farming lands, you should take the time to drive around the impoundment to see where any former cleared lands existed. This will not only show you areas where trees are lacking, but will show the potential structure in the area. This journey will also give one of the most important observations that you can make, and that observation is the COLOR of the water that is present in the different parts of the reservoir. In the final analysis, fishing the best available water color could be the control as to whether or not fish are caught on that particular fishing trip.

Working the former farming lands, both casting and trolling, would present no problem. Finding good productive structure could also be done easily, if available.

The importance of the old river or feeder stream channels (No. 2), cannot be stressed too much. They represent the deepest water in the reservoir and in most all of the reservoirs of this type and nature, these channels ARE THE HOME OF THE FISH. There will be very few instances where the deep water sanctuary is outside of these channels. As stated previously, reservoirs that appear to be covered with standing trees are relatively shallow impoundments which are located in flatlands, and the only deep water in the entire lake will be found in the old stream channels.

The breaklines, breaks, structures and trees that will produce fish are found along the edges, or near edges of these channels. Note that this includes the tree areas that will be productive.

In No. 3, man-made structures produce some of the better structures found in reservoirs. These structures are usually very easily observed and located, and are usually cleaner of brush and debris than any other areas to be found. Presenting lures on man-made structures, both casting and trolling, normally requires less skill and presents fewer problems than on natural structures.

Man-made structures would be listed as:

(1) Old submerged roadbeds.

(2) Causeways, or roads, that were constructed across certain portions of the reservoir during construction.

(3) The dam area.

(4) Power lines or boat trails.

It is surprising how the old roadbeds (1) in the immediate area of the newly formed reservoirs were constructed on good structure. Long sloping bars and ridges that led out to the channel of the gullies, creeks, or rivers were used since this was the easiest approach to crossing these areas. Then when the area was flooded, these old roadbeds became ideal structure and migration routes for the fish to use. They produced visible structure and breaks from the deepest water to the shallowest. Some of my fondest memories are those of fine catches made

while trolling a clanking lure up or down one of these old roadbeds. Some of the hard roadbeds give walking lures a lot of abuse, but this is much better than staying continually hung up and losing lures in a tangle of trees or brush.

When trolling these areas, there is no doubt as to whether or not your lures are in position. All that is necessary is to make straight line runs, covering all sections. It is hardly possible to cast the wrong areas when casting an old roadbed, provided you cast all sections and work all depths with different retrieve speeds. Efforts, both casting and trolling, should be concentrated where the roadbed crosses any channel. The fish movement originates here, and most of the time the migration will not reach far from the channel.

(2) The causeways and roads that cross portions of the reservoir are too often overlooked. You will find in many instances that entrance to the dock facilities is located adjacent to an existing causeway or road; and often these are passed up as you zoom across the water headed for the trees. Not only will the adjacent areas of the causeway be clear of trees, due to construction procedures, but the structure and riprap may be the most productive fishing spot in the whole lake. Normally, these causeways will have a bridge at some point, and usually the bridge spans the old river channel. There are cases where the bridge portion does not cross the old channel, but it crosses a man-made or a dug channel, and the surrounding water will be the deepest in the area. These causeways give structure immediately from the deepest water in the area to the shallows. The causeway and its riprap gives a clear route for migration.

I normally look at a road map before arriving at the reservoir to see if a service road (causeway) crosses the reservoir at any place; and the longer it is, the better. If one exists, this is normally the area I head for. Working the causeway and riprap is one sure way to be assured of good structure—structure that is clean and workable. Many times. I do not have to go to any other area to get fish. There have been times when other areas would not produce, and I would ride quite a distance to locate a causeway, and fish. These are also excellent areas to escape from heavy wind and wave action; in fact, at times these are the only areas that can be fished if extremely high winds prevail.

To fish these causeways trolling, each size lure is "jammed" right up against the rocks, with each one walked or skipped along the top of the rocks, or whatever material was used in construction. You will soon find that a certain section, or sections (depending upon the length of the riprap) will be more productive. This is due to a bottom condition being created during construction that made that particular area a little different from the surrounding area, causing the fish to move up to or on these particular spots.

When casting the sides of a causeway, I prefer to locate the boat very close to shore so that I can make the casts up and down the shoreline. In this way, all depths can be checked thoroughly, and the lures held in position for the total length of the retrieve. The boat can be moved along the shoreline with little effort, and if there is a slight wind blowing, the boat will move satisfactorily by itself with little work on the part of the caster. The boat may bump the sides of the riprap once in a while, but, so what. About the only time I position the boat out from the shallows, and make the cast in toward the shoreline, is when I have a group of fish located in the shallows.

No. (3), the dam area. Normally, in reservoirs that contain large areas of standing trees, you can just about assume that the area where the dam is located will be quite a wide area since a long dam is usually constructed. This means that, due to the construction process, this area was cleared of trees, making quite a large area with clean structure available. The dam area will have the deepest water in the lake, and in general will contain older and larger fish.

If at all possible, I try to drive into the dam area and look at the size of the dam, the type of construction used and determine the color of the water. Sometimes, the best water color will be located in the dam area, as well as the cleanest and most productive structures. In very few instances have I found these clean areas not workable, and this was in those isolated instances when moss on the bottom, due to pollution, made presentation of lures difficult. The clean structures found in the dam area allows presentation of lures to be made both casting and trolling with a minimum of trouble. The long dams provide good riprap fishing, the old ramps, borrow pits, etc., provide some of the best structure to be found. And, as is often the case in flatlands, when the wind is a problem the dams can serve as sheltered areas when the need arises.

No. (4), power lines and boat trails. Although, these could not rightly be called structure, they are listed here as they provide areas clear of standing trees and will at times contain or cross productive water. Too often, though, these trails are cut through trees which are located on large flat areas, void of any deep water or structure, and you end up fishing in the trees or the edges of the trees where there are no fish. It's too bad that these trails were not cut to productive structure, and the areas marked in some way to show where fish could be caught. These trails could then serve as great aids. But if you use these trails only in the light of expecting to stumble upon a productive spot, then your chances are very unlikely and these trails will serve no useful purpose. In this case, it would be better if no trails were cut at all. If you gotta fish them, work the areas where they cross a channel of some description.

To emphasize some of the points brought out, note Figure 16 and comments.

Note that the drawing is a top view of a typical flatland reservoir in which masses of trees were left standing.

In observing the depths on the sketch, they indicate typical depth situation for a reservoir of this type. While these depths can vary in different reservoirs, the depths among the trees is relatively shallow, very seldom exceeding 15–20 feet. The depths in the trees could be greater or less, and the depths in the channels could vary accordingly. But, in most cases these depths are about what should be expected in reservoirs of this nature.

The normal main stream channel winds and turns as it crosses the reservoir. The overall depth of the channel will not vary a great deal from one section to that of another. The best structure on the channel will exist at all "turns" and where the feeder stream channel enters the main channel. You should check these areas thoroughly.

The deepest water in the channel is found on the turns, and the portion of this structure that normally produces best will be found on the "outside" of the turn. However, in the overall picture, the structure that will be the most productive spot along the channel is the structure that is adjacent to where the side feeder stream enters the main channel. At times some of these may have a "delta" condition.

Note the areas where the boat trails were cut through the standing trees. This is typical of most reservoirs. The trails go out across the large flats with no regard to structure or to the most productive spots along the channel. In most reservoirs these tree areas have an overall depth that is normally under 15 feet, and, in many cases, much less.

Often, where a sizeable pond or lake has been submerged, the trails will lead to these areas. At other times they will not. You should be aware of any deep water pond or slough that may be located back among the trees, as they often contain fish.

The two areas that should get a lot of attention are the causeways and the area adjacent to the dam. These areas have clean workable structure. The dam area, especially, requires a lot of attention. The deepest water in the lake occurs here, the structure is normally better and more varied, and it would be in this particular area that clumps of standing trees may be observed. In most instances,

these clumps of trees represent a hump or some break in the structure, the meandering of channels, and so on.

Most of the reservoirs built today have a map of some nature available. Sometimes these maps may be purchased at the dock facilities or at an area sporting goods dealer. Many of the maps show great detail. Some are in color with all of the three areas, channels, boat trails, causeways, cleared areas and water depths all clearly marked. It is always wise to purchase one of these maps if they are available, and they should be carefully studied before going on the lake.

Figure 16

My closing comment is to take with a grain of salt any suggestions from those around the boat dock who tell you to take off back into the trees if you want to catch fish. In most cases, it's a bum steer, as far as locating the most productive structure in the reservoir. Just keep in mind that you can do a lot better by "getting the heck out of the trees"!

* * * * * *

When I classify reservoirs, I put them into several groups; 1—Highland, 2—Lowland, 3—Flatland. I go further and break these groups down into several types. The major differences between these groups and types is water color, depths, bottom conditions, structure—where it is likely to be, it's features, and how best to work, etc.

In the material thus far, and in these "Fishing Situations" I have not covered all these groups and types, BUT, I have tried to condense them down into Typical Structure, and Typical Situations and Conditions **found in all of them.** In choosing the Typical Situations, I have used those I consider of more importance at this time, and to drive home as many Basic Facts as possible. If you "get" the Basic Facts in these illustrations, you need have no fear of having trouble in ANY of the others.

I have always felt, that more people have more trouble with **"Flatland"** reservoirs, than any other type. I also feel that these type conditions, **will teach more,** than any other.

Figure 16 (Get the Heck Out of The Trees) is a typical Flatland Reservoir. To make sure you have gotten the points I was trying to make, and also to convert this reservoir into one more likely to be fished **by the most people,** I am going to change it slightly, and proceed from another direction.

A "Flatland" reservoir is exactly what it says—it was built in Flatlands. Not in a hilly country, nor in the mountains. The reservoir has rather definite features and conditions.

1—**A long Dam.**
2—**Short shallow structure along shorelines.**
3—**Wide flats.**
4—**A channel winding through the flats.**
5—**Very little deep water outside the channel.**

Figure 17 is a side view or a cross-section of a typical flatland reservoir. When observing this figure you might be inclined to say I am repeating myself, and that I used this when I was talking about the "Delta" situation. If you will observe closely, **there are no humps or ridges along the edge of the channel.** The big flats go right on out and drop into the channel.

The Flats can be very wide at times, and as you go out across them, they appear to be as flat as the top of a table. The widths of the flats can vary, as the stream channel winds around as it moves through the flat.

The relatively short shallow structure along the shorelines, are normally in the form of "bars" as shown.

Figure 18 is a top view of a typical Flatland Reservoir. Note carefully what we have—the wide dam, the huge flats (note depths carefully), and the winding channel up through the flats (note depth). You should see that this condition exists over the whole reservoir, the only change being in the depths. A reservoir of this type can be quite large. It can be several miles wide, and a dozen miles long.

You note that I do not show any structure or depths along the shorelines, neither do I show any feeder stream channels that might cut through the flat and join the main channel. But, I have added several features, that are likely to be present in a reservoir of this type, and which will play an important part in your being able to fish it successfully.

I have added a road crossing the lake (causeway); an old roadbed (submerged); structure at the Dam; and I have marked particular areas. I hope you have already seen, that all bottoms were "clear cut" (trees removed),

Figure 17

with the exception of the upper shallow sections, and back in the shallow sections of coves (feeder streams).

When you arrive at this big flatland reservoir, you will then see the various features that have been added. The question immediately arises—"**Where will I fish?**" or "**Where and what is productive structure?**"

The first thing you should do is try and find a Map of the reservoir showing as much detail as possible. Today, most reservoirs have some type map available for

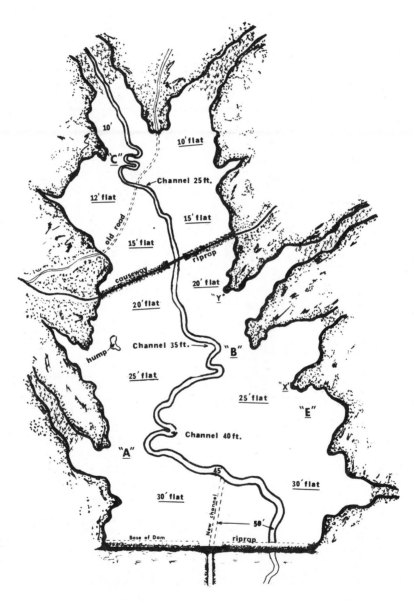

Figure 18

the fisherman. Usually it can be obtained at the Dock or Marina.

When you look at your map, you find that it looks practically like Figure 18. It may have some differences, but for all practical purposes Figure 18 is your fishing situation.

The first thing you note are the depths involved. A quick glance tells you, THE HOME OF THE FISH IS THE CHANNEL. You can't escape this fact. To think otherwise results in failure. This is especially true as the lake gets older, and when weather and water conditions are not **ideal.**

When the fish are in their deep water sanctuary (the channel), they are quite dormant—non-chasing, etc. They are extremely hard to locate and make "take". Usually there is no indication of structure in the channel that would tell you where to present lures. This being the case, you are not likely to present your lures correctly by just going in there and wandering around.

Therefore, you are faced with the fact you are not likely to make contact with the fish until the movement period occurs and the fish migrate toward shallower water.

Here is where the rub comes in a Flatland reservoir. How do the fish move? What are the migration routes? What shoreline structures produce? Which will be good? Which bad? In other words, **where do I fish?**

When looking for productive structure and migration routes in a Flatland reservoir, I break them down into two groups. 1—**Man-made,** 2—**Natural.**

I look first for the man-made structures, for **they are the ones most likely to "go all the way".** That is, these are the ones that will give the fish a visible route across the flats. They are:

1—**The Dam**
2—**Causeway (a road crossing the lake)**
3—**Old roadbeds covered when the area was flooded.**

The natural structures, or possible migration routes, would consist of:

1—**Humps**
2—**Bars or ridges that extend out from the shorelines.**
3—**Side feeder stream channels**
4—**Breaklines along the edges of the channels**

With Figure 18 in view let's look at the possibilities. I will start with the man-made.

1—**Dam:** I have already pointed out that the dam area must not be overlooked when fishing a reservoir of this type. This area contains the deepest water in the lake. It has good structure, which is clean and workable due to construction activities. I have pointed out the importance of "trolling" the riprap (with the different lures "stacked" with each size skipping along the tops of the rocks). Etc.

In Figure 18 I have noted several things that you should be aware of that can exist in the Dam area. Often, the Spillway or the "Outlet" will not always be at, or in, the old river channel. Often it will be built to one side, and a new channel cut. When this occurs, it increases greatly the potential of the area. It produces more deep water, and more structure. At the same time, it provides a perfect condition for the fish to have access to the riprap. The old channel comes right up to the base of the Dam.

Figure 19 shows a cross section of the Dam. The thing to note here is the **Base of the Dam.** When constructing a "Dirt Filled" Dam, often a wide base (or foundation) must be made upon which to build the upper portions of the Dam. It creates a situation such as shown in Figure 19. The importance of you being aware of this condition, is due to the Depths, Breaks, and Breaklines that may be present.

You should see, if there is no depth of water on this base, or if there are no "breaks" along the breakline, or on the flat base, there is likely to be no migration of the fish to the riprap.

In a Flatland Reservoir such as this, the water level, can play a very important part in the movements of the

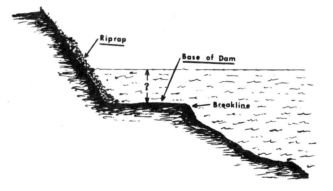

Figure 19

fish. Often just a few feet will make all the difference in the world. In the case of Figure 19, **if there is no deep water (more than 8–10 feet) on top of this base, and there is no "cut" or wash through the flat base leading to deep water, it is not likely there will be any fish along the riprap.** In this case, you move to the edge of the Base, and work along the breakline. Trolling is the best way to check it.

2—Causeway. I believe I have already expressed my thinking about the importance of working the riprap along any road that might cross the lake. These are perfect structures in Flatland reservoirs. In the case of Figure 18, this particular causeway will be productive (when the fish move). This is due to the flats and the depths involved. The lower side (toward Dam) will be more productive than the upper side. With water only fifteen (15) feet deep (the flats) on the upper side, and since most of the causeway is a long distance from the channel, movements of the fish will be confined primarily to the riprap adjacent to where the road crosses the main channel. On the lower side, with the depths involved (20 feet), there could be movements, at times, to all sections of the riprap. But, during bad weather conditions it could also be confined to the area where the road crosses the main channel..Trolling the riprap with lures tipping the rocks, will show you if movement of the fish is in progress and just where, and how they use the causeway.

3—Old submerged roadbeds. Any submerged roadbeds give the fish a visible route across the flats toward shallower water. In our case (Figure 18) the only submerged road we have is in the upper end where the water on the flats is only 10–12 feet deep. This means, that the movements of the fish will be confined primarily to the area where the road crosses the channel. At times under good weather conditions, and at certain periods of the year, there can be migrations up along this road for quite some distance. This is easily checked out, but most of the time, you would concentrate your efforts at the channel.

Now let us look at the Natural Structure found in this reservoir, that will receive migration of the fish.

1—Humps. In many Flatland Reservoirs, there will be no humps or underwater island available. In Figure 18 I have placed one (1). From the map it appears it is located on a flat, a long distance from the channel, with no visible "breaks" that might lead the fish. There is no indication that a feeder stream channel is in the area. In the early life of the reservoir, there might have been yearling fish around this hump, and there might be a remote possibility that "breaks" in the form of bushes or brush might lead the fish across the flats to the hump, but in this case, it is too far from the channel. The flats are too wide. I might go look at it, but I'd spend no time there.

2—Bars or ridges that extend out from the shorelines. These are the more important natural structures to consider. In discussing them, and when viewing our map for shoreline structures, we will have to look at them in terms of our number 3 item—**feeder stream channels.** These channels with their breaklines, will be a major factor in guiding the fish across the flats to a structure along the shoreline. We will also have to look at them in terms of the edges of the channels—our number 4 natural structure listed.

When looking at a map of a flatland Reservoir and trying to determine what Natural structure might be good, the first thing I look for are the areas where the channel comes in close to the shoreline. In Figure 18 there are three areas where this occurs—"A", "B", and "C".

In observing these areas, I look to see if there are any feeder streams or feeder stream channels in the near area. In this case, both "A" and "B" have them. "C" is located in the upper shallower area, so I'm not too concerned whether any side channels exist.

The next thing I look for is any unusual twisting or turning of the channel. This is an indication that something, or some different bottom condition exists. It could indicate **structure.** In looking at Figure 18 there are three areas where this occurs. Here again it is at "A", "B", and "C". It is uncanny how these three conditions will exist in the same area. That is; a—where the channel swings in close to shore, b—the presence of feeder streams, c—the main channel has some unusual twist or turn.

After I get on the water, **I try to locate the SHALLOWEST running "point" or "bar", that runs the FARTHEST into the lake. The narrower** this point and bar, the better I like it. At times my map may show the depths, and I can locate them BEFORE I go on the water. In the case of our map (Figure 18) the depths are not shown. BUT, it does show the most likely places where this type structure may exist. AND, here again, they appear to be at "A", "B", and "C". In looking at section "E", it would appear any structure in this area, would not be good. There is no indication of good structure in the light of the above. I would certainly take a look at the point 'X', for our map indicates there is a feeder stream channel on the upper side, and the shoreline indicates a "point". Probably a pretty good "bar" exists, but if the fish moved to it, the "contact" point would be at some point on the upstream side of the bar. I would check it out.

Of course our Main points of interest would be Areas "A", and "B". Area "C" is shallow, and the place to work would be the breaklines along the channel.

When working area "B", I would certainly spend time on the point marked "Y". There is deep water on two sides, and the structure most likely would be long, and extend quite some distance toward the main channel.

Earlier I stated that it was uncanny how all the **features to look for,** seemed to congregate in particular areas? Actually it isn't any mystery, these things come together naturally, each is related to the other. In times past, the flow of the main channel was interfered with, or affected by the flow of the side feeder stream. This in turn, caused the unusual bending of the main channel. These actions, also built up the "point," and the long underwater bar extending out toward the main channel. If the side feeder stream didn't exist, the area "B" wouldn't even exist. The shoreline would probably be as far away from the main channel as section "E", and the main channel would not have any unusual bends.

Now let us assume that we found a structure, or a bar, at "B". We would most likely find that it does not "go all the way" to the channel. There still exists a 20–25 foot flat between the end, and the channel. But due to the fact the side feeder stream channel shows the way to the structure, and the fact that the end of the bar isn't too far away, and the likelihood there will be "breaks" on the flat to show the way (in the form of bushes most of the time), the structure should produce. The only hitch is to find what part of the structure produces. To help clarify this better let us look at a couple more Figures. I might add, that in a Flatland reservoir, your productive "bars" will be viewed the same way **regardless where they may exist.** The depth of the flat may vary, but the features of the structure (bar in this case) will be the same.

Figures 20 and 21 are two cross sections, or side views, of a "bar" (structure) that runs out from the shoreline in a Flatland reservoir. In this case the flat has a depth of 20 feet. Figure 20 has a breakline that breaks at 12 feet to the flat. Figure 21 has a 9 foot breakline that breaks to the flat. One can be productive, and the other will not. There are two main differences between these two bars.

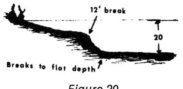

Figure 20

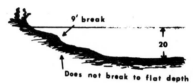

Figure 21

The first thing to examine is the depth of the break. As is often the case in a Flatland reservoir, the bars along the shoreline will break off rather shallow. This creates problems for the unknowledgeable fishermen. As stated earlier, just a few feet difference in water level can play havoc with a productive structure. You must keep in mind that 8–10 feet is the separation point of the shallow water from the deep water. Fish are very reluctant to pass this depth. Many times a fisherman is having success on a bar where it breaks at 11 feet. Then the water drops a couple feet, and he can't understand why he no longer catches many good fish. **The breakline (or break) becomes too shallow to receive the bulk of the moving fish.**

When interpreting a structure (bar) in a Flatland Reservoir Figures 20 and 21 shows a **very important feature.** That being; when the breakline occurs, **it must break all the way to the depth of the flat.** The distance from the breakline to the area where it is as deep as the flat, must not be very great. It cannot break a foot or so, and then slowly get deeper and deeper. OR, you can't expect a bar to produce if it just gets deeper and deeper over a long distance until it reaches the flat. (For a bar such as this, to produce, it would have to be very narrow and ridge-like, and this is not likely to occur in a Flatland Reservoir.)

Figure 22 is a top view of a long shallow running structure off a point such as "A" and "B" in Figure 18. **It is quite big,** and has "fingers" at different spots. A typical situation. A breakline is shown running around the greater structure. Let's interpret it.

Finger "A" breaks at nine (9) feet, but it does not break fast or very far. The area off this finger slopes off gradually, until it reaches the Flat depth of 20 feet. Doesn't look very good.

Finger "B" also breaks at nine (9) feet. It breaks very good, and drops to the flat depth in short order. This finger has possibilities.

Finger "C" breaks at 12 feet, and drops to Flat depth quickly also.

On good weather and water conditions, both "B" and "C" should produce. BUT, in the overall picture Finger "C" would be the "contact point" of the mass of the fish. Finger "B" has too shallow a break, and when weather and water conditions are not good, it may not get any fish—while "C" would. In any case, when movement does not come up to the breakline, you would concentrate your efforts off (deeper) these two fingers.

A major reason why the structures must have the feature of the break dropping quickly to the flat depth, is the fact, **the FLAT may have water deep enough to hold the fish BEFORE migration.** In other words, although the Channel in this case is the "home" of the fish, the depth is such (20 to 30 ft.), that under **extremely** good weather and water conditions the fish may not go all the way back to the channel after the movement period, but settle down somewhere on the flat. As you can see, if this occurs, the structure (or bars) "go all the way" and are readily available and visible for the movements of the fish.

Above the causeway, this will not happen, as the depth on the flat is too shallow. Each migration in this area would begin at the channel.

By no means take my statement about the fish "settling down" on the flats, as meaning this is the "home" of the fish. The "home" is the channel, and any bad weather condition, such as a cold front, can cause them to scoot back to the channel, and it may be a week before they get back to the structure (bar).

This return to the channel is the reason the Man-made structures in a Flatland Reservoir are so important. **They reach the deep water.** You could be catching fish for days on the man-made structures before the first fish showed up on the natural ones. (bars)

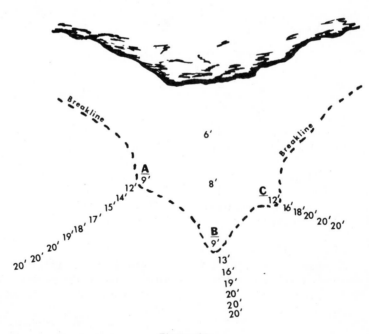

Figure 22

This brings us to the 4th item listed in the Natural structures or areas to find fish. These are **the edges, or breaklines found along the channels.** These are very important for those times when weather and water conditions are not for good migration. AND, **this will occur a great deal of the time throughout the year.**

In the section above the causeway (and probably in all feeder streams) the water on the flats is not very deep and the troller can work these breaklines (edge of channel) without too much trouble. When casting the breaklines he may be confined to a "jump type" lure, but this should produce the fish once they have been located—which is easier done by trolling.

Major effort would be made where the old road crosses the channel, and where any side feeder stream or wash has cut into the main channel. Any time that two major streams come together in this upper area, you would thoroughly check where they join.

Below the causeway, where the edge of the channel is quite deep, the troller should go to "wire" line to reach all the breaklines. The caster would have a pretty hard time doing a good job of finding the fish. Once they are found (by trolling the wire), then casting can be tried. Here again, concentrated effort would be made where side feeder stream channels enter the main channel.

Probably when you were looking at Figure 18, you kept looking at those standing trees up in the upper end, and in the coves. I suppose you kept looking for me to get around to them, and couldn't quite understand why I did not bring them in when listing the potential areas. This was no oversight. There might be some fish in these areas at certain periods of the year—such as late fall or early spring, but in the overall picture of the Reservoir, these areas would not attract much of my attention. They are not worth the time or the effort. There are too many other places that produce good fish, there is no guessing about it.

This Fishing Situation on the Flatland Reservoir, has taken up a lot of space. It probably created hard reading, due to continued reference to Figure 18. The reason I went into great detail on all the possibilities—it gave me a chance to drive home again the basic facts concerning fish behavior, and what part structure plays in your search for fish. My suggestion would be for you to study this material several times. I feel sure, each time you will find a Fishing Fact you had missed.

✿   ✿   ✿   ✿   ✿   ✿

Probably it would be appropriate at this time, after study of the Flatland Reservoir, to bring out again some of the things said with Figure 5 page 15. In some large natural lakes and some large Reservoirs, there exist large shallow areas, **long distances from any appreciable deep water.** These areas may be represented by coves, sloughs, and some may be viewed as "swampy". There may be fish in these areas (provided there is cover) that stay here all the time. This is "home", they are not aware there is any deep water in the lake. I refer to them as "grass" bass.

Too often, I see too many fishermen going straight to these areas for "straggler" fishing. They pass right over the deeper water, where the mass of the lunker fish will be found. This is due in part to their not "knowing" fish, or how to fish "open" or "deep" water.

There are several things wrong with this approach. 1—There is no "mass" of fish in these areas in most instances. 2—Lots of small fish. 3—Weather can affect these fish just as it does the fish in deeper water, and in most cases **more**—they do not have the deep water to help offset some of the ill effects. They lie very dormant under the cover, and cannot be reached. 4—Normally the water is "clear." 5—The fisherman is "straggler" fishing. He is fishing blind, other than casting to visible objects. 6—He will give total credit for his success (or failure) to some AID, such as size, color, action, equipment or skills—this is bad. 7—He (the fisherman) **will resist accepting the facts—that lunker fish "school"; the deep water is the "home" of the fish; structure; movements of fish; and how weather and water plays a part in his success or failure.** 8—He could fish for a hundred years and never get any better—as far as catching fish. 9—Etc.

I get no satisfaction in working these areas for the reasons given above, but primarily due to the fact I cannot "learn". I will fish structure and deeper water at the expense of no catch at all. If I have to "straggler" fish, I'll do it in deeper water.

These areas **do** have their advantages at times. When the weather and water conditions of the main or deeper sections, are so bad as to be unfishable, these areas can often provide protection. At times when the main body of water is too muddy, these areas will have more clarity. Some of these areas will contain lots of fish during the spawning season—**if not too far from deep water.**

Any problems encountered in farm ponds is due to several things; but all, a result of the features normally associated with these small bodies of water—primarily depth.

I have already discussed some of them (Figure 55) under this section; so I will not make further comment on those covered with weeds, or those where the weeds go deep.

In farm ponds, as in other waters, you must keep in mind that the **deepest** water is the home of the fish. The fish HERE, are likely to become MORE dormant under certain weather and water conditions, than in lakes where greater depths will help offset the ill effects.

Many of these type ponds, are not suitable for good reproduction of bass. They are most always overloaded with small pan fish, and some get so loaded, there will be NO reproduction of the larger fish.

If the pond contains larger bass, and difficulty is had in catching them, it is due to **improper depth and speed control. These are the only controls available to you.** Many fishermen will catch fish with a particular lure—when they are "biting" or during the early spring spawning period. They continue to use this style lure all season, whether it will give the necessary Depth and Speed control or not.

Due to the forage fish available to these fish, you better always figure you have to make them 'Strike'. This means, you have to check your speeds at all depths —**free running or walking.**

One of the more often remarks I hear—"I try to catch fish out of the pond, but I fail most of the time. Now, take Grandpaw for instance, he can really catch them."

This should give you the 'key'. By this time you should be well aware of the fact that fish do not move constantly nor consistently. Probably, you decide to go down to the pond to fish for a spell. As is in most cases you don't have much time, especially if the fish aren't biting.

Ole Grandpaw, most likely spends the **whole day** at the pond.

I have built several farm ponds in my life. I always found it advisable to place a nice 'break' in the deepest water—one that I could reach on the cast. The material used was such that I could **bang** my walking lure against it without hanging up. This normally solved any problems of "finicky" bass.

CHAPTER 2

Mapping and Interpretation

Buck Perry Reveals His Bass Fishing Secrets!

If I were to place the importance of knowledge on any one given area, the highest degree of importance would probably have to be placed in your ability to read and interpret bottom conditions.

Success on any given fishing trip will be determined by how well you understand how fish move on structure, the effects of water conditions, weather conditions, and how well you can evaluate these conditions at the time you're on the water.

The degree of understanding that you have will determine how and when you arrive at the fish. Your interpretation of structure, and of conditions affecting fish at the time, will direct you into the procedures necessary to put fish on the stringer. The approach to catching fish will not always be exactly the same, so you must react to the conditions which you face at that particular time.

All good Spoonpluggers take ample time to evaluate the water to be fished. This means BEFORE and AFTER he gets on the water. For example:

. . . Is this a steep canyon lake, heavy with timber, rock, etc?

. . . Is it a natural lake? Man made lake?

. . . Was this farm land? Was it all timberland? Is it part farm land, part timberland?
Are there any well established feeders, or dry gullies, which lead into the lake? What kind of terrain did they come out of?

. . . Etc.

Additional information, which would be useful, can be obtained by asking a few questions of the local people, such as:

. . . Where does the main river go through the lake?

. . . Is there a secondary river, or big streams, joining the main river?

. . . Where do you catch fish when 'they're biting'. (This quickly gives the near area of productive structure).

. . . Etc.

Total interpretation of structures, weather and water conditions, to arrive at the fish, will not come overnight. Each trip will be an improvement over the previous trip. Once mastered, you can concentrate your efforts in key areas. There will be less water to work, and less time will be needed to check the water. One hundred percent of the time will be spent in working productive water, which will keep you on top of the fish. You will be the first to become aware of any fish activity and migration. Not only that, but you will be in a position to take advantage of any activity.

In the final analysis your mapping and interpretation ability will decide your future as a fisherman. This is the major area where you can always get better.

BEFORE YOU GET ON THE WATER

Interpretation of the fishing potential of a smaller body of water, be it natural or artificial, is not too difficult to the average Spoonplugger. It is when he comes to a BIG body of water that the men are separated from the boys. A NATURAL lake, in most instances, does not present too big a problem for the "knowledgeable" fisherman. It is the big ARTIFICIAL reservoirs that give him trouble.

Most fishermen just can't wait to get on the water when fishing a strange lake. Most likely the lake was reported to be a "real fishing hole"; anticipation is at a high pitch, so he hurries to get "fishing". Hurrying to get on the water can be a great error, and later when he begins to wonder if there are any fish in the water, he is puzzled as to why his catch is zero.

Taking a little time to drive around a lake or reservoir; observing the water conditions, the terrain, and the type of bottom conditions likely to exist, is well worth your time and effort.

By this time, you should be well aware that there are good conditions and bad conditions for the fish, and your ability to fish for them in the best manner. Then it should be obvious that you had better do everything in your power to look the situation over and see if you cannot eliminate some of the water, and come to a conclusion that conditions appear best in this area or that area for you to do your fishing. You must stop doing your fishing by wild guesses, but instead, go about it in a sound intelligent manner. And if you do this, you should have the battle at least half won.

You might say, 'Yeh, but the dang thing is so big, and there is so much water out there. Just where do we begin to make our study?"

Let's break down your pre-fishing studies into three (3) headings—as you go around the lake asking questions and observing.

1—Water Color.
2—Available structure.
3—Can it be fished properly?

In studying water color, you should be aware that most of the time your main concern will be one of too much clarity. In some sections, during certain seasons of the year, you may be faced with water being too muddy and you will need to look for water with more clarity. But, most of the time you will be faced with finding an area with dingy water. Your past studies should give you clues as to what color of water you would normally **expect to find in certain areas.** Now your actual observation can verify or disprove your prediagnosis.

In studying the "lay of the land", or terrain, around a body of water, you can see the areas with potential structures. Instead of picking out a deep gorge-type water, you pick the former farm areas, or areas with obvious structures such as islands, long flat bars, flats with streams or channels running through them, or a road bed that may cross the lake, etc.

If the reservoir was formed by a dam that is quite long, then it is a sure bet that the dam area will contain structures, deep water, and riprap.

The third (3) heading above, "Can I fish it properly?", is actually an additional heading that need not be included for the "educated" fisherman. If a good job is done on the first two items, the answers will be had concerning the third.

A particular exception to this might occur when making the color selection. The **preferred** color could take you into an area with brush, or other features that may limit presentation. For example; you have a reservoir where the dam was built in a narrow gorge. The shorelines are steep, with little visible structure, and the bottom is covered with bushes. Normally the water is too clear for good migration—so you passed it up. But due to rain, or spring run-off, the water has become dingy, and you have decided to give it a try.

If you should pick such an area (due to water color) and run into problems of presentation of lures, you are not entirely dead, due to the fact that at the time this occurs the fish are likely to be up and moving, and fishing wouldn't necessarily have to be "right on the money". So again, the Spoonplugger would be wise to stick to his acceptable water color.

You must remember that these normally too-clear-areas, with all of their questionable bottom conditions, are not entirely void of fish. You know that fish are there. It is just a question that for most of the time there is not sufficient migration or you can't fish it well enough to make contact. If you find one of these deep-gorge areas, even with all of its toughness, and it has a decent water color, you had better fish it, for the fish certainly haven't been disturbed or harvested. I often keep my eyes on a situation such as this. When the water color gets right—in I go.

If you will observe the water color, and observe the structure possibilities in a given body of water, you will most likely find the "workable" areas. The relationship between them is too great to miss.

Figure 1 shows a portion of a reservoir where the channel of the original stream wound around, or where "bends" occur. Few reservoirs will be fished, where you will not find where the original stream curved in some fashion, or to some degree.

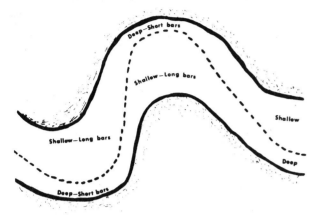

Figure 1

One of the most important, and most often encountered, observation and interpretation that you will face, will be in the nature of that shown in the sketch. A quick glance should tell just where the steeper banks, deeper water, and shorter bars are located, also where the flatter sections, long structures and shallower water is located.

The above information, along with additional observations of terrain—such as coves, hills, and distances—should give a fair estimate as to where and what type of structure exists in the area, before it is ever checked out.

One of the best ways to improve mapping and interpretation is to make a calculated guess as to what is present, before checking it.

One of the best mapping tools that you will find, are the lures in your tackle box. Other tools, such as contour maps, depth sounders, etc., can be used to SOME DE-GREE. But, in the final analysis the use of lures is the only way to get final interpretation of a structure, and that is—**by catching fish.**

The mapping and interpretation process will not be complete until every little detail about a structure is known. Lures, run at their proper depth, with correct gear, will tell every detail. It is important that you be rigged to carry out this important phase. It may take years to understand fully how fish use all these little details, under all weather and water conditions. But here

again, is a reason you can get better and better in your fishing.

When I designed the Spoonplugs so many years ago, the use of it in mapping and interpretation, was a major factor. This, along with its ability to control depth and speed at the same time, left no doubt in my mind as to the results I'd have in catching fish.

Let's map a structure (bar) in a lake, and at the same time show the use, and importance of "markers".

Usually when mapping the **shallows**, it is not necessary to throw out markers except when marking a weed-line or brushline. The shoreline will contain objects that are close enough to give location, such as an extrusion in the shoreline, tree, house, etc., however, at times, the shallows may extend so far into the lake that markers are needed. These can be tossed out as the crown of the bar or structure is worked with the smaller lures. Note all features in the shallows.

It is when you get to the deeper sections of structure

After you get on the water

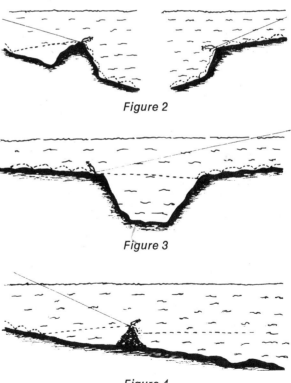

Figure 2

Figure 3

Figure 4

MAPPING AND INTERPRETATION   43

that markers become important. This is normally farther away from shore, and you need to have additional reference points for establishing breaks, breaklines, drop-offs, or the "contact" points on structures.

Noting Figure 5. Trolling pass #1, in the deeper section, will establish that a bar exists. You drop a marker. This first marker can't be thrown back to where the lure made contact with the bar, and at this point there is no need to place it exactly where the lure came over the structure.

placed at the last breakline or slightly back from the breakline so it will be out of the way for subsequent trolling and casting.

Before any marker is picked up, you must be sure that you know what the structure looks like. For future reference, and to fully implant it in your mind, you should put it down in black and white—draw a map. Before picking up the final marker you must establish your sight bearings.

To establish sight bearings, note the sketch. If you

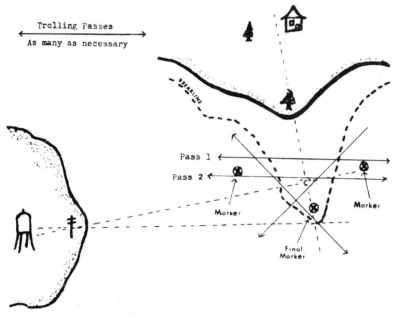

Figure 5

Trolling pass #2. As soon as the lure makes contact with the bar, you again throw a marker.

You now have the structure positioned between these two markers. A quick glance toward the shoreline will further note its position.

Subsequent trolling passes (and markers—if needed) will allow you to throw the final marker. You must establish the exact crown of the bar, and how far out it extends, all positions of features such as breaklines and drop-offs should be noted in relationship to the markers.

With these things firmly established in your mind, you now place the final marker. This final marker should be

line up the tree on the shoreline to a position slightly left of the house, the line of sight will fix the position of the drop-off in this direction. It also fixes the casting position "C" of the boat.

Now you must establish the position of the drop-off and the casting position from another direction. You should establish the second sight bearing as near as possible to 90 degrees (right angle) to the first sight bearing.

To select two objects to line up for a sight bearing, remember that the farther apart they are, the more accuracy you will have in your position on the structure.

On the shoreline to the west—if you line up the telegraph pole with the center of the water tank, you have a line of sight that positions the drop-off in this direction.

Where the two sight lines cross is the exact position of the drop-off.

If you move the telegraph pole until it lines up with the edge of the tank on the left side, you have a line for the casting position.

In future fishing trips to this area, all you have to do to be in the correct trolling or casting position is to **proceed along one of these sight bearings, until the other bearing lines up.**

Most important of all in the mapping and fishing process, is for the Spoonplugger to RECORD what he finds.

The drawings and markings on your first structure map may not be complete and in correct detail. You may find that there will be slight changes to be made on every trip. These changes may be something you missed, such as a small detail or break, or it could be a depth factor. Even a slight direction and distance change will have to be made. This will call for an additional change in your trolling and casting patterns, and your shoreline sightings will possibly be altered.

A proper record of structure will not only tell you where it's located and what some of its particular features are, but most important is that in making this record you increased your knowledge about proper interpretation. This is the important factor in your fishing know-how and growth. THIS IS THE TEACHER THAT YOU CARRY WITH YOU.

You may ask, "Do I have to have **exact** depths, distances, and scale when preparing structure maps?"

The answer is NO.

The important thing in mapping and recording the findings, is to show LOCATION, SHAPE AND DETAILS. Having **exact** depths, or **exact** measurements in feet, of the different dimensions of a structure is not necessary. It is not likely you would gain any knowledge, or that it would help you to present lures correctly, if you had exact measurements.

If exact measurements are desired, there are several methods which could be used to get them; the use of contour maps prepared by engineers, depth sounders to secure depth readings, and even a tape to measure the distances.

Having everything to exact scale isn't important. In preparing your detailed structure maps, you would be using a certain section of the shoreline as a reference point. You would be using a certain object on the shoreline as a reference in determining location of the structure. With very little effort you will relate these things and a satisfactory SCALE will fall into place.

After all, the purpose of the map is to allow YOU to know where it is, how it is shaped, how far out it runs, how trolling passes are to be made, what size lures to use to reach certain sections, and where to position boat for casting, etc. What do you care if your map does not give a true picture of actual measurements.

The same thing applies in your shoreline sightings for locating certain areas on structure, trolling paths, or casting positions.

You might ask, "Why am I told to keep checking the shallows, especially since I know they will not contain big fish in quantity, and particularly after I learn where the deep structures are located?"

There are two main reasons why you are advised to keep checking the shallows:

1—Because fish are there part of the time. Even though you normally expect small fish, these fish can be 'indicators'. They can indicate the area is productive. In fishing strange waters, one of the easiest and fastest ways to find potentially productive water is to troll the shorelines. Small fish caught along the shoreline also indicates movement. Several small fish picked up in succession is indicative that movement is occurring, and that the larger fish are at a reachable depth on structure. Never assume that fish are at a particular depth, break or breakline—you could miss them, they could be at a deeper or shallower one. But by starting in the shallows and working out, there is no guesswork.

2—In interpreting bottom features in a body of water, one of the key observations is the shoreline, and what is found in the shallows. The first 8–10 feet of water will tell you a lot about what to expect in the way of bottom conditions.

By working the shallows repeatedly, you begin to relate the features observed to things found below this depth, and, at the same time, relate it to fish caught. Pretty soon, just a brief observation will tell you the fishing possibilities of an area. You may get the relationship sooner than others. But, even those who are not quite so observant will, in time, subconsciously relate shoreline and shallow water features to good productive structure.

* * * * * *

"You might say, the lake I fish has very tall weeds. The depth at the weedline is 14 feet, and the weeds come completely to the top of the water. We are not allowed to motor troll, and I have been unable to find a contour map of this lake. I also do not own a depth meter. My question is, how do I go about mapping the lake? In fact, how would I fish the structures once they are found?"

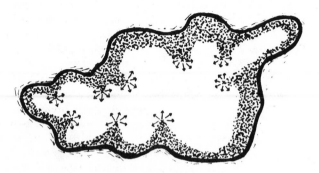

Figure 6

You can get the answers to both questions at the same time. Let the weedline be your guide. Locate the extrusions in the weedline, such as shown in Figure 6. Place your boat at the edge of the weeds, and 'fan cast' the area out from the point in the weeds. If any productive structure exists it should be in these areas. Note carefully the depths. **How long it takes the lure to sink, will give you the depths.** I have already discussed how to fish it correctly.

You might ask yourself, "Can a weedline tell me anything about the structure, or the bottom make-up of a particular lake?"

I have already discussed, and stated, that the weedline will tell you lots about the water color, type of bottoms present, and how it can indicate just how easy or tough the fishing will be. But, it can go further, and indicate just what TYPE of structure is present.

Figures 7 and 8 are top views of the same lake. Figure 7 shows the WEEDLINES in the lake. Figure 8 shows the interpretation of structure that I made. Probably your interpretation will be different, and in fact when the truth is known—both of us may not be right. BUT, neither of us would be far off, and this type interpretation will surely put us on the best spots. After all, our working of the best potential spots is important—if we expect consistent catches.

Your analysis of a weed condition in a lake, is just as important to your future **growth as a fisherman** (Knowledge), as any other phase of Spoonplugging.

❋   ❋   ❋   ❋   ❋   ❋

Let's say Figure 9 is a structure (bar) that you have just mapped. You have correctly, and wisely, left out all contour lines, and only show the one **breakline.** I take for granted there were no other breaklines on this structure, for if there had been, I am sure you would have put them in.

As you look at this big structure—the long crooked breakline, the 'fingers', and the many depths involved—you realize that you must now **INTERPRET** the structure.

Finger "A" has a three foot break. The bottom off this finger is rather flat—a long, sloping bottom. It appears to be too far from the deep water. The break is rather shallow for good migration.

Finger "B" appears closer to deep water. It has a three foot break, and it breaks deeper—at 10 feet. The

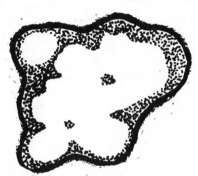

Figure 7

Figure 8

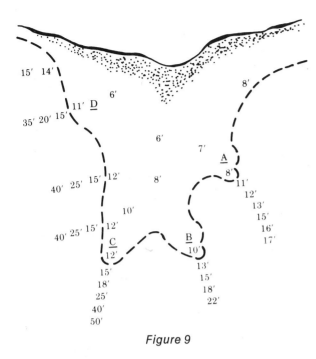

Figure 9

bottom is rather flat, but somewhat better than finger "A".

Finger "C" has a three foot break, and it occurs at a greater depth. The bottom goes off rapidly into deep water after the breakline.

Finger "D" is not well defined. In observing the total left side of the structure there appears to be a breakline all down the side, which drops off into deep water. A channel, or deep hole, is indicated on this side of the bar. Since there is no **break** SHOWN on the breakline you would say the fish would not make contact with the side of the bar.

Finger "C" would be the best choice. It would provide the most likely contact point at the very tip of the finger.

From what is shown, your interpretation that Finger "C" would be the migration route of the fish, would be correct. BUT, there is one area on the greater structure that would require more study. This is the sharp breakline into deep water on the side of Finger "C".

You must use lures to fully check all the small details along this breakline. On certain weather and water conditions, the fish may use the side as a contact point to

the structure. This would be especially so; from a SEASONAL point of view.

CONTOUR MAPS

Many fishermen are not aware that a contour map can provide **valuable** fishing information. To many, these maps are just a bunch of lines; to others, the lines have a little more meaning in that they show something about water depth; and, some few fishermen may occasionally check one for some specific information such as an underwater island. But, for the vast majority of fishermen these maps play no part in their fishing, or at the most a very limited part.

Contour maps are worthy of far more than a quick glance! There is a great deal to be gained from these maps, provided they are studied and **interpreted** correctly. Most bodies of water have some type of contour map available. These maps may not show the small details that are important to the fish, and to the fisherman, but they will, in most cases, show the larger picture. And from this the fisherman is able to pinpoint the areas for a more detailed study.

A contour map can be of tremendous help in eliminating most of the lake **before** you get on the water! Many lakes have good fishing areas, or productive water, in only a **fraction** of the total area of water available. So, in addition to providing useful information they can be a time-saver as well. No time need be **wasted** in areas that will **not** produce fish.

Why then are contour maps not being utilized fully by fishermen and the information they provide put to use?

I find that the average fisherman, first of all, **does not know how** to read the map correctly; and, secondly, he does not know how to **interpret** it! This fact is borne out by the large number of maps that are sent to me to be marked. This lack of knowledge is certainly understandable, for a great many do not understand fully the basic habits and movements of fish, and how the lake or reservoir bottom conditions affect him.

To show what information is available in a contour map and how this information can be used to good advantage, let's take as an example a typical map, and from it extract and digest the information it provides. But, in order for you to understand more fully how the results are arrived at, a review of basics, plus additional tips, or information, is called for.

(1) The home of fish is deep water, the deepest water in the area.

Anytime a fish is caught, it must be remembered that this fish **originated** from the deepest water in the area. This could be a deep hole in the center of the lake, or it could be a deep channel in the area. The immediate reaction to a strike or a fish should be, "**How** did this fish get here? **What** lead him here? **What route** did he take in arriving at this particular spot?"

(2) Fish use bottom STRUCTURE to arrive at a particular spot. The most common structure that fish use is a BAR; a ridgelike formation that extends out from the shallows into deep water. The structure must EXTEND ALL THE WAY TO DEEP WATER! Fish must be able to see the route they are to take IMMEDIATELY upon leaving deep water, and the route must be marked by visual SIGN POSTS (breaks) for the movements, or migrations, from deep water to shallow, or vice versa.

(3) **In order to fully "read" a contour map,** there is one feature that you must be aware of, as it is of great importance in arriving at whether or not a structure is worth working, and to pinpoint to some degree, the CONTACT POINT (or the NEAR contact point) of the fish as they begin migration.

This particular feature is a BREAKLINE; that is, a position on structure where there is a rather **sudden increase** in depth.

Normally, in reading a map this feature is overlooked, and unless searched for and determined, you have no way of knowing which is the BEST structure to work, or if the structure is very large which area of it should be worked.

In fact, a practical interpretation of bottom structure is not possible without noting this feature.

If there is any question in your mind as to what exactly is a breakline, and how it relates to interpreting a contour map, go back and re-study, "Breaks and Breaklines."

In studying a contour map, you may have no trouble finding the breaklines, but you may have some difficulty in determining the area, or section, **where fish first make contact with the structure, or breakline.**

Let us view a few sketches that may clear this up.

Figure 10 is a cross-sectional view of a structure with the breakline shown.

Figure 11 is a top view of the same section. Note that I have drawn in all the 5 foot contour lines. In this case, the contour lines do not run around the structure in a uniform manner, and they form a breakline at only one spot. In this case, this area could, and should, be called a "break" instead of a breakline. In most bodies of water

the breakline is not located around the entire structure, but is located on only a portion or "spot" of the main structure as shown. In this instance, the breakline is more accurately referred to as a "break." Figure 11 would be described as a 10 foot "break" occurring at the 10 foot depth.

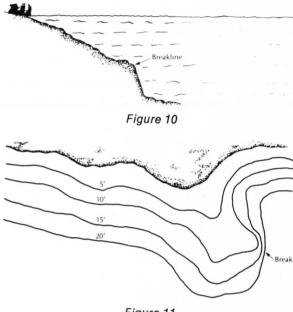

Figure 10

Figure 11

When studying an average contour map in an effort to determine: (1) where your efforts should be concentrated; (2) the worth of an area; (3) the location of the contact point, **the only clue that you will have is given by the breaklines.** The breaklines **determine** if these conditions are present.

When the breakline occurs at only one spot (break), such as in Figure 12, you consider **this** the contact point.

However, on a LONG breakline (where no break is shown) you will have to check the breakline thoroughly to determine the contact point. In this instance, the breakline contact point would be at breaks in the form of a rock, an eroded spot, a hump, stump, weeds, bushes, sunken objects and so on.

There are three main ingredients that an average contour map gives which serve to show you the fishable spots. They are:

(1) Deep holes or channels.

(2) Structures, such as bars and underwater humps (islands).

(3) Breaklines.

No contour map will show the small details on structure, such as any small projections, eroded spots, rocks, stumps, small humps, dips, logs and so on. **These are the details you must determine by actually working the area!** But, most maps will show the main features listed.

In any **interpretation** of structures shown, you should keep a few things in mind when considering depth. Do not be too deeply concerned about HOW deep the **deepest** water is. I personally prefer that the depth be at least 35 feet, and deeper if possible. In many bodies of water this much depth is not available. In this case, the deepest water whatever it is, is the home area.

You may become confused about water depth. When mention is made of the 30–35 foot depth being an important depth, you react by pointing out that your lake has 80 or 100 feet of water. I do not care how much water is BELOW the 30–35 foot depth. However deep your water may be, you assume that the deep water sanctuary of fish is around this 30–35 foot depth, until proven otherwise. At times, under certain weather conditions, the fish will be down to the bottom of that 100 foot lake. But, as conditions become more normal, the fish move back to the 30–35 foot zone. It is this position that you must visualize as the STARTING point of fish movement, and subsequent migration.

In observing the breaklines on contour maps, you should observe all breaklines that occur shallower than 30–35 feet (except in the case of Muskie—then you have to note those from 50–55 feet).

The 10 foot depth (Figure 11) is rather shallow, and

only in exceptionally good migrations will a school of lunker fish move up to this breakline. This type of migration does not happen very often. Any breakline deeper than 10 feet becomes more important, especially those from 12–20 feet. The deeper breaklines in this range will receive more frequent migrations than those with shallower depths. But, the shallower breaklines will be more easily identified and more easily worked, as fishing will not be quite so EXACT as those in deep water, and usually the fish are more active.

If it were possible to pick out an ideal breakline it would have to be at around 14–17 feet (Fig. 74). This range gives good depth for lunker fish migration and, more importantly, you can work it easily—both casting or trolling.

With all of these various facts in mind let us look at a sample contour map. We will approach it as if you have never seen a map before. We will observe all features and then put an interpretation on what is shown.

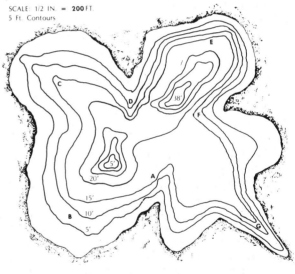

Figure 13

Figure 13 is a typical Contour Map.

The scale shows that ½ inch equals 200 feet.

Just what does this mean, and how can it serve any purpose?

First, every ½ inch of the map represents 200 actual feet of the lake. Either by actual measurement, or by an approximate guess, the distance and size of the structures

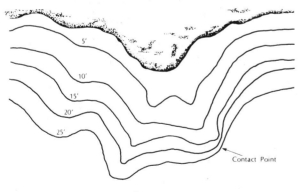

Figure 12

can be determined. The quantity of deep water can be determined, and the length of any particular breakline as well. All of these measurements will serve in determining the position of any structures in the lake, and how best to make presentation of lures or bait.

Five foot contour lines are mentioned. Just what does this mean?

You will note that a line is drawn all around the lake and is marked five (5) feet. This means that this line follows a path around the lake that is actually five feet deep. If you get inside this line, toward the shore, the depth of the water would be shallower. If you stepped outside this line, toward the center of the lake, the water would be deeper than five (5) feet. If you were ten feet tall and wanted to walk around this lake with just the top of your head sticking out, you would have to follow the path of the line marked ten (10) feet. If you did **not** take this path, your head would be either sticking out of the water or you would go out of sight!

Many maps will not be marked with the footage shown on the lines. Instead, the map will show only at the bottom, or over in one corner, that the lines are five foot contour lines. In this case, you must carefully **count off** the lines to a certain section to determine just how deep this section might be.

With the information given as to contour depth, you can now determine the water depths of this particular section and the deepest water in the area noted. A picture of the area now begins to emerge.

At the section marked "B"—This is a shallow, flat sloping bottom; the depth does not drop off very fast. Contrast this with the section marked "E" where the bottom falls off fast, sharply creating deep water very close to shore.

The section marked "C" is not a bar, but a washed out gully.

The section marked "G" (right hand, bottom) is a deep cove, or bay, with steep banks.

The section at "D" is a nice bar, or ridgelike structure, that runs out for some distance into the lake, toward deep water. This bar runs rather constant until it reaches the fifteen (15) foot depth, then it rapidly drops off to twenty (20) feet on the end and on both sides. You will note that on the right side of this bar (facing it) is a short "finger" on the twenty (20) foot contour line that extends out toward the twenty-five (25) foot contour line of the thirty-eight (38) foot hole. Keep this particular spot in mind, as later on we will call attention to this particular feature.

Structure "A" runs out nicely, but note the area just in front of the fifteen (15) foot depth. Here is a great big flat area that runs most of the way across the body of water. On the left side the five (5) foot contour has a slight "break" down to the ten (10) foot contour. Then farther out, on the ten (10) foot contour, another "break" occurs to the fifteen (15) foot contour. You could call these two 5 foot "breaks" a breakline; but, in a situation such as this it is preferable to refer to them as a "break" since there is not a continuous break along the whole area, but only a sharp break at one particular place on the contour. If the break had extended for some distance, such as in section marked "D", it would be referred to as a break**line.**

Out from the small "breaks" on the structure marked "A", the bottom flattens out until it reaches the twenty (20) foot contour, and this represents the deepest water in the entire left end of the lake. It is assumed that you have already observed that the section marked five (5) feet is not a deep hole, but a hump or underwater island. (On most maps the top of humps will be marked with the depth.)

Section "F" is another bar. It is a better structure than "A", because the twenty (20) foot depth water swings in fairly close and, subsequently, drops off into the thirty-eight (38) foot hole.

In studying a contour map remember that if the contour lines run far apart, this is more of a flat sloping area; where these lines swing in close, there is a sharp increase in depth. If the two lines come close together for quite a distance, this would be called a breakline. If the two lines come close to each other at a point or spot, you would refer to this spot as a "break". It is in these areas that you place emphasis when reading a map. These are the areas where fish will be found.

Each area should be studied carefully and the study should follow a pattern. First, find the deep holes or channels. Next, note any underwater islands. Then, search for bars or narrow running ridges that extend out **toward** the deep holes. Note if any large flat areas exist between the bars and deep water. Then, carefully study the contour lines to see where a "break" occurs, such as the "break" at "A" and on the finger at "D". In establishing this type of study pattern, all of the pertinent details will be determined.

We have now carefully studied the map and a good mental picture is in mind. The time has come to evaluate the information.

What does the map tell you?

If I were to evaluate the areas marked, it would be thus:

(A) A nice looking structure, but not likely to get a good migration. The flat area directly off the end of the bar (between the fifteen (15) foot and the twenty (20) foot contour) would hinder any migration toward this particular structure. Fish must be able to see their route and destination.

(B) A big flat. There is no indication that any "breaks" exist in this area, it would be **passed up** as a fishing area.

(C) This is more or less a flat area which has a slight depression caused by washing or erosion. There is no break**line** any where in the area, so, again, this area would be eliminated.

(D) This is the best structure in the area. It has a nice "break" on the end and sides, and in addition has a "finger" in the direction of the deepest water (home of the fish). This "finger" should be the first contact point of the fish!

(E) Section "E" is a steep, deep area. This particular section could be important under certain conditions and during certain parts of the season (colder). But, during most of the season (warmer) this area would be passed by.

(F) Structure "F" would be the second choice as a productive structure. The contour lines do not show any particular "break" that would give a clue as to its worth, but upon inspection certain "breaks" could exist that would make it a better structure than "D". "F" was given second choice from a study only of the contour map. Though no "breaks" show on the map, there is a good possibility that some exist. Thus it's always wise to **check the structures that show possibilities.** In so doing, you get the "big" picture.

(G) Here again, this area may be of importance during short periods of the season (colder), but in the overall picture, this type of area would not be of great importance.

Any underwater hump, or island, is always important structure. Most of them have some access to deep water.

In looking at the hump on the sketch, it could have possibilities. The fish could move up through the 20–25 foot section off point "D" and, in turn, arrive at the top of the hump. If the fish took this route, it would be entirely due to the small "breaks" found in the twenty (20) foot section. If this rather large, flatter area did not contain any "breaks", you would draw a blank on this hump. This could be determined by checking out the area.

In Section "D", reference was made to a short "finger" found on the twenty (20) foot contour line that extends out toward the twenty-five (25) foot contour line, and it was noted that special attention would be called to this particular feature.

Quite often, a structure will have not one "finger" but several, such as shown in Figure 12. Your job is to recognize which one of the fingers would best produce. The **key** to determining this is to find the one with **the sharpest break to deeper water!**

As fishermen, you should always be looking for **the contact point** on a breakline in the form of a "break," as illustrated. In studying contour maps, this is one of the prime features to look for.

As you can see, quite a bit of useful information can be determined by studying a contour map. But, in order to get this information, it is essential to learn exactly what contour lines mean. You must be able to **interpret** what you find, or it is of little value.

Every good fisherman has a map of the water he fishes. Some have the map on paper, some have it in their heads . . . but all have a map. If you are trying to fish your waters without buying or making yourself an accurate map, you are wasting a lot of valuable time. You could be wasting a whole season, you could even waste a lifetime of fishing!

FOOD FOR THOUGHT

The following figures and questions (76 thru 83) are not tests, nor quizzes. I am putting them in FOR YOUR STUDY. These cover only a part of the material studied, but they should indicate to you what parts should be reviewed. They could also indicate to you, if you need more expansion, and detail, on each section. Do not write and ask for answers. All the answers are in the book.

Figure 14 is a side view of a structure. It is quite long. I have enlarged the 'breaks' for your convenience.

1—At how many spots would you look for the fish?

2—Migration has not yet started. Where would you most likely find the fish?

3—Where would you most likely find the fish:
   a—1st day after a cold front? 3rd day?
   b—Temperature rises—starting to haze up and a few high cirrus clouds observed?
   c—Where on—a fair migration? A good migration? Excellent migration?

4—Where would the scatter point be?

5—If you hit a lot of small fish along the weedline—where and what would you do?

6—Would the color of the water make any difference in your answers?

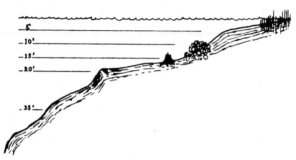

Figure 14

Figure 15

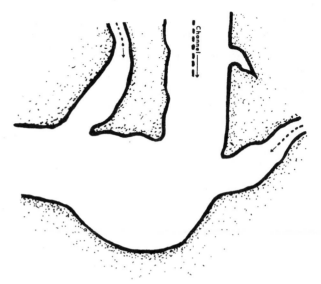

Figure 16

1—Pin-point them after migration.

2—What is the water color likely to be:
   a—If the weeds go to 7 feet? 15 feet?

3—This is a deep natural lake with very clear water. It has big bass and lunker northern. The time is 3 or 4 days after a cold front:
   a—How is the best way to fish this lake?

Figure 15 is a side view of a reservoir. It is quite large in area. Before this lake filled (wet weather reservoir), it was bulldozed all over to even out, or smooth, all bottoms. It has very clear water. Tall thick Moss covers all bottoms. The shallower water also contains tall weeds.

1—How would you fish it?

Figure 16 is a section of a reservoir (top view) which has some 'delta' conditions. It is located in rather hilly country.

1—Finish drawing in all channels.

2—Draw in bottom structure likely to exist in all areas.

3—Mark "X" on the spots likely to be productive.

Figure 17 is a top view of a natural lake with lots of weeds. This lake contains two schools of fish.

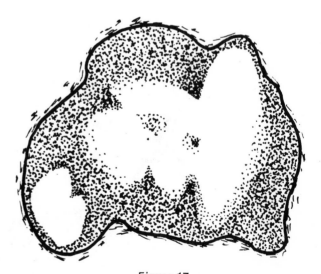

Figure 17

b—What type fish are likely to be caught in large numbers?

Figure 18 is a top view of Flatland reservoir. The area at the dam is over a mile wide.

1—Draw in the channels.
2—Where is the boat dock likely to be found?
3—When would you fish in the standing trees?
4—If the wind was coming out of the northwest, where would you fish?
5—If any clean bottom exists, where would it be found?
6—In working shorelines with the bottom covered with bushes, how would you work the lures on the troll?
7—In what areas of the lake should the edges of the channel be worked?
8—Indicate the best spots, and how would you work them?
9—Where are you likely to find the best water color?
10—Give 4 reasons why the dam areas, such as this, are good areas to fish.

Figure 19 is a top view of a large natural lake. The scale is ½ inch equals 400 feet.

1—How many migration routes are possible?
2—How many 'Home' areas are there?
3—In any home area, is there one particular structure you think fish would use above all others?
4—Which is the best structure in the lake?
5—Would any structure be difficult to find, if you did not have a depth sounder? How would you find it?
6—Would fish appear to come up on the side of any bar?
7—Which structure would casting be better than trolling? Why?
8—Can you see evidence of an ideal bar, which would contain no fish?
9—What would the color of the water be if the weeds went to 8 feet?
10—If this lake was located in an area that had frequent cold fronts, which would you consider fishing it for—bass or walleyes—?
a—If the weedline went to 17 feet?
b—How would you fish it?
11—If the water was clear, and there was a restriction of "no boats". Would it be easy to fish? If so, what structure would you work?
12—You cannot motor troll, how would you go about finding the best spots, without a contour map or a depth sounder?
13—If you had no restrictions on presentation, is there any particular structure you would concentrate on if you were fishing the 2nd or 3rd day after a cold front?
14—Draw a side view of all good structures.

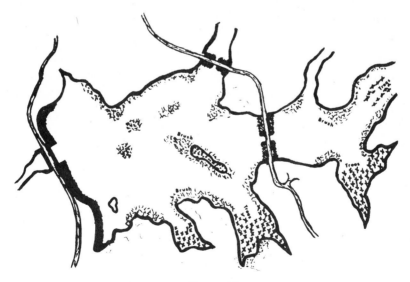

Figure 18

15—Would you consider this a good lake? Why? Under what conditions?

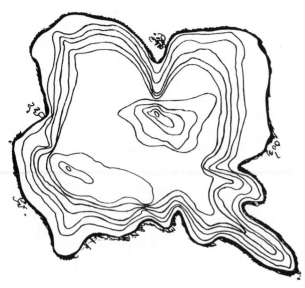

Figure 19

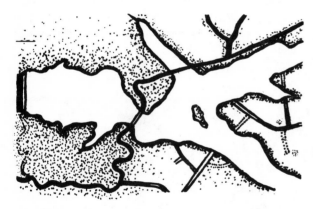

Figure 20

Figure 20 is a top view of a reservoir, **such as found on a ROAD MAP.** I have enlarged the roads for convenience of 'seeing'. They can tell you lots about the fishing potential of a lake.

1—Where are steep deep shorelines likely to exist?
2—If there are any underwater humps, in what section should they be located?

3—Where is the best water color likely to be found in the late summer?
4—List the visible structure to be worked.
5—What indication do you have about the region where the dam is built?
6—Where are you likely to find former farming lands?
7—Where would you start, or where would you launch your boat if you had a choice?
8—This is an old lake, the bottoms are clean and hard, would you pick this lake over one where the bottoms are covered with brush?
9—How would you go about 'finding' the fish in this type lake?
10—You are fishing this lake in early spring, you are working a **steep** shoreline. The predominate fish in the lake is smallmouth. You are moving along casting in **toward** the steep shore. You are using a light spincast reel, your lure is a small jig. In full detail, describe the cast and the complete retrieve.

Figure 21 is a top view of a natural lake. When you arrive at the water, your interpretations tell you that if fish are caught on this particular day, they will have to be caught in a period of about 14 minutes, at one particular spot.

1—What is the color of the water?
2—Are the weeds tall or short?
3—What weather conditions exist?
4—What method of lure presentation is used, casting or trolling?
5—What type, or types, of lures would you consider best?
6—Draw a detail of the **spot** and locate its approximate depth.

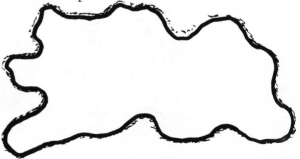

Figure 21

Earlier I stated, that a GOOD Spoonplugger could walk up to a lake, observe the features, ask a few questions, and come up with some answers, BEFORE he gets on the water. If you have been able to answer all "Food for Thought", (Figures 76 thru 83) to complete satisfaction, you are well on your way to becoming a good fisherman. This part, however, should show, you still have a long way to go, and that you can always get better in your interpretations.

Let me give you an example of what I mean by interpretation.

Recently, my wife and I were in Florida on business. While there, I had time to run by and fish a lake I had in some way missed. It was a very large lake, being several miles in diameter. I knew that it was a shallow lake, and when I got there I was informed that the deepest water was 9 to 10 feet in depth. I noted that the water for quite a distance from shore was covered with weeds and lily pads.

After asking a few questions, I told my wife that we would have to find a "break" or a spot that broke from 7 to 9 feet if we wanted to catch some fish. We found three such spots and each was working with big bass. We had a ball. To make it more satisfying we had the whole thing by ourselves, although there were lots of other boats and fishermen on the lake.

Probably you are wondering how I figured we had to find that particular spot. In the first place, I heard the man say 9–10 feet was the deepest water in the lake. The second thing he said was fishing hadn't been so good the last week or so. In the third place I had quickly noted all those other fishermen on the lake working the daylights out of the weeds and pads. I figured this had been going on for the last week or so which clearly indicated **the fish were not in the weeds or pads.** I noted also the weeds and pads cut off at 5–6 feet, and since the **bottom was flat with no "breaks" or structure beyond the weedline, the fish HAD to be in the deepest water.** I picked the 7–9 foot section as the weather conditions told me the fish **would not move very far.** This type of break would be large enough for me to see, and if there happened to be a deeper break it would be so close by I'd have no difficulty finding it.

It was easy pickings. (The spots are so far out in the lake I suppose the only ones who will ever pass over them will be the water skiers.)

During the preparation of this section, I have wondered what I could include that would "stick in your craw" and make you realize the importance of mapping and interpretation. **But of more importance,** would drive home the fact that the knowledge found in this book, is absolutely necessary, if you desire to become a good fisherman.

I have picked out one particular statement I have made—**MOST of the time MOST of the water contains no fish.**

Figure 22

In order for you to better understand the factors that contribute to **most of the water not being productive,** let's take a lake, and eliminate all the water that does not contain enough fish to warrant any time or effort. When viewing the amount of water in a lake or reservoir, you should view it from all directions. Not just the surface area, but all the water below. In other words, length, width and depth—all the water.

off at approximately 5 ft. (Good water color). Outside the weedline some bottoms are clean, while others are dirty. The predominant large game fish in the lake are Largemouth Bass, and Northern Pike.

Take a close look at Figure 22, and try to figure out where the good structure might be. Where would you start, or do your fishing? How would you go about fishing this lake?

Figure 23

Figure 22 is a aerial view of a well known lake in the midwest. I might add that the last time I heard, this lake was scheduled to be "reworked". Due to the "bitching" of the unknowledgable fishermen, about the lousy fishing, the "State" is going to pull it down, poison out, and restock. If this is done, most Spoonpluggers will pass it up as a fishing hole in this generation. If EVERYTHING goes perfectly right, it may someday have the amount of lunker fish it has today—**but I doubt it.** Too bad, the lake isn't stocked each year with small fish, and the fishermen taught how to catch them—**after they grow up.** I have often wondered which would be better for the "State"—drain, poison out, and restock; or educate the fishermen? I am sure the educational route would be cheaper, faster, and especially **more lasting.** For in just a few years the fishermen are "on their backs" again.

You will note the lake is quite large. I do not know how many acres or miles of shoreline it contains, but whatever it is, there's quite a lot of water down there. The maximum depth is around 35 ft. The weedline cuts

Figure 23 is the same view of this lake, but here, I have marked the areas that contain the fish. ("A" and "B"). Although big bass and northerns can be caught in either area, if you wanted to go after big bass in quantity, you would work section "A". If you wanted lunker northerns, you would concentrate in section "B".

Look at Figure 23, wouldn't you say the amount of water to be fished has been **reduced?**

Hold on, we're not thru yet. We gotta reduce the water that contains fish still further.

Figure 24 is a top view of section "A". The solid line represents the breaklines in this section where the fish will be found.

The overall size of this section isn't too big, and the areas that will produce fish **are still smaller.** You will note that the fish do not come to all parts of the breakline. Neither do they use all the "fingers" or projections.

Wait just a minute, we got a couple more steps to take. First, the fish will not be on these spots all the time. They do not move or migrate constantly or consistently. On a

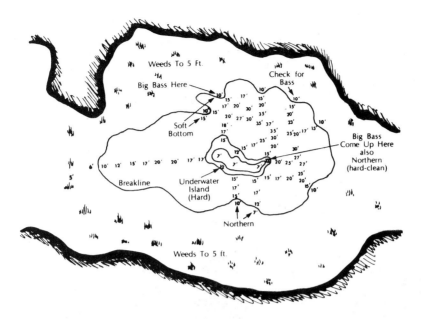

Figure 24
(Section "A")

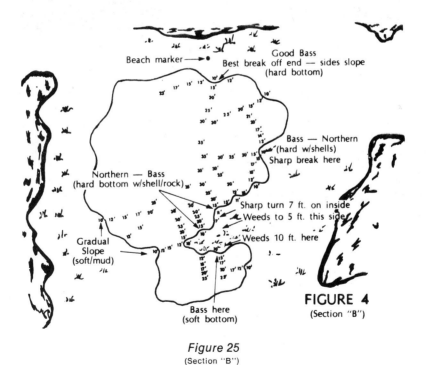

Figure 25
(Section "B")

FIGURE 4
(Section "B")

normal fishing day, you can't expect the fish to move to these areas more than one or two times—and for only a short period. Second, weather conditions in the area may be such, that days may pass before any quantity of fish move toward the spots.

Note very carefully all the depths—the breaklines, and the sections below. Study these depths, and see if you can figure out why the fish are caught on these particular spots (also in Figure 25).

Figure 25 is a top view of the larger section "B". Here again, not all the parts of the section produces. If you were to take the areas where fish can be caught in quality and quantity, and overlay them on the total lake (Figure 22) they would most likely appear as small dots.

By this time you should begin to see what I mean when I say, MOST of the time MOST of the water contains no fish. You should also begin to realize why you can't fish blindly, or haphazardly, and expect to "stumble" upon a fish. You should see if you do not understand the instincts and habits of the fish, and what part "structure" plays, MOST of the time, you will be fishing where they AIN'T.

Your reaction to the above might be, "He isn't talking about my fishing water, he is talking about one isolated instance in the Midwest."

You wanta bet I'm not talking about your fishing hole? This particular lake is rather a small body of water, when compared with most important fishing lakes and reservoirs. I would go further, and say, if you compared the productive areas for lunker fish in this lake, to the overall size, percentage wise, it has more productive water than your lake! Furthermore, this particular lake was easy to work out. I can't say the same thing about your lake.

All through the book, I have tried to impress upon you that the **deepest water in the area, was the home of the fish.** Here, I have tried to hammer home the fact, that **most of the water contains no fish.** Both are such basic fundamental fishing facts, that unless you grasp both of them fully, you will never be a successful fisherman! I'm not using the word "never" carelessly, I mean just that. The word is NEVER.

It is only **after** you accept and fully understand these two basic principles of fish behavior that you will be able to go about solving the problems of the waters you fish. Do they apply to your lake? You can bet your life, they apply to **ALL** lakes.

*   *   *   *   *   *

Mapping is the key to interpretation—
Interpretation is the key to knowledge—
Knowledge is the key to success—
Success is the key to satisfaction.

*   *   *   *   *   *

CHAPTER 3

Presentation of Spoonplugs

Buck Perry Reveals His Bass Fishing Secrets!

Many fishermen gain a degree of proficiency after many years of experience, and begin to feel the urge to create a lure of his own design. Subconsciously, he is looking for a lure that will perform magic, and secretly he thinks his brainchild will do just that. The proverbial path will then be beaten to his door, and the clamor of fellow fishermen for his product will give him untold riches.

I once heard a well known writer make the statement, "Boy, if I could design the perfect lure, I could retire tomorrow." He, too, harbored the desire to have a lure that when thrown in the water—no matter where— would cause the fish to rush with a frenzy to gobble it up.

Many years ago I had the desire to design a lure, but my reasons differed from those of my writing friend in that I had no thought of monetary value. Neither did I, for a minute, think that a lure could be designed that would catch fish without effort on the part of the fisherman. My reason for thinking of a new lure design was for the purpose of having a lure for my own **personal use** that would allow me to have some control over my fishing. The lures available could offer little more than action to a limited degree, and in a variety of colors.

I was considered a rather successful fisherman using the lures that were available, but I fished hard and for long hours to get my catches. Observations made, had convinced me that if a lure could be designed that would allow control of speed and depth—**at the same time**— then this, combined with color, action and size could make my desire for consistent catches a reality.

With this objective in mind, I turned to my tin snips, and from sheets of metal began the task of trying to create a lure that could be **trolled** or **cast.** It had to maintain depth, whatever speed, while free running or bottom bumping. Actions had to be built in that would vary according to the need of the speed being used; and so balanced that it would come to the top of the water when fouled. Most important of all, it had to WALK and TALK regardless of speed or bottom conditions (mapping, etc.).

I soon found that I had set for myself no small task. If I got speed, I lost depth; if I got depth, the action was gone, and so on and on.

After arriving at a model that proved satisfactory, I began making some for my own use. Later, friends were given samples, and when my friends became too numerous to supply, the idea of making lures to sell was born.

I am glad my desire to create a new lure was not born from the idea of getting rich. This dream would have been totally destroyed. Today, I am sure of one thing, if I had built the lure to sell I certainly wouldn't have made it look like it does. Many fishermen and writers refer to it as a shoe horn that has been stepped on by a horse.

I have never had the heart to tell my writer friend that his dream is "all wet". Dreams are to be fostered—not shattered. He will pass many happy hours contemplating his dream of fame and riches, never realizing the sad truth that fishing habits follow generation after generation in the same manner, and are not easily displaced; and that you can show a fisherman how to catch a bushel basket of fish, and he will only shake his head and say, "I don't believe it"—**and he helped catch the fish.**

The remark is often made that most other lure manufacturers come out with something new each year, so why haven't Spoonplugs been changed or updated, or replaced with some new design. Originally, Spoonplugs, as stated, were not designed to be sold. They were built for many reasons; the main one being that no such lures were available that allowed control of depth or speed to any great degree. There was a need for a lure that could do a specific job in casting and trolling; one which could be used in mapping to determine what the bottom of the lake looked like, and how it was made up. A lure that would allow fishing knowledge to be transferred to others. You can tell a fisherman how to fish properly, but without the tools to allow implementation, this knowledge is of little value.

Over the years the present lures have done their work superbly. There has never been any doubts that the original designs were correct, nor have I felt the design could be improved, or that another lure would do a more thorough job. Spoonplugs will catch anything that swims. But above all, they are teaching and disciplinary tools which enable catches to be made, which are the important things a lure must do.

That's why I ask the question, "Why should I change or build new lures? What would be the purpose? Gimmick sales? Every tackle box has more than it needs of these. Change, for sake of change? This doesn't always make a better product. I could design a dozen new lures a day—and they'd all catch fish—but so what? All Spoonplugger items, such as lures, rods, lines, etc., were designed especially for SPOONPLUGGING. They had to be, none existed. Every item was made to do a specific job—not to appeal to the fisherman.

If there are any who are critical of these specific tools, then so be it. It is unfortunate that a study of fishing must, at times, be associated with the sale of fishing tackle. But I feel that proper explanation as to how this has come about is quite sufficient. My rewards have been largely from those who write to say, "Thanks to you, my fishing has taken on a new meaning". Or from being able to help the many who write and wish so fervently to catch fish for a change. All I can say to the critic is, let the results speak for themselves.

I teach fishing. If proper equipment is used, I care not what the brand name might be.

After a quarter of a century, I have my doubts if you have ever heard of Spoonplugs. I further doubt if your local dealer has any in stock. I have no salesmen. I do no advertising, nor do I call on any dealers or jobbers. I attend no sport shows to display my 'creations'. My policy is, "take 'em, or leave 'em". It doesn't matter one iota to me. But, if you desire to try them, Buck's Baits, P.O. Box 66, Hickory, N.C. 28601, will be happy to serve you.

In this section on the Presentation of Spoonplugs we are going to see WHERE, WHEN, WHAT, WHY and HOW—"tools" should be used.

I can go to great lengths to explain what makes a fish tick, but in the final analysis your ability to become "expert" will require practice and experience. **By utilizing the BASIC procedures for the Presentation of Spoonplugs,** you will present lures correctly. And from the very beginning start catching fish in quantity and size, or both, as never dreamed of before. This gives the incentive to gain further knowledge and really become good at the game.

In some sections of this book necessity dictates repetition. It is not possible, in a study as comprehensive as fishing, for you to remember all the basic points. And since some of these points **are applicable in many areas, many will be repeated for clarity and for the purpose of tying together all information as closely as possible.**

These basic approaches to casting and trolling structures have been proven to work without a shadow of a doubt, and with tremendously satisfying results. But above all, these Basics are the MEANS by which YOU LEARN the important things for your FISHING KNOWLEDGE AND GROWTH.

Figure 1 shows perspective sizes, series numbers, weights, length, and running depth, of the first 5 sizes of the standard free-running, bottom bumping Spoonplugs. The number system may confuse you for a spell, but just keep in mind that you control **depth** by the size lure. That is; the smaller the lure the shallower it runs. The larger the lure, the deeper it runs. The 700 and 800 series (not shown) are larger lures. The 700 series is 4 inches long, and its trolling depth is 15–20 feet. The 800 series is 5 inches, running depth 20–25 feet.

The length of line being used in trolling will affect the depth at which lures run. For instance, if 60 to 80 feet of line is first let out additional line will allow the lure to run deeper.

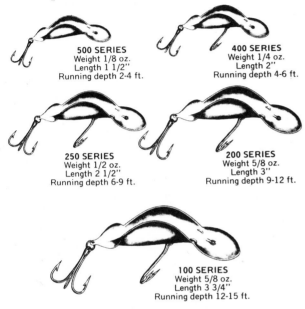

500 SERIES
Weight 1/8 oz.
Length 1 1/2''
Running depth 2-4 ft.

400 SERIES
Weight 1/4 oz.
Length 2''
Running depth 4-6 ft.

250 SERIES
Weight 1/2 oz.
Length 2 1/2''
Running depth 6-9 ft.

200 SERIES
Weight 5/8 oz.
Length 3''
Running depth 9-12 ft.

100 SERIES
Weight 5/8 oz.
Length 3 3/4''
Running depth 12-15 ft.

Figure 1

Let's set up some categories of line length:

1—Short line   10–20 yards
2—Medium line   30–40 yards
3—Long line   50–80 yards

When trolling shallow water, a shorter line length is normally desirable over a long line; depth control can be accomplished better with lure size rather than line length. When deeper sections are fished with the larger lures a long line is necessary, and in order.

Spoonplugs were designed with a limited depth range, this was desired so the lures would not vary their depth too much with a change in line length. This design allows the smaller, shallow working lures to hold their depth range with a **minimum of line length;** and the larger sizes, which call for a longer line length, would have their depth range limited to a **controllable line length.** In other words, the lures were designed to get their maximum depth range on a minimum of line length; additional line not adding any appreciable depth to the lures.

Spoonplug sizes and their running depth as per recommended line length is as follows:

500 Series	2 to 4 feet	Short to medium line length
400 Series	4 to 6 feet	Short to medium
250 Series	6 to 9 feet	Short to medium
200 Series	9 to 12 feet	Medium to long
100 Series	12 to 15 feet	Medium to long
700–800 Series	15 to 25 feet	Medium to extra long

It should again be noted that the diameter of the line will affect lure depth. The larger diameter will give a greater line drag which results in a depth loss. The above figures on depth were based on the smaller diameter lines (.019–.021 inch).

The medium line length (30–40 yards) is a good length to run on Spoonplugs. This length will give good control and depth. Before the 100 Series lure is removed, extra, or long line should be used to get the maximum depth of this lure. Any water shallower than this will have already been "strained" by the other lures on a medium line length.

Normal trolling will not scare fish. They may be more "skittish" in the early part of the season with its colder water, but as weather warms and water temperatures rise, the passing of a boat is sometimes an aid. Different line lengths would take care of these conditions if they should appear—longer lines in the early season, less as it warms.

In this light, let me emphasize the shorter line length in hot weather. During hot weather, many times the troller does not run through the lure sizes with a short enough line. This is especially true when working for smallmouth bass. At times the line should be no more than 5 to 10 yards behind the boat; in or beside the "boil" of the motor. A good rule to follow under hot weather conditions is to go through the lure sizes with a short line before using the recommended medium lengths. In areas where shad are plentiful, the correct line length under these hot conditions, could be the distance the shad are observed breaking in the wake of the motor.

I would suggest at this point you go back to "Presentation of Lures" and "Tools," and review what I said concerning trolling lines—"how to control lines," "how to sit in the boat," etc.

Figure 2 is a cross section view showing where different size Spoonplugs are used in fishing the various sections or depths, of water.

ZONE A (shallows). You will note that the 500, 400, and 250 Series are used to test the shallows. The larger lures, are used when testing the deeper water area (Zone B). This does not mean the larger lures will not be used in the shallows. When casting the different types of shoreline waters, the size lure necessary to maintain Depth control must be used. Again, often the fish will be found when trolling a small lure. This does not mean you have to go back and cast with the same lure size. Pick out one big, or heavy enough to do a good job. But when trolling, you can visualize Figure 2 as being the areas in which to troll the different sizes.

Many fishermen consider the Spoonplug unique due to the fact it will maintain its depth regardless of speed **on the troll.** Most are amazed at how it will go down and walk bottom, even over rough bottom conditions. They are flabbergasted at its ability to attract a strike when other lures fail.

Some consider its greatest asset is its performance **on the cast.** It will allow the speeds necessary to cover all ranges. It comes to the surface in a hurry when fouled, but when it comes to speed and depth control, on the cast to deep water, there is no substitute. **There is no other lure which will give bottom control as well.** To a great many, the control on the cast over-shadows the control on the troll—including myself.

After hard use the Spoonplug may need minor adjustments to keep it down or to make it run true at any speed. If the lure runs **to the right,** place a pointed object, such as a knife blade, beside the metal loop where the ring is attached. Bend this loop **very slightly to the left.** Do the opposite if the lure tends to run to the left. Do not kill the action by using too large a snap or snap swivel. A No. 2 snap is best. If you "have" to have a swivel, use no larger than a No. 10. Most of the time a swivel is just excess baggage. Retie the snap after a hard pull, and periodically check your line for nicks or frayed spots.

Some basic rules for handling rods in casting and trolling would include:

1—Do not point rod toward the line (line of retrieve).
2—Let the lure work against the rod tip.
3—Keep the rod tip **low** most of the time.
4—Palm the reel. Do not hold it in a "pistol" grip.

To get into the subject of presentation, we will proceed as if you and I are on a fishing trip to a lake neither of us has fished before. **On this trip I want to set up a procedure for you to follow on every fishing trip on every lake.** There must be no doubts in your mind about the things you are going to do, or the way you are going to do them. The purpose is to find out everything about this water, as soon as possible, and as successfully as possible. **This trip is to set the pattern for THE BASIC PRESENTATION of lures, both casting and trolling.**

Depth is the one thing that we must CONTROL by some means. The only effective way I know to do this is by letting lures do it. We will use the different size Spoonplugs. This is the tool that is going to enable us to fish from the shallowest water to as deep as we can go; and

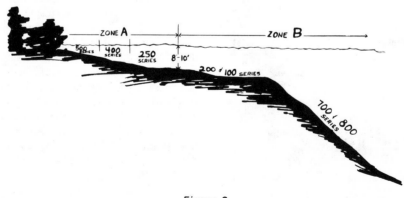

Figure 2

somewhere—in the shallow water—in the deep water—or somewhere in between, we are going to find the fish. If we don't find them on the first try—we'll try again.

In working out a lake to determine where the fish are, I like to begin by trolling with a motor. As stated before, trolling has many advantages. It allows a greater portion of water to be covered, and the water can be checked faster. It allows for a greater speed variance, and in many instances, will locate and catch fish where it would be impossible to do it by any other means.

Since most casting outfits are no good for trolling, we will use a short, stiff rod, rigged with a line that is not only heavy and stiff, but it is metered so we know how much line we have out at all times. With a rig such as this we will be aware of what is going on at the other end of your line. We will use a NO-BO trolling line, a T-45 trolling rod and a 101 Spoonplugger reel.

If you have lures and gear that will do the job, that's fine, you won't have to use mine.

Figure 3 is a top view of the lake we have decided to fish. What should we do first? How do we start? How do we use the lures?

When fishing a strange lake there is one thing I try to find out before leaving the dock. That is, where are the "hot" spots located? Knowing this will greatly expedite our work. The dock owner tells us the northern end is where a lot of fish are caught from time to time. This is good news to us, for we know that somewhere in this area is potentially good water. We will waste no time in getting to that end of the lake.

In looking at the north shoreline (Figure 3), it appears to be about a mile long. We were not told where on this north end to fish, or where the fish were caught. Therefore **every lure** we use for testing the shallows **will be kept on until the TOTAL length of this north end has been covered.**

The first Spoonplug we will use will be the small, 500 series. Figure 4 shows the path and position of this first lure size (as well as the other two series we will use in checking the shallows).

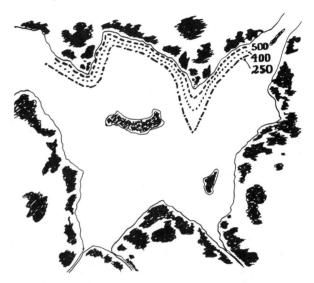

Figure 4

We will let out 60 to 90 feet of line. This can be judged accurately because we are using metered, No-Bo line which has different color markings every 30 feet. We just let out 2 or 3 colors. The 500 series Spoonplug has a depth range of two to four feet. The shorter line length will give the minimum depth, and the longer length maximum depth. We could run longer line lengths, but normally, the short to medium lengths will be sufficient during our trolling of all lures in the shallow zone.

When you first see this smallest Spoonplug, your reaction might be, "What are we fishing for—minnows?" Although this Spoonplug is small, it does a man-sized job in working the depth of water for which it was designed. It does catch a lot of smaller fish, but when the large fish are in the zone—it catches them also. Too

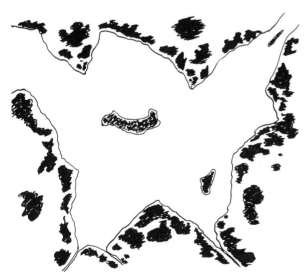

Figure 3

many fishermen will not run this 'deadliest' of lures. In lots of areas and types of waters, this lure used on the troll, is all that is needed to obtain consistent catches.

We will start our troll with enough speed to give the lure some action—a tight wiggle. At intervals we will increase the speed. Before the lure is let back, take a gander at it to see if it is running correctly. The 30 to 40 yards will not be so far, that you can't feel every little wiggle. At intervals, a slight pull with the rod, will enhance the "feel". If the 'feel' is just a steady pull, with no wiggle, the lure has become fouled. Normally all it takes to get it cleared, and running again, is a quick jerk with the rod. Some types of grasses and weeds, will require several quick hard jerks to clear. Too many fishermen spend half their time reeling in, to pick some small debris from the lure. When working areas with lots of weeds, the rod is used to RIP the lures through the weeds, if you come too close.

This rod action, to keep lures clean and running correctly, will be utilized on ALL sizes of lures, in ALL depths of water. I might add, though, it is oftentimes hard to clear a deep running lure with rod action. In this case, hold a steady pull, and as soon as the lure comes to the top, then apply the rod action—quick hard jerks. As soon as the Spoonplug is clean, down she goes, and she stays there until fouled again—regardless of speed.

In determining the Speed factor, remember the hand rule is according to temperature. The colder it is, the slower the speed. The hotter it is the faster it is. I never have any trouble getting fishermen to go slow enough. It's the fast speeds that give trouble. When working shallows in warm water, the correct speed TO START WITH, is about the time you begin to think the fish can't catch it. Then increase it.

Whatever speed is being used at the time, **when the lure hits bottom, reduce speed** so the lure will walk—not plow. Then **when it comes off running free again, increase throttle.** This means, you are changing the throttle rather constantly when working the shallow water. In deeper water, when working bottom, the throttle is used less often, but even here, the best speed must be found.

The worst mistake the troller makes is not keeping his lures in position. Each size lure MUST run in its proper place. What is the proper place? The bottom will be the guide. If the lure runs 4 feet deep—try to keep it in water 4 feet deep. If it runs 8 feet deep on the troll, keep it in water 8 feet deep, etc.

This north shore, as well as other lakes, will have sections where the bottom slopes off gradually with a lot of shallow water, while other sections will have steep banks where the bottom drops off rapidly with deep water close to shore. Our trolling must be done so as to keep each size lure in its proper position, even though the bottom contour may be changing constantly.

In the section where the bottom slopes off gradually, we want to get our 500 lure as close to shore as possible, so it will be bumping bottom at times. If this area contains bushes, or has standing trees, we will get our lures back among them, if at all possible.

In the section which has the steep banks, and the bottom drops off rapidly, we will run this lure "Jam-Up" against the bank, or skipping along the rocks, or whatever the bottom might be. In some waters the shallows contain weeds. When this occurs we will get the lures as close to the weeds as possible, and maneuver the boat so we **are not continually fouled.** If we are continually fouled, we are not following the contour of the weedline, or we are in too close. However, if we are never fouled, we are possibly too far away. As stated, the lure can be cleaned by a quick jerk of the stiff rod and hard line. This cannot be done if a limber rod and stretchy line is used.

After the entire length of the shoreline has been covered with the 500 series, and no strikes resulted, we now change to the next size lure. It is important to use the different sizes in sequence, as they will allow the water to be "strained" thoroughly, leaving no section or control unchecked.

The next size lure we will use will be the 400 series. This runs at a depth of 4 to 6 feet. We will fish this lure along the **SAME shoreline.** It would be rather foolish to check another shoreline with another depth. Again, we must keep this lure in its proper position as stated before; this is done by maneuvering the boat. To maneuver the boat, we first move in toward shore until the lure starts bumping bottom. (When working in some lakes the lure will come in contact with weeds instead of bottom.) When this happens, **slowly** head the boat towards deeper water. Then, as the lure starts running free, slowly head back toward shore until the lure starts bumping again. By continually moving the boat in this manner, the lures will always be in position and the contours of the bottom will be followed, regardless of shape.

The degree of correction of the boat is so slight, that the lure is never more than a few degrees from directly behind the boat. What would happen if you moved your boat until the lure started bumping, and you continued to let it bump without ever turning toward deeper water? If you did this, you could come into a large flat area; and find yourself going out across the flat getting farther and farther away from fishable water.

Now let's suppose you slowly maneuver the boat away from the shallows and the lure starts running free. If you did not begin to correct your heading, and slowly start back toward the shallows, you could find yourself out over 50 feet of water, and the lure would be completely out of position.

It is not necessary to bump bottom at all times with the first few sizes of Spoonplugs. When fish are in the shallows they will take a free swimming lure. It is necessary, though, to hit something once in awhile, be it weeds or bottom, to assure yourself your lures are in position and not out over deep water. This way your lure is free running at times and bumping at times. But, you also must bump the bottom to make the fish take. At times they may refuse a free running lure, but strike a bottom bumping lure savagely. I am usually surprised when a bass takes a free-swimming lure.

In teaching trolling, one of the main problems is that the fisherman OVER-CONTROLS. He does not correct SLOWLY, but hastily moves the boat putting it completely out of position. When the lure makes contact or comes off running free, the boat is so far out of position that a lot of water has been missed. It takes time to get the lure back behind the boat again. If you use a depth sounder in the shallows—which you shouldn't—the boat will be out of position most of the time, as well as your lures.

When maneuvering the boat in trolling, you have four things to accomplish: First, keep lures in position; Second, keep lures fishing at all times; Third, learn your waters—know the bottom contours and find the breaks, structure, etc.; Fourth, arrive at the fish. The above procedure will accomplish this.

After checking speeds and varying line lengths (10 yards—1 color) with the 400 series, and still no strikes, we will go to the 250 series. The 250 will run from 6 to 9 feet. We will fish this size like we did the others. It will be kept in position by maneuvering the boat as previously explained. Its position and path is also shown in Figure 4.

By the time we are into this third series you should begin to know something about the bottom make-up. By maneuvering the boat you should begin to see the shape of the area we are fishing.

If any fish are caught along this shoreline, on any of the three sizes, the immediate area would be checked thoroughly at that time by **casting** or **additional trolling** to determine if other fish are in the area. **Thoroughly** means depth, speeds, and colors. If weeds exist, and fish are caught along the weedline, it could mean fish are back in the weeds, and the weeds should be checked.

If you stop and cast any area in the shallows with Spoonplugs, **be sure your retrieve is FAST and STEADY.** This holds true when using or casting Spoonplugs in any free-swimming way. If you think the fish are sick or something, then use a lure that you have to retrieve slow. Don't poke around in the shallows with Spoonplugs. If you use them you must work them fast and steady—that's the only way.

Let us say we have covered the whole north shore (Figure 4), with three sizes of Spoonplugs and we haven't caught a single fish. What next?

First, let's look at what we've accomplished: From the "catching" standpoint it might seem like a wasted effort. This is not true. In trolling the three sizes, three things were accomplished.

1—We have eliminated all of the shallow water in the area. We caught no fish so we must assume the fish are not in the shallows at this time. Now we have only the "in-between" water and the "deep" water left.

2—We have found the types of structure in the area and the bottom conditions. Normally, the contour of the shore itself would indicate if any structure exists. But now our lures have given us the whole picture.

3—We have established the only migration route in the area—a long underwater bar. So now instead of fishing a mile or more of shoreline, we have come down to a narrow structure, or path, leading to deep water.

At this point we make a definite change in our lure presentation. From now on our main purpose is **to work bottom.** This is done by keeping the lures walking or bumping right on bottom. The fish will ignore a free-swimming lure—just watch it swim by. But, a bumping lure will cause every fish in the school to out-do each other trying to get at it. All of the controls become insignificant here in comparison to the walking or bumping of the lure on structure.

Figure 5 shows the point of land and the underwater bar upon which we will now concentrate our efforts. It also shows the series of Spoonplugs we will use.

We now go to the 200 series. We will walk or bump this lure on the structure we have found. In order to cover all the contours on this structure, we will make trolling passes in several directions across it. On each pass, as soon as the lure runs free, we will immediately turn the boat around and make another pass so the lure will be back on bottom. This size lure will reach 11 to 12 feet.

We must make enough passes to feel reasonably sure that as much of the structure as possible has been reached with the 200.

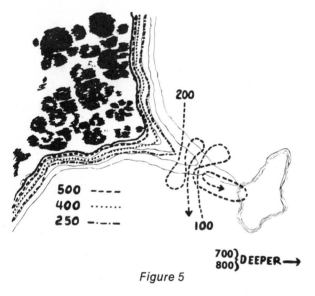

500   - - - -
400   . . . .
250   - · - · -
200
100
700}
800} DEEPER →

Figure 5

If the 200 does not produce a strike, the next move is to the 100 series Spoonplug. Now we can work deeper on structure as this lure will go to 14 or 15 feet. The 100 will be used exactly as we used the 200. Trolling passes will be made in several directions, and the lure will bump bottom as far out as possible on the structure.

When working this structure by trolling, maximum line can, and should be used. On the final passes, as much as eighty to ninety yards might be needed to allow the lures to reach maximum depth. If a small diameter line is used (.019″ or less), the depth range can be extended beyond the 14–15 feet.

As stated previously, we start running into difficulties at this depth in our controls. So now we have come to a point where we must assume the fish were caught, or not caught. If no fish were caught, it means the fish are deeper than we are fishing.

There are several possibilities open to us now. (1)— We can exercise patience for the fish to move up, or (2) —**Since we are rigged properly,** we can go to the 700 and 800 series, and go deeper to see if the fish can be located. These lures go deep, but handling them separate the men from the boys, and you would not try it if you were not rigged as we are. (3)—We can go to another section of the lake which shows, from looking at the shore, there might be other spots which could have good structure, and proceed to work out these areas by following exactly the same procedures. If we decide to move then we would return periodically to this known area and re-check it to determine if any movement has occurred. **On a normal fishing day we would repeat our trolling procedures many times to check and re-check both the shallows and the deep structures.**

If we decide to exercise patience and to stay with this structure until the fish move, our efforts would be concentrated as deep as we could effectively reach. This could, in most instances, be done effectively by casting.

Let's take the brighter side of the picture. Let's say we picked up a nice fish with the 100 or 200 series on our first trolling passes. It was caught in deep water, and this normally means a school. We want to immediately position our boat for casting.

At the time of the strike we quickly noted the position of the boat with reference to the shore. This is important, because the fish are "schooled," the area they cover is not too large, and we must get our lures back to the same spot. Sometimes this is a little difficult to do unless an additional pass or two is made, or a marker thrown to serve as a guide.

You might ask, "why stop and cast? Why not continue trolling?" There are several reasons why the casting position should be taken when fish are located on a troll. You can more easily control speed (and depth) on the cast, and when handling the fish. You HAVE to keep these fish in a so-called frenzy or competitive spirit. You can't allow them to quiet down. It's sort of like throwing a grain of corn to a bunch of hungry chickens. You also have a TIME period in which to make the catch. The time lost in making the trolling run, the handling of the fish, etc. would eat up most of the available time. In other words, you got little time to make a catch. Furthermore, the fish are already "spooky" by being this shallow, and repeated trolling runs over this shallow area, could send them into deep water.

Figure 6 shows the position we will assume for casting to a school of fish. We want to anchor the boat just as shallow as possible, but yet near enough to allow the casts to reach immediately beyond the fish. If we anchor over water too deep, difficulty will be encountered in keeping the lure on bottom for its walk through the school of fish. The steep angle of the retrieve will pull the lure off bottom and you'll lose depth control.

Figure 6

Many fishermen have trouble determining the size lure to use on the cast. At times they may find the fish while trolling a small lure. They stop to cast and they become flustered when they find they can't control the small lure. IT IS NOT NECESSARY, pick out a larger Spoonplug that you **can** control. The **fish** couldn't care less. But, to be more specific, in this case (Figure 6), the position the boat is anchored, will determine the best size lure to cast. THE SIZE WILL BE DETERMINED BY THE DEPTH OF THE WATER UNDER THE BOAT. If you are anchored in DEEP water, it will require a LARGER lure to maintain depth and speed control, than when anchored in shallower water.

If you are anchored in water less than 4 to 5 feet, you may get good performance from a 250 series. If you are anchored in water 6 to 8 feet in depth, you will have to go to the 200 or 100 series to maintain a good walk along the bottom. At times when working extra deep on the cast—30 to 40 feet—you may have to go to the 700 or 800 to maintain depth control.

Anytime you anchor in water 12 to 15 feet, or better, you begin to run into trouble maintaining good depth and speed control with a free-running bottom bumping lure. You will then have to switch to a jump-type lure such as a jig, worm, spoon, etc. You will sacrifice speed

control, but you can retain depth control, and of the two, depth is the more important.

In casting a Spoonplug toward deep water, you make the cast slightly beyond the spot you are trying to work (a school of fish, hump, breakline, etc.) and let it sink to the bottom. Watch the line, when it becomes slack, the lure is on the bottom. When letting the lure sink, keep a slight tension on the line. Do not feed a lot of loose line, this will allow the lure to tumble as it sinks, and the lure could foul with the line. This would be true of any lure with multiple hooks—one of the reasons a single hook lure works better on spinning gear, where the snap cast produces a lot of lure tumble and excess line.

As soon as the lure reaches bottom, take a few turns of the reel handle to sink and remove the excess line in the water. This gets you directly to the lure. With the rod tip **low,** and pointed toward the side (not toward line of retrieve) a few fast turns of the handles will get the lure up on its nose 'walking'. Regulate your retrieve speed to maintain a steady walk. If the lure leaves the bottom for any reason, stop the retrieve and let it go back before continuing the retrieve. If it doesn't walk, you are either anchored too deep, or trying to use too small a lure. While casting to a school of fish there are a few do's and don'ts. When a strike occurs, and after the hook is set, you should get the fish from the school as quickly as possible. You certainly don't want him floundering around where he might spook the others. You don't want to play around with him at all, during any stage of game. The other fish in the school have a tendency to follow the hooked fish, and should they see the boat, the school is prematurely lost. They will drop back into the deep hole since depth is their only escape. This is one of the reasons why I recommend the heavy casting gear. Light gear will catch only a fraction of the fish, that can be had with heavier tackle.

The fish we have found are schooled and they could be large. We want to do everything possible to keep from losing any of them. Too often, if the biggest fish of the school is hooked and lost, or if too many are lost, the school will spook. When we get into one of these *groups* don't be surprised if you seem to be all thumbs and start shaking like a leaf. Just play it cool, and keep 'em coming.

Today's school may be four pounders, but it could be close to six pounders tomorrow. But no fisherman has really lived until he has a school of these big beauties where each successive cast puts one on the stringer. A stringer full of these is truly a memorable experience.

Finding migration routes, and **where** and **how** the fish use them, is not accomplished without time, effort, and patience. It will be difficult at first, but as experience is gained and additional knowledge is had, this becomes just a routine part of fishing. Finding these routes, however, is well worth the time and effort expended. Once they are found you can take your grandchildren there and catch fish. Once these home areas and migration routes are established they will remain there until the water level, or bottom changes, force the fish to look elsewhere.

After a lake has been **worked out** and the productive areas **known,** then it could be checked out fairly well, by casting alone (with no pre-trolling). Figure 7 shows the boat position for doing this on a bar, such as we just worked.

By anchoring the boat rather close to shore, long casts can be made along the shoreline. In this way, the lure is fishing the shoreline for the entire length of the retrieve. If the shallows do not produce, long casts can be made on the deeper migration route. But remember—this deeper section is the area for bottom fishing, and your lure must sink to bottom at all times. To work further out on the migration route, move the boat progressively further out so your casts will come as near to the drop-off as possible. By casting all sections in this manner, you can determine if any fish are on the move.

It might be a good idea to repeat—**Fish do not move constantly or consistently.** You might make contact with

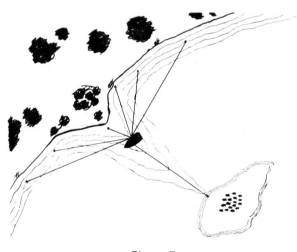

Figure 7

the fish on the first cast today, but tomorrow you go out at the same time and sit for three or four hours before you get a movement. This is normal. I like to get there ahead of the movement. It means the good fishing is ahead of me and not behind me. At another time you may have to spend three or four days before they show on your favorite spot.

The fishing trip we have just completed was for the purpose of establishing the basic way that you should go about your fishing. In this instance we used Spoonplugs, and were working a particular shoreline; but, regardless of what lures you use, or what type of water you fish, you must have procedures that will enable you to work the water quickly and thoroughly. The procedure as outlined, and with Spoonplugs, is the best way I know to check out any water to eventually arrive at the fish. I found I had to have these "Tools" many, many years ago. I believe you will find they are still needed today.

If you go to strange waters, or big waters, where do you start? What do you use? How do you fish it? If you use Spoonplugs, and go to work as outlined, it won't take long to find what, where, why, when and how. Then, catch them anyway you like, using any gear you desire.

Remember on all the structure types—bars, humps, breaklines, weedlines, Delta, etc., and in all the fishing situations—rivers, sloughs, deep lakes, shallow lakes, brush and muck bottoms, etc., the Spoonplugs have their place. They eliminate no lure in your tackle box. They just make all the others more valuable. Spoonplugs were designed for depth and speed control—nothing else. I can't say the same thing about most lures on the market.

YOU MIGHT SAY:

When fishermen are first introduced to Spoonplugging, and the presentation of Spoonplugs, most are exposed to trolling for the first time. Most do not know why it is important, nor what it is all about or how to go about it. Most have associated trolling with "dragging" a lure through the water with the boat and motor.

I recall when fishing with Dad years ago, we would be casting every little nook and corner in the shoreline. We'd see a fisherman trying to troll (actually he wasn't, he was in 100 feet of water, pulling a lure that ran at 5 feet.) Dad would look at him and comment, "Look at that lazy rascal, he's too lazy to cast".

Years later, when we would observe a good troller, he would say, "Look at that guy trolling. You know, he's a pretty smart fellow".

When fishermen are learning to troll, two questions normally are asked. 1—What do you do, or how do you handle that boat when the lure gets hung on a snag? 2—What do you do, or how do you handle the boat and motor when you hang a **fish?**

In answering these two questions, I am going to say a lot, and in detail. If you are wondering why I am doing this, it is for the simple reason, **I want you to learn how to troll.** Too often fishermen will not learn how to troll due to the very things you have asked. There are more reasons, but just loss of lures alone will scare many off. It has always amused me, that a fisherman raises a big squawk if he loses a Spoonplug. He belly-aches to me for telling him to fish the bottom or other places where he might lose lures. But, you never hear a peep out of him when he goes hunting and shoots a pocket full of shells. He will fire at something, even if it's a tree.

Trolling is not only a skill, but it becomes a great pleasure when done correctly.

Figure 8 shows two trollers proceeding down a shoreline (Position A). The motorman fishing inside (next to shore) gets his lure hung on something. He realizes that he has a secure snag because of the immediate action which he took at the moment he became aware of (or felt) the impending hang. His first reaction was to immediately apply pressure to the rod. The purpose of this action was to rip the lure through the hang, or off of the hang. Since this did not work, he vigorously worked the rod back and forth in an attempt to throw back loose line so as to allow the lure to drop free.

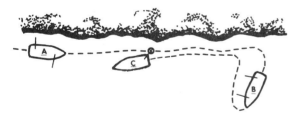

Figure 8

Many times when the reel is trolled in the anti-reverse position, it is hard to throw back sufficient loose line to free the lure. If the reel is on light drag, you can pull forward enough with the rod to get additional line off the reel and then rapidly throw the rod tip backwards. This method of getting loose line is preferable to that of releasing the anti-reverse, because if the anti-reverse is released with tension on the line a bad backlash can result. If you are one of those that troll with the reel on free spool (with the anti-reverse disengaged), and "thumb" the reel, loose line can be obtained immediately and thrown backward in an attempt to free the hung lure.

All of the initial efforts involved in trying to free the lure takes place in a few seconds. If these efforts fail, there is no doubt about the severity of the hang.

The moment that the hang is determined, the motorman should quickly cut the throttle, and turn the boat toward deep water. This will kill the forward motion of the boat. As the boat comes perpendicular to the shoreline the motor is thrown into neutral gear.

As the turn of the boat is made, BOTH fishermen swing their rods over, and swivels his body so as to face the hung lure—Position B. **The person not hung, IMMEDIATELY winds in his lure as fast as he can.**

When he's ready to go back to the hung lure, the motorman turns (swivels) the boat and proceeds back ALONG THE PREVIOUS PATH OF THE BOAT. While going back toward the hung lure, he keeps TENSION on his line. The speed going back, is determined by how fast he can take up the line. If he over-runs the line, he can add to his troubles. If he is not sufficiently skilled to run the boat and wind in line at the same time, he should hand the rod to his partner.

It is important that the boat proceed back along the path of the taut line. If the line gets wound around any brush or debris when proceeding back, the lure will be difficult or impossible to free. By proceeding back along the path of the line the additional problem of a wrapped line can be avoided. The taut line also serves as a guide for the motorman.

When the boat reaches the position of the lure (Position C) it should proceed slightly beyond, and then with vigorous rod action an attempt is made to jerk the lure free. At this point, a **steady pull normally will not free the lure,** unless it happens to be under an object such as a rock. But for a hang on debris or brush, heavy rod action (jerks) will be needed, and even this may fail to free the lure.

If all of the above fails, then there is another tactic that can be quite effective, and that is "shooting" the lure loose. This in no manner requires the use of a real 'shootin arm', but merely makes use of the line to do the shooting. This is done by taking the line loosely in the left hand and then using the right hand to apply a great deal of pressure on the line, as if shooting a bow and arrow. When the pressure of the right hand is released, the line is "shot" toward the lure with considerable force. If the line is merely plunked, such as plunking a banjo string, no effective force will reach the hung lure. **The loose line must be shot to the lure to be of value.** The best position to apply this action is DIRECTLY ABOVE the lure.

If several attempts to shoot the lure loose has failed and the water is shallow enough, try to reach the lure with the tip of the rod. Stick the rod down in the water as far as possible, taking up the line with the reel. If the lure can be reached with the rod tip, the lure can be pushed free from the hang.

If all of these attempts fail, then a plug-knocker can be used if one is available. Most commercial plug knockers have a ring, or some device, that allows the knocker to slide down the line. They also have a line attached for working the knocker and for pulling the lure loose.

Most of the time you will be faced with a lure that is hung but no plug-knocker in the tackle box. It is wise to save a few old spark plugs for such an emergency. A rather effective plug-knocker can be made by using an old plug. The line can be placed between the points of the plug, and a slight tap on the top point will close the gap. The spark plug can then be worked down the line with a little rod action (small jerks). This can be a great tool for releasing hung lures.

If no spark plug is available, a heavy sinker with a snap or snap swivel attached, can be used in much the same manner.

Earlier, the point was made how the boat should proceed back to the hung lure. The question might arise as how to determine if the boat has reached the hung lure, or if it's only to where the line is wrapped around a limb or some protruding object. This can be determined by grabbing the line, beyond the rod tip, and applying **heavy pressure** to the line. Be careful to note if the line is "stretchy", and try to feel any "sawing" action on the line. If it is stretchy, or you feel a slight 'sawing,' then the boat has not reached the point of the hung lure, you are only to where the line is wrapped around something. You must now get the line free before the lure can be recovered.

First, try to determine in what direction the line is wrapped. Then back the boat off 8 to 10 feet, all the while keeping steady pressure on the line. Circle the obstruction in the opposite direction of the "wrap". If the line does not come free after the circle is made, go

around it in the other direction, and again keep plenty of tension on the line.

Now let us assume that the fisherman in the front of the boat is fishing on the inside (next to shore) as the trolling pass is made. The boat is traveling down the shoreline in the opposite direction—Figure 9, position A. The motorman, who is fishing on the **outside**, on this pass, gets hung again.

The forward motion of the boat is killed as described above; and the boat immediately swings to a perpendicular position in respect to the shoreline (Position B). **As the boat turns, the fisherman in the front of the boat raises his rod tip and swings his line over the head of the hung partner in the back of the boat,** and IMMEDIATELY retrieves his lure. His lure will now approach the boat on the opposite side of his partner's snagged line. He merely leans forward and lifts the retrieved lure across the motorman's line.

Figure 9

Now, let's assume the fisherman in the front of the boat, and who is on the inside, gets hung. The boat is immediately swung out and its forward motion killed. The fisherman whose lure is hung lifts his rod tip high, swivels his position and passes his line over the head of his partner in the stern (motorman). The motorman is now in the position to retrieve his lure quickly and without any complications.

In all cases, whether the fisherman in the front or the one in the back gets hung, both of them bring their rod tips up, and swivels his position so he is facing toward the hung lure. You should not be concerned if the lines cross over each other. The fisherman that is not snagged can immediately retrieve his lure with ease.

Figure 10 is a similar situation with two fishermen shown trolling a shoreline. In this instance, the fisherman on the inside hangs a **fish**.

The "drag" should never be so tight that the line could break if there is a hang, or if a fish strikes. The short interval of time that occurs between a strike and getting the forward motion of the boat killed can, at times, exert enough pressure to tear a lightly hooked fish loose.

My own personal policy is not to use anti-reverse, or the star drag, when trolling with small lures, as the smaller lures are normally equipped with small hooks. I prefer to use thumb tension, as this allows me to release line while the forward motion of the boat is being stopped. I use just enough tension on the line to assure control of the fish and to hold the hooks firm. The only time I use anti-reverse is when trolling the larger lures which have bigger hooks and heavier pull.

When the strike is made, the same procedures are followed as in the case of a lure hang; the motor throttle is closed, and the boat swiftly turned to position B, with both fishermen facing toward the hung fish.

The only change in procedures now is in the maneuvering of the boat from Position B. When the boat is swung out perpendicular to the shoreline the throttle should be thrown to the absolute minimum, or the motor thrown into neutral. THE MOTOR SHOULD NOT BE KILLED.

By leaving the motor running, you are in a position to maneuver the boat if it becomes necessary. Normally, the forward motion will carry the boat into deeper water and away from any shoreline obstructions that may exist, but in many instances the boat will have to be maneuvered farther out into deeper water, especially if there is an adverse wind blowing or if heavy weeds or brush is present.

There is rarely an occasion in which I feel it necessary to kill the motor. I have it either barely ticking over, still in gear, or I throw it into neutral. There are very few times that I do not have to use the motor to further position the boat so as to be on the safe side when fighting a fish. If I have to swing further out into the lake as in Position C, Figure 10, I swing slightly back toward the fish as indicated. Very often, I find it necessary to go quite far out and a good distance back toward the fish, in order to pull the fish free of weeds and brush.

Not killing the motor when a fish is hung is a good habit to get into. Whether fishing the shoreline or some underwater island in the center of the lake, there should never be any more or any less power on the motor than necessary to keep the boat in a desired position. There are times when a strong power will be needed, either forward or backward, to maintain a desired position such as in a strong wind or strong current. Whatever the situation, a running motor enables it to be handled quickly and easily.

Invariably, when talking about procedures such as above, the question is asked, "What do I do when the fish jumps?"

Unless you are one of those who had rather see the fish jump than put him on the stringer, there are several things that you might try. The first effort made is to **try to keep the fish from jumping.** This is not always possible and there is no sure-fire method that will prevent the jump. At times, quickly putting heavy pressure on the fish when he is observed rising to jump will work. At times, I have found a complete reduction of pressure stopped the jump. Sometimes, if the fish is close to the boat, jamming the rod tip down into the water as far as you can reach with a downward pull, seems to work.

The best procedure that I have found, after all attempts to stop the jump has failed, is to PRAY he is solidly hooked. Because, all of the fine points of retrieving your lure and maneuvering the boat on a strike is for naught—if the rascal gets away.

YOU MIGHT SAY:

"I can use Spoonplugs to outline a structure, and I can tell fairly well the depths by using the different sizes. Where I run into trouble is that I am never quite sure I know where the "breakline" or the "drop-off" is. For instance, I can make a long trolling pass with the larger sizes toward a structure. I start this pass from quite a distance out in deep water, and sometimes the pass is made at an angle, at other times straight in on the bar or structure. I can note where the lure makes con-

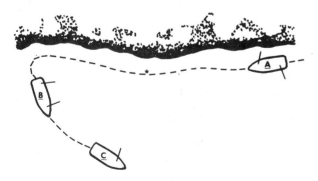

Figure 10

tact, but can I be sure this is the breakline? Could I not be hitting 'up on the structure' rather than at the breakline?"

Yes, you certainly could be hitting up on the structure itself, rather than at the breakline or drop-off. Here would be one of those times where a depth sounder could serve as an aid. However, previous interpretation and knowledge of the lake could give a partial answer. What does the study of other sections tell you? Do you have structure that normally breaks into deep water by the time you use the larger lures? Just how deep do other structures run before they drop into the hole or channel? Just how deep is the channel? How far out? Relate these things.

A simple check as to whether the lure is hitting 'up on structure' or whether it is hitting the "breakline" is to **reverse** your trolling run. By reversing your trolling pass, you are utilizing your tool to a greater degree so that it can tell you as much as possible about the structure. On your reverse pass the lure would make contact with the bottom on a shallow section of the structure. The lure would begin to walk DOWN the structure, as the boat direction would be toward deep water. As long as the lure keeps walking it keeps going down. The lip is digging into the bottom, greatly increasing the downward pull. If you feel the walking becoming lighter, decrease speed to a minimum (never below a 'walking' speed, and never just a drag) and drop back more line. If you keep the lure walking, it keeps going down the structure, much deeper than previously. The thing that pulls a lure UP is the line pressure. You are pulling UP while the lure is pulling DOWN. If you increase the size and pulling power of the lure, you get greater depth.

When handling lures in this manner, any breakline or drop-off will be noted quickly. If there occurs a short breakline anywhere on structure the lure will tell you by running "free" for a short spell. If the lure suddenly stopped walking and continued to run free, you have passed a greater breakline or the drop-off. Relate these positions to your previous trolling passes.

In most waters the larger lures used on a 'reverse pass', will reach the breakline or drop-off. In some water, bars will extend below the depths you can reach in this manner, and the drop-off or breakline cannot be reached. This would normally be the case where a steeper deep-section of the lake is being fished, and you maybe shouldn't be there in the first place. It would depend upon how well you did your "home work" before you went fishing.

YOU MIGHT SAY:

"I do not have a Depth Sounder. I am trolling Spoonplugs to locate a "bar" (or structure) that runs quite far out into the lake. I have established the shape and how it changes depth, etc., but I do not know the exact depths on the structure. However, I do know that a certain lure size will reach just so far, and beyond this point, I have to use a bigger deeper running lure. I have used all of my lure sizes and have a pretty good idea what the structure is like. Since I have no depth sounder and the structure is quite large, is there any way for me to establish the approximate depths without taking a lot of time to measure each structure?"

Let your lures do the job. Each size will run at a given depth with a given amount of line being used on the troll. Go back to Figure 1 and restudy the Spoonplug sizes, and their running depths.

To verify these depths, make a trolling pass with a noted length of line. Get the particular size Spoonplug just skipping the bottom. Go back and measure the depth. After a few tests you will know fairly accurately what depth they all run, or, more correctly, at what depth they all come in contact with the bottom.

YOU MIGHT SAY:

"I fish primarily in a man made reservoir. The lake is quite large, containing about six hundred miles of shoreline. The reservoir near the dam is large, and most of the fishing is done in this area. When the lake was first built, it was quite easy to catch a limit of fish. In recent years, the water has become quite beautiful and you can see bottom in fifteen feet of water—but the catches of fish keep going down. Today, I am lucky to catch one fish— much less a limit. And, I figure I can use Spoonplugs pretty darn good. My question is, "what happened, and what can I do about it?"

First, you didn't ask one question, you asked two. The most important question of the two is the second one, "What can I do about it?" Before attempting to answer this question though, we need to take a look at 'what happened'. Three things should be considered when trying to arrive at the answer to this.

First, as the lake became older, fish began to eliminate large sections of the lake that were not suitable for their habitation. They began to adapt themselves to certain areas of the lake. The result being—large sections that once contained a great quantity of small fish no longer have them.

Second, since the reservoir was built the fish have increased in age and size. Small yearling fish have a tendency to run around in the shallows, but after they reach approximately three years of age, or have reached around two to two and one-half pounds, they are no longer 'teenagers'. They now have become compatible with the larger fish in the area, and spend more and more time in the deep water sanctuary.

Third, the water color is a determining factor in this case. The statement concerning "beautiful water" would indicate this reservoir is more for drinking purposes than for fishing. In this case, the clear water is producing extra deep sanctuaries, and the movements are not bringing the fish within reach.

Structures in the lower sections of large reservoirs, such as this, are oftentimes not too good. Some of the shoreline structures, at first glance, appear to be 'good looking'. A closer check will show that most have breaklines which are too shallow, they do not extend far enough toward the deep water, and the majority of them have a big flat between them and the channel (a 'Delta' situation). The big problem presents itself at this point— **the breaklines at the channel are too deep to work effectively.**

There are two routes you can take, in trying to solve the problems. First, you can spend more time in studying the extra deep breaks and breaklines. Then spend a good bit of time in learning how to present your lures on these structures. This particular route is work, and it will take time to completely work it out.

The second approach, and it is clearly the best and wisest one for you to make, is to leave this large clear area near the dam, and go toward the headwaters. You should continue toward the headwaters until workable structure and decent water color is found. Oftentimes, a long 'cove' or arm on the reservoir will contain decent workable structure and a better water color.

As far as your ability to handle Spoonplugs, it appears you are working the wrong end of the rod. Instead of expecting a piece of metal to solve your problem, you should use your head a little.

YOU MIGHT SAY:

"I fish a deep clear lake that is loaded with big northern and muskie. I can catch plenty of northern, and ever so often a legal size muskie, by trolling Spoonplugs fast along the tall weedline. But, I can't seem to catch the BIG northern, or many muskie. I practically draw a blank on any good size muskie. What am I doing wrong?"

I wouldn't say you are doing anything wrong. Stacking the lures along the weedline on a fast troll is the BEST way to catch the northern and muskie **that have moved up.** Your problem seems to be you didn't carry your Depth Control deep enough.

First, let me say more about the deep water sanctuary of the fish. The 30–35 foot depth is the normal depth that you view as the starting point of migrations for most fish. In your situation; the deep clear water, BIG northern and muskie, you have to increase the 30–35 foot depth down to 45–55 feet.

The myth that the muskie is an elusive fish, and that only the expert can catch him, can easily be dispelled by working the deep structure. Large lures (700–800 series Spoonplugs) trolled along the deep breaklines, humps, etc., should solve any problems you might have with big northern and lots of muskie. The BIG muskie will be in this area, most of the time.

In order for you to reach these depths (45–55 feet) you will have to use a monel line (wire). Fifteen to seventeen pound test line should be adequate.

YOU MIGHT SAY:

"Boy! Have I got a lot to remember. Where, or how in the world do I start to become a good fisherman?"

YOU HAVE ALREADY STARTED BY READING THIS BOOK. Now go back and STUDY it.

Probably when you asked this question you had in mind **what you do first on the water.** You do just like I did, and as all good Spoonpluggers did. YOU LEARN TO TROLL THE SHALLOWS. You learn how to troll the first three sizes of Spoonplugs. By doing this, you immediately start to discipline yourself on Depth and Speed Control. You start your mapping and interpretations, what and where structure exists. The effects of weather and how it controls the movements of the fish. You will become aware of water color, and how it affects the lake conditions. You also start catching fish as never before. This coupled with what you have observed gets you started. I know of no other way to mesh all the gears, in a reasonable length of time.

You should spend time on every trip trolling the shallows with these three lures, AND, in as many different lakes as possible. If you don't keep them in position, as discussed, you will miss the whole point, and will be fishing just another lure—not a "teaching" tool.

You will know when the time comes to go deeper, or to the cast. But, don't be in a hurry. It may take several trips and several lakes before you are confident you are ready for the next step.

If you will do as I say, you will become as good as the best, before you realize it. BUT, if you are lure crazy or lure biased, or won't troll—forget everything I have said in the book.

I have traveled, and fished this country for a great many years. Very little water has been missed. Just this past year I traveled thousands of miles to work reservoirs that had been built since the last time I was in the areas.

In all this time, and in all this water, there were only a few times where I saw the fishermen catching enough fish. The very few times was in new reservoirs, where the water was working with yearling fish.

Whatever the situation, or wherever I found the fishermen catching fish pretty good, I moved on and came back at a later date (when they weren't catching fish). This didn't happen very often, for, as a whole, fishermen are a greedy bunch, and I could still "shake" them up, even though **some** fish were being caught.

In many many waters I made sensational catches, but I moved on without opening my mouth, or showing the fish to a single person.

Why did I leave the area, without saying a word, or showing the fish? It was due to the fact THE FISHING WAS TOO DIFFICULT FOR THE AVERAGE FISHERMAN. If I had told them I caught the fish on Spoonplugs, and they tried it and drew a blank, **I would do more harm than good.** I would lose this group entirely, and probably permanently. I had already lost thousands, primarily due to the fact, the fishermen **did not hear what I said.** All they were interested in was a shortcut to success, and they figured my lures were the answer. They soon found out they weren't—**although successful fishing was EASY in their case.**

The predominate situations where the fishing was too difficult for the local fishermen was, the DEEP CLEAR LAKES AND RESERVOIRS. The situation was such, that the movements of the fish did not bring them within range of the average fisherman—spoonplugs or not.

In so many many cases, I had to go to wire line to catch the fish. It would have not only been unfair, but would have been a completely lost cause, had I done anything other than leave the area.

You should have noted at several places in this book, I have mentioned "Wire" lines. I did not dwell on this, because: 1—Most fishermen do not have wire. 2—It can be difficult to use. 3—To be effective, it is very very important, that you know structure, can read deep water, weather, and know where the fish will be. You just can't go out there in deep water and wander around like some lost dog. Deep water means "exactness" in both interpretation and presentation.

Earlier, I stated I wouldn't be caught out fishing without a reel filled with wire line. I have found, if I have the wire, no lake or no species can give me trouble—for long.

When a monofilament (nylon) is used in trying to reach extra depths you are faced with larger lures, and extra long lines. You are still limited to around 25 feet. But with a monel wire line, you not only can run short lines, but you can run smaller lures to reach depths. When trying to reach the 25–50 foot depths, you can still reach them with the 200 and 100 series lures with a **controllable** line length.

There are three type lines that can be used to obtain extra depth on the troll. 1—Weighted (lead core); 2—Solid steel (monel); 3—Stranded steel wire. I personally prefer the wire over the weighted (lead core), although the weighted may spool better. However, either type will get the lures to deeper structure.

The solid wire has a greater diameter per pound test, than the stranded. I use both, with the solid wire around 20 lb. test, and the stranded from 20 to 30 lb. test. The smaller diameter on the stranded has more tendency to "get behind the spool" if care isn't taken, and more line may be called for than with the solid to reach a particular depth. Probably the stranded, in the long run, may be easier to handle for most fishermen. You can try all of them, and see which works better.

I use the wire on the same type trolling reel as I do the monofilament. One hundred (100) yards is sufficient in most all cases, but I still use "backing" to insure a fairly full spool.

I use a monofilament leader (No-Bo) of 17–20 lb. test, between the wire and the lure. This leader is approximately 3–3½ feet long. I insert a small swivel between the wire and the leader. I use just a snap on the leader for attaching the lures. A number 10 snap-swivel can be used. Separate the snap from the swivel. The swivel is small enough to run thru the guides on the rod. The snap is strong enough to use on the leader. This leader is used for several reasons. It is a flexible joint between the heavy wire and the lure. It allows the lures to function better. It helps in control of proper line length (see below). It makes it easier when changing lures or handling a fish at the boat. Situations will exist when it becomes necessary to "break off" the lure. The leader will protect your line, and make it easier.

When properly rigged, the swivel should stop before it hits the reel. If you find when handling the rig, the swivel tends to butt or hit the level wind—shorten the leader.

In order for the wire to "spool" correctly, it is important that you use care in letting the line out. Let it out slowly—at all times "thumbing" the wire on the reel, so that the lure is pulling the line out under pressure. If you do not do this, the wire will loosen up on the spool, and you could be in trouble.

By letting the lure out in this manner, you accomplish two things. You keep your line straight, and you also control **the amount of line let back**. It is very important, when working wire, that you **do not run excess line**—just enough to get the lure down (bottom). If you run too much line, you lose control. Wire sinks, and if you run too much, the wire will hit the bottom (and "breaks") before the lure (a major reason I prefer the wire, over the "weighted" lines). This creates problems—loss of control, lure doesn't function properly, etc., etc.—and you hang up too much.

With a wire—any action on the part of the lure is clearly felt, and when it hangs, you receive a big jolt. There is no give or stretch, and you can lose a lot of lures. Being sure you run "just enough" line is very important. You may have to adjust the length, by winding in or letting out, but proper line length will normally correct any troubles you are having with wire.

At all times, check your wire for kinks. In most instances, when these occur, you can carefully remove the kink, without breaking the wire.

Proper use of wire will raise your score tremendously. Most of the time, if you are not catching fish, you are not fishing deep enough. As I have said before—you better go to the fish, as he may not come to you. BUT, DO NOT USE WIRE, UNLESS CALLED FOR.

Many lakes and reservoirs have holes and channels, with no visible structure. **By no means go out there and wander around.** It is much better to wait on shallower structure for the fish to appear. **You do not use wire to go deep. You use wire to reach deep STRUCTURE.** If it's not there, or if you don't know it's there (and where)—don't go.

A few years ago, I would not have advised fishermen to go to wire line on the troll. But, today, with the many Depth Meters available, the fisherman can "see" structure in deep water. He doesn't have to wander around in deep water "hoping" he might run across a deep breakline, hump, etc.

BUT, the Depth Sounder can create problems in deep water. In the first place, most fishermen will not take the time to check maps, or ask, if structure exists in deep water. He will too often forget all about structure, and spend his time running around looking for suspended fish, and will waste the whole time, trying to catch some forage, rough, or small pan fish he might see on the Meter.

Too many times the fisherman is not knowledgable enough to know what to look for, and most likely could not interpret what he saw, anyway. I am sure he wouldn't be observant enough to distinguish between those bodies of water that **contain** structure in deep water, and those that **do not.**

If you know what you are doing, wire line can be one of the more important items in your tackle box.

CHAPTER 4

All About Rods

A complete and definitive guide to rod actions, design, fittings, materials, workmanship and performance.

SELECTING THE RIGHT ROD

There are many different kinds and types of fishing rods. For example, there are one, two, three, and even four piece rods; there are rods of bamboo, glass, steel, and graphite; and there are fly, spinning, spin-cast, bait-casting, surf-casting, deep sea, pier, and boat rods. Then too, there are rods with different "actions," and, of course, rods of varying quality.

Choosing the right kind of rod for the specific type of fishing to be done is vitally important. One could not expect to be very successful fighting 100 pound tarpon with an ultra-light rod designed for small stream trout fishing, nor could one hope to properly cast three ounce lures with a rod meant to be used with lures weighing no more than ⅝ths ounce.

Beginning fishermen should seek the aid of an expert in selecting a rod, perhaps a friend who is a veteran angler, or the proprietor of a reputable tackle shop. Experienced fishermen can recommend not only the type and design of rod best suited to the kind of fishing to be done, but also can suggest several manufacturers of suitable rods.

In most kinds of fishing, rod "action" is vitally important. "Action" is the flex of a rod, and it will vary according to the weight of the lure or bait being cast. What kind of "action" a rod has depends upon the rod material, its taper, length—and even upon the number and spacing of the guides.

Generally speaking, most rods are rated as having actions that are light, medium-light, heavy, medium-heavy, or extra-heavy. A rod with "medium-light" action would be proper for casting light lures for smallish fish in snag-free waters; a rod with "heavy" action would be appropriate for casting large lures for husky fish in weed-filled waters.

A rod should be chosen first of all for its action, secondly for its quality. A rod may be made of the best materials, and its craftsmanship may be superb; but if it lacks the proper action for the angling job to be done, it will perform less than well under actual fishing conditions.

Quality rods are properly tapered for the best action. They are of the correct weight for their size, and for the type of fishing for which they are primarily designed. Finally, quality rods have snug ferrules, comfortable, well-designed handles, smooth-working reel seats, and a suitable number of long-wearing guides.

In many ways fishing rods are about like other merchandise; usually you get what you pay for. There are inexpensive rods on the market that have excellent actions, and they offer fine value commensurate with their prices, but as a rule-of-thumb it is wise to purchase the best rod you can afford. Moreover, "brand name" rods are recommended. Rod manufacturers having a widely recognized, widely accepted "name" (for example, The Shakespeare Co.) got their reputations by marketing quality rods, at fair prices, and then standing behind their products.

ROD NOMENCLATURE

Rods of all types generally are made up of the same basic components. They may differ in design, size, and actions, but all have handles, blades (shafts), guides, reel seats, etc.

ROD MATERIALS

Rods have been made of various kinds of woods (such as greenheart), of bamboo (a cane), of metals such as steel and copper, and of solid and of hollow glass. Recently a brand new innovation in rod materials has been developed—high-modulus carbon graphite.

Graphite rods are new on the market, and it will probably be some time before they are readily available in large selections. Rods of wood and copper are no longer made, and even rods with steel blades are very scarce. The most popular rods today are made of glass, but many premium grade rods are still made of bamboo. (Those by The Orvis Co., for example).

Glass rods are most in demand because they are resilient, providing excellent "action," do not take a "set" (that is, suffer warping or permanent bending), are practically impervious to sun, heat, cold or salt water, withstand hard use and, compared to rods of some other materials, are inexpensive.

Solid glass rods are not as popular as hollow glass rods. For one thing, solid glass rods are a bit heavier, and do not have actions as smooth as fiberglass rods that are hollow. However, solid glass rods are very sturdy, can take quite a lot of hard action, and they are not as expensive as hollow, fiberglass rods. Solid glass rods are selected frequently by fishermen who want a tough, serviceable rod that is moderately priced, for boat or pier fishing, for trolling, or even for big game, deep sea fishing.

Most hollow glass rods are made by weaving glass fibers into cloth. The fine cloth is cut into patterns, then rolled around calibrated steel templates or tapered wooden dowels. They then are placed in ovens and receive heat treatment, under pressure, that forms the

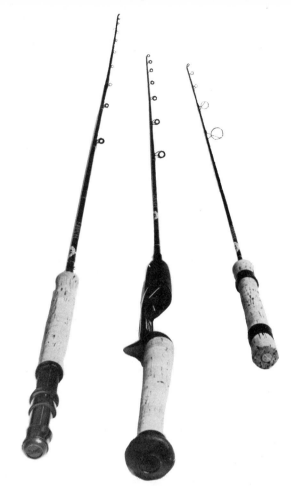

Graphite is the newest rod material. These are by Fenwick. From left, a 2-piece fly rod, bait-casting rod, and ultra-light spinning rod.

permanent hollow glass shaft (steel templates or dowels are removed).

Rods of hollow glass are very light, yet they are very strong. They can be readily broken through *carelessness* (slamming one in a car door), but seldom will one snap under normal stresses due to casting or playing fish.

In general, it would be difficult nowadays to find a better buy than a hollow glass rod, regardless of rod type or manufacturer. Any hollow glass rod—from the least expensive to the top premium grade—will almost certainly be well worth its selling price.

Some fishermen still prefer bamboo rods, especially for certain kinds of fishing, such as fly fishing small streams for trout. Quality bamboo rods have exquisite actions, and their "fittings" (ferrules, reel seat, guides) are usually of the best materials.

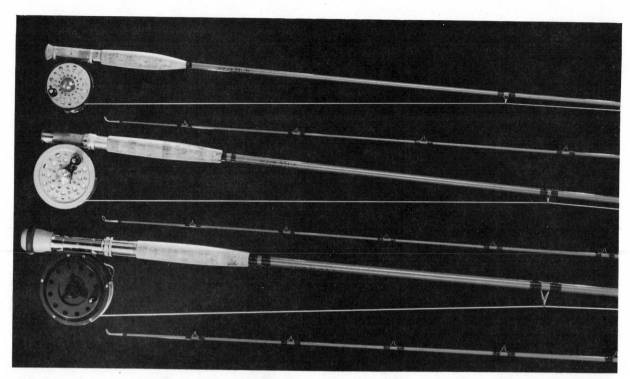

Three premium grade hollow glass fly rods by Orvis.

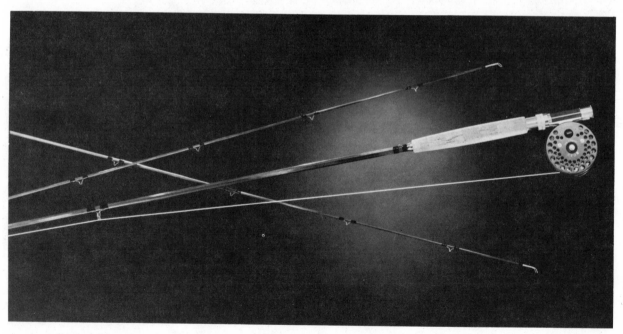

Rods of bamboo impregnated with bakelite resin, such as the Orvis line, resist taking sets.

Bamboo rods are heavier than hollow glass rods, and most makes can take "sets." At least one line of bamboo rods (Orvis) are impregnated with bakelite resin, however, and not only resist taking "sets" but also withstand the normally damaging effects of heat, extreme cold, and salt water.

Rods of bamboo require better general care than glass rods, and most are far more expensive than glass rods.

Only a comparatively few tackle companies currently are manufacturing graphite rods (Shakespeare, Fenwick, Cordell, Scientific Anglers, Pflueger) but doubtlessly graphite is an important "coming" rod material. Rods made of carbon graphite fibers are at least 25 percent lighter than comparable glass rods, and sometimes 40 percent lighter. They are 50 percent lighter than comparable bamboo rods. Too, graphite rods are very strong, and a graphite fly rod is capable of performing satisfactorily with a wide range of fly line sizes.

Currently only fly rods, spinning and bait-casting rods are being made of carbon graphite, and they are very expensive, well over $100 apiece. It is probable, however, that other kinds of rods (surf, trolling, etc.) will soon be made of graphite, and also that prices will be greatly reduced.

TIPS, GUIDES, AND FERRULES

The tips, guides, and ferrules are very important "hardware" on any rod. If a rod's tip top, or its guides, are not of quality material or well designed, they will quickly wear and can then fray and cut a line—causing the loss of lures or of hooked fish. And guides that are not properly designed can interfere with casting ease.

Ferrules of cheap material or poor design will not be serviceable for very long. They will wear quickly, and loosen so much that it is impossible to keep the rod sections properly joined.

Rod tips and guides are made of various metals, or metal alloys, and sometimes the metal tip top or guides are ringed inside with agate. Agate is very hard and glass-like, and while it may withstand many years of ordinary line wear, it can be easily cracked or broken. Sometimes agate guides receive a blow that causes the agate to suffer a hairline crack, invisible to the naked eye, but the minute crack will fray or cut the line. In addition, agate is expensive.

Nowadays only a minority of rods are available with agate guides and/or tip tops. As explained, agate is very serviceable, but rods with agate tops/guides must be handled with care—and the agate should be checked frequently for nicks or cracks.

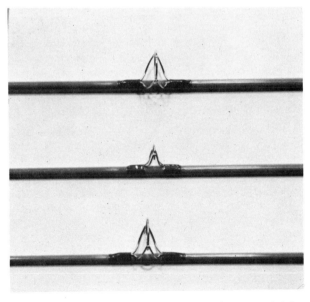

Carboloy is generally the most popular material for rod guides. Quality guides are well-designed, properly mounted.

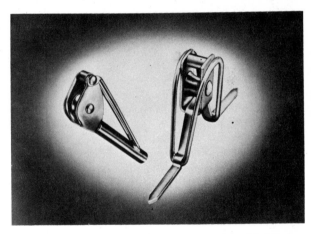

Roller type tip tops (left), and guides (right) are needed on many rods for deep sea, big game fishing. Roller guides greatly reduce line friction. These Allan Tackle Co. guides are chrome-plated and have "Oilite" bushings.

Carboloy is the most popular material for guides and tops. It is super hard, hence longwearing, and is corrosion resistent. It, too, is expensive.

Stainless steel guides and tops are good, as are guides/tops of other metals when heavily chrome-plated. What is most desired in guides and tips is that they be made of a metal or other material sufficiently hard to take considerable wear, and that they be rust-proof. It is most important that the guides/tip tops on salt water rods be corrosion resistent.

The best kind of tip top for rods other than fly rods is one having supporting bars. These little supports keep a tip top from breaking loose at the slightest bump and, moreover, help prevent the casting line from wrapping around the tip, something that can be very aggravating in the course of a day's fishing—particularly when it happens time after time.

Roller tip tops are ones having rollers within the guide that are mounted on oilless bushings, or on greased

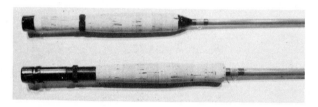

Two samples of fly rod handles and reel seats: at top is a "Cigar" grip with cork skeleton reel seat and, below, a "Perfectionist" grip with full screw-locking reel seat.

but sealed ball bearings, so that friction is kept to a practical minimum when big gamefish are running out line. Such tips will be found on all quality deep sea, or big game rods, because heavy, powerful fish such as marlin and bluefin tuna can streak away with line so swiftly that friction would build up dangerously in any rod tip top that did not have a built-in roller.

For the same reason, roller guides also are built into some big-game rods. There are a few different kinds of roller guides, but essentially each of them simply allows the line—taut under the pull of a heavy, powerful fish—to pass through the guides with a minimum of friction, thus helping assure the angler that the rated strength of his line will remain true throughout his battle with the "fish of a lifetime." Roller tips and roller

guides are most desirable, in fact are essential, in big-game, deep-sea rods.

Fly rods are mounted with spiral type guides called *snake guides,* and the best are made of hardened wire which may be chromeplated, black, or of stainless steel. Most important is that fly rod guides be sufficiently large to allow easy passage of the fly line.

Guides for spinning, spin-casting, and bait-casting rods are, fundamentally, similar in design—in that what the guides are expected to achieve is control passage of the casting line along the length of the rod, with a minimum of interference (friction).

The guides on a spinning rod should be very large, since line "balloons" off a spinning reel, and they should be only slightly smaller on a spin-cast rod, since line also "balloons," although less so, off a spin-cast reel. The guides on a bait-casting rod can be comparatively small, because the line coming from a bait-casting or "level-wind" reel does not come off in spirals when a cast is made.

Quality rod guides—whether on spinning, spin-cast, or bait-casting rods—should be of sturdy metal, rust-proof, and lightweight.

The best rod ferrules are made of nickel silver, or, as a second choice, of brass. Both metals are strong, long-lasting, lightweight, and corrosion resistent.

Quality ferrules fit tightly when a rod is new, so much so that it is difficult to join the rod sections totally without considerable effort and perhaps some "greasing." A new rod whose ferrules fit quickly and loosely should not be purchased.

HANDLES AND REEL SEATS

There are as many different kinds of rod handles as there are types of rods. Regardless of the kind of rod or type of handle, a rod handle must be FUNCTIONAL; that is, it must be comfortable, strong, and accept the proper reel in an easily tightened, secure reel seat.

Fly rod handles and reel seats are uncomplicated. The cork grip can be one of many different shapes: for example, it may be "cigar" style, "half Wells," "Fishtail," and so on. All that is really important about the shape or style of the fly rod grip is that it be comfortable. The most popular fly rod cork grip is the "cigar" shape.

A screw-locking type reel seat is the best on fly rods. With this type the fly reel can be held firmly in place, and even after hours of casting the reel should not loosen. An improvement over the screw-locking type reel seat is the double screw-locking reel seat—which is just what the name implies; there are two (instead of one) opposing threaded washers which are screwed down to lock the fly reel in place.

Fly fishermen who want the lightest possible fly rods buy ones with "skeleton" reel seats. Those have cork reel seats, with a simple sliding band to secure the reel, rather than heavier metal reel seats.

Be sure, when purchasing a fly rod, or for that matter any other kind of rod, that the reel seat will accommodate the reel you will be using. The reel seats on some fly rods will not accept some fly reels, and the reel seats on certain bait-casting, spinning, and other kinds of rods will not handle all casting, spinning, and other reels.

The handles and reel seats on bait-casting and spin-cast rods are basically similar. Usually they are of the "offset" type, which means the handle is recessed where

An "offset" casting handle by Browning.

And Shakespeare's long-famous "double offset" Wonderod handle.

the reel is mounted, or they may be of the "double off-set" type, which means that not only is the handle recessed where the reel is mounted, but the cork grip, too, is at an off angle, instead of being in a straight line with the rod blank.

The only real difference between a "double offset" handle and a standard "offset" is that the cork grip fits better into the caster's hand—or so think a lot of fishermen. The difference is slight, indeed.

A typical spinning rod, with typical spinning rod handle, is this medium-action, two-piece Shakespeare tubular glass Wonderod.

Some bait-casting rods are made with straight handles to satisfy the few casters who believe straight-handled rods provide greater casting accuracy.

Spinning rod handles all are straight, but the shapes of the cork handle, and the foregrip (which may be of cork or composition material) can vary. So can the reel seat, which may only have sliding bands to secure the reel, or it may be screw-locking or double-screw locking.

What is most important is to select a spinning rod having a handle that is comfortable to the hand, one that will mount your spinning reel properly, and which will hold the reel securely through a day's fishing. Most fishermen avoid spinning rods having sliding bands to hold the reel, since such bands work loose. However, one advantage to sliding band reel seats is that they are considerably lighter than other types of reel seats.

The handles on salt water spinning rods, and salt water "popping" rods (heavy action, straight-handled bait-casting rods), are usually quite long, 15 inches or more, so that the angler may utilize a two-handed casting technique.

Long, strong handles also are the rule on surf fishing rods because two-handed casting is necessary. Boat, pier, and deep-sea rods are others having long, sturdy handles because two hands are needed in using them. Too, the handles of such rods are frequently placed in rod holding sand spikes, rod holders mounted on the gunnels of a boat, or in special sockets in "fighting" harnesses or belts worn by deep sea fishermen when they've hooked tackle busters such as bluefin tuna or marlin.

Many surf rods, as well as most pier, boat, and deep-sea rods have handles made of a hardwood, most often hickory. Wood handles on such rods are usually preferred because they are rugged and withstand years of hard usage. Some rods in those categories, however, have handles and foregrips made of neoprene or other synthetic material, and they are quite serviceable.

Rod reel seats, incidentally, may be made of tough plastic, chrome-plated brass, or anodized aluminum. All those materials are satisfactory.

CANE/GLASS POLES

The so-called "bank pole" or "rod" is the simplest kind of fishing rod. Most such poles are made out of heavy Calcutta cane, some made of metal are available, and still others are made of fiberglass.

One-piece poles are stocked by many tackle shops, as are two and three piece poles, and ones that telescope. Too, some are mounted with tip tops, or tip tops and a series of guides, and some even have small cork handles built in, along with a simplified kind of little reel that comes filled with monofilament fishing line.

What kind of "pole" is best suited to the specific angler's need is up to the individual to decide. Actually, any of these so-called "bank" or stillfishing poles will do a job, and undoubtedly will be worth whatever small amount the fisherman pays for one.

The best "pole," however, is the more sophisticated one. That would be a telescoping fiberglass pole, with a

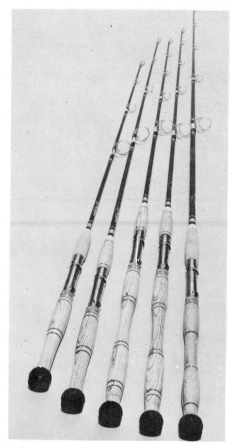

An assortment of wood-handled salt water rods by True Temper.

built-in reel and line supplied. The glass poles are more resilient, light in weight, cannot warp or bend, will not rot, and are longlasting.

Bank poles come in various lengths, and which length is best depends upon individual preference. Children do best with the shorter poles, 8 to 12 feet, while adults can easily handle the longer ones of 16 to 20 feet.

SPIN-CAST RODS

Spin-cast rods, as indicated earlier in this book, are very similar in style, "action," etc. to bait-casting rods, but there are differences.

While a spin-cast rod may be used with a bait-casting reel, and a bait-casting reel may be used on a spin-cast rod, a spin-cast reel operates best on a spin-cast rod.

Spin-cast reels, also called "push-button" or closed-face spinning reels, mount higher on a rod's reel seat than do bait-casting reels. For that reason, some spin-cast rods have low-profile reel seats—which puts the spin-cast reel's push-button within easy reach of the caster's thumb.

Too, monofilament line tends to balloon a bit when leaving a spin-cast reel (though not as much as from a spinning reel), so the guides on a quality spin-cast rod are larger than the guides on a typical bait-casting rod.

In selecting a spin-cast rod check its handle first, to be sure that it is comfortable, then its reel seat, to be certain that it will properly mount the spin-cast reel you intend to use with the rod. It's a wise fisherman who takes his reel along when he goes shopping for a spin-cast rod.

Next check the rod's guides. They should be on the large side—to reduce line friction on the cast—and the best guides will be made of carboloy. Quite a lot of rods, however, are made with all guides of chromed stainless steel, while the tip top will be made of carboloy. A rod's tip tops are far more subject to wear than are its guides.

An inexpensive spin-cast rod, as well as other types of rods, can be quickly recognized by its insufficient number of guides. There should be enough guides on the rod to permit uniform bending, and they should be properly spaced. However, there should not be too many guides, as they increase the rod's weight unnecessarily, and also stiffen its action.

Spin-cast rods are available in different actions and lengths. In general, fairly long, whippy spin-cast rods are preferred, because they balance out best with light lines and light lures. The most popular lengths are 6 and 6½ feet. Shorter, stiffer action spin-cast rods are needed in heavy fishing, for example, muskie fishing or fishing for the smaller salt water species.

The most important thing in selecting a spin-cast rod for its action is the weight of the lures to be cast. If the rod is to flex and "work" it must be limber enough to respond to the weight of the lure and provide maximum momentum at the instant the lure is delivered, or "cast."

SPINNING RODS

There are countless models and various designs in spinning rods, but all have at least a few things in common; the reel seats are near the center of the handle, guides are over-sized, and the rod shaft is, comparatively speaking, long and whippy.

Spinning was designed, originally, for casting lures too heavy to be used with fly outfits, and too light to be cast with standard bait-casting outfits.

What's important in buying a spinning rod is that it be appropriate for the kind of fishing the angler will do, and that it be of a quality commensurate with its price. Those things, of course, apply to the selection of any kind of rod.

The ideal spinning rod is lightweight because of the lures used, and this lightness also reduces casting fatigue. Spinning rod lengths may range from a minimum of 4 feet to 14 feet, and weight may be 1½ to 30 ounces. The range of rods would run from ultra-light to extra heavy.

Some spinning rods are of one-piece design, others two-piece, and still others are three-piece. For the ultimate in casting, a one-piece rod is best, since it has no ferrules to interfere with the natural flexing of the rod's shaft. The take-down rods, whether 2-piece or 3-piece, are for transportation conveniences.

Spinning rod handles are designed for one- or two-handed casting. In general, rods meant for one-handed casting are for use with lures weighing ⅝ths ounce or less. All spinning rods have long handles, but surf and other rods intended for two-handed casting have handles 15 inches or more in length.

A high quality spinning rod has a comfortable, well-designed handle.

Most spinning rod handles have fixed reel seats, and this type is the most secure and therefore the most popular, regardless of the size or style of the spinning rod. The best fixed reel seats are double screw-locking, the next best single screw-locking. These seats are heavy, however, and less comfortable than sliding-band reel seats.

Sliding-band seats, being the lightest, should be chosen when purchasing an ultra-light spinning rod, since light weight is the UL angler's prime consideration.

Some spinning fishermen prefer sliding band seats on any size spinning rod, because of their lightness and comfort to the hand. Sliding bands have a knack for loosening, though, and usually must be secured with tape wrapped around the rod handle and reel foot if the spinning reel is to be kept in place.

An important feature of any spinning rod is its guides. A proper set of spinning guides is graded in size from the one nearest the tip top to the one nearest the reel. If the guides are selected properly as to size, and are mounted at the right places on the rod, one can sight from the rod butt to its tip and see an elongated cone. If the guides do not line up that way, the rod is poorly designed.

This guide situation is of particular importance on a spinning rod because line pours from the open-faced spinning reels in large spirals when a cast is made. The first, and largest guide, chokes down part of this whirl and passes the line on to the next guide, which reduces the size of the spiral further. If the rod guides are correct, the line will be moving without any spirals by the time it reaches the end of the spinning rod.

Guides that are properly selected for any spinning rod also will be elevated certain distances from the rod's shaft. The butt guide will be highest from the shaft, the other guides decreasing gradually in elevation. The elevation of guides is to reduce "line slap," which occurs when the spinning line whirls off the reel spool.

BAIT-CASTING RODS

The bait-casting rod, sometimes also called "plug-casting rod," is used in conjunction with a revolving spool reel, usually one having a levelwind mechanism that spools the line evenly onto the reel.

The bait-casting rod, as with all other kinds of rods, must be selected according to the fishing to be done. A long, light, whippy-tipped bait-casting rod would be best for fishing with light line, and light lures for, say, smallmouth bass in some Ozarks stream. On the other hand, a fairly stiff, "heavy-action" bait-casting rod would be wanted for tossing large lures at tarpon and, in fact, such a stout rod would be needed in order to drive the hooks into the bone-hard mouths of tarpon.

A new type bait-casting rod designed strictly for plastic worm fishermen. This one has an off-set handle with "pistol" grip.

Bait-casting rods and reels are preferred by many fishermen who believe these outfits provide greater casting accuracy, allow more "feel" in working lures, and are superior to other tackle in fighting fish.

Plastic worm fishermen, in particular, enjoy using bait-casting rods, and many tackle companies make bait-casting rods that are designed solely for "wormin'." Most bait-casting rods for plastic worm fishing are fairly stout, and their actions will be classed at least as "medium" and more often as "medium heavy." Fairly stiff bait-casting rods are wanted by most fishermen because they strike hard and very fast, repeatedly, when a bass picks up their plastic worm.

The best lengths for "worming" rods are 5½ to 6 feet. Just be sure the rod has plenty of backbone.

The beginner at bait-casting would do well to purchase a medium-action rod of 5 or 5½ feet, since such actions and lengths are easiest with which to learn the art of "plugging." Longer, "softer" action rods require more experience and greater skill to handle them properly.

A light bait-casting outfit—which would be ideal for fishing clear lakes and rivers for smallmouth bass, or for fishing the big western rivers for trout—would be a fast, free-spool, tournament type reel on a 6 or 6½ foot, light-tip action bait-casting rod. The best line weight would be 6 to 10 pound test.

For medium fishing—such as largemouth bass and northern pike in weedy waters, and for lures ranging in weight around ⅝ths of an ounce—a medium-action bait-casting rod, or a "medium heavy," ranging 5½ or 6 feet in length, would be good. Such an outfit would best handle lines testing 12 to 18 pounds.

In choosing a bait-casting rod a fisherman must decide not only upon the length and action best suited to his needs, but also the kind of handle, whether straight, offset, or double offset. Which is best is a matter of personal preference.

Should the bait-casting rod be one-piece, 2-piece, or even 3-piece? Ferrules or "joints" alter the normal action of a single piece rod blank, so the fewer pieces the better—where action is concerned. Also, the more ferrules, the heavier the rod. A rod that "breaks down" into several pieces is, however, the most portable.

Bait-casting rods in 2 or 3 pieces are available that are "ferruless," that is, they do not have a metal ferrule. The smaller tip section simply fits directly into the larger butt section. Such "ferruless" rods are strong, very light, and have actions far superior to rods having metal ferrules.

A quality bait-casting rod will have a reliable means of locking the reel to the reel seat. Be certain the reel you use properly fits any bait-casting rod you buy, and that the reel can be quickly, easily, and solidly screwed and locked into place on the reel seat. Too, most bait-casting rods—even those that are 1 piece—have detachable handles. The rod blank, or shaft, is joined, for fishing, to the handle via a male ferrule on the shaft butt which goes into a locking female ferrule on the foregrip of the handle. Such locking devices should be checked carefully to see that they work properly, and that the rod shaft will not loosen when locked in place in the rod foregrip.

FLY RODS

Fly rods may be of one-piece design, two piece (the most popular), or three piece. Some are avaliable with extra tips, some with only one (an extra tip is desirable, of course, to replace a tip that may be broken, but second tips add considerably to the price of a rod).

Some fly rods have extention butts, most being removable. An extension butt is fixed to the bottom of the rod, adding 3 or 4 inches to the handle section, and it may be used as a second hand grip or pressed against the angler's belly to provide leverage when fighting a husky fish. Extension butts are found only on the heavier fly rods, such as those used in fishing for salmon or in salt water fly fishing. Unless the angler is likely to hook fish of those species that take considerable time to "play out," extension butts are generally unnecessary. Many experienced fly fishermen never use extension butts under any circumstances, feeling they add some weight to the rod and are not needed anyway. Some other fishermen prefer them, believing they take up some of the strain when fighting heavy fish for long periods.

There also are two-handed fly rods, the second "handle" being a long butt extension, which may or may not be removable. Two-handed rods are found chiefly on the world's salmon rivers, though some also are used in salt water fly fishing.

Whether the heavy duty fly rod should or should not have an extension butt or be two-handed is a matter of personal choice.

The biggest selling fly rod is one made of hollow fiberglass, which is strong, lightweight, will not warp, and can be designed or tapered to produce almost any kind of rod "action" desired. Next in popularity are bamboo rods, custom grade, which often have exquisitely smooth "action," and are in special demand by serious trout fishermen.

Solid glass fly rods in general are not up to the quality of most fiberglass rods, and tend to be considerably heavier. The carbon graphite fly rods now on the market are super light, very strong, have excellent "actions," and accept a variety of line weights; but at this printing, graphite fly rods are very expensive.

Three important features of any fly rod are its guides, ferrules, and reel seat. All guides should be of a fairly large size, especially the ring or butt guide (first guide), so the heavy fly line will pass through with the least friction. Excepting the butt guide, and tip top, guides should be of the "snake" type, and the harder the material used in the guides the better. Carboloy, or tungsten-carbide guides are the best, but guides of hardened wire, or ones with hard chrome plate, also are long-lasting and serviceable.

Good ferrules are made of nickel silver or plated brass, and they should fit extra snug. Check to see that the fly rod's ferrules are not loose, neither when joined nor disjoined. Shaking the tip section, then the butt section of the rod, will reveal any looseness between the ferrule and the rod blank.

Many high quality fiberglass fly rods have no ferrules, the graduated tip section(s) simply fitting inside the end of the butt or next larger section. These "ferrules" arrangements are much desired, since they are strong, weightless connections. There is nothing to loosen or twist off the rod when there are no metal ferrules. Too, rods sans metal ferrules not only are lighter than rods with ferrules, but they have an uninterrupted, smoother "action."

Fishermen wanting the lightest possible fly rod, for its length and action, should purchase one with a "skeleton" reel seat; these usually are cork, with a couple sliding metal rings to secure the reel. Similar reel seats have walnut "fillers," with screw-locking nuts and hoods.

The reel seat on any fly rod should be well designed and long-lasting. The seat must properly accept the fly reel, that is, it should be possible to mount the reel quickly and easily, without a great deal of pushing and forcing to get the reel seat hood over the reel foot, or the rear reel foot into the rear hood of the seat. Once in place, the reel should not be loose and "wiggly" in the reel seat, and, finally, screw-locking type nuts should be on the seat to tighten down and keep the reel firmly in place.

Reel seats made of anodized aluminum are long-lasting; they are corrosion and rust resistant, stand up to hard wear, and are very light yet strong.

In a sense, fly rods are "sized," and must be selected for length, weight, "action," weight of line they will use, and the fishing purpose for which they will serve.

The fisherman who will use one fly rod for all of his angling—which may be bluegill fishing one day, bass fishing the next, and walleye or northern pike fishing another day, would probably be happiest with an 8 or 8½ foot rod, weighing 4 to 5 ounces, and taking a No. 7 or 8 weight line, in level and 3-diameter sizes (L8–F, WF8–F).

For very light fly fishing—panfish in lakes, small stream trout—a rod weighing 2½ to 3½ ounces, ranging in length from 6 to 7½ feet, and taking lines No. 5 or 6, would be preferred by most anglers.

In heavy fly fishing, such as in bass bug fishing or in salt water fly fishing, a rod 8½ to 9½ feet, weighing 4½ to 5½ ounces, is about right. Such a rod should have a slow "action," and work with a size 8 or 9 weight line.

It should be pointed out that no fly rod, regardless of its quality and cost, cannot, even in the hands of an expert caster, perform properly if it is not matched with the proper weight line. Most fly rods today are marked by the manufacturer as to the size fly line suited to the rod, and buyers should adhere to the manufacturer's line recommendations.

SURF RODS

With almost no exceptions, tubular fiberglass is generally considered to be the best possible material for building surf rods. The typical surf rod, even the shortest and lightest, is something of a heavy-duty, long-distance weapon, so those made of the lightest possible materials are most in demand.

The most popular surf rods today are big spinning sticks, but some anglers still prefer to do their surf casting with revolving spool reels, so there are actually two

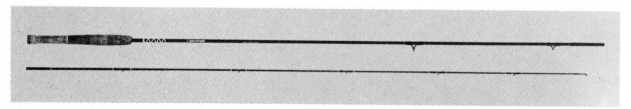

Lightest fly rod on the market is the spanking new Shakespeare, all graphite rod. This 8 footer weighs less than 2 ounces.

kinds of surf rods—the long, two-handed spinning rods, and the powerful, lengthy, "conventional" surfin' rods.

A good surf rod, whether "conventional" or spinning, has an action that balances between power and flexibility. "Power" is needed to set hooks in fish that may be striking a lure 150 feet away, and rod "flexibility" is needed to cast a lure those 150 or more feet.

One-piece surfin' rods are preferred by most beach veterans, since they have smoother casting action and are lighter, but when transportation is a problem, two-piece rods are necessary. Some surf rods are available with one-piece shafts, but with detachable handles.

Surf rods are available in lengths from 7 to 14 feet, but the conventional type is most popular in lengths of 9 to 10 feet, measuring from the butt to tip top. The action of such rods is designed to handle lures weighing 2 to 4 ounces.

The heavy surf spinning rod usually is 8 or 9 feet, and while the butt action may be quite powerful, the most serviceable of these rods have whippy or so-called "fast" tips, which aid in handling a wider range of lure weights, and also reduce the fatigue factor in casting.

The guides on a surf spinning rod are far larger, comparatively, than the guides on other spinning rods. The butt guide, in particular, is of giant size, and necessarily so to gather in the looping monofilament line as it leaves the spinning reel spool. Always check the surf spinning rod to be certain the butt, or first guide, is of adequate size.

The quality of guides, ferrules, reel seats, and handles are especially important in the surf rod, conventional type or spinning.

The guides should be the best, with quality rings and strong bridge supports. The best guides will be of tungsten carbide, carboloy, agate, or hard chrome-plated stainless steel.

Ferrules of reel seats on a good surf rod are of heavily plated brass or anodized aluminum, and they've got to be solidly mounted to take the rigors of surf casting. The glass shafts of quality surf rods go all the way through the rod handle, right to the butt. This builds a very strong handle, one that will not break or loosen in the normal course of casting or playing hooked fish.

BOAT AND BAY RODS

Boat and bay rods, which might also be called pier or trolling rods, encompass an unbelievably vast variety of rods. The one thing they all have in common is that they are meant primarily for salt water fishing, although some rods of these types frequently are used in deep trolling for lake trout (especially wire line trolling), and for coho and Chinook salmon fishing in the Great Lakes.

Most boat-bay-pier-trolling rods also are uniquely short, have stiff, powerful actions, large reel seats built to accept the larger salt water revolving spool reels, and long, husky, two-handed handles—usually made of wood but sometimes both foregrip and handle will be cork.

The exact model or type of boat or bay rod the angler selects will depend entirely upon his personal preference, and what he desires most in a rod—which in turn depends upon his fishing habits and experience. In almost all cases the boat-bay rod may be considered a "meat stick"—a powerful rod by which to put the fish that bites into the boat promptly, with a minimum of ceremony. However, the fisherman who wants a rod for bottom fishing with heavy sinkers from a boat for flounders in Maryland's Sinepuxent Bay likely would prefer a rod quite different from one used by a fisherman "walk trolling" for tarpon and snook from a Florida Overseas Highway bridge.

The fisherman must decide for himself, or with the assistance of an experienced angler or qualified tackle store clerk, on the length, weight, and degree of "heaviness" in the boat-bay rod he buys. The fisherman who does mostly bridge or pier fishing will do best with a lengthy rod, such added length enabling him to reach well away from bridge structure, not only to better control his bait but also to keep hooked fish from fouling line in bridge supports. The fisherman who will do chiefly boat trolling may want a much shorter rod, for ease in handling in the confines of a boat.

If finicky, wary, easy-biting fish are to be the angler's primary target, a rod with a "soft" sensitive tip should be selected. It will assist the angler in detecting light bites. A boat-bay rod with a short, extra-stiff shaft is in order when fishing from a party boat that is crowded with fishermen, and when it is necessary to deck hooked fish quickly to avoid tangled lines.

The most common deficiency in boat-bay rods is loosening of the lower handle, where it mounts in the reel seat. The glues used in fixing butts to reel seats often dries and crystallizes with storage, so check the butt and foregrips to be sure they are secure before purchasing the rod. Handles that are loose, however, can be readily repaired by the tackle dealer.

DEEP SEA RODS

The rod used in taking big gamefish from a boat varies according to the area fished and the species of fish involved. For example, a much lighter, longer rod may be appropriate in fishing for Atlantic sailfish out of Stuart, Fla., where the fish doubtlessly will weigh under 70 pounds; whereas, a heavier, shorter rod would normally be called for in trolling for black marlin off Panama,

where the average fish encountered will weigh 250 pounds or more.

The big gamefish, deep sea rod must by necessity be more solidly built, more dependable than any other fishing rod. When a prized Pacific sailfish of 130 pounds goes greyhounding over the surface, or an 800 pound Atlantic bluefin tuna sounds to the bottom, are not times for a rod handle to split, or for guides to rip off the shaft.

Most manufacturers grade their deep sea rods according to line test classifications; in other words, if one hopes to take a record fish that would be eligible in the "under 30 pound line test classification," he would be wise to purchase a rod rated as a "30 pound class" or less rod. Such classifications of rods really is just another way of identifying their actions, from "light," to "medium," to "heavy." In this vein rods usually are listed as 30, 50, or 80 pound class. The International Game Fish Association, which maintains the world records for marine gamefish, in addition to listing records according to line tests, stipulates in its rules that rod tip lengths may not exceed 5 feet, so that is an important factor to consider in purchasing a deep sea rod, assuming that one might like to be eligible for world record status in the event he should hook and land a prize winner. I.G.F.A. rules also encourage, but do not demand, certain limitations in rod butt lengths. For 12, 20, and 30 pound test outfits, the rod's butt length usually is a maximum of 18 inches; for 50 and 80 pound gear, the butt shouldn't be more than 22 inches, and for 130 pound outfits (the heaviest) the butt should not exceed 27 inches.

Deep sea, big game anglers who are not particularly concerned about angling for records might remember that the longer the rod the more easily and more quickly large fish can be beaten and brought to boatside.

Insist upon quality construction when buying a big game rod. The handle, ferrules, reel seat, and guides must be top grade. Guides are especially important. They should be heavy-duty, well supported, and of roller type. Roller guides usually have, and *should have*, self-lubricating bearings that can be readily disassembled for cleaning.

PACK RODS

Pack rods originally were designed for hikers and campers who wanted a light, compact rod that would be easy to carry and to stow. Pack rods are still in great demand among "backpack" fishermen and campers, but other fishermen, too, have use for pack rods.

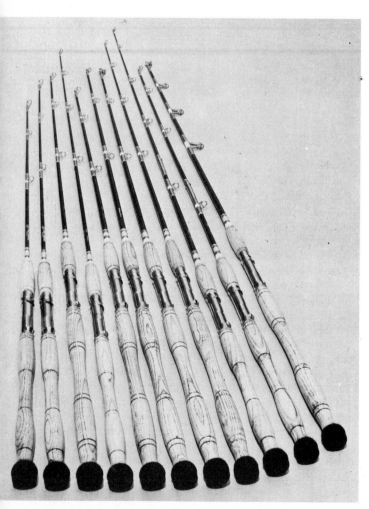

An elaborate selection of boat and bay rods, plus a couple of "big game" sticks.

Pack rods are nothing more than "take anywhere" rods, rods that can be taken apart into many small pieces, or telescoped into a single, short length. Many traveling businessmen use them because they can be carried conveniently in a suitcase or even an attaché case.

There are many different kinds of pack rods. There are pack rods for spin-casting, spinning, bait-casting, and fly fishing. And there are pack rods that are "combination" rods—ones that can be put together for use as a fly rod, or as a spin-cast or bait-casting rod, or as a spinning rod. It all depends upon the rod design.

Some pack rods break down, or telescope, into much smaller sections than other pack rods. But the more sections, the poorer the action is likely to be. So the fisherman wanting a pack rod first of all must decide whether he wants a spinning or other type rod, and whether he wants the smallest possible rod, or merely an average size pack rod. He'll have to decide, too, whether or not he wants a combination pack rod, one he can use for a couple different kinds of casting methods. Some combination kits are available that even make up into more than two kinds of rods. You can, for example, buy a rod kit that contains a couple separate handles—one for fly fishing, and one that can be used for spin-casting or bait-casting.

Pack rods, no matter what type, also come in various containers. Some are ordinary zippered vinyl cases, some are plastic cases, and some are fancy aluminum containers designed to look like a businessman's attaché case. There are so many varieties of pack rods it is not possible to describe them all. Moreover, each fisherman has to decide for himself what type pack rod will most perfectly satisfy his needs.

But regardless of the kind of pack rod selected, its price will pretty well reveal its quality. The one thing to be careful of in selecting any kind of pack rod is the rod's action. If the rod is telescope type, extend it to its full length and check its action. Be sure that it will provide the action needed to perform a proper casting job. If the pack rod is the sectioned type, join all the sections and check the action. Finally, it is wise to be sure that the pack rod's reel seat will correctly mount the reel of your choice.

ICE FISHING RODS

Ice fishing rods come in different shapes and sizes, but in general almost all are of simple design and measure under 4½ feet, and most also are "light action," suitable primarily for taking panfish.

The unique design of ice fishing rods is for a purpose; they must be short to permit the angler to work close to his ice hole, construction must be simple because the fisherman will be wearing heavy gloves, and the "action" of the rod should be light because the bulk of ice fishing is for panfish such as bluegills and crappies.

Experienced ice anglers also want ice rods with "soft" or sensitive tips since so many fish taken through the ice "mouth" baits very gently, and it would not be possible to detect strikes unless the ice rod had a sensitive tip by which the fisherman can "feel" strikes.

Most ice fishing rods do not have reel seats, simply because ice fishing often is done without a reel. Reels with small moving parts can freeze up in ice fishing weather, so most ice fishing rods merely have wire line winders attached to the handle. The fisherman winds line he is not using around the line winder.

Ice rods, which are comparatively very inexpensive, usually have wooden handles although some are made with cork handles. The best ice rods have 1 to 3 guides (depending upon length) and a tip top.

CHAPTER 5

How To Bait-Cast—better!

*Follow these proven instructions
and your bait-casting technique
will improve overnight.*

Bait-casting is as American as Huckleberry Finn.

With the exception of spin-casting (an innovation of spinning), bait-casting is the only popular casting method that originated in America.

Sometimes called "plug-casting," bait-casting was well underway in the United States in the early 1900s, shortly after Jim Heddon whittled the first wooden plug on Dowagiac Creek, in Michigan. Immediately following World War II spinning became a big thing, and for a time bait-casting seemed almost forgotten. But during the last 15 years there has been a major revival in bait-casting. Today a man is not considered a "finished" angler unless he is adept at fly casting, spinning, and bait-casting.

Perhaps the reason for increased interest in bait-casting is the greatly improved plugging tackle that's available today. The bait-casting gear seen in tackle stores now is a far cry from what was available years ago.

Cumbersome, slow-starting and slow-stopping casting reels are generally a thing of the past. Short, stiff rods are out too, as are thick, rough casting lines. Not only has American-made casting tackle been vastly improved, but several U.S. firms now are importing foreign-made bait-casting reels that are dandies. Even though tackle manufacturers abroad had little knowledge of bait-casting 15 years ago, many of the finest casting reels available these days are imports.

Advances in glass and graphite rod construction have helped, too. Manufacturers are turning out glass bait-casting rods having superb action, durability, lightness, beauty—as well as appealing price tags. Same is true of graphite sticks, although they're expensive.

And we now have monofilament lines, almost translucent, ultra-smooth, soft and waterproof. Braided lines are better too, with most of them now made of tough, long-wearing nylon.

But despite the fact that bait-casting equipment is better than ever, many fishermen still outfit themselves poorly. There are certain factors to consider in selecting bait-casting tackle.

The weight range of lures you will cast should determine the action, and to a lesser degree the length, of the rod you select. The actual weight of the rod is almost meaningless.

For very light lures, long rods with "fast" tips are best; for heavy lures, shorter rods with stiffer actions are needed. To cast lures ¼ ounce or less, a rod with a very "soft" or "fast" tip, about 6½ feet, and used with 4-pound test line would serve well. For lures ½ ounce or heavier, select a stout-action rod, preferably one of about 5 feet.

Generally it is not necessary to have a rod shorter than 5 feet, or longer than 6. Since most lures used by bait-casters range ⅜ to ⅝ ounce, the most popular rods have fairly flexible tips but their action "slows" or becomes heavier toward the butt. Most popular rod length is 5½ feet.

A friend of mine uses a chuck-type, universal rod handle with one of four glass rod blanks he fitted with guides. Each tip is different in length and action. He selects the one which best handles the lures he wants to fish at a given time.

Rods with one-piece tips normally have the best action. When there is no ferrule-break in a rod shaft, its action is continuous from tip to butt. Many bait-casters prefer rods having one-piece tips, with the tips removable from the handle. There are, however, lots of two-piece rods that have superb action.

Guides on a bait-casting rod should be evenly spaced, and there should be enough of them so that the rod bends uniformly. Breakage can result, when playing a fish, if a rod does not have the proper number of guides. Guides should be reasonably large too, so that line-friction is reduced when casting.

Plug rods come with three types of handles; straight, off-set, and double off-set. Most have off-set handles, ones in which the reel seat is low. Double off-set handles, sometimes called "angle off-set," have the low reel seat, and a cork grip that is angled downward slightly. An off-set handle allows easy thumbing of the reel and reduces wrist fatigue. The angled grip of a double off-set handle fits the contours of the hand well, and is preferred by many fishermen.

The cork grip of a plug rod should be shaped to fit the hand, and should be on the thin rather than the thick side. The fore-end of the rod handle should be of decent shape and size, so you can get a good grip on it when reeling. Rod handles should not have sharp nuts or lugs around the reel seat. They can be uncomfortable when gripping the rod with your left hand as you work a lure or pump-in a fish.

The bait-caster's most important equipment is his reel. Buy the best you can afford. The typical casting reel is quadruple-multiplying, meaning the spool revolves four times with each complete turn of the handle. The reel is but a tiny winch and must be well made.

The heavy metal reels of the past have given way to light reels with aluminum-alloy or plastic spools. Quality modern reels have fast-starting, fast-stopping spools. They revolve with ease, and operate with watch-like precision.

The big bug-a-boo in bait-casting reels is friction. A bait-casting reel's level-wind device creates friction and thus slows the cast, but it is generally necessary. Many "free-spool" reels (originated by tournament casters) are available now. With these it's possible to disengage some of the reel's gears so the handle does not revolve during the cast. Most free-spool reels disengage the handles but not the level-wind. A "total free-spool" reel also disengages the level-wind so that nothing moves, on the cast, except the spool. Total free-spool reels eliminate all gear-and-handle inertia, making it possible to cast lures as light as ⅛ ounce. With all free-spool reels, a turn of the handle usually re-locks the gears so the retrieve can be made.

The spool of a bait-casting reel should fit snugly into the reel-frame, otherwise line may slip over the spool flange and jam the spool. Casters using monofilament line must be especially careful to select reels having tight spools; mono' is worse than braided line for slipping between a reel spool and frame. Reels specially designed for use with monofilament, having extra-tight spools, are available.

Spools *must* be well made. One-piece construction is best, because such a spool will not get "out-of-round" nor will it collapse from the pressures occasionally exerted by monofilament line. (When playing a heavy fish for some time on monofilament, the line is stretched and its diameter reduced. If respooled this way, the mono' will return to its original diameter on the spool. If the spool is poorly made the swelling mono' may push its flanges out and cause a jam.)

Many new bait-casting reels come with or without star drags. A star drag is helpful in fighting big fish. However, there's at least one major annual angling contest in which fish caught on bait casting reels having star drags may not be entered in the plug casting division; they must go in the open division.

Some reels are made with elaborate anti-backlash devices. But the fisherman who learns to use his thumb to slow down the reel spool when necessary, instead of relying on the anti-backlash, is better off. All bait-casting experts agree there is no substitute for an "educated" thumb.

Take good care of your casting reel. Oil it regularly, 2 to 3 times in a day's fishing. Follow the manufacturer's lubricating instructions, and never use too much oil. Keep the reel clean by washing it frequently in a solvent such as gasoline.

The smaller the diameter of the line you use, the longer, smoother your casts will be. Most bait-casters use lines much too heavy. Unless you're fishing for large fish with heavy lures in snag-filled water, extra strong line isn't necessary. For ordinary bass fishing six or eight pound test is adequate. If you want one line for all-around bait-casting, use 10 or 12 pound test.

Do not use soft-braided line. It takes on too much water, which retards movement of the line through the rod guides. The best lines are round, hard-braided, waterproof nylon—or nylon monofilament.

Many plug casters use monofilament exclusively. Its finer diameters, strength, smoothness—plus its ability to

The overhead cast is the bait caster's "workhorse" throw. It is the safest and most accurate cast, with the rod brought up and back directly over the caster's shoulder.

shed water—offer the bait-caster special advantages. Round mono' used on bait-casting reels should be pre-stretched and of the "limp" or pliable type.

In filling a reel's spool, see that the line comes within about ³⁄₁₆ inch of the spool-edge, or within ¼ inch or so of the reel's crossbars. Too little line on the spool will cause poor casting. If the line is deep down and the line-core narrow, you won't be able to get out much line without forcing your casts.

If you use a braided line, rather than monofilament, tie a nylon leader to the line. Use limp nylon so lure-action will be unaffected. Tie the leader to the line with a small barrel knot, which will pass through the rod guides okay. The leader should be 12 inches shorter than the rod, so the leader-line knot isn't wound onto the reel. If the knot is wound onto the reel it will brush the level-wind on the cast, adding unnecessary friction.

The size snap, or snap-swivel, you tie on the leader depends on the kind of fishing and type lure being used. Use the smallest snap practical, or none at all if you can get by without one. I never use snaps on surface lures. I think they retard the action of top-water baits.

Most plug casters do not hold a rod right. They hold the rod, and make their casts, with the reel spool up; their thumb is pressed straight down on the line. The correct way, for a right-handed caster, is to place the thumb on the left side of the spool, then turn the hand so the palm faces down and the reel handles up. (For a left-hand caster, handles face down). Turning the hand so the palm is down gives you freer wrist movement when casting, and provides for best rotation of the reel spool.

The casting motion in nearly all casts combines forearm and wrist movements, but most of the power comes from the wrist. The rod grip should not be held too tightly. The handle of the rod must be allowed to "rock" over the fulcrum of the skin-web between the thumb and first finger. As the rod goes back, the last two fingers relax on the rod grip, even opening a bit, then are closed in a squeezing motion to rock the rod forward on the wrist "hinge."

Right-handed casters must switch the rod from right to left hand to retrieve. Cup the reel comfortably in your left hand, and take the line between the thumb and index finger of your left hand. Run the line between your fingers as you respool it. This will clear the line of some water, will respool it under even tension, and will keep you prepared for the strike of a fish. When a hooked fish runs, the left thumb can be used to brake the turning spool.

In retrieving, you can push the rod butt against your stomach. Or you can hold the rod out, with the reel and part of the reel-seat cupped in your left hand. Holding the rod handle against your body gives added support, but it can be awkward when working a lure.

The overhead cast is the bait-caster's workhorse throw. It's the most accurate cast, the safest to use when fishing from a boat with companions, and it gives good distance. (All instructions following are for hight-hand casters; the opposite holds for left-handers.)

Begin an overhead cast by grasping the rod properly, as explained earlier, with the palm down and reel handles up. Face the target with your right foot forward and extend the casting arm. Your right elbow should not touch your body and, in fact, should not even be close to your body.

Aim by looking over the tip of the rod to the target, or raise the rod and look *through* the rod, past the first or second guide, to the target. Keep your eye on the target, using secondary vision to sight along the rod.

The thumb is kept pressed against the reel spool during the backcast, and part of the forward cast, to keep the lure from flying out prematurely.

Start the backcast by raising your forearm slightly to lift the rod up and back. The wrist then takes over, acting as a pivot-point or "hinge" for the rod. Your wrist becomes the rod's axis. As the wrist "rocks" back, the lower fingers relax on the grip, allowing the rod to pass no more than 10 degrees beyond the vertical. If the rod has good action, and a lure of the proper weight is being used, the rod should develop a deep casting bend as the wrist checks the rod's backward movement.

With a ⅝ ounce lure, the tip of a medium-action, 5½ foot rod should bend to about the 3:00 o'clock position on the backcast, even though the rod handle does not go farther back than 12:00 or 1:00 o'clock. Actually, there's no precise point on an imaginary clock-face that will apply to all rods and all lure weights. But if the tackle is well-designed and matched, the backcast should be stopped near the vertical, and the rod tip will continue on to develop a proper casting bend.

As the rod reaches its deepest bend, close your lower fingers in a firm squeeze on the rod handle. At the same time, bring your forearm down a little and turn your wrist toward the target, to bring the rod tip forward in a sweeping arc. The forward cast should be made with twice the speed of the backcast.

As the rod "turns over" on the forward cast, ease your thumb pressure on the spool so that the plug shoots out. The proper release point normally is between 11:00 and 10:00 o'clock, or when the rod is at an angle of from about 45 to 35 degrees. The thumb stays on the spool throughout the cast, controlling the speed of the spool and the out-going line. As the lure travels out, "follow through" with the rod, gradually lowering it so that it is near its original starting position when the lure nears the target. Just before the lure hits, "thumb" the spool, first lightly, then enough to stop the spool, and halt the lure as it drops into the target area.

Strive to make the arc of your cast flat as possible. A cast with low trajectory is most accurate, least affected by wind. If the cast is too high, you released too soon; if the lure dives into the water, you released too late.

Most casters put too much power into a cast, swinging the rod forward with full-arm punch. Let the rod,

Right-hand side cast has rod moving parallel to the ground. It is a useful cast under many conditions but not the most accurate.

pivoting on your wrist-hinge, do the work. The force
that bows the rod is in the wrist, which rocks first back,
then forward. If the rod handle doesn't "rock" a little in
your hand, you are too tense. It is the bend of the rod,
under full load, that straightens and propels the plug.
There's a snap-application of wrist power (coupled with
closing the fingers on the grip) at the peak of the forward cast that must be mastered.

Try always to make a smooth cast, as though the rod
is part of your arm, by a graceful, merging action of the
wrist and forearm, with wrist movements predominating.
Once you've accomplished this, you'll have the coordina-
tion that is the foundation for all bait-casting.

Other important casts to learn are the side-casts, underhand, and bow-and-arrow. To these should be added
the catapult, flip, backhand, and lob casts.

The side-cast is the most difficult to do accurately, but
with practice you'll be able to side-cast a lure into tiny
pockets beneath overhanging trees. It's a valuable cast

*Left-hand side cast is same as right-hand, except
executed from left side of caster's body. If caster
held rod as shown here, but at shoulder height,
cast would more properly be called the "backhand" cast.*

*The underhand cast looks tricky but is easy, and often is the way to deliver a rea-
sonably effective cast when standing on a brushy bank.*

The catapult cast is an inverted bow-arrow cast, and, like the bow-and-arrow cast, it is very useful in delivering flat casts that drive lures beneath overhanging tree limbs.

when you are forced to work under tree limbs, and when you want to drive a lure under wind.

The basic motions used in the overhead cast also are used in the side casts. For a right-side-cast, face the target with your left foot slightly forward, the rod held parallel to the ground about waist high and pointing to the target. The palm of the hand should be turned up, so the reel handles face down. Bring the rod back briskly, keeping the real handles down, and stop the rod when it is at a right-angle to your body. The rod tip will continue back, acquiring a casting bend. Come forward immediately, using both wrist and forearm, and lift your thumb from the spool at the peak of the forward stroke. Learning the proper release point is important. Releasing too soon will send the lure right. Releasing too late will send it left.

The left-side-cast is done by holding the palm of the hand down, reel handles up as you face the target and point the rod at it. The rod is brought back to the left side of the body by quick wrist and forearm movement. Your forearm must pivot sharply on your right elbow. When the rod is at a right-angle to your body, stop its

backward progress. Bring the rod forward without hesitation, using lots of wrist-snap and forearm motion. Release the lure as the rod nears its starting point. On this cast, a too-early release will send the lure left; one too late will go right.

The underhand cast is easy. While it looks like a "trick" cast, sometimes it's the only way you can cast out of brush. It's an accurate cast, but not good for much distance. The underhand cast can't be done well with rods that are too stiff, or if a lure is too light to create a decent casting bend in the rod.

Face the target with your right foot out, casting hand extended, and rod pointing to target. The rod, your wrist, and forearm should form a straight line toward the target. The rod is gripped palm-down, reel handles up.

Using your elbow as the pivot-point, "kick" the rod sharply upward by raising the wrist and forearm. Keep the stroke short but brisk, so that the rod tip bows up, and then rebounds as you turn your wrist and lower your forearm for the downward stroke. Make the tip of the rod "work," going into a deep casting bend at com-

A bow-arrow cast may be delivered from the angler's left side, as is being done here...

... or from the right side. Crossing-over of caster's arms looks cumbersome but isn't.

pletion of the downward stroke. As the rod recovers from this bend and starts upward, lift your thumb from the reel and the lure will zip toward the target.

It is the weight of the lure that makes the rod tip flex up, then down and in toward your feet. All you do in the underhand cast is give propulsive speed to the lure so that it creates a casting bend in the rod—which flips the lure out.

The bow-and-arrow cast shoots a lure low, with accuracy, and will get you out of tight spots. Let out about ½-rod length of line, and take the lure in your left hand. Hold the lure at a hook-bend, being careful of the barbs, and draw the lure back so that the rod is put into a tight bend. You should be holding the rod with the reel handles up, palm down. Release the lure, the rod tip will snap forward and propel your lure to the target.

You can get good distance with the bow-and-arrow cast by bending the rod well back. The initial speed of the out-going lure is great, so be sure to maintain good thumb-control on the reel spool.

Don't ease thumb-pressure on the spool until the rod has nearly straightened, and don't aim too high. These faults will send the lure too high or too low, instead of straight out.

The catapult cast is an inverted bow-and-arrow, the rod bent down instead of up. It's done the same as the bow-and-arrow, but be careful not to aim too low.

You can do a bow-and-arrow cast from the left or right side. Done on the left, the reel should be at belt-level, handles up, palm down. On the right side, handles go down, palm up. A right-side bow-and-arrow cast looks tricky, with the caster's arms crossed, but it's easy and efficient.

The flip cast is done best with a short, whippy rod. Hold the rod pointing down, reel handles facing the target. Using mostly your wrist, snap the rod tip down and in so that it goes into a casting bend near your feet. The lure should pass within a few inches of the ground.

As the rod rebounds out of its casting bend, straighten your wrist and release the lure as the rod aligns with the target. The release must be at the right moment. If it isn't, you won't get any distance. And at its best, the flip is only a "pitch" cast, good for 40 to 50 feet with the average bait-casting outfit.

The backhand cast is useful for getting a lure under trees when you're required to cast from the left side but must hold the rod high. The cast is like a regular left-side-cast, except that instead of holding the rod waist-high it's held at shoulder level. The lure is cast by flick-

The lob cast—this is the right-hand lob cast—is meant for maximum distance. Long, arcing sweep gives the lure great propulsion. Tournament casters use this cast to achieve distance.

right-lob cast, only more wrist and less arm is required.

Two-handed rods are used for heavy bait-casting, especially in musky and tarpon fishing. Two-handed rods are generally short and stiff, except so-called "Texas popping rods." These are 6½ to 7½ feet long, with 10 to 15 inch butts.

In two-handed casting the end of the rod handle is held lightly with the left hand. The right hand raises the rod up and back to about the vertical position, where the rod is stopped and develops a casting bend. The left hand then pulls on the rod butt, starting the rod on its

ing the rod tip behind your left shoulder, then bringing it forward.

The lob casts, both right and left, are the best throws for distance. Good distances can be had with the overhead and side casts, but a properly executed lob cast will give more. It's the cast tournament champions use to win distance events.

For a right-lob cast, stand with your left foot slightly forward as you face the target. Hold the rod out to your right side, the reel handles down, and your palm up. The rod tip should be close to the ground so the rod will make a long, sweeping arc when you cast. Swing the rod back fast and low, pivoting at the waist as the rod goes into a casting bend. Put all of your arm and wrist into the cast as you start the rod forward, pivoting back toward the target. Swing the rod high on the forward cast so the rod points to about 10:00 o'clock when you let the lure go. In the lob cast the rod planes from a very low to a very high position.

To do a left-lob cast the right foot is forward, the rod held across the body. Reel handles are up, rod tip points down. The casting motion is the same as for a

Backhand cast is little used, but can be helpful when casting from shoreline brush or when required due to boat positioning.

Long, two-handed rod is best for heavy-duty bait-casting. They are most popular among tarpon fishermen, but have a place of value in other forms of angling.

Long, accurate casts, with heavy lures, can be delivered with the two-handed bait-casting rod. Left hand can be used to "kick" rod butt.

forward downstroke. The rod handle rocks in the right hand, and as the thumb is removed from the reel spool, the left hand forces the cast with a sharp inward pull against the rod butt. Casts of 300 feet are possible.

Only rarely, of course, is distance of real value to the bait-caster. Accuracy should be your first objective, followed by a mastery of all the practical casts. In the end, these are what put fish in the pan.

CHAPTER 6

How To Spin—Properly

*Any spinning enthusiast, beginner or expert,
can learn from the detailed casting and
tackle instructions presented here.*

Most spin fishermen can do overhead casts fairly well. Most also use right and left side casts, at least occasionally. But few know about, or utilize, the many other excellent casts available to them. The result is that frequently they are unable to put their lures into promising water, they catch fewer fish, and have less fun.

Even the basics of spinning—such as the rod hold and aiming the cast—are done incorrectly by the average fisherman.

Before getting into the mechanics of spinning, here are a few tackle tips overlooked by most fishermen.

It is difficult to recommend spinning rods by length and weight. The weight varies according to length, grip, type of reel-seat, hardware, and the kind and quality of rod material. Generally speaking, a rod 6½ or 7 feet long, about 5 ounces, will serve most spin-fishing needs. It should have good whip, with a fairly "soft" or "fast" tip, but it must have ability to "recover" quickly without excessive tip vibration. A too-fast tip cuts distance of the cast and impedes accuracy.

A screw-locking or "fixed" reel-seat keeps a reel from shifting or falling off. Some fishermen consider such seats uncomfortable to grasp, and fixed reel-seats prevent positioning a reel anywhere on the handle. Reel-seats with sliding rings or bands enable you to position a reel where it balances best. Also, you will be able to mount

the reel forward when using heavy lures, nearer the butt (to lengthen the rod) when using light lures. However, sliding bands sometimes work loose from a reel's "foot."

Large, light, strong guides are needed on the spinning rod. The butt, or "gathering" guide should be at least an inch in diameter on light rods, larger on medium and heavy rods. This butt, or first, guide must be mounted at the right spot, usually near the female ferrule on a two-piece rod. Also, butt guides on the best rods are slightly "off-set," so they face away from the reel spool. Remember that the "face" or spool of a spinning reel is not at right angles to the reel leg. The reel shaft is on a tilted axis. The spool faces up toward the rod and the rod's butt guide. The proper placement and off-set features of a butt guide reduce friction on the line during a cast, and prevent the uncoiling line from "slapping" the rod.

All true spinning reels are of the "open-face" type. (Thumb-controlled reels with housings covering the spool are properly called *spin-casting* reels). A quality spinning reel has a smooth, reliable drag or "brake"; a good rate of retrieve; and a well-fitted spool.

A skipping or faulty drag will keep line from paying out evenly when a hooked fish runs, and the fish may break off. The drag should have wide latitude of adjustment too, since the drag must be finely set to give a fish just the right amount of pressure without excessive strain on the line. Following proper adjustment for drag, a mere ¼-turn of the drag nut on some reels can lock the spool, or completely release the brake if turned the other way. Such small latitude of adjustment does not allow the varying range of drag tensions that are frequently needed.

To check drag latitude, turn a reel's drag completely off. Next, tighten the drag nut until you feel the drag beginning to grab. Now continue tightening the drag nut, counting each complete revolution, until the spool is locked. Well-designed reels have a minimum of four complete turns; less than three may not be enough latitude of adjustment, which one day may mean a broken line and a lost fish.

The best reels have lock-washers or such separating the drag nut from the reel spool. This keeps the brake from "creeping" out of adjustment when the spool is turning.

Your reel should have a fast rate-of-retrieve. Without good retrieving speed some lures can't be worked right, nor can hooked fish be handled properly. The rate-of-retrieve, or gear-ratio, should be at least 3.5 to 1— meaning the reel-spool housing or "cup" makes 3½ turns for each revolution of the handle. With most medium-size reels this would bring in about 22 inches of line with each complete turn of the handle. A large-diameter spool aids in speed-of-line-retrieve, and helps minimize twist in the line. A big spool also makes for easier, longer casts since fewer coils of line are taken from the spool on any given cast.

The reel-spool should fit snugly in its housing. If there's much space between the spool and housing, line may slip behind the spool and foul. Some reel manufacturers prevent this by lining the spool edge with chenille; others build "skirts" of metal or plastic over the housing.

The handling of spinning tackle is uncomplicated, yet it's easy to develop bad habits that hinder your casting.

Hold the rod with your thumb on top. The thumb, and heel-of-thumb, power your cast.

Most anglers place two fingers in front and two in back of the reel post. However, you may want to place one finger in front or even three, depending on the reel's design. Use whichever grip is most comfortable, but be sure the tip of your forefinger can easily reach the reel-spool.

Here's the proper way to line up for a cast with a spinning outfit. With thumb on top of the rod grip, caster aims his cast by lining target up with the butt or second guide.

With a reel having the usual line pick-up bail, the bail is opened and the line secured on the *tip* of the forefinger preparatory to casting. The line should not be hooked around the finger point or held against the rod.

There's another way to secure the line with the index finger prior to casting. Catch the line on the tip of your finger, open the bail, then drop your finger to the spool. The line will rest *on the spool*, but is kept from unwinding by your fingertip. The line is released on the cast by raising your finger. This way, you get better control and accuracy because at no time during the cast is the line actually on your finger. This method works with any bail-type reel, but best with ones that wind clockwise since the line is more easily secured with the fingertip. (Some spinning reels wind counter-clockwise.)

A lure shooting toward a target can be stopped instantly by turning the reel handle and closing the bail. A better way to halt the lure is dropping your forefinger to the spool flange, thus preventing more line from going out. Use your finger also to "feather" a cast; that is, to retard the flight of the lure slightly. Do this by lowering your finger just enough so that the uncoiling line brushes against it.

When necessary, you can use your fingertip for added braking. Most spin-fishermen deliberately set reel drags low. When a hooked fish runs out line against the drag, they press their forefinger against the revolving spool, thus slowing the fish. This system of braking is essential when using hairline and ultra-light tackle, as the slightest hesitation of the reel's mechanical drag would cause the fine line to snap.

When using a large outfit with heavy line for tough salt water fish, finger pressure on the revolving spool sometimes isn't enough. You can get additional pressure by holding the thumb and forefinger of your left hand on the spool.

As in other casting, accuracy is most important in spinning. Next in importance is having a good repertoire of "working" casts; and, finally, being able to get distance when it's needed.

The overhead cast is most accurate. Start by reeling a practice weight or a lure to within an inch or so of your rod tip. If the lure-weight is right for the action of the rod, it will not be necessary for the lure to hang more than three inches from the rod tip. If the lure is too light, it must hang farther down. Reason for this is that a light lure, hanging well down from the rod, has a

In spinning, as in all other forms of casting, the overhead cast is the most accurate. Multiple exposure photograph shows correct rod positions, and rod flex, from beginning of cast to delivery.

pendulum effect and creates greater pull against the rod tip during the casting arc, thus imparting more of a working bend to the rod.

The instructions that follow are for right-handed casters; for southpaws, the opposite will be true.

Face the target with your right foot slightly forward, aligned with the target. Now raise the rod and extend it toward the target. Reach out with your rod arm, keeping elbow and forearm away from your body. You can aim by centering the rod tip on the target, or by raising the rod higher and centering the butt guide or second guide on the target. Aiming should be done with *secondary* vision. Look directly at the target, but line up the rod tip or lower guide with the target by secondary vision. In other words, the cast is aimed by looking *through* or *beyond* a point on the rod. (This is how a good wingshot aims. He looks only at the flying bird, but he sees his shotgun barrel with secondary vision.)

One of the easier ways to get a lure tight up under overhanging foliage is with the underhand cast, and this cast is especially useful when standing in thick brush.

The bow-and-arrow cast is no "trick" cast, but rather a very useful casting technique. It will fire a lure a good distance, even when casting from cover much too heavy to permit a normal backcast.

Casting is done chiefly with the wrist and forearm. All movements are smooth but brisk, which brings out the action of the rod. The rod does all the work, pivoting on the axis of your casting hand.

Start the overhead cast by lifting the rod sharply, raising your rod hand slightly but with most movement only in the wrist. Wrist action, with the thumb-on-top grip, prevents the rod from going back much beyond the vertical position. Most casters err by making sweeping motions with their whole arm, which allows the rod to travel so far back that the hanging lure nearly touches the ground. By stopping backward movement of the wrist at a position about 10 degrees off the vertical, the swinging lure will put a good working bend into the rod. It is the rod's springing out of this bend that propels the cast.

When the rod reaches maximum bend on the backcast, bring the rod forward crisply and throw the rod tip into the cast. Release the line from your index finger when the rod is at about the 10:00 o'clock position. Keep the rod pointed at the target while the lure is in flight.

On a proper overhead cast the lure will sail out in a fairly flat trajectory, about 15 feet above the water. If the lure is released too soon it will arc out in high, looping flight; then wind may belly the line, slow the cast, and carry the lure off-target.

Some casters take their eyes from the target and watch the sailing lure. It's better to keep your eye on-target and watch the lure with secondary vision. If it appears you will over-shoot, "feather" the cast or stop it altogether by dropping your finger to the spool, as explained earlier. You can also pull the cast up short by raising the rod tip, at the same time using your forefinger to control the outward flow of the line.

Develop instinctive forefinger control. Finger control should be used on *every* cast. Many fishermen do not understand this. They cast and allow the lure to fall without using their fingertip at all. This causes excess coils of line to drop off the reel after the lure has landed. The result is a great deal of slack line, which means the lure may sink too deeply, a striking fish may be missed, or loose line may even foul on the reel or rod. By touching the reel-spool just before your lure reaches the target, or soon as it hits the water, you'll have a taut line and maximum control.

The underhand cast is one of the most useful. It permits you to cast from the tightest spots, provided there's room to poke your rod-tip through the foliage.

It's an accurate cast, but its distance is limited to about 60 feet.

Point the rod horizontally at the target, holding the rod about waist-high. Using mostly forearm and little wrist, flex the rod sharply upward. Let the rod rebound downward, giving it some "kick" by pressing down with your thumb on the rod handle. When the rod has maximum downward bend, let it spring back toward the horizontal, releasing the line as the rod tip rises and straightens. If your release is correct, the lure will shoot out low, 4 or 5 feet over the water.

Catapult cast, also occasionally called the "arrow" cast, is used when it's desirable to keep the lure closer to the water than can be accomplished with bow-arrow cast.

The bow-and-arrow cast fires a lure much like the underhand cast but can be used in tighter quarters. Let out line about half the rod-length. Grasp the lure at a hook-bend (avoiding barbs) with thumb and first finger of left hand. With the reel-bail open and the line on the tip of your index finger, point the rod at the target and pull the lure up and back until the rod has a tight bend. Release the lure, allowing the rod tip to snap forward. Do not straighten your forefinger, as you would in other casts, to release the line. Instead, let the outgoing lure pull the line from your finger.

The distance achieved with the bow-and-arrow cast depends on the amount of bend put into the rod. For maximum distance, shorten the length of line dropped from the tip as much as possible, so you'll have more pulling range with your left hand. Try to get good delivery by releasing the lure cleanly, and don't aim too high.

The catapult or "arrow" cast is simply an inverted bow-arrow cast. It's done the same as the bow-and-arrow but with rod bend reversed. In doing the catapult, don't aim too low.

Both the bow-and-arrow and catapult cast can be done as left or right side casts. About any cast wanted can be made by bending the rod tip.

The flip cast is one of the most difficult, particularly if rod action, lure weight, and line diameter are not prop-

Executing a right side bow-and-arrow cast.

The right-hand side cast is good for getting under wind or for sliding a lure beneath overhanging tree limbs.

Left-hand side cast has rod parallel to chest and horizontal to the ground.

erly matched. This is a short range cast, but useful under certain conditions.

Raise your arm to eye-level, pointing the rod downward at about a 30 degree angle. Snap your wrist down and in, making the rod flex sharply toward your feet. When the tip bounces back, nurse the rod forward, up, and out by wrist and arm movement, releasing the lure when the rod is pointed at the target.

The side cast, either right or left, is less accurate than other casts but is good for getting under wind or for putting your lure beneath over-hanging trees. And under some conditions, such as when in brush, the side cast is best. It throws a lure great distances, and keeps it in a low trajectory with minimum "belly" in the line.

Begin a right-side-cast by facing the target, weight on your left foot (weight on right foot for left-side-cast) and left foot slightly forward. Hold the rod horizontally, waist-high, and pointing at the target. Sweep the rod back quickly, stopping it at a right-angle to your body. When the rod attains its deepest bend, start it forward by turning your wrist and pushing against the rod handle with your thumb and thumb-heel. The lure should be released as the rod nears its starting point. Throughout the cast the reel should be *parallel* to the ground. Holding the reel vertically will give you freer wrist ac-

The lob cast is the one used for greatest distance, chiefly because it permits great application of thumb and heel-of-thumb power.

Left lob cast, like the standard right lob cast, is executed with snappy wrist action.

tion in the side casts, but it will prevent application of power with the thumb and heel-of-thumb.

The wrist is used almost exclusively in powering the side casts, the forearm very little. Accuracy depends on releasing the lure at the proper moment. In a right-side-cast, a too-early release will send the lure right of target; a release too late will send it left.

The backhand cast is occasionally useful when fishing from a boat with companions, and you want a cast that will go low under trees. The rod is held horizontally,

Big, two-handed surf spinning rod is built for distance casting. Pushing the left hand solidly downward on the rod butt during the forward stroke greatly increases rod speed and lengthens the cast.

When striving for maximum distance, surf caster's rod should drop far back so that there is full bend of rod and sweep in the cast.

head-high, and the lure is cast by a quick flip of the rod tip behind your left shoulder. Another backhand cast is made by holding the rod across the chest, pointed up at about 45 degrees, but this cast puts the lure into a higher arc.

The lob cast, either right side or left, is best for distance. It's the cast tournament champions use for distance because the rod goes into a long, sweeping arc, and because it permits great application of thumb and heel-of-thumb power.

The reel must be held at an angle of about 45 degrees to the ground. Snappy wrist action, as well as full arm movements go into the cast. Start a right-hand lob cast by holding your rod arm out to the side, slightly below shoulder height. Swing the rod back fast and low, so the lure nearly touches the ground, and pivot some at the waist. When the rod bends deeply come forward without hesitation, swinging the rod higher on the forward cast. The lure is released when the rod is pointed over the target.

Distance depends upon the action and length of the rod, diameter of the line, weight and design of the lure, trajectory of the cast, and the power put into the cast.

For heavy spinning, two-handed rods and large reels are used. Most commonly an over-the-shoulder cast is used—something between a straight overhead cast and a side cast. In addition, more body movement is put into two-handed casting than in conventional one-hand casting. Most two-handed rods are longer than regular spinsticks; hence the arc of the rod is higher on the cast, which sends a lure greater distances. With good tackle and the right wind conditions, casts of more than 200 feet are easy with two-hand spinning outfits.

For a loping, side-of-the-shoulder cast, start with the rod in about the 11:00 o'clock position. The left hand should be poised near the rod butt, or holding the butt of the handle loosely. Swing the rod far back. Bring it forward smartly, pushing your left hand solidly against the rod butt, at the same time shifting your weight and putting your shoulders into the cast. The lure is released when the rod tip attains top speed, which should be at the point where the rod is aimed over the target, and the rod is at an angle of about 45 degrees from the ground. The lure should soar out on a trajectory affording maximum distance.

How you use your left hand is important in two-handed casting. The left hand acts as a fulcrum, holding the butt of the rod. The left hand should pull on the butt, while the right pushes.

Many fishermen make unnecessary work out of spinning. Sometimes poor casting is due to badly matched tackle, but more often it's because the fisherman doesn't allow his tackle to do the casting for him.

CHAPTER 7

How To Fly Cast—Expertly!

Practice the tips and instructions given here and not only will you enjoy fly fishing more but you will be more successful at it.

Fly casting easy?

Pure nonsense.

Skilled fly casters often explain away their skills by saying "it's easy," or they think that it IS easy because they've been at it for so long, and they've forgotten the years of experience behind them. Some of the non-fly casters who claim fly casting is easy are simply misinformed, or they deliberately knock fly casting because they themselves are inept at it.

It does not, of course, require much talent to toss a fly 30 or 40 feet. And it is not difficult to make ordinary, short casts with small flies under good weather conditions, in an open area, for a short period of time. But how many fly fishermen do you know who can cast large, wind-resistant flies or bugs in a bad wind, from a small, bouncy boat, 80 or 90 feet—and do it all day long without fatigue?

A good fly caster is capable of much more than merely putting out an ordinary overhead, "wide-bow" cast to 70 or 80 feet. With typical light trout tackle, a skilled fly caster is able to execute all the practical casts—such as the overhead "wide-bow," the wind-cheating "tight-bow" cast, left and right side casts, back-hand cast, roll casts both left and right, and he can execute both left and right curve casts.

A skilled caster can make a roll cast pick-up of his line, as well as a snap pick-up. He can "mend" line, as well as send out a perfect "Lazy S" cast. He can put a dry fly down on a slick pool so lightly that the fly settles like goose-down. He can put his flies accurately to within inches of close targets, to within feet of distant targets. He can cast under almost any wind condition, and seldom is there a wind so strong as to force him to bait-casting or spinning.

An accomplished fly caster is a master of the double-haul. He can shoot 20 or 30 feet of line, can shoot line on both the forward and back casts, and he can execute a long cast—100 feet or more with a "heavy" outfit—with a minimum of false casts. Most of all his casting is effortless, untiring, done automatically, gracefully, almost unconsciously—so that the angler is able to concentrate not on his casting, but on his fishing.

Being a good caster isn't show-off" stuff. Casting ability is the skilled angler's Ace-in-the-hole, it's some of the edge he has over the ordinary guy that consistently puts fish in the pan for him. Thus anyone who takes his fishing seriously—whether it be fly fishing, spinning, or bait-casting—will enjoy his sport much more by working on his casting until he becomes expert.

Tackle details won't be mentioned here, but naturally you can't become a good fly caster if your gear isn't right. The rod should be a quality one with proper action,

Fly caster here has 60 feet of line in the air, but it's only a false cast. On final cast an additional 30 or 40 feet of line will be "shot."

Famed fly fisherman Charles Ritz of Paris watches as Tom McNally casts. Note high-held arm.

The proper way to grip a fly rod. The hand is Johnny Dieckmann's, who believed strongly in the role the thumb and heel-of-thumb play in powering the cast.

and the line or lines you get for it must be of the correct weight to "work" the rod. Any experienced fly fisherman can check your tackle for you, or the tackle salesman (if qualified) in the local sporting goods store *may* be able to help.

If you hope to polish your fly casting, start by checking your rod hold. A firm, solid grip on the cork is necessary. While the thumb-on-the-side grip is preferred by many accomplished casters, few tournament fly-rodders use that grip. Instead, they use the thumb-on-top grip.

The reason for this is two-fold. For one, the thumb-on-top aids in halting a rod at about the 1:00 o'clock position on the back cast, while still allowing a necessary "drift" of rod from 1:00 o'clock to about 2:00 o'clock as the back cast straightens. Secondly, the top-side grip allows a certain application of power on the forward cast.

The heel of the thumb *pushes* against the cork, giving power that can't be obtained with a thumb-on-the-side hold.

Now to the left hand (assuming you're a right handed caster). This is your "line controller." You use it to keep the fly line taut at all times and, of course, for the double haul. Take a good grip on the line with your line hand. Don't merely pinch-hold the line between your thumb and index finger, as some casters do. The line should be secured across the four fingers and under the thumb, with the hand nearly clenched.

Once you have properly matched tackle, know how to properly grip the rod and hold the fly line, the first cast you should work on is the ordinary overhead or "wide-bow" cast. This is the simple, work-horse toss of all fly-rodders.

A "wide-bow" cast should be started by extending a "working" length of line on the water. This would be about 40 feet with a WF9 line.

The late Johnny Dieckmann, one of the best professional casting champions, sighted his casts this way when super accuracy was called for.

For maximum distance on "shoots," Dieckmann held rod high, arm straight out.

"Up casting," as opposed to "down casting," should become habitual.

Now strip about 30 feet of line from the reel and drop it loosely on the ground, taking care that it doesn't tangle. Then, reaching out with the rod tip (keeping the tip low near the water), grip the free line with your left hand near the bottom guide on the fly rod. You pick line up for the back cast by making a quick, upward movement with the rod, at the same time tugging back sharply with the left hand.

This application of power with the left hand on the line pick-up takes much of the line load off the rod, and gives you line speed that is needed to start the line back fast enough that it will carry the proper length, and unfold with enough authority to "work" the rod at termination of the back cast.

At the top of the back cast the rod should pause between 12:00 and 1:00 o'clock, and as the line unfolds on the back cast the rod should then drift to about the 2:00 o'clock position.

The first movement in starting the forward cast should be a nursing-forward of the rod. The rod is started slowly forward while the back cast is straight as a needle. A good "wide-bow" cast is delivered by releasing or "shooting" the line when the rod is at about the 10:00 o'clock position on the forward cast. If the wind is directly behind you, or is quartering from behind on the left or right side, then utilize the wind and toss the line higher into the air, releasing or "letting-it-go" when the rod is in about the 11:00 o'clock position. By throwing the line high, the wind will carry it out much farther and give you a longer forward cast.

Strive for a big, wide loop when making the "wide-bow" cast. This is achieved partly by a slower flexing

Back casts, and forward casts too, should be "hump" free. The mark of an accomplished fly caster is a needle-straight line.

of the rod during the forward cast, that is, using the rod's power slowly rather than forcing the tip to turn over quickly as you would in delivering a "tight-bow" cast. If a "wide-bow" cast is one having a very wide loop on the forward cast, a "tight-bow" cast is, naturally, just the opposite—and the tighter, or narrower, that you make the forward loop, the better. It helps to throw a very tight loop into the line by bending low at the waist as power is put into the cast. At the "power" moment if you exaggerate and speed up the "turning over" of the top 1/3 of the rod, this will drive the line forward in a low, tight loop. A properly executed "tight-bow" cast has the line shooting out close to the water, and this is the sort of cast to use when it's necessary to cast directly into wind, or when you have to put your fly or bug up under overhanging tree limbs.

Side casts, either left or right, are casts in which the rod is held parallel to the ground, or to the water. Neither cast is difficult, but it's often helpful to cast either from the left or right side when bank foliage makes a standard cast impossible.

The back-hand cast is, for right-handed casters, a cast in which the line is tossed back over the caster's left

Reach high with the casting hand when you want an especially high back cast.

shoulder, then the forward cast done by rolling the casting hand over, in a backhand style. Turning some at the waist and looking back while making the backcast, then swiveling forward on the back-handed forward cast, is helpful. This cast is the one to use when it's desirable to put the backcast into an opening in trees behind you; or when the wind is coming from your right side so strongly that it would throw an ordinary backcast, executed on the right side of your body, into your scalp when you brought the line and fly forward.

The only difference between a left and right roll cast is the side of the body on which the rod is tilted. The standard roll cast is a very valuable cast, a cast that small stream anglers sometimes use almost exclusively. It's easy to learn. Just get 15 or 20 feet of line laying on the water out in front of you, then raise the rod to past the vertical position, canting it out somewhat from your right side. The rod's tip should be at about a 1:00 o'clock position, the line hanging loosely down from the tip. The cast is delivered simply by slowly starting the rod tip forward then increasing speed as the rod tip reaches the 11:00 o'clock position. From 11:00 to 10:00 o'clock, the rod tip is "thrown" hard into the cast. These movements will cause a large loop to pick up and roll down the line, turning the forward line over and carrying it out and on toward the target.

Curve casts often make the difference between catching a trout or not catching one to the stream fisherman who finds himself in a situation where a trout is unreachable, perhaps rising behind a rock, unless he can cast a curve. Curves left or right can be delivered by canting the rod almost to the horizontal position, left side or right, and then sending out a weaker-than normal forward cast. A better way to throw a curve into the line is by tilting the rod slightly right or left (depending on the curve wanted), delivering a normal cast but to the proper side of the target, then lifting up and back with the rod just before the forward cast unfurls and is completed.

A roll cast pick-up is simply an incompleted roll cast. Follow the usual moves necessary to make a roll cast— BUT—as the line lifts off the water and rolls forward raise your rod sharply, start a backcast move with the rod, at the same time tugging down on the line with your left hand. These moves will keep the forward-rolling line from dropping onto the water as it would in an ordinary, completed roll cast and, instead, will send it backwards into a normal backcast.

A snap pick-up is done by lifting the rod straight up in front of you to about the 11:00 o'clock position. From that position the rod tip is snapped quickly downward, with only the tip action of the rod allowed to influence the cast. This will put a large hump in the line which will continue down the line to the leader, at which moment you lift the rod straight up quickly. The leader and fly will then pop off the water, vertically, to a height of three or four feet, and all you need do then is execute a normal backcast.

It's advantageous to mend line when strong cross current will sweep your fly line and cause the fly to drag unnaturally. Mend line by canting the rod to one side (either left or right), then sweeping the rod across your chest in the opposite direction. That will cause a large loop to form in the line, and to be thrown out in the direction that is up-current. Before the current washes out the large loop you've put into your line by mending the cast, your fly will probably get a natural float—at the same speed as the current—for 10 or 20 feet.

There are two ways to deliver a "Lazy S" cast. One way is to overpower an ordinary forward cast so that the line jumps against the reel at the end of the cast, kicks backward, and falls slack to the water with some curves or "S's" in it. A better way is to make a typical forward cast, and just as the line straightens and begins to fall, to waggle the rod tip from side-to-side while the rod is held horizontal. This method puts a perfect and lengthy series of "S's" into the line as it settles on to the water.

The best way to deliver a delicate cast, usually desirable when dry fly fishing, is to be an "up" caster and not a "down" caster. A "down" caster throws his cast low over the water so that the forward part of the line hits hard just as the cast loses steam. An "up" caster throws his cast high so that the line straightens like a needle then falls flat to the water. In "up" casting you can help the fly and line to drop gently by lifting back slightly on the rod just as the line begins to fall after losing its forward momentum.

The double haul or double-line haul separates the accomplished caster from the mediocre because it is NOT easy to learn. The double haul is the *only way* to get real distance, but more important, it takes the drudgery out of fly casting. When you know how to double haul you can use a heavy rod and cast big, wind-resistant flies or popping bugs all day without fatigue. The fly-rodder who tires quickly isn't casting properly—he's doing the work instead of his tackle.

Knowing how to double haul also has other advantages. It improves your casting accuracy, and makes it possible for you to more easily throw an extra tight loop on the forward cast and put your fly beneath overhanging tree limbs. The double haul will help you get your fly out very quickly, with a minimum of false casts. And, in addition, it will let you drive your fly line into the teeth of a strong wind.

The double haul alleviates the necessity of out-sized fly rods. Years ago many salmon and salt water anglers believed that big rods (some were 16 feet long and weighed more than 8 ounces) were absolutely necessary to make long casts and to handle flies and poppers. However, the fact is, a very long line and heavy fly can be more easily cast with just an 8 foot rod when the double haul is employed.

The double haul takes much of the "load" off a rod. A rod can support only so much line in the air. To get more line up, the left hand must tug or haul on the line at the start of the back and forward casts. This increases line speed, cuts air resistance to the bug or fly, and reduces the line's weight or "load" on the rod. A right-handed caster executes the double haul by a series of movements of his left hand, all of which coordinate with movements of his right or rod hand. For a left-handed caster the opposite is true.

To learn the double haul, rig an 8 to 9½ foot rod with a WF8 or WF9 line, whichever is proper. You can double

Watching the fly line sawing back-and-forth when deliberately false casting is a good way to improve timing.

Caster completes "haul" on forward cast with left arm well past his thigh. This indicates a long hauling "stroke."

haul with any rod and any line, but heavy, three-diameter tapers are best since they're designed for distance casting.

Start by extending a "working" length of line, and proceed as you would normally when making a "wide bow" cast. As you pick up the line from the water with the rod, your line hand should make a quick, downward motion. On the back-cast, when the rod has been brought back up to between 12:00 and 1:00 o'clock, it will come under full load of the line. No real power has yet been put into the forward cast, but as the full weight of line is felt, start driving the rod ahead forcefully, at the same time tugging keenly downward with the line hand. This final yank with the line hand should be a long one, with your hand ending well below your waist. At this point the

Camera catches fly rod under "full load," with left hand "haul" completed, and fly line (humpless and straight) well on its way. This cast, with a standard weight-forward line, went a measured 110 feet after a single false cast.

cast and double haul are actually complete, with both line-hand and rod-power having been transferred to the line, which now is zipping forward on a tight, hump-free loop. All that remains is to extend the rod and let the line "shoot" through the guides. Once you get the basic double haul moves down pat, all it takes to become skillful is practice.

Although it is possible for a good caster to make a 70 foot cast *without a single false cast*, some false casting is necessary for longer casts. However, a good caster employing a 9 foot rod and WF9 line can cast 100 feet with a single false cast. He would start with about 50 feet of fly line, false cast once extending the line to 70 feet, then on the forward cast he'd double haul sharply and easily shoot another 30 feet of line on the forward throw.

Shooting line on the backcast is a good way to lengthen line and to get a cast out in a hurry. It's done in conjunction with the double haul.

When your backcast unfolds properly, you'll feel the weight of the line pulling against your line hand. As your line hand comes up, following along with the rod hand, ease your grip on the line when you feel the line pulling in your hand. This will permit several feet of line to "shoot" on the backcast. As the backcast slows and starts to drop, tighten your grip on the line, and start into the forward cast as usual.

Once you develop an educated line hand, you'll discover it does more than give you extra distance. Throughout the casting routine, your line hand can compensate for any errors in timing. It will increase or decrease the distance of your cast—by tugging sharply when more distance is desired, or not so sharply when you decide to shorten the cast. If you should be false casting with considerable line toward a target and then realize, just as you shoot, that you have fired too much line, you can pull the cast up short by tugging with your line hand—braking the cast in mid-air.

Tournament casters use their line hand to achieve greater accuracy. Just before their fly drops to the target ring, they tug slightly on the line, causing their leader to straighten perfectly.

One of the easiest ways to learn the double haul is to practice with just a rod tip. Lengthy casts with a rod tip are not possible unless you haul with your line hand. Using a tip literally forces you to develop hauling.

The tip of a two-piece, 9 foot rod will throw about 35 feet of WF9 line without the caster using the double haul. Such a 54 inch tip cannot "carry" or support more than that amount of line. But when you get 35 feet in the air, you'll feel the little tip bending and the line pulling hard in your hands. You'll tend to tug with your line hand, increasing the line's speed, holding it up, lengthening it—until you find you can keep around 60 feet of line in the air. Then you can shoot about 20 feet of line, for a cast of 80 feet—all with a "rod" only 54 inches long.

The double haul isn't easy to learn, and most fly fishermen never master it. But it does so much to improve your casting, and your fishing, that every fly-rodder should strive to get it down pat. Without the double haul most fly fishing is hard work.

When you can do the things discussed briefly in this article, and do them effortlessly, and when you can cast accurately with any type fly tackle, you'll be a pretty darn good fly caster. Not great—just good.

After you've mastered what's been outlined here you can learn such things as the Belgium cast, the spey cast, the parachute cast, the switch cast, the snake pick-up, the bow-and-arrow cast, the Galway cast, the steeple cast, how to cast well using leaders 20 feet long, and how to deliver a cast making no false cast whatever—just to name a few. When you can do all these things, and more, then you are a good fly caster. All you'll need to do then is to become a good fly fisherman.

CHAPTER 8

Deadly New/Old Bass Lures—And How to Fish Them

Twelve Deadly Lures
Here is the "Deadly Dozen" lures no bass fisherman should be without.

Any fisherman brash enough to make a special selection of lures is going to face criticism from many fishermen and lure manufacturers. Somebody's pet lure is sure to be omitted.

But at risk of being dubbed an angling dodo, I'm going to name my "Deadly Dozen" lures. However, some qualifications must be made.

First, these lures are chosen chiefly for largemouth black bass fishing in lakes. Secondly, they are selected as casting lures (any method of casting), as opposed to lures that are especially effective when trolled. Finally, they are lures that make it possible to utilize various systems or techniques of fishing.

When bass are in the shallows, it has been my experience that nothing takes them better than a fly rod popping bug. That's my first choice lure. But the bug has got to be a good one, and the bass have got to be in water less than 12 feet deep, and preferably around shoreline stumps, brush, and weeds.

A GOOD bug is one that pops well, casts well, and has a proper hook so fish that strike will not be missed. To cast well the bug shouldn't have too much hair or feathers. To hook well, it should have a long-shank hook that hangs on the water at about a 30-degree angle from the surface.

Fly rod popping bug is "first choice" lure when fish are in the shallows.

117

Well-made, commercially produced bugs are hard to find. The best are homemade, or turned out by skilled professional tyers like Jim Poulos (411 Stone Pl., Wheeling, Ill.).

My second selection for bass is the black porkrind eel. I use them in a variety of lengths, from four to nine inches, and usually in conjunction with a leadhead jig, preferably black. Jig weights, type (whether weedless or not), and color vary according to specific fishing conditions. Normally, a particular length eel, and particular jig, is settled upon through trial and error.

Generally, I start by fishing a small jig with a short, four-inch eel, working shoreline shallows. Then I go to larger jigs and larger eels, and to deeper water. The eel should always be fished on bottom, or very close to it. Cast, let the jig-eel sink, lift the rod tip, let it sink, and so on.

Bass most often slam the eel right at the jig head, so are readily hooked. Sometimes, though, they'll mouth the eel, and I've had bass up to the boat (not hooked) that were still holding onto the porkrind eel and wearing it like a mustache.

A third selection has to be a plastic worm. There are so many good ones on the market today that it's hard to make a selection by manufacturer. Worms by Creme Lure Co. are excellent and so are those made by Butch Harris (1125 E. Morehead St., Charlotte, N.C.).

The "flaptail" kind of worm is preferred, in purple, blue, black, green, and they should be rigged with a leadhead, and made weedless. The technique of fishing them is much like that used with the porkrind eel—snake 'em along the bottom, with a slow, tantalizing, up-and-down hop. Set the hook hard as you can when a bass hits.

My fourth selection is a green-specked, white, porkchunk frog, or an all-white porkchunk frog with red yarn protruding from its sides. This lure can be fished with a weedless hook and tossed into weeds and lily pads, and fished to look more real than a genuine live frog. For somewhat deeper fishing, the frog can be rigged

There are many varieties of plastic worms, most of which are good. Plastic worm is one of expert's top lure selections.

with a spinner, and of course whatever lead weight is needed can be added.

A spinner bait, such as the Twin Spin or Single Spin, would be a fifth choice. Such lures have lead on them, a spinner or two, and usually "winging" of impala, bucktail, marabou, nylon, or saddle hackles. Spinner baits should be fished rather swiftly through shallows, but with slow hops and jumps when worked deep.

Spinner baits like these are "musts" in bass angler's kit.

A sixth selection would be the Buck Perry Spoonplugs. Incidentally, except for the first two lures, there is no particular order in this listing of the "Deadly Dozen." The Spoonplugs, for example, are chiefly for deep fishing, and certainly would be a first choice for deep fishing.

Black porkrind eel.

Buck Perry's "Spoonplugs" dig deep and take bottom-hugging fish.

A jig made in Florida that's called the Salty Dog could be a seventh lure selection. It's a plastic bodied lead-head, and not a very attractive bait. Its action in the water, though, is spectacular. When stroked on the retrieve, the Salty Dog jumps, hops around, sinks, and slips left and right—acting just like a shrimp that's been hurt and can't swim properly.

Dardevle.

The eighth choice is a Dardevle spoon—in various weights, sizes, and finishes. The famed Dardevle has superb castability, can be fished many different ways, and it has a fish-getting "action" that has endeared it to fishermen for generations.

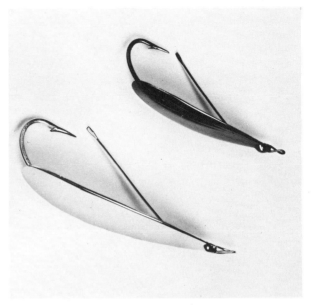

Johnson "Silver Minnows."

Same is true of the Johnson Silver Minnow—another famous spoon, and one hard to beat when fishing weeds or lily pads. It's one of the most weedless lures made, and is especially deadly when fished with a strip of porkrind or with a porkchunk frog. It's ninth on my list.

Art Wallsten's "Salty Cisco."

In tenth place is Art Wallsten's great Salty Cisco, one of the Cisco Kidd line of lures. I like it in the deep running model, because it gets down in a hurry, casts beautifully, and the fisherman can give it whatever action he wants.

In 11th and 12th places are the popular Creek Chub Darter and Plunker surface lures. The Plunker is a finely balanced popping plug that will bring bass rushing when it's worked slowly and when the fish are sufficiently shallow. Same is true of the Darter, which can be worked over the top or periodically yanked under water.

"Sting Ray Grub" is one of unusual, fish-getting new baits.

Creek Chub's "Plunker."

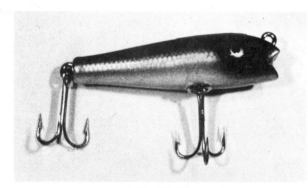

Creek Chub's "Darter."

This list includes only some of the super bass lures available today. But just about every one of them has stood the test of time—and they'll be catching bass for years to come.

FOUR NEW ONES

The "Sting Ray Grub," and all its imitations, is one of many new types of lures that have been causing largemouth and smallmouth bass considerable damage. The "Sting Ray Grub" is nothing but a short, chunky, meaty-feeling piece of plastic produced by Mann's Bait Co., Box 604, Eufaula, Ala., 36027. So far as is known, Mann's makes the plastic grub body and markets it; you attach it, like a plastic worm, to whatever kind of leadhead jig you prefer.

The "Sting Ray Grub" has that chunky little body, ending in a flattened "tail," and there's nothing else about it, so far as can be seen, that makes it any different from a bunch of other lures of the same type. But bass find it different!

The Mann's "Grub" has an unbelievably life-like feel, when you're handling it—but then, so do a lot of similar plastic baits. Too, a bass striking the "Grub" has no idea how it "feels" until he hits it. So "feel" has nothing to do with the attractiveness of the lure to bass.

It should be retrieved in 4-foot-long "strokes" of the rod, but it also catches bass when drawn steadily through

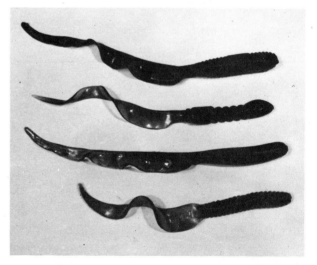

Plastic worms with crooked tails are something new in an old line of bass baits.

the water. No one really knows why bass go for it—but they do!

Also new on the bass fishing scene are plastic worms with crooked tails. These worms are just like the traditional plastics, except that their tails are flattened and curled, twisted, and corkscrewed. Experts have been fishing these new worms for some time, and while they feel the new curly worms will not replace the standard plastic worms, there is no denying that the new worms are unusually effective. The worms with the screwy tails do, indeed, have a special, lively, added action in the water.

Most of the plastic worm manufacturers are turning out crooked tail worms. One of the better known firms making them is Cordell Tackle Inc., P.O. Box 2020, Hot Springs, Ark., 71901. Cordell calls the new worms "Pigtail Worms."

Bagley Bait Co., P.O. Box 110, Winter Haven, Fla., makes a plastic worm called the "Screw Tail," and the Lindy/Little Joe Tackle Co., Box 488, Brainerd, Minn., 56401, markets crooked tail worms they call the "Swirl Tail."

New "tail spinner" lures cast like bullets, sink like rocks.

Another new kind of lure getting a lot of attention from bass fishermen are the "tail spinner" variety. Several companies make them, and all are similar. These are small, lead-body lures that cast like bullets and sink like rocks. They have a spinner attached, which wobbles and flashes, attracting bass, even as the lure sinks. What makes these little lures so effective is their quick-sinking characteristics; they get down to bass in a hurry.

Mann's Bait Co., as well as Lindy/Little Joe, are two firms manufacturing a line of very good "tail spinner" lures.

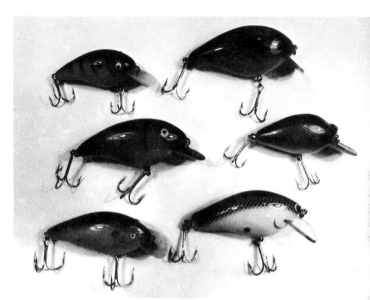

"Fat baits," also called "alphabet plugs," today are in every bass pros' tackle box.

No report on new bass fishing lures would be complete without mentioning the unique "fat baits." The "fat baits," also called "alphabet plugs," are included in the group of wobbling plugs bass anglers now like to refer to as "running baits." There's nothing new about "running baits," but the "fat baits" certainly are different.

There's a whole bunch of these new chunky plugs, all having come after the original, called the "Big O," which was handcarved of cedar by a Tennessee fisherman. All the "fat baits" look alike, more-or-less, in that they are tearshaped, pudgy, doublehooked, and have a lip up front that makes 'em wobble.

Cordell Tackle Co. is marketing a factory model of the "Big O." A lure called "Big B" is being turned out by Bagley Bait Co.; and "Big N" is offered by Norman Mfg. Co., Ft. Smith, Ark.

Those are just some of the "fat baits" around today. All of them are weird looking, but they take bass!

AND WEEDLESS WORM TECHNIQUES

The art and science of plastic worm fishing has come a long way since the late 40s and early 50s. Both fishing methods and equipment have improved, yet there are new developments that continue to make this method even more deadly. Nearly every season, some smart angler figures out a new way to fake-out a fish with a hunk of soft vinyl (please, they are *not* rubber!) plastic.

During the last 20 years, one plastic worm fishing system has become basic. It's called the "Texas Rig" and involves using a single large (4/0 to 6/0) hook, a sliding bullet-type sinker, a fairly stiff rod, and at least 15-pound test line.

Born of necessity in the brush-and-timber-filled river reservoir impoundments in the South, the "self-weedless" hooking method is the standard with most Dixie bass anglers, and it is slowly migrating North as Yankee fishermen find out just how deadly this "slip-sinker system" really is.

Newcomers to this system wonder how just one hook, regardless of how big, way up there in the front of a plastic worm, can possibly snag a bass. They often favor the old, original three hook worm harness, complete with

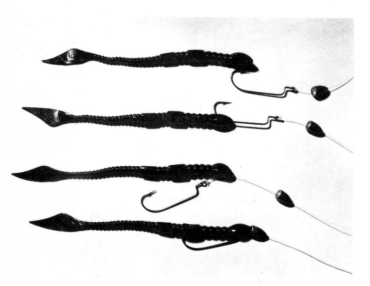

How to rig "the perfect weedless worm."

beads and propeller. There's no question that rig has caught many bass—and will continue to do so, as long as the fish aren't in extremely dense cover. But hooking fish with a single-hook rig is really no problem because of the way a bass takes a plastic worm—they inhale it with one swift sucking motion. In other words, they eat the "whole thing!"

Years ago a guide on Greers Ferry Lake in Arkansas developed the "Three tap method." The guide, named Smitty, said, "That first tap you feel is the bass pickin' up the worm. The second tap is when he drops it. The third tap is me tappin' you on the shoulder, just to let you know *y'all missed the damn bass!!*"

The moral is to hit 'em fast! When you feel that telltale tug, it's time to reel-in-slack-and-strike-hard!

Setting the hook hard is vital when fishing plastic worms, because you have to drive the hook point through the worm and into the bass' jaw. That takes more *oomph* than most anglers realize. Remember, a rod bends and gives—even a stiff rod. And the monofilament line stretches, too. It's no exaggeration when some accomplished bass anglers say you should "try to break the rod" when setting the hook. There's no way you can strike *too* hard.

There's another practical reason why you must hit hard; and that's to get a bass out of heavy cover before he can "get his head," turn and get back to the brush, stump, weed bed, or wherever he'd been hiding. Give a hooked bass just a little leeway and you'll wind up with a busted line every time.

Bill Dance, a man who has won more major bass fishing tournaments than anyone, typifies the "hit-'em-hard" school of fishermen.

Bill works *just* his rod and line, *not the reel*, when he crawls a worm along the bottom. He begins a retrieve with his rod held at about a 45 degree angle. Then he raises it with a slow, deliberate motion to the vertical position, then as the rod is lowered back to 45 degrees, the reel is used to take up the slack line. The reel never is used to impart action to the worm.

This system was developed because plastic worm fishing is basically a "feel" type of fishing. The rod telegraphs what's happening down there on the lake bottom, and the "feel" is far more precise with the lift and retrieve method. A good worm fisherman can "feel" his lure all the way back to the boat. He can tell if the worm is crawling up a stump, tree branch, log, or weed bed.

Becoming a good plastic worm fisherman isn't difficult —it's just a different kind of fishing. Plug and spinnerbait anglers usually apply the simple "cast-and-crank" method of retrieving. The lure itself has action and it sure isn't hard to tell when a fish hits. There's little "feel" or judgment necessary when a bass takes those kinds of lures.

Therefore, "feel" is the main difference between fishing plastic worms and other types of artificials. An angler must be able to tell whether a snag is tugging at his plastic worm or a big bass. But when in doubt, strike! You may look foolish occasionally and set the hook in a stump or two, but you'll also put a lot more fish in the boat than the guy who waits until he's "sure" a fish has struck.

If you haven't yet fished plastic worms you're missing a lot of fun. More important, you're not catching your share of fish. "The worm" is one of the most popular *bass catching* methods that guides and pro fishermen employ. They fish worms because these lures consistently produce bass. Careful surveys reveal that during the last six years, plastic worms took 85 to 90 percent of all fish weighed in at major bass tournaments.

So, rig up "Texas-style," work the worm with your rod, "feel" your way along the bottom and, when in doubt, strike hard! Your bass fishing's bound to improve!

CHAPTER 9

1975 Saskatchewan Fishermen's Guide

Where to go for what, when, and how much to pay.

If you find the "locals" almost reluctant to tell you about Saskatchewan's great fishing, it's only because some tourists tend to be suspicious when a Saskatchewan native proudly tells about his experiences—getting tired hauling fish into the boat or throwing back all pike under 10 pounds.

But it's true, fish are really *that* hungry in Saskatchewan, especially in the far north.

This western Canadian province is a big one, stretching from Montana and North Dakota's northern borders almost to Eskimo-land. Its 30,000 lakes, rivers, and streams offer some of the finest fishing you can find on this continent, whether you are looking for a family fishing vacation, or a rugged "he-man" adventure.

Saskatchewan waters have northern pike, walleye, perch, lake trout, brook trout, rainbow trout, brown trout, splake (a fast-growing cross between a brook trout and lake trout), sauger, goldeye, whitefish and Arctic grayling.

In an article for Fishing Yearbook, Hank Bradshaw calls Saskatchewan's Churchill River "Pike Paradise." This is how he described his introduction to June fishing on the Churchill River:

Sundown on Saskatchewan's Lac La Ronge.

Fly fishermen works for grayling on the Cockrane River.

"I didn't think it would ever happen to me. I am a fishing fool, but I had been catching fish so fast and furiously that I had grown tired of taking them off the hook and releasing them. So I reeled in, laid my rod across my lap, and took what I thought was a well-deserved rest. Inadvertently, I let my lure dangle over the side of our freight canoe. Suddenly, something came out of the water, jumped almost to the gunwale, smashed the lure and would have made off with my rod if I had not scrambled quickly and grabbed it.

"I complained to Daniel Mackenzie, my Cree Indian guide, 'you can't even relax on the Churchill River.'"

He went on to say that he soon learned that was not merely a "lucky day," but that fishing like that is almost a regular occurrence in Saskatchewan.

PARKLAND FISHING

Looking at Saskatchewan with an angler's eye, the center of the province in particular attracts attention.

Sail-like dorsal fin, dark spots, and metal-gray sheen are characteristics of the Arctic grayling.

This is rugged country, the home of moose, elk, and lots of fish. You will find good, all-weather roads, cabins, campgrounds, service stations, and supply centers throughout the area.

Four parks fan out across central Saskatchewan. In Prince Albert National Park, which lies in the geographical center of the province, Careen and Kingsmere lakes offer excellent pike, walleye, and lake trout fishing. The province's record lake trout, a 51 pound, 10 oz. fish, came out of Kingsmere Lake.

To the east is the Hanson Lake Road. This all-weather road was built less than 10 years ago and opened up hundreds of square miles of new fishing waters, previously accessible only by air. Along the Hanson Lake Road's 225 miles, you can fish for pike and walleye on the big lakes, like Jan and Deschambault, or stick to the smaller waters. Little Bear Lake has trout, pike, and walleye. If rainbow and brook trout are your forte Piprell, Sealey, and Shannon lakes are for you.

Northern pike are thick as weeds in many of the province's wilderness lakes.

Whitefish are abundant in most of these northern lakes and in early June you can catch them on ultra-light spinning tackle, with small spinners, or by fly-fishing.

On the western side of the province is Meadow Lake Park. Here, pike and walleye are abundant in the bigger lakes; such as Pierce, Lac des Isles, Waterhen, Greig, and Flotten. But you need not look far to find a secluded trout stream. Fishing in these streams is generally good year round, but best in May and June.

Lac la Ronge Park, slightly farther north, is becoming known as the jumping off point for those heading beyond the end of the roads.

You can catch northern pike, lake trout, and walleye on Lac la Ronge, Nemeiben and Wapawekka lakes. A 10 minute boat ride to Downton Lake leads to the province's most southerly Arctic grayling grounds.

When you aren't out fishing, you might look around the hustling, bustling mining town of La Ronge. Drop into a handcraft shop to browse over the Indian beadwork and hand carved furniture. There are no longer many prospectors in America, but if you drop into the La Ronge Hotel you are sure to find at least one or two old-timers talking about the "latest uranium rumors."

There are plenty of cabin accommodations throughout the parkland area, and the prices are reasonable. A light housekeeping cabin for two ranges between $5 and $10 per day. Most camps have weekly rates as well. You usually find at least some form of plumbing and many have now installed comforts such as modern washroom facilities.

Tent and trailer sites, stores and restaurants, motor and boat rentals, and guide services are available. Many camps have quick freezing and filleting plants as well, so you can take some of those delicious fish back home.

Guides are needed on some of the larger lakes such as La Ronge, Jan, and Deschambault and they can be hired from the fishing camp operators and outfitters for between $10 and $15 per day. These guides are almost all Indians, native to the area, and have been familiar with the waters upon which they guide since they were youngsters.

THE FAR NORTH—FLY-IN LAND

Charter flights from Saskatoon or Prince Albert, which can be reached by paved highway; or from La Ronge, will take you beyond the end of the roads.

Here camps with modern facilities offer you three days, a week or two weeks of fishing at its *best*. You find northern pike, walleye, and lake trout in most of the lakes up here. Some of the big waters are Athabaska,

Black, Cree, Hatchett, Lloyd, Tazin, Waterbury, and Wollaston.

In the fast cold streams, Arctic grayling fishing is excellent. You find grayling in the Fond-du-Lac River which flows out of Black Lake, the Grease River leading into Lake Athabaska, the Cree River and streams leading into Reindeer Lake; and in the Clearwater, Virgin, Blackbirch, and Geikie rivers.

The Churchill River system is great for pike and walleye fishing.

Far northern fishing camps offer a package rate (American plan) which includes return air fare from the point at which you choose to start your charter flight, lodging, meals, boat, motor, and guide. The cost runs between $200 and $595 per person per week with an average price in the $300 range, depending upon how far north the camp you choose is located, and just how luxurious the accommodation. Some are genuine rough-it camps and others boast modern facilities.

Fishing here is really tops. Not only do men come this far north, but every year more ladies are signing the guest books, and dads are choosing this as the spot for a father and son vacation. Some of the camps offer reduced rates for youngsters accompanied by dad.

After a hearty early morning breakfast, you set out with your guide to fish for the species of your choice. In the morning you might want to cruise a bit looking for the spot where the "really big ones" lie. But be sure to keep enough of the medium-sized fish you haul in for a tasty shore lunch. As soon as your party returns to camp in the evening, your guide will take the day's catch, and clean, fillet, and quick-freeze them.

Many of these fly-in camps have what they call outposts. Charter planes will fly you to one of these cabins and pick you up two or three days later, for only the cost of the air fare. Many fishermen taking these trips do so to reach the best Arctic grayling streams, or to wet their lines in a virgin lake.

When is fishing best in northern Saskatchewan? It's excellent throughout the summer. The ice leaves the lakes around the first or second week of June, and they remain open until late September or October. The ice is off the lakes in the central portion of Saskatchewan by the end of May.

If you're after lake trout, they come to the surface just after the ice goes out and again prior to freeze up. You can catch them throughout the fishing season, but during the hottest part of the summer they are in

Working upstream on the Clearwater River for grayling.

Streams such as this feeding into lakes congregate walleyes.

deeper water, for lake trout seek a water temperature of 45 degrees.

Ed Lennox hefts modest pike from Wollaston Lake.

SOUTHERN SASKATCHEWAN

In the South Saskatchewan River are walleyes, pike, goldeye, sauger, and sturgeon. In the Qu'Appelle Valley, less than an hour's drive from Regina, the capital of the province, lies a chain of lakes with pike, perch, and walleye. Lost Mountain Lake, also in this vicinity, is the home of some pretty good-sized walleye, up to seven pounds, and quite a few pike, too.

In the southwestern portion of Saskatchewan, many streams hold brown, brook, and rainbow trout.

Parks are scattered throughout the south and the waters have plenty of fish; mostly pike, walleye, and perch.

HOW TO CATCH THOSE LUNKERS

Northern pike are best caught by casting spoons or plugs in shallow, reedy bays, three to twelve feet in

depth, or by shallow water trolling. On windy days, when the waves make it rather rough in the middle of the lake, head for one of the calm bays or inlets and cast into the reeds for northern pike. These voracious fish are always ready to snap at the lures offered, and it seems they are always hungry. And when you hook them, they put up quite a struggle.

For walleyes it's best to cast with jigs, spoons, or plugs, in water eight to twenty feet deep, and preferably where there is a rocky bottom.

Cast near the surface, not deeper than six to twenty feet for lake trout, if it's June or late August to September. In July and early August the trout head for deeper

The Fond du Lac River is broad, with heavy water at Black Lake and produces grayling of exceptional size.

water and you have to troll to find the big ones. The best method is to use deep-sea tackle and monel line. Some fishermen prefer heavy monofilament. Lake trout can also be caught by jigging, that is, by dropping the spoon or jig right to the bottom, raising and lowering it several times, and reeling in quickly. For rainbow trout, which are found in small waters where there is usually plenty of natural food, your best bet is trolling. Use spoons, or whatever your favorite lure happens to be. (Veteran Saskatchewan rainbow fishermen claim miniature marshmallows are the best bait.) Live bait, except worms and frogs, is illegal in this province. When fishing for "brookies" or rainbow trout in streams, many anglers use grasshoppers and small spinners.

Arctic grayling are caught by fly-fishing or using small spinners or spoons.

REGULATIONS

The Saskatchewan fishing season is open for 50 weeks of the year. It costs non-residents $5 for an angling license if they fish south of the 55th parallel, in waters not holding trout or grayling. To fish throughout the province, it costs a non-resident $10. Under 15 years of age, no license is required. Within Prince Albert National Park a special $2 license must be purchased. However, one may fish in the park without holding a provincial license.

An angler's daily catch may not exceed eight fish, and his possession limit is twice the daily limit. When the fish are filleted, two fillets count as one fish.

If you are fishing for pike, walleye, sauger, goldeye, whitefish, grayling, or lake trout, you may catch eight fish of one species in a day. If it's brook, rainbow, or brown trout, or splake, you can only take five of a single variety.

You have to call it a day, as far as fishing goes in Saskatchewan, within two hours after sunset, and you may not begin again until one hour before sunrise. Sunset, however, comes late in the North—around eleven p.m.

Minnows and other small fish are taboo as bait in Saskatchewan, as are fish eggs, unless they have been treated so they will not hatch when placed in the water. Frogs and worms may be used, but it is illegal to import into the province any live bait intended to be used for taking fish.

Cabins at Wollaston Lake camp. Wise fisherman is placing rods out of harms way on roof top.

Saskatchewan's best fishing can be reached only by "bush" planes.

SASKATCHEWAN'S PROVINCIAL RECORD FISH

Lake Trout—51 lbs., 10 oz., caught in Kingsmere Lake in 1958 by H. J. Thorimbert of St. Louis, Sask.

Northern Pike—42 lbs., 12 oz., caught in Lake Athabasca in 1954 by F. W. Terry, Prince Albert.

Walleye—13 lbs., 9 oz., caught in S. Saskatchewan River in 1953 by D. Snieder, Burstall, Sask.

Perch—2 lbs., 7 oz., caught in Struthers Lake in 1953 by A. Simon, Yellow Creek, Sask.

Goldeye—3 lbs., 2 oz., Saskatchewan River in 1964 by Alex Riba of Prince Albert, Sask.

Arctic Grayling—4 lbs., 5 oz., Fond Du Lac River in 1966 by Karl R. Gallauer of Oconomowoc, Wis.

Brook Trout—5 lbs., 12 oz., Echo Creek in 1968, John Fiddler of Prince Albert.

Brown Trout—15 lbs., 8 oz., in Duncairn Dam in 1951 by E. P. Lowe, Gull Lake, Sask.

Rainbow Trout—18 lbs., Piprell Lake in 1967 by Reinhard Thiese, Success, Sask.

Rainbow Trout (Stream Fish)—6 lbs., 8 oz., in 1962, in Frenchman Creek by H. Oslen, Eastend, Sask.

CHAPTER 10

The Caiman Caper

*Is this the first crocodilian
ever taken on a fly rod?*

It was a fish-filled afternoon on Brazil's Araquaia River, an Amazon tributary. Jack Parry and I had been taking pavon, or peacock bass, one after the other. In addition, our surface lures periodically drew slashing strikes from such exotics as red piranha, primitive trahira, and needle-toothed payara.

Now we were working 70 feet out from the jungle-coated shore with our Caraja Indian guide, Joao, paddling slowly along. Jack was in the bow, plugging away with a bait-casting outfit. I was near the stern hauling on a fly rod and tossing a 5-inch-long saltwater popper.

As we neared the gnarled limbs of a fallen tree, I made a cast and deposited the big white popper close to the bank. I popped the bug once, let it rest, then popped it again. On the second *pop* the water rippled four feet from the bug and a long, dark shape appeared on the shadowed surface.

"*Look there!*" I shouted to Jack. "Something's stalking my bug."

I twitched the popper, and suddenly a 4½-foot caiman lurched across the surface, jaws agape, and engulfed the bug. The line tightened and then went slack as the crocodilian wrenched its head furiously from side-to-side and threw the popper five feet away. The bug floated idly as the caiman, his poppy eyes and long snout showing clearly on the surface, glared at it.

I had no desire to hook a hungry, irritated caiman, so I took slack out of the fly line preliminary to lifting

Tom McNally draws caiman, or crocodile, towards skiff after frisky reptile hit fly rod bug on Brazil's Araquaia River.

131

the bug and getting it out of there. But the bug wobbled a bit, and *THAT QUICK!!!* the caiman launched himself through the air and again had the popper securely in his snapping, tooth-filled jaws. The 2/0 hook imbedded itself in a soft, fleshy corner of his mouth, so there was nothing to do but to "play" him in and release him.

At first the caiman barely resisted the pressure of the rod, and allowed me to draw him directly to the boat. I believe the croc' was so wild that he had no fear. Finally, however, as he looked us balefully in the eye only a few feet away, he decided all was not in his best interest and he began to scrap like the devil unchained. He surged across the surface of the water, half in, half out, powerfully ripping line from the reel. Like a small tarpon, he pulled 30 yards of line out before I was able

. . . popping bug is worked loose, and critter is released—ruffled, but unharmed.

to pull him up just short of brush where surely he would have popped the leader. It got to be hilarious; a fly fisherman fighting a snaggy-tooth caiman as though it were a good-size snook or northern pike.

At last the pressure told, and I drew the caiman within reach of Joao, who leaned over, grasped him behind the head, and swung him aboard. Jack Parry made a few photos since, after all, this might have been the only crocodilian (or alligator, for that matter) ever taken on a fly rod.

We handled the little caiman gently, removed the bug, then returned him to the water. For long minutes he just lay there, glaring at us. Then he kicked that long, scaly tail and scooted away—ruffled, perhaps, but unharmed for the experience.

Caiman is boated

CHAPTER 11

What You Should Know About Lake Trout

The full story on laker habits, distribution, where, when, and how to catch them by trolling, casting, or fly fishing.

The finest lake trout fishing is in the wilderness waters of Canada. Lake trout thrive in some cold, shallow lakes, and in certain rivers providing the lake-like qualities required by lake trout, but they rarely do well in lakes not having depths of at least 100 feet. Lake trout need water with a high oxygen content. Therefore large, deep lakes are most suitable. Wide, open lakes are frequently wind-thrashed, and turbulent, and such heavy wave action aeriates and "turns over" lake water—thus adding to and distributing oxygen. Very small and protected lakes, even though clean, deep, and cold, seldom maintain respectable lake trout populations. Lakers cannot prosper where temperature rises above 65 degrees Fahrenheit, and 45 degrees is the preferred range.

Lake trout are common to many waters in Alaska, but Alaska as a rule does not provide trophy-size lake trout. Certainly the finest of North America's lake trout angling is in selected lakes in Alberta, Ontario, Manitoba, Saskatchewan and the Northwest Territories. It is at hard-to-get-to wilderness lakes where trophy fish abound. It takes a long time to grow a lake trout of 40,

50, or more pounds, so one shouldn't anticipate mountable fish from waters that are seasonally pounded by numerous anglers.

It is impossible in limited space to name all the Canadian lakes that offer extraordinary lake trout fish, but among the best is Great Bear Lake in the Arctic Circle in the Northwest Territories. This is a comparatively "new" lake, but it has been "opened up" with the establishing of comfortable camps on its shores, and as of this writing there are four camps on Great Bear that provide five days' fishing, transportation to and from Winnipeg, and all other usual "package" items (guides, meals, etc.) for about $900 per person. Top fishing for Arctic grayling also is available at Great Bear, and fly-out trips to places like Tree River can be made for Arctic char.

Saskatchewan has many prime lake trout waters and, in fact, its Lake Athabaska once gave up a 102 pound laker, the largest known, though it was not caught on rod and reel. (The world's record lake trout, taken by angling methods, weighed 63 pounds, 2 ounces and was caught from Lake Superior in 1952 by Hubert Hammers.) Lake Athabaska remains a superior lake trout angling spot.

The Province's Black Lake, near the bush town of Stoney Rapids, is another good lake. It is ideal for the angler who prefers to cast for trout rather than troll deepdown with wire or lead-core or heavily weighted line. Simply by casting out, allowing the lure (usually a lead-head jig) to sink 15 feet or so, it's possible to take lakers weighing 8–12 pounds on every-other-cast at Black Lake in late June and July.

Other famed laker spots in Saskatchewan are Wollaston, Cree, Reindeer, and Lac La Ronge. All, except La Ronge, are fly-in lakes, and all have some excellent northern pike and grayling fishing, and fishing for lake or common whitefish, in addition to the lake trout angling. Wollaston Lake fishing is particularly enjoyable since it has some exceptional grayling fly fishing in the Cockrane River, which feeds the lake, and also some fine shallow bays where an angler can easily boat a dozen or more northern pike of over 15 pounds in a single afternoon. Lac La Ronge you can drive to, and put up in the town of La Ronge, and either fish there or arrange for trips to distant points of the 450-square mile lake.

Many of Ontario's lakes are more readily accessible

Bob and Tom McNally wrestle with huge lake trout Bob hooked casting from dock at Manitoba's Nanjelini Lake.

With net not sufficiently strong to hold fish's weight, pair seize netting to swing fish up and out.

than those of some of the other Canadian provinces, therefore Ontario waters are highly attractive to thousands of anglers, especially those coming from mid-America population centers such as Chicago, Detroit, Milwaukee, Minneapolis-St. Paul, Des Moines, etc. Numerous Ontario lakes, such as Rainy Lake at Fort Frances, can be reached by auto, have been fished by both expert sport and commercial fishermen for years, and therefore provide only smallish lakers. Remote Lake Simcoe, in northern Ontario, is one of the province's best, having a heavy population of good-size lake trout.

Manitoba's lake trout fishery closely approaches the excellent angling available at some lakes in the Northwest Territories and Saskatchewan. Gods Lake, a wilderness fly-in spot, long has been known for its prime laker fishing. Even today it consistently gives up lake trout ranging from 30 to 50 pounds. There are at least two camps operating on Gods Lake; the oldest and probably best known is Tom Ruminski's Gods Lake Lodge, which is ideally located on the lake shore at the head of Gods River, famed for its large brook trout. Ruminski's camp is comfortable and has all modern conveniences, and can be reached by float or land planes, since in the mid-60s Ruminski constructed a sizable landing strip.

An "out camp" has been established by Ruminski a few hundred miles north of Gods Lake on the Wolverine River. The river drains large Nejanilini Lake, and while the lake has a good supply of trout the most interesting fishing is in the river. The river is broad, has a swift current (there are even rapids in some areas), and has a series of large, wide, shallow pools lake-like in character. The pools are stiff with trout 10, 15, and 20 pounds, and there are 30-pounders, too. The pools generally range 5–15 feet deep, with perhaps the deepest holes no more than 20 feet.

Because the trout in this section of the Wolverine are large, because there is strong current, and because the water is shallow, there are few places where an angler can enjoy greater sport with lake trout. Trout here are caught by casting lures, rather than by trolling or bait fishing, and light spinning or bait-casting tackle—such as might be used in bass fishing—can be employed. This is also the place for the fisherman who wants a respectable laker on a fly rod. By drifting with the current and fly casting with six-inch long, yellow-red "McNally Magnum" streamers, it's possible to catch dozens of Wolverine lake trout ranging from 6 to 25 pounds.

Hoooppla! *Laker, 28 pounds, is secured at last.*

Tom McNally drags fish to camp, as Bob follows. Leading the way is veteran Manitoba camp operator Tom Ruminski, who pioneered sport fishing at Nanjelini Lake.

Ruminski's Wolverine camp naturally is somewhat primitive, without the usual luxuries such as hot and cold running water, but it is a practical and very comfortable camp. Presumably it is being improved annually, but at last report accommodations consisted of a large, general "bunk house" with canvas-tenting for a roof, and plywood sheeting for siding and the floor. Beds and bedding are excellent, as is the food. Boats, motors, and the Cree guides also are good.

The laker is the largest of the trouts, and coloration varies greatly, depending upon area where caught and even the season. The majority of lake trout are uniformly dark grey, with irregular pale checking or spotting. The thin laterial sensory line is distinct, running from the top-most edge of the gill plate to the tail, which is deeply forked.

Canada's northern wilderness waters produce fish like this at the drop of a line. This lake trout was taken from Great Slave Lake, Northwest Territories.

The flesh of lake trout may range from a soapy or creamy white to a bright orange-red. Many people consider lake trout something of a table delicacy. The smaller lakers, ranging 3 to 6 pounds, taste the best— and at no time are they better eating than when quick-fried in deep fat over a wood fire on the rocky shore of a northern lake.

Large lake trout, 15 pounds or more, usually are steaked for cooking, or baked whole. Lakers of such size tend to be extremely oily, and actually are best if smoked. Smoked lake trout, properly done, pleases the palate of the most discriminating gourmet.

Lake trout feed primarily on smaller fishes, especially smelt, chubs, ciscoes, lake whitefish, yellow perch, suckers, and even grayling and smaller lake trout.

Lake trout spawn in the fall in very deep water over rocky reefs or gravel bottoms, often spawning at depths of 100 feet or more, although in some suitable areas in the northern edges of their range they will spawn successfully in shoalwaters. Naturally, spawning time varies according to locale, earlier in the fall in the far northern lakes, later in the winter in the more southerly part of the lake trout's range. Generally speaking lake trout spawn from the latter part of August to early January.

Because the lake trout *is* a *trout*, *is* a product of clean, cold water, *readily* strikes lures and *is* good to eat, it certainly rates as a desirable gamefish. But the lake trout is not one of the world's *great* gamefish. First off, it most frequently is caught only by very deep fishing, usually trolling, and such techniques do not permit for maximum sport. Too, lake trout rarely jump when hooked. The typical scrap with a laker involves the strike, a short but fairly fast dead-away run, then a gradual twirling resistance as the fish is drawn close. Lake trout are notorious for rolling over-and-over, fouling the leader or line around the body as the fish gradually wears down.

None of which is to say that lake trout aren't fun to catch. They are. When they can be taken by casting lures, even if leadhead jigs must be fished very deep, lakers provide sport. In some waters lake trout are in comparatively shallow water all of the open-water season, and so can be fished for with light tackle and cast to, much as one might fish shoreline rocks, steep bluffs, peninsulas, and shallow reefs, and such fishing can be exciting, especially if the trout are ranging 10 pounds or more.

Too, the angler seeking maximum sport with lakers can gear his tackle accordingly. In other words, if the

Tom McNally hoists "small" 15 pound lake trout hooked in Manitoba's Wolverine River . . .

. . . then promptly releases it. Fish under 20 pounds are simple routine in the far north.

trout are running smallish, 3–4 pounds or so, ultralight spinning tackle may be used, say a rod of 1½ ounces measuring 4½ feet, and line of 2, 3, or 4 pound test. Lake trout of any size will be a rodful on such equipment.

Even when deep trolling is required to take lake trout, and heavily weighted lines are necessary to get the lures down where the fish are, wise fishermen still can rig so that they get some action out of the fish they hook. First, no extra heavy, deep-sea tackle is necessary. An ordinary medium-light bass outfit will do, either bait-casting or spinning, and the line can be rigged with whatever lead weights are necessary, plus a sinker-release mechanism. When a fish strikes, the sinker-release will free the lead, and the fisherman then fights his hooked lake trout on a "free" line—thus getting maximum action from his fish.

Great sport can be had with lake trout by fly fishing. Granted, reasonable opportunities to take lake trout on flies are not everyday occurrences, since the fish most often are at least 20 or 30 feet down, but at many lakes

in the far north lakers can be readily taken on flies. A lake trout of even modest size, say 6, 8, or 10 pounds, can provide a lot of action for the fly-rodder.

Of course, there are numerous lake trout angling methods, and therefore the variety of tackle that can be used is considerable.

The majority of lake trout caught are taken by deep trolling, no matter if the area fished is Great Bear Lake in the Northwest Territory or one of the Finger Lakes in New York State. Deep trolling methods, and tackle, are fairly standardized and in some places trout are being caught today just as they were 75 years ago.

Stiff, deep-sea type rods, with big reels mounted with wire line, and large spoons for lures, is typical lake trout tackle for the average angler in most parts of the U.S. and Canada. Even at famed Great Bear Lake, where most trout are hooked at depths of 50 feet or less, many fishermen use heavy gear. A very common outfit seen at Great Bear is the salt water type spinning rig, a stout spinning rod (surf type) of 7½–9 feet, huge open-face spinning reel designed for surf casting, and several hundred yards of monofilament line testing no less than 20 pounds. The popular lure always is a spoon, one as large as your hand, and it will have treble hooks large enough to belt out a 150 pound tarpon.

Some fishermen using wire line, which naturally takes the lure or bait down deeper than conventional mono or braided line, use special reels designed for wire line fishing. They are narrow-spool reels, but the diameter of the spool is great so that line can be recovered (reeled in) quickly. The reels are made with narrow-width spools so that the layers of wire line will not "dig in," and so that the line is spooled onto the reel in wide turns. Wire line that is tightly wound onto a narrow-diameter spool will kink and become unserviceable.

Lead-core lines also are used by some fishermen for deep trolling and, as when wire line is employed, additional lead sinkers occasionally are used. Wire and lead-core lines usually are selected by fishermen striving to do away with lead sinkers. Lead is needed, of course, to get monofilament or braided lines down deep.

While the rod selected for deep-trolling is chiefly a matter of preference in so far as "action" (stiffness), length, weight, and type (whether deep sea, heavy fresh water, boat or "bay" rod) are concerned, most fishermen who troll 'way down for lakers choose a stout glass rod of about 5 feet in length. Usually it will have a strong handle long enough to grip easily with two hands, or to place solidly in a rod-holder mounted on a boat's transom or gunnel.

If trolling is to be done with lines other than wire or lead-core, then large-capacity, multiplying reels with level-wind mechanisms are preferred. Light salt water reels are excellent, since they normally are sturdily made and have good line capacity. The reel for laker trolling should accommodate at least 250 yards of 15 or 20 pound test line. It must be remembered that at times the angler may have to put a lure down to a depth of 300 feet and, with bowing of the line, it may be necessary to pay out 400–450 feet of line. Then, should a fish be hooked, it may run off another 100 or 200 feet of line before gradually succumbing to rod pressure. Consequently, plenty of line frequently is needed in deep trolling for *Namaycush*.

Monofilament is preferred over braided line by many veteran lake trout fishermen. They believe mono takes on very little water and so spools onto a reel better than braided line, and also sinks more quickly than braided line. Other seasoned fishermen select braided line (of nylon, Dacron, etc.), because they do not want the stretch that often exists in monofilament lines. Too much stretch, especially when yards and yards of line are out, makes hooking fish difficult.

Terminal rigging used in deep-trolling for lake trout is variable. As a rule, a monofilament leader is desirable, it's length and test depending upon conditions. When fishing for trout in very clear water, in hard-fished areas, it's best to use long, fine leaders. For most laker fishing a leader six feet long, testing 10–12 pounds, is fine.

Leaders usually are tied with improved clinch knots to a three-way swivel, with the fishing line tied to one part of the swivel, and a weaker line tied to the other part of the swivel and the sinker tied to it. Having the sinker or sinkers tied to weak line will make it possible to break off the sinker should it become fouled, *without losing all* of the terminal tackle.

Preferred sinkers for such trolling are bell types, or "Dipsey" sinkers, if the angler intends to bump bottom. Dipsey sinkers do not easily foul on snags. "Keel" and "Drail" sinkers are especially designed for trolling, and are good. But some anglers prefer "Clinch-on" and "Diamond" sinkers. "Clinch-on" sinkers are bad because they are pinched onto a line rather than tied, and so frequently loosen and are lost.

A barrel-swivel, or a barrel-swivel with snap, is desirable as a leader-lure connection. Just about any lure that is trolled will put twist in the fishing line unless a swivel is employed. Swivels sometimes spook fish, however, so many anglers prefer to tie in a single barrel-swivel in the leader about two or three feet up from the lure. So located, a swivel will prevent line twist yet is not likely to be noticed by a striking fish.

To get maximum fight out of hooked fish, when trolling deep with weights, use one of the many sinker-release mechanisms on the market. A sinker-release is a simple gadget which, when fixed to the fishing line and the line leading to the sinkers, releases the sinkers at the strike of a fish. The jolt caused by a lake trout hitting the lure or bait triggers the sinker-release mechanism so that the sinker falls away, leaving the fish to fight without the hindrance of dragging a heavy weight.

Keels are great aids for deep lake trout trolling. They're made of metal or plastic, shaped much like the deep keel of a sailboat, and are tied into the line not far above the lure to prevent twisting. When one considers that the lake trout angler may troll for hours, frequently circling, doubling-back, and criss-crossing previous tracks, a well-designed keel in the rigging can be well worthwhile.

Planers are unique little devices designed to get a lure or bait down to the desired depth without the use of lead weights, or with a minimum of lead weight. They're made of metal or plastic, and while there are various designs they generally are thin, rectangular units equipped with rings, snaps, etc. so that they can be tied into the fishing line, or into a separate line used to take the fishing line down. By virtue of their design and construction, planers dig deep and dive when pulled through the water. They are effective, and are very popular among Great Lakes region trout fishermen.

"Down-riggers" are used, also, to get lures or baits down to about any depth desired. A down-rigger is a strong separate line, that is attached to a very heavy lead weight, iron window sash, or even a coffee can filled with cement. A clothespin or similar item is attached to the down-rigger line just above the weight, and the fishing line is secured in the clothespin or some kind of line-release. The down-rigger takes the fishing line down to the desired depth, and the fishing line is payed out and trolling done. When a fish strikes, the fishing line is automatically released from the down-rigger and the fish is played on a "free" line.

Some other gadgets used by the deep-trolling lake trout fisherman are "flashers" and similar fish-attractors such as "cow bells." The normal haunt of a lake trout is a vast one indeed, possibly involving several dozen square miles of very deep water. So it is not easy to locate lake trout, and sometimes a boat trolling a couple lures or few pieces of bait may pass close to lake trout but not get the fish's attention. Fish "attractors" are used to help draw trout from great distances to the lures or bait.

A "cow bell" rig is simply a group of large spinners which usually are mounted several inches apart on a length of heavy wire. Normally the spinners are of different finishes and coloring, and big ones 2–3 inches long are preferred. There'll be barrel swivels and snaps at either end of the rig so that the "cow bells" can be tied into the fishing line several feet ahead of the lure or bait. Some fishermen drop "cow bells" down on separate lines.

"Flashers" are rectangular pieces of metal or plastic, generally 6 or 10 inches long, and 2–3 inches wide. They're thin, mounted with swivels, and can be used in the fishing line or on a separate line. Bright chrome "flashers" are most popular, but brass and bronze ones are

available, as are some of plastic that have bright fluorescent red or yellow finishes.

Spoons are the most popular lake trout lures. The size of the spoon used depends chiefly on the average size of the trout present, as well as on the sizes of the forage fishes available to the trout. Small spoons, say 2 or 3 inches long, are about right when the trout seldom exceed 3 pounds; ones 3–5 inches are better for trout in the 6 to 12 pound class; and when large trout are expected, fish of 15 pounds or more, most anglers use spoons ranging in length from 6 to 8 or 9 inches.

Sometimes bright spoons are the best choice on dull days, and darker ones—even those finished in black—on bright, sunny days. Some of the colors that have been notable for taking lake trout over the years are orange, red-and-white, black-and-white, green, green-and-white, yellow, and all of those colors with contrasting diamonds or circles of other colors.

Artificial plugs also can be trolled successfully for lake trout. Large plugs, either one-piece or jointed, are generally best, and most quality deep-running plugs will take fish. As with spoons, though, the angler should keep switching plug types and finishes until he finds the one that takes the most fish.

Some lake trout fishermen troll with bait. Live smelt of 6–8 inches long are an excellent bait, and dead ones of the same size are a top second choice. Also good are suckers, ciscoes, alewifes, chubs, and lake shiner and golden roach minnows. There are countless methods of attaching minnows to hooks for lake trout trolling. But in general tandem hooks and wire minnow "harnesses" are utilized because minnows rigged those ways seldom tear free while trolling.

Fishing with cut bait—which can be portions or halves of any of the bait fishes mentioned—is sometimes done by trollers but more frequently cut bait is used by stillfishermen or those who drift slowly in boats. The bait is fished at different depths and, of course, in different places until a laker bites. Drifting over deep reefs and bars, over sunken islands, in the vicinity of known spring holes, and off rocky peninsulas and bluffs is a good way to take trout on cut bait.

Experienced anglers seeking lake trout head for typical "lake trout water," that is, deep reefs, rocky bars, submerged islands or rock piles, and similar bottom formations that are known to be attractive to lakers. They begin trolling at moderate speed, and start checking depths, as the boat is guided over the likely spots, and from one promising area to another. Initial fishing may be at a depth of only 15 feet, then lures are consistently fished deeper and deeper, until, at some lakes, they may be fished as much as 500 feet down. Trolling speeds are altered continually, too, since at any given time modest speed may take fish, or very slow or very fast.

Cree guide swings the net at Great Bear Lake (Northwest Territories) and another lake trout is in the mesh. This is a small one, at least at Great Bear, which rates as one of the finest spots for trophy trout.

Trolling should be executed with some sort of pattern. Helter-skelter, aimless, non-directed trolling is illogical and a waste of time, with any catch made chiefly being luck. It's best to strike a straight-away trolling course, with a definite objective or "target" area in mind. One should project his thinking to the lake trout holding areas *beneath* the surface, deep down, and visualize the pattern of his fishing. A reverse course can be taken when the "target" area is reached, and that run also done on a straight line. If neither of those runs produce fish, then a criss-cross trolling pattern may be assumed, sort of saw-tooth shaped, and finally long, curving, "S" shaped trolling patterns may be run over the area. Presumably during all trolling runs different depths are tried, as well as various lures. If no fish are taken from a specific area following tactics as outlined, then another area should be fished.

"Drift-fishing" often is a good way to take lake trout.

It involves motoring up-wind, then drifting back with the wind while "trolling" baits or lures. The skiff is turned broadside to the wind when starting the drift down-lake, and all persons aboard sit toward the down-wind side of the boat. This will raise the up-wind side slightly, 3–5 inches, enough for the wind to grab under the boat and push it steadily down the lake. Rods are held over the "high side" or up-wind side of the skiff, lures are released and allowed or reach fishable depth, then reels are thrown into gear and "trolling" begun. This system can be particularly effective on some lakes because it allows lures to reach maximum depths and to be fished slowly and tantalizingly. This same system can be used to fish lead-head jigs very effectively, with the fisherman yanking his rod in proper cadence to give his jig good action as it hops over the bottom.

Jigging, incidentally, is a different, effective, and comparatively new system for taking lake trout.

It involves the use of lead-head jigs, those weighted lures that have been used in salt water fishing for years but which are considered "new" in fresh water fishing. The jig's ability to get down deep in a hurry is the feature that makes them so popular with so many lake trout fishermen.

Deep-jigging can be done with spinning or bait-casting tackle. The jig is cast out, allowed to sink to or near bottom by paying out line, and then is fished on the bottom. The "pumping" routine is most commonly used in "bottom bouncing" with jigs. That is, the rod is twitched sharply upward to make the jig hop off the bottom a foot or so; slack line is quickly re-spooled, then the rod twitched or yanked again so that the jig hops again. The results, with cadencical repetition, is that the jig hippity-hops along, fished in a very life-like manner at precisely the depth the angler chooses. Few techniques involving repetitious casting can be more effective on lake trout.

Modern fish "finders," fish "locators," and similar electronic devices are a real boon to the lake trout fisherman.

Most electronic fishing aids reveal water depth, which is of major importance to the lake trout angler. Some, too, show the kind of bottom present, whether it is mud, gravel, weeds, or rocks. And still others, the better ones, will reveal the location of any fish present, showing the precise depth.

Such "fish locators" are invaluable to the serious lake trout fisherman since they will reveal whether or not the fisherman is working over productive or at least promising lake trout water, i.e. rock, sand or gravel bottom as opposed to mud, weeds, etc., saying nothing about such electronic aids actually pin-pointing the locations of fish.

In spring and sometimes again in early fall lake trout will be found on or near the surface at many lakes, even those in the southern extremity of the fish's range. And at many far-northern lakes, trout can be taken to the surface throughout the open water season.

When lakers are within 15 feet of the surface they are set ups for the angler who wants to spin for them, or to use bait-casting tackle. And they also can be taken at that depth by fly fishing if the fly-rodder uses a sinking line, or a weighted fly and gives the fly time to sink. At times such fishing is just like working a shallow lake shore for largemouth bass.

The tackle used for this fishing is not unlike bass tackle, either, with the ideal spinning outfit being a rod of 6½ or 7 feet, medium action, mounted with a medium size fresh water open-faced spinning reel. A line testing 8 or 10 pounds is perfect. The bait-casting outfit also should be medium, with the rod 5 to 6 feet long, carrying quality level-wind reel with good drag, and line testing from 10 to 15 pounds. Nylon monofilament line is preferred by most experts to braided line because it casts better—much smoother going through the guides, with less friction, and it is certainly less visible in the water than most braided lines.

Good lures for this type of lake trout fishing are wobbling spoons, sinking plugs, spinners and spinner-feathers or spinner-bucktail combinations and lead-head jigs. Such lures should be retrieved rather slowly, although change-of-pace retrieves with quick jerks and stops sometimes trigger hesitant trout to strike.

Many fishermen, unfortunately, never consider trying for lake trout with flies. This is pathetic considering that a lake trout likes nothing better than a big, lively streamer fly, and that such great sport can be had with lakers by fly fishing.

Appropriate fly tackle for lakers is a bit on the "heavy" side. An ideal outfit is a bass-bugging outfit or, say, a "light" salt water fly outfit such as you would use for bonefishing. The rod should be 8½–9½ feet long, weighing 5 ounces. It should have a fast-tip action but a slow, powerful butt so that short casts can be made with ease, yet long casts can be made very quickly with a minimum of false casts.

A quality fly reel should be used in fly fishing for big lake trout. The reel should be single-action type, with a strong, dependable drag. At least 50 yards of 15–18 pound test backing line should be on the reel, behind the fly line which should be three-diameter, or triple-taper type, of a size to match or "work" the rod, which for the rods mentioned earlier would be at least a WF8 or WF9 line.

The leader for laker trout naturally depends upon overall fishing conditions, i.e., clarity of the water, time of day, wariness of the trout, size of the fish, etc., but generally a leader 9–12 ft. long and tapered to a tippet of 6, 8, or 10 pound test will do.

The most productive flies are streamers, which is not to say that lake trout cannot be taken on wet flies, nymphs, and even dry flies. However, streamers are best, and any good streamer of a decent size, say at least three inches in length, when properly fished where lake trout are, is going to catch fish. Hook sizes for lake trout streamers should be 1/0, 2/0, and 3/0, with the latter plenty big enough to handle any lake trout most fishermen will ever encounter—which means a laker of 60 pounds or more.

CHAPTER 12

Bass Boats

*Never has there been a fishing machine
like the modern bass boat.*

"Bass boats," comparatively new on the fishing scene, are serviceable for many different kinds of fishing, but they originally were designed to give the bass angler a craft particularly suited to his type of fishing.

Forrest Wood, a former guide at Arkansas' Bull Shoals Reservoir and the White River, turned bass boat designer and builder. His "Ranger" boats are well worth checking into.

There's a variety of Ranger bass boats, in 14, 16, and 18 foot lengths. Most feature carpeted decking for quietness, rod storage compartments, wide foredecks for easy mounting of optional equipment (such as electric motors), trays for lures, a raised forward casting deck (with no screw eyes, cleats, etc. to foul line), live well, padded bucket seats, covered storage boxes, and running lights.

I bought an 18-foot Ranger bass boat from Wood, and what a fishing machine it is!

After the first hour of fishing from the boat, a companion, Casimir Popielewski, sighed and said to me: "I am so comfortable I can't fish good."

That's one feature of a bass boat—comfort. My 18-footer will easily fish three persons without crowding. The boat is equipped with three removable luxurious, upholstered chairs, two of which even have arm rests. The chairs are mounted on swivels so that you can quickly turn in any direction to deliver a cast. The seats

Bass fishing "pros" really go for bass boats. These are Ranger boats in use at a Bass Masters Classic tournament.

142

Forrest Wood, former Arkansas fishing guide, turned boat builder to produce the popular Ranger line of bass boats.

This 14 ft., 4 inch bass boat is well powered by a Johnson 50.

Three fishermen fish comfortably from this 18-footer.

are spaced far enough apart that one fisherman never is in the way of another.

The design of the boat's hull is such that it is unbelievably stable. Three men can walk around the thing at the same time, all on the same side, and there is no lurching, no tilting, no slipping or swaying. The boat is heavily carpeted throughout with colorful soft, super-tough "astro-turf" so there is no chance of slipping. Moreover, the decking is flat throughout, so you're not standing or walking about with your feet turned askew as they ususally are in small boats having "V" shaped hulls.

Upholstered, "swing-about" seats are one of the modern bass boats features.

Bass boats trail easily and launching, too, is no problem.

The stability of my boat is so great that a man can stand on a gunnel and the boat hardly tips perceptibly. (Try that sometime with an ordinary rowboat or runabout.) This remarkable stability, incidentally, is of great help when reaching to land fish, and it also is of tremendous benefit to a photographer. When shooting angling photos, a cameraman frequently must reach far out to one side, or have his subject lean this way or that, and such actions in an ordinary small boat can result in dunkings.

Speed and maneuverability are other important features of a quality bass boat. The main powerplant on my boat is a 115 h.p. Johnson outboard. The boat is not rated for anything larger. The 115 will push the boat at

Bass boats are unbelievably stable; almost impossible to tilt or capsize.

better than 50 m.p.h., plenty fast enough. Flat out, the boat skims the water like a shingle, and gets from one fishing spot to another in a hurry. No time is lost from fishing because of traveling delays and, too, when tired after a day's hard fishing, and wanting for home, you can be at the dock in minutes.

The 115 Johnson is equipped with "power steering," and is operated at a console amidships. You sit there as

Even the larger bass boats (this one is 18 feet) can be easily maneuvered in tight areas.

Roominess, lots of storage compartments, live wells, even plush carpeting are just some of the features of this 18-foot Ranger.

comfortable as in an auto, and "drive" the boat with a steering wheel—just like in a car.

The "fishing motor" I use is a Shakespeare electric, model 812, which is probably one of the most powerful of the electrics. It is bow-mounted, has a remote control foot pedal, three speeds, and is whisper quiet. When plugging along a shoreline, we run the electric, moving in and out of likely spots, as silently as a floating leaf, as our cast lures check out this flooded tree, that stump, or that sunken log.

The Shakespeare electric can be turned to run in any direction, all by a simple turn of the foot, which rests on the control pedal. The boat can be made to turn silently in a full circle, and go forward or backwards at one of 3 speeds. The man in the bow, running the electric motor, can move the boat in and out of tight little bays, maneuver it around stumps and brush piles—go anywhere—and all the time be fishing himself.

The fantastic interest in "bass boats" has resulted in countless queries from fishermen seeking further information on them.

Following are letters, or portions of letters I've received having to do with bass boats, along with replies:

"Is it necessary to have an electric motor with a bass boat?"

Roger Admanski
Chicago

Bow-mounted electric fishing motor, with remote foot-control, silently moves this bass boat as anglers cast for crappies.

It is not "necessary" to use an electric motor with a bass boat, but certainly desirable. My 18-foot Ranger, in fact, does not have oar locks. To move it around for fish, paddling would be necessary if no electric motor was used.

Paddling or rowing a typical bass boat would be strenuous and difficult, since most are big, heavy boats. But a good electric motor moves them easily, at various speeds, in complete silence, and with great maneuverability.

Bass boats really are designed for use with electric motors. A large outboard motor is used for the long runs, traveling from the dock to fishing grounds, then the electric—which can be mounted anywhere and, by remote control devices, operated from any spot in the boat—are employed as the "fishing motor."

"What does a good bass fishing rig cost?"

Sal Savaglio
Lombard, Ill.

The 18-foot Ranger boat at this writing sells for about $2,300–$2,500, depending upon accessories and how it is "fitted out." The trailer for the boat sells for about $550, and the 115 horsepower Johnson motor sells for around $1,700. If you add to the basic boat, trailer, etc., such things as 3–4 life-preservers (costing $50 or more apiece), lines, horns, lights, etc., you will have a rig running somewhere around $5,000. However, what such a rig will do for your bass fishing will make the cost well worth while.

"Why is an electric fishing motor so important? We've done without them for years."

Paul Mulhanns
Milwaukee, Wis.

The man running an electric motor rarely has his fishing interfered with. He plugs away as continually, as effectively, as other fishermen in the boat.

It is these great new electric motors that have added to the popularity of bass boats. In the days BBB (before bass boats), and electric motors, fishermen had to row— sometimes laboriously with a bad boat or wind—and only one man could fish at a time. They had to take turns fishing and rowing, but bass boats and electric motors have changed all that.

"I do mostly bass bug fishing. Is it easy to fly fish from a bass boat?"

Dave Whitlock
Hibbing, Minn.

Bass boats are superb casting platforms for ALL fishermen. Their stability is unbelievable. You can stand up, walk all around, even on the gunnels, with no tipping. The Ranger bass boat has a wide, clutter-free forward deck so that the fly fisherman can drop fly line anywhere he likes, and there's nothing to foul it when he casts.

"Do bass boats have live wells to keep fish or bait alive? What about rod racks?"

Chuck Wirz
Springfield, Mo.

The 18-foot Ranger has a big live well, as well as a long, large insulated ice box for food, drink, or for fish to be iced. Moreover, with lining removed, it can be used as a second live well.

There's a large capacity rod storage compartment along one side of the boat, so rods never are bouncing around or in the way. The storage compartment has a lid, and it can be locked.

There's a covered rear storage compartment (concealing batteries, gas tanks, etc.), and yet another storage compartment forward. It can be locked. Even lure trays are molded into the fiberglass hull, so an assortment of favorite plugs, spoons, etc. can be at the fishermans' fingertips at all times.

"What are the launching and trailering characteristics of bass boats?"

D. M. Lattenouse
Detroit, Mich.

Bass boats are remarkably easy to launch and to recover. And in my opinion they are more trailerable than boats with "V" or other types of hulls.

"We've done without bass boats since James Heddon whittled the first bass plug. Why need them now?"

Eric Fox
Belvidere, Iowa

The thing about modern bass boats is that they take fishermen to and from the fishing grounds in a hurry, in safety and comfort. They make it possible to fish with a kind of efficiency never had before, in a lot of places, in a minimum of time, with a minimum of effort.

Bass boats have, in short, done for fishing what electric carts have done for golf.

Persons interested in Ranger boats might write for a color brochure to Wood Mfg. Co., P. O. Box 262, Flippin, Ark. 72634.

CHAPTER 13

Florida

*The Sunshine State has angling on both coasts
—and a lot in between.*

Board a deluxe fishing cruiser at one of many Gulf of Mexico ports on Florida's northwest coast, sail out into the smooth, blue Gulf, start trolling a lure or bait—then steady yourself and be prepared for anything.

Out there in the sun-spanked Gulf, not far from the sandy Florida shores, is a fish-filled, ecological wonderland that has only recently been discovered by sport fishermen. Previously it was felt that the best of Florida big-game fishing was along the Sunshine State's Atlantic Coast, and while that fishing remains among the best, many experts believe world-record fish are soon to come from upper Gulf waters.

What makes the upper Gulf a fisherman's wonderland is a nearly bottomless area known as the "DeSota Canyon," and swirling currents caused by the Mississippi Delta Flow and the Yucatan Current. The unusual, strong currents create a plankton concentration which draws small baitfish and, ultimately, the larger gamefishes which feed upon the smaller fishes.

So it is that the angler trolling a lure or dropping a baited hook over in these Gulf waters can reasonably expect to catch anything from wahoo to sailfish, from broadbill swordfish to marlin, and from snappers to bluefish—which is to name just a few of this ultra new fishing ground's popular species. Both white and blue marlin are available which, along with sailfish, are probably the blue-water angler's most sought-after "trophy" fish. Some other important gamefish taken regularly

An extraordinary new deep-sea fishing grounds has been discovered off Florida's northwest coast which produces giant blue and white marlin.

147

here are huge kingfish (king mackerel), Allison, blackfin, and bluefin tuna, plus dolphin, oceanic bonito—even the rare and prized Atlantic spearfish.

Anglers were totally unaware of the potential of Gulf fishing until the United States Fish and Wildlife Service conducted a survey to determine whether or not Gulf waters might support a commercial fishery. The survey showed that the Gulf was, indeed, quite stiff with fish. The DeSota Canyon is a deep trench in the northeastern part of the Gulf, and the Yucatan Current is a strong, persistent flow that comes into the Gulf from the south, passing between Mexico's Yucatan Peninsula and the western edge of Cuba. Where the Yucatan Current meets the Mississippi Delta Flow, part of the current turns eastward and develops a clockwise movement around the DeSota Canyon. With this sort of continuous ecological set-up, there almost is no "best time" to fish the area—the angling can be as good in June as in January.

Florida's big-game Gulf fishing is done chiefly by trolling rigged baits, which might be small squid, bluefish, ladyfish, mackerel, or strips of fish flesh. The tackle used is generally heavy, and such outfits can be expensive. But the fisherman who doesn't have his own big-game fishing outfit for a Gulf fishing trip needn't worry; complete fishing rigs, baits, etc. are provided by charter boat captains at no extra cost.

A lot of fishing skill isn't needed, either, for a Gulf fishing excursion. The captain or his mate on the boat that you charter will rig the tackle, put the baits over, then troll in likely areas and keep their eyes peeled for fish. When a strike comes, the mate or captain will even hook the fish for beginners. Skilled blue-water anglers, however, will insist on hooking, and playing out, their own fish. These same veteran fishermen, in fact, often have their own deluxe "offshore cruisers," which they may have sailed down for them from home ports such as Breille, N.J., Ocean City, Md., Richmond, Va.—or wherever.

Florida's tarpon fishing is legendary, and silver kings can be taken along either coast.

Florida's inland lakes and rivers produce largemouth bass exceeding 10 pounds. George Seaman tussles with a good one at Lake Okeechobee.

All told, sports fishermen have learned that there is some 615,000 square miles of first-class, blue-water, big-game fishing grounds sprawling off the northwest Florida coast, roughly lying between Panama City and Pensacola. As a direct result of the discovery of this new fishing area, motel-hotel accommodations, restaurants, and charter boat facilities have been greatly expanded at Destin, Panama City, Pensacola, and Fort Walton. Often when there is a rush for charter boats, and there are too many fishermen for the local skippers to handle, charter skippers from other areas of Florida will bring their cruisers to the upper Gulf Coast.

Two good billfish—a white marlin and a sail—from upper Gulf waters.

Possibly there is one major difference between fishing for upper Gulf billfish, such as the marlins and sailfish, and fishing for the same fish in the Atlantic and along the Atlantic Gulf Stream. In south Atlantic waters those fish normally are taken right on top, with the bait just skimming along the surface. In Gulf waters, however, it appears that the prized billfish hang much deeper, possibly because of those unusual currents described earlier. Whatever the reason, upper Gulf fishermen have found they must work their baits much deeper to be consistently successful.

So anglers who bring their own craft to this new fishing country should be prepared to do some deep trolling. And those who come to the upper Gulf Coast area intending to charter boats, had best be prepared financially; this is no penny type, pier or dock fishing.

On the average, expect a charter cruiser to run about $150 for a full day's fishing. A full "day" usually is from about 8:00 A.M. to 4 P.M. and that is from dock to dock. Counting the time used up in running from the dock to the fishing area, then back again, you and friends would get in about six hours of actual fishing. Realistically, that is plenty of fishing for anyone, and especially when you hang into a couple of hard-fighting, wearing-you-out-type of fish. The average angler who hooks and fights down a sailfish, for example, or still better a nice, big blue marlin, is more than anxious to call it a day—to sit down and watch his buddies do the same.

That average price of $150 for a charter cruiser for a day, is, of course, broken into at least four parts—when you charter with some friends. The $150 a day average is for four anglers, with a slight additional charge for each fisherman beyond four. Most charter skippers dislike groups of more than six fishermen.

So, with a $150 a day charge, and four fishermen involved, the per-man rate comes down to about $40. That isn't much for a day's fishing that might result in a 400-pound blue marlin on the dock, plus a couple sailfish, dolphin and wahoo.

Florida's east coast has superb saltwater fishing. Although somewhat overlooked, the northeast coast of Florida has great surf fishing for red and black drum, spotted seatrout, whiting, sheepshead, croakers and even for bluefish, Spanish mackerel, and tarpon. Fishing can be excellent just about anywhere along the coast, but especially good spots to headquarter are Jacksonville, St. Augustine, Daytona, and farther south at the town of Cocoa Beach. The best times for bluefish and Spanish mackerel are in winter; other species are caught mostly during the warmer months.

Florida's Atlantic coast blue-water fishing is legendary. All along the Gulf Stream, from the town of Stuart south, offshore cruisers take large numbers of sailfish, white and blue marlin, dolphin, wahoo, amberjack, kingfish, barracuda, and many other species.

Atlantic sailfish are the "glamour" fish of the east coast —and fishing for them can be very good. The best sail-fishing usually is from December 1 through the end of February. Fishing is done from charter boats. Charters can be had at just about any one of the larger East Coast ports. Rates vary with the time of year, size of boat, crew, etc., but usually prices range from $100 to $200 per day for a party of four anglers.

Surprising as it may seem, huge, metropolitan Miami also has good saltwater fishing within the shadows of its concrete skyscrapers. Both private charter boats cater-ing to a few fishermen, and "party boats," that take up to 50 anglers per trip, work offshore out of Miami. Miami is the chief Florida port for sailfishing, and other species such as wahoo, dolphin, kingfish, amberjack, blue and white marlin, etc., are taken, too.

Anglers in the Miami area also take a wide variety of saltwater fish from bridges and causeways. Fall and winter usually are best for pompano, bluefish, snook, kingfish, crevalle, and Spanish mackerel. Not all bridges and causeways are open to fishing, however, so visiting anglers should check with local tackle shops for current information.

South of Miami stretch the Florida Keys. There is almost always good fishing of some kind, somewhere in the Keys throughout the year. The better Keys to fish, and also where there are excellent guides usually avail-able, are Islamorada, Marathon, Big Pine, Key Largo, and Key West.

There's first-rate inshore fishing throughout most of the Keys for tarpon, bonefish, permit, spotted seatrout, ladyfish, barracuda, numerous species of snappers and groupers and red drum. Blue-water charter-boat-fishing also is popular in the Keys for sailfish, dolphin, kingfish, wahoo, and amberjack.

On Florida's extreme southwest tip the Ten Thousand Islands offer excellent light-tackle fishing. The islands are a labyrinth of mangrove outcroppings and a good guide is a must. Guides for Ten Thousand Islands fishing can be had at Everglades City or Marco. The principle fish are tarpon, snook, spotted seatrout, red drum, and a variety of snappers and groupers. Best fishing is May through September.

Some of the best tarpon fishing found anywhere in the world is along Florida's southwest coast. Principle areas are Boco Grande Pass, Tampa Bay, and also near the town of Crystal River north of Tampa. The best times for tarpon vary, but normally early May through July are tops. During the peak of the fishing activity it's not un-usual for anglers to hook as many as 6 tarpon in one

One of Florida's greatest angling attractions is the bonefish, best described as a silver bullet sporting fins.

Soon to be boated—and released—a sailfish oggles a charter skipper.

day—averaging about 70 pounds with many fish weighing in excess of 100 pounds.

Charter boats and experienced guides are recommended for this type of West Coast Florida tarpon fishing. Rates average around $100 per day and charters can be made easily at most marinas.

Freshwater canal fishing is very popular among Florida anglers. Thousands of miles of canals and drainage ditches criss-cross much of Florida—particularly in the southern part of the state. There literally is no man-made waterway in Florida that doesn't have largemouth bass and various species of panfish in it—although, of course, there are some canals and ditches that have larger populations than some with poor fish-spawning areas.

Conservation Area 1, located in Palm Beach County in the southeast part of the state, is one of the best canal fishing spots in Florida. The area has many miles of wide canals alive with largemouth bass, bluegills, shellcrackers (redear sunfish), black crappies, and warmouth. To the south, Conservation Areas 2 and 3 also have superb canal fishing for a variety of freshwater fish.

All three areas have many good boat launching facilities, parking lots, rental boat and motor marinas, guide service, etc. For more information, maps, etc., on south Florida canal areas write: Director of Recreation, Central and Southern Florida Flood Control District, Evernia St., West Palm Beach.

Florida has good fishing for a variety of fish in its freshwater lakes and rivers. And although the Sunshine State produces heavy stringers of chain pickerel, various sunfishes, catfishes and gars, the most sought after freshwater fish is the largemouth bass.

Every year hundreds of bigmouths are taken from Florida waters that weigh between 5 and 10 pounds, and plenty of bass between 12 and 16 pounds are caught annually.

There's no closed season on largemouth bass in Florida. Bass can be taken year-round, but October through June is the peak of the big bass fishing.

Of the thousands of good largemouth lakes in Florida, some of the better ones are: Lakes Talquin, Jackson, Iamonia, and Miccosukee, near Tallahassee in the north; Deer Point Lake and Dead Lake near Panama City;

Schools of king mackerel swarm periodically in offshore waters.

Lakes George, Little George, and Crescent near Welaka; good bass waters near the town of Leesburg are Tsala Apopka, Griffin, Dora, Panasoffkee, Eustis, Harris, and Little Lake Harris; Lake Istokpogo at Lorida, Lake Martin near Haines City, Lake Lena at Auburndale, and Lake Seminole close to Clearwater.

There's also good bigmouth fishing in many of Florida's streams and rivers. Among the best are the St. Johns, Chipola, Caloosahatchee, Oklawaha, Withlacoochee, Chassahowitza, Suwanee, Homosassa, Crystal, and Rainbow Rivers, and Dunn's and Murphy's Creeks.

American or white shad fishing is occasionally quite good in the St. Johns River during winter, particularly between Lake Monroe and Lake Harney.

For more information, maps, brochures, etc. on Florida fishing write the Florida Game and Fresh Water Fish Commission, Farris Bryant Building, 620 S. Meridian St., Tallahassee, 32304.

CHAPTER 14

Michigan

Coho and Chinook salmon get the spotlight in Michigan these days, but there's lots more fishing on the state's thousands of inland lakes and streams.

By Stan Lievense

Michigan's fishing is simply a dream that has come true. A nearly disastrous tumble of Michigan's Great Lakes fishing sparked a rejuvenation that has never been equaled in any lake management history. Rounding out the total program is Michigan's exciting, greatly diversified inland fisheries. Michigan can proudly boast of 11,000 lakes and 28,000 miles of streams; 13,000 miles of this stream length is classified as trout water. Michigan's sport fishing is big and is getting bigger.

Great Lakes fisheries management was changed from a staid commercial fishing emphasis to a radically new sport fishing emphasis. Coho salmon were introduced from the Pacific, followed by an introduction of Chinook salmon. Later, massive plantings of steelhead and brown trout were made possible by Michigan's far sighted Legislature's approval of a new large capacity trout-salmon hatchery. Meanwhile, the U.S. Department of Interior has been waging an effective fight to control the once dominant parasitic sea lamprey and has been making large recovery plantings of lake trout. Top this all off with the further fact that this new, almost unlimited Great Lakes fishing has eased the fishing pressures on Michigan's inland waters. Stream trout fishermen have

exclaimed, "It's like it was ten years or more ago; even during the 'caddis hatch,' you can have a good chunk of a stream to yourself."

Lake trout are native to the Great Lakes and have been a very treasured fish primarily because they reach large sizes and have superb table quality. The heavy recovery plantings started in the early 60s in Lake Superior and the mid-sixties in Lake Michigan, have replenished the species to old time levels and sizes, except in Lake Huron. Lake Huron's lake trout fishing is still a few years away from being a quality fishery. But lake trout are now the "bread and butter" fish of the charter boat fleet on Lakes Michigan and Superior. Seldom do experienced fishermen go out on these two lakes without getting some action and limit catches are common. In any catch of a few fish at least one is likely to go to 10 lb. in size or more!

An experienced lake trout fisherman knows well that lake trout are very light sensitive, are bottom huggers ordinarily and are most active when water temperatures in the 45°F. to 55°F. range are available. The knowledgeable angler will start fishing the depth level of these temperatures when possible. In the spring and fall, when these temperatures are near the surface and on the shoals, lake trout will move in only during the low light intensity periods of early morning and the evening. Catches of lake trout are more routine in the summer months because the water temperatures are more stable then.

Silver-sided, alewife-stuffed coho salmon taken in fall in Lake Michigan off the Manistee River.

Since the innovation in the Great Lakes of the downrigger, sportsfishermen have found positive depth fishing works out very well in taking lake trout, especially when using a Herring Dodger as an exciter, followed by a sensitive action, thin metal spoon or a fly. In mid-summer, when the cool water is deep, another good technique for lakers is to use a wire line trolling outfit, with a single hook spoon as a lure. A must technique for fishing such a hook-up is to constantly pump the rod causing a quickened retrieve to the lure and then, a drop back. A pumped rod will greatly outfish one in a rod holder.

There's excitement a'plenty fly fishing Michigan streams for giant coho and Chinook salmon.

Coho, and then Chinook salmon, were introduced in the Michigan waters of Lakes Superior, Michigan, and Huron in 1966 and 1967 respectively; and large annual maintenance plantings have continued. Both species have survived well and their growth has been spectacular. Cohos have been the easiest to catch, but this is changing. Michigan's Lake Huron fishermen fish specifically for Chinook and are very successful, especially in August. Chinook, in Lakes Michigan and Superior, are caught more as incidental fish.

The most dependable fishing for cohos is in the spring, while the fish are small, and again in the fall when they congregate off their parent streams. Coho start to move in April, feeding right on top, recklessly hitting most flashy, wiggly surface-trolled lures. This easy fishing lasts until about June. As the upper water warms above 55°F., the cohos go deeper, staying with the 53°F. temperatures, and they start to migrate northerly. In mid-summer cohos are often stratified in their preferred temperature level over depths of 150' to 200'. By September, the fish are usually found in schools in the general area of their home streams. By this time they are a chunky 7 lb. to 15 lb. in size. The record Michigan, angler-caught coho is 30 lbs., 8 oz.

Cohos are easy to catch, once located. Conventional spoons and plugs and a dodger with a trailing fly work equally well. Positive depth trolling, off a downrigger weight, in the 53°F. temperature level is most successful.

It appears the Chinook in Lakes Michigan and Superior are missed by most fishermen because they go after easier targets, such as lake trout and cohos. The different habits of the Chinook indicate why most fishermen are missing them. Chinook differ from other trout and salmon in these ways: 1. Although they have a 53°F. temperature preference, as do cohos, they like to orient where that temperature is near bottom. This ordinarily puts the Chinooks well shoreward of cohos and lake trout. 2. They are a very wary fish. It pays to fish a light line, if the boat traffic allows; as light as 8 lb. test! A heavier line can be used, but then a cowbell or a dodger must be used with the fly or lure, to excite strikes. 3. Chinook prefer a slow trolled lure. 4. Chinook are light sensitive. It's best to start fishing at the break of day and to fish again at dusk. 5. Chinooks are long runners when hooked. Most inexperienced anglers panic when one gets hooked, and they try to force them.

Besides the coho and Chinook open water fishing, each offers a considerable fishery for mature spawners in inland waters, including some lakes and streams. The peak time for this fishing is October.

Michigan has some of the finest smallmouth water in the country. Hundreds of miles of clear-water shoals in northern Lake Michigan support an immense smallmouth bass fishery.

Michigan offers more open water lunker steelhead and brown trout fishing opportunities than can be found anywhere. We're talking about fish weighing 15 lb. and more! The official state record brown trout and steelhead, at the time of this writing, is 27 lb., 12 oz. and 22 lb., 6 oz. respectively. The Department of Natural Resources, with its $4,000,000 trout and salmon hatchery now on the production line, is annually pouring out rainbow and brown trout in numbers so great even Michigan fishermen haven't yet adjusted to them. In 1973 for instance, more than 1½ million brown trout and salmon over 5 inches in length were planted in Lakes Superior, Huron, and Michigan; and they were merely supplemental fish to large natural reproduction.

In spring, fall, and winter trout and salmon offer a prime challenge in the many specially designed trout streams that remain open for this special fishing. (The MICHIGAN FISHING GUIDE, obtained at license dealers, lists key streams open for the extended seasons.)

The "big ones" in Michigan are not limited to salmon and lake trout. In recent years, the State has embarked on an intensive inland lake muskie management program. The value of the northern pike—especially the "lunkers" in the warm water bays of the Great Lakes—has also gained increasing attention since 1966 when

Lightly hooked, a Lake St. Claire muskie is drawn close.

they were removed from the commercial species list and declared a sport fish.

Lake St. Claire is world renown amongst veteran muskie fishermen as a prominent potential area for a future, record-breaking muskie. A good two dozen or more inland lakes have proven so outstanding it has been said a good fisherman now can expect to catch at least one muskie a day in them.

The warm water bays of Michigan's Great Lakes, such as Big and Little Bay De Noc, in Lake Michigan, and Thunder Bay and Saginaw Bay in Lake Huron, have responded to protection from commercial netting—both in their abundance of northern pike and in sizes. In the spring of 1974, fisheries biologists in the Escanaba area, netting Big and Little Bay De Noc for northern pike, for egg-taking purposes, were amazed at the numbers and sizes of the fish taken. A high percentage of the northern pike netted were 18 to 25 lbs., with the biggest tipping the scales at 35 lbs.!

A 30 pounds plus Chinook salmon—from Lake Michigan.

Perch fishing in Michigan offers the excitement of fishing for numbers and the delight of a delicious taste treat. Yellow perch, fried crisp and crunchy, are hard to beat as a main course. Angling for perch is very relaxing because the techniques are simple. A good day is catching a bucketful of 10 to 14 inch jumbos, occasionally two-at-a-time.

The phenomenal success of Michigan's salmon program has brought international attention.

Small boat fishermen stay with the salmon schools spring, summer, and fall.

MICHIGAN   155

Remarkable photo of porpoising salmon shows these fishermen are working the right area.

Michigan's perch population is almost unlimited. It's the most bountiful species in Michigan's inland lakes, and bumper crops are now the rule in southern Lake Michigan, Michigan's Lake Erie shoals, and Lake Huron's Saginaw Bay.

Great Lakes perch bite well all summer and fall, but most consistently starting in early June and lasting through July. In huge, shallow Saginaw Bay; Lake St. Claire and Houghton Lake (Michigan's largest inland lake), winter ice fishing is especially exciting.

In open water fishing, a cane pole is ideal gear for perch. However, most fishermen use a spinning outfit. Since perch are a school fish and there is no creel limit, two hooks are used as droppers off a main line, with a sinker at the terminal end. Minnows, baby crayfish, leeches, and wigglers are popular baits.

Natural populations of largemouth bass and bluegills are common in almost every lake in the lower ⅔ of lower

Michigan, and in some northern lakes, including those in the Upper Peninsula. Bluegills may be caught the year-around, and bass during the period between the Saturday before Memorial Day each year and December 31.

Bass and bluegills are most active during the summer. In the heat of August, the larger fish drop a bit deeper, especially in the big lakes.

Bluegills are commonly caught still-fishing from an anchored boat off an extensive weed-bed and over a mud bottom. They are a fish that "suspends," often several feet off bottom. A long cane pole, rigged with a light monofilament line, small bobber, split-shot sinker, and hook baited with crickets, red worms, or catalpa worms, is unbeatable for summertime bluegill fishing. Early in the summer, fly fishing a sponge-bodied, rubber-legged spider while wading shoals is most exciting.

Michigan offers outstanding opportunities for inland

trout fishing, both in its vast stream system and in lakes. The trout streams come in all types. There are small feeder creeks with pure stocks of native brook trout; some streams that are remote, with soft bottoms and overhanging brush, where canoes only are recommended; profuse miles of firm-bottom, wading waters, including some that require a cautious approach because of deep holes, slippery rocks, or a clay bottom; and, finally, big waters that lend themselves best to float fishing. Michigan's stream trout populations are mostly self-sustaining from natural reproduction, but the lakes are planted on an annual basis.

Although the brook trout is the only native trout in Michigan, the brown trout has become the dominant trout. The state's stream rainbows have evolved almost entirely into an anadromous fish, and live in the streams until smolting time—which occurs when they reach 5 to 10 inches.

Michigan is unique in having excellent access situations to its trout streams. Much river frontage is State-owned, or owned by large corporations that are cooperative with fishermen.

Some of the better trout streams are listed below:

UPPER PENINSULA

Sturgeon River and tributaries—Baraga County—brown and brook trout
Ontonagon River and tributaries—Ontonagon County—brown and brook trout
Upper Escanaba River and tributaries—Delta and Marquette Counties—brown and brook trout
Fox River System—Schoolcraft County—brook trout
Two-Hearted River—Luce County—brown trout.

NORTHERN LOWER MICHIGAN

Jordan River—brown and brook trout—Charlevoix and Antrim County
Manistee River—brown trout—Kalkaska County
Boardman River—brown trout—Grand Traverse County
Platte River—brown trout—Benzie County
Pere Marquette River—brown trout—Lake County
Sturgeon River—brown trout—Otsego County
Au Sable River—brown trout—Crawford and Roscommon Counties
Black River—brook trout—Cheboygan County

Michigan actively manages well over 500 lakes for one or more species of trout. These lakes are planted with either brook, brown, or rainbow trout, splake, lake trout, or combinations of these fish. Those lakes where the fishing quality drops off are eliminated from the planting program. All managed trout lakes have public access. Trolling or still-fishing are the most popular fishing techniques. Fly fishing both wet and dry is an excellent method for spring and fall trout fishing when the surface waters are cool. However, this exciting technique is seldom utilized.

Most of the managed lakes are open to fishing any time. Designated trout lakes having a limited open season from the last Saturday in April through September are listed in the annual MICHIGAN FISHING GUIDE.

Michigan's better fishing waters by lake or stream, by species of fish, and by county, have been cataloged completely as an aid to fishermen. This "Catalog of Michigan Summer Fishing," and other additional information on Michigan fishing, can be obtained by writing MICHIGAN TOURIST COUNCIL, 300 South Capitol, Lansing, Michigan 48926.

The BEST largemouth lakes in southwestern Michigan are: in *Ottawa County*—Springlake, and Bruce's, Lloyd's, Strens, and Pottawatomie Bayous; *Berrien County*—Big Paw Paw Lake; *Allegan County*—Hutchins, Ely Swan, Silver, Duck, and Miner Lakes; *Kalamazoo County*—Gull, Sugarloaf, Long Gourdneck, and Sherman Lakes;

St. Joseph County—Mud Hole, Noah, Long, Palmer, Klinger, Corey, Fish, and Fisher Lakes; *Barry County*—Crooked, Wall, Fish, Pine, Thornapple, Gun and Middle Lakes; *Van Buren County*—Saddle, Muskrat, North and South Jeptha, Van Auken, Gravel, Eagle, and Cedar Lakes;

Branch County—Long, Loon, Silver, Lime, Cary, Marble, South Craig Chain, Union and Gilead Lakes;

Calhoun County—Duck, Cedar, Lane, Nottawa, Prairie, Ackley, Graham, and Goguac Lakes; *Cass County*—Stone, Eagle, Juno, Dayton, Painter, Fish, Magician, and Whit Lakes; *Eaton County*—Narrow Lake.

For smallmouth bass in southwestern Michigan, the best waters are in *St. Joseph County*—Fawn River, *Kent County*—Thornapple, Flat, and Grand Rivers; *Cass County*—Diamond Lake; *Calhoun County*—Duck Lake and Kalamazoo River; *Barry County*—Thornapple River, Gun and Gull Lakes; *Berrien County*—St. Joseph River.

The LAKES and rivers in the southwestern part of the state for northern pike include: in *Branch County*—Silver, Rose, Marble and Union Lakes; *Cass County*—White Pond and Diamond Lake; *Allegan County*—Kalamazoo River, Dumond and Swan Lakes; *Barry County*—Thornapple Lake and River; *Eaton County*—Smithville Dam and Lacey Lake; *Ottawa County*—Grand River bayous and Pigeon Lake; *Kent County*—Flat, Grand, and Thornapple Rivers, Wabasis, Murray Lincoln, and Reeds Lakes; *Calhoun County*—St. Joseph and Kalamazoo Rivers, Lee, Prairie, and Duck Lakes.

The southwest corner of Michigan isn't exactly a walleye hunter's heaven, but there are a few lakes with good walleye populations. Among them are: *Calhoun County*—Duck Lake; *Kent County*—Grand River.

Muskies? Southwest Michigan's got them, too. Three kinds, in fact. Some waters have the northern muskellunge, others the Great Lakes muskellunge, and most others have the tiger muskie, which is a hatchery hybrid between the northern muskie and northern pike.

Lakes recommended for muskies: in *Branch County*—Marble and Rose Lakes (both have tiger muskies only); *Barry County*—Thornapple Lake (northern muskies); *Kent County*—Dean, Murray, Lincoln and Campan Lakes (each has tiger muskies).

CHAPTER 15

North Carolina

From trout to tarpon, and bluegills to blue marlin,
North Carolina has it all.

North Carolina offers anglers a wide variety of both fresh and salt water fishing. The state has high mountains laced with many small streams, flat plains with huge man-made reservoirs, brackish water tidal estuaries holding both fresh and salt water gamefish, and a barrier reef offering excellent blue water offshore fishing. Fishermen can catch just about everything from brook trout to blue marlin in North Carolina.

Offshore salt water fishing—for fish such as dolphin, blue marlin, sailfish, yellowfin tuna, and cobia—in North Carolina is done from large specialized sport fishing cruisers with twin engines. They usually are manned by a captain and a mate, and the boats are fully equipped with tackle for both light and heavy fishing. The fishing is normally done well beyond the sight of land, and occasionally as far out as the Gulf Stream.

Six people is an ideal number for an offshore fishing party. Rates range from $135 for a 12-hour trip to $300 for a 24-hour trip. Tackle is provided but food and beverages are extra. Charter rates vary according to the services provided.

The deep water fishing grounds are located off North Carolina's three capes—Hatteras, Lookout, and Fear.

The offshore waters of the northeast coast are fished by fleets of charter boats based at Oregon Inlet and at Hatteras. Oregon Inlet boats fish Platt Shoals (directly off the inlet), Wimble Shoals (20 miles to the southeast),

and the Gulf Stream water beyond. Hatteras boats fish the 12 miles of turbulent shoals—Inner Diamond, Hatteras, and Outer Diamond—and the Gulf Stream waters which begin at the Diamond Light Tower, stationed on the east tip of the shoals.

North Carolina's hundreds of miles of hard sand beaches afford the surf fisherman prime sport. These anglers are after bluefish at Cape Hatteras.

159

Lookout Shoals and the blue water beyond them are fished by the charter boat fleet based at Morehead city. Here, as at Hatteras, excellent fishing is sometimes found over reefs and the wreckage of ships.

Anglerette ties into a white marlin off Oregon Inlet . . .

Frying Pan Shoals off Cape Fear are fished by charter boats from Southport, Wrightsville Beach, and Carolina Beach. Deep sea charters working Frying Pan Shoals also are available from Calabash, Shallotte, Sneads Ferry, Swansboro, and New Topsail Beach.

Most offshore fishing is done from the first of May through the last of October. During that period an astonishing variety of blue water gamefish are available.

Amberjack are taken from May through early autumn. "Jacks" average 10 to 20 pounds, but fish up to 123 pounds have been taken.

North Carolina's dolphin fishing is excellent. Dolphin weighing over 20 pounds are common catches, but the average is 5 pounds and the record is 66½ pounds. The best fishing runs from May into the fall months with big catches reported from Cape Hatteras in late autumn. Like amberjack, dolphin are taken along the entire coast

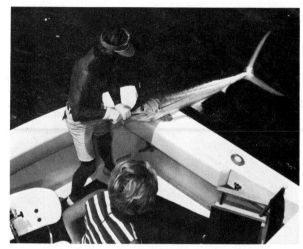

. . . and sleek, powerful billfish soon is boated.

but the best fishing for both species is located beyond the three "capes" already mentioned.

Blue marlin are the "glamour" fish of North Carolina. Fish up to 810 pounds have been landed off Hatteras and the average fish weighs 300 pounds. The first marlin ordinarily is taken late in May and these great gamefish continue to strip line from reels on into late October. Blue marlin are taken out of Hatteras, Oregon Inlet, Morehead City, Wrightsville Beach, Carolina Beach, and Southport. Dare County waters (Oregon Inlet and Hatteras), besides being one of the world's great marlin centers, are famed for producing particularly large fish, as is the Morehead City area.

North Carolina's white marlin average around 60 pounds, but fish weighing 100 pounds sometimes are caught. The best white marlin fishing runs from July through September. Charters fishing just off Oregon Inlet have excellent white marlin fishing, with one boat occasionally catching as many as 10 marlin in one day.

Good angling for sailfish is available from late summer to early fall. Charter boats working from Morehead City, Wrightsville Beach, Carolina Beach, and Southport regularly produce sails.

North Carolina has become a blue marlin fishing mecca. This blue was hooked off Hatteras.

Barracuda up to 44 pounds (but averaging around 10 pounds) are caught along the entire Carolina coast, particularly off Cape Fear.

Cobia fishing can be excellent. Cobia weighing more than 90 pounds have been taken. The best fishing is in May and June when these fish begin spawning.

Big Hatteras blue comes aboard. Note remora attached to fish.

Yellowfin tuna are found off Dare County waters year around. So-called "school tuna," which are really small bluefin tuna, also are taken. Atlantic big-eye tuna—weighing up to 253 pounds—are caught in North Carolina waters. Gulf Stream waters off Oregon Inlet yielded a 203 pound yellowfin tuna in 1960.

Dolphin abound in North Carolina seas.

Anglers who don't want to go the expensive, private charter boat route can still fish big open water from a "party-boat." "Party-boats" take large numbers of fishermen (up to 90) out to blue water where they drift and bottom-fish coral reefs. For about $15 per person anglers can catch porgies, groupers, grunts, sea bass, trigger fish, red snappers, and an occasional amberjack or dolphin.

North Carolina ranks as one of the world's best areas for catching big red drum or channel bass.

While there is some surf fishing for channel bass in the spring—late April through early June—the prime season begins in mid-to-late September and runs into November and even December.

The first fish of the spring and fall runs ordinarily are taken from the surf of Smith Island at the mouth of the Cape Fear River. Most are small "puppy drum." The first of the big channel bass usually are caught near the inlets north of Cape Lookout—Drum, Ocracoke, Hatteras, and Oregon. The last of the big drum usually are taken from the surf at Hatteras in late November and, sometimes, December.

The very best fishing—particularly for the slab-sided lunkers—is in the area north of Cape Lookout and south of Oregon Inlet.

Along the entire coast, from Calabash to Currituck, the best surf fishing is near the inlets. The four top spots are Drum Inlet, Ocracoke Inlet, Hatteras Inlet, and Oregon Inlet.

Drum Inlet, reached by boat from the town of Atlantic on the mainland, offers simple but adequate housekeeping cabins. Parties furnish their own food. There are similar facilities on the banks near Davis, just south of Drum Inlet.

There is good channel bass fishing on the Currituck Banks which run north from the Nags Head beaches to the Virginia line. However, this roadless area, reached only by boats crossing Currituck Sound or by beach buggy, is fished sparingly. The same is true of the Banks south of Drum Inlet to Cape Lookout.

Only productive fishing ever fills a pier like this. Most of these fishermen are after Norfork spot, but bluefish, sea trout, etc. also are caught.

Farther south, all of the inlets—Bogue, Bear, Brown, New River, New Topsail, Masonboro, and half a dozen others—provide surf fishing for channel bass that ranges from fair to very good.

At the top of the fall surf season puppy drum (up to 6 pounds) are common and so are yearlings in the 6 to 20 pound class. Adult channel bass weighing 20 to 50 pounds are taken each season. Anglers are limited to two

large fish (32 inches and up) per day. There is no limit on pups or yearling channel bass.

Channel bass anglers favor the points of inlets and, on the straight beaches, the deeper sloughs with openings in the offshore bar that connect with the sea.

While the channel bass is the king of the North Carolina surf fish, there are other species available. Bluefish sometimes are caught in large numbers. Hatteras is particularly famous for bluefish.

Spotted seatrout also are taken in the surf, particularly on the rising tide of brisk, fall mornings.

Joel Arrington shows a fine 5½ pound sea trout.

Pompano, most of which are in the 1 to 2 pound class, are taken in September and October with small spoons or shrimp on small hooks. Flounder are common in the surf and so are northern kingfish (also called whiting and sea mullet) and black drum. Smith Island at the mouth of the Cape Fear River, is a good spring and fall spot for surf fishermen. There are no accommodations on the island, so parties commute by boat across the river from Southport.

Pier fishing is, in a sense, an extension of surf fishing. All of the surf fish mentioned are taken from piers. Because these piers reach out 1,000 feet or more from the beach they generally provide more consistent sport for bluefish, Spanish mackerel, spot, and other species which are not tied by their feeding habits to the surf sloughs. The pilings of the piers provide habitat for wary fish such as sheepshead. Northern kingfish provide fine sport for pier fishermen during balmy spring nights.

North Carolina has numerous ocean piers. There are a number of other piers located in the inland sounds. The fee for pier fishing runs about $1 per person. Tackle can be rented ($1 to $1.50 per day with a $20 deposit required) and all piers sell a variety of bait.

While most of the pier fishing in North Carolina is done with live bait, a growing number of sportsmen use the piers as platforms from which to cast artificials. Lures account for good catches of bluefish and mackerel when schools of those fish move within casting range.

An Oregon Inlet channel bass soon to be gaffed. North Carolina's coastal waters provide some of the finest channel bass fishing in North America.

The ocean waters up to around 10 miles off the coast, the inlets, and the 2,000 square miles of inland sounds provide another important type of salt water fishing. This variety of fishing is reflected in the fact that it is done from a range of craft that includes both Gulf Stream cruisers and flat-bottomed skiffs.

The blue water cruisers fish these protected waters when weather conditions make it unwise to venture far off the coast, and when certain species of fish, such as Spanish and king mackerel, bluefish, channel bass, and striped bass, are running through inshore waters.

Also, there is a large fleet of fishing craft which is not equipped for Gulf Stream fishing but caters to inshore parties. Sport fishing boats of this class are found at all of the places where the blue water cruisers dock.

Channel bass, or red drum, average very large in North Carolina waters. Ones 3-50 pounds are not unusual.

Most of the inshore, inlet, and sound fishing is done by trolling. Charters average about $60 per day—$30 to $35 per half day—for a party of six. Boats taking out parties to bottom fish in the sounds charge around $20 to $25 per day. Tackle is provided but bait, lunch and beverages ordinarily are extra.

There are protected waters in the vicinity of all of North Carolina's sport fishing ports that offer wonderful opportunities for casting, trolling, and bottom fishing from small craft. Skiffs and outboard motors are available on a rental basis and there are launching areas for private boats.

The best time for inshore, inlet, and sound fishing varies with the species. There is good fishing for channel bass, Spanish and king mackerel, cobia, tarpon, striped bass, spotted seatrout, weakfish, croaker, spot, hogfish, pompano, sheepshead, black drum, and flounder.

North Carolina is endowed with tremendous reaches of brackish waters that produce remarkably good sport fishing for fresh water gamefish. Enormous volumes of fresh water enter the upper sounds—Currituck, Albemarle, and Pamlico—daily and support astonishing populations of freshwater species such as largemouth bass.

Currituck Sound is widely famed for the quality of its brackish water fishing. From its beginning south to the Point Harbor Bridge, where Currituck opens into Albemarle Sound—a distance of more than 75 miles—this sound provides some of the finest bass fishing in America. The same brackish water conditions—and the same fishing—extend beyond the mouth of Currituck into Kitty Hawk Bay and the Colington Marsh which fringes on the Outer Banks just above Roanoke Island.

All of the streams feeding into Albemarle Sound—the North, Pasquotank, and Chowan Rivers, to name a few—have good brackish water bass fishing.

Below where the Outer Banks swing back to the mainland at Morehead City, the upper tidal waters of streams such as the White Oak, New, and Cape Fear Rivers also offer excellent brackish water fishing.

Currituck Sound and sections of Albemarle Sound year-after-year continue to produce bass up to 5 pounds in record numbers. The peak of the season is from mid-April to early June and again in September and October.

North Carolina's tidewater areas have excellent fishing for largemouth, panfish, and pickerel. This tidewater section is a vast, low-lying belt of swamp forest spotted with pocosins and savannahs and laced with the black-water streams typical of southern swamp country. This area extends from the Dismal Swamp near the Virginia line south to the broad bottoms of the Cape Fear River.

North Carolina's natural lakes are found in the tidewater belt. Mattamuskeet, some 30,000 acres, is the largest. Lake Phelps in Hyde County (Pettigrew State Park) and Lake Waccamaw in southeastern North Carolina, also are large and well known to anglers. The 1,100 acre Merchant's Mill Pond in Gates County is a good spot known mostly to local fishermen. These lakes, and the black swamp creeks and canals which surround them, provide prime fishing for bass and panfish.

Some of the best fishing in this area isn't in the main rivers but in the tributaries which flow into them. Tranter's Creek, a tributary of the Tar near Little Washington is one of these. Others are Batchler's Creek, joining the Neuse near New Bern; Black River below Lock #1 on the Cape Fear; Cashie Creek off the Roanoke River; and Indiantown Creek off the North River. Yeopin and Chowan Rivers and Perquiman's and Pembroke Creeks, flowing into Albemarle Sound offer excellent fishing for largemouth, panfish, and stripers.

Fishermen trying these areas for the first time are advised to hire a guide. Guide service usually is available locally, and the fee is $25 to $35 per day for a party of two anglers.

Each year great schools of striped bass move up the Roanoke River from Albemarle Sound to the edge of the Piedmont Plateau near Weldon to spawn. Ordinarily the run begins in early April and continues for about 45 days. Good catches are made in the mouths of the rivers feeding the Roanoke early in the year on cut

An "ordinary" string of largemouth bass from the brackish waters of Currituck Sound.

bait, bucktails, spinners, and spoons. Trolling and casting from small skiffs produces fish in the Roanoke River below Weldon later in the year.

In the feeder streams of the Coastal Plain each spring there are spawning runs of both white and hickory shad. Spin fishermen and fly-rodders take these gamefish with jigs, small spinners, and streamer flies—principally from the Tar, Neuse, and Cape Fear Rivers and from Pitch-kettle Creek.

The Roanoke River's Kerr Reservoir, with some 50,000 acres of water and 800 miles of shoreline, which lies in both Virginia and North Carolina, has excellent largemouth and land-locked striped bass fishing. Too, Gaston Reservoir and Roanoke Rapids Lake are both good spots for largemouth bass and panfish.

The Yadkin River has a string of man-made "power lakes," including 15,000 acre High Rock and, below it, Badin, Tillery, and Blewett Falls. These big "power lakes" produce largemouth bass and panfish. Walleyes up to 10 pounds are taken from Lake James where this fish, first stocked in the late 1940s, has thrived. There are launching areas, marinas, and accommodations on or near all of these reservoirs.

Fishing is best on the Piedmont power reservoirs in May and June, and again in September and October.

North Carolina's mountains—the Blue Ridge on the east, the Great Smokies and Unakas on the west, and transverse ranges such as the lofty Blacks creating a step-ladder effect in between—offer a wide variety of fishing.

There are small creeks, big streams, and lakes loaded with largemouth and smallmouth bass, panfish, walleyes, white bass, and brook, brown and rainbow trout.

In North Carolina's 25 mountain counties there are 1,800 miles of clear, cold waters which produce trout ranging in size from 12-inch brookies to 10-pound browns, and in the lakes rainbows weighing over 10 pounds are taken.

Much of this water is stocked with trout. However, many of the smaller, less accessible back country mountain streams aren't stocked because natural reproduction keeps these trout waters near their carrying capacity.

Many of these streams, such as Forney, Eagle, Hazel, and Noland Creeks in the Great Smokies, are accessible only to anglers crossing Fontana Lake by boat. These creeks stretch back through the roadless forest towards the spine of the Smokies.

Transylvania County streams like Horsepasture, Whitewater, and Toxaway are lightly fished because their rugged, deep gorges discourage most anglers. The same is true of the wilderness areas threaded by the white runs of the Linville River. Great brown trout streams such as the Slick Rock, which feeds Calderwood Lake, are visited only by fishermen willing to walk the 6 miles of mountain ridges to reach this water.

In the river valleys, there are some top-quality small-mouth bass streams. The New River, including both the North and South Forks, in Ashe and Alleghany Counties, is one of the best. So is the Watauga River in Watauga County, the Upper Yadkin, Elk Creek, the Johns River, lower Wilson's Creek and a number of others. While these streams don't produce big fish—anything over 4 pounds is huge—smallmouths are plentiful.

Some of North Carolina's best bass and panfish angling is found in the mountain lakes.

Fontana Lake, Hiwassee Reservoir, and Lake San-teetlah are extraordinary bass lakes. Fontana Lake is particularly well known for its white bass fishing and its walleye fishing in the spring.

Lake Chatuge offers particularly good crappie, large-mouth and smallmouth bass fishing. Lake Lure, in Polk County, Glenville (Thorpe) Lake, and Cheoah (a trout lake directly below Fontana), and Lake Calderwood below Cheoah, can be just as good.

This lake fishing is best in May and June and again in September and October. At those times big bass—10 and 12 pound fish—are in the shallows.

There also are a number of small trout lakes scattered through the mountains. Price's Lake, off the Blue Ridge Parkway near Blowing Rock, Bee Tree Reservoir near Asheville, Tater Hill near Boone, the Sparta Reservoir in Alleghany County, and the rainbow trout lakes located on the headwaters of the East Fork of the Tuckaseigee River, are good for trout.

Accommodations of all sorts—swank resorts to modest rooming houses and motels—are available throughout western North Carolina.

No license is required for salt water fishing in North Carolina, and there is no closed season on any species of salt or fresh water gamefish except in designated public mountain trout waters. In brackish waters of coastal sounds and the lower portions of certain coastal rivers, fishing is permitted without a license.

Detailed information on licenses, seasons, creel limits, methods by which fish may be taken, designation of fishing waters, etc. is available from the North Carolina Wildlife Resources Commission, P.O. Box 2919, Raleigh, North Carolina 27602.

CHAPTER 16

Shad—Super Gamefish

*On both coasts, the American or white shad
is a delight on rod or table.*

By Robert Warner

Fly fisherman on Maryland's Deer Creek, a Susquehanna River tributary, holds his rod high as he allows his shad fly to swing in front of a school of hickories.

My wife, Sylvia, and I had just fished the fly-fishing-only stretch of Connecticut's Housatonic. We had fished it hard for three days to wind up with five brown trout, the largest a thirteen incher. Not much of a record.

Sylvia said, "The way I analyze it, you and I are both crazy. Here we are, an hour's drive from the world's best shad fishing, and what are we doing, we are getting covered with worms hanging off the trees chasing a lot of little hatchery browns. Since you only have two days of vacation left, tomorrow let's go to the Enfield Dam and get some shad. I want some roe and I want the fun of catching some decent sized fish."

No argument. I had forgotten that the shad run had started a couple of days earlier in the Connecticut and its lower tributaries, the Eight Mile River and the Salmon River.

I have been a trout fisherman for fifty-nine years, longer than I like to remember, but since I got my first shad on a fly eight years ago, I have no quarrel with the tens of thousands of Americans and Canadians who follow the sport.

For my money, the shad is one of the world's best fresh water gamefishes. Pound for pound, with the current behind it, which the shad knows how to use, it is every bit as fine a scrapper as a trout of its own weight. Like the snook, it has a soft mouth so if you try to horse it in you lose it. It strikes hard and its runs downstream are powerful. In quiet water it is not as strong as the trout or smallmouth but it still gives a very good accounting. The top of its head and back are a bluish green and the sides and belly a bright silver. Equipped with a sizeable dorsal fin and large tail, and a prize fighter's disposition, it keeps on battling until it is in the net. The shad needs no apologies to any of its finned brethren.

Moments later a plump two pound hickory shad is held aloft.

It is about the only fish I know of that does not have to be hatchery raised to keep up with the demands of our population increase. All it asks of man are enough fish ladders and/or an occasional elevator to negotiate man-made dams. Its requirements closely parallel those of the Atlantic salmon and when they come in from the sea on their spawning runs, they are inclined to inhabit the same waters, at least from the Connecticut River north. And now that we have at least wakened up to these facts and started cleaning up our streams and building the needed ladders, both the salmon and the shad are starting to return to our northeastern rivers again. The shad, which managed to survive in spite of the obstacles of man's "progress," had a sizeable base to take off from, so it is coming back a great deal faster than the salmon. Presently in our northern coastal streams you should get hundreds of shad to every salmon. While our human population is growing at much too fast a clip, the shad, thank God, is increasing even faster.

I called Cole Wilde, Director of Connecticut's Fish and Water Life Unit, an old friend who had introduced me to the sport back in 1964, and he said, "Sure! Tomorrow's Saturday, count me in."

We went about fifteen miles north of Hartford on Route 91, turned right on Route 140 and, at the end of two hundred yards, went north on Route 5. Then we went about three miles on a two-lane highway until it became a four-lane divided highway and at the end of a quarter of a mile of that we reached Dunn's Motel, a long-time hangout for shad fishermen, with an excellent restaurant and bar where the majority of the customers are in fishing clothes. Across the highway, and south, a country road turns off to the right and a couple of hundred yards farther brought us to the public boat launching.

It is a half mile upstream from the launching to the Enfield Dam, one of the world's premier shad grounds.

Hefty American (white) shad can be taken on a variety of artificial lures, from flies to jigs to spoons to spinners.

Premier because here the shad are not passing swiftly through but mill around in the huge pool below the dam (as they do at Conowingo Dam, on the Susquehanna, in Maryland) before going on up to spawn. We could see a line of fishermen casting lead darts and flies from the dam—only the spillway was more than ankle deep—and there were lines of fishermen wading both shores below the dam. We dropped anchor with a dozen other boats and went to work.

Cole was fishing a small lead dart while Sylvia fished a weighted fly. I tried an unweighted salmon fly. Cole, who was running the motor, cast directly downstream into the heavy flow from the spillway while Sylvia and I cast at thirty degree angles from the sides, let our flies swing below our rod tips and worked them slowly, very slowly, upstream.

Cameraman shooting over fly-rodder's shoulder catches a shad flip-flopping in Maryland's Wicomico River. Shad do not strike artificials well except in water with good current.

"Got one," Sylvia shouted. Her rod whipped forward and line peeled off the reel. Her four-ounce fly rod was bent in a half circle as the shad, with the current behind it, sped on downstream. "This is fun," she announced, slowly recovering line.

As Cole picked up the net he had a strike and, with the net in his hands and the rod under his arm, jerked back and managed to set the hook.

I reeled in and grabbed the net just in time to scoop Sylvia's fish up, a two-and-a-half pound buck. I took the hook out and threw the fish overboard. In the Connecticut, we only keep the roes. The roes are larger and they have the eggs, which are about as good eating as Beleuga caviar.

Cole landed his fish, another buck, and tossed it back. Then Sylvia hooked our third, the strongest fish so far. It made three good downstream runs and jumped before it splashed on the surface and I got the net under it. A fat four-pound roe. I knocked it on the head and tossed it in the bow.

After Sylvia and Cole had each taken two more, Cole said, "Bob, take that salmon fly off and try a sinking one."

I nodded. "I was thinking the same thing." Half a minute after I switched, I had my first strike. And this one, another roe came out of the water twice before I brought it in. It was around 3 pounds, a bit on the light side, so I tossed it back. While the roes are almost always larger than the bucks, because they usually do not return to fresh water until they are five years old and the bucks normally come back as three or four year old fish, you still occasionally pick up a two-and-a-half to three-pound roe.

The fish were everywhere, thousands of them. Looking down into the clear water, as thick with schooled fish as a hatchery truck, milling around our boat, I wondered why we didn't get one with every cast. But a hundred or more would let the flies and Cole's jig go by, then suddenly one would take. Why? No one knows, because the shad, like the salmon is incapable of digesting food following its return to fresh water. Curiosity, anger, or a memory of the river where it grew up and fed before it took to the sea—one guess is as good as another.

At the end of a few hours, or days, something moves them and one by one, or in small schools, they leave the big pool below the dam to drive through the racing spillway and upstream to spawn. Some continue on up to the elevator, a free ride to the top of the big Holyoke Dam. But a sizeable majority spawn in the main river above Hartford and below Holyoke. The elevator now handles sixty thousand shad annually. In another year or two, it will be rebuilt and greatly enlarged, at a cost of over a million dollars, so it will take care of at least twice the present number of shad, plus the much larger Atlantic salmon which, hopefully, will shortly be back again in the Connecticut in worthwhile numbers. And fish ladders are planned at Turner's Falls, Massachusetts, and far upriver in Vermont at the Wilder and Bellows Falls dams.

"There's one of your tags, Cole," Sylvia said, pointing to a shad with a long yellow streamer attached to its back.

He nodded. "Not ours really, they are put on by the Essex Marine Laboratory. You'll see one every four or five minutes if you watch. To study the fishes' migratory habits a great many thousands are tagged every year. Happily, the sport fishermen are wonderful about turning in the tags with exact information on where and when the fish were taken."

By noon, when we pulled anchor and headed for Dunn's Motel, we had kept eight good sized roes from three-and-a-half to five pounds. And we had thrown back nineteen males and small females. That gave us ten to go as Connecticut has a six-shad-a-day limit per person.

The combination restaurant and bar at Dunn's Motel was full of fishermen, many of them wearing hip boots and waders. Apparently, everyone had gotten fish, though this was close to the end of April, a bit early for the peak of the sport. The commercial fishermen, who net well below the Enfield Dam, normally do not start their operation until mid-April when, they claim, the larger shad are coming into the river to spawn and the larger ones are much easier to bone. Commercial fishing is legal from the first of April, whereas sport fishing does not open until the third Saturday of the month.

Although not nearly as powerful as the Atlantic salmon, the shad is a damned sight smarter. When you run a gill net most of the way across a river, the salmon swims into it and is bound for the market. Connecticut, by chance, learned that the shad are not so easily fooled. The Essex Marine Laboratory and the State of Connecticut Fish Department stuffed two-inch long sonic transmitters down a number of shad's throats, at a cost of forty dollars a fish, to learn what effect the Yankee Atomic Power Plant and the heated water effluent was having on the shad's migratory pattern. They also learned why such a tiny proportion of shad wound up with their heads in the mesh when the transmitter equipped fish set off on their travels. The transmitters sent out beeps for about a thousand yards which were recorded on mag-

netic tapes and hydrophones. The biologists could tell the direction in which the fish were traveling by which hydrophones they hit first. And they learned that when the shad came up to the thousand to sixteen-hundred foot long gill nets, they almost always turned and swam the length of the mesh, then around it, in preference to taking it head on and getting caught.

When we got back to the dam after lunch, the river was inches higher as they were releasing water thirty-five miles upstream at Holyoke. The current now was too strong for flies so Sylvia and I switched to spinning rods with the heavy lead darts. In two hours, we had one short of our limit in roes and started tossing even the larger fish back.

Sylvia asked about the hickory shad, as she has only fished the Connecticut and has never caught one. Hickory, while not as great a table delicacy as the white shad, is a lot smaller and, unlike its larger cousin, can be distinguished by its protruding lower jaw. The American or white shad occasionally gets up to twelve pounds

Bill Bevis unhooks a nice shad he took from Florida's St. Johns River, near the town of Sanford.

while six is about the hickory's limit. Cole added, "Hickory generally prefer the smaller streams, at least when up north. It swims right by the Connecticut. It is found in rivers all the way from Long Island Sound south to the Saint John's in Florida."

More shad, both American and hickory, are caught in the Saint John's than in any other American river, about a hundred thousand a year, around twice the present catch in the Connecticut. All of the shad from Florida north through the Carolinas are small, regardless of the species, as the southern fish are all one-time spawners. Both the hickory and the American are caught from Florida to Long Island Sound and the American all the way to the Saint Lawrence and beyond to Nova Scotia's Bay of Fundy. While Maryland's Susquehanna and Potomac have both the American and hickory, now few of the American are taken by sport fishermen due to commercial overnetting. But the sportsman's catch in both rivers is still enormous.

"Hey! I have a striper," Sylvia called as we resumed fishing. "A nice one."

I saw the fish roll, a five or six pounder, big for the Connecticut where they average about a pound. The fish ran across the river, then upstream. It came to net in half the time of a shad the same size. I took the hook out. "Want to keep it?"

"Nope. Let it go. We'll catch it a couple of years from now at Cuttyhunk when it's out of the diaper age."

The Connecticut, long famous for its shad, is pretty close to a gamefish aquarium, pike up to twenty-five pounds are caught close to Hartford. Smallmouth and largemouth bass are all over the place though you seldom get really big ones. Brown and rainbow trout get up to five pounds in the upper reaches where the river forms the Vermont-NewHampshire boundary. This water offers some of the best trout fishing in the Northeast. At one time, there was a commercial sturgeon fishery close to Enfield and sturgeon of over two hundred pounds were taken. Apparently, the sturgeon are still there but no one bothers them. The same is true of the forty and fifty pound carp you almost always see rolling just below the Enfield Dam. The carp, which fight hard, are excellent game fish. The Europeans pursue them with a vengeance while here they are almost never fished. Every year I plan to go after them with a small hook baited with a kernel of corn, then I get involved in the shad and forget them. The Connecticut also boasts an annual run of twenty to fifty million glut herring, plus a run of alewives, both great table delicacies. And

White shad pops through the surface trying to shake a Dart lure from its jaw.

once the State of Massachusetts gets down to business and forces the Holyoke Power Company to build an adequate elevator, the Connecticut presumably once again will be one of North America's finest salmon rivers.

I counted a hundred and twenty-nine fishermen, all within a quarter of a mile of our boat. In May I have often counted over three hundred. Sounds like a lot but considering that twenty million people in Connecticut, New York, New Jersey, Rhode Island, Massachusetts, Vermont, and New Hampshire are within a three hour drive of the Enfield Dam, the numbers are really very small. I once drove eight miles along the Battenkill in New York and Vermont, one of America's finest trout streams, and counted a hundred and ninety-seven fishermen wading after that river's hard to catch browns. When you multiply the number on that eight miles by the same number of anglers times the hundreds and hundreds of eight-mile stretches of trout water within a couple of hundred miles of Hartford you get some idea of the fishing pressure, on the trout as compared to that on the shad.

Aaaaaahhh! *The gourmet's delight! Sauteed shad roe, and baked shad, are delicacies.*

So the question is not why there are so many shad fishermen but why so few. I am sure that on any given day within two hundred miles of Hartford, you will find fifty fishermen after trout to the one who is after the shad. And for the man who enjoys eating fish as well as catching them, the shad fisherman's creel will average at least five times the weight of the trout fisherman's, not counting the shad played and released.

The shad was eaten before the American Revolution and was introduced successfully along our West Coast in the nineteenth century. The fish is now found from Alaska to southern California. But no one fished for it as a sport fish until the 1930s when some enterprising angler went after it with a bright lead dart fished deep in Connecticut's Salmon River. He whispered the secret to a friend who whispered it to another and the shad bonanza was under way.

With our limit of eighteen fat roes caught, we headed back for shore and a final beer before Cole returned to Hartford and we went south to Washington. I wrapped up our twelve shad in wet burlap, knowing that if you let the shad's skin dry you need dynamite to scale it.

Back home in time for a cocktail before a huge dinner of shad roe, Sylvia said, "You take the trout, but while the run is on, I'll take the shad."

I piled my fork high with roe. "Thanks sweetie, I'll take it with you. Let's go back to the dam tomorrow."

She nodded, her mouth too full to answer.
(Orvis News)

SHAD DATA

THE BEST RIVERS—(East) Salmon, Connecticut, Scantic, East, and Eight Miles Rivers, Connecticut; Hudson and Delaware Rivers, New York; Susquehanna, Potomac, Pocomoke, Wicomico, and Patuxent Rivers, Maryland; Chickahomoniny and James Rivers, Virginia; Roanoke River, North Carolina; Cooper River, South Carolina; St. Johns River, Florida. (West) Umpqua and Coos Rivers, Oregon; American, Russian, and Feather Rivers, California.

FLIES AND LURES—Weighted flies, fast sinking lures generally best. Popular fly patterns, Silver Yank, Dillon's Shad Fly, McNally's Joobie. Popular lures, Shad Dart, Huntington Spoon, small Marabou Jig, most other small spoons and lead-head jigs.

FISHING TECHNIQUES—Fly fishermen do best after locating a school of shad "holding" in a bottom depression by strong current, and then casting so that flies swing slow, and deep, in front of the fish. No action is imparted to the fly. The "swing" of the fly in the current triggers strikes. Sinking fly lines can be helpful. Lure fishermen cast down and across current, allow lures to swing deep, and retrieve steadily and slowly. In certain current situations it is wise to pay out line, retrieve, pay out line, and so on—so that the lure remains active in or near shad holding area. Trolling, with either flies or lures, also can be productive.

TACKLE—Fly tackle for most shad fishing should be on the heavy side, 8½ or 9 ft. rods, with matching WF8 or WF 9 lines. Full sinking lines, or sink-tip lines are excellent, although frequently good fishing can be had with floating lines provided flies are sufficiently weighted. Single-action reels are preferred. Bait casting tackle, bass weight, is ideal, although more fishermen prefer spinning gear. Rods 6 to 7½ ft. in length are adequate, and lines should be 6 or 8 pound test. Ultra-light spinning tackle not only is productive but fun to use on shad, particularly the smaller Hickory shad.

TABLE PREPARATION—The roe of American or white shad is a world-renown delicacy. In spring, 1975, shad roe where available in Chicago markets was selling for more than $8 a pound. Roe should be washed, salted and peppered, and simmered slowly in butter. Nothing more. Simple baking is one of best ways to prepare whole shad. Cleaned fish should be salted, peppered, coated with bacon grease, covered with a few sliced onions, and baked slowly 1½ to 2 hours.

(T.McN.)

SHAD—SUPER GAMEFISH   171

CHAPTER 17

How and Why to Use Pork-Rind Baits

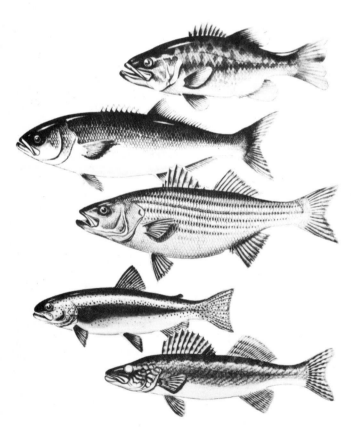

Uncle Josh porkers are multipurpose baits. They have been for more than fifty years. They're used alone on plain and weedless hooks, hung on saltwater bait-rig tippets as teaser/trailers and they ride shotgun on hooks dressed with killies, clams and sandworms. Our hook strips bag the short-strikers. The big ones! And there's hardly an artificial lure on the market . . . wet flies, poppers and streamers to big plugs and spoons . . . for which there isn't a number of colorful Josh patterns capable of giving it more clout than the manufacturer built into it.

Around the "hot-stove" league, discussions on *how* to use pork baits are apt to run the gamut of great deeds and monster fish to dismal confessions of "I couldn't catch a cold with pigskin!" Whatever your experiences have been, good, bad or indifferent, try the following tactics. The experts use them and they'll work for you.

THE PORK FROG

This venerable old patriarch of the Josh clan is a creature of the "edges": weedy shorelines, mossy bays and backwaters, reed beds, lily pads and other types of rough cover. Of four sizes available, Model No. 11, green-spotted, is the most widely used of this prime bass and northern pike bait. Generally, he's fished as we build him: color side up, chunky body and beveled face. But if the going gets rough and you're dredging up bales of moss on retrieves, thin him down by cutting off his belly. And for the "dead frog" variation in any water, work him with the color side down.

Where you fish the pork frog depends on a number of circumstances, but here are three methods that often produce fish. Try them with weedless hooks and spoons. And remember, always, to approach shallow water in dead silence.

Early morning, dusk and cloudy days:
Cast frog *onto* weedy shore. "Hop" it into the water and let it rest on the bottom. Take in slack line and retrieve frog in short, "swimming" jerks with frequent pauses to let it rest. Cast again and repeat. If you have no takers after awhile, switch tactics and cast parallel and close to shore and maintain same retrieve.

Any time of day:
Cast frog deep *into* lily pads or reed bed. Keep your line high and off the water to avoid entanglements. Work frog across open water to a lily pad or drape it in the reeds and let it rest. Repeat, until you're clear of cover. Watch for a sudden movement in the reeds, a bulge in the pads or a wake at the edge of the cover!!! Alternately, cast into pockets at the edge of surface cover, at points that poke out in irregular beds and, finally, parallel to the edge of the cover. Work the area for all it's worth!

Midday:
When the sun's high and hot, look for bass in deep water. Cast and let the frog settle to the bottom. Then, "crawl" it slowly back to the boat along the bottom or bounce it with a stop-and-go retrieve, until you're ready to cast again. And don't overlook the pork frog, when you're on the flats for bonefish. Its soft, resilient body will handle any crusty, variegated bottom and it does a creditable job of coming out "alive", after a session with the bonefish's specialized grinders.

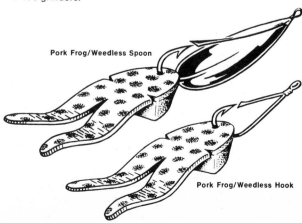

Pork Frog/Weedless Spoon

Pork Frog/Weedless Hook

THE BLACK WIDOW EEL ®

The Widow was developed, originally, as a largemouth bait. Because that spells BASS!, it wasn't long before the old girl became a regular employee of striper fishermen, who troll her on plain and bucktail leadhead jigs. Hooked to heavy jigs and trolled at night along jetties and around pilings, the 9" black eel also will take big snook. Put up in three sizes, this chunky, segmented strip can be used with any number of artificials. However, most fishes are taken on weedless hooks and jigs which do not interfere with the pattern's extremely natural action. For largemouth, eel length is optional. Color's another matter. Start with black, which is most natural. Then, reverse your pitch and try white. In many areas, purple is very productive, so give it some action, too. Like this:

Early morning, dusk and cloudy days:
On an unweighted, weedless hook, cast your eel smackdab into the skin-thin shallows on a weedy shore. Let it sit; you're in no hurry. Then, ever so gently and slowly, take the slack out of your line and give the eel a twitch. Take up slack and twitch it again. Repeat. Retrieve and place your cast within a foot or so of your first target. This technique requires extreme stealth. So, remember the rule: approach the shallows in dead silence, make accurate casts.

Day and night:
Anchor off a rocky point or deeply sloping shore with lots of brush. Cast the eel (on a plain or bucktail jig), right against the waterline and work it slowly down the bottom. Stop reeling when you feel it touch something, put your reel on free spool and wait. If nothing happens, continue retrieving. If you feel a tug, count slowly to three with your rod tip low . . . and let 'im have it!

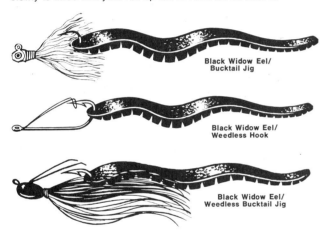

Black Widow Eel/
Bucktail Jig

Black Widow Eel/
Weedless Hook

Black Widow Eel/
Weedless Bucktail Jig

THE PORK RIND STRIPS

All of our stock rind patterns are cut from top grade hides, only. Pure, thin, back flesh, they're extra-ordinarily "tough". No bait can touch them for durability. And because they are a natural product, they have a flexible, fluid, life-like action which remains constant, whether you retrieve them in open water, fire them willy-nilly into a thicket or bring them back at a lazy amble along the bottom.

Their numerous colors, sizes and shapes adapt them to a multitude of artificials which, in turn, makes them appealing to a wide variety of fresh and salt water fishes. Despite their muscular texture, anyone with a single-edged razor can alter a large strip to match the size of forage fishes in the area, to match a lure size or to vary the rind's action by fork-tailing, puncturing, slitting or otherwise modifying its original form.

Because space limits us to no more than a handful of the many artificial lure/pork rind strip combinations possible . . . and which are used . . . we have confined the following descriptive text to a group of popular, but short to medium length "skins".

Fly Strip

The pork rind "fingerling" is used, for the most part, as a teaser/trailer on small artificials and plain and weedless hooks. It's tops for wet flies, streamers, light spoons, poppers, plugs, jigs and spinners. And it takes pan fishes, seatrout, shad, bass, bluefish, pompano, snook, walleye and trout, including the lunker browns and rainbows in the Great Lakes.

Spinning Strip

Not unlike a pair of "dutchman's britches", the spin-cut has a relatively broad-based and flowing action that makes it a natural on spoons, jigs, streamers, plugs and wobblers for bass, walleye, stripers, trout, sea bass, cobia and amberjack.

Bass Strip

Don't let the name fool you; the bass strip's at home, anywhere. On a weedless spoon, it's the end of the line for any bass, muskie or northern pike that takes a poke at it. In the salt, on a wobbler, or nylon jig, you'll pick up flounders, amberjack, bluefish and seatrout. And, with a bit of luck, you'll boat a trophy tarpon.

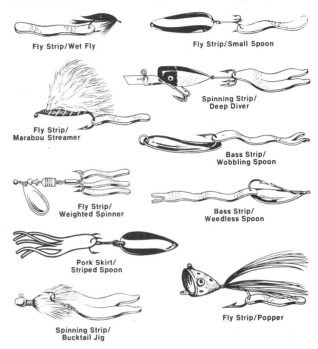

Fly Strip/Wet Fly

Fly Strip/Small Spoon

Fly Strip/
Marabou Streamer

Spinning Strip/
Deep Diver

Bass Strip/
Wobbling Spoon

Fly Strip/
Weighted Spinner

Bass Strip/
Weedless Spoon

Pork Skirt/
Striped Spoon

Fly Strip/Popper

Spinning Strip/
Bucktail Jig

THE TWIN-TAILS

Introduced in 1972, the U3 and U4 Twin-Tails have already acquired a secure niche as prime pork rind baits for the single-spins, the skirted "throbbers" whose popularity as bass killers is sweeping the country like a Fundy Tide. Essentially, the single-spin is a deep water lure designed for bottom-bouncing in lakes and reservoirs with a diversified structural terrain, a phenomenon not often encountered in many natural southern lakes. When bass retreat to deep water, they're attracted to various structures or holding points and they gang up. (With no structure, they scatter). At such points, the Twin-Tail/single-spin combination . . . it's noisy, colorful and active . . . is most effective. During the slow retrieve, the Twin-Tails' super-soft bodies move along at a lazy, undulating gait that completely belies their toughness. Infinitely more durable than plastic worms, they can take punishment all day long and go back for more. As further evidence of the Twin-Tails' ability to draw a crowd, early in '73 the U3 pattern chalked up two bass tournament wins. But coming off head hog wasn't enough; "he" did the job riding on an Uncle Josh pork rind Kicker! It, too, is a great combination. It can be skittered on the surface, retrieved at varying depths and bottom-bumped like a jig.

U3 Twin-Tail/Single-Spin

CHAPTER 18

Great New Salmon River

*Norway's Reisa River is one good
place for Atlantics.*

The scenery on the Norway coast, nearly 250 miles north of the Arctic Circle, is breathtaking. I had been in Norway for several weeks and now, with Erik Myhre, Oddvar Kjelsrud and Frode Johansen (all Norwegians), was heading for the Reisa River.

I'd had good salmon fishing on the Driva and at Malangsfoss, and now we were driving from Alta south to the town of Sorkjosen. Erik was driving. It was raining, and Arctic mist swirled in from the fjords and Norwegian Sea. Occasionally Laplanders herding reindeer crowded the road.

"You'll like the Reisa," Erik said. "So far as we know, you'll be the first American to fish it. We're anxious to see how you do. The river is owned by the government but for years the salmon fishing rights have been in the hands of Lapp landowners on the river. Netting has been going on in the lower Reisa and in the fjord, and the Lapps do some rod-and-reel fishing."

"But few fishermen," Oddvar injected, "other than the Lapps, have fished the river. They use heavy tackle with shrimp or spoons. The Lapps tell us no fly fisherman nor any American has ever fished it."

"The government, as well as the Lapps, feel it might be best if netting is stopped and the Reisa turned into a sport fishing river," said Erik. "But we do not know if it is a good river for fly fishing. We hope you'll find out."

Now we were on the Arctic Highway and nearing the

Reisa. The road twisted through snow-tipped peaks and plunged into green valleys. The fjord country was beautiful, even though cold wind and rain whipped in from the sea.

We reached the town of Burfjord, ate lunch, then continued on to Sorkjosen. Numerous Lapps were on the road. These nomads roam northern Norway, Sweden, and Finland. They do not have a country of their own, although northernmost Scandinavia is referred to as "Lapland."

Dressed in colorful tunics, Lapps follow wild reindeer herds and subsist almost entirely off them. In winter the reindeer migrate inland. In summer they leave the mountains for the coast. The Lapps pitch tents along the coast roads, and sell reindeer meat, hides, horns, knives, and boots to travelers.

Before long we reached Sorkjosen and the Reisa. The cold had me shivering. "The weather is seldom this bad in summer," Oddvar said. "The Gulf Stream is close to Arctic Norway, so July and August usually are warm and pleasant. But this has been a crazy summer. Last winter was the worst in years and, as you've seen, the snow pack still is big in the mountains. As the snow melts the water runs down and keeps the rivers high."

"It's too cold for good fishing," added Frode. "Look how high the Ray-zzaaa is, and how cold! The salmon will not take well."

Gillie gaffing fine Reisa salmon is silhouetted against the midnight Arctic sun.

The river was about 300 feet wide, a great, powerful stream that twisted down from distant peaks then poured into the salty fjord. Upriver I could see long gravel bars and rocky shores. There were slick pools, the kind salmon rest in, fast runs, and riffles. I thought of the river as a highway for salmon, an expressway from the sea to their distant spawning grounds. I was anxious to fish it.

In Arctic Norway in summer there is no full darkness, so a fishing day can be 24 hours long under the "midnight sun." Since it was only 8:00 P.M., I suggested getting settled in the Sorkjos Hotel, then going fishing. "We can't," Erik said. "The townspeople are giving us a dinner party. But you can go first thing in the morning."

The whole town turned out to welcome us. The food was excellent and included goat cheese, reindeer steaks, smoked salmon, and yellow cloud berries smothered in cream. Later I fell into bed and dropped off to sleep to dream of giant salmon arching up out of the Reisa, my flies hanging from their jaws.

In the morning it was still cold and blowing. The temperature was about 35. It wasn't much of a day for fishing. Oddvar, Frode and I bundled up and drove to the river. A road parallels much of the Reisa. We went upriver several miles, passing a lot of spots that looked good to me.

"Where are we going to fish?" I asked.

"Wherever you like," Oddvar said. "We have permission to fish anywhere."

We went on about a mile, to where the river funneled into a short rapid then broke into a broad pool.

"There!" I pointed. "Let's try there!"

We stopped and I got out tackle and waders. I rigged a 9-foot glass fly rod, with WF-9F line, a 15-foot leader tapered to a 10-pound tippet, and tied on a 4/0 Black Doctor. In Oslo, I'd bought several dozen Norwegian salmon flies, in the typical large sizes that are used on their big rivers. The flies ranged from 3/0's to 8/0's and cost $3.00 to $4.25 apiece.

"Ready?" I said to Oddvar.

"Yes," he replied, "but I won't fish yet. I'll just watch, and Frode will assist you if he can."

We walked down to the river and I waded out. At the head of the pool I could see a big submerged boulder. "Near that boulder is where the salmon should be," I thought. I cast to the spot and mended line as the fly drifted down so that any salmon there would see the fly broadside. I made several casts but nothing happened. I then lengthened line, and cast above and beyond the boulder. The fly came down fast, swung into the eddy behind the rock, then suddenly the line tightened and the rod bowed. The fish ran 30 feet then came out in a curving leap.

"A sea trout!" I called to Oddvar and Frode. "A sea-run brown."

"Usually we get no sea trout before August," Frode yelled back. I played the 3-pounder out, walked ashore with him, showed him, then released him.

The Reisa gets a big run of sea trout in August. They average 7–8 pounds, with some to about 12 pounds. The Reisa and many of its feeders also have resident brown trout. While July normally is the peak month for salmon, August is best for resident and sea-run browns. Non-migratory browns in the upper river and side streams average a pound, but ones 12–15 pounds are possible. Once a 36-pound brown was netted in the lower river. Arctic char and grilse come into the Reisa in August.

I fished on through the pool but didn't raise another fish, so we went to the car and drove upriver. We came to a Lapp village and went into a cafe for coffee, then we returned to the river. Several Lapps were there tending long river boats and outboards, and they oggled my tackle as I started fishing.

The wind was really lashing now. I wore a windbreaker over a woolen shirt, a thermo-type vest and a fishing jacket, but was still cold. My hands turned blue after the first few casts but I kept at it, covering the water as best I could. The Lapps were watching intently, since they'd never seen a fly fisherman before.

Above me a small island split the river. Strong current rolled down along the shore where I was and formed a deep hole. I checked my leader, tied on a Blue Charm, a big 7/0, and made a short cast. A couple more casts, then I moved a few yards upstream. Another cast, and this time I saw a flash under the fly that made my mouth drop open. What I'd seen reminded me of a strip of aluminum four feet long and a foot wide. "A salmon!" I said aloud, "THAT big?"

I tried to steady myself for the next cast. The big fly hit with a little splat, swung down, and again I saw that long, silvery fish. He came under the fly, turned away, swam back, followed, and then I saw his cotton-white mouth open. When the line tightened, I raised the rod tip. I felt the fish's weight as the hook went home. For a moment the salmon didn't budge. I put pressure on, but all he did was swim in lazy turns. Finally he took off downstream for 100 feet, came out in a straight-up leap, turned over, and plunged back. It was a magnificent leap! A shout went up from in back of me. All the Lapps were running along the bank, heading downriver as though they hoped to turn the salmon back. Keeping my rod high, I eased into shallow water to follow the fish. He was 300 feet away now, and dogging it along the far bank. I reached a gravel bar that made a great place from which to fight the fish. Oddvar, Frode, and the Lapps crowded around.

The salmon turned back and I recovered yards of line. When he was opposite us, 50 feet away, he made two beautiful leaps. I'd caught plenty of salmon in Norway, up to 24 pounds, but this was the biggest yet.

"He is a giant," Frode yelled, "maybe 20 kilos!"

Twenty kilos? I quickly calculated that in pounds. Two-and-a-quarter pounds per kilo, times 20, over FORTY pounds! I paled and tightened my hold on the rod.

For a long while the salmon sulked in deep water, swaying with the current. He'd drift downstream, then power his way back. After 25 minutes I figured he was tiring. I put pressure on, trying to get him to shallows by the gravel bar. He was right on top of the water, in close, when suddenly he kicked his broad tail and shot to the head of the pool. He was lolling in the heavy current up there, near where I'd first hooked him, when the line went slack. Everybody went "Ooooohhhh!" I knew what had happened. That big 7/0 hook had worn a hole in the salmon's jaw and fallen out.

"*Det var en helvetes rusk!*" moaned Frode. "That was a helluva fish!"

"Too bad," said Oddvar, sadly. "That *was* a great fish. But perhaps we can get another."

That afternoon some Lapps took us upriver in their boats. We came to a pool where three Lapps were fishing. They had a fire going and some hot coffee. We visited with them, warming ourselves and gulping coffee. The Lapps were using 16-foot cane poles fitted with guides, and big fly reels with 30-pound test mono' line. They had 1-ounce drail sinkers on their lines, and three-inch long red shrimp on tandem hooks. The rigs looked deadly, and the Lapps could toss their shrimp a mile. They'd cast upstream, let their sinkers bump along bot-

Tom McNally lugs an 18-pounder up a Reisa bank.

tom, and in that way work a lot of water on a single cast.

"The Lapps say fishing is no good," Frode reported. "They say there are many salmon in the river, but they are not taking well because it is so cold and the water is so high."

The Lapps had two salmon on the bank, a 22-pounder and one 18. "How long have they been fishing?" I asked. "About two hours," Frode replied. "Well," I said, 'it's too bad fishing is so poor. Imagine—just two big salmon in two hours!"

We got into the boats and motored farther upriver, stopping at places the Lapps said were usually good. Oddvar and Frode fished too, using big salt water type spinning outfits with spoons. At one pool they each caught a salmon while I drew a blank. Oddvar's went 14 pounds, Frode's 21. They were bright, strong, firm— fresh from the sea.

Finally we came to a place where the Reisa was only 60 feet across. "The Lapps say this is an excellent spot, that there always are salmon here, and that the water is shallow so you should do well with your flies," Oddvar told me.

"Then you fish it," I said.

Tight banks force the fly fisherman to execute long roll casts at many of the river's best pools.

"No," Oddvar insisted. "I have had no experience fly fishing. Besides, I will fish here many times when you leave."

The river bottom sloped out like a beach. I looked hard but could see no salmon. I cast my 3/0 Silver Doctor to the edge of the main current. The fly swung down, there was a glint of silver, a *"tic"* on the fly, but no salmon. I fished for 20 minutes without another rise. So I waded ashore and dug out another reel.

"Why have you changed reels?" Frode asked. I explained that this one had a sinking line, and that if I got my flies deeper I might do business. On my fourth cast I hooked a salmon. He went 12 pounds. In the next hour, fishing that one spot, I took three more fish—14½, 15¾, and 19 pounds!

Reisa River rises in Finnmarks, Norway's most northerly county, and is about 225 miles north of the Arctic Circle. It rolls for some 80 miles through mountains, alpine parks, and meadows. Despite netting, the Reisa gave up nearly 1,000 salmon in one year to the few Lapps who fished it with rod-and-reel. Average weight of the fish was 18–22 pounds. The best was a whopping 59 pounder. The rod-reel record for the river is 70½ pounds! The largest taken while I was on the river was 37 pounds.

Early next morning I started at a pool in the lower river while Oddvar, Frode, and Erik watched from the bank. The weather was nippy but the sun was shining. The pool was 200 feet across, about seven feet deep. I started at the top and worked all the way through without even seeing a salmon. I waded ashore and went up to my Norwegian friends.

"I have fished this pool many times," said Frode. "It always has salmon. Perhaps you need a bigger fly."

"Pick one," I said, holding out my fly book. Frode fingered the flies. Oddvar and Erik began looking, too. Frode selected an 8/0 Jock Scott. Oddvar and Eric suggested other patterns. They started arguing over what I should use. "Okay," I said at last. "Each of you choose a fly, and I'll try them all."

I started with the Jock Scott Frode had recommended. I'd covered about 30 feet when a salmon titled up and sucked it in. Frode shouted triumphantly, bragged about the fly he'd picked, then waded out with a gaff. As he gaffed the salmon I said, "This one is for Frode." It went 18 pounds.

Pulling the Jock Scott off, I tide on a Night Hawk fly, 5/0 size, that Erik had selected. Before long another

A 24-pounder—still with sea lice.

And a sleek 16-pound Atlantic, also with some sea lice.

salmon was tearing up the pool. "This one," I shouted happily, "is for Erik." Frode handed me the gaff, and I hauled him out—a 21-pounder so fresh from the ocean that sea lice still clung to his sides.

Back I went, this time with the 5/0 Silver Gray Oddvar had chosen. Taking those first two salmon must have shook the pool us, because it was a long time before another fish rose. But finally one did. When, at last, he swam nearly lifeless at my feet, I "tailed" him by hand. I waddled ashore, dumped him at Oddvar's feet, grinned and said: "And this one is for *you!*" That third salmon was 19½ pounds.

That was the start of the best day's salmon fishing I ever had. I took four more, 8 to 12 pounds, and lost two even though I spent a lot of time watching Oddvar and Frode spinning. Oddvar got three, including one 24 pounds; Frode two, each about 15.

The following day—another with wind, cold, and rain —we whipped the river hard. Yet only Oddvar scored, with a salmon of 14 pounds. The two days I fished after that blank day, I caught six salmon ranging from 11 to 26 pounds.

On the last day I said good-bye and Oddvar drove me south to Tromse. From there I flew to Oslo, then back to the states. Weeks passed, then a letter arrived from Erik, in Oslo. He wrote:

"Friend Tom:
"We met with government officials and Lapp landowners, and now the Reisa will be sport fishing water for the public. The Lapps formed a fishing association. There will be no more netting of salmon.

The Reisa starts up in heady canyons, boulder strewn and well forested.

"The annual season will be June 23 to August 15. Fishermen can fly from Oslo to Tromse, then for $25 each go by seaplane to the Reisa. The weekly cost of fishing, everything included, each man, will be about $750. Each angler will have two miles of water to himself.

"Spinning will be allowed June 23 to July 10, as the river is usually high then. July 10 to Aug. 15, only fly fishing.

"With no more netting and only rod fishing allowed, the Reisa soon will be one of the world's outstanding salmon rivers.

"One thing more. Remember the pool where you lost the big one? The Lapp fishing association has named it 'McNally Pool.'"

Regards,
Erik

I replied to Erik's letter right away. I wrote that I was glad the Reisa was now officially classified as an angler's river, and that most of the season it would be for fly fishing only Then, joking, I added: "I hope you'll keep people out of 'McNally Pool,' because I want to come back."

Only I wasn't joking about that last part!

A. J. ("Al") McClane, author of revised and enlarged "McClane's New Fishing Encyclopedia and International Angling Guide," is framed by a brace of tullibees he caught on a single cast witn a two-jig rig at Manitoba's Crow Duck Lake.

CHAPTER 19

McClane's New Fishing Encyclopedia

In 1965, Holt, Rinehart and Winston, Inc. published a massive angling text entitled "McClane's Standard Fishing Encyclopedia." The product of several years' work by A. J. McClane, Executive Editor of *Field and Stream* Magazine, the book ran to 1,072 pages. It was the most complete, most comprehensive, highest-quality "fishing book" ever produced—and it sold for $30 a copy. And sold. And sold. And sold.

The extraordinary world-wide acceptance of his "encyclopedia" immediately put McClane back at his typewriter, producing a larger, more concise, more complete, revised edition. Late last year, almost 10 years from publication of the first edition, Holt presented "McClane's New Standard Fishing Encyclopedia and International Angling Guide." It dwarfs the first edition and, in effect, because of its enormous size and quality, makes the initial "encyclopedia" obsolete.

The all-NEW McClane Fishing Encyclopedia has 1,176 pages, several hundred full-color fish paintings and photographs, sketches—and sells for $40.

By special permission from the author and publisher, "The Fishermen's Bible" here presents a random selection of pages from McClane's NEW encyclopedia.

ALGAE Man and his domestic animals, and many populations of terrestrial animals are largely dependent on members of the grass family for their food, either directly or indirectly. Similarly the animal life of aquatic environments is dependent for food on several groups of photosynthetic plants collectively known as the *algae*. Although 25,000 species of algae have been described and given scientific names, relatively few have common names. One may refer to such conspicuous examples as rockweeds, kelps, Irish moss, pond scums, mermaid's tresses, and a few others, but the remainder have not been called sharply to the attention of laymen. Their important place in the natural world has not been generally recognized. These numerous, abundant, diverse, ubiquitous, and fascinating organisms are well worth study for many reasons. Perhaps the recent concern with problems of pollution will serve to direct proper attention to them.

Terrestrial plants possess roots, leaves, stems, and reproductive structures such as cones and flowers; and we utilize these as recognition marks for the various groups included among the 350,000 species known the world around. The algae do *not* possess any of these organs. Although they carry on the same fundamental processes as the terrestrial vegetation, they are organized in a wholly different manner. Their forms range from simple, single cells, to colonial aggregates, to simple and branched filaments, to structures resembling higher plants, and some are very complex. They include some of the tiniest plants as well as some of the largest, such as the giant kelps. Their sexual organs are unicellular in contrast to those of the terrestrial types which are always multicellular. They lack the vascular systems by which land plants transport materials from one part of the plant to another. Finally, they do not have embryos, although all land plants do.

The cells making up the bodies of both land plants and the algae are very similar in general features, but they differ from one another in a number of distinct ways. The major differences lie in the nature of the photosynthetic pigments, the cell walls, and the food reserves which they produce. These features are useful in distinguishing the 8 recognized groups of algae.

CHARACTERISTICS

Algae are essentially aquatic organisms, growing in all our natural bodies of water from the smallest to the largest, the coldest to the warmest supporting any kind of life, the freshest to the supersaline, and surface to hundreds of feet in depth. A large number of kinds grow on moist surfaces such as the soil. Others grow on or in other types of plants and animals. Some species grow in close association with certain fungi to form those numerous, varied, and widespread growths known as *lichens*.

Spirogyra

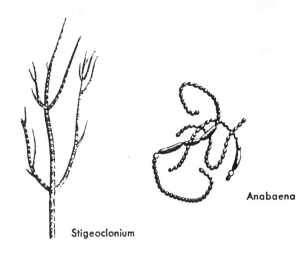

Stigeoclonium

Anabaena

Many single-celled and some colonial representatives of green algae, yellow-green algae, euglenoids, and dinoflagellates are motile; they can move about by means of hairlike structures called *flagellae* which are normal cellular features. The reproductive cells of many algae are also motile.

Most species of algae are not motile, and thousands of kinds spend most of their lives attached to solid objects of great variety. Intertidal algae, such as the rockweeds, are excellent examples. Some of the larger algae, such as the *Sargassum*, float about and pass most of their lives in this state. Indeed, the Sargasso Sea, an area as large as Texas, is named for and characterized by the presence of great floating masses of gulfweeds.

Of special interest are thousands of small species whose members float about at the mercy of winds, waves, tides, and currents. Collectively known as the phytoplankton, they are extremely important as primary producers. In oceanic waters, two groups of unicellular algae, the diatoms and the dinoflagellates, carry on most of the photosynthesis essential to all nongreen organisms. The products of this process serve to feed small herbivorous animals, these in turn are consumed by larger animals, and these in turn furnish food for still larger forms. The algae are the starting points for many of the food chains and food webs which have been recognized. When one considers the vastness of the oceans as compared to the land surfaces of the earth, the idea that these tiny algae carry on more photosynthesis than does the terrestrial flora is not unreasonable.

In addition to their extremely critical role as primary producers, the algae are important to animal life in other ways. As a by-product of photosynthesis, they release oxygen and, thus, aerate the waters to the benefit of the animal life which requires it in its respiratory activities. The plants provide protection and shelter for the many small animals which live among them. They provide breeding grounds in which eggs may be laid, the young produced, and the juvenile stages developed until they seek wider horizons for their activities. In light of these considerations, the necessity for obtaining algae in aquatic life becomes very apparent.

Almaco Jack, 12-pound Male,
Fort Lauderdale, Florida

ALMACO JACK *Seriola rivoliana* This Atlantic species has also been called falcate amberjack and, much less appropriately, bonito, and has previously been recorded by the scientific name of *Seriola falcata*.

The nuchal band of the Almaco jack extends from the eye to the origin of the first dorsal fin. The five bars on the body of young fish are split and irregular and disappear at lengths larger than eight inches. The body is relatively deep, but the depth decreases proportionally with growth. The greatest body depth goes into the standard length about 2.7–2.85 times in specimens up to 16 inches in standard length, about 2.85–3.1 times in specimens 16–24 inches, and about 3.1–3.3 times in larger specimens (standard length is measured from the tip of the snout to the end of the bony plate of the tail). The dorsal-fin lobe is relatively long; its length goes about 4.6 times into the standard length, but there is considerable variation in the lobe length. The total number of gillrakers on both limbs of the first arch is relatively high, and this number decreases with growth of the fish; there are about 24–28 total gillrakers in fish up to 16 inches in standard length, and about 21–25 in fishes larger than this size, and sometimes as few as 18 gillrakers in very large individuals.

The first dorsal fin has 7 spines (but rarely 8). The second dorsal fin has one spine and 27–33 softrays (usually 28–32). The anal fin has two detached spines (which may be covered by skin at large sizes), followed by one spine and 19–22 softrays. There appear to be several color variations in the adults. The nuchal band is usually olivaceous with golden reflections, but the basic body color may be predominantly dusky or brownish, or more steely-blue, or olivaceous. Frequently the sides also have a lavender tint.

This species occurs on both sides of the Atlantic and in the Mediterranean. In the western Atlantic it extends from Buenos Aires, Argentina, to Cape Hatteras and northward to the offing of New Jersey, in the West Indies, and at Bermuda. Fish up to about 32 inches in length and 14 pounds have been recorded.

ANGLING VALUE

The almaco jack is of some interest to sport fishermen, particularly in the Bahamas, in the West Indies, and at Bermuda. There is no large commercial fishery of this species. *See also* Amberjacks, Carangidae.

—F.H.B.

AMA-AMA The Hawaiian name for mullet (*which see*).

AMBERJACKS Twelve species of four genera are listed for amberjacks occurring in American waters.

They are distinguished from other carangids by having elongated, usually thickened bodies; no scutes in the lateral line; usually 7–8 spines in the first dorsal fin; and the anal fin is appreciably shorter than the dorsal fin (the dorsal fin has 7–19 more rays than the anal fin). *See also* Carangidae, Greater Amberjack, Lesser Amberjack, Pacific Amberjack.

—F.H.B.

AMERICAN CASTING ASSOCIATION (ACA) A national nonprofit organization composed of affiliated clubs, regional (state and district) associations, and individual members, which lists among its objectives the promotion of casting and angling as a recreational activity, co-operation with and assistance to groups desiring to initiate classes in casting, training of casting instructors, research and experimental work in the development of improved angling and casting equipment, and the promulgation of standard rules governing tournament fly- and bait-casting in the United States. ACA is affiliated with the Amateur Athletic Union and is recognized by that organization as the sole governing body of all tournament casting in the United States.

HISTORY

ACA was originally formed in 1906 under the name "National Association of Scientific Angling Clubs" (NASAC), although at least two other national organizations had preceded it (National Rod and Reel Association, 1882–1890, and American Fly Caster's Association 1891–1906). Another national organization, the National Amateur Casting Association, was organized in 1913.

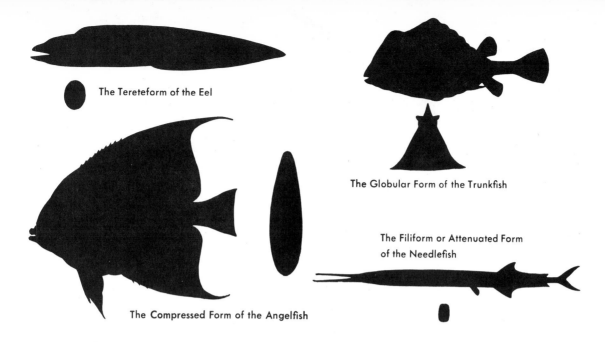

The Tereteform of the Eel

The Globular Form of the Trunkfish

The Compressed Form of the Angelfish

The Filiform or Attenuated Form
of the Needlefish

ANATOMY OF FISH

Color and color patterns are used in concealing behavior, aggressive behavior, and reproductive behavior. In many freshwater fishes, bright spawning colors are apparent only during the reproductive period, and are involved in courtship, nest-building, and care of the young. Intensity of color and patterns are important in marine fishes. The color of most fishes changes with growth, the young being colored differently from the adults, and, for example, in the bluehead wrasse the male and the female are very differently colored, both being distinct from the juvenile.

SKELETAL STRUCTURE

The body of a fish has a supporting framework of connective tissue which holds the body parts together and supplies a place for muscle attachment. The skeleton may be considered to be modified connective tissue.

The elements of the skull are of diverse origin. Sharks have a cartilaginous "skull" (chondrocranium) and branchial or throat arches (branchiocranium). In bony fishes, the neurocranium, or brain case, consists of a membranous covering strengthened by cartilages to protect the brain, and the branchiocranium comprises the jaw and associated bones. The three paired organs of sense are enclosed in cartilaginous capsules. The parts, together with the jaws, tongue, and gill arches, form the skull. This can be seen in at least the embryos of all vertebrates above the lampreys. The lampreys and hagfishes are fishes without jaws. Their skull, as well as the rest of the skeleton, is cartilaginous as in the sharks and rays. In bony fishes, the cartilaginous portions of the skull are more or less ossified and strengthened by outside dermal bony plates making a complex structure.

The vertebral column is flexible and covers the notochord, the dorsal neural canal, and, in the caudal region,
the ventral hemal, or blood-carrying, canal. Fibrous rings and tissue connect the parts or vertebrae. In addition, interlocking spines assist the fast swimmers by providing a solid axis on compression and a unit more loosely held together in an opposite bend. Ribs help give strength to the fish's swimming and hold the viscera in place, as well as being a site for muscle attachment.

In all fishes the longitudinal notochord persists as a definite feature. It is a stiff flexible rod or beadlike structure occurring beneath the central nervous system. It is the main skeletal axis in the more primitive forms. In higher animals it forms the basis for the vertebral column. More than other skeletal features, it probably serves most strongly as a basis for the development of the form of body in fishes and for the genesis and continuance of the lateral movement as a propulsion method in early vertebrates.

The dorsal and anal fins are also known as the vertical or median fins, and are important in maintaining balance. There may be a single soft dorsal fin, containing no spines, as in minnows, herrings, and tarpon. Perchlike fishes, such as bass, groupers, and snappers, have two dorsal fins, a spinous, or first dorsal fin, as well as a soft dorsal fin. Sometimes these are united (groupers, grunts, snappers) or are separate (barracuda, snook, striped bass). In some of the cods, there may be three dorsal fins. In freshwater trout and chars, and in deepsea relatives of these salmonlike fishes, a small, fleshy adipose fin is present between the dorsal fin and the tail. It contains no bony supporting rays or spines.

The anal fin is behind the vent or anus, on the lower surface of the body, and may be soft or spinous. In the cods and marlins there may be two anal fins. In some pelagic fishes, a series of small detached fins called finlets follow the dorsal and anal fins.

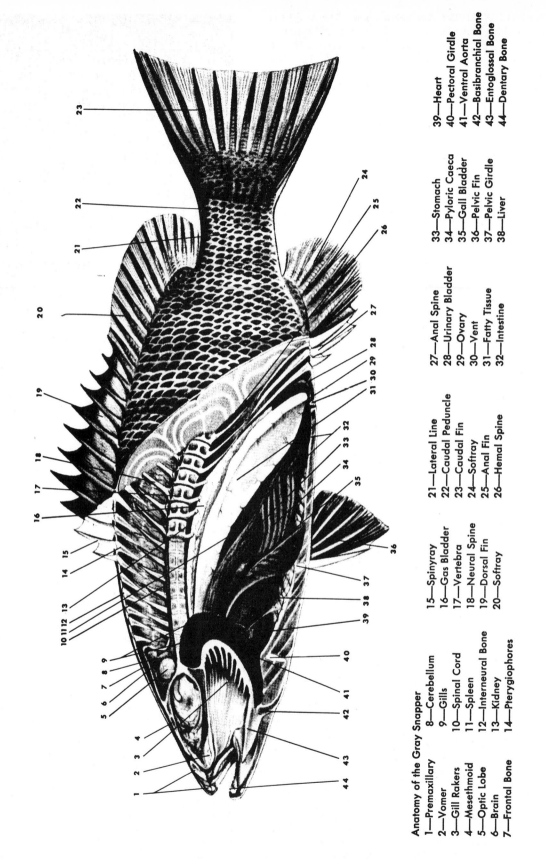

Anatomy of the Gray Snapper

1—Premaxillary
2—Vomer
3—Gill Rakers
4—Mesethmoid
5—Optic Lobe
6—Brain
7—Frontal Bone

8—Cerebellum
9—Gills
10—Spinal Cord
11—Spleen
12—Interneural Bone
13—Kidney
14—Pterygiophores

15—Spinyray
16—Gas Bladder
17—Vertebra
18—Neural Spine
19—Dorsal Fin
20—Softray

21—Lateral Line
22—Caudal Peduncle
23—Caudal Fin
24—Softray
25—Anal Fin
26—Hemal Spine

27—Anal Spine
28—Urinary Bladder
29—Ovary
30—Vent
31—Fatty Tissue
32—Intestine

33—Stomach
34—Pyloric Caeca
35—Gall Bladder
36—Pelvic Fin
37—Pelvic Girdle
38—Liver

39—Heart
40—Pectoral Girdle
41—Ventral Aorta
42—Basibranchial Bone
43—Entoglossal Bone
44—Dentary Bone

ATLANTIC WOLFFISH *Anarhichas lupus* The wolffishes are large blennylike fishes occurring in the cold waters of the North Atlantic and North Pacific. They have well-developed canine teeth and large molars on the vomer and palatine bones. Thus, they are well adapted to feeding on mollusks. The Atlantic wolffish is sometimes called the striped wolffish or loup (France). It is found on both sides of the North Atlantic; in the west it occurs from southern Labrador to Cape Cod and occasionally as far south as New Jersey; in the east it has been taken at western Greenland, Iceland, Faroes, Spitzbergen, and from the White Sea to the west coast of France.

Its color varies from slaty blue to dull olive-green to purplish-brown. Usually 10 or more dark transverse bars on the anterior two-thirds of the body, some of these extending on the dorsal fin; underside of head and belly to vent dirty white, tinged with general tint of upper parts.

Other distinguishing characteristics of the Atlantic wolffish are body compressed and elongate, greatest depth 5½ in total length, occurring about middle of pectoral fin; body then tapering to a small caudal peduncle. Head 5 in total length, heavy, blunt, profile rounded; mouth terminal, oblique, angle somewhat behind posterior edge of eye; a row of about 6 large, stout, conical teeth at front of upper jaw with a group of 5 or 6 smaller canine teeth behind them; these opposed by 4-6 large tusks at the front of the lower jaw, 3 series of crushing teeth in roof of mouth, 2 rows of rounded molars in lower jaws, small scattered teeth in throat. Eye small, 7½ in head.

Dorsal fin with 69-77 spines, fin begins over posterior part of head and extends to base of caudal; caudal fin small, very slightly rounded; anal fin with 42-48 softrays, a little more than half length of dorsal and ending under posterior tip of dorsal. Pectorals heavy, rounded, base low in sides, a short distance behind gill openings; pelvics absent. Lateral line absent. Head scaleless, body covered with poorly developed scales.

This species lives in moderately deep water (10-85 fathoms) over hard bottom. Individuals are apparently solitary and are caught in the same areas at all times of the year. Their food consists primarily of whelks, mussels, clams, and other mollusks. Crabs, hermit crabs, sea urchins, and starfish have also been found in their stomachs. The eggs are about ³⁄₁₆ inches in diameter and are attached to the bottom in large, loose clumps.

FOOD VALUE

The Atlantic wolffish is a good food fish and catches of about 1½ million pounds per year are made in the Gulf of Maine and on the Georges Bank. It is popular table fare in Denmark and Spain. It grows to a length of about 5 feet and a weight of about 40 pounds. *See also* Spotted Wolffish —J.C.B.

AUFWUCHS *See* Freshwater Ecology

AUSTRALIA The most arid continent on earth, Australia nevertheless has claim to some of the world's best fishing in its surrounding oceans and its island state of Tasmania. While Australia appears to be small, a mere spot on the underbelly of the globe surrounded by the Pacific and Indian oceans, the country is immense. In general shape and total land area (approximately 3 million square miles) Australia is comparable to the United

An over-thousand-pound black marlin comes out of the sea off Cairns. No other area produces such large billfish today

States. Despite the kangaroo and Outback image, it is one of the most urbanized nations in the world, with two-thirds of its population living in cities. But sports-minded Aussies are well aware of their outdoor heritage. Numerous black marlin of over 1,000 pounds have been caught in North Queensland, which fronts the Great Barrier Reef. The boats working out of Cairns have made the area one of the most important fishing centers in the Pacific. Blue marlin, striped marlin, sailfish, swordfish, yellowfin and bluefin tuna, wahoo, and dolphin are also seasonally abundant in Australian waters. Shark fishing, which has always been an Aussie preoccupation, is popular among local anglers, and some exceptional white, mako, gray nurse, bronze whaler, and hammerhead sharks have been boated. The estuaries and tropical rivers of Australia also produce excellent angling to the light-tackle caster for barramundi, ox-eye, jungle perch, black grunter, riflefish, mangrove jack, flathead, Australian bass, and Murray cod.

Australia is south of the equator; summer begins in November, autumn in April, winter in June, and spring in September. Climates vary greatly, but in general you can expect mild weather with temperatures in the 60's and 70's. The trout season runs from January to the end of April, with February a prime month.

NEW SOUTH WALES

Sydney, the major port-of-entry for most travelers, is a big city with a kaleidoscopic population (2½ million) drawn from all over the world. Aside from the usual tourist offerings Sydney also provides some offshore fishing for striped marlin and yellowfin tuna just outside North and South Heads, the massive rock bluffs guarding its harbor.

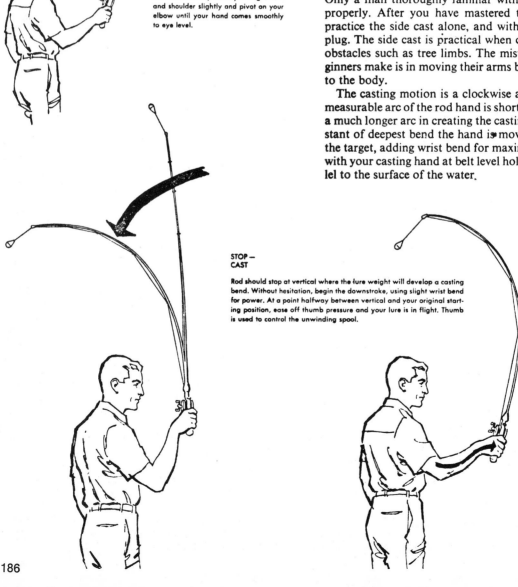

AIM

Face target with left foot rear of right foot and tip at eye level. Elbow doesn't touch body.

BACK

Start backward phase by lifting elbow and shoulder slightly and pivot on your elbow until your hand comes smoothly to eye level.

STOP — CAST

Rod should stop at vertical where the lure weight will develop a casting bend. Without hesitation, begin the downstroke, using slight wrist bend for power. At a point halfway between vertical and your original starting position, ease off thumb pressure and your lure is in flight. Thumb is used to control the unwinding spool.

Do not let the rod drift back over your shoulder. Without hesitating begin the forward phase by moving the rod downward following the same path it made on the upward stroke. This motion should be a crisp forearm chop using a slight elbow-and-wrist pivot for added power. At a point halfway between the vertical rod position and your original starting position release the thumb pressure from the spool to start the lure in its flight. Control the spool speed with your thumb while continuing the down stroke; ordinarily, this requires a gradual *increase* of pressure until the lure hits the surface at which point the spool is stopped completely. Through practice you will learn the minimum pressure required to prevent a backlash.

All movements in the overhead cast should be made smoothly. Do not attempt long casts at first, but concentrate on blending the backward and forward phases without jerkiness, so that the rod tip bends and literally "kicks" the plug out.

The Side Cast The side cast is of limited value and not safe to use when fishing with a companion in a boat. Only a man thoroughly familiar with casting can use it properly. After you have mastered the overhead cast, practice the side cast alone, and with a rubber practice plug. The side cast is practical when casting from under obstacles such as tree limbs. The mistake that most beginners make is in moving their arms back at right angles to the body.

The casting motion is a clockwise arch. Although the measurable arc of the rod hand is short, the rod tip makes a much longer arc in creating the casting bend. At the instant of deepest bend the hand is moved slightly toward the target, adding wrist bend for maximum power. Begin with your casting hand at belt level holding the rod parallel to the surface of the water.

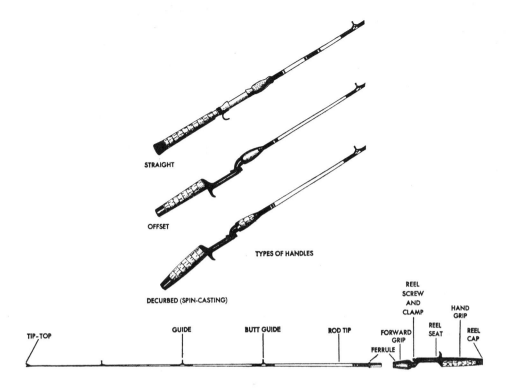

STRAIGHT

OFFSET

TYPES OF HANDLES

DECURBED (SPIN-CASTING)

TIP-TOP · GUIDE · BUTT GUIDE · ROD TIP · FERRULE · FORWARD GRIP · REEL SCREW AND CLAMP · REEL SEAT · HAND GRIP · REEL CAP

Bait-Casting Rod Nomenclature

DEVELOPMENT OF BAIT-CASTING REELS

The Kentucky Reel   The bait-casting reel prior to 1880 was entirely a handmade mechanism. Yet every one of them was crafted with painstaking exactness. No two screws were alike, and as a result every screw had to be put back in its proper place after the reel was taken apart. The lathe work, fitting, and filing were truly perfect. Reel handles were chopped out of sheet metal with a cold chisel and then filed to shape. The gears were slotted on Swiss cutting engines and then filed by hand. The main gear wheel was always made of brass casting or a section of brass rod that was hammered on an anvil, while the small wheel or pinion gear was made of the very best tempered tool steel. This resulted in a gearing that was almost indestructible. However, considering the labor involved, the average monthly production for a skilled builder was about seven reels, and these would sometimes bring $60–$70 apiece. Customers didn't ask the price—they ordered and were charged what the builder throught it was worth. The best a sporting goods dealer could hope for was a 10 per cent discount, and the order was filled when the "manufacturer" was in the mood. Oddly enough, fully 90 per cent of all bait-casting reels made came from the state of Kentucky. These were great reels. While none of them is made now, the modern bait-casting reel owes its existence to the craftsmen of Frankfort, Paris, and Louisville. Many of their original reels, now over one hundred years old, are still in use today.

George Snyder   The modern bait-casting reel was developed in the nineteenth century by a group of Kentucky watchmakers. Foremost among these was George Snyder, who made the first multiplying reel in 1810. Until that year, there were only two kinds of casting reels available—the English single-action reel made of brass or the domestic wooden kind made from a discarded sewing spool mounted on a frame by the local tinsmith. The rods used by these pioneer bass fishermen were native woods such as bethabara, Osage orange, and hickory; they were nearly 10 feet long but comparatively light, weighing 5–8 ounces. This was nearly one hundred years before James Heddon was to manufacture the first bass plug; so Snyder's customers were actually looking for a very sensitive spool with which to cast live baits. The inertia of a heavy single-action brass spool or the crude wooden type was too much for a bait to overcome. With a fine raw-silk line they could cast live minnows about 50–60 feet, provided the wind was right. The "cast" was what we know today as strip-casting. The angler would lay coils of line in the bottom of the boat or, if he was adept, hold the loops in his hand and propel the bait with a sideswiping motion.

Having a watchmaker's knowledge of gearing, George Snyder was able to make not only a delicate spool but one that revolved several times for every turn of the crank handle. In his reel the steel ends of the spool shaft were beveled to points, which in turn fitted in beveled recesses of pivots that screwed into the center caps of the outer disk plates of the reel. This compensating measure would take up any wear, and the running of the reel could be regulated by a turn of these screw pivots. How sound Snyder's methods were is best shown in the reel he made for the Honorable Brutus Clay in 1821.

FILLETING A FISH

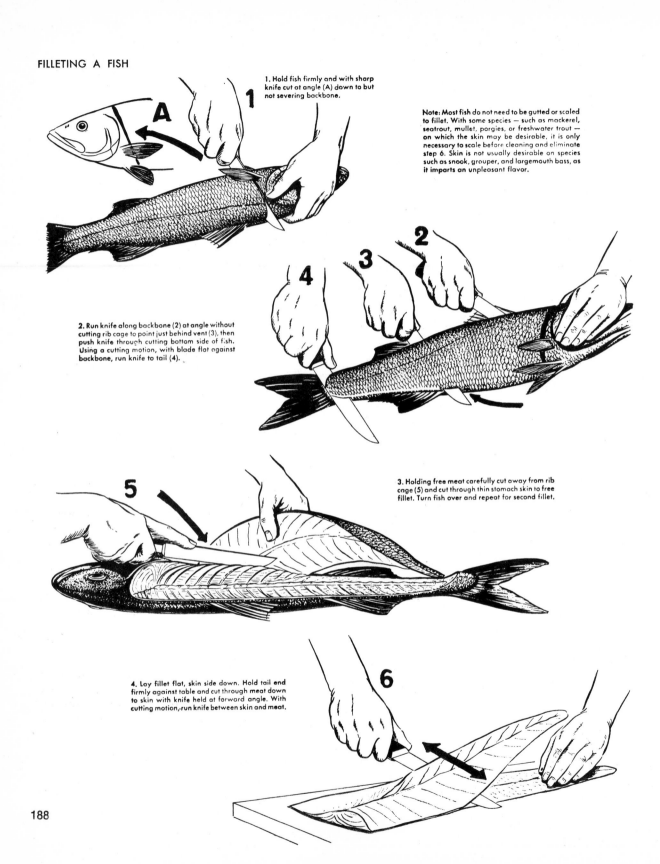

1. Hold fish firmly and with sharp knife cut at angle (A) down to but not severing backbone.

Note: Most fish do not need to be gutted or scaled to fillet. With some species — such as mackerel, seatrout, mullet, porgies, or freshwater trout — on which the skin may be desirable, it is only necessary to scale before cleaning and eliminate step 6. Skin is not usually desirable on species such as snook, grouper, and largemouth bass, as it imparts an unpleasant flavor.

2. Run knife along backbone (2) at angle without cutting rib cage to point just behind vent (3), then push knife through cutting bottom side of fish. Using a cutting motion, with blade flat against backbone, run knife to tail (4).

3. Holding free meat carefully cut away from rib cage (5) and cut through thin stomach skin to free fillet. Turn fish over and repeat for second fillet.

4. Lay fillet flat, skin side down. Hold tail end firmly against table and cut through meat down to skin with knife held at forward angle. With cutting motion, run knife between skin and meat.

CHAPTER 20

Old Fly with a New Twist

*One of America's outstanding fly fishermen
presents new ideas on "The Trude" fly.*

By Ed Curnow

ED CURNOW, author of the accompanying article on the Trude or "Sofa Pillow" fly, is a life-time western fly fisherman, fly tier, and owner-operator of "Ed's Tackle Shop," Ennis, Montana. He has also been a full-time western fishing-hunting guide, and even today (when properly approached) may be enticed to guide fishermen to the "big ones" sulking in Montana's Madison River, and other waters.

The illustrations for this piece were done by GLEN WEST, professional fly tier at Ennis. (T.McN.)

"IT WORKS! It really works! I've caught three fish, all over two pounds!" My excited friend Joe Pflebis had just tried one of my *special* flies.

I started to reply with "I told you so," but a large brown trout interrupted.

"I can't believe it," Joe called out, "that fish you have must weigh four pounds!" I pulled the brown out, and then carefully released it. We were fishing the Jefferson River in southwestern Montana, and using my special Trude flies.

I discovered the Trude when I moved to Montana ten years ago. As a boy growing up in western Nevada, I had spent many hours trying to make an imitation of a small yellow caddis and a yellow-gray stonefly. My hours spent over a fly-tying vise were never very successful. One day, however, while fishing a Sofa Pillow (another name for the Trude), an idea came to me—why not use the Trude pattern and try to match the size and color of those Nevada yellow caddis and yellow-gray stoneflies.

I tied up a bunch of my new Trude flies, and went to my favorite Nevada river to test them. The stonefly hatch was beginning to wane—a time when the trout are usually selective. I cast the Trude into a good pool. It started a perfect float, but then the current caught the belly in my line and the fly began to break the surface, forming a wake. As most fishermen do, I started to pick up the line to recast. Just then a fourteen-inch rainbow jumped clear out of the water and bombed the fly. I was so startled that I missed the fish and slipped off the rock on which I had been standing. With a half a gallon of water in my waders and a nice rainbow jumping out there, my fishing pace quickened, and so did the fishing. That evening I caught and released fourteen fish ranging from a pound to two-and-one-half pounds—a fantastic catch for that modest water.

That fishing proved that my theory was correct. I had finally found a good imitation for the stonefly, and had

189

also discovered that the Trude properly imitated stone-fly, caddis *and* terrestrials.

The origin of the Trude is told by William Sturgis, a proponent of this fly, in his book, "Fly-Tying" (Charles Scribner's Sons, New York, 1940). The Trude was originated by Carter H. Harrison, once Mayor of Chicago. In 1901 Harrison was a guest of A. S. Trude on the Snake River. Trude had insisted upon using a large fly, so Harrison, as a joke, picked up a piece of carpet, used it for the body of a fly, and plucked some red hair from Trudes' spaniel dog to use as winging. He then added brown hackle, Palmer style, at the head of the fly. Harrison named it the A. S. Trude and, after really close examination decided it ought to be a killer pattern. It was proving to be a very successful, extraordinary fly. In his book, Sturgis commends Harrison for his innovation and concludes the story of its origin: "Thus was born the A. S. Trude Fly, the forerunner of all hair-wing flies of today, and it is an outsanding contribution to the art of angling."

The Trude pattern has been sort of eclipsed by the Wulff patterns of today, even though the Wulff flies are not necessarily a better fish taker. To the contrary, for many waters, the Trude is much better than Wulff patterns, but most commercial tiers making Trudes have never used the proper color and sizes that are necessary to match the countless varieties of stonefly, caddis, and terrestrial hatches occurring in western rivers.

Western fishermen are just beginning to discover the Trude, and to realize that it is an excellent imitation of caddis, stonefly, and various terrestrials. The true importance of this is only realized when fishermen recognize that these natural flies named make up sixty to seventy percent of all the surface trout food in any Western stream. Many Eastern streams also have good hatches of those insects.

Historically, classic fly patterns were designed for English chalk streams or Eastern United States limestone streams where the mayfly is the dominant surface food. The Eastern syndrome has actually retarded the development of Western flies. Only recently have fly tiers begun to match our Western natural insects. The simple Trude—with its small dubbed body, tied-down wing over the top of the hook, and short stiff hackles, offers the Western fisherman a whole new group of flies with which to match Western "natural" hatches. Eastern fishermen will also find the Trude a welcome addition to their fly boxes.

Natural stonefly, from nymph (bottom left) to freshly-emerged adult, are shown in various stages of development in left column. Pen permits size comparison. Artificial flies in right column are popular stonefly imitations including Trude patterns (1st, 2nd, and 4th flies from bottom).

(For details of Trude pattern types, materials used, and tying instruction, see illustrations accompanying this article).

Two factors are very important in the Trude's fish-taking success. First, and most important, is its profile. Caddis, stoneflies, and terrestrials have an oblong profile on the water, while the mayfly is slender, straight, and upright. The mayfly sits on top of the surface film while the caddis, stonefly, and terrestrial actually rests well down in the surface film. This also contributes to the larger oval shape of terrestrials. From the fish's view, the flies look considerably different.

The profile of the Trude is oblong. The tied-down wing, sitting on the water, looks like the wings of a caddis or stonefly. Made out of hair, the Trude's wing also has a transparent look—as do the wings of the insects it imitates.

The Trude wing is important to the flotation of the fly. Because the wing is tied back, it catches tiny air bub-

Ed Curnow whips one on at the Madison River near Ennis, Montana.

Pro fly tier Jim Poulos used a Trude fly to blitz these Big Hole River browns.

bles and holds the hook nicely parallel to the water. At the same time, only the hair is on the water. This actually allows the fly to float in the surface film, as does the live insect.

The Trude is a fly-tier's delight. It is so simple anyone can tie it. No mystical or unusually difficult tricks are needed to make a good Trude fly. Each tier can use the colors and sizes (6 to 26) which match the particular hatches in his own area. I use eleven basic ties and they seem to cover most of my western fishing. Some of the patterns have similar names, and use similar materials, as the Wulff flies. The Blond, Gray, and Royal Trudes are made from about the same materials as the Wulff flies by the same names. The Olive, Black, and Brown Trudes are simply mono-colored ties. The Yellow Trude and the Hopper are yellow-bodied with gray wing and grizzly hackle. The only difference between these two flies is that the Hopper is tied with a heavier body, usually made out of polypropolene, and has a brown hackle and one grizzly. The Spruce Trude is much the same as a Blond Trude except the body is larger and the wing is splayed—or spread—to give a larger profile on the water. The Pine Butterfly Trude has a white body, ribbed with black thread, pure white hackle, and a white wing of impala (calf tail). The wing is splayed very wide to give the profile of a butterfly. I must add that the Sofa Pillow is still a favorite of mine to match our super large Montana stonefly.

Fishing the Trude is as easy as tying it. It is hard to fish it wrong. Its versatility can only be matched by that of the famed Muddler Minnow.

When I started fishing the Trude, I had the "dead drift" syndrome. That method of fishing a fly on a natural float was successful, but a dimension new to me was added one day while fishing with Russ Ward, a Missoula, Montana, sporting goods dealer. We were fishing slicks and tail-outs of a large river. There was a hatch of size sixteen light brown caddis flies on the water. I could not catch a fish, even with a very fine tippet. Russ put a small, (size 16) blond fly on his large 1 X tippet. The leader was so heavy that he could hardly get it through the eye of the fly. I laughed and changed flies hoping to land at least one of the fish that were rising all around us. Suddenly, Russ had a nice rainbow. Luck? It *had* to be! Soon he had another trout, and then another. I began to feel frustrated. With all the nonchalance I could muster, I asked, "What are you doing right?"

"Skating," came the reply.

I had skated Muddlers and Spiders, but never a size sixteen dry fly. I tied on a sixteen dry fly, skated it, and it worked!

Remembering my early experiences of taking fish as my dry fly broke through the water, I began to analyze the situation and ask why? Again, the answer was in the fact that most Western insects are not mayflies that perch jauntily on the surface. Caddis, stoneflies, and terrestrials are actually *trapped* by the surface water. Once on the water they cannot break free, as a mayfly might, but rather must struggle to a nearby bush or a shoreline rock to dry their wings before they once again can take flight. This frantic movement, this struggling by the fly to get to shore, creates a riffle and disturbance on the surface. By skating or twitching his dry fly, the angler simulates the exact movements and disturbances caused by a fly trapped in the surface film.

Twitching the fly has been my most successful technique in fishing the Trude. I use it about sixty percent of the time. In quiet water, both during the day and late evening, I have exceptionally good results. Twitching is best done with a long, fairly flexible rod. Try casting straight across the river or stream and mend the line once; then actually twitch the rod so that the fly takes a little jump upstream or sometimes across stream. Allow the fly to dead drift in between twitches, and it looks exactly like an insect attempting to become airborne, struggling frantically to get off the water.

Skating often works when nothing else will. When skating the Trude, I cast slightly upstream, mend, and then strip the fly toward me. The fly should make little jumps and hops when bouncing over the surface. When skating a Trude, allow it to come all the way around in the current, and retrieve it with a few snappy jerks before picking the line up to recast. Often a fish will follow the fly and wait until it is actually moving upstream before he decides to hit. When skating in riffles, put line dressing on your leader; this keeps the leader up and allows you to work the fly better. Remember, if all else fails—SKATE!—even if you don't use a Trude pattern.

About fifteen percent of the time, I fish a Trude wet. My favorite trick is to cast above a large rock and allow the fly to dead drift down to the rock. If a fish doesn't hit the fly, I allow the line to catch in the current and pull the fly under water just as it passes the rock. Often fish that are above the rock will chase the fly and take it just as it goes under water. If no fish takes the fly then, I allow it to stay underwater until the line and leader straighten out. Sometimes fish will dart from beneath the rock and hit the submerged fly that way.

As a wet fly, the Trude is effective because many more caddis, stoneflies, and terrestrials are sucked underwater than are mayflies. When fish are lazy or the water is a little off-color the Trude, fished wet, will produce excellent results. Remember, though, not to be afraid to fish the Trude as a *dead drift dry fly*, as well.

The Trude should appeal to every fly fisherman, everywhere. Its profile allows it to be used to imitate a wide variety of insects found both in the East and the West. Its versatility permits it to be fished wet or dry. It can be twitched or skated. Fly tiers will approve of it, too, because it is easy to tie with many variations in color and materials. But best of all, the Trude is a WORKING fly that takes fish.

The Trude

Some Trude types have a Royal Coachman look.

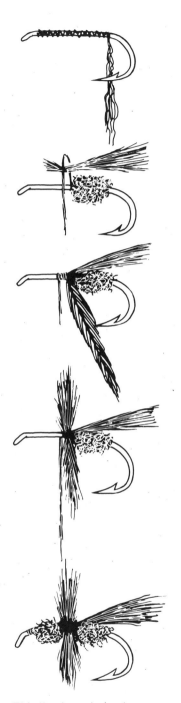

Standard Trude has dubbed fur body, hair winging, and short, stiff hackles.

Hair-bodied Trude has body of clipped deer or moose hair.

This Trude variation has dubbed body, short hair winging, and center hackling.

Grasshopper

May Fly

Caddis

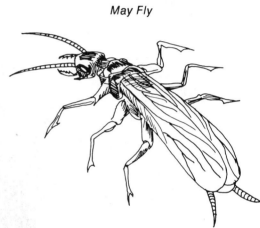

Stonefly

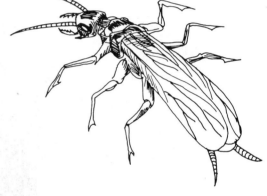

Flying Ant

Spruce Moth

Trout commonly mistake the Trude Fly for these natural insects.

CHAPTER 21

Mann's "George" Baits and How to Fish Them

ABOUT TOM MANN

Tom Mann has been a serious bass angler all his life. He is one of the nation's top professional bass fishermen—having placed in the top three of B.A.S.S.'s national point standings for three consecutive years, 1971, 1972, and 1973.

Mann has fished in dozens of bass tournaments all over the country, and usually places high. Many fishermen consider Tom Mann one of the most knowledgeable and outstanding bass anglers in the nation.

Mann was an Alabama Fish and Wildlife Officer when he started a lure manufacturing business as a side-line. His 30 years of fishing experience helped him develop superb lures that fishermen nation-wide praise highly. His lure manufacturing business prospered quickly, so Mann today devotes his full time to making "Mann's Baits,"—except when he's fishing.

Tom Mann's uniquely designed lures, such as the "George baits," are among the most original and productive bass baits marketed today. This feature presents Mann's own techniques for fishing his "Big George" and "Super George" lures. (T. McN.).

Tom Mann created the "Little George" in 1960. He wanted a lure that would cast easily, get down deep quickly, resemble a small forage minnow, and yet be versatile so that it could be used under various angling conditions. Mann whittled the first "Little George" out of lead. And after dozens of tests he finally perfected the "Little George" so that it was balanced properly and had just the right action Mann wanted.

Mann used his "Little George" with great success on largemouth bass at Lake Eufaula, Alabama. Soon anglers throughout the South were employing the "Little George," and they too found this little bass lure to be extremely effective.

Tom Mann—a leading bass "pro."

193

The "Little George" has been such an excellent bass bait that Tom Mann recently developed two more "George" lures which he calls the "Big George" and the "Super George."

"Big George" and "Super George" are a pair of fast moving, vibrating "sound" lures that should add many pounds of bass to your stringer.

"For several years I realized the need for a really effective vibrating lure that would catch all species of bass under all kinds of fishing conditions," Tom Mann recalls. "Often, in both tournament and pleasure fishing, I found that bass would strike a vibrating lure more readily than any other type.

"After many hours of research and testing, I believe I have come up with the best vibrating lures made. I originally hand-carved 'Big George' and 'Super George,' and after many tests, I was finally satisfied they would run exactly the way I wanted them to.

"Sound is very important in a vibrating lure," explains Mann. "To increase the sound waves created by 'Big George' and 'Super George' I designed a special built-in chamber with a rattling, sound device. These lures have been tested hundreds of times and I am satisfied we have created the most effective, quality-made sound lures available to sportsmen."

HOW TO FISH "BIG GEORGE"

The "Big George" is one of the best-balanced, vibrating lures made today. It can be fished at all depths and at any speed. Tom Mann has thoroughly tested "Big George" and caught countless bass with it. Following are some of the ways he suggests using this lure:

" 'Big George' is great for fishing very shallow water. Simply cast the lure out and start your retrieve the moment it hits the water. Hold your rod high and retrieve the lure so that it will swim just under the surface. The clearer the water the faster the retrieve should be, unless the water is very cold. When the water is cold slow the retrieve. Too, a slow retrieve is necessary when water is dingy or muddy.

" 'Big George' is ideal for fishing structure such as rocks, stumps, tree tops, etc. Cast past the snag and start retrieving as fast as you can—remember it's usually not possible to retrieve a lure too fast for bass. Often when you see a fish follow your lure and turn away, you're reeling too slow—make another cast and speed the retrieve.

"Submerged points of land are superb places to fish 'Big George.' Just cast the lure across the point and bring it back. Begin working the lure close and parallel to shore, then slowly move toward deeper water. With a normal retrieve 'Big George' will run 3- to 5-feet deep, depending on the line test used. The lighter the line the deeper the lure will run. When fishing deep water you should pause after the cast and let the lure sink. For example, if you're working 'Big George' in 10 feet of water, and want the lure to be retrieved along the bottom, wait 10 seconds after the cast before retrieving. If you want the lure to run at 12 feet, pause 12 seconds; 15 feet, 15 seconds, etc.

"Schooling bass are set-ups for 'Big George.' When you locate a surface-feeding school of bass simply cast 'Big George' beyond the school and retrieve the lure through them. Vary the speed of retrieve until the right one is found. If the surface fish disappear let 'Big George' sink several feet on your next cast before retrieving. Often when feeding bass leave the surface they will stay in the same area but just drop to a lower depth.

" 'Big George' is an effective lure for fishing weed beds. The best way to fish this lure is to make it skim just over the tops of the weeds. This way, bass laying in the weeds will dart up and hit 'Big George' as it's brought over the fish. If the lure picks up weeds during the retrieve, on your next cast hold your rod higher, and retrieve the lure faster.

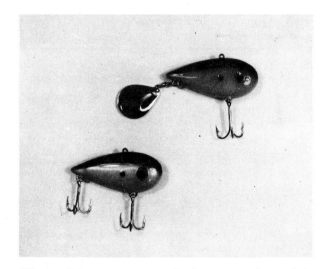

"George" baits are not particularly attractive to fishermen, but they get bass.

"The design of 'Big George' makes it difficult to 'hang-up.' The lure runs with its nose down so its hooks are protected from most obstructions by the lure's body. Therefore it's possible to fish 'Big George' in snag-filled water where it would be impossible to fish many other plugs.

"When running, 'Big George' actually stimulates a shad—a natural forage fish to bass," Tom Mann explains. "This lure is most effective on largemouth bass. However, I have found while field testing this new lure, that it also is very good for spotted (Kentucky) bass, smallmouth, white bass, and even crappie."

HOW TO FISH "SUPER GEORGE"

"Super George" has the same body as "Big George" but there is one exception—the tail hook is replaced with a spinner bade.

"'Super George' can be fished several of the same ways that I fish 'Big George,'" says Tom Mann. "I use 'Super George' in muddy water, cold water, over weeds, for schooling fish, across points, through flooded timber and tree tops, buzz it on the surface, and fish it at night."

"Super George" puts out tremendous sound waves when retrieved, and this is very important when fishing muddy water because it helps bass locate the lure. Fish "Super George" very slowly in dirty water and work this lure close to shore because bass frequent the shallows in muddy water—regardless of water temperature.

Bass are more lethargic in cold water, and consequently "Super George" should be retrieved very slowly when working water such as that. Often, in early spring, bass will "suspend" in flooded timber (cedar trees are particularly good) near the surface. This is an ideal situation for fishing "Super George." Cast the lure beyond the trees and retrieve "Big George" right alongside them—

even make the lure bump the trees if possible. It's sometimes a good technique to retrieve "Super George" right to a tree then stop reeling and lower your rod tip—this will cause the lure to sink near the tree trunk and often bass will hit "Super George" as it's falling. When fishing flooded timber it's usually necessary to experiment with different rates of retrieve and lure depths to locate bass.

"The 'Super George' probably is one of the best lures I've ever used for schooling bass," Tom Mann says. "When I find a school I cast 'Super George' over the fish and retrieve the lure back through them with a medium to fast speed. If this doesn't work I cast again, and when the lure is in the middle of the school I lower my rod tip and stop reeling. 'Super George' will sink slowly and bass will usually hit the lure as it falls."

"Super George" can be used as a "buzzing lure." During spring and fall, when bass frequent the shallows, "Super George" is deadly when retrieved very fast so that its spinner blade churns the surface. The best method is to fish parallel to shore and cast "Big George" toward shallow, shore line "structure." After the cast raise your rod high and retrieve "Super George" fast.

Many avid bass anglers prefer night fishing. "Super George" is very effective for that type of fishing because this lure produces many sound waves. Generally speaking "Super George" should be fished very slowly at night, but it's wise to try different rates of retrieves and depths, and fish various types of structure until you get fish.

"The techniques mentioned here are the most productive bass-catching ways I've found to fish 'Big George' and 'Super George,'" Mann explains. "But there are many other techniques that can be employed with these two baits—just keep experimenting and you'll find dozens of ways to fish these lures that'll help you take more bass!"

The head-down position of "George" lures on the retrieve helps make them snag proof

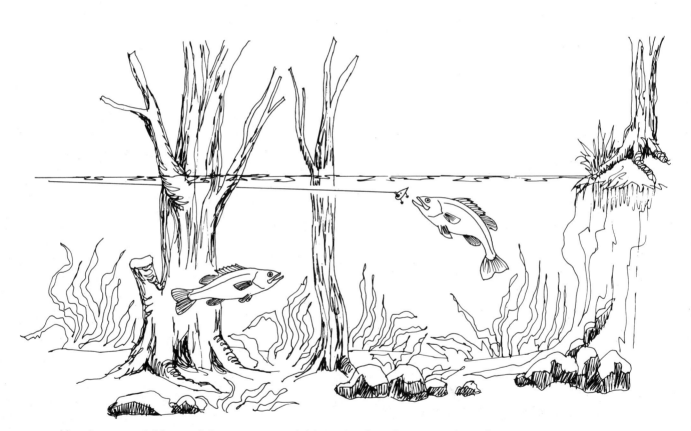

Mann's unusual ''George'' lures are especially productive when worked carefully through flooded timber.

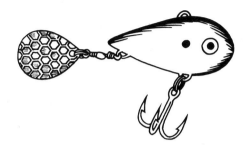

Mann's "George" baits are available with or without spinner attachments.

A fast jerk-and-pause retrieve with a "George" bait over weeds often brings hard strikes.

CHAPTER 22

Glossary of Knots

The knot-tying section in this Third Edition, "Fishermen's Bible," is one of the most complete presentations of knots of practical use to fishermen ever done. The knots illustrated, along with the descriptive copy, are, however, taken from a new book, "Tom McNally's Complete Book of Fishermen's Knots," and they are only a fraction of the knots presented in this latest and most complete knot-tying book. "Fishermen's Knots," for example, is the first and only guide containing *all known* fishing knots—nearly 150 of them. "McNally's FISHERMEN'S KNOTS" sells for $4.95 and is available at most book and tackle stores, or direct from the publisher, J. Philip O'Hara, Inc., 20 E. Huron, Chicago 60611.

LEADER KNOT (Sometimes called Knot Canada)

This knot is an excellent one for tying two nylon lines together, and some experts feel it's much easier to tie than the Blood Knot.

Fig. 1   Lap the ends of the strands as shown, holding with thumb and forefinger where marked.

Fig. 2   Loop end around both lines and poke end through all three loops.

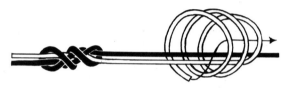

Fig. 3   Now twist the other end around both strands three times and stick end through all three loops.

Fig. 4   When both sides of knot look like this, slowly pull the knot tight and use your fingernails to push the loops together.

Fig. 5   Finished knot looks like this. Trim ends close to knot.

FISHERMAN'S BEND KNOT

This is an excellent knot for joining two lines of equal diameter. However, it is difficult to tie and other knots, such as the Blood Knot, are more often used by knowledgable anglers.

VARIATION OF FISHERMAN'S BEND

Some anglers still use this variation because the ends of the knot are in the center, and the knot passes through rod guides easily. Although it's much easier to tie this knot than the regular Fisherman's Bend, there are many other knots for joining lines of equal diameter that can be tied much more quickly.

MULTIPLE CLINCH KNOT

This is the ideal knot for bait casters who use nylon leaders six or eight feet long, because they need a knot joining leader to line that isn't bulky. This knot passes from reel through rod guides easily, and is extremely strong.

SHOCKER KNOT

This is a good knot for tying two lines of different diameters together. It's easy and fast to tie, yet strong and secure.

Fig. 1   Make an Overhand Knot in the light line. Form a loose Overhand Knot in the heavy line and pass the end of the light line through the Overhand Knot.

Fig. 2   Tighten the Overhand Knot in the heavy line.

Fig. 3   Make three wraps with the light line around the heavy line, and pass the end back through the first loop.

VARIATION OF THE NAIL KNOT

This knot was only recently developed. It's best used when tying a heavy leader butt to a fly line. Because there are only a few wraps, some anglers feel this knot is easier to tie than a conventional Nail Knot. However, some other Nail Knots, such as the Fast Nail Knot, are even easier to tie than this one, and moreover, are stronger. Thus this Nail Knot should be used only by fishermen who have difficulty tying the other types.

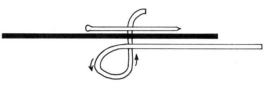

Fig. 1   No tying is done with the fly line. Hold the nail parallel to the fly line and form a loop with the leader butt.

Fig. 2   Hold the loop below the fly line and wrap the leader's butt end twice around the fly line, nail, and standing part of the leader.

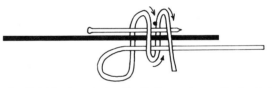

Fig. 3   Put the butt end through the last wrap and the first loop, as shown.

Fig. 4   Push all the wraps tightly together with your thumb nail, and withdraw the nail slowly.

Fig. 5   Pull on both ends of the leader, then trim the leader and line tag ends.

BLOOD KNOT

This knot is valuable to all fishermen, particularly fly fishermen who use it to join nylon strands in making tapered leaders. Its only drawback is that the nylon strands to be connected must be of equal, or nearly equal, diameter. The Blood Knot provides a small connection, and when properly tied it cannot pull loose no matter how close its ends are clipped.

Fig. 1   Cross the two lines, and wrap one line three times around the other. Now place the end through the loop formed by the two lines.

Fig. 2   Turn the other line around the standing part of the first three times, and put its free end through the loop from the opposite side.

Fig. 3   The turns should look like this. Now slowly pull on both long ends of the lines.

Fig. 4   The finished knot looks like this, with its loose ends trimmed closely.

198   GLOSSARY OF KNOTS

MODIFIED NAIL KNOT

Although this type Nail Knot can be used to join almost any kind of lines, it was originally designed for connecting lead-core trolling line to monofilament line. Too, fly rodders use the Modified Nail Knot for joining lead-core fly lines to leaders and backing.

Fig. 1   Lay two lines next to each other, alongside a plastic or metal tube, just as you would if tying a standard Nail Knot.

Fig. 2   Wind one line around the tube, as well as around the second line.

Fig. 3   After three wraps with the first line, take *both* lines and wind them once around the tube.

Fig. 4   Then continue wrapping with the first line, as shown in the illustration.

Fig. 5   Next pass the first line back through the tube, pull the lines snug, slip the tube out, and tighten the knot.

Fig. 6   This is how the completed knot looks.

TRIPLE FISHERMAN'S KNOT

This is just an improved version of the Fisherman's Knot. It is used for joining two strands of nylon monofilament and is a good knot for making fly leaders. Although it does take some practice to tie it properly, it is a superb connection.

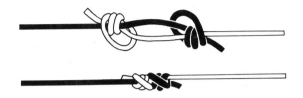

IMPROVED BLOOD KNOT

This is a superb knot for joining two lines of different diameters—for example, tying 12-pound test line to 80-pound test line.

Fig. 1   Double the smaller diameter line. Wrap it five times around the larger diameter line and bring it back between the two strands.

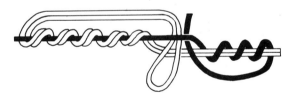

Fig. 2   Twist the larger diameter line around the doubled line three times, and place its free end back through the loop in the opposite direction.

Fig. 3   Pull the knot slowly to tighten it. Use your fingernails to push the loops of the knot together. Trim all loose ends one-fourth inch from the knot.

VARIATION OF THE ANGLER'S KNOT

This connection is simply a regular Angler's Knot carried one step farther. The extra tie in the knot makes it more secure than an ordinary Angler's Knot.

This Variation of the Angler's Knot is used primarily for tying a dropper line to monofilament leaders.

SINGLE WATER KNOT

The Single Water Knot is a simple Overhand Knot using both lines for the tie. It is not as secure as some knots, such as the Surgeon's Knot, when used to connect two pieces of monofilament. However, the Single Water Knot is fast and easy to tie.

ALBRIGHT SPECIAL KNOT (Also known as Key Knot Splice and Key Loop)

This is an excellent knot for tying light monofilament to heavy monofilament line, wire cable, nylon-coated wire, and even to small diameter single-strand wire leader.

Although it takes time to learn to tie the Albright Special well, this is a very useful and strong knot that passes through rod guides with ease.

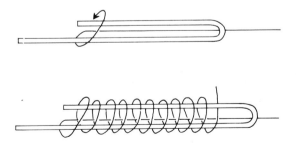

DOUBLE IMPROVED CLINCH KNOT

Fig. 1   Double the line, bringing the line end back parallel to the standing line so there is about eight inches of double line. Take the end of the double line and push it through the hook eye. Wrap the doubled line end five times around the doubled standing part of the line, and push the line end back through the loop formed near the hook eye.

Fig. 2   Pull the doubled line end through the loop in front of the hook eye, then push the end through the large loop, as shown.

Fig. 3   Moisten the knot with saliva, then pull tight.

DOUBLE TURLE KNOT

This is merely a standard Turle Knot carried one step farther. Instead of making a single wrap with the Overhand Knot, as when tying the standard Turle Knot, two wraps are made with the line end around the standing part of the line before passing the hook back through the loop.

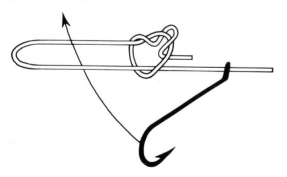

The regular Turle Knot originally was designed for tying gut leaders to hooks with turned-up or turned-down eyes. The Double Turle Knot, however, was created for use with nylon monofilament lines. It is stronger and more dependable than the Turle Knot.

DUNCAN LOOP KNOT

Here is an excellent "sliding loop" knot. When the knot is tied, it can be tightened anywhere on the standing part of the line, which means an angler can adjust the knot to form any size loop he desires. The loop will remain open during normal casting and retrieving. However, when a fish is hooked, the knot will slide down the line and "jam" tightly against the hook eye. After the fish is landed the knot can be moved up the line and the loop opened once again.

Fig. 1   Put the line end through the hook eye, bringing about eight inches of line through the "eye" with which to tie the knot. Keep the line end parallel to the standing line.

Fig. 2   Turn the line end down, so that it comes back underneath the two parallel strands. Wind the line end around the two parallel lines and through the loop, as shown.

Fig. 3   Make five wraps around the two parallel lines, inside the loop. Then pull the tag end and standing part of the line to tighten the knot.

PALOMAR KNOT

Many anglers, particularly those with failing eyesight, find it difficult to tie the Clinch Knot or the Improved Clinch Knot. For those anglers the Palomar Knot is the answer for tying line or leader to a hook, lure, or swivel "eye." This is a strong, yet easy-to-tie knot. Some skilled anglers can even tie the Palomar Knot in complete darkness, using only their sense of "feel."

Fig. 1 Double the end of the line and pass the loop through the hook eye.

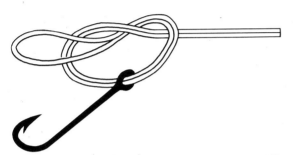

Fig. 2 Double the loop back, then make an Overhand Knot around the standing line, leaving a loop large enough for the hook (or lure) to pass back through.

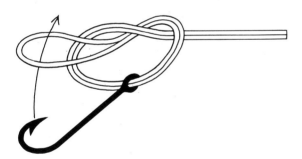

Fig. 3 Put the entire hook (lure) through the loop, as illustrated.

Fig. 4 Pulling on the standing line will draw the knot tight. Trim it, and the knot will be compact and effective.

BUMPER TIE KNOT

The Bumper Tie is becoming increasingly popular with anglers who snell their own hooks. The Bumper Tie is a more complicated knot to tie than the "Snelling A Hook" Knot, or the "Quick Snell Knot." However, some fishermen prefer the Bumper Tie when using natural baits for fish such as steelhead and Chinook salmon; they feel the Bumper Tie is a stronger knot.

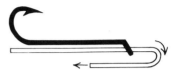

Fig. 1 The leader end is pushed through the hook eye.

Fig. 2 The standing part of the leader is wound three times around the hook shank and the leader end. Then the *butt* end of the leader is pushed out through the hook eye.

Fig. 3 A loop of about four inches is left under the hook shank, and then is wrapped around the hook shank.

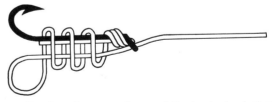

Fig. 4 The loop is wrapped around the hook shank three times, forming a series of coils.

Fig. 5   Now the standing part of the leader is slowly pulled tight, and the knot is completed.

HOMER RHODE LOOP KNOT (Sometimes called Flemish Loop or Loop Knot)

This is an easy knot to tie, and very popular among salt water and Great Lakes anglers who do considerable trolling. The Homer Rhode Loop makes the use of "snap-swivels" unnecessary, and allows lures to have more "action."

The knot forms a loop through the "eye" of a lure, so the lure "swims" more freely than if a knot were tied tightly to it.

Although this knot is normally tied with monofilament line or nylon-coated wire, it also can be used effectively with braided lines.

Fig. 1   Tie a simple Overhand Knot about four inches from the end of the line. Push the end of the line through the hook eye, then back through the center of the Overhand Knot.

Fig. 2   Next, with the end of the line, make another Overhand Knot around the standing part of the line. Now slowly pull the two knots tight, at the same time sliding them together so they "jam" or lock against one another.

WYSS TURLE KNOT

This is an ordinary Turle Knot, with an extra step before the knot is pulled tight. Many fishermen use the Wyss Turle Knot rather than the regular Turle Knot

because the Wyss Turle Knot is less likely to slip and break from pressure exerted by strong fish.

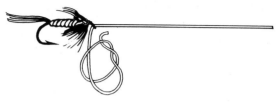

Fig. 1   Thread the leader through the hook eye. Bring the end of the leader back and tie an Overhand Knot around the standing part of the leader.

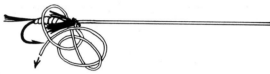

Fig. 2   Slip the loop formed by the Overhand Knot over the hook shank, and bring the end of the leader through the loop that's now around the hook shank.

Fig. 3   Hold the tag end of the leader against the hook shank, and slowly pull on the standing part of the leader to tighten the knot.

DOUBLE-LOOP CLINCH KNOT (Occasionally called Double Jam Knot)

Few anglers are aware of this fine version of the standard Clinch Knot. The Double-Loop Clinch Knot is somewhat new, and has only recently become popular among trolling fishermen.

The Double-Loop Clinch Knot is used chiefly for tying on various types of swivels when trolling. The knot takes a little more time to tie, so it is most practical when using the same terminal tackle over a long period, as is normally done when trolling.

Fig. 1   Turn the line end through the hook eye twice.

Fig. 2   Wrap the line end around the standing part of the line three times, then put the line end back through the two loops in front of the hook eye.

Fig. 3   The finished knot pulled tight.

THE END-LOOP KNOT (Sometimes called the Buffer Loop)

This is a good "loop knot" for anglers who use heavy test "shock tippets." It forms a loop with heavy mono much easier than other knots.

The End-Loop Knot is not recommended, however, for use with light lines since it weakens the line more than do some other "loop knots," such as the Nail Loop.

Fig. 1   Tie an Overhand Knot about six inches from the end of the line, then pass the line through the hook eye.

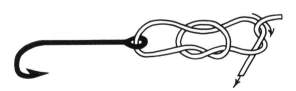

Fig. 2   Put the line end through the open Overhand Knot and tie a Half-Hitch with the line end onto the standing part of the line.

Fig. 3   Now slide the Overhand Knot either up or down the standing part of the line. This will determine the size of the loop that the knot will form. Slowly pull the line's end and its standing part to tighten the knot.

Fig. 4   Trim the knot, leaving a tag end about one-eighth-inch long.

ROUND-TURN FISHHOOK TIE

This knot is often used by anglers using heavy nylon while fishing natural baits. The knot holds best with stiff, heavy nylon rather than with wispy monofilament or braided line.

Too, the Round-Turn Fishhook Tie is a better connection when there is a constant pull or pressure from the standing part of the line to the knot, as when trolling or stillfishing.

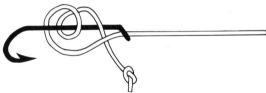

Fig. 1   Thread the line through the hook eye. Make a wrap around the shank of the hook toward the hook eye, then tuck the line end under the wrap. Now tie an Overhand Knot in the end of the line.

Fig. 2   Pull on the standing part of the line to tighten the knot.

SNELLING A HOOK (Commonly called Salmon Hook Knot)

Originally, Snelling A Hook was necessary because many hooks did not have "eyes." However, some expert anglers still insist today on snelling their "eyed" hooks because they feel snelling makes a strong, permanent connection.

Snelled hooks usually are used in fishing natural baits, especially for fish such as coho and Chinook salmon, and steelhead trout.

Most bait fishermen prefer snelled hooks because bait can be slipped right over the leader knot. Too, a properly snelled hook will give a direct pull from leader to hook, often essential to consistently hook fish.

Fig. 1   Thread the leader through the hook eye, and lay the leader along the hook shank.

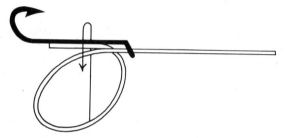

Fig. 2   Pull about six inches of leader through the hook eye, and form a loop below the hook shank, as shown.

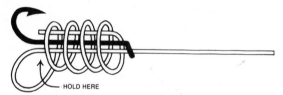

HOLD HERE

Fig. 3   Hold the two lines parallel to the hook against the hook shank. Then wrap the loop over the entire hook so that the line of the loop that's closest to the hook eye forms a series of coils.

Fig. 4   After six tight coils are formed on the hook shank, slowly pull on the standing part of the line. This will bring the loop through the coils and tighten the knot.

Fig. 5   The completed Snell.

LARK'S HEAD KNOT

The Lark's Head Knot is used extensively by natural bait fishermen for tying on hooks, and by some other anglers for attaching swivels and lures to line or leader. It can be tied and untied quickly, which is advantageous at times when it is necessary to change lures fast.

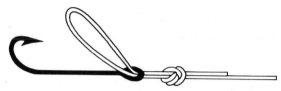

Fig. 1   A loop is formed at the end of the line or leader, and then the loop is passed through the hook, lure, or swivel "eye."

Fig. 2   The loop is passed over the lure or swivel.

Fig. 3   The knot is then pulled tight.

DOUBLE EYE KNOT

The Double Eye Knot is a quick, secure tie that is often employed by fishermen using natural bait.

It is a satisfactory knot for use with all types of hooks, however, it is especially good on hooks having turned-up or turned-down "eyes."

Fig. 1   Double the line, forming a loop, then tie a simple Overhand Knot over the standing line. Pass the loop through the hook eye.

Fig. 2   The loop now goes over the bend of the hook, and is pulled up to the hook eye.

Fig. 3   Take the "tag end" of the Overhand Knot and pass it under the loop, against the hook shank, and draw the knot tight.

Fig. 4   The completed Double Eye Knot.

DOUBLE-LOOP IMPROVED CLINCH KNOT

This is a Double-Loop Clinch Knot carried one step further. The line end is passed through the hook eye twice. The line is wrapped four times around its standing part, then it is passed through the two loops near the "eye." The final step is to put the line end through the large loop, as shown.

The Double-Loop Improved Clinch Knot isn't difficult to tie. It's a very strong connection. Moreover, one very large fishing tackle company even recommends the use of this knot with all of its lures.

DOUBLE SNELLING KNOTS (Commonly called Double Salmon Knots)

Many coho and Chinook salmon anglers in the Great Lakes area and on the West Coast use two, three, four—sometimes even six—snelled hooks at the same time, each threaded with a natural bait. This is the best knot to use when snelling more than one hook on a leader.

The Double Snelled Knot takes time and is difficult to tie, but it is an extremely durable connection.

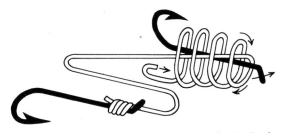

Fig. 1   Snell the lower hook first. Then take the leader from the hook already snelled and loosely wind the end of the leader over the standing part of the leader and the shank of the second hook. Push the leader end through the loose loops.

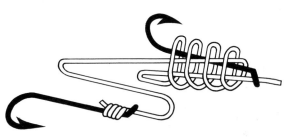

Fig. 2   The leader end must be passed through all of the loops to make the knot secure. Then the tag end and the standing part of the leader are slowly tightened.

RETURN KNOT

This knot was designed for tying monofilament leaders to a fly, lure, or hook eye. Although comparatively few anglers are familiar with the Return Knot, it is very strong and not difficult to tie. This is a particularly valuable knot for tying heavy test nylon to flies or lures.

Fig. 1   Put the end of the line through the hook eye. Wrap the line around the hook, and hold the loop between your thumb and forefinger.

Fig. 2   Make a second turn, like the first, and again hold the loop.

Fig. 3 Pass the end of the line under both loops, and slowly pull on the standing part of the line. As the knot tightens be sure both loops are on the shank side of the hook eye.

Fig. 4 The completed knot, tightened and trimmed.

CRAWFORD KNOT

The Crawford Knot often is overlooked by even the most skilled anglers. It is a very versatile knot for tying most types of hook, swivel, or lure "eyes" to a leader or line.

The Crawford Knot is not nearly so difficult to tie as it looks, and it makes a solid, firm connection.

Fig. 1 Insert the line through the hook eye, leaving about eight inches for tying the knot. Bring the line end back around the standing part of the line to form a loop.

Fig. 2 Now bring the line end under the standing part of the line, and *over* the two parallel lines, as shown.

Fig. 3 The knot has formed a "figure 8." Bring the tag end of the line under the two parallel strands, then back over all three lines.

Fig. 4 The knot is completed by tucking the tag end between the standing line and the front part of the loop. Pull the knot tight, slide it down and "jam" it against the hook eye and trim.

END LOOP KNOT

This loop knot is much easier to tie than it appears. With very little practice it can be tied in just a few seconds.

The End Loop works equally well with braided lines or monofilament. And, too, this knot is often used by some anglers who want a double line that is stronger than the standing part of the single line.

Fig. 1 Double the end of the line, leaving about six inches of doubled line with which to tie the knot.

Fig. 2 Wind the doubled line back over itself five times.

Fig. 3 Take the end of the doubled line and pass it through the first loop. Now tighten the knot by pulling on the standing line and the tag end, as well as on the doubled line.

Fig. 4 The finished End Loop.

BIMINI TWIST KNOT (Often referred to as 20 Times Around Knot, Rollover Knot, and The 100 Percent Knot)

Although some knots perform equally as well as the Bimini, and are easier to tie (such as the Spider Hitch), many anglers still prefer the Bimini Twist for making a double line that will have 100 percent knot strength.

The Bimini Twist is often used by salt water anglers who want a double line for use with offshore trolling rigs. Too, some fishermen use this knot for making a "shock tippet" to use with fly or bait-casting tackle.

The Bimini Twist is valuable because it doubles the test of the single strand of line with which the knot is made.

Although this knot can be tied by one person, it's much easier to make it with the aid of an assistant.

Fig. 1 Double the end of the line along the standing part of the line, for about four feet. Then twist the line 20 times, creating loops, as shown.

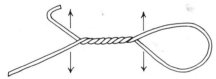

Fig. 2 Pull all four ends apart so that the 20 twists will be forced tightly together, leaving a wide loop.

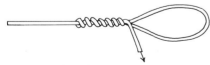

Fig. 3 Keep the twists tightly together, and begin winding the end of the line back over the twists.

Fig. 4 Continue winding the end of the line over the twists until the line reaches the loop.

Fig. 5 Hold the end of the twists with one hand, and make an Overhand Knot around one side of the loop.

Fig. 6 Make an Overhand Knot around the other side of the loop. (Some anglers make this Overhand Knot around the two lines of the loop rather than around just one side and then the other.)

Fig. 7 Wind the line end three times around the two lines of the large loop, and push the end back through the small loop just made.

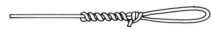

Fig. 8 Slowly pull on the standing line and the large loop to draw the Bimini Twist tight.

DOUBLE LINE LOOP KNOT

The Double Line Loop is difficult to tie. It can be used to make a permanent loop in the end of a line, to which leaders may be tied. Too, this knot may be used to create a "double line" that's stronger than the single line.

Fig. 1 Double the line and wind the end of the line four times over the standing part, leaving a large loop.

Fig. 2 Wind the line end four times back over the wraps just made. Then, with the end of the line, make a simple Overhand Knot around one side of the loop, and tie a Half-Hitch around the other side of the loop.

Fig. 3 Now the two ends of the line are drawn slowly tight. A finger or pencil placed in the loop will prevent the the loop from pulling out.

Fig. 4 The finished Improved Dropper Loop.

IMPROVED DROPPER LOOP (Also known as Blood Dropper Loop)

In recent years some inventive fishermen have begun using the loop with bait casting and spinning equipment. A deep-running lure is tied to the fishing line's end in the conventional manner, then one or two Improved Dropper Loops are tied above the first lure. Other leaders with lures attached are then tied to the loops, and such a rig can make an unusual and often productive trolling outfit.

SPIDER HITCH KNOT

Many anglers around the country are now using the Spider Hitch instead of the Bimini Twist when they want a knot that will double their line. The Spider Hitch can be quickly tied, it has superb knot strength; and it can be tied easily by one person (the Bimini Twist is best tied by two people).

The Spider Hitch can be tied effortlessly—with either nylon monofilament or braided lines—to form a double line having twice the strength of a single strand.

Fig. 1 A two- or three-inch loop is formed in the line. The two lines that cross to form the loop are pinched, and the loop is twisted five times around the two crossed lines. When this is done correctly the loop should appear as in the illustration.

Fig. 1 Double the line, then put a small reverse loop in it.

Fig. 2 The center of the twisted lines is opened and the loop is pushed through.

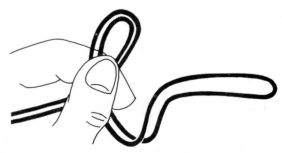

Fig. 2 Hold the reverse loop with thumb and forefinger.

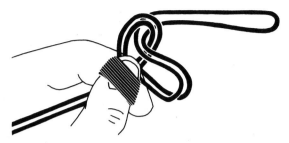

Fig. 3 Wrap the doubled line five times around the thumb and the reverse loop. Then pass the large loop through the small reverse loop.

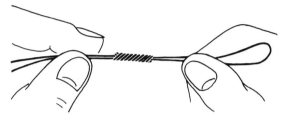

Fig. 4 Slowly pull the large loop so that the line unwinds off the thumb, pulling until the knot tightens.

HAY-WIRE TWIST

This is one of the best ways to link solid wire to any type of connecting ring. The number of wraps and the two different kinds of wraps in the Hay-wire Twist may seem elaborate to many fishermen, but for numerous varieties of salt water fish this tie is absolutely necessary to keep the wire from "pulling out."

Fig. 1 Thread the end of the wire through the hook eye, pulling about five inches of wire through the "eye."

Fig. 2 Bend the end of the wire back over its standing part, forming a small loop.

Fig. 3 Wrap the end of the wire over the standing part of the wire about six or seven times. Then hold the standing part of the wire straight out from the hook eye, and wrap the wire end tightly around it six times at a 90 degree angle.

Fig. 4 Bend the tag end of the wire back and forth until it breaks, and the Hay-wire Twist is completed.

SINGLE-SLEEVE RIG

To rig this connection thread wire through a metal sleeve, pass the wire through the hook eye, then back through the sleeve. Crimp the sleeve and trim the tag end of the wire.

The Single-Sleeve Rig is one of the most popular ways of connecting wire to a hook eye or to a lure. It is commonly used by salt water anglers for light "inshore" fishing.

(Wire and metal sleeves are obtaainable at most tackle shops.)

JOINING WIRE TO BRAIDED LINE

This connection is used by anglers, when fishing for toothy fish such as barracuda, who want to tie wire leaders to braided bait-casting line.

This knot can be difficult to make because the wire tends to kink unless the tie is made with the utmost care.

Fig. 1 Tie a loop in the end of the braided line (use the Spider Hitch or the Perfection Loop). Put the end of the wire through the loop and wrap the end around one side of the loop.

Fig. 2   Wind the wire completely around the loop twice.

Fig. 3   Bring the wire back out through the loop, and wrap it four times around the standing part of the wire.

OVERHAND WIRE WRAP (Occasionally called Barrel Twist)

This is merely the second part of the Hay-wire Twist. The wire end is put through the hook eye and wrapped around the standing part of the wire four or five times at a 90 degree angle.

The Overhead Wire Wrap is a fine connection for use in light salt water fishing. However, when large fish may be encountered a Hay-wire Twist or a Single-Sleeve Rig is usually preferred.

METAL SLEEVE SECURING A LOOP OF WIRE

This is another variation of the Single-Sleeve Rig. It can be used to connect wire to a hook or lure "eye," or it can be used to form a simple wire loop to which a leader or line may be attached.

Fig. 1   Pass the wire through the sleeve and double the wire back toward the sleeve.

Fig. 2   Put the wire through the sleeve again, leaving whatever size loop is desired.

Fig. 3   Turn the end of the wire back into the sleeve.

Fig. 4   Crimp the sleeve firmly and the connection is finished.

QUICK-CHANGE WIRE WRAP

The Quick-Change Wire Wrap is the perfect connection for anglers who need a wire wrap for use with light tackle, yet want the convenience of being able to change lures quickly.

Although this wire wrap is not as strong as some other wire connections, such as the Hay-wire Twist, it is adequate for most light salt water angling.

The trick to making the Quick-Change Wire Wrap is to make the "wraps" of the wire end onto the standing part of the wire somewhat apart. The wide wraps make the tie much stronger than if "tight" wraps were used.

Also, because the wraps are made far apart, the connection is easy to unravel. Thus a lure can be put on or taken off very quickly.

METAL SLEEVE AND KNOT

This is a superb connection for joining heavy wire or cable to a hook. The Metal Sleeve And Knot is adequate for most types of salt water trolling. However, this is a permanent tie that is most practical when used with trolling outfits that will not be "broken down" after each day's use.

Fig. 1   Thread the wire through the sleeve and hook eye.

Fig. 2   Wrap the end of the wire around the standing part of the wire.

Fig. 3   Pass the end through the hook eye again.

Fig. 4   Now bring the wire end through the open loop, through the sleeve, crimp the sleeve tight, and trim the excess wire.

DOUBLE-SLEEVE RIG

This connection is slightly more elaborate than a Single Sleeve Rig, however, the Double-Sleeve Rig is much stronger. For that reason, it is favored by many anglers for attaching cable to large hooks for offshore trolling.

To make this connection, insert wire through two sleeves. Pass the end through the hook eye, then back through one sleeve. Now wrap the wire end once around the standing part of the wire, and push the end through the second sleeve. Crimp both sleeves and trim the excess wire end.

KNOTTING NYLON-COATED WIRE TO MONO LINE

Many veteran anglers believe that this is the best, most secure knot for tying nylon-coated wire line to nylon monofilament line.

It's important when tying this knot to keep the wire line straight while the knot is being pulled tight. This will keep the wire from kinking when the "wraps" of nylon mono are drawn together.

Fig. 1   Form a loop with the wire line and a loop with the mono line. Place the two loops on top of each other, as shown.

Fig. 2   Wrap the monofilament line six times around the wire loop. Then insert the mono end through the wire loop.

Fig. 3   To tighten the knot, slowly pull on the standing parts of both the mono and wire lines.

Fig. 4   The finished knot.

SPECIAL SPOON WRAP (Sometimes referred to as Trolling Spoon Wrap)

This is an excellent way of attaching wire to a spoon or other artificial lure. The Special Spoon Wrap forms a wire loop through the lure's connecting ring and allows the lure to "swim" more life like.

This wire connection is used by many salt water fishing guides for such fish as king mackerel. And, too, it is used by many northern anglers in deep trolling for lake trout.

Fig. 1   Put the end of the wire through a lure's connecting hole or ring twice, leaving about four or five inches of wire with which to make the wrap.

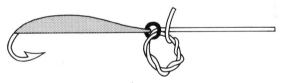

Fig. 2   Wrap the wire end four times around the wire circle formed through the lure's connecting ring.

Fig. 3   Wind the wire end loosely around the standing part of the wire twice, then make several tight wraps around the standing wire, similar to the way a Hay-wire Twist is made.

CHAPTER 23

Feeding Bluegills Betters Bass Fishing

When you draw bluegills to "fish-feeders"
in ponds and lakes, largemouth bass are sure to follow.

By Bob McNally

Fishermen cast to floating plastic ring which supports tray (underwater) filled with fish-food pellets.

A system of artificially feeding bluegills developed recently by Leo Pachner of Kankakee, Ill. has proved to also greatly benefit fishing for largemouth black bass.

Pachner, publisher of *Farm Pond Harvest Magazine*, has demonstrated that by placing fish-feeders in the water and periodically filling them with inexpensive, high protein fish-food pellets (marketed by Ralston Purina Co.) it is possible to maintain a top population of large bluegills (up to three pounds), and thus provide consistently good bluegill fishing.

"Many people who started a bluegill feeding project on a pond, lake, or river, not only have had fine bluegill fishing just beyond their cottage doorsteps, but also great largemouth bass fishing as well," Pachner says with enthusiasm.

When fish-feeders are put out bluegills take up residence right around the feeders. Both big and small bluegills remain near these feeders to eat the pellets they contain. Some largemouth bass also move in to feed on floating food pellets, but what draws really *big* bass to the bluegill feeders are the bluegills themselves. Small bluegills are a *vitally important* food supply for bass.

Leo Pachner with hefty string of bass and bluegills taken by working popping bugs around fish-
feeder.

Food pellets (marketed by Ralston Purina Co.) are
placed in a floating "fish-feeding station" by can
attached to lengthy cane pole.

What this means to the average angler is that not only
can he, his wife, and children catch plenty of scrappy,
good-eating bluegills around these feeders most anytime,
but they also can catch bass that visit the feeder to eat
the bluegills it attracts.

A lot of black bass weighing over six pounds have been
caught "accidentally" by bluegill anglers while fishing
near these fish-feeders. Often, youngsters dunking worms
for bluegills have come up with bass that even would
make serious bass fishermen envious.

Many bass anglers have perfected special techniques
for catching bass around these bluegill feeders. They
set floating bluegill feeders well out from shore over
deep water where big bass lay, and fill the feeders with
fish-attracting food pellets. They're careful, however,
when filling the feeders with pellets, not to alarm any
bass that may be lurking nearby. Feeders can be filled
from shore or a boat. But in either case these fishermen
use a 20 foot pole with a tin can attached to the end to
pour the pellets into the feeder. This way, the fisherman
can stay well away from the feeder when filling it, so he
won't spook bass.

When food pellets are placed in the feeder, bluegills
usually begin a feeding frenzy—then any bass around
move in to gorge themselves on the bluegills. That's when
knowledgeable bass fishermen cast various lures around

the feeder, and frequently they land out-size bass! Other
good techniques that work for bass anglers fishing around
bluegill feeders include night fishing with black plastic
worms, and some bait fishermen even go so far as using
a small three or four inch bluegill as bait.

The first time I experienced this unique type of bass
fishing was at a small six acre farm pond in southern
Illinois. The owner of the pond contacted me and insisted that he had some of the best and most unusual
largemouth bass fishing in the state, and wanted to know
if I'd join him for a day of fishing. Naturally that was an
offer I couldn't refuse.

When I arrived at the pond I was surprised to see several of the new floating bluegill feeders bobbing around
the lake at various spots.

"How do you like the bluegill feeders?" I inquired.

"Just great," he said with a smile. "They're the best
bass attractors I've ever seen!"

"This I've got to see," I thought.

We loaded all our bass fishing gear into a small rowboat, along with a bag of fish-food pellets and a long
cane pole with a tin can attached to its end.

We rowed to the middle of the lake, dropped anchor
near a "bluegill feeder," and he began pouring pellets
into the feeder with the cane pole.

In a few minutes bluegills of all sizes were feeding on
the pellets.

"Just cast that lure of yours to the other side of the bluegill feeder, let it sink a few feet, then reel it in," he said confidently.

I made a cast about 20 feet beyond the feeder, let my lure sink, then retrieved it. As the lure passed the bluegill feeder I felt a good strike, set the hook, and soon landed a two pound bass. After that it was a simple matter of casting to the feeder to catch largemouths—literally one after another.

When the action slowed at one bluegill feeder we'd row to another, put in fish-food pellets, the bluegills would start churning the water, and we'd have great bass fishing.

We caught over 40 largemouth bass that day, weighing from one to 5¾ pounds.

Since that day on that southern Illinois farm pond I've had many people tell me about the fantastic bass angling they've experienced around Pachner's specially designed bluegill feeders. And some of the best and most memorable bass fishing I've had has been on small lakes and ponds where there were several fish-feeders.

Farm pond owners, bluegill fishermen, and bass anglers wanting additional information on this revolutionary "instant bluegill and bass fishing" should write to Leo Pachner, 372 S. East Ave., P.O. Box 884, Kankakee, Ill., 60901 or contact any Ralston Purina dealer.

Here's solid proof that largemouth bass relish bluegills. This 3 pounder went hard for a small bluegill served as bait.

Innovator and impresario of new bluegill, bass "feeding" program is Leo Pachner—shown here nonplussed over a 5-pound bigmouth.

CHAPTER 24

How to Plan a Fishing Trip

Many important factors add up to make, or break, a fishing trip. The tips presented here could save you time, money, and great disappointment.

There s a classic story about a well-known angler who planned a month-long fishing trip to Alaska. Everything was great when he reached Alaska except that his big parcels of fishing tackle were in Brazil! Somehow the airline goofed, and the famed fisherman never received his favorite, specialized equipment in Alaska. He had to content himself with using borrowed fishing gear, but in a professional sense that does a pro-angler no good.

And there's another sad tale of a fisherman who spent a bundle getting to a famous river in Chile. In corresponding and making plans for the trip the camp operator told him to bring "boots." The man brought hip boots instead of chest-high waders, and consequently used up two weeks fishing virtually from shore, unable to wade the rivers properly.

Anyone who has fished much has had experiences similar to the ones outlined above. No matter how carefully fishing trips are planned there are going to be some foul-ups. It seems to be the name-of-the-game. There's no denying though, that thoughtful and careful planning greatly reduces the chances of your having a bad trip. Fishing trips cost money—big money when the trip is for exotic species in distant places—so it's simply good common sense to plan a trip as carefully as possible, and well in advance of departure day.

Experienced fishermen would be surprised at the number of novice anglers who decide overnight they want to go someplace, right away, and "catch a blue marlin," or "take a bonefish on a fly," etc. Few neophytes realize that many fishing camps and guides are booked solid months in advance, and that two days before you want to leave is no time to line up a fishing camp or a guide.

The importance of early planning for fishing trips can't be stressed enough. Where South American trips are concerned, most are planned about six months ahead. It takes that long to make all arrangements. A Florida Keys bonefish or tarpon guide should be booked equally far in advance, and it doesn't hurt to start working on a Canadian fishing trip at least 3–4 months ahead of time.

In planning any fishing trip certainly a few basic factors must be considered. *When* the trip will be made, *how far* you are willing to travel, how much *time* you can afford, and how much *money* you are willing to spend. In other words, given ample *time*, the opportunity to go *when* the fishing will be best, more-or-less unlimited *time*, and when *money* is no account—you have a better than average chance to come up with a world-beating trophy.

In starting to plan any major fishing trip (obviously this doesn't include the guy who intends to go walleye fishing in his own back yard) the first step should be to contact experts in the area, and experts in the kind of fishing you intend doing.

It takes more than clean water and scenery to make a successful fishing trip. There have got to be fish, too.

For example, let's say you are intent on going largemouth bass fishing, but you don't want to just catch some bass, you want a chance to catch a really big one. Assuming you have no leads whatever, you might first write to the angling editors of *Field & Stream*, *Sports Afield*, *Outdoor Life* and *Fishing World* magazines for advice. They've fished for trophy largemouth bass many times in many places, and can recommend various states and lakes, as well as possible fishing camps and guides.

From your correspondence with the angling editors in the outdoors-mag field you've learned that Florida, California, and Texas (merely abritrary choices) look very good for big bass. Your next step, then, should be to write outdoor writers in Florida, California, and Texas, as well as the chiefs of the fishery divisions of the conservation departments of each state.

It's easy, this type of correspondence. You simply write that you are contemplating visiting their state for a bass fishing trip, and tell them what it is you want—whether a huge, mounting-size bass, or that you'd just like a pleasant trip, on a picturesque lake, with a reasonable chance of catching some nice bigmouths.

Contrary to what many people think, you may be surprised how direct both state outdoor writers and conservation department people will be. For the most part, the outdoor writers have nothing to sell, and most of them know what fishing's all about. They'll give you the facts. They'll tell you if this particular spring things don't look very good at such-and-such a lake or elsewhere in their state, and that you'd probably be better off going to Florida, or somewhere. The fisheries biologists of the conservation departments are equally direct, and they'll tell you flat out whether or not prospects are good for fishing in their state that particular season.

These fishermen have come a long way, at great expense, to fish for Arctic char in the Tree River, Northwest Territories. The success of their trip is dependent almost wholly upon the abilities of their outfitter.

Other sources of where-to-go information are state or provincial or national fishing information departments, ads in outdoors magazines by guides, camps, etc., and sport and travel shows. When checking on a fishing camp exhibiting at a sportsman's show, try to meet and talk with the camp operator. You can learn more about his place, and about him, in a few minutes conversation than in long hours of studying brochures—which might even contain photos of fish caught somewhere else.

If you read an account of fabulous fishing at a spot in June, it doesn't follow that you'll experience the same angling there in August. In fact, the opposite is probable. Try to arrange trips so that you'll be at a place as close to the right time as possible.

When you get lined up with a camp operator or guide, and are corresponding, try to pin him down to specifics. Make him tell you precisely *how* his fishing is done. Is it all trolling? Does he recommend live bait when what you want to do is fly fish? Will the fish be deep or shallow while you're there? How far is the fishing from camp? Must you run three hours by outboard to get where the fish are, or will you have to make time-consuming portages? Has the camp owner trained his guides? Has he taught them how to handle the boat for casters, and how to land fish properly? Has he told them that the fisherman who is paying the freight is damn well captain of the ship and not the guide? Exactly what kind of fishing and conditions can you expect?

It's usually best to shy away from any camp whose owner *guarantees* that, day after day, you will fill the boat with contest-winning lunkers. Nowhere is the fishing so good that it can, day by day, be "guaranteed."

Much to be preferred is the camp operator who says, "Look, friend. We've got a damn good lake. It may not be the best in the world, but if the weather holds and the fish behave as usual, and if you work at it a little, you should get some pretty good action."

Bad weather can foul up many a "fly-in" fishing trip so that there is no "fly out" for many days. Fishermen shouldn't plan such trips on tight schedules.

Certainly the best recommendation for any fishing camp is that the operator is an astute and dedicated fisherman. Prospects for your personal enjoyment are even better if the camp operator likes the kind of fish you like, and prefers catching them the way you do.

As a general thing, the camp owner who is a serious sport fisherman (as opposed to meat fisherman) will not operate a camp where the fishing usually is poor or where other factors make it less than par. Such sincere operators normally will close a poor camp and find a better one elsewhere.

In getting details from your prospective camp operator or guide, have him describe the "housekeeping routine." You're going to live in a houseboat on the lake, right? Okay, fine. But what kind of houseboat? How old

An offshore fishing trip can be only a boat ride if the captain, mate, boat, or tackle do not come up to par.

or new is it? How many men stay in one room? Do you sleep on bunks, cots, air-mattresses? What? Learn what sort of living and sleeping arrangements there will be, and you'll know better what to expect and exactly what little extras of equipment to take along.

How many guides and boats will there be? Many fishermen have taken off on trips presuming that, for the price quoted them, there was to be one guide and one boat for each *two fishermen*—only to discover that there was one guide and boat for each *three* or *four fishermen*. If you want a guide and boat for each *two fishermen*, be sure the camp-operator understands that well in advance. He may have to make special preparations for extra guides and boats.

What about the cooking and food? Is someone in the fishermen's group expected to handle the cooking, or will a cook be provided? It's usually cheaper when the fishermen handle their own cooking, but that usually means one angler will have to stay behind in camp each day to prepare meals. And you'll probably have to make arrangements for provisions, too.

Knowing something in advance about the area you'll be fishing is very helpful. For example, the lake might be such that hooking 5 and 6 pound bass in a jungle of flooded timber is not unusual. Knowing that will help you select the proper rod, reel, and line. Have the guide or camp owner suggest what he considers a "proper rod," along with reel type, correct clothing, quantity and type of lures, monofilament or wire leaders, footwear, etc.

It's always a good idea to check with camp owners regarding the possibility of mishaps. For example, what if a member of the party suddenly suffers appendicitis, a broken leg, heart attack, snakebite, etc. A good guide or camp operator anticipates emergencies. Usually it is possible for them to get an ill person out of the "bush" or off the lake and to safety in quick order, or to have help brought in.

It's a good idea, too, to take along a quality first-aid kit of your own. A kit of this nature should include not only the obvious things such as aspirin and Band-aids, but several kinds of antibiotics, butterfly closures, medicines to fight diarrhea, food poisoning, nausea, etc. A plastic tackle box is perfect to carry this stuff in, and a first-aid box such as this comes in mighty handy on many trips.

Once you've pretty well settled on a particular guide or fishing camp, ask for names of some recent former clients or guests, and their addresses. You should then contact those people and ask for a recommendation on the camp, querying them about results of their trip, quality of the fishing, etc. Remember that the very best information on a fishing area, guide or camp comes from the man who's done it before you.

Something else to be dead certain of before committing yourself finally to a camp or guide is price—that's spelled PRICE! Many a sportsman and his fishing host have had serious falling outs because of misunderstandings over costs. If you're making a major trip, such as a South American fishing jaunt, ask the camp owner you're dealing with to give you an itemized cost sheet.

If you've queried properly and planned properly there should be no unexpected charges at the end of any fishing trip. And don't be afraid to ask about costs. A lot of

Fishing trips cost money—big money when the trip is for exotic species such as Arctic grayling, so it's smart to plan trips as carefully as possible. This fisherman on Saskatchewan's Clearwater River is there at the height of the black fly season, but the grayling are wonderful!

sportsmen who may be rather financially well-fixed sometimes don't bother inquiring about what they think will be incidental costs, and later when it comes time to pay find that the cost is anything but "incidental."

Package fishing trips are becoming increasingly popular, and in general they are bargains, with the camps and the fishing checked and tested by the various organizations involved in working up the package. Airlines, sportsmen travel agencies, camp owners, and sometimes governmental agencies cooperate in arranging such trips. As a result, these trips normally work out well.

Many wilderness fishing lodges book their parties months before seasons start. Making reservations early is the name-of-the-game.

If you'll not be fishing out of an established lodge or camping out, but rather using in-town facilities such as motels or hotels, make your reservations well in advance. Remember that there may not be three people in that motel in Hayward any day in March, but the day before the walleye season opens it's filled to its closets and, in fact, there's not a room available for 100 miles around.

In planning any fishing trip that you'll be conducting "on your own," that is without benefit of guides, check in advance with wardens, park rangers, "local residents," etc., in the area you want to fish, asking about lakes, rivers, where to fish, etc.

Catches like this are not routine when rivers are too high, too low, too clear, or too muddy. When you go fishing is as important as where!

Finally, be most sure of your fishing partner. Old friends will know each other well and will get-along, but if your angling trip will be with someone "new," try to be sure ahead of time that he'll make the kind of companion you prefer. If possible, go on a couple of short, near-to-home fishing trips with your new pal—before the big one—so that you can get to know him better.

It's not important whether the fishing partner be a banker, baker, or barber. What's important is that he be enthusiastic, of even disposition, willing to take some physical discomforts without griping, polite, honest, and willing to accept his share of the responsibilities. A good fishing companion also is one who enjoys the trip, without complaining, even when few fish have been caught. You have a right to expect those traits of your fishing partner—just as he has a right to expect them of you.

A successful fishing trip with good company is one of life's treasures; a fishing trip with bad company, regardless of fish caught, is pure misery.

CHAPTER 25

Florida's Ten Best Bass Lakes

Here's an up-to-the-minute guide to Florida's trophy largemouths

By Elgin White

Florida, in all modesty, claims to be the "bass capital of the world."

This must be so. After all, there are several areas within the borders of the Sunshine State that lay claim to that title, and if you put them all together, then it must be valid.

This claim has been shot at for years by other areas in the nation that also boast their lakes and streams produce as many black bass as Florida.

Maybe so. But where else but in Florida are you going to catch a preponderance of black bass that reach up to 16–18 pounds?

True, the world's record catch of 22 pounds, 8 ounces came from an obscure lake in Georgia way back in 1933, but that was before Florida bass began reading the papers. As a matter of fact, there have been stories (and when you discuss fishing anywhere tall tales figure into the conversation with regularity) that have some bass as high as 24–25 pounds being caught in Florida lakes, but the fish were devoured before being weighed for all-star records.

Some skin divers who have found a mecca for their particular activity in many Florida clear-water lakes, claim to have had an eye-ball-to-eye-ball confrontation with black bass that could qualify for a movie about Jonah.

Be that as it may, Florida still ranks at the head of the class when it comes to bass fishing, and among the state's 30,000 named lakes and streams are some of the fightingest denizens in the annals of the sport of bass fishing.

Suffice it to say not all those 30,000 lakes have swarms of sportin'-size bass. So, let's take a look at what might be considered Florida's top ten bass lakes.

For lunker-size bass, Lake Jackson, on the outskirts of Tallahassee, has to be considered numero uno. This 4,000 acres of clear water has disgorged fish up to 18 and 20 pounds in the decade since it went dry and then returned to near normalcy.

Lake Jackson has a habit of that. It happened last time in 1955 and 1956, and the land of large lunkers simply meandered away, leaving a mere pothole in dead center where folks from miles around came and picked up bass and panfish by the bucketsfull.

Jackson came back in 1957, and in the interim, thousands of fingerlings that survived in other potholes around the big lake grew to some size, and by 1959 and 1960, Lake Jackson was teeming with bass big enough to pull a boat.

Lake Jackson, near Tallahassee, is one of Florida's outstanding big bass waters . . .

. . . and lunker largemouth being boated here is ample proof. Fish weighed just under 10 pounds.

It still is THE place for huge lunkers, although you probably won't catch as many total numbers of fish in Jackson as in other Florida lakes. Jackson is weedy, and it takes a good fisherman to haul a prize winner aboard. But the prize winners are in there—some claim the new world champ is among those weeds.

There are a number of fishing camps at Lake Jackson, with a convenient one right on U.S. 27 leading into Tallahassee. Guides, bait, boats, and motors are available at all camps. Accommodations are scarce, but Tallahassee abounds in fine motels and hotels and all are within easy driving distance from Lake Jackson.

Another famous fishing lake in North-Central Florida is Lake George, on the famed St. Johns River. Lake George is situated in Volusia County just north of State Road 40, midway between Daytona Beach and Ocala.

Covering better than 46,000 square acres, Lake George has long been a mecca for bass anglers from all over the world, and in spite of a great increase in people living around the periphery of the lake, it is still one of Florida's top bass spots.

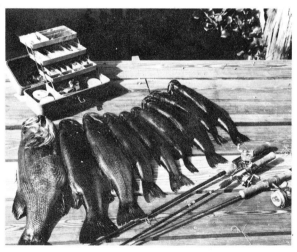

Nine bass from Lake George—from five to 12 pounds!

Just north of Lake George on the St. Johns is the Rodman Pool. To say this is an area of controversy is putting it mildly. The Rodman Pool was born during early construction of the Cross-Florida Barge Canal. This project has subsequently been placed in abeyance by executive order of the President, and there are still arguments pro and con on whether or not that waterway ever will be finished.

But fish could care less. When the Pool was first filled and the impoundment settled into an area of 1,800 square acres, fishing was fantastic. Bass and panfish spilled into the Pool from the waters of the scenic Okla-waha River and in spite of periodic drawdowns of the water level of Rodman, it still remains one of Florida's ten best spots.

Accommodations abound in several nearby communities, including Palatka, Welaka, Fruitland, Georgetown, and Salt Springs. Principal access is by boat from the St. Johns River through the lock that operates at regular intervals, starting at daylight.

Another prime bass fishing lake in northern Florida is a primeval stretch of water that flows from the upper reaches of the Chipola River. The Chipola meanders down through some really wild country to near Wewahitchka, where an impoundment there forms the mystic and magnificent Dead Lakes.

The Dead Lakes is close to the Apalachicola River in Gulf and Calhoun Counties in Northwest Florida. It is easily reached by State Road 71, which parallels the lake between Blountstown on the north and Port St. Joe on the south.

The lakes cover 3,659 square acres and harbor some of the most beautiful, placid waters anywhere in the world. Magnificent stands of cypress trees accentuate the stillness of the entire basin, and bass, panfish, and fresh-water catfish mosey around the bark of those trees in deep, black water.

There are numerous fish camps at various points along the 10-mile-long lake where boats, motors, bait, and guides are available. Many of these camps have fine accommodations, too.

The Dead Lakes are in a section of Florida that is a far cry from some of the densely populated regions in the peninsular section of the State. Good farmlands surround the lakes, and it is an area that is ripe for industrial expansion that is compatible with Florida's program of development. In fact, the State's Division of Commercial Development has instituted such a program for this area of the State, and recreational lures such as the Dead Lakes and the nearby Florida Gulf Coast make the region outstanding for industrial growth.

The coffer dam that creates the impoundment of the Dead Lakes also creates a bustling activity in February and March each year. Salt-water striped bass move into the Apalachicola River and over to the coffer dam in numbers, and anglers have pulled stripers out of those waters weighing up to 60 pounds.

Another prime Florida bass fishing lake is found in Sumter County, farther down the Gulf Coast. Interstate 75 feeds into Lake Panasoffkee, which is just a cast away from the junction of 75 and the Sunshine State Parkway.

Lake Panasoffkee covers 4,460 square acres, and the water levels are controlled by the flow of the Withlacoochee River through a large canal.

Numerous camps dot the shoreline of Lake Panasoffkee, and there are a number of communities within short driving distance, including Leesburg, Wildwood, and Inverness.

Just a stone's throw west of Lake Panasoffkee is Tsala Apopka, another of Central Florida's top bass areas. This lake lies entirely within Citrus County, and is actually a series of lakes interconnected at three separate levels or pools in order to keep a constant water level.

Tsala Apopka, like Panasoffkee, is connected to the Withlacoochee River by canals. Three communities on the lake also lend their names for the various pools. At the south is Floral City, Inverness is in the middle, and Hernando is to the north.

Each community has a number of motels and fishing resorts that cater to visiting anglers. U.S. 41 passes the lake to the west and Interstate 75 is about 20 miles to the east, with State Road 44 the exit turn to reach the lake.

The combined Tsala Apopka chain of lakes cover better than 19,000 square acres, and long has been considered this area's best bass fishing region.

Lake Poinsett, just west of Cocoa in Brevard County, lies near the headwaters of the St. Johns River. The lake covers slightly more than 4,400 square acres, and its periphery is dotted with good fish camps and accommodations, with boats, guides, bait, and abundance of fishing information.

If accommodations around the lake do not suit your fancy, there are plenty of good motels, hotels, and apartments in Cocoa, the southern anchor city to Cape Kennedy.

Interstate 95 is the most convenient route to Lake Poinsett, with famous U.S. 1 just a few miles to the east. The closest exit from Interstate 95 to the lake is State Road 520.

numerous wading possibilities, particularly those who like to use a fly rod.

Tohopekaliga covers 18,810 square acres, but that is only half the size of Lake Kissimmee, a few miles south. Kissimmee is 34,948 acres of really good bass-fishing country. In between lakes Kissimmee and Tohopekaliga are lakes Hatchineha and Cypress, the other two bodies that make up the Kissimmee River basin chain of lakes.

Central Florida is dotted with dozens of superb bass lakes. This is a view of Tsala Apopka Lake.

Kissimmee bass came out of heavy stuff to wallop surface plug.

There is a chain of four lakes in the Kissimmee River basin that forms still another of Florida's treasure chests of bass fishing.

Lake Tohopekaliga (don't try to pronounce it), in Osceola County, is the second largest lake in the chain and rests on the outskirts of the town of Kissimmee, up until a year or so ago just a thriving cattle town.

But along came Mickey Mouse and Kissimmee and environs have become an outpost to Walt Disney World and as a result is a fast-growing bustling city.

That hasn't changed the fishing. Tohopekaliga has numerous fine fishing camps around its perimeter, with some of them offering outstanding accommodations. There are many excellent motels in Kissimmee, too, especially since the opening of Disney World.

The eastern shore of Lake Tohopekaliga is fairly shallow and the firm bottom will allow a fisherman

Lake Kissimmee is about 20 miles east of the city of Lake Wales, where the famous Singing Tower and Mountain Lake Sanctuary are located. There are a number of good fishing resorts on the lake, offering every facility to satisfy the most finicky angler.

And last, but certainly not least or smallest, on our list of Florida's top ten bass lakes, is the biggest of them all, Lake Okeechobee.

Known for years as one of the nation's best for bass angling, this 448,000-square-acre lake, the second largest fresh-water lake wholly within the boundaries of the United States, lures fishermen from all corners of the nation.

Okeechobee features a huge dike, or levee, better than 85 miles in length, along the north, southeast, south, and southwest shorelines, that contains the shallow lake water.

The dike was constructed back in the 1930s to prevent a recurrence of the tragic hurricane in 1928 when thousands of lives were lost, mostly to flooding.

Outstanding fish camps, accommodations, and complete marine facilities dot the entire shoreline of Lake Okeechobee, for within its shallow depths is some of the finest bass fishing in the world.

Okeechobee is almost fifty miles across, and from the air resembles a huge silver dollar plopped into the edges of the Florida Everglades. When bass fishermen first started coming into Florida, Okeechobee was their first destination. Partly because it was so big you couldn't miss it and partly because it was the only lake anybody knew anything about, Lake Okeechobee became synonymous with black-bass fishing in the Sunshine State.

The towns of Clewiston, Belle Glade, Moore Haven, Okeechobee, and South Bay are well equipped with some of the finest fresh-water fishing camps and marinas to be found. Motels are abundant as are some really outstanding restuarants. Little wonder, then, that Lake Okeechobee remains one of Florida's prime bass-fishing lakes.

The lakes listed herein do not constitute Florida's total supply of good bass fishing areas by a long shot. But they are what many Florida anglers consider the Top Ten in number of fish, size, availability, locale, and facilities.

Broad, immense, reed-filled Lake Okechobee has long been a mecca for the nation's bass anglers. George Seaman shows a seven pounder that hit a porkrind eel.

FLORIDA'S TEN BEST BASS LAKES

1. JACKSON
2. GEORGE
3. RODMAN
4. DEAD LAKES
5. PANASOFFKEE
6. TSALA APOPKA
7. POINSETT
8. TOHOPE KALIGA
9. KISSIMMEE
10. OKEECHOBEE

CHAPTER 26

Fly Fishing for Seatrout

You do not have to be an expert to catch dozens of seatrout on flies, bugs.

By Bob McNally

Spotted seatrout (*Cynoscion nebulosus*) are one of the most abundant and sought after "inshore" salt water gamefish. And although the most common methods of angling for these fish are with artificial plugs and jigs and also with a variety of natural baits, fact is, spotted seatrout will *readily* take streamer flies and popping bugs.

It shouldn't surprise knowledgeable anglers that fly rod streamers and poppers are pure poison for spotted seatrout. These fish feed primarily on small forage minnows and shrimp, and no artificial lure resembles real fish food better or is more life-like in the water, than a fly or popping bug. Streamers and poppers are versatile and can be tied many different ways so that they resemble *any type* of natural forage food. Too, there's something about the way a fly or bug can be slowly, and tantalizingly, retrieved, with its hair or feathers gently undulating, that drive spotted seatrout wild.

These fish—which are commonly called seatrout, spotted squeteague, spotted weakfish, speckled trout, corbina, "spots," "specks," or just simply "trout"—are abundant from the Chesapeake Bay all along the Eastern Seaboard, and throughout the Gulf Coast states to the Mexican border. However, a few places have particularly good seatrout fishing and deserve special mention.

Fly-rodder works a shallow bay for seatrout.

The area around Cocoa, Florida, on that state's east coast, has exceptional spotted seatrout fishing. The Cocoa region produces more large "seatrout" than any other section of North America. Every year hundreds of "trout" between 6 and 12 pounds are taken, which is why Cocoa residents refer to their town as the "world's seatrout capital."

Large trout also will take the fly fisherman's offerings. This 6-pound trout took a popping bug in Florida's Loxahatchee River.

Trout of this size, about ¾ pound, will readily hit a variety of flies and bugs. Streamers and shrimp patterns shown are ideal.

The Texas coast has many excellent areas for seatrout. One of the best places is San Luis Pass, at the lower end of Galveston Island, which is a favorite spot for wading-anglers coming from the nearby city of Houston. At certain times, particularly during the winter months, it's nothing to see wade-fishermen with enormous stringers of spotted seatrout, with many fish exceeding 5 pounds.

Another superb location for trout along the Texas coast is a bay-like area known as "Laguna Madre." This protected shallow "bay" extends from Corpus Christi Bay almost to the Mexican border. "Laguna Madre" averages 3-miles wide and is 100-miles long, so there's plenty of elbow room for fishermen. This area is well known for its outsized spotted seatrout and is a popular place among both wading and boating anglers.

A nice string of Galveston Island, Texas trout, weighing 4 to 6½ pounds each, all hooked on streamer flies.

One of the most overlooked places for seatrout, but certainly one of the best, is the Tampa Bay region on Florida's west coast—right in the back yard of cities such as Tampa, St. Petersburg, Clearwater, and Sarasota. The best trout fishing in this area is during the winter months. When temperatures drop and the water gets chilly seatrout school in shallow water areas and are set-ups for light tackle fishermen—especially fly-rodders.

One winter I fished this region with Roger Cavallo, proprietor of a restaurant in Tampa, and good friend Herb Allen, Outdoors Editor of the *Tampa Tribune*. We worked sand bottom flats and "turtle-grass" shallows around the Anclote Keys near the town of Tarpon Springs. Cavallo and Allen both fished plastic bodied "shrimp" jigs with spinning outfits, while I worked streamers.

Although both Allen and Cavallo complained the fishing was poor because of unusually *warm weather* for that time of year, in a couple of hours we caught *dozens* of seatrout ranging from 1 to 4 pounds. By casting my streamers out, letting them sink a couple of feet, and then retrieving them with foot-long hauls, I took as many "specks" on flies as my two companions combined caught on jigs.

Most large streamers will take some spotted seatrout. Bucktail, marabou, and saddle hackle streamers all take fish, and expert anglers switch from one type streamer to another until one type produces well. Accomplished salt water fly-rodders also prefer streamers with a bit of mylar (a non-tarnishing silver material resembling Christmas tree tinsel) tied in. They believe the added flash of the mylar helps attract hungry seatrout.

Streamers for seatrout should be tied on size 1, 1/0, or 2/0 quality stainless steel (non-corroding) hooks. The large, heavy hooks won't rust, and they sink quickly —getting down to where the fish are.

Best streamer colors are all yellow, all white, pink, blue, or green, or combinations of those colors. Although most streamers can be productive, some experts favor patterns such as the Micky Finn, Grey Ghost, Black Ghost, Light Tiger, White Marabou, Yellow Marabou, and Yellow Butcher Streamers.

Spotted seatrout are especially fond of moving in with a rising tide to search grassy bottom areas for shrimp, and because of this many competent fly rod anglers use flies imitating those crustaceans. Most small flies used for bonefish, such as Phillips' Shrimp Fly and their Bonefish Fly, are very good for seatrout seeking shrimp.

Often, spotted seatrout are found close to the bottom in areas dense with "turtle-grass." Under these conditions a weedless fly is extremely valuable.

Streamers tied on "keel fly hooks" are good weedless flies. The bend and barb of these hooks are turned up, rather than down, so few weeds foul your fly when its retrieved. And striking fish are easily hooked because nothing obstructs the hook point, as is the case with many weedless popping bugs and other artificial lures.

Another excellent weedless streamer is the "Ruffed Neck." This fly was developed only recently. It's a bucktail streamer that's tied with the bucktail underneath the hook shank, rather than above the shank. The bucktail is tied at the hook eye as usual. But before the fly is completed the bucktail is bunched up behind and underneath the fly's "head" and several wraps of tying thread are wound around behind the bulged bucktail to form a ¼-inch ridge.

At first glance the fly doesn't look any more "weedless" than any other streamer. However, because the buoyant bucktail is tied *under* the hook shank the hook point rides *up* in the water rather than down. And, too, the clump of bunched-up bucktail helps deflect weeds and snags away from the hook point. Some fishermen tie weighted "Ruffed Neck" flies, which helps the fly get down to seatrout very quickly.

Occasionally seatrout feed almost exclusively on needlefish. In south Florida this happens quite frequently

Even the smaller trout often will hit a large salt water type popping bug.

in tidal bays at night, and it's at these times that a fly-rodder needs a fly that will resemble a needlefish. Streamer flies that have a long, slender silhouette get the most strikes from seatrout working on needlefish. Fly patterns such as the Ugly Duckling, Balsa Streamer, Hamada Silversides, and Bluefish Streamer are especially good.

When "spotted squeteague" move into shallow bays, and when the water's surface isn't whipped by the wind, working popping bugs is an exciting way of taking fish.

Most quality, salt water popping bugs work well for "spots," and some fresh water bass bugs are okay. But experienced fishermen insist that poppers be made on large, 3X long, 1/0, or 2/0 stainless steel hooks. Poppers painted all white, pink, yellow, and red, or combinations of those colors are preferred.

Finding good quality poppers can be difficult, so most fly-rodders make their own.

Not only are pan-size trout fun on a fly outfit but they are delicious in the pan.

Several years ago I designed a popper for spotted seatrout. It's made to simulate a wounded needlefish floating injured on the surface. It's called the "Pencil Bug." This bug has a 3-inch long pencil shaped cork body with a pointed head, and several long saddle hackles tied in for a tail. The "Pencil Bug" is tied on flat or ball-eye hooks which help keep the bug from "diving" when retrieved. Because of its pointed head and long, slender body this bug has an erratic action when retrieved.

Bill Gallasch, a Richmond, Virginia fly-tier, commercially makes a popper called the "Skipping Bug." This is a well-made balsa-body bug with bucktail affixed into the rear-end of the bug. It's available in several sizes and is a good one for seatrout.

Another excellent, "home-made" popper that should be in every fly-rodder's kit is the "Bullet Bug." My dad, Tom McNally, developed this bug years ago for striped bass and bluefish in Chesapeake Bay, then discovered it worked like magic on spotted seatrout. When retrieved this bug doesn't "pop," but skitters along just beneath the surface like a wounded minnow. Overall the bug measures 4-inches long, has a bullet-shaped cork head and flowing saddle hackles. Two feathers are wound palmer-style behind the cork body.

When seatrout are in fairly shallow, clear water a big streamer or popping bug will produce as many fish or more than conventional casting lures.

For daylight fishing, flies and bugs usually should be retrieved rather fast. The fly or popper should be cast to "fishy" spots such as the mouths of inlets, the edges of tidal rips, against reefs and over grass beds or along jetties—then brought back in long, quick hauls. A short, jerky retrieve will sometimes do the trick but spotted seatrout usually prefer a fast moving fly—they like action.

When your streamer or popper alights point your rod tip at it, then with the left hand haul in line in big, quick strokes. That makes the lure jump along—and if there's a "speck" around he'll jump right after it.

When night fishing for trout retrieve flies and poppers *super slow*. For the most part, at night real forage fish hang motionless in the water, and move in quick spurts. But seatrout normally take them only when they are idle. Give spotted seatrout plenty of time to strike by imparting a stop-and-go retrieve to all your poppers and streamers.

Seatrout are school fish. Consequently, some anglers fish two or more streamers simultaneously. The flies are tied to the fly leader with Extension Blood Knots. Many times two or more trout are hooked at the same time when this technique is employed.

Many clever seatrout fly fishermen use a popping bug with a weighted streamer fly rigged on a length of monofilament and tied to the popper's hook shank. The popper-and-streamer are blazes to cast, but it is an excellent method of taking trout. The popping bug on this rig should be "popped" very loudly which attracts fish to either the streamer trailing below or even to the popper. This technique is very much akin to the "popping-cork-rig" used by many commercial seatrout fishermen, and it is particularly effective when "squeteague" are scattered over a wide area and difficult to locate.

Drift-fishing is the most common method of fishing for spotted seatrout. Anglers motor upwind and then drift and cast until they take a fish. Because trout are school fish it's usually true that "where there's one, there's more." Therefore most fishermen anchor and cast until the action slows. Then they drift with the wind again until they find more fish. Fly fishermen working from boats prefer vessels with large "casting decks" that are free of fly-line-fouling obstructions.

Wade-fishing also is a popular way of catching "spotted weakfish." Because much less water can be "covered" by a wading-angler, fishermen should be well familiar with the area fished if they want to be very successful. Too, wade-fishing can be dangerous. A fisherman unfamiliar with tidal changes and undertow in the area he's wading easily can get into very serious trouble.

Fly casting while wading normally is very easy because there's nothing to tangle fly line, and there's plenty of room for long back casts. But some anglers like to use "shooting baskets," which hold their fly line neatly and make distance casting quite simple.

More trout are taken at distances of 40 to 60 feet than are caught on casts dropping within 20 feet of the boat. So while it's not necessary to be a tournament-type caster, you must be able to handle your tackle reasonably well.

The fly-rodder who masters the "double-haul," and can cast a streamer or popping bug 70 or 100 feet, letting his tackle do the work, won't suffer casting fatigue and will be far more successful than the inept caster who, after only an hour or two of casting, is completely worn out. Tiring from fly casting forces the poor fly-rodder to pick up a spinning or bait-casting outfit.

Generally speaking, typical bass bugging tackle is perfect for spotted seatrout. Rods 8 to 9½-feet long, weighing about 5 ounces, with a rather heavy action built for handling WF8 or WF9 lines, are great. Some salt water buffs equip their fly rods with special guides that help prevent salt water corrosion. However, if you thoroughly wash your fly outfit with fresh water after every excursion in the "salt" it won't rust.

Big, expensive, specialized salt water fly reels with superb quality drags aren't needed for trout. Good single-action reels with interchangeable spools, such as those normally used for bass bugging, are perfect. These reels *must be washed* with fresh water after each use in salt water to prevent them from corroding.

Serious spotted seatrout fishermen equip themselves with several different type fly lines for different angling situations. Floating lines are used with popping bugs. "Sink tip" fly lines are employed when "specks" are down a few feet, and these forward sinking lines take a fly down adequately. Some fly-rodders even use fast-sinking "shooting-head" lines, making it possible to take trout when they are 20-feet down.

Nylon leaders from 9 to 12-feet long, tapered to 6-pound tippets, will do for most spotted seatrout fishing. Seatrout have dozens of small, needle-like teeth, plus two very large canine teeth at the tip of the upper mandible. However, heavy-test "shock tippets" usually aren't needed.

Many experienced salt water anglers consider fishing for spotted seatrout pretty "tame." But, by using a fly rod with streamers or poppers, fishing for seatrout takes on a whole new, sporty outlook!

CHAPTER 27

How and Why to Use Salmon Eggs

Salmon eggs are a natural fish food. They attract by feel or texture, odor, taste and color. They are gulped down by fry and fingerling and consumed in vast quantities by mature fish, providing forage for all species inhabiting the same waters. Hordes of trout and char follow salmon runs, as they pour into their natal streams from the ocean and the Great Lakes, to feed on loose eggs, swept by the current from the spawning nests. Brown trout, notorious cannibals, shake hands and raid brookie beds, one brown gorging on eggs, while its companion plays stand-off with the frantic parent. And even those happy little warriors, the bluegills, gang up like dead-end kids and hustle lunker large mouth bass off their nests to get at the clutch.

Although crudely processed, salmon eggs have been used by Indians, inhabiting our coastal waters, since time immemorial. Their cooked, opaque eggs, prepared at streamside to toughen them for the hook, hardly match the colorful and more natural roe produced by modern technology. But, they knew a great bait, when they saw it!

FEEL OR TEXTURE

Feel, texture and consistency are words you will hear quite often, during any discussion of salmon eggs. But they all mean the same thing: the egg's degree of firmness, important because firmness has much to do with the effectiveness of the egg as a bait.

Hatchery studies have shown, for example, that trout will mouth, then drop, hard food pellets. Conversely, they are quick to grab and swallow soft foods. Occasionally, processed eggs may appear to be too firm. They can be softened by gently rolling them between thumb and forefinger. In other instances, they may be too soft and more like fresh eggs, which are difficult to hold on the hook. Usually, they will take on body, firm up, if exposed to the air for awhile. If exposure doesn't produce the desired feel or consistency, add a few grains of salt to the jar. The saline touch, with its side contribution as a taste/smell additive, is very effective.

TASTE AND ODOR

Anyone who has done his homework knows that most fish have acute senses of taste and smell which enable them to find their food, often when they can't even see it. And, in the case of smell, frequently from a considerable distance.

Uncle Josh salmon eggs cater to these dual senses with cheese and fish oil scents, flushed into the water by the milking action of the eggs. Cheese and cheese scent are, of course, old trout standbys. The oil scent, comparable to the odor we smell in a hatchery tank full of yearlings, is the same odor fish smell, as the eggs drift in the current.

COLOR

One way or another, color attracts, adding the visual factor to those of egg texture, odor and taste. However, its influence will vary from day to day, water to water and from one area to another. To compensate for these variations in time, place and preference, Uncle Josh salmon eggs are processed in several life-like colors.

You will find them bottled in natural, light and medium shades, in red, fluorescent red, in light fluorescent red and dark fluorescent red. Once the eggs have been deposited, however, and exposed to the water, they assume the paler hues, referred to as "light," "medium" and "natural." If you are uncertain about which color or colors to use, take a tip from the old timers and carry an assortment in your tackle box.

FISHING THE SINGLE EGG

Spawned eggs, jarred from the nest by the current or some other disturbance, generally tumble downstream as singletons. While it's a lonely trip for the little embryos, a single egg, impaled on a hook, is the most natural way to fish them. Here's how the experts do it, matching hook size to the size of the egg to be used:
1. Insert point of *sharpened* hook just under the egg skin. Make hole as small as possible.
2. Work egg up shank and over eye. 3. Rotate egg over hook point. 4. Push egg down onto hook point. 5. Leave only bend of hook, supporting egg, visible.

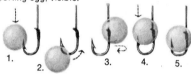

If tactics call for more than one egg, use a small cluster or several singles, which can be slipped onto a larger hook like beads.

For trout, in most situations, a 6 lb. test monofilament line and a 1 to 3 lb. leader are sufficient. Before joining the line and leader, slip a small, egg-type sinker . . . it will have a hole bored down the middle . . . onto the line. Then, between the line and leader, tie in the smallest swivel available. The center hole in the sinker lets it ride up and down the line, but the little swivel prevents it from sliding onto the leader.

This type of rig will allow fish to grab the egg, turn and move off, without feeling any undue drag, because the slack line will play through the sinker which, normally, will be lying on the bottom.

FISHING CLUSTER EGGS AND EGG SACS

Clusters and sacs are "gob" baits, put up, primarily, for large fish. They are especially effective in the spring and fall for coho, chinook, steelhead, rainbow and brown trout, sea-run cutthroat and Dolly Varden. Hook sizes 1/0 and 2/0 are appropriate.

Cluster eggs, fished loose, are a tacky mass bottled without any artificial covering. They also are the stuffing for egg sacs, which are made by wrapping a cluster the size of a thumbnail in a 3-inch square of maline cloth, a light netting available at dry goods stores. Pulled snug and tight around the cluster, the netting is secured at the top with thread or a piece of bright yarn. Both baits are fished the same way, with sinkers, and allowed to drift freely and close to the bottom.

For clusters, use a strong, extra short shank hook. Tie the leader down the shank of the hook, leaving a loop. Impale the cluster on the hook, then work the leader loop around it and pull tight. For sacs, many fishermen prefer the same general pattern, but with a slice in the shank to hold the sac in position.

STREAM FISHING

Because salmon eggs are a natural food, your presentation should follow, with all the magic you can muster, the free-wheeling pattern of a single egg or cluster, traveling the current and close to the bottom. Ideally, the sinker will touch bottom every few feet, while the current lifts and floats the bait. Depending on your ability to read water and to detect and avoid snags, you may expend several casts and many long moments observing the action of the current, before it carries your bait at the proper speed and into the proper areas.

As in all stream fishing, strive for accuracy and cast to cover . . . brushy and undercut banks, logs, boulders, rocks and every nook and cranny of fishy-looking water in the drift. Work each thoroughly and systematically and in small areas at a time, for these are the holding grounds where fish lie doggo, waiting for the current to bring them food.

LAKE FISHING

Catching fish in lakes calls for techniques different from those used in rivers and streams. The fish are often extremely wary and light leaders and small, hidden hooks are essential. Equally important, eggs should be worked around springs and over gravel and sand bottoms near cover. Despite their color and smell, they won't produce for you, if you promptly dunk them in mud or hide them in a weed bed.

Use the rigging described under FISHING THE SINGLE EGG and, just as you do in stream fishing, watch your rod tip and the point where your line enters the water. The pick-up may be very subtle and a slight movement will be the only sign you'll get that you're "on." If action is slow, when fishing the bottom, strip in the line a few inches at a time; this will give the effect of natural movement.

Remember to check water temperature, particularly at the depth you're fishing. Trout, salmon and other fresh water sport and game fish have relatively narrow temperature ranges in which they are most active. Readings above and below the range preferred by a specific fish are pretty good signs that you won't see much action.

SALMON EGG HOOKS ARE A SPECIAL BREED

Successful "egging", particularly in rivers and streams, requires a number of brain-busting disciplines, but none is more important to the fisherman than the hook on the end of his line. For that hook must produce in a rough-and-tumble world of brushy and undercut banks, logs, rocks, boulders and in, around and behind every other fishy-looking area and obstruction in a drift. The hooks at right are old hands at the game. All have hollow points, reversed (offset) bends and are forged for extra strength.

Nos. 92167 and 92168, 3X strong, have sliced shanks to hold an egg sac in position. No. 92162, 3X strong, is a cluster hook; the loop on the shank-tied leader is snugged tight, after the cluster's impaled on the hook. No. 92553, X strong, is used for single and cluster eggs. And No. 79792, 5X short shank, is the tiny wire shown under **FISHING THE SINGLE EGG,** above.

BEAK HOOK No. 92167, nickel-plated. No. 92168, turned *up* eye.

BEAK HOOK No. 92162, nickel-plated.

BEAK HOOK No. 92553, nickel-plated.

VIKING HOOK No. 79792, gold-plated. **No. 9479,** bronzed.

Hook Drawings Courtesy O. Mustad & Son.

CHAPTER 28

Tuning Up Tackle

The time to tune up and ready your tackle is NOW!

New flies should be tied or purchased, lines checked for wear and possible replacement, and rods, reels, kit bags, waders, etc. checked over carefully.

If flies were put away where moths could get at 'em, some of the hackles or wool parts of your pet "killers" may have been ruined. Dry flies can be made like new again if they are steamed over a tea kettle or coffee pot spout. Wives of fishermen are adept at this chore!

If the finish of fly lines are cracked, buy new ones.

Old dry flies can be made "like new" again by steaming.

Otherwise a thorough greasing and drying to straighten kinks will put your line in top fishing condition.

Nothing is more disturbing to a trout fisherman than leaky hip boots or waders. Test them by filling with water, being sure to turn them inside out for drying afterwards. Stuffing with dry newspapers will hasten drying. If there are leaks, take your boots to a service station and have rubber patches applied. "Hot" patches are no good for boots and do not hold up. The old type put on with rubber cement last indefinitely, so are much better.

Fly, spinning, and casting rods should be examined for frayed wrappings; broken, twisted, or missing guides, and loose ferrules or reel seats. If a rod needs rewrapping you can do a professional job with nylon thread (size 00), turning it on tightly. Apply a color preservative after wrapping, then clear varnish. All these items can be obtained at tackle stores.

Loose ferrules are common rod ailments. Winter storage dries out the glue in ferrules, crystalizing it, so the first time you flex your rod one or more ferrules may loosen. Usually a ferrule can be reset just by turning it slowly over a small flame. If this doesn't tighten it, remove it, clean the rod, apply some ferrule cement, and then reseat the ferrule.

Bamboo rods, and some cheap glass rods, may need varnishing. Take the old coat off bamboo rods with varnish remover, not a knife or razor or you may sever the strong outside fibers of the bamboo. Warm the rod varnish in a pan of hot water before you apply it with a finger tip, and afterwards put the rod in a dustproof closet to dry.

Fly and spinning reels are simply constructed and easy to prepare for fishing, but casting reels, having several moving parts, need more attention. Disassemble your plugging reel and clean all parts with kerosene or gasoline. Then use gear grease and fine oil sparingly where recommended by the manufacturer, and reassemble. Fly and spin reels also should be cleaned and oiled.

A few minutes spent sharpening hooks of plugs, flies, and bass bugs will help you hook more fish when you finally get into action on Big Bass Lake.

And, for most fishermen, tending to tackle is a labor of love, and, like old friends, the more time spent with it the greater the affection.

Guides should be checked for wear, and replaced when necessary.

Time is well spent sharpening hooks on plugs, fly rod bugs, spoons, etc.

CHAPTER 29

Jig Fishing

*The lead-head jig, in all its variations,
is the best all-around gamefish lure ever
devised.*

By Bob McNally

One black July night Tim Sampson of Omaha, Neb., and I were fishing Grindstone Lake in far northern Wisconsin. It was about 1 A.M., so dark we could hardly see shoreline rocks only 40 feet away from my Ranger Bass Boat.

We moved slowly along the shore casting our lures right into the rocks, sometimes tossing them onto the rocks, then sliding them gently into the water. We worked our lures super-slow, merely nudging, hopping, and twitching them along the lake's bottom.

Some smallmouth bass and walleyes struck the instant the lure touched the water, frequently taking in mere inches of water, tight up against the bank. Others would hit a few yards out and 30 feet down, and still others would strike near the boat, just as the lure was being lifted for another cast.

The two of us caught 26 smallmouths and nine walleyes that summer night, fishing from about 10 P.M. to 3 A.M. The bronzebacks weighed from just under one pound to just over four pounds, and the walleyes averaged around four pounds, although Tim landed one of about 6½ pounds. The lure we used was a ½-ounce all-

black marabou jig, its hook tipped with an Uncle Josh three inch long black pork-rind "eel."

The lead-head jib is, in my opinion, the best all-around gamefish killer ever contrived. If, in fact, I had to select just one lure or bait for all of my fishing (including salt water) it would undoubtedly be the jig.

There is nothing new about jigs. Primitive tribes the world over have been using crudely fashioned jigs made of bone and shell for centuries.

I first learned about jigs in 1958, and of all places on an Arkansas trout stream. It had been a week-long summer trip, fishing with my dad, Tom McNally, and a friend of his whose name I can't remember. We'd had tough fishing because the weather was scorching, and the fish were "sulking" in the deepest water they could find.

Late one morning dad and I were fishing a small Ozark mountain stream, and almost immediately he hooked a big rainbow trout on light spinning tackle. I went over to watch the action. He played the fish with absolute skill, then finally reached down and swung the rainbow out—a thick-bodied 2½ pounder. What looked like a three inch long yellow marabou streamer fly with a big head hung from the trout's jaw.

"What's that?" I asked.

"It's a jig," dad said. "On gamefish it's pure poison, particularly when it's hot and sunny and the fish are laying on the bottom and near cover, trying to stay away from the sun's rays."

some. The point here is that gamefish *everywhere* will, at some time or another, and particularly during the "dog days" of summer when fish are often deep, slap lead-head jigs with relentless enthusiasm.

Many years ago when jigs first hit the sportfishing world, and received well-earned publicity, many fishermen used them with excellent results. But when "flashy"

Herb Allen, popular Outdoor Editor of the Tampa (Fla.) Tribune, removes a plastic-tailed jig from a seatrout. Neither jigs nor trout are anything new to Herb.

Plastic-tailed jigs, comparatively new on the market, account for a lot of bass. Bob McNally took this modest Arkansas bigmouth on a "Sting-Ray Grub."

Since that day the jig has been a standby lure for me, especially during the broiling summer months when most fish are hugging bottom. With various kinds and sizes of jigs I've caught dozens of different salt water fish species and just about every type of important fresh water gamefish in North America. The fresh water species includes brook, brown, rainbow, cutthroat, and lake trout, splake, muskie, northern pike, largemouth and smallmouth bass, walleye, coho and Chinook salmon, arctic and Montana grayling, and even lake or common whitefish and Rocky Mountain whitefish—just to name

new plugs and artificial lures arrived, and promised anglers everything but the moon, most fishermen turned to the new lures and forgot the "lead-heads." It's been their loss, because although fancy plugs and other new lures take their toll of gamefish, lead-head jigs continue as effective today as they were when they first came out.

Jigs are available in various sizes, shapes, weights, and colors. They can be had in weights from 1/64 ounce to 5 or 6 ounces, and in almost every color or combination of colors imaginable.

Jig heads are made slanted, keeled, bullet-shaped,

oval-shaped, coin-shaped, and other variations too numerous to name. Weight and shape of a jig is what's most important to an angler.

Simply stated, flat or coin-shaped jigs sink more slowly and are more resistant to underwater snags. Bullet, ball, and keel-shaped jigs sink quickly, but are more prone to "hang-up." Thus, what shape and weight jig you should use depends upon the "snags" and depth of the water you're fishing. For example, it's best to fish lightweight jigs with flat heads in shallow, weed, or stump filled waters, and heavy jigs with bullet, ball, or keel-shaped heads in deep rivers and lakes that have mud, sand, or rocky bottoms.

Jigs also are available with a variety of body "dressings." Popular jig bodies are made from synthetic materials (such as nylon and Dacron), saddle hackle

Jigs are made in many shapes and sizes, and with a variety of materials used for the "winging" or "body." Body material may be nylon, bucktail, impala, marabou, mylar, plastic, feathers—or combinations of those materials.

Pike hit 'em too! Here's a 21-pounder that hit a Jack Crawford jig tied with saddle hackle winging.

feathers, marabou stork feathers, bucktail hair, polar bear hair, impala hair (hair from a calf's tail), soft plastics (similar to the material used for plastic worms), and Mylar (thin, shiny silver metal strips). Too, some jigs have bodies made from two, three, or even four of these different materials.

At times jigs made from one of these types of body dressings will out-fish jigs made from any other type material. Therefore, skilled anglers carry an assortment of jigs made from different body materials in a variety of weights and "head-styles."

Jig color is not too important when those lures are fished deep (below 25 feet). Because very little sunlight penetrates in deep water, lure color is almost indistinguishable. Therefore, for all practical purposes, color of jigs used for deep jigging is relatively unimportant. However, when jigs are fished in shallower water (less than 25 feet), lure color can make a significant difference. Although every fisherman has his own preferences of jig colors, I've found that black, blue, purple, white, yellow, and red jigs are most productive for my fishing.

Because a jig is a compact glob of lead molded around a specially designed hook, it casts like a bullet and sinks like a rock—which makes it a deadly lure for deep fishing. However, some brands of jigs are better than others.

A quality jig should ride hook-up in the water, and rest nose down on a lake's bottom—this helps avoid snags and assures easier hooking of fish.

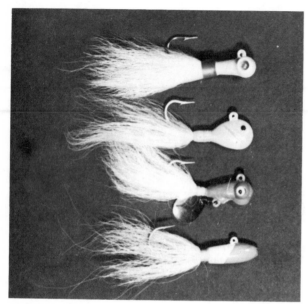

Typical "salt water jigs," which have become fresh water fishing favorites. Each of these has bucktail winging.

For the most part you won't go wrong if you select the jigs of a manufacturer who has been in business for some time. For quite a while, and with excellent results, I've been using an assortment of jigs made by the Lindy Tackle Co., in Brainerd, Minn. Lindy specializes in a wide variety of jigs and they are excellent, particularly their "Dingo" jig. This jig is specially designed so that the jig head rests on the bottom with the hook pointing upward at about a 45 degree angle. The "Dingo" is superb for deep, bottom-bouncing, and it's much easier to consistently hook fish with it than with some other jig styles made by other tackle companies.

When selecting jigs be sure to pay close attention to the hooks they have. The best jigs are made with lightweight, properly tempered wire. These hooks can and should be honed to needle-like sharpness before being

fished. More so than any other type lure, the jig requires an extra sharp point because fish often strike a jig when it's "free-falling" or when it's resting motionless on the bottom. Thus, fish rarely hook themselves when they strike jigs, and consequently jig hooks *must* be supersharp so that the barb easily penetrates a fish's jaw when you set the hook.

You can fish jigs with spin-cast, spinning, or bait-casting equipment. If you are fishing a small, light jig in comparatively open areas with few snags, light spinning outfits are ideal. If you employ heavy jigs in weedy or brush-filled water, a medium-heavy spinning outfit, or medium-heavy bait-casting outfit should be used. As a rule I prefer using bait-casting gear whenever possible because I can work a jig better, and more easily hook and play fish in deep water.

There are many excellent ways to rig and fish "leadheads" for "jigging."

You can tip a weedless or open-hook jig with a variety of different pork-baits, a minnow, leech, nightcrawler, small plastic worm (the floating type "worm" is particularly good for deep jigging), or even a small piece of freeze-dried shrimp or a cut chunk of flesh from a fish you've already caught.

The so-called "spinner-baits" which have been so popular among bass fishermen recently, are just ordinary jigs rigged with spinner attachments. The ways to "doctor-up" jigs with spinner blades for deep fishing are virtually limitless.

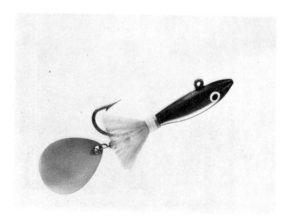

"Earl's Pearl" is representative of jig-and-spinner types.

A jig has exceptional "action" on the bottom when rigged and fished properly. The jig will dive-and-rise when the angler imparts a jerk-and-reel type of retrieve to his lure. Each time the rod is twitched the jig darts forward and up, then, as the fisherman spools line, the jig dives quickly, nosing down, its body dressing wiggling and shivering as it goes. It's action that bottom-hugging fish find hard to resist.

However, imparting action to a jig is much more limited if the angler ties his line to the jig with a "snug-fitting" knot, such as an Improved Clinch Knot, than if the fisherman uses a "loop-type-knot," such as the Homer Rhode Loop, Dave Hawk's Drop Loop, or the Buffer Loop (consult the Glossary of Fishing Knots chapter in this book). Because a jig doesn't have built-in action like most plugs, spoons, and spinning lures, it's imperative that the jig is able to "swing" freely on a "loop" when the lure is activated by the fisherman. A "loop-knot" allows a jig to have much greater action when it's retrieved.

Too many anglers employ wire leaders when fishing jigs for toothy fish species. It's been my experience that wire leaders shy fish away, and too, a stiff piece of wire tied or fastened to a jig greatly impairs the action of the lure—which is particularly important when working jigs. Almost every expert fisherman I know (not the self-pro-claimed type of expert that there seems to be an abundance of these days) prefers using a heavy piece of 30 to 100-pound test monofilament "shock leader" instead of wire. Heavy mono is less likely to spook fish; it holds up well against even the castanet, tooth-studded jaws of fish such as northern pike, muskies, and walleyes; and heavy mono can be tied to jigs with "loop-knots."

A quality jig with pork-rind "eel" attached is death on bass, walleyes, northern pike, muskies, and a myriad of salt water species as well. Use an appropriate style and weight jig with a three or four inch long "eel." Toss it into a likely looking "hole" or "drop-off" and retrieve slowly, letting the jig-and-eel snake its way through weeds and over obstructions on the bottom. Fish it right along the bottom, or lift your rod with quick jerks, which will make the lure flutter and quiver just off the bottom.

Another way to demolish deep-living gamefish is to let the jig settle slowly to the bottom, in, say, 20 or 30 feet of water. Remember to keep a taut line as the jig sinks, and watch the line for any unusual twitches or jerks signaling a strike. Often, fish will pick up a jig as it's plummeting toward bottom, and a slack line will cause missed strikes. Once the jig has reached bottom lift the rod gently, and ease the jig forward a foot or so, then stop. Repeat, making the jig squirm over the bottom—putting

Whether these rate officially as jigs or "spinner baits" is open to conjecture. They are, however, lead-heads —with weed guards, spinners, and plastic tails. They get fish, too.

Just another largemouth gone bug-eyed over a jig.

up little puffs of mud or sand, just as a live, feeding crayfish or some other bottom-living forage food might do. Gamefish, particularly bass and walleyes, will come to a jig fished thusly and hover over it, their tail up and nose down. Then suddenly the fish will suck the jig in, and you set the hook hard!

Knowledgeable anglers occasionally fish two or more jigs simultaneously when working deep water. First one jig is tied to the end of the fishing line, then a second jig is either tied on a "dropper line" a foot or two up from the first jig, or the second jig is tied to a length of monofilament that's attached to the hook shank of the first jig. Both methods of rigging two jigs are good, and are very effective when casting for school fish such as bass, walleyes, crappies, etc.

Two or more jigs fished at the same time are meant to simulate a group of baitfish, and should be fished as such —with a snappy, jerky, erratic retrieve.

One skilled proponent of the double-jig rig is the eminently prolific writer, superb angler, and Executive Editor of *Field & Stream* Magazine, Al McClane. When fishing gets tough one of the first things Al does is tie on a pair of bucktail jigs.

One spring Al, his charming wife Patti, my father and I were fishing famed Crowduck Lake in central Manitoba. Although Crowduck is jammed with smallmouths, northern pike, and walleyes, due to horrid weather and water conditions we had an extremely poor morning's fishing. When we finally stopped fishing at noon and beached the boats to prepare a shore lunch (which of course no Canadian trip is complete without), we didn't even have enough fish to feed the four of us plus our two Indian guides. It appeared as if canned food would make up the balance of our luncheon menu.

As the guides built a fire and Patti, my dad, and I lounged on shore, Al rigged two bucktail jigs and fished. He'd make a long cast with his spinning outfit, wait for the two jigs to settle to the bottom, then retrieve them erratically and *fast!* In 20 minutes Al caught more fish with his jigs from shore in an area only about 100 feet long than we had caught all morning fishing around the entire lake! He landed smallmouths, northern pike, walleyes, and *even tullibees* (more commonly known as ciscos)—which were not known to inhabit Crowduck! With the use of a double-jig rig Al saved us from a canned lunch. He released all fish he had caught except the tullibees. Then Al poached those fish for lunch— delicious!—far superior to the normal shore lunch fare of fried walleye and pike, and certainly better than canned spaghetti and baked beans!

Little grouper hit a little nylon jig, fed to him on ultralight.

And trout, too, are readily fooled by jigs. This is a sea-run brook trout, fresh from northern Manitoba's Machichi River.

The double-jig rig is particularly effective during the scorching summer months when many species of gamefish are in large schools and deep. Schools of gamefish often "herd" and feed on giant schools of forage fish. To gamefish, the double-jig set-up often triggers an instant response because the fish see more than one "forage minnow." I've often fished two or three jigs at the same time for white bass, largemouths, and walleyes, and have had two or three fish hooked simultaneously.

Another good way to fish jigs for some species of fish is with a large bobber or with a popping cork or float. This method is particularly deadly for white bass, crappies, bluegills, and in salt water for seatrout or spotted squeteague. It's a simple but very effective system of fishing.

One, two, or several jigs may be employed. The jig or jigs are tied to the fishing line as usual, and the bobber is attached above the jigs. Where the bobber is put will determine how deep the jigs will be fished. Usually some time must be spent fishing the jigs at different depths (this is done by re-positioning the bobber) until the most productive depth is found.

Essentially, the angler just casts the bobber-jig arrangement out, and periodically twitches and slowly retrieves it. Some anglers, particularly Gulf Coast fishermen pursuing spotted seatrout and red drum or channel bass, prefer to use a popping type float rather than a conventional bobber. Those anglers slowly retrieve the rig with hard yanks and jerks, making the float "pop" loudly on the surface and thus attract any gamefish nearby to the jigs hanging below the float. A few knowledgeable fishermen use this same technique on largemouth bass and they are quite successful.

Bobber fishing with jigs also lends itself very well to drift fishing from a boat. This method is especially good when an angler is fishing a large body of water for the first time because it will speed the search for fish by enabling the fisherman to cover a lot of water in a short time. Bobber-jig fishing also is used effectively by some stream and river fishermen for trout, bass, and panfish.

One of the most important parts of jig fishing is to always know or "feel" what the lure is doing. A skilled jig angler will know what his jig is doing every time he imparts some type of action to it. He'll know when the jig is twitched off a rocky, underwater ledge or into a deep creek channel and is bouncing down toward bottom. He's able to dance and swim a jig so that it's just above submerged brush and trees. And most important, he'll know when a fish has hit his jig—sometimes the strike is a hard jolt, at other times the line just goes slack as the jig is "free-falling," and occasionally the line merely tightens—but in every case the expert "jigger" *will know what his jig is doing at any depth!*

Jig fishing isn't like any other type of fishing, because a certain sense of "timing" or "feeling" must be learned if the jigging angler is to be consistently successful. And this "timing" isn't something that's easy to learn nor easy to explain to the neophyte jig fisherman. It's something that an angler will only learn through experience.

Jig fishing isn't a magic-method of angling, it isn't always fast sport, and anyone who thinks he can just tie on a jig, cast it out and catch fish will find out quickly it just doesn't work that way. To be good at jigging and consistently catch fish you've got to work at it—it's that simple. However, throughout the fishing season, you'll discover that when fished properly there's nothing more deadly for most gamefish than a "lead-head" jig.

Lead-heads tipped with Tom Mann's "Sting-Ray Grub" plastic bodies are among the deadliest of jig-type lures.

CHAPTER 30

How to Hook, Play, Land, and Boat Fish

What you do from the instant of the strike on makes the difference between a lunker landed and just another big one that gets away.

Experienced anglers and veteran guides from the Caribbean to Ontario agree that about 80 percent of fish hooked-and-lost are lost because of human error. Either the fisherman doesn't set the hook, doesn't handle his tackle correctly, or otherwise plays the fish wrong. The other 20 percent are lost due to tackle failure, the fish's peculiar structure or fighting ability, or some outside interference such as another boat cutting one's line, a mangrove root getting in a tarpon's way, or a bonefish slicing a leader on sharp coral.

It's obvious more top gamefish would be caught if more fishermen knew something about playing fish. Guides say that not one out of ten sportsmen have any real understanding of how to fight fish. Most just grunt and reel and hope—turning what should be a well-controlled, exciting scrap into a tug-of-war.

Each species of fish has certain characteristics and fighting styles that call for special tactics by the fisherman. The environment of some fish poses special problems. And the limitations and competence of your tackle should be understood, too, if you're to land most of the fish you hook—whether they be bluegills or blue marlin.

Don't hope to land any decent fish unless you've set the hook properly. Sinking the barb is partly your job, partly the job of your rod. Some people use rods that have action like wet spaghetti. The fish they catch usually hook themselves by the force of their strike. Select a rod with enough backbone that it will drive hooks into fish when you pull back sharply on the rod.

For fish that have hard mouths—such as tarpon and muskies—use a rod having considerably more backbone than one you'd use for soft-mouthed fish like bass. If you do a lot of spinning or spin-casting with monofilament, use a line that will not stretch to China when you try to drive-home a hook.

Many fishermen do not realize it takes a solid jerk to sink hooks past the barb. The larger the fish and larger the hook, the stronger yank needed. And often speed in striking is essential.

Some bass fishermen using surface lures always pause after the strike before setting the hooks. However, most experts believe it's imperative to jerk hooks into fish the instant they hit or else a large percentage of bass will be lost. Some skilled anglers set fly rod poppers so fast and hard that if a bass misses, the bug comes sailing back through the air.

Fish usually hook themselves on underwater lures—particularly if you're trolling or retrieving fast. Even so, it's smart to give the rod a quick, hard yank. In fishing dry flies for trout, all you normally need do is tighten up and the barb goes home. But if you're bouncing dries on fast water, and a trout takes, set the hook fast.

Some fish are slow, deliberate hitters, so your strike should be delayed. When an Atlantic salmon sucks in a dry fly you can get your barb in the corner of his mouth by letting him turn after the rise, and hook himself on a tight line.

The surest way to lose bonefish is to be anxious and set the hook when you see the fish clobber your fly. Bonefish have pebbly growths on top of the tongue and roof of the mouth. If you try to sink your fly soon as a bone' grabs it, the hook point may hit these hard growths.

The average angler has very little understanding of drags and how to set them, and how to employ them in playing fish correctly.

A lot depends, of course, on the kind of fish you are after and overall fishing conditions, but generally speaking there is a "striking drag" and a "playing drag." In other words, you want enough resistance against your reel's drag that your fish will be solidly hooked when he strikes your lure, then you want to reduce the drag so that he will fight against sufficient tension but not pop your line.

Some species of fish—muskies for example—are particularly difficult to hook. Skilled muskie anglers will hit back at a striking muskie 3, 4, 5 times or so—just like tarpon fishermen—because they know that a muskie, like a tarpon, has a bone-hard mouth and it's tough to set those hooks. Once their muskie is hooked, though, they reduce the drag because they know a hard-fighting muskie can snap even heavy line if the fish is held up too tight.

Fish that make long, fast, hard runs should be played on light drags once they are hooked. Line creates drag in the water, and naturally the more line out the more drag. Too, the heavier the line the greater the drag. A fly line sawing through the water, for example, creates immense drag, so when some fish has taken out a lot of your fly line you should reduce your reel's drag to nearly zero.

There are times, of course, when the angler is forced to screw down on his drag and attempt to hold a fish up tight. If you've hooked a big bass in a maze of flooded timber there's nothing to do except tighten up, hang on—and hope.

Before the first cast is made, a reel's drag should be adjusted to provide the correct amount of resistance so that a striking fish can be hooked. Thereafter, throughout the fight, the angler should make whatever alterations in drag are dictated according to conditions. In the course of playing a hooked fish many skilled anglers will adjust their reel's drag half-a-dozen times or so.

Salt water fishermen, used to fighting big, bad stuff, know the tremendous importance of correct drag, but drag can be vitally important in fresh water fishing, too. Fishermen who enjoy light tackle angling in fresh water —ultra-light spin-fishermen, for example, MUST be careful to keep drags adjusted properly. The UL spin-fisherman using 1, 2, 3, or 4-pound line who is careless and tightens his drag too much is going to break off one fish after another.

After hooking a fish, many anglers go to extremes in playing it. Some "horse" fish—others coddle them. Applying too much pressure is a good way to get a busted leader or pull out hooks. But coddling a fish for fear of losing it is worse.

A sportsman *fights* a fish. He doesn't bull it, but he doesn't baby it either. A fish should be worked steadily, without putting undo strain on your tackle. Of course a fish should be "played out" when you try to land it, but don't be so afraid of losing a fish that you don't give it something to pull against. Anyone could land any fish if they took hours, or days, to let the fish swim itself into exhaustion.

Regarding ultra-light tackle, it's no great achievement to land big fish unless the terminal gear is fine. Taking hefty salmon on short, light fly rods, for example, isn't difficult if you use a stout leader, point the rod at the fish, and play him off the reel.

Many fishermen are ignorant of what their tackle can do. With a 3X leader tippet you can pull a small trout to you in nothing flat; a 4-pound tippet is heavy enough for most of the bass you'll run into; and the whippier your rod, the better your chances of landing a fish provided you have room to play him.

Fish exert a pulling force in the water that is considerably less than their actual weight. So when selecting tackle consider the problems of setting the hooks, what rod is best to cast the lures you'll use, whether or not the fish you're after have hard mouths or run out line, and the kind of place you'll be fishing—open water or snag-filled.

When you've got a fish hooked right, half the battle is won. But if it's a good fish, you'll still need know-how to put him in the boat.

Press the rod butt against your middle while you pump-and-reel. Pumping and reeling is standard technique for fighting strong fish, regardless of tackle used. To pump a fish, lower your rod tip, reeling fast to keep a tight line, then pull up smoohtly, repeating the process. Never attempt to handle a good fish by steady reeling. This doesn't fully utilize the rod's action, so will wear you down and prolong the battle unnecessarily.

On Manitoba's Kississing Lake, Tom McNally pumps a 20 pound northern pike to the boat.

With casting tackle you can apply additional drag by pressing on the reel spool with your thumb. Some fishermen cross one thumb over the other to hold a fish up tight. Be sure to let go if the fish runs, or you'll get a burned thumb. In playing most fish with casting tackle, experts hold the rod away from their body. Toward the end of a tarpon fight, when they've got the fish coming, they put the butt against their middle and pump-and-reel. Whenever the tarpon takes off, they extend their arms again so the rod gets the play.

Holding a rod butt against you reduces the strain on your arm and wrist, but you can accomplish the same thing by holding the rod so that the butt comes under your forearm. Your forearm serves as a support for the rod butt.

Fly fishermen have trouble with big fish because they have a single hand-hold on the rod, yet a lot of leverage.

It's impossible to exert maximum pressure with a fly rod by using a one-hand hold. For run-of-the-pond fresh water fish, this doesn't matter. But take your fly outfit to salty water, where fish come big and tough, and you'll learn quickly that fresh water rod-handling techniques don't work.

Most fly-rodders tying into strong fish grip the rod with two hands. It's the proper hold while a fish is running, but when you've got him coming, or when you want to exert pressure to turn him, lay one hand across the rod butt and push down, at the same time pulling up with the rod grip hand. This system for pumping with a fly rod isn't tiring, doesn't require much strength, and your "push-and-pull" is on a short axis so that you get maximum leverage.

Let your rod do the work. It's built for it. A rod "works" (flexing forward under pressure, recovering when the pressure weakens) best when it is held nearly vertical. Never point your rod at a fish to play him from the reel. You might as well fish with just the rod handle and reel. Don't point the rod tip at the water, either. Wrong rod angle is a common mistake.

Properly "played out," pike rolls on his side . . .

It's especially important to hold a rod high while bonefishing, or when taking any strong, fast fish in shallow water where there are obstructions. The high rod is the trademark of bonefishermen, because these fish streak over flats full of sea fans and coral. Holding the rod high helps raise the line and keep it free of snags.

Some musky fishermen dip their rods into the water and hold them straight down while playing fish. They believe this low rod angle slows a musky and hinders him on jumps. Nonsense. When fish want to jump, they jump. There's no way to stop a fish from leaping—and who'd want to? Watching 'em jump is half the fun.

A fish should not be given anything solid to pull against. Your rod, held nearly vertical, bucks and bends under the pull of a fish and takes most of the strain. But if you reel a fish too close to your rod tip he'll get a more direct pull, and may break away.

When possible, stop a fish from running out too much line. If you get a billfish or tarpon on, and he takes off, follow him. The boat shouldn't be "backed down" on the fish. But it should be kept close enough that you can fight your fish on a fairly short, tight line.

When a fish gets out too much line the pull you exert with the rod is minimized. To test this, hand your buddy a rod and reel. Take the end of the line between two fingers and walk away 50 feet. Let him reel up while you hold the line tight. Then have him raise the rod smartly as though he were trying to set a hook. The

. . . and, spurning a net or gaff, McNally quickly grasps pike firmly behind gill plates.

line will jump from between your fingers. Now take the line and walk out 100 feet. If your pal has a light casting outfit, he won't pull the line free.

Try this with different kinds of tackle and you'll discover that the farther you get from the rod, the lighter the pull. This is why, when you let a marlin, sailfish,

tarpon, or wahoo get out too far, it's blazes doing anything with him.

Experienced tarpon fishermen know the value of playing silver kings on a short line. They boys who consistently win contests are the guys who fight tarpon from *above*. They nearly run over a tarpon when he sulks. A constant upward pull is exerted on the fish, so the tarpon thinks his head will be pulled off unless he moves. The system can be dangerous, because when a tarpon decides to leap near your boat he may fall into your lap.

Some guides back down on hooked billfish so fast the angler hardly knows he has a fish on. Soon as the boat is close, the mate grabs a "flying gaff" and may chuck it 30 feet to impale the fish. This technique puts marlin flags on a captain's boat, but it's unsportsmanlike and doesn't give an angler the sport he's paid for. Captains should keep boat transom's turned to fish, backing up only enough so the fisherman can keep a tight line.

A fish that's hooked right will not escape in open water if you give him slack, but a fish getting slack near roots or stumps may break off. Always keep a tight line to have constant pressure on a fish.

If a fish darts for snags, give him the butt—all you dare—to keep him out. And if you hook a good fish near brush or coral, turn for open water. Once you've got him clear, he won't be able to cut, tangle, or fray your line.

Slack line should be given deliberately when fish jump. Most fishermen recognize this as an old rule, but they don't know the reason for it. It's simple. You've got a nice 8-pound largemouth bass on. He jumps, pulling the line with him. At the top of the leap he flips over backward. You failed to lower your rod tip to give slack, so now you have 8 pounds of mossback muscle falling on your leader. The fish's weight snaps the leader or rips the hook out.

When you start fishing, be sure there's nothing in the boat that may catch your line. Don't let ropes drag in the water. If you're anchored and hook a good fish, haul in the anchor. The fish may run around the anchor line.

Sight of the boat usually spooks a fish into a last-ditch run, so be ready for it. Let him go if he wants, being sure not to "horse" him. A "green" fish is hard to boat, and you'd probably injure it during handling—which is no good when you want to release it.

Many anglers lose fish that dive under a boat because they pull from one side, trying to haul the fish back.

Now totally subdued ...

... big pike is unable to bat a fin as he is admired by youngster. Pike landed this way can be released unharmed.

When a fish dives under the boat, let out line, move to the bow, and work the line around so that the boat no longer is between you and the fish.

A landing net isn't needed for most fresh water fish. If your fish is played out, he'll come in on his side, so tired all you have to do is pick him out. Guides and many fishermen sweep landing nets after fish the wrong way, and so miss. The fish, startled by the flashing net, makes a last-ditch dash against the short, tight line and breaks off. The antics of some fishermen trying to net fish would be comical if they weren't so sad.

They literally chase fish with nets. They make pass after pass as the hooked fish darts one way then another, including under the boat. The correct way to net a fish is to play it out, then to lower the net into the water, hold it motionless, and lead the fish into the net *head first.* Handled properly, a hooked fish will actually swim into a net. The netter does not hoist the net until the fish is well into it; then he sweeps it forward and up, not just up.

Most highly skilled anglers dislike nets and never use one, not even when fishing for toothy species. Nets tangle lures miserably, and expert fishermen find it just as easy to land fish by other means.

When the fish is whipped you can land it yourself, or have a *skilled* companion or guide to do it. Leave a little more than a rod's length of line out, and ease the fish to you. If he doesn't come easily you haven't worn him

down. So let him go, and let the rod's action wear him out. When he tires bring him toward you. If the fish is a bass or other species with no sharp teeth, put your thumb in his mouth and other fingers under his chin. Push down and in on his jaw, temporarily paralyzing the fish, and swing him abroad. Always be careful when landing a fish that he doesn't shake his head and bury a hook in your hand. Take a look as the fish is brought close to see where and how it's hooked.

Fisherman dressed for rigorous Hudson Bay weather plays a nice sea run brook trout. Note rod is held in proper position to best play fish.

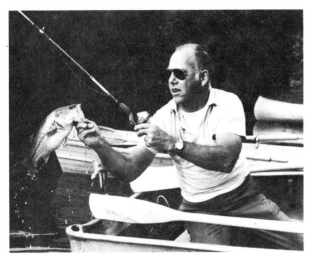

Thumb-and-forefinger grip on bass' chin half para-lyzes fish and makes handling simple. This grip does fish no harm, either, if it is to be released.

Northern pike, muskies, walleyes, and such toothy species can be landed easily by grasping them from above just behind the gill covers. Some fishermen grab northerns with a thumb-and-forefinger grip in the fish's eye-sockets. This hold isn't necessary, is not as good as a behind-the-gill plates grip, and should *never* be used if the fish is to be released. Fingers in a northern's eyes can damage his eyes!

"Tailing" is another way to safely land certain kinds of gamefish. Bob McNally has reason to look startled over this 22 pound "steelie" he took at British Columbia's Babine River.

Really large muskies—played out—can be landed with a hand in the gills, gaffed, or beached. Best way to gaff a fish is to nail him in the mouth, preferably in the lower jaw.

Shooting a fish is unsportsmanlike, unless the fish is a shark. The fisherman who pumps a muskie up to his boat and then shoots it hasn't caught a muskie. He's merely killed one!

Quite a lot of experienced fishermen and guides still use clubs to subdue fish. In some instances the practice is probably okay, such as when applying the coup de grace to a marlin that is to be mounted or, even, to a muskie that is to be killed. But a club shouldn't be used until the fish is in the boat. Swing one sooner and you might lose your fish and, worse, a clubbed fish knocked off the hook will sink away almost surely to die from the blow.

Regardless of how skillfully you play fish, you're going to lose some. But you'll lose fewer if you follow these few simple rules of "playing" fish.

Fish to be killed, such as this big rainbow, needn't be coddled. A hand thrust under the fish's gill plate makes escape impossible.

CHAPTER 31

Finding the World's Greatest Fisherman

The many fishermen claiming to be "the best" should check out their qualifications more closely.

There has been a great deal of talk about the "world's greatest fisherman." Some angling writers have pronounced flatly that so-and-so is the "world's best fisherman;" certain TV shows have arbitrarily identified so-and-so as "America's best angler;" and until recently a Chicagoan conducting a radio outdoors show called himself (with tongue in cheek) "the world's best fisherman."

What nonsense!

There's been enough talk now of the "world's best fisherman," and of the "world's best fresh water fisherman," that perhaps the time has come to identify, or at least to define, the quality of angler who might, indeed, justify the title of "world's best."

To be considered the "world's best," a fisherman certainly needs far more experience than simply angling for bass, walleyes, pike, lake trout, Great Lakes salmon, and various panfish. To rate as the *"world's* greatest angler," our hero would need world-wide fishing experience—rainbows in New Zealand, salmon in Norway, grayling in Yugoslavia, brown trout in Argentina, pike in the Baltic, bluefins off Cat Cay, marlin at Pinas Bay, and certainly he would have taken one or more of

the many species of pavon, and dorado, too, in South America's jungles.

Lugging tackle and a net full of sea-run brook trout, two fisherman climb the bank of Ten Schilling Creek, a tributary to Hudson Bay in far northern Manitoba. Could one of them be "the world's greatest fisherman?"

246

SINCE IDENTIFYING ANY INDIVIDUAL AS THE *WORLD'S* BEST ALL-AROUND FISHERMAN OBVIOUSLY IS ABOUT IMPOSSIBLE, LET'S HOLD IT DOWN TO WHO IS AMERICA'S GREATEST FRESH WATER FISHERMAN. THAT WILL BE PROBLEM ENOUGH!

Our country's best fresh water angler will have vast fishing experience. He will possess great personal skill in handling all types of tackle. He will be knowledgeable on all angling techniques, and have much more than passing biological information on the various species of fresh water fish and their habits. He would know about the best places to fish, where to go and when. He'd be well traveled, a necessity to acquiring meaningful angling experience.

Since our best fresh water angler has fished many years in many places, he surely has caught: largemouth bass exceeding 10 pounds; smallmouth over 6; northern pike, 20; lake trout, 25; walleyes, 9; muskies, 25; cohos, 20; Chinook, 25; steelhead (true salt water variety), 15; brown trout, 6; brook trout, 3; rainbows, 5; cutthroats, 4; Arctic grayling, 3; and Montana grayling, 1 pound.

In addition, our hero would have fished for, and caught, countless other fresh water species of fish, including all the panfishes, eastern chain pickerel, Rocky Mountain and common whitefish (there's a difference), Atlantic salmon, ouananiche (landlocked salmon), and, finally, Kentucky bass, and maybe also redeye, Suwannee, Guadalupe, or one of the other of more than 15 species of black bass.

To rate as our best fresh water angler, this top fisherman would also have caught at least the important "exotics," such as Arcatic char and grayling, and possibly sea-run brook trout, Kokanee, Aurora, and blueback trout.

America's Number One fresh water fisherman would have to be a skilled caster—with ALL tackle, not just one casting method. He'd be skilled at spinning, spincasting, bait-casting and fly casting. He'd be able to execute all practical casts—such as the overhead, left and right side casts, bow-arrow, catapult, lob, flip, backhand, and with a fly rod the wide and tight bow casts, roll cast, roll pick-up, "S" cast, left and right curve and side casts, Spey cast, reverse-direction cast, snap pick up, left-right roll, the single and double haul, and, of course, the technique of shooting line on both the forward and back casts. He could throw a fly, or bass bug, 100 feet, effortlessly, and do it all day long without fatigue.

The country's leading fresh water fisherman would, naturally, have experience at all phases of fresh water fishing in America. That means he'd have to know about fishing alpine lakes in the Rockies, and the tide affected fresh water estuaries of our three coasts. Catching hickory and white shad would be nothing strange to him.

He'd have a thorough understanding of spoonplugging, and other techniques of deep-water structure fishing. He'd know about fishing bass bugs *on the bottom* of lakes, of skimming spoons *on the surface*, the methods of fishing jassids and other terrestrials, and naturally he'd be expert at working midges in the meniscus.

America's best fresh water fisherman would be a skilled fly tier, and if not experienced at all phases of rod making (including construction of bamboo rods), surely he'd be qualified in the assembly, repair, and maintenance of rods. He'd be a knot-tying expert, capable of instantly whipping out a Bimini twist or speed nail knot. He'd know how to design and build a proper shooting head, how and why to fish a double lure tandem rig, and, surely, how to make his own leaders.

Our best fresh water angler would be completely familiar with lake stratification, knowing the importance of the thermocline, epilimnion, and hypolimnion, and that oxygen inversion can occur in lakes so that fish can at times live comfortably at depths far below the thermocline. He'd understand how each fish species would relate to the various water conditions.

This best fresh water fisherman also knows that in most situations the color of a lure is meaningless at depths beyond 35 feet, and that certain colors at certain depths become neutral to fish. He also is aware of the fact that, due to variations in bone structure, certain fish species better detect the "sound" or vibrations of lures than other species—and therefore "sound" lures are more useful in fishing for them.

Our fresh water fishing expert can identify at a glance brown and black bullheads, and channel, blue, flathead, and other catfishes. He can readily discern a Snake River cutthroat from the Yellowstone strain. He's familiar with the dozen or more species of rainbow trout, knows that each has different spawning characteristics, temperature, and oxygen requirements, and continually live and feed at varying levels.

America's best fresh water fisherman assuredly understands the alkaline and acidic requirements in the water for trout, and he knows the makeup of all the hybrids, such as splake, tiger trout, trousal, and brownbow (a new one).

Without delving too deeply into this area, our expert angler knows something of stream improvement techniques—such as the design, construction, and implantation of log diverters, "wing" dams, and other fish conservation tools. And, of course, he is at least an amateur entomologist, naturalist and ichthyologist—and is fully familiar with the overall ecology of river, lake, and stream.

The things listed are, of course, only SOME of the experience, skill and knowledge that must be possessed by *America's best fresh water fisherman.*" There's more, lots more, behind the man who honestly wears that title!

NOW LET'S MEET AL "A.J." McCLANE

In the weird world of fishing writers there are some who couldn't catch fish in a hatchery, some who are good fishermen but bad writers, a few who are both good fishermen and good writers, and at least one who not only is a master fisherman and master fishing writer, but an angling innovator, casting engineer, tackle technician, skilled photographer, and by formal training a professional ichthyologist (fish zoologist).

He is A. J. "Al" McClane.

The by-line "A. J. McClane" is known to millions of sportsmen the world over. McClane, 53, was Fishing Editor of *Field and Stream* Magazine for 25 years, and recently became the magazine's Executive Editor so he would have time to produce more "in depth" angling articles.

In addition to his association with *Field and Stream*, McClane is noted for his production of outstanding books on fishing, the most recent being "McClane's New Standard Fishing Encyclopedia," an angling classic.

I first met Al McClane at a New York sportsmen's show in 1952. As *Field and Stream*'s Fishing Editor, he was conducting a free public casting clinic. I stepped up, confident of my casting ability, and with tongue-in-cheek asked McClane to help me with my fly casting.

"Let me see you cast," he said, passing a rod. I made a 90-foot cast with a single backcast—and grinned. "That's good," said Al, "but I noticed you didn't double-haul. Try it like this." He then cast, using the double-haul technique of increasing line speed, and tossed out a cast of 110 feet.

That was the longest, smoothest, best cast I'd ever seen with regulation fly fishing gear, and I walked away determined to learn the double-haul. Today I can easily do 110 feet, maybe a little more, but probably never would have if I hadn't met A. J. McClane—and learned of the double-haul.

Since that day in New York it has been my good fortune to visit and to fish often with "A. J." With due respect to other fishing writers, and to various fishery biologists, Al McClane is the only one from whom I always can learn something. Any session with Al, anywhere, is productive. He is the most knowledgeable "fishing writer" *(what a horrible term for a complicated, professional field)* this country has produced.

As a fishing writer reading other fishing writers what I enjoy most about McClane's writing is that it rings true. He knows enough about fishing not to be ashamed to report that "today I caught nothing." Unlike some so-called "big names" in the angling world, who never will let the facts interfere with a good story, McClane doesn't fabricate.

He feels no compulsion to write that he caught a 120-pound sailfish on 4-pound line, or boated a fly-hooked 150-pound tarpon in 12 minutes. Neither does he expound on catching 20-pound Atlantic salmon on 6-foot fly rods weighing 1½ ounces—since anyone who knows anything about fishing knows that is no great feat. (It's the leader tippet test that counts and not rod structure.)

To gather material and to broaden his own knowledge and experience, McClane roams the world's fishing fronts. McClane is usually in no more than transitory residence, but he makes his "home" in Palm Beach, within casting distance of fish-filled Lake Worth—a long tidal lagoon short steps from the sea. One year he spent eight months abroad. He fishes every corner of North America, South America, and Europe. He makes about six major angling trips yearly, totaling around 100,000 miles traveling to and from fishing spots.

Al McClane averages more than 500 letters a month from readers, and spends days dispensing fishing advice and information to his readers, airlines people, tackle manufacturers, and governmental agencies. He has caught every kind of North American gamefish, and more than 50 varieties of salt water gamefish. In the course of duty (which is fishing) McClane has survived a plane crash in Alaska, earthquakes in Peru and Chile, and revolutions in Colombia and the Belgian Congo.

What about McClane's fishing? Well, he's not one to make big noises about his catches, but consider the following: I once watched Al take 11 brown trout on 11 successive casts on the Yellowstone River in Montana; he has taken snappers to 50 pounds; in Norway with standard fly gear he got an Atlantic salmon of 48 pounds; in 1951 at Walker Cay he caught a world record 44½-pound barracuda on 8-pound line; he beat a 112-pound tarpon on a fly in the Florida Keys; took a 16-pound largemouth bass at Haw Creek, Fla.; and a 33-pound northern pike in Saskatchewan. In Africa, McClane once caught tree walking fish by casting dry flies into trees and onto mud banks.

Al McClane skillfully works a small Montana stream for trout.

McClane sold his first fishing story for $15 to *Outdoor Life* Magazine on taking trout on flies using dental floss to catch the wind and bounce the flies realistically over the water. He was 16 years old.

In the world of fishing "personalities" there are others who are better known to the average fisherman than A. J. McClane. That's because they are "fishing publicists," actors, you might say, who expound on any angling "feat" simply to build a "name." A. J. never does that.

Arnold Gingrich, publisher of *Esquire* Magazine and a skillful angler himself, wrote recently of McClane ". . . to me in my time, there are no anglers beside McClane. McClane is unique."

I don't know that A. J. is all that damn good. But I'd be happy to know half of what he does about fish—and fishing.

CHAPTER 32

Streamer Tactics for Bass

There are times when nothing draws strikes like a streamer fly.

By Bob McNally

Much has been written about the effectiveness of popping bugs for largemouth and smallmouth bass. And no one can deny that bugs do take bass. But it's common knowledge that under conditions of riffled water, or when bass are deep, bugs usually don't score. So most fly-rodders hang-up their buggin' rods and resort to bait-casting or spinning to fill the stringer with fish. But what many fishermen don't realize is that fly rod streamers often will take bass under such conditions.

I recall one day fishing with a friend on Florida's Lake Okeechobee. Okeechobee is on the northern end of the Everglades, and has some of the most interesting largemouth fishing found anywhere. It has shallow weedy bays, deep open canals, and some clear water areas without weeds, thus offering a wide variety of bass fishing.

It was a calm, sunny day when we started bass bugging and we caught several nice bucketmouths. But around noon the wind came up, and our action with poppers quickly slacked off.

My buddy picked up a bait-casting outfit, and began plugging a drop-off near a weed bed. I just changed from a popper to a weighted Yellow Marabou Streamer fly.

On his first cast my companion hooked a fine 2½-pounder, which he released. After several fruitless casts with my streamer I connected, and soon had a 5¾-pound largemouth along-side the boat. The rest of the afternoon we both had action. Me using a weighted fly rod streamer, my friend using a bait-casting rig; but by

What it's all about—this bass comes right out of the water after piling into a streamer fly.

the end of the day I had out-fished him 2 to 1, and on the average my largemouths were bigger.

The point here is not to discount plugging for bass, but rather to show that a fly-rod fisherman shouldn't resort to bait-casting or spinning gear simply because fly rod popping bugs aren't producing fish.

The best streamers for bass are large 3- to 6-inch long, salt-water type bucktail, marabou and saddle-hackle flies. Some of these flies are weighted to make them sink faster, others are not.

Life-like appearance of streamer flies in the water is what draws strikes from bass. This is the "McNally Smelt," shown dry at top, wetted below. Note realistic smelt shape.

"Bead-head" multi-wing saddle hackle flies are particularly good. These were originally designed for snook, but are death on bass. They are tied on plated, size 1/0 Mustad hooks, and are dressed with fuzzy wrappings of chenille, and extra hackles are wound palmer-style around the fly's head to give it added color and bulk. Usually about six saddle hackles—the long, webby feathers growing over a rooster's shoulders or "saddle" —make up the wing.

Also, there are many standard streamer "patterns" that are very effective for bass in most reservoirs, lakes, ponds, and streams. Among them are the Black Ghost, Grey Ghost, Royal Coachman, Black-Nosed Dace, White Marabou, Yellow Marabou, Mickey Finn, and the famed Muddler Minnow. Many fly fishermen feel that if a bass is around he'll take their streamer—no matter how

smallish the fly or how big the fish. Sometimes big fish will take small flies, but *as a rule* you're going to need streamers in extra-large sizes for big bass.

An assortment of streamers that will do a job on bass, both largemouths and smallmouths.

When a weedless fly is desired, most veteran fly-rodders use the same streamer types mentioned, but tied on the new "keel" fly hooks. The bend and barb of these hooks are turned up, rather than down, so few weeds and snags foul your fly. Also, many experts use bucktail streamers when fishing weedy areas. Because bucktail is more buoyant than other fly materials, it will make a fly "ride" near the surface, yet you *can* let it sink enough to attract bass even on wind-swept days.

While you may not be able to get the same streamers mentioned above, or duplicate them exactly, any decent fly-tier can turn out streamers that will take bass. And, in addition, there are *some* good commercially-made streamer flies you can buy that are similar to the favorites already discussed.

Buy bucktail, marabou and feathered streamers in various patterns and colors. Then purchase some "keel" fly streamers also in assorted patterns. Too, it's wise to have weighted streamers in your fly box. The streamer flies you buy should be of good quality so they can take repeated strikes from good-size bass.

Few lures or baits are as versatile or as life-like in the water as a streamer fly. Possibly only the pork "eel"—

which is recognized all over the country as a bass killer
—has more built in wiggle and wobble. But the pork eel
falls somewhere between lures and bait, so the streamer
fly still gets the vote by many veteran anglers as the
liveliest of all artificial lures.

*Bass fisherman should use fly reels with interchange-
able spools, so that when one line starts to sink another spool with dry, high-floating line can be quickly
substituted. Often streamers skimming along just under the surface bring more strikes than ones running
deep.*

Because of its long "hackles" and "wings," and general weight-forward construction, a properly made
streamer does not travel horizontally through the water.
Unless a constant, steady retrieve is used, a streamer
dips forward on its nose and dives each time the angler
strips line. The result is an up-and-down, or sawtooth
kind of movement by the fly as it is retrieved. As the fly
is jerked forward it rises, but falls again on a short dive
due to the slight slack in the line occurring as the fisherman reaches forward to strip fly line.

The action is akin to that transmitted to a bottom-
scratching "lead-head" jig when the caster "works" or
"pumps" his rod to raise and lower the jig tantalizingly
in the water.

In addition to this sawtooth passage through the
water, a streamer "breathes." The long, wavy hackles
open and close with each rise and fall of the fly, and
even the wings of bucktail-type streamers have this un-

dulating action. The pulsating-action of a marabou wing
is more constant, without the specific separations of motion so noticeable with hackle-winged flies.

Another major credit on the streamer ledger is the
ability of these lures to transfuse light. Many bait fishes
are nearly transparent—or seem so when observed in
clear water against bright surface glare. At best an
angler's offerings often merely *suggest* food to gamefish.
But the overall appearance of a streamer fly is about
as close as an artificial can come to looking like a real
forage fish.

The speed at which a streamer is retrieved should be
varied until the right one is found. Best technique is to
point the fly rod at the fly and strip line with the left
hand in yanks that may range from about 6 inches in
length to a yard. The rod tip should be kept low so that
you have plenty of room to raise it when striking bass.

Generally speaking, on calm days streamers should be
worked very slowly. But on windy days, when the water
is white-capped, a fast retrieve usually is best. It seems

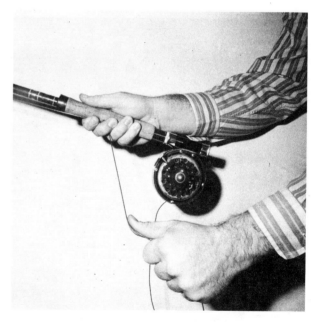

*Here's the right hold for stripping in a streamer. Most
important is that the fly line is held tightly beneath
fingers pressed against the rod handle, which means
a striking fish always will hit against a taut line.*

that under windy conditions the added movement made by a fly fished hard and fast is more likely to attract bass.

Often it's possible to see a bass trailing behind your streamer, trying to make up his mind whether or not to hit the fly. When a bass trails your streamer, vary the retrieve quickly before the fish gets so close that he spies you or the boat. A following fish often can be made to hit by slowing the fly, or stopping it altogether so that it flutters toward bottom. Other times speeding the retrieve works. You should do all three maneuvers—slowing, stopping, starting up again, and going fast—until a following bass hits.

Most knowledgeable fly-rod bass anglers use weighted streamers whenever it's blowing so hard that a regular fly won't go deep enough to be seen by bass. Weighted bucktail, marabou, or saddle-hackle streamers sink very quickly, and are "working" even when going down. Many bass are caught just by letting a weighted fly sink, because when diving the hairs or feathers wave and flow—making the fly act as if it was an injured, struggling minnow.

Even when using lead-bodied, weighted flies it's occasionally necessary to add extra weight to the leader to quickly get the fly down deep to bass. The best way is to attach one or two BB split-shots to the leader, right at the head of the fly. There are two reasons for placing the shot there instead of up the leader. For one, a fly is more active in the water when the sinker is near the hook eye, since each time you twitch your rod the fly will have an up-and-down darting action that can't be accomplished any other way. This murders bass.

Placing the shot at the fly's head also makes casting easier. If you put it on the leader well above the fly the streamer does flip-flops when you cast that can snarl your leader.

Streamers can be fished *very deep* when a sinking fly line is employed. Depending upon the fishing conditions and the depth you want to fish, a "sink-tip" fly line or a regular sinking line can be used. At times when bass are really deep—15 to 25 feet—some fly-rodders use a "high density" sinking, "shooting-head" fly line. A "head" is used not because long casts are necessary, but because a short (30-foot), heavy "shooting-head" sinks like a chunk of granite—much faster than does a conventional sinking line.

A good trick to use with marabou or saddle-hackle streamers is to pull the fly's wing around and under the bend of the hook. If it's marabou wet it, stroke it thin,

then set it under the hook. This puts a curve in the streamer's wing and causes the fly to zig-zag as it's pulled through the water. This kind of action can net big bass when other methods fail miserably.

You can get much the same lure action by tying your leader to the streamer with a riffling hitch (Portland Creek hitch), a knot that puts leader pull from below and to one side of the hook eye. Or you can use a conventional knot, then loop the leader back under the fly's wing. Only fault with the latter is that it's hard to hook and hold bass, especially large ones.

Still another way to get bass-killing action with your streamer is to alter the arrangement of the wings. Tie some streamers with offset wings. Offset wings are tied out of alignment 20 or 30 degrees with the hook shank. As you pull the fly through the water, that cock-eyed wing kicks the fly around in a crazy, crippled-minnow action.

A few fly-tiers put tiny metal cups or wiggle-disks on the head of a streamer to make it wiggle, as does a mouthpiece on a "floating-diving" jig. Too, lightweight spinners even can be attached to the fly's head to give the streamer bass-attracting "flash."

More of what it's all about—fly-rodder lips a nice 3-pounder that mistook a streamer for a minnow at a Nags Head, North Carolina pond!

Some anglers often fish two, three, or even four streamers at a time for bass. The flies usually are tied on dropper lines from the leader with extension blood knots. The idea is to make the streamers appear as a school of minnows, and the system is often very effective for schooled bass.

Be sure to work your streamers where bass are. Don't cast blindly over open water, figuring fish will spot your fly. Let your streamer sink near rocks, logs, undercut banks, reservoir creek channels, around stumps, brush, flooded timber—anyplace where bass hide and escape sunlight. Don't drop your fly on top of these places; cast beyond them, and then retrieve the streamer past the spot. It's not natural for a minnow to fall out of the air onto a bass' nose, but it is normal for one to swim to a log, boulder, or other cover.

At dusk, when shadows creep over the water and bass come out of hiding, cast to more "open water" areas. Cruising, hungry fish may be anywhere. This is a particularly good time to use streamers since you can "cover" a lot of water with them.

Streamer bass fishermen don't need a lot of elaborate tackle—which is a "God-send" in this day of "mechanized" bass fishing. All he requires is a good fly rod, reel, line, leaders, and streamers. The rod should be about 8 to 9½-feet long, weighing about 5 ounces, and with a rather heavy action. The line should be torpedo-tapered, size WF8 or WF9. Leaders should be at least 9 or 10-feet long, tapered to 6 to 10-pound tippets. Single-action reels are preferred by most experienced fly fishermen, primarily because they are light and have interchangeable spools. With such a reel a fly-rodder can change from a regular floating line to a sinking line or even to a "high-density" shooting-head fly line without changing reels.

Streamer flies definitely are not a sure cure for all of a bass fisherman's ills. Streamers or not, there'll be times when no matter what you do you can't put a bass in the boat. But there are lots of days—through any season anywhere—when streamers will take bass like nothing else.

CHAPTER 33

Exotic Game Fishing Guide

New information on tarpon, bonefish, permit, dorado, marlin, sailfish, and Atlantic salmon.

By Jim Chapralis

The definition of an exotic fishing place is variable. To one fisherman exotic fishing may be traipsing off to the Ventuari River in Venezuela or to some other little-explored area. To others, it may represent any trip outside North America.

The places we're going to examine here belong to the latter group: Unfamiliar places which provide good fishing, and a reasonable amount of comfort. With so many American anglers seeking fishing outside the country, there are numerous fishing camps sprouting up which are now operated more or less to American standards.

But the American sportsman ought to realize that operating a camp miles away from nowhere does present problems: Occasionally a charter plane will be late; a generator may cease to operate; and one is not going to be able to always get the best steaks. Guides may not be sophisticated either, but the itinerant angler learns to overlook such shortcomings. After all, the American sportsman has always been interested in fishing those places which have not been overrun by a small army of anglers.

ICELAND—LAND OF SALMON

The first impression a visitor to this tiny country has is that Iceland is not covered by sheets of ice but is, in fact, very green. If the visitor happens to visit nearby Greenland, he is due for some head-scratching, for that country has very little greenery, and a great deal of ice. Whoever named these countries when they were discovered must have been thoroughly confused. At least a few people have suggested that "Laxland" would have been a more appropriate name for Iceland since "lax" means salmon, and the country is fairly well laced with Atlantic salmon rivers.

Iceland might be the least polluted piece of real estate in the entire world. For one thing, this country is practically naked of trees, so you're not going to find any wood burning going on here. The total population of this country numbers less than 250,000 and the majority of these people live in or near Reykjavik. Reykjavik is unique in that the Ellidáar River, which flows through its suburbs, produces over 2,000 salmon per year. No other capital city in the world can approach that claim!

Although there is some very good brown trout and small char fishing, Iceland basically offers Atlantic salmon fishing. There are 60 salmon rivers, of which a couple dozen could be considered very good, and maybe a half dozen fall into the premier quality.

At the top of the list are Laxa i Kjos, Nordura, Laxa i Adaldal, Thvera, and probably Grimsa and Langa.

Laxa i Dolum can be very good and sometimes sensational but it is extremely sensitive to water heights.

If you are looking for huge salmon, the size that one encounters in Norway or at Quebec's Moisie River, forget about Iceland. Most of the Icelandic rivers produce salmon in the six to 10-pound class, with enough in the teens to make things interesing. The exception is Laxa i Adaldal, which produces heavier fish, but during some weeks, this river has a weed problem so it may not provide the very best fishing.

Jim Chapralis grips a 13-pound Atlantic salmon taken in Laxa i Kjos, Iceland.

Since the waters are shallow, these six to 10 pounders are very active indeed; they jump often and can streak off plenty of line. The real pleasure lies in the fact that the angler can use very light tackle (8-ft. fly rod, lightweight reels with fair capacity for backing, and smaller flies)—tackle that one associates more with brown trout fishing than with salmon. Never mind long casts, they

are not necessary in Iceland for the most part, and, in fact, distance casting may be a detriment.

It's not so much the size of the fish that dictates the use of light tackle, so much as the size of fles. In Iceland, hook sizes of 4, 6, 8, and 10 are most popular, and often 12's and 14's are the answer in clear waters. Favorite salmon flies include: Hairy Mary, Blue Charm, Black Doctor, Rusty Rat, Sweep, Night Hawk, and other traditional patterns. The English tube flies and Muddler Minnows have also produced heavily. Most Icelandic rivers are shallow so they can be logically fished with hip boots.

Salmon from Iceland's rivers are small compared to many Continental rivers, but they're acrobatic, gamefish.

Icelandic rivers offer a 90-day season and the best time is the end of June to the first part of August, with July being the best month.

One is quick to notice a certain amount of regimentation on the rivers. By law, the rivers are restricted to 12 hours of fishing per day. Most rivers offer a morning fishing period from 7 A.M. to 1 P.M. and an evening period from 3 P.M. to 9 P.M. (bear in mind that this is the land of the midnight sun), and these hours are religiously followed.

Every river is also designated as to how many anglers can fish it at a time. A "ten-rod river" means that no more than ten persons can fish it at one time. A river is divided into sections or "beats" and these are reserved for the sole use of one angler. Fishermen rotate beats usually after two-hour periods, thus everyone has a chance to fish different parts of the river every day. It sounds chaotic, but it works, and preserves that intimacy between angler and his own water, which after all, is one of the trademarks of Atlantic salmon fishing.

The potential of Icelandic fishing might be quickly gathered by looking through the annual statistics of one river—the Laxa i Kjos. During the 1973 season, the river produced 2,082 salmon. The best single day of fishing produced 84 salmon for ten anglers. One pool provided 22 salmon in a single day's fishing. The best pool produced 224 salmon for the season.

While most American sportsmen more or less adhere to fly fishing, Icelandic laws do not prohibit use of other gear. Icelanders are practical in their fishing attitudes, and are quick to try a spoon or even a worm when their favorite flies do not work. Oddly, sometimes big spoons work very well, which doesn't substantiate the old theory that salmon don't feed once they ascend fresh water rivers, but only rise to flies through a reflexive habit.

The whole catch to the Icelandic salmon fishing deal is the price. The top rivers command, and get, from $1800 to $2000 per week's fishing. One can shave this price somewhat by sharing a rod with a friend. This cuts the price down by approximately 40 percent, but your fishing time is cut in half. Thank God for the reasonable air fares offered by Icelandic Airlines, which happen to have a monopoly on the U.S.-to-Iceland market. A round-trip excursion fare from New York to Reykjavik is only $352.

No one especially gets rich despite the high cost of Icelandic fishing. A good chunk of the money goes to the farmer associations which own the land on either side of a river, and therefore the fishing rights. With the cost of Atlantic salmon sky rocketing to $7 a pound on the market, the farmers are quick to point out that they can "farm" their waters with nets and receive a substantial sum of money. Rightly so. The farmers are very quick to do everything possible, such as construct costly fish laders, stocking the rivers with smolt, build artificial pools (which incidentally have worked tremendously well), and, of course, see to it that poachers are not fishing the waters.

To the fisherman who feels that fishing starts and ends with *salmo salar*, Iceland represents his best bet. But he ought to be aware of one thing: Even in the super rivers

of Iceland, salmon may or may not be cooperative. Icelandic salmon are governed by such variables as weather, water clarity, temperature, and other conditions. But then, the real salmon man knows, otherwise he would have given up on salmon long ago.

ARGENTINA AND ITS GOLDEN FISH—DORADO

Separating Argentina and Paraguay is the sprawling Parana River, home of the dorado, possibly the world's best-fighting, strictly fresh-water fish. The dorado must not be confused with the dolphinfish, which is a marine species, but also called "dorado" in Latin American countries. The dorado averages 10 to 25 pounds, but the Parana River produces fish weighing well over 30 pounds, and there are records of dorado over 60 pounds.

The dorado smashes a plug hard, and almost immediately leaps in the air, and some of his jumps are five or six feet high! One can well appreciate the dorado's fantastic leaps when viewing a movie film shot in slow motion. He twists, turns, tumbles, and often jack-knives four or five times. He comes equipped with very powerful jaws capable of destroying plastic plugs and mangling strong hooks. He has a jawful of small, thick teeth giving him tremendous gripping power. The dorado's body is thick, obviously powerful, and quite different from

Cartwheeling dorado almost shakes its scales off trying to throw angler's plug.

other great leaping fish found in fresh water—such as the slender Atlantic salmon, steelhead, and muskie.

The dorado's spectacular jumps are his trademark; but his bag of tricks include long powerful runs, vigorous head-shaking, and an ability to change directions quickly. The dorado does not sulk like many species but fights very hard from the moment he feels a mouthful of hooks until he is landed, expending every ounce of energy.

The dorado is a river fish, and like the Atlantic salmon, likes to lie in front of a big boulder in current. Unlike the salmon, however, he is not very shy, and if he is inclined to feed (and he nearly always is), he'll smack any plug that approaches his lair.

For the most part, the Parana River is very wide, and in many places it may be a couple of miles wide. The river is broken up with islands in places, or huge rock piles. There are a number of tributaries which are not as deep as the main river, and if an angler wishes to wade he would have to concentrate on those areas. For the most part, the Parana is fished from skiffs powered with outboards.

The success of a dorado trip is determined mostly by two variables. The most important seems to be water levels. Flooding conditions mean poor fishing on the Parana, but the angler may salvage his trip somewhat by fishing the smaller tributaries. The second factor is the quality of the guide. A good guide knows the exact location or holding positions of dorado for various seasons and water conditions, especially water height. Boat positioning is very important and a good guide, after observing an anglers' casting ability, positions the boat so that the fisherman's average cast is likely to swing right in front of a dorado before the lure is retrieved against the current.

As in other remote areas, lighter gear is replacing heavy tackle. At one time the recommended tackle would resemble a 4/0 ocean trolling outfit with a heavy line, long, strong, braided-wire leaders, and huge spoons or plugs. Trolling was considered the most effective method, no doubt by process of elimination since it would be impossible to fling a lure with the above outfit.

But visiting sportsmen, especially from the United States, have done much to change that. Americans have always been more interested in casting for fish, and this means lighter, more manageable tackle. The large plugs of six to seven inches have given way to smaller lures. When I fished the Parana, I quickly lost most of the bigger plugs and was reduced to a few small bass-size lures. Our guide, Virgilio Magri, was convinced that these lures were not only too small, but the delicate hooks would never hold the brawling dorado. He was wrong. The lures proved not only to be excellent producers, but had another distinct advantage too; the smaller lure was taken deeper into the mouth of the dorado, so in addition to hooking better, the lure was beyond the powerful jaws so the fish could not grind the plug with its teeth.

An ideal dorado outfit would consist of a 6½-foot sturdy plug-casting rod, a good casting reel (preferably with a fast retrieve ratio) loaded with quality 15- to 20-pound test line (150 yards or more), six-inch cable-wire leaders with good snaps, and an assortment of plugs such as Creek Chub Pikie Minnows, Wiggle Diver, Cisco Kid, and a few spoons.

Open-face spinning gear can also be used effectively on doardo, and even fly fishing. There have been an increasing number of Americans who have successfully used fly fishing gear for dorado. A size 9 or 10 fly fishing outfit is fine, and tarpon streamers work well.

The season on the Parana River is from June to late October. The last half of August until mid-October is best. The weather tends to be chilly in the morning and evening, so some warm clothes are in order as well as the inevitable two-piece raingear.

Virgilio Magri, Laddie Buchanan, and George Wenckheim are three excellent Parana River guides. Virgilio does not speak much English, but knows how to communicate with Americans. Magri has his own camp, called Apipe Safaris, located at Apipe Rapids, no doubt among the best waters of the Parana. Laddie and George fish any number of places along the Parana, using small inns as a base camp. Places like Corrientes draw at times a large number of fishermen, especially during the much-publicized dorado tournaments, but downstream from Corrientes there's very little pressure. Luis O. Schultz is a good guide who specializes in fishing near Corrientes. The rates are approximately $70 per day, all inclusive, but don't look for luxurious accommodations.

To reach these areas, you must fly to Buenos Aires and from there local airlines fly you to Posadas, Corrientes, and other towns along the Parana.

If there is one disadvantage to dorado fishing (in addition to the hefty air fare, i.e., $640 round-trip excursion fare Miami to Buenos Aires), it is that this fish is very sensitive to water heights and it is a long way to go for casting practice. Laddie Buchanan, however, will

Apipe Rapids, on Argentina's Parana River, is one hot spot for dorado.

set up a trip with the stipulation that if everything appears unfavorable he will cable or call a week prior to the scheduled trip and postpone it. There are a couple of other species of fish at the Parana, but I don't think they are worth going all that distance for unless, of course, one has a good chance for the dorado.

The dorado is an excellent table fish. It is generally barbecued, with constant basting with various sauces. The people along the Parana River are very friendly, and are heavily flattered that a North American would travel so far to fish in their country.

CLUB PACIFICO—INFINITE VARIETY

If Zane Grey were alive today, and if he wanted to do a sequel to his famous "El Dorado" book, he might want to concentrate his efforts at Coiba Island, located on the Pacific side of Panama, not far from the Costa Rican border. For one thing, he might never find a

In most good areas dorado range 10-15 pounds; this 28 pounder is trophy class.

better wahoo fishing spot than this area; certainly he would be impressed with the great abundance and variety of fish. And since he loved big-game fishing, no doubt he would enjoy trolling Hannibal Bank and several other nearby areas which are emerging as outstanding black marlin places. Sailfish? Zane would have loved to tangle with these speedsters, forsaking his heavy gear, for some of today's lighter, sophisticated tackle. No doubt about it, Zane Grey would have loved the Coiba area!

One of many attractions of fishing at Panama's Club Pacifico is that long runs are not necessary to get into good fishing, even for billfish. Jim Chapralis here has a sailfish hooked on fly fishing gear—and within a few hundred yards of shore.

For the first time this fantastic area is available to any sportsman who has the time, inclination, and money, of course. Previously this entire area was unavailable to sportsfishermen, except for a very few hardy souls who had the energy and a good boat loaded with provisions, fuel, and water to safari to this section.

Happily, today there is a modern camp built right smack in the heart of these productive grounds. From this base, sportsmen can fish such exciting areas as Hannibal Bank, Jicaron, Contreras, Secas, Montuosa, and other groups of islands and reefs.

Club Pacifico de Panama was developed by Bob Griffin, a young, energetic sportsman who searched for his "El Dorado" and finally found it at Coiba. Club Pacifico was at first going to be a minimum-comfort lodge capable of handling a half dozen fishermen, who wouldn't mind a number of discomforts and fishing from outboard powered boats. A couple years later, however, Club Pacifico emerged as a luxurious fishing camp that sported such amenities as spacious cottages, wall-to-wall carpeting, air conditioning, a fine main lodge, outdoor patio, cement sidewalks, and a fleet of swift, roomy, 24-foot cruisers equipped with 225 horsepower diesel engines. The investment is probably close to $500,000 and still rising!

The future looks bright indeed for Bob Griffin, who has been able to package that unusual combination of a very comfortable lodge, miles from civilization, in a breathtaking setting, and in an area that just might contain more fish per-square-mile than any other piece of aquatic real estate. That's one heck of a statement, but there's plenty of proof to back it up!

Take the catch of Charles Eberle and his son Clay. In a week's fishing they landed 24 different species totaling 174 fish. This included 39 wahoo, sailfish on plugs, roosterfish, dolphin, amberjack, rainbow runners, barracuda, all varieties of snapper, and other desirable fish.

For the black marlin fisherman, one need only look at the accomplishment of Walter Hidding fishing from one boat with his sons and one of their friends. They had over 20 strikes from black marlin, boating five, with the largest weighing approximately 600 pounds (released). Amazingly, they only concentrated on marlin a fraction of the time since the youths were equally interested in testing some of the other smaller species.

Or consider the results of Dr. Joe Van Cura and Dr. Frank Lhotka. In one day off Coiba Island, they hooked 15 billfish, nine of which were black marlin. What makes this even more spectacular is that those fish were all hooked on artificial plugs and light gear intended for other species. One wonders what that particular day would have produced if bonito had been trolled as bait.

For those who do not wish to brawl with black marlin, they can certainly find happiness with the Pacfiic sailfish. These fish range from 80 to over 100 pounds, are deceptively fast, and among the sea's most acrobatic denizens. Their fast and furious fight allows the angler to use light tackle; in fact, an increasing number of Club Pacifico's clientele are using line tests generally

Natives struggle under the weight of a huge black marlin taken off Coiba Island.

Bob Griffin, owner of Club Pacifico, with sailfish he took on plug casting gear and 6-pound test line.

associated with freshwater bass fishing. Numerous "sails" have been landed on 12-pound test lines and conventional plug-casting gear, and this has been done by "average" fishermen, not the experts who specialize in that sort of thing. In fact, a number of sailfish have been landed on six-pound test line, but this tends to become more theatrical than practical.

The fly fisherman has good opportunity for practicing his sport on these Coiba sails, because these fish have a penchant for following trolled, hookless, plastic squids. These lures are pulled away from the fish continuously, bringing the sail closer and closer to the boat, and at the same time infuriating him. At the proper time the engine is stopped, the squid is pulled out of the water and the fly fisherman plops a popper or big streamer near the sail. The fish is so angry by this time that he sucks in the popper or fly.

Snapper fishing is generally unexciting elsewhere in the world since this species is a bottom feeder. At Club Pacifico, however, they are often taken on the surface on top-water plugs and by casting. The spring fishing is especially good, because the cubera snapper are feeding on crab, and that's the time to fish a surface plug. The average cubera is probably from 20 to 40 pounds here, and the record at the camp is 77 pounds, caught by George Markham. Bigger ones have been hooked, some say over 100 pounds, but it is difficult to bring them in even on heavy gear.

At times Coiba Island waters are covered with thousands of dolphin—a fish which always provides a fantastic aerial fight. The surface plug-caster or fly fisherman is in his glory amidst a school of dolphin.

Roosterfish are an enigma at Club Pacifico. At times they are easily found and hooked, but often they are difficult to locate. One reason might be that every roosterfish taken at Club Pacifico has been hooked on artificial lures, and no one has tried bait fishing, a very productive method employed in the La Paz area of Baja California.

When Griffin is asked how come bait has not been tried for "roosters," he shrugs and explains: "Look, we have only scratched a small fraction of these waters and haven't even started experimenting. We hardly have become acquainted with 5 percent of the area we fish. For example, we know that there are good snook in a number of areas and we haven't been very successful with them. This past season we discovered black marlin in good quantity that we were not aware of previously. We found tremendous quantities of sailfish just a couple of hundred yards offshore. Before we were looking for them miles from shore with only fair results. I hope that Club Pacifico becomes what Christmas gifts are to a child. Each time a guest returns to Club Pacifico we want him to unwrap a new fishing adventure. It was thought at first that these waters were mostly good for trolling. Now even fly fishermen are doing well."

Roosterfish, taken along rocks at Panama's Coiba Island, are supreme light-tackle fish for anglers using casting, spinning, and fly gear.

Here's a 30-pound cubera snapper, courtesy Club Pacifico. Camp record, however, for cuberas, is 77 pounds!

There's a great deal that must be learned about seasons, too. Basically Club Pacifico is a good year-round fishing ground, with the exception of September, October, and maybe the first half of November, when heavy rains can be expected. It is even good during those months for wahoo, but the weather is too uncomfortable for most guests.

All species of fish have been taken year-round off the island, but wahoo fishing is best from mid-June to mid-January. The summer months in Panama tend to be the coolest, and although one can expect showers, summer is a very comfortable time to fish. Sailfish seem to be very thick at that time. As an example, Dr. Richard Reilly and his party, fishing from one boat, raised *40 sails in one afternoon!*

The rates at Club Pacifico for their weekly package (two persons fishing to a boat) are $800 per person. While at first this may appear higher than some camps in Latin America, one should consider that accommodations are far superior and offer air conditioning and other comforts, plus the fact that the anglers fish from brand new, expensive boats with powerful motors.

Bookings are accepted on a Friday-to-Friday basis. Clients fly to Panama City, Panama on Thursday; stay at one of the fine hotels available, and the next morning are flown by charter plane ($75 per person round trip) to the island of Coiba.

Club Pacifico is not all things to all anglers. It is a place where the potential runs very high for a variety of fishing, but an occasional poor week pops up. However, that is less likely to happen at Club Pacifico than at other places.

PARISMINA—THE PLACE FOR TARPON AND SNOOK

Parismina is hardly a new, exotic fishing area. Possibly this camp has been featured in more articles than any other fishing camp. But there's a new look to Parismina, and another dimension has been added to the fishing there.

Previously Parismina was a very rustic jungle camp with limited comforts, but since Jerry Tricomi and his wife purchased it the camp has been completely renovated. Individual cottages with private washroom facilities, cement sidewalks, floral garden, and new boats and motors have been added to Parismina. While still not luxurious, it is as comfortable as most typical Canadian fishing camps. At one time the clientele was more or less confined to males; but today men are taking their wives to Parismina.

The camp is located on the Parismina River, on the east coast of Costa Rica, 25 miles north of the port town of Limon. This is tarpon and snook country, and when conditions are right it would be difficult to find a better area. Most of the fishing takes place in the freshwater lagoons and intricate network of waterways. Often tarpon can be found by the hundreds in such famous spots as California Creek, Pacuare, or the mouth of the Parismina River itself. Tarpon can actually be seen entering the mouth of the river as they porpoise and roll.

What makes Costa Rican fishing so appealing is that, first of all, northern fishermen can escape the climes of winter, since some of the best fishing takes place from mid-January to mid-May. Secondly, just about every method of fishing can be used: spinning, plugcasting, fly fishing and surf casting. For those unskilled

at casting, trolling is a very effective method and a solution for the wife who has little fishing experience.

Fishing is done from 16-foot skiffs powered with 18- to 25-horsepower motors, with two persons sharing a boat and guide. There is an increased tendency to use lighter tackle at Parismina, and today probably 20-pound test lines are preferred, despite the fact that few of the tarpon weigh under 60 pounds and probably average close to 70 pounds. The most important aspect of tarpon fishing is knot-tying and, of course, hook-sharpening—but Jerry Tricomi has all his guides trained to tie proper knots.

Parismina has added something different for 1975. It is Tricomi's pontoon boat, which should solve the problem of finding tarpon in the ocean when they are uncooperative in the lagoons. During the winter and spring season, the mouth of the river is dangerous to negotiate because of the out-flowing current, sand bars, and surf. Heretofore ocean fishing was practically impossible on all but the calmest days.

Tricomi's new boat consists of two 38-foot fiberglass floats. A sturdy platform is constructed six feet above

True to form, a nice Parismina tarpon comes up and out—too close to the angler and the boat.

the pontoons. Guests and smaller boats can be placed on the platform, and theoretically the surf breaking underneath the platform should be of no concern. Beyond the mouth of the river, the ocean is often sufficiently calm to fish from smaller boats.

The attraction of ocean fishing is that nearly always one can find huge concentrations of tarpon, hundreds and sometimes thousands of tarpon. Actually, these fish are not very far from the mouth of the Parismina, and most of the time they are only a few hundred yards offshore.

In addition to tarpon, Parismina guests fishing the ocean take good kingfish, and some of the kings are taken on fly-fishing gear. Other species include jacks, Spanish mackerel, barracuda, and possibly some reef fish

In fall Costa Rica's Parismina River is a top spot for large snook. Dave Carley took this 30-pounder.

farther out. Between the mouth of the Parismina and the port town of Limon, there's a big reef several miles offshore, and at least several knowledgeable persons claim that it contains Atlantic sailfish, dolphin, cubera snapper, amberjack, and other species. With the pontoon boat, there's some thought of exploring this reef for these desirable species, which of course will widen the variety of Parismina fishing.

While the tarpon seems to grab most of the headlines along the Caribbean coast of Costa Rica, there's excellent snook fishing at every river mouth. The big snook, those weighing 25 pounds and more, are caught chiefly during the "fall season," which starts at the end of August and continues to late October. At that time big snook come to the beaches and are best fished by wading the surf and casting out. Carlos Barrantes, previous owner of Parismina Tarpon Rancho and the man who put Costa Rica on the angler's map, feels it is important to pick a likely spot and continuously cast, if not energetically, certainly mechanically. It does seem monotonous, but when the snook start to feed, the results can be extraordinary. I have seen Carlos do just that: Cast to one spot for several hours. I once left him for some excitement from tarpon and when I came back a couple of hours later, he had taken six snook. The smallest was 18 pounds, and the largest 28 pounds. In those two hours, Carlos had taken more big snook than some snook-chashers take in several years of fishing in Florida.

Dr. Fred Novak in two hours of fishing at Parismina landed four snook. They weighed: 5, 14, 23, and 30½ pounds. That, of course, reperesents unusually good snook fishing, because there are many slow periods, even at Parismina.

Parismina is open during the fall season to take advantage of the snook run, but this is also a great time for tarpon because the ocean is often calm then. As an example, Dr. Rod Neubert boated 19 tarpon on a fly rod in one week, and that was only his second try at tarpon fishing. During another week in September, Winston Moore landed a dozen tarpon on a fly rod, and when you consider that these fish run well over 60 pounds on the average, that is quite an accomplishment.

There's also good snook fishing during the "normal tarpon season" which runs from mid-January to mid-May. Late January often produces very fast snook fishing, but these snook run from only four to 12 pounds on the average. On light bass tackle, however, they provide great sport indeed.

After the "school" snook diminish, snook are caught less frequently, but they are larger. Even during the tarpon season there usually are a number of snook close to, or over, 30 pounds taken. Happily, one of the best snook holes is just across from the camp, and after a day's tarpon fishing, many anglers like to stop off and fish snook there for a few minutes.

The rate at Parismina is $500 per person, double occupancy, Saturday to Saturday. This includes all accommodations, all meals at camp, seven days' fishing, boat, motor, guide, and fuel. There are some attractive excursion air fares from a number of cities or gateways in the United States. As an example, from Chicago, New York, Boston, and other northern cities one can fly to San Jose round-trip via Miami for $303. There are even more attractive fares for a party of ten or more sportsmen traveling together.

While a high percentage of anglers fishing Parismina are rewarded with top-drawer tarpon or snook action, a poor week of fishing now and then can be expected. Weather conditions and heavy rainfall are certainly determining factors, but since they are unpredictable, you better go to Parismina (or on any fishing trip for that matter) when you can!

PEZ MAYA—FOR BONES AND PERMIT

Those who have fished Pez Maya Resort might ask: "What is a nice comfortable camp, so close to Miami, doing in an article on exotic fishing?" True, Pez Maya is easily reached via a short flight to Cozumel from Miami, and then a 20-minute hop right to the camp's airstrip by light plane. True, Pez Maya also offers very comfortable facilities, and, moreover, the chances for a trophy fish are indeed slim.

Pez Maya is included here, however, because it provides some fast bonefishing as well as good potential for permit, and the area is certainly not overrun by tourists. Pez Maya has the distinct advantage of offering short trips (three days minimum), the air fare is small, and the resort is ideal for the person who is planning a business or pleasure trip to Miami and who has a few days for fishing.

Pez Maya might well represent the very best place for a fisherman who has been completely frustrated in his pursuit of bonefish in other areas. The catch is that these bonefish run two to four pounds and probably average three pounds or less. However, the "bones" are not anywhere near as spooky as their Florida Keys or Bahamian counterparts. If you happen to be there dur-

Spin fisherman tosses one out for bonefish at Pez Maya.

ing favorable conditions, it would take a good deal of bad luck, or a very uncoordinated fisherman to terminate his trip without catching a few bones.

This writer, for example, in one-and-a-half days, took a total of 27 bones on a fly rod, and previously had only modest experience with the species.

Pez Maya is probably the very best place to hook a permit, which is no doubt the wariest of all marine species. Yet fishermen of only mediocre skill have sometimes taken several permit in one day. The same fisherman might spend a number of weeks fishing in the Keys without hooking one. Like the bonefish, permit run considerably smaller at Pez Maya than in the Keys or Bahamas. Most of them will go from seven to twenty pounds.

Cubera snapper are taken at an outlet, a few hundred yards from the camp. The area is best fished with top-water plugs in the evening after supper. There are a number of places in the inside lagoons where one can take barracuda, and occasionally small tarpon and snook. But conditions for tarpon and snook must be ideal for them to come into the lagoons. So anyone going to Pez Maya specifically for snook or tarpon is likely to be disappointed.

Pez Maya fishing resort offers comfortable accommodations.

On the ocean side, there are good runs of wahoo, but not so consistent that one can definitely plan on them. Water conditions must be ideal. The camp owner is procuring bigger boats to explore some of this ocean fishing.

Basically, if one goes to Pez Maya with the hope of getting some good bonefishing and a chance at permit, and possibly pick up a couple of other species, he is not likely to be disappointed. If he plans his trip toward the end of April, May, or June, he might want to spend a couple of days at Cozumel and charter one of the boats there to sample some fine Atlantic sailfishing.

As far as tackle is concerned for Pez Maya, it should be on the light side. If you enjoy fly fishing, and if conditions are not too windy, you can get by with an eight-foot fly rod equipped to take a size six or seven shooting-head line. Most of the bonefish fly patterns work well, but the shrimp keel fly is hard to beat. Spinfishermen should use a light rod (6½- to 7- feet), and a good spinning reel equipped with at least 150 yards of six-pound monofilament. "Wiggle Jigs," in ⅛ to ¼ ounce sizes, will work fine. Slightly heavier gear is suggested for permit fishing.

It would be hard to find a fishing camp with more tasteful architecture. When owner Mauro Gonzalez designed his camp, he blended Mayan architecture with the modern, and came up with a very attractive camp. Most of the stone used for the construction had to be taken from the ocean by divers and shaped by hand.

Pez Maya is most popular from December until the end of June and this represents the entire season. Probably April and May provide the best bonefishing, because the winds are not as heavy during this time.

The rate per person at Pez Maya is $300. This includes the charter plane service from Cozumel (round-trip), three days' fishing, all meals, boat, motor, fuel, and guide. It also includes an overnight at the Cabanas del Caribe in Cozumel prior to going to Pez Maya. The round-trip air fare from Miami to Cozumel is $117 per person.

CHAPTER 34

The "Shooting Basket"

Buy one ready-made or make your own "basket"—then cast a country mile.

Fly fishermen who do much angling on large rivers might be interested in trying a casting aid used by many steelheaded fishermen in the West. It's called the "shooting basket."

Commercially-made "shooting baskets" are available from firms such as the Orvis Co. (Manchester, VT) and Eddie Bauer Co. (Seattle, WA).

A shooting basket is a vinyl or plastic tray-like device that is strapped around the angler's waist. They are five or six inches deep, and are used to hold the backing or "shooting" line, and part of the fly line, when a cast is delivered.

Angler at left.wears "shooting basket" fashioned from a cardboard box. Better line holders can be made from plastic "bowls" used for dishwashing, etc. Fisherman on right has a commercially-made vinyl basket.

Backing line used with "shooting head" fly line is stripped loosely into "shooting basket."

267

With yards of fine backing line coiled loosely in box, steelhead fisherman on British Columbia's Babine River starts long cast across and downstream.

Belt passed through slots cut in cardboard box holds "basket" in place. "Baskets" of this type do not last long but are easily replaced with no expense.

Long casts are the rule in steelhead fishing, whether it be in Washington, British Columbia, Michigan, or Wisconsin. Too, the fisherman usually is forced to wade very deep, in heavy water. As he retrieves line normally, following a cast, he must either drop the loose line to the water—where it will be grabbed and pulled by the current—hold it in loose coils or, as some fishermen do, hold coils of line in their months. All of those methods add to the difficulty of casting 90 to 100 feet or more.

But with a shooting basket strapped to his waist, the deepwading fisherman merely strips loose line into the "basket," then "shoots" it on the forward cast. The fly line and backing literally zoom out of the "basket," and casts of 100 feet become a simple routine.

Satisfactory "home-made" shooting baskets can be fashioned from heavy cardboard boxes or plastic dish pans. Make two slots in the back of the box or pan, and slip a heavy belt through. If you use a cardboard box and it finally falls apart, from getting wet, just get another box and make another "basket."

"Shooting head" line zips away and hauls running line out of basket. Casts of 120–150 feet are not difficult.

CHAPTER 35

Gulf Coast Rig Fishing

By McFadden Duffy

Recent World Records caught at the Gulf oil rigs off Louisiana include a 44 lb., 5 oz. king mackerel landed by John R. Peters, Jr., on February 10, 1974, for a men's 12 pound line class record; and a 30 lb., 4 oz. red drum caught by Priscilla Jordan in April, 1973, for a women's 6 pound line class record.

In November of 1972, there was a relatively quiet but important celebration in Morgan City, Louisiana, USA, just a two hour drive west from New Orleans. Presidents and senior executives of the country's major oil companies gathered to participate in ceremonies marking the 25th anniversary of the first offshore oil drilling completion. Gathered with these distinguished visitors were heads of the many construction, fabricating and service companies which make possible exploration and production of oil and gas from the depths of the Gulf of Mexico.

Out in the gulf on these two important days in the annals of offshore petroleum operations, several thousand fishermen—completely unmindful of what was taking place in Morgan City—were enjoying what is known in Louisiana today as "rig fishing." At that time of the year they were hauling up red snappers, battling slashing king mackerel, tangling with toothy bluefish, reeling in Spanish mackerel, white trout (weakfish), spadefish, cussing lookdowns and occasionally snapping lines on stubborn amberjacks. Perhaps, here and there, a group would be tied up to a rig over a school of pompano, deftly catching these cautious nibblers that command a better price on the market than prime beef.

In the March-April issue of "The International Marine Angler" it was reported that the first international conference to explore artificial reef construction and use had been held March 20-22 in Houston, Texas. Panel discussions, designed to provide for maximum sharing of information, opinions and ideas, focused on artificial reefs around the world; scientific aspects, materials and methods of construction; physical, economic and legal considerations, all vital to construction of reefs to attract and concentrate fish for marine anglers.

It can be assumed that this was a meaty series of discussions because construction of artificial reefs embraces a number of responsibilities. This has been demonstrated in the northern Gulf of Mexico where several of Louisiana's sister states decided they would construct artificial reefs to provide the start of ecosystems that would attract and concentrate fish.

In one instance, old automobile bodies were towed offshore and dumped from barges. This proved to be a dismal failure because the tidal action soon moved the cars around. Thus, they not only ceased to be an artificial reef, but they presented a hazard to shrimp trawlers who snagged one of the old automobiles from time to time, ruining the expensive trawls.

Eventually the U.S. Coast Guard entered the artificial reef picture and came up with specific regulations for their establishment. They called for buoy marking for night and day maritime traffic, fog-sounding devices, and minimum clearance, along with the lacing together of reef material and proper weighting to name just a few of the expensive items in which reef builders would have to invest.

Good-size bluefish are simple routine when fishing offshore Louisiana.

It soon became obvious that building an artificial reef wasn't as simple as it sounded to the enthusiastic fisherman. There were other vested interests and even a small artificial reef could prove costly.

It was really by accident that fishermen discovered that offshore oil wells served as artificial reefs. When the first offshore well was being drilled, just over a quarter century ago, it attracted numerous sightseers and a few brought tackle along. Some of them tried fishing near the first well and they caught quite a few fish. Some ventured the opinion that the noise of the rig operation attracted the fish. This might seem foolish to biologists, but the fact remains that even today fish can be taken around a working rig shortly after it has been

moved into position and before the ecosystem can be established that will eventually make the offshore platform a permanent home for fish.

At the present time there are thousands of offshore drilling platforms, producing wells and gas completions strung out along the coast of Louisiana from Texas to the Mississippi Sound. These, and the huge offshore sulphur mine near Grand Isle, Louisiana, provide "artificial reefs" costing untold millions of dollars. As the rigs move ever outward from shore, not unlike a horde of mighty steel spiders, the cost of the drilling rigs becomes greater. But this cost is borne by the oil companies and the side benefits of the rigs accrue primarily to sport fishermen.

Wherever the rigs, platforms, producing structures (all lumped together and referred to as rigs), and pipe line centers are found, there are ecological changes that take place. Contrary to some people's beliefs, they are not harmful changes, as fisheries statistics for Louisiana and other northern Gulf states readily reveal.

In a sense, Louisiana took a gamble and won as far as sport fishermen are concerned. The vast oil and gas production off the Louisiana coast has proved that oil and water do mix—not in the laboratory sense, but in practicality. Any look at federal fisheries statistics will show this to be true. As oil and gas development took place in the Gulf, fisheries products increased. The increase may be partly due to the fact that individuals in the coastal fisheries have increased numerically, as have petroleum and gas activities, but the fact remains that observation over a quarter of a century has proved that the rigs do produce fish.

More properly, it should be said that the rigs collect fish and make them available to anglers. The welded steel stanchions that criss-cross the huge structures underwater soon begin to collect algae, which are basically primitive chlorophyll-bearing plants that start a food chain cycle. The algae attract little bait fish, which in turn attract bigger fish, and then even bigger fish. In short, the oil platforms that fishermen call rigs become artificial reefs offering housing to varieties of fish that probably have been present in the Gulf of Mexico for centuries but have never felt the sting of a baited hook or the steel shaft from a spearfisherman's gun.

It might be appropriate at this time to say that offshore oil production, especially in its relationship to marine and estuarine ecological problems, most of which are not related to oil operations, has become the center of considerable debate in recent years. The controversy still goes on between well-meaning environmentalists and advocates of multiple use of natural resources. Probably much of this debate developed from and was focused on the effects of certain accidental oil spills which were of great size but of generally short duration.

These accidents, staring with the Torrey Canyon incident in England, the Santa Barbara (California) spill, and the Chevron, Shell and Amoco platform fires, attracted the attention of the world press, television, the public and political leaders. Just as an indictment makes headlines and a "not guilty" is often buried in the want ads, so to speak, such accidents do not represent the true impact of the petroleum industry on the basic marine ecological systems, nor is there much evidence that after the hue and cry have been raised that the accidents have actually affected the environment to any degree, or permanently.

In the offshore deep-water areas off Louisiana where the oil rigs now extend, the ecosystem is more stable than it is close to the coastline, and the placement of physical structures such as platforms appears to have little effect on marine fauna in the area. The fact is that the numerous offshore platforms have been highly beneficial to recreational and sport fishing off the Louisiana coast, as they would off any oil-producing coast.

Rig and flare fishing (fishing around the light of burning natural gas flares at night) represent a new and valuable industry to the state. Fishing success near the rigs is phenomenal, and night fishing in the area of the structures where waste gas is burned is excellent. There is little doubt in the minds of Louisiana fishermen that the almost countless offshore structures serve as the most expensive and productive artificial reefs in the sea. For the small-boat fishermen and the charter boat captains the rigs in the Gulf have opened up whole new areas of relatively safe and highly successful fishing.

Species of fish which had never been caught by sport fishermen before the advent of the oil rigs are now plentiful. Of the 28 species of fish eligible for trophies in Louisiana's Grand Isle Tarpon Rodeo, for example, more than a dozen of them have been added to the eligible fish categories since the ecosystems developed around the offshore platforms. The mighty, tailwalking, leaping tarpon—the most prized fish in these contests—is not a result of petroleum platforms in the Gulf, but it has numerous other companion fish that are a direct result of the platforms and flares. These include

hefty amberjack, cruising barracuda, bluefish, king mackerel, Spanish mackerel, red snappers, sheepshead, spadefish, tripletail and blackfin tuna.

Fishing the oil rigs is something anyone can do, and enjoy. There's bait fishing for the novice, but experts can cast lures or flies and take bluefish, mackerel, etc.

In the case of the barracuda, for example, early records kept by the Louisiana Outdoor Writers Association showed no entries by rod and reel fishermen until an angler named John Dofter entered a 37 pound, eight ounce 'cuda in 1965. It was tied four months later by a barracuda caught by Richard Glynn. Today, the top barracuda is a 50 pounder, caught by A. C. Mills in August 1970. There was only one thing that caused barracuda to take up summer residence around the platforms. It was the food chain ecosystem developed by the rigs. Prior to the two early catches, no barracuda had been recorded by the Louisiana Outdoor Writers Association, and it has been keeping records for more than 25 years.

There are also seasonal visitors to the rigs such as pompano, considered the prince of game and food fish when taken on light tackle. Each year finds more cobia lingering in Louisiana's waters as well, generally around the petroleum rigs. In short, there was a time when Gulf fishing was a warm weather sport. Now, it is an annual sport, bringing economic benefits as well as unrivaled recreational benefits.

The unfortunate thing for U.S. Atlantic and Pacific coast anglers is that today's environmental groups, private for the most part, have made the petroleum industry the whipping boy for everything that stands for pollution. They are just now seeking out what might be called the major polluters for assault; but they have not released petroleum as a primary source of pollution.

What is needed is an in-depth study of 25 years of offshore operations in the Gulf off Louisiana's coast, showing the upsurge in commercial fisheries production and the benefits that have accrued to the sport anglers. It is said that there is not a single offshore petroleum platform from Maine to Florida, and those coastal states do not want to see refineries either. In reality, they are failing to take into consideration multiple uses of natural resources.

Additionally, they are depriving marine anglers of excellent fishing, leaving needed petroleum resources untapped in an energy-hungry country, and paying no heed to years of research and evaluation that have been conducted in Louisiana since the first drill bit began boring into the bottom of the Gulf of Mexico.

Louisiana has not suffered from offshore drilling for oil and gas. It has gained economically, with one of the now dollar-important side benefits—marine sport fisheries.

The point to keep in mind in regard to oil rig fishing off the coast of Louisiana, USA, in the Gulf of Mexico, is that for slightly over a quarter of a century, oil and water have mixed. Anyone doubting that is invited to sample Louisiana's rig fishing. The petroleum structures are there by the thousands and the fish are there by the millions! It would be a safe bet to wager that as the petroleum industry probes deeper into Louisiana's offshore waters, there will be better fishing. This is true not only of commercial fishing in which Louisiana leads the country, but also in sport fishing. The factual data is available to anyone, and not only from state sources. Federal statistics will reveal the same information!

The advent of fast, twin engine sport boats have opened the entire oil rig angling frontier in the Gulf of Mexico to the average fisherman. Some venturesome anglers think nothing at all about running 25 miles offshore. They keep an eye on the weather and make a dash to safe harbor if the weather turns sour. Traveling in pairs is an accepted practice.

To fish a rig, it is necessary to "tie on" to the lower stanchions. Boats are never anchored at the rigs because of the danger of the anchor line becoming entangled with the lower section of the structure, which in many cases slants outward and is actually under the boat. The rig must be approached with caution, and of course the boat must be tied so that it will swing free away from the structure on the current or wind and will not bang against it. Most coastal sporting goods stores carry light, long aluminum poles with huge, bent, hooklike front ends to facilitate boaters in catching on to a stanchion and holding their position until a mooring line can be fastened, allowing the boat to drift back the desired distance.

There are three basic types of rig fishing and two of these involve being tied to the rig. These two are bottom fishing and casting.

BOTTOM FISHING

In bottom fishing, the anglers tie up as close to the rig as possible and fish straight down, using cut bait, shrimp or squid. Your bait may be anywhere from 30 feet down to 100 feet or more. Some anglers use as many as three drop lines, although two baited hooks is the general practice. Catching two fish at a time is common and these are called "double headers" by bottom fishermen.

The fishing tackle used in bottom fishing is generally heavy. The rod is sturdy and not too long. The reel is sturdy and spooled with not less than 30 to 50 pound test line. There's no telling what species of fish will take the bait, and hauling up an amberjack requires heavier tackle than taking two bluefish or a pair of snappers.

CASTING

An altogether different form of sport is found in casting around the rigs. For this, the boat is allowed to drift back on the mooring line and light tackle is used. Spinning gear seems to be the favorite tackle in this type of fishing, although some anglers prefer casting tackle. Artificial lures are best in this sort of rig fishing. Good advice is to bring plenty of lures. Bluefish are a nuisance at times and will either slash a big piece out of a hooked and fighting fish, or cut the swivel and line. Black swivels are recommended for rig fishing.

One of the choice targets at the rigs in the summer months is cobia, a large fish which is not too difficult to

To most anglers a "double" of small snappers is nothing to get excited about, but it can be exciting sport to many fishermen.

Fly fishing from boats anchored at oil rigs for bottom fishing often takes bluefish 2 pounds and better.

land on light tackle. They may be seen swimming leisurely around the edges of the platforms, generally on the shady side, and will hit just about anything tossed their way. Catching a single cobia is always a good omen because where one is hooked there are usually more. Curiously, when a cobia is hooked, often others will swim out and around it seemingly wondering what is going on. Other fishermen aboard can cast for them and it is not uncommon to have two or three cobia hooked and battling at the same time. But if the first fish is hauled in too quickly, the others will swim back under the rig.

The same is true of what Louisiana fishermen call "school dolphin" or large schools of young dolphin. Experience has taught that keeping one on a line in the water will hold the school near the boat for a half hour at times. When a second and third fish are hooked the first is taken aboard. They are about the most beautiful fish taken around the rigs, but immediately lose that spectacular coloring when boated and iced down.

TROLLING

The third method of rig fishing is trolling, with from two to four lines out. The boat lazily circles the rig and there's no telling what fish will take the lure or bait, as the case might be. Many king mackerel are taken in this fashion and they're battlers from the first strike. They'll make a long run and sometimes take to the air in an effort to free themselves. While the most sought-after quarry in trolling are king mackerel, a swing around an offshore platform may produce anything from Spanish mackerel to bonito. These are school fish and when the action starts it usually lasts a long time.

DRIFT FISHING

While trolling is a good way to raise king mackerel or tangle with Spanish mackerel, bonito and a half-dozen other species that can be found around the rigs including redfish (channel bass) and speckled trout (spotted sea trout), there's another way to get kings. This writer thinks this manner of fishing produces the most king mackerel action. You can try it even while you're tied to a rig for bottom fishing or casting.

Along the Louisiana coast they call it "drift fishing." You rig your line and leader and fit it with a good hook on a swivel at the business end of the leader. Then take a small white trout (weakfish) or some other bait fish and put it on the hook. Toss it out in the direction the current is moving and let it drift. When it's out 50 to 65 yards, set the drag and put the rod in a holder. Then go about your business of bottom fishing or casting.

We like king mackerel because they do not mess around with a bait. They take it on the run and keep running. It's a good idea to let a mackerel run with the bait, mouthing it while you hasten to grab the rod from the holder. In the time that it takes to do that, the bait is swallowed and the time has come to set the hook. There are those who will not agree, feeling that four lines out with spoons, dusters or other lures, will get the most action. It is a debatable question but whenever a fine catch of kings is unloaded at the dock, chances are that the anglers will readily admit the fish were taken drift fishing.

OTHER SPECIES

Spadefish are so numerous around some rigs that they might rightfully be called the fish to which parents should introduce their youngsters. A young person can become sour on fishing if he doesn't get any action. Adults want bigger and better fish, but for those taking young anglers out for the first time, it might be well to ask a charter boat captain for the location of a rig where spadefish are plentiful. They will be glad to obilge and after a couple of hours, an adult has converted a potential fisherman into a dedicated angler for the rest of his life. There's no frustration for young folks around the rigs.

Red snappers are the most popular fish with charter groups. They want fish for the freezer and the snappers are there for the taking. In this writer's personal opinion, the red snapper is more a commercial fish than a sport fish. For one thing, the snapper schools are down deep and it takes a lot of lead to get down to their depth because of current flow. When hooked, sometimes three at a time, it is a matter of cranking them up. Not much sport, but plenty of food.

Along with the brick-red "Pensacola" snappers, rig fishermen also take mangrove snappers and lane snappers from time to time. At the rigs, one just can't predict what will be in the day's catch, although it's fairly certain that the fishing party will not go home empty-handed.

CHARTER FLEET

Louisiana's charter fleet isn't as large as some states can boast. In fact, Louisiana is missing a bet as far as the tourist-fisherman dollars are concerned because there is ample room for more boats. A good guess is that there are less than 40 charter boats in Louisiana waters, and only one "party boat" out of Empire that takes persons out to the rigs at a nominal charge of about $11.00 a head, renting tackle and bait for $2.00.

FOR FURTHER INFORMATION

On Louisiana salt water sport fishing, write to: Information Section, Louisiana Wild Life & Fisheries Commission, 400 Royal Street, New Orleans, Louisiana 70130, USA.

CHAPTER 36

Newest Taxidermy Twist— "Freeze-Dried" Fish

An Illinois taxidermist no longer "stuffs" fish. He literally dehydrates them, and claims it's the best possible way to preserve your important angling trophies.

By Bob McNally

Taxidermy has been around almost as long as man has angled for fish and hunted game. Through the years certain refinements have been made in taxidermy so that more life-like mounts could be produced, and also so that sportsmen could keep their decorative trophies longer without having them deteriorate.

Conventional taxidermy requires hours of tedious work. The taxidermist often labors for days to get everything "perfect" on a mount before it's completed. And usually it takes months before a taxidermist can get to do a fish because of the backlog of specimens he has.

But "Buzz" Meyers (Route 3, Box 215, Sand Bar Road, tel. 815-933-9455), of Kankakee, Ill., has found a new method of mounting all types of fish and game. His technique is similar to the freeze-dry food process.

Meyers got the idea of freeze-drying fish from the Smithsonian Institution in Washington, D.C. The Smithsonian was freeze-drying fish and animals for use as

Freeze-dried bowfin, appearing very life-like, gets finishing touch with lacquer spray.

275

specimens, Meyers read an article about it, and wrote to the Institution.

After some lengthy correspondence, the Smithsonian sent Meyers the detailed information he needed to build his own freeze-drying unit.

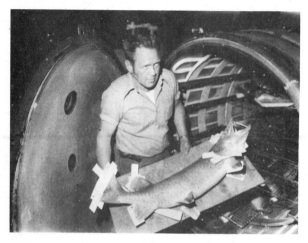

Taxidermist "Buzz" Meyers of Kankakee, Ill. prepares to place a muskie in his freezing, drying chamber.

Meyers built this freeze-drying chamber himself, but got the idea from Smithsonian Institution, Wash., D.C., which had been using the process for mounting fish and animal specimens satisfactorily for years.

Building the unit was extremely complicated. However, with the help of some friends, and a local college class studying refrigeration techniques, he was able to build a small freeze-drying chamber.

There were problems with the freeze-drying operation at first, but eventually most of them were ironed out and Meyers began turning out excellent mounts of fish for sportsmen. However, it soon became apparent that his freeze-drying chamber was too small. Because his fish mounts were so good he had more business than his small freeze-drying chamber could handle, and also the electrical cost to run the small unit far outweighed the profit from his work.

Determined not to give up, this innovative taxidermist purchased an old 1,000 gallon steam boiler, got his friends together again, and went back to work. They made the tank into a huge freeze-drying chamber which was seven times the size of the original model. Thus, Meyers was able to reduce the cost of running his freeze-drying equipment because he could place many more specimens in the larger tank than he could in the smaller original. This made freeze-drying a practical, economical tool of his taxidermist's trade.

Meyers' freeze-drying chamber works like this. One compressor keeps the large steam boiler "specimen" tank at approximately 10 degrees below zero. Another compressor keeps a condenser tank at approximately 50 degrees below zero. The "specimen" tank and condenser tank are connected by a large pipe. A vacuum pump also is connected to the large "specimen" tank. When the machinery is turned on the moisture from the fish in the "specimen" tank is drawn to refrigeration coils in the condenser tank where it turns into ice and is disposed of. The vacuum pump keeps the fish from shrinking while all the moisture is being drawn out.

Most fish are about 70 percent water, and when freeze-dried, they have the texture and weight of styrofoam. Since the water has been extracted, the specimen will not deteriorate in the open air, and Meyers injects his fish mounts with a special type of chemical to prevent the mount from being destroyed by bacteria.

"Usually when all of the moisture has been withdrawn from a fish the mount is finished," Meyers says. "Some fish, however, require proper color restoration or a thin coat of a special lacquer that gives the mount a beautiful, natural shine. But all of this depends upon the type of fish, and the care the fish was given after being caught. Fish should be frozen as soon as possible. Then it's usu-

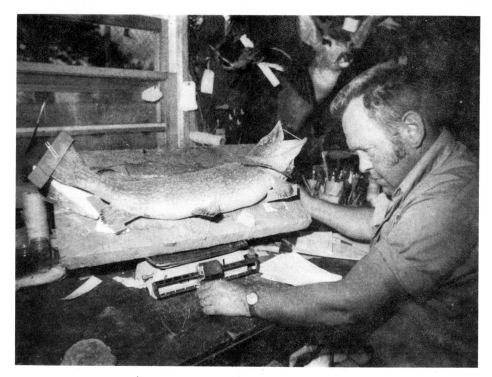

Meyers weighs a northern pike in the mounting, uh, *freeze-drying process.*

ally no problem for me to mount the specimen any way the customer wants."

When Meyers first receives a fish he positions it the way the customer wants the mount to look. He does this in a unique way. When he's beginning to work on a fish he "paper clips" pieces of cardboard to the fins and under the gill-plates. This way the fins and gills can be positioned any way Meyers wants for a more life-like mount. Then he freezes the fish. After it's frozen, he weighs the fish, records the weight, and places it in his freeze-drying tank. Every few weeks he takes the fish out of the chamber and weighs it. The mount is "done" when it has weighed the same two or three different times—which means all of the moisture has been drawn out.

Fish usually take from one to five months to be completed, depending upon the size and type of the specimen.

Meyers' freeze-drying process saves him many hours of actual bench work, which is required when using normal taxidermy methods. However, he must pay large electric bills, and also for maintenance upkeep on his freeze-drying operation. Yet, his taxidermy prices are very reasonable and are comparable to, or even lower than, other taxidermist's fees.

Meyers explains that his freeze-dried fish specimens stand up better to heat and humidity than do many mounts done the old taxidermy method. "Many conventionally mounted specimens have preserved skins, so they dry out and the skins shrink on the specimen forms," Meyer says. "But with freeze-dried specimens this can't happen."

Some taxidermists dislike Meyers' new freeze-dry method of mounting fish. "They say it isn't true taxidermy," Meyers states with enthusiasm. "But I don't care how the mount is done as long as the specimen is life-like. With the normal method of taxidermy some type of body form must be used, but all fish are built differently, and often pre-made forms are too big or too small for a specific specimen. But with the freeze-dried technique you can't get a better form—because you use the actual fish. All you need is the ability to place the specimen in the proper position before beginning to take the moisture out of it."

With his freeze-dry process Meyers has mounted everything from ciscos to cohos and from 4-ounce bluegills to 40-pound muskies. People from all over the country have been contacting Meyers about his new freeze-dry method. It's without question one of the biggest steps forward in the field of taxidermy in many years.

CHAPTER 37

Fishing Frontiers: British Columbia

Steelhead, grayling, rainbows, salmon—
all are available in picturesque British Columbia.

The variety and quality of British Columbia's sport fishing borders on the unbelievable. This western Canadian province has it all. One day you can fish salt-water tidal bays from a large luxurious charter boat for giant Chinook salmon weighing up to 80 pounds. And the next day you can wade waist-deep in vodka-clear water, on a tree-lined virgin mountain stream, and catch sea-run cutthroat, Dolly Varden and brook trout, and even steelhead that may weigh as much as 30 pounds!

The top five (and the most sought after) gamefish in British Columbia are the rainbow trout (locally called "Kamloops"), steelhead trout (sea-run rainbow), cut-throat trout (both anadromous and freshwater residents), coho salmon, and Chinook salmon (in British Columbia this fish is known as tyee, spring, king, and blackmouth salmon).

Rainbow trout are native to British Columbia and are the most popular gamefish in the province. Thousands of lakes and streams throughout B.C. have been stocked with this high-leaping trout.

Enormous rainbows have been taken from British Columbia's waters. Fish weighing more than 25 pounds occasionally come from some of the province's better inland lakes, such as Kootenay and Shuswap, but most

"Kamloops" average around 1½ pounds, although a monster rainbow weighing 56 pounds was taken from Jewel Lake—but not on rod and reel.

Angling for rainbow trout in British Columbia is done similarly to rainbow fishing elsewhere. Fishermen do well in rivers and streams with light spinning tackle and small spoons and spinners, and also with light fly rod gear. Most fishermen troll British Columbia's inland lakes for rainbows, although some intrepid fishermen cast with spinning gear, and fly-rodders can occasionally cast to rising trout during the early morning and evening hours.

The Kamloops Region, located in the south-central part of the province, has some of the finest rainbow trout fishing found anywhere in B.C. The city of Kamloops is the hub of the district and is a good place to head-quarter for visiting anglers.

Huge, 16-mile long Kamloops Lake has good rainbow fishing in spring with fish up to 6 pounds common. Hihume Lake, northwest of Kamloops, has fine fishing with boats, motors, and resorts available right on the lake. Fountain Lake, north of the town of Cache Creek, has excellent rainbow fishing but there are no accom-modations—only a launching ramp and a campsite. The

Rivers like this—the Similkameen—are what lure anglers to British Columbia. The Similkameen in south-central B.C., is accessible by road, yet provides extraordinary rainbow fishing.

Canim River, northeast of the town of 100 Mile House, has very good stream fishing for rainbows averaging around 1½ pounds. Mahood River, north of Little Fort, has superb late summer and fall trout fishing. Paul, Hyas, and Pemberton Lakes, north of the city of Kamloops, all have top spring fly fishing for rainbows to 8 pounds, with boats, motors, and accommodations located on each lake. Little Shuswap, Shuswap, White, and Arrow Lakes, east of Kamloops, all provide good rainbow fishing, with fish up to 10 pounds taken. Resorts, boats, motors, etc. can be had at all lakes. The Adams River, which flows into the lower end of Shuswap Lake, has extraordinary rainbow fishing along its entire 8-mile length.

The Okanagan District, located just south of the Kamloops District, in extreme south-central British Columbia,

also has some very good rainbow trout fishing. Some of the better "Kamloops" spots in the district include: Sugar, Round, Postill, Penask, Hatheume, and Allendale Lakes, and the Dee Lake Chain. All lakes have resorts, boat and motor rentals, private boat launching facilities, etc.

Some of the best rainbow trout fishing in the Kootenay Region of B.C., which borders Alberta in the southeast part of the province, is in Whatshan, Slocan, Kootenay, Edwards, Moyie, Premier, Quartz, Whiteswan, Cartwright, Cleland, Cub, Topaz, Jade, Wilbur, North Star, and Fletcher Lakes, and in the Slocan River and the Kootenay River below the power dams. All facilities are available at most lakes.

There are a number of very good rainbow lakes located west of the town of Williams Lake. Some of the better lakes are Elkin, Vedan, Charlotte, and Nimpo. Good "Kamloops" trout lakes near the town of Quesnel include Horsefly, Quesnel (rainbows here go over 20 pounds), and Dragon.

The area between the towns of Prince George and Smithers has many superb "Kamloops" waters. The better ones are Nulki, Lavoie, Germanson, Nation, Babine, Taltapin, Tchesinkut, Francois, Uncha, Stuart, Takla, and Trembleur Lakes (rainbows in the last three lakes weigh up to 15 pounds), and the Tachie, Driftwood, Stellako, and Fulton Rivers.

Tweedsmuir and Wells Gray Provincial Parks also are well endowed with excellent "Kamloops" rivers and lakes.

Vancouver Island has topnotch rainbow fishing. Most lakes, streams, and rivers on the island have good fishing for rainbows, but Nahmint Lake, which is a fly-in lake near the town of Alberni, produces the biggest trout on the island. Other good spots for 'bows on Vancouver Island are Elk, Prospect, Durrance, Council, Dougan, and Cowichan Lakes, and the Cowichan River.

The migratory, sea-run rainbow or steelhead resembles the native inland British Columbian rainbow or "Kamloops" trout. However, the difference between a "Kamloops" and a steelhead is that the steelhead only lives the first 1½ or two years of its life in its natal sweetwater stream, then heads down-river to the ocean. Sea-run rainbows live in the Pacific Ocean one, two, or three years. In saltwater they grow quickly, waxing fat on the abundance of aquatic sea food, before returning to their "home" freshwater rivers to spawn. Unlike West Coast salmon, all steelhead do not die after spawning. In fact, many live to spawn a second time. Most steelhead return to their rivers to spawn during late fall and winter—but there are some rivers in B.C. where there are "summer runs" of fish.

Most "steelheading" is done during the cold weather months, but there is steelhead fishing available every day, somewhere in British Columbia's myriad creeks, streams, and rivers. Steelhead are an extremely wary fish and are therefore very difficult to catch, particularly with fly rod gear. Due to their great size and gameness, "steelies" are world-renown for their tremendous high-jumping fighting ability.

Probably the greatest lure to fishermen is the British Columbia steelhead. Bob McNally hoists a 22 pounder he took in the Babine River.

Methods of steelhead fishing are extremely varied. Fly fishing is the most difficult, though the most rewarding. High-density shooting-head lines usually are needed along with "shooting-baskets," special weighted fly patterns, long 8- to 9½-foot rods, and a good, strong casting arm. It seems almost every B.C. river has a special fly that works remarkably well on that particular river, (so visiting anglers should consult local residents on choice of flies).

Spinning and bait-casting anglers also take steelhead on spinners, spoons, and a variety of special "bobber-type-lures." Bait fishing (it's illegal on many B.C. rivers) with spawn-sacks also is very effective for sea-run rainbows.

British Columbia has a multitude of fine steelhead rivers. And despite the fact that some seasoned steelheaders believe that environmental encroachment by man, and increased commercial netting, have seriously hurt the B.C. steelhead runs, thousands of sea-run rainbows—many of 20 pounds—are still taken yearly. The largest steelhead caught in B.C. was a 36-pounder from the Kispiox River, and a 47½-pounder was netted in the Babine River. Both rivers are part of the famous Skeena River drainage system, which is well known for producing outsized steelhead.

Vancouver Island has remarkable steelhead fishing. Just about every sizeable river flowing into the sea gets a run of steelhead. Some of the best "winter run" rivers are the Cowichan, Nanaimo, Little Qualicum, Puntledge, Campbell, Caycuse, Courtenay, Englishman, Eve, Keogh, Kluxewe, Kokish, Oyster, Quatse, Salmon, Sarita, and Tsolum Rivers. The Ash, Stamp, Gold, Heber, San Juan, Somass, and Sproat Rivers receive good summer and winter runs of "steelies."

A large number of steelhead rivers on the lower mainland of British Columbia no longer support runs of steelhead for various man-caused reasons. However, excellent winter runs of "steelies" still occur in the North and South Alouette, Campbell, Chilliwack, Squamish, and Vedder Rivers.

Some "feeder streams" in the upper Fraser River system have good sea-run rainbow trout fishing. The Chilko and Chilcotin Rivers have fall-winter-spring runs of large steelhead. And the lower reaches of the Thompson River, from the mouth of the Nicola River south, has a fine run of big steelies from early October on into May.

The many rivers in the famed Skeena River drainage probably have the finest run of huge steelhead in British Columbia—if not the world. The best rivers include the Babine, Bulkley, Kispiox, Kitsumkalum, Kloyah, Lakelse, Morice, Suskwa, Telkwa, and Zymoetz Rivers. The fishing in all of these rivers is very good during fall and winter, although the Babine occasionally has good steelheading in spring, as does the Zymoetz in late summer.

Good winter run steelhead rivers along British Columbia's north coast are the Atnarko, Bella Coola, Kitimat, and Wolfson Rivers.

The Queen Charlotte Islands, off British Columbia's north coast, have fine steelhead rivers. Most support winter run fish, with the top rivers being the Copper, Deena, and Yakoun.

Cutthroat trout are found in just about all streams, rivers, and lakes along the coastal portion of British

Scenery and salmon! This is salmon-rich Bute Inlet, with snow-topped Mount Smith in the background.

Qualicum River, good fishing throughout the year; Big Qualicum River, with good sea-run cutthroat angling spring and fall at the river's mouth; and Puntledge, Tsolum, Oyster, and Campbell Rivers have great cutthroat angling all year long.

Of the hundreds of lakes and streams in southern-mainland British Columbia with good populations of cutthroats, some of the better ones are: Buntzen, Alouette, Stave, Harrison, Big Bar, Pitt, Loon, Hayward, Rolley, and Lindeman Lakes; and the Nicomekl, Campbell, Serpentine, Fraser, Coquitlam, Pitt, and North and South Alouette Rivers. In the northern part of the province the best cutthroat trout rivers are the Bella Coola, Brem, Dean, Atnarko, Elk, Wigwam, Goat, and St. Mary.

Coastal Brtish Columbia waters contain coho, Chinook, chum, pink, and sockeye salmon. All five species are caught in great numbers by commercial fishermen, but only the coho and Chinook are enthusiastically pursued by anglers.

The prime fishing for cohos and Chinooks is from early summer on into late fall. However, there is some excellent fishing offshore along the lower mainland from December through March.

Angling methods for both coho and Chinook salmon are similar. Early in the year, before the salmon enter

Columbia. Both anadromous and nonmigratory cutthroats can be found in hundreds of streams along the coast. British Columbian cutthroats average 2 to 2½ pounds, although they've been taken as large as 17 pounds. Lake-living cutthroats average larger than sea-run or resident stream fish. British Columbia anglers pursue cutthroats successfully during every month of the year, but September through November are peak months for sea-run cutthroat fishing.

Vancouver Island is loaded with quality cutthroat waters. Some of the best are: Sooke River, where top fishing is in February and March with sea-run cutthroat fishing peaking in spring and fall at the mouth of the river; Cowichan River and Lake with fine fishing year-round; Somass River, best angling April through July; Sproat Lake, good April to November; Taylor River, May to October; Great Central Lake, March through October; Ash River, very good year-round; Nahmint Lake, outsized "cuts" at the upper end of the lake; Little

Coho or "silver" salmon—common in B.C. waters.

their freshwater natal rivers to spawn, fishing is done from power boats offshore in various saltwater bays and sounds.

Most fish taken in saltwater are caught by trolling herring baits or artificial lures behind special fish attractors called "dodgers."

Another popular method of taking salmon while they're in saltwater is "mooching." "Mooching" gear consists of a rod 10- to 12-feet long with a light-action tip, and a large capacity reel that can hold 400 yards of 15-pound test mono (Shakespeare's Windex reel is a good one). A heavy 1- or 2-ounce keel sinker is attached to the line about 8 feet above a number 6 treble hook, and a live herring is attached to the hook. Anglers drift or stillfish with "mooching" rigs, and they're death on big salmon. Some Chinooks weighing in excess of 50 pounds have been taken while "mooching."

Once the cohos and Chinooks enter the rivers fishermen do well with bait-casting and spinning tackle and artificial lures, and also with fly rod gear and streamers.

The rod-and-reel record Chinook was taken in British Columbia's Skeena River and weighed 92 pounds. The Chinook is an extremely important gamefish in B.C., and is sought by anglers year-round.

Vancouver Island hosts some superb Chinook fishing. These fish can be found in most inshore saltwater areas and in numerous freshwater rivers. The best towns to headquarter from are Campbell River, Qualicum, Port Alberni, Duncan, and Victoria.

British Columbia's coastal mainland has extraordinary Chinook fishing. Some of the better areas include: Howe Sound, Point Roberts, Eagle Harbour, Horseshoe Bay, Furry Creek, McNab Creek, Christie Cove, West Bay, Long Bay, Snug Cove, Powell River, Philips Arm, Rivers Inlet, Bella Coola, and in the Skeena River estuaries near Port Edward.

Mount Robson Provincial Park is jammed with good fishing rivers.

Coho salmon are numerous in British Columbia waters, and although these fish are much smaller than Chinooks, cohos are excellent sport fish. Cohos average 6 to 12 pounds in B.C. waters, and the world record of 31 pounds was taken from Cowichan Bay. Some accomplished coho fishermen believe there are two separate groups of cohos caught in B.C. These fishermen believe there are "coastal" cohos that spend most of their lives in saltwater but stay near their natal freshwater

Salmon fishing is good year-round in Bute Inlet, north of the famed Campbell River. Heaviest runs are from June 15 to October 1, in a normal year.

rivers. And they also think there is a different group of much larger "northern" cohos that ventures far out to sea and only comes into British Columbia's coastal areas in late summer and early fall. Whatever the case, the coho salmon is a spectacular, hard-fighting, high-leaping gamester.

Vancouver Island provides good coho fishing along both coasts. Most noteworthy areas are Barclay Sound, Cowichan Bay, Duncan Bay, and Oyster Bay.

Top mainland areas for B.C. coho fishing are Howe Sound, Jervis Inlet, Powell River, and Toba Inlet. There's

also good fishing near the towns of Bella Coola, Prince Rupert, and Kitimat.

Throughout various portions of British Columbia there are also kokanee (land-locked sockeye salmon), lake trout, Dolly Varden trout, brook trout, Rocky Mountain whitefish, and Arctic grayling. There are excellent, viable populations of all of these cold water gamefish species, and fishing for them in certain watersheds can be superb.

Smallmouth and largemouth bass also have been introduced to certain British Columbia waters. Smallmouths up to 11 pounds, and bigmouths to 6 pounds have been caught. Very good smallmouth bass fishing can be had on Vancouver Island. The best largemouth fishing is in the lakes of the Columbia River drainage system.

For detailed information, maps, brochures, regulations, etc. on British Columbia's fishing write: Fish and Wildlife Branch, Department of Recreation and Conservation, Parliament Buildings, Victoria, British Columbia, Canada.

Arctic grayling are just one of many exotic species to be taken in British Columbia's clear, clean rivers.

CHAPTER 38

Guide to Wisconsin Walleyes— Plus Walleye Tips

Here's a complete directory to Wisconsin walleye waters, along with walleye techniques used by experts everywhere to take more fish.

By Bob McNally

My Ranger bass boat bobbed gently on vodka-clear water in the middle of the lake. The "depth-finder" showed we were fishing 25 feet above a submerged island, and the lake bottom around the island gradually sloped down to a depth of 45 feet. From the bow I cast a ½-ounce yellow, bucktail jig toward the deep water. Slowly I began an erratic retrieve—making the jig jump, hop, and wiggle up the slope from the deep water. Fishing a jig from the boat's stern was Charlie Biladeou, of Des Plaines, Ill. On my second cast a fish hit the lure. As I set the hook, Charlie struck another fish hard with his rod, and we both had fish on.

The fish darted back-and-forth deep beneath the boat, sometimes nearly causing our lines to cross. But slowly I pumped my fish close, until I had him by the gill-plate, hauled him aboard, and backed the jig out. He was only a small, 1½-pound fish, but he'd fought in typical tough, bottom-boring walleye style. Charlie had landed his walleye too—a 3½-pounder. These two fish had filled our limits, so we kicked the outboard motor over to head for home.

This type of fishing wouldn't be anything special on a remote, under-fished Minnesota or Canadian lake, but we were on a Wisconsin lake only 200 miles from one of the world's largest cities—Chicago!

There are hundreds of excellent walleye lakes and rivers in the Badger State, yet comparatively few anglers know about them. And usually the few intrepid anglers who try for Wisconsin walleyes don't know the proper techniques for catching those fish, so they become discouraged and quit—and instead fish for other species such as northern pike, bass, and panfish—all the while believing that the walleyes are too tough to catch.

One of the most important aspects of walleye fishing is knowing where to fish. And while there are countless, superb walleye waters in the Badger State, a few deserve special mention because every year they consistently produce many large walleyes and also "limits" of fish.

Nelson Lake, located just north of the town of Hayward in Wisconsin's Sawyer County, is an exceptionally good walleye lake.

Nelson Lake (sometimes called Totogatic Flowage)

A mixed string of walleyes and sauger, with a few white bass, are a hefty load for this young-ster, but such catches are not unusual at some Wisconsin lakes.

and-minnow combinations. Also, because Nelson is such a remarkably clear lake, many fishermen prefer night fishing when the lake's walleyes move into the shallows to feed. Night fishing on Nelson is a particularly deadly method of catching walleyes.

Nelson Lake walleyes, taken at night on spinner baits.

is a large, 3,000 acre rock-and-sand bottom, man-made flowage. The lake is shallow, averaging about 15 feet, but it's loaded with good "structure" such as islands, vast expanses of flooded timber, deep holes, river channels, sand bars, and rock outcroppings—perfect walleye water.

Although fishing pressure on Nelson occasionally is heavy, walleyes are abundant. Motor trolling is permitted on the lake and is a common method of taking walleyes. However, because there's so much flooded timber, trolling with deep running lures almost is impossible. Most experienced trollers on Nelson employ balsa wood "diving" plugs or shallow running spinner-

Incidentally, Nelson Lake also is excellent for large-mouth bass, crappies, and bluegills. Every year many bass weighing over 4 pounds are caught. Too, sometimes northern pike fishing is good, with outsize fish weighing up to 20 pounds taken.

Nelson Lake has many resorts, boat and motor rental marinas, and quality boat launching ramps. For more information on Nelson Lake contact the Nelson Lake Resort Association, Hayward, Wis. 54843.

Lake Winnebago, in Winnebago County, is the largest lake in Wisconsin and it's one of the best walleye lakes in the state.

Surprisingly few walleye fishermen concentrate on Winnebago—probably because the lake is so big (215 square miles, with an 85 mile shoreline) and big water confuses most anglers because they don't know where to begin fishing.

Motor trolling is allowed on Winnebago and, of course, it is a popular way of fishing for walleyes. Winnebago has many reefs, rocky points, sand and gravel bars, and underwater islands, all offering a wide variety of "structure" fishing. And, in addition, walleye angling is legal on the lake year-round.

Although Lake Winnebago is huge, its maximum depth is only 21 feet. This makes it comparatively simple for fishermen to get lures down deep, where walleyes are most of the time.

The first time I ever employed the now famous system of trolling "Spoonplugs" was on Lake Winnebago. My companions and I tried everything for Winnebago's big walleyes, but didn't connect until we trolled copper and silver, series 200 "Spoonplugs." We tied on the zany looking lures and they worked like magic. By deep trolling over rocky points and reefs with those "Spoonplugs" we filled our stringers fast with bottom-loving walleyes.

Boats and motors can be rented, private boats can be launched, and excellent camping facilties and fine motels and restaurants are available around most of the lake. Good towns to headquarter for Lake Winnebago fishing are Neenah, Menasha, Fond du Lac, and Oshkosh. For more information on the lake's walleye fishery and its angling facilities contact the Wisconsin Conservation Department office in Oshkosh.

Northern Wisconsin has many prime walleye waters, and the Flambeau Flowage, located in Iron County northeast of the town of Park Falls, is certainly one of the best. This flowage is noted for consistently producing big walleyes year after year.

The 13,500 acre Flambeau Flowage is dotted with numerous islands, and has a varied bottom terrain with gravel bars, sandy points, and rock ledges that drop off to depths of 50 feet.

Flambeau Flowage is noted for its large walleyes, and these are not exceptional for Flambeau.

There are dozens of motels and resorts around this flowage that cater specifically to fishermen. Al's Place, a marina located on the lake 16 miles east of the town of Butternut, is one of the better marinas and they have camping facilities, boat and motor rentals, boat launching ramps, and guide service.

Lake Geneva, in Walworth County, has a large population of walleyes, yet the lake hosts mostly pleasure boaters and panfish anglers, with few serious fishermen trying for its walleyes.

Huge Lake Winnebago is one of the state's most consistent walleye grounds. Some white bass and sauger are "incidental" catches, always, at Winnebago.

Geneva is the 6th largest natural lake in Wisconsin, covering more than 5,000 acres. It's over 140 feet deep in places, it's air-clear, and is surrounded by high, glacier-made hills, some of which tower almost 300 feet above the lake. The lake is completely surrounded by mansions, resorts, and homes of the wealthy.

Lake Geneva can be tough to fish. During mid-summer days irresponsible pleasure boaters and water skiers make fishing almost impossible. Also, Geneva is extremely deep, clear, loaded with "natural structure," and in places it's jammed with long, stringy weeds that grow to the lake's surface in even 30 feet of water!

However, skilled walleye anglers do well on Geneva when working the lake at night by "drift fishing" or trolling across points with natural baits, and also by casting jigs to "cribs."

"Cribs" (as local anglers call them) are old, dilapidated cement and wood dock foundations. They can be found to depths of 40 feet and are perfect man-made "structures" for walleyes. Locating "cribs" can be difficult, but with the help of local anglers or a "depth sounder" it can be done—and this is the way to go for walleye fishermen.

The broad Mississippi, often wind-swept, is one of Wisconsin's most underrated, underfished walleye areas.

Boat and motor rentals and good boat launching facilities are available at the town of Fontana on the lake's west end.

Probably the most underrated and under-fished Wisconsin walleye water is the Mississippi River. The "Father Of Waters" provides over 200 miles of good walleye fishing—from the Illinois state line north to the town of Prescott in Pierce County.

Many novice anglers find the Mississippi difficult to fish because it's such an immense river. However, the river is much easier to fish than it appears, because only certain areas will consistently "hold" walleyes and knowledgeable fishermen concentrate their efforts in these places.

The fast current water directly below man-made locks and dams on the Mississippi are excellent places to find walleyes, particularly during the spring months when walleyes swim upriver to spawn. The dams block the walleyes' upstream progress, so consequently many fish congregate below the man-made obstructions.

Also, "wing dams" usually are great places to fish for walleyes. Wing dams are man-made, underwater, rock-sand-and-gravel structures that extend from the river's shoreline out into the main-stream of the river. The wing dams were built to control and slow the river's current during periods of high water and also to help stabilize the river chanel for safe ship traffic.

Wing dams draw walleyes because small forage minnows are attracted to the "dams," so walleyes go there to feed. Usually, anglers who know how to locate wing dams and then fish them properly will take walleyes.

Some maps show where the submerged wing dams are, but usually it's simple to find the dams merely by looking for ripples or surface disturbances in the river's flow. Wing dams ordinarily are only a few feet underwater, so the river's current deflects off rocks and gravel and boils the surface.

Casting natural baits and various artificial lures to wing dams from a boat anchored 50 or 60 feet away is a good way to catch Mississippi River walleyes. And trolling with bait and diving-plugs along the edges and above the wing dams works, too.

There are hundreds of camping sites, motels, and restaurants along the Mississippi, as well as boat launching ramps, and boat and motor rental marinas.

The Wisconsin River is well known for its excellent walleye fishing. And although there is good walleye angling throughout most of the river, one of the best areas is the stretch from just below the Castle Rock Dam down to the town of Wisconsin Dells. Every year huge walleyes in the 10-pound class are taken from this part of the river. There are fine lodging, food, and boating facilities in this section. A good place to headquarter is the town of Wisconsin Dells.

Two damned lake areas of the Wiscinsin River which have exceptional walleye fishing are the Castle Rock and Petenwell Flowages. Both are located in central Wisconsin south of the town of Wisconsin Rapids in Juneau County.

The 16,000 acre Castle Rock Flowage has a maximum depth of 30 feet, and is a superb lake for deep trolling. Petenwell Flowage is the larger and deeper of these two flowages. It covers 23,000 acres and drops off to depths of over 40 feet. Motor trolling also is legal on Petenwell.

Excellent county and private camping areas, public boat launching sites and boat rental marinas are available around both flowages.

Few lakes in Wisconsin produce as many large walleyes every year as Grindstone Lake, in Sawyer County.

Two fishermen prepare to put another Wisconsin River walleye on the stringer. For very large walleyes, probably the Wisconsin River is the best in the state.

Grindstone is a 3,000 acre, crystal clear, rock-sand-and-gravel bottom lake. And although Grindstone doesn't give up as many walleyes as do some other lakes, most of the walleyes that come from Grindstone are big. Walleyes of 6, 8, and 10 pounds are not particularly uncommon catches for skilled anglers.

At first glance Grindstone appears to be a tough-to-fish, round, saucer-type glacial lake. However, by checking a hydrographic map or by using a "depth sounder" it's easy to see that Grindstone is loaded with excellent underwater structure which, of course, helps anglers locate walleyes and makes for easier fishing. Grindstone is also a very good smallmouth bass and muskie lake.

Motor trolling is allowed on Grindstone. There are many fine fishing resorts located around the lake, and the Blue Spruce Resort, Rt. 5, Hayward, Wis., is a particularly good one.

Walleye fishing can often be good in the Wolf River, especially in the section of river between Lake Poygan in Winnebago County and Partridge Lake in Waupaca County.

Every year (usually in mid-April) hundreds of fishermen throng to the Wolf for the annual spring spawning "run" of walleyes. The best fishing is usually between the towns of Fremont and Orihula, and although the fishing at times can be tough, often good fishermen can take limits of walleyes.

All lodging, camping, restaurant, and boating facilities are available in Fremont. More information on the Wolf River can be had by contacting the Chamber of Commerce, Fremont, Wis.

Quality, balanced tackle is just as important for walleye fishing as it is in most other types of sport fishing. Serious walleye anglers are equipped with several different outfits for use in different walleye fishing situations.

When casting lightweight bait rigs and artificial lures in fairly open, deep water (as so many walleye lakes are) a light or medium action 6½ or 7-foot spinning outfit rigged with 6- or 8-pound test monofilament line is ideal. However, when working ultra-clear water it's wise to have a spare, interchangeable spinning-reel-spool loaded with 4-pound test line handy.

Bait-casting tackle is excellent for walleye fishing too, particularly when working large plugs, jigs, or heavy-weight natural bait-rigs. Bait-casting gear is great for fishing weedy, stump-filled walleye water because with it you can control fish much easier than with any other type tackle. A 6- or 6½-foot, medium-stiff action rod, coupled with a good reel spooled with 8- to 12-pound test mono is about the best combination for most "heavy" walleye fishing.

Although some walleye fishermen use short, stiff rods for trolling, many skilled trollers swear by long, 6½ or 7-foot, super-stiff action rods. The so called "Texas popping rod," equipped with a bait-casting reel and 15-pound test mono is a great ttrolling outfit. A long rod enables a troller to keep his line well away from the boat, thus preventing his line from being tangled in the motor's propeller or with another angler's line.

There are many natural baits, artificial lures, and angling techniques that are very effective for walleyes.

The most popular natural baits for walleyes are nightcrawler worms, minnows, and leeches. All of these baits can be fished many different ways.

One of the best methods of fishing bait for walleyes is with the famed "river-rig." A "river-rig" consists of a three-way· swivel which connects a lead sinker on a one foot leader, a hook on about a 3- or 4-foot leader, and the fishing line. There are many variations of this rig. All types of natural baits can be used, and even artificial lures can be substituted for live bait.

Most fishermen use the "river-rig" when drifting or stillfishing. The rig is lowered until it hits bottom, then it's "reeled-up" about 1 foot. The idea is to keep the bait down deep where most walleyes are. Various size weights (from BB split-shot to 3-ounce sinkers) can be used so the rig can be fished easily at any depth.

Another excellent natural bait rig is the Lindy Rig, manufactured by Lindy Tackle Co., Brainerd, Minn. Lindy makes dozens of different bait rigs for a variety of different kinds of fresh water fishing. And they make at least 8 different models designed specifically for walleye fishing.

The Lindy Rig is a masterpiece of simplicity. Essentially it consists of a specially designed "walking" type slip-sinker, a unique type of barrel, snap-swivel, 24 inches of light test monofilament leader, and a short-shank, off-set hook that's snelled to the leader.

The sinker is threaded onto the fishing line, the line is tied to the snap-swivel, the leader is attached to the swivel, and the rig is ready for fishing. The special swivel has a clip-type piece at one end which enables the angler to quickly change the 24-inch piece of mono (which has a loop tied in its end) and snelled hook if the leader becomes frayed during fishing.

The rig was designed by Ron and Al Lindner for trol-

ling or drift-fishing natural baits. The specially designed "walking slip-sinker" (which looks like a flat piece of lead with a hole in it and bent up at both ends) enables the angler to troll with the rig and not have the lead weight "hang-up," which is so common with most weighted bait rigs.

All types of natural baits (and even artificial lures) can be fished with the Lindy Rig, although the walleye Lindy Rigs are designed specifically for either minnow or worm fishing. The rig is available in a variety of different weight "walking sinkers" so it can be fished properly at any depth.

The Standard Lindy Rig

SPECIAL SWIVEL CLIP

SPECIAL 24" SNELL VARIES BY RIG

on bottom

ROCK PROOF NO DRAG "WALKING SINKER"

SPECIAL BAIT HOLDER HOOK

snells

swivel clips

walking slip sinkers

The "Lindy Rig" is one of most effective bottom fishing rigs for walleyes. It consists of "walking sinkers" (available in different weights), special swivels with clips attached, and snelled hooks with leaders. Top illustration shows the "Lindy Rig" set up and ready for walleyes.

Other types of good bait rigs include the old, reliable June-Bug-Spinner, Prescott Spinner, and Strip-On-Spinner. All of these rigs are spinner-and-minnow combinations and are used usually for trolling or occasionally for casting. Spinner-and-worm combinations are employed sometimes by walleye anglers and they take fish too.

Other good natural baits for walleyes, that are often overlooked by most so-called "expert" walleye fishermen, are nymphs (Mayfly larva) and hellgrammites (larval stage of the dobson fly). Nymphs and hellgrammites are particularly good baits when fishing for river walleyes below rapids or in turbid water. These baits are most effective when hooked onto a small, short-shank hook and a small split-shot is pinched about 2 feet above the bait. Then the nymph or hellgrammite is cast upstream and allowed to bounce along the bottom downstream. At times this method is deadly on walleyes.

Most expert walleye fishermen insist that when using natural baits it's very important *how the bait is impaled on the hook*. They insist that worms, leeches, nymphs, and hellgrammites be hooked *just once* through the "head" or tip of the bait. Minnows (no matter what type) should be hooked *once*—up through the bottom lip and out through the top lip.

Some fishermen also maintain that there are necessary, special techniques for consistently hooking walleyes. One of the best ways is to fish the bait with either an extremely light "drag-setting" or with the bail open (spinning) or the reel set in "free-spool" (bait-casting). This way when a walleye takes the bait the fish will feel very little, if any, tension so he's less apt to drop the bait before he's hooked. Experienced anglers will allow the fish to "run" with the bait for several feet before setting the hook.

Knowledgeable artificial lure fishermen know that to catch walleyes they always must adapt their lure fishing techniques according to water and weather conditions. Too, they know that although there isn't one lure or angling method that will *always* catch walleyes, nonetheless there are *some* artificial lures and fishing procedures that *often* are consistently productive for walleyes.

Because walleyes are bottom-hugging fish, what's usually (but *not always*) needed is a lure that will scrape the lake or river floor. Deep-diving, "large-lipped" plugs and spoons often are good, as are bottom-bouncing, lead-head jigs, and occasionally "spinner" type lures. Color of lures and jigs vary with the preference of the angler. However, many accomplished walleye enthusiasts find

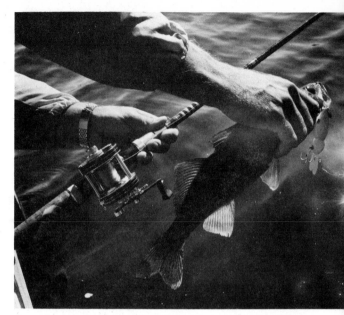

A variety of deep-running plugs work well on walleyes.

that drab-colored plugs work best; while copper, brass, and silver spoons and spinners, and yellow, pink, and chartreuse jigs are good.

Probably the most consistently successful walleye lure is the lead-head jig. It's an excellent lure because it's extremely versatile and can be rigged and fished many different ways. Also the jig is a fine walleye lure because it can be fished effectively right on the lake or river bottom, even in 30, 40 or 50 feet of water.

A common method of rigging a jig is to "tip" it with a natural bait—usually a minnow, leech, or nightcrawler worm. This combination is particularly effective for walleyes because it combines the color and life-like movements of a jig, and the "smell" of a natural bait. Jig-and-porkrind arrangements also are great walleye takers.

One of the best jigs to use in conjunction with a natural bait is the Dingo Jig, made by the Lindy Tackle Co. The Dingo has a specially designed "head" that enables the jig to "stand-on-its-head" when it's resting on bottom—with the hook pointing up at about a 45-degree angle. When the Dingo Jig is tipped with a bait, porkrind or even a plastic worm, and fished along the bottom, the "material" the jig is tipped with hovers above the rest of the jig. Thus, the bait, porkrind, or plastic worm flutters and wiggles enticingly about the Dingo Jig when it's retrieved, and of course aids in attracting walleyes.

Most accomplished walleye anglers fish jigs in a "sawtooth" fashion by pumping and reeling the lure during the retrieve. The speed of retrieve is often the deciding factor for consistently taking walleyes on jigs. Sometimes a fast "jigging retrieve" is necessary, at other times the jig must be fished *very slowly* right along the bottom.

Many walleye anglers fish two, three, or more jigs (rigged tandem style) simultaneously. The idea is to make the jigs simulate a school of baitfish, and often the method works quite well.

Jigs also can be equipped with spinners, which occasionally add to their effectiveness. The now famous "spinner-baits" are simply jigs rigged with spinners, and they are great for walleyes.

Another type jig that's very effective for walleyes is a "home-made" model that's used extensively by fishermen along the Mississippi River. The jig looks exactly like an ordinary "lead-head" bucktail jig, except that the "head" is made from either cork or styrofoam.

This floating "jig" is fished with a heavy slip-sinker that's positioned above the jig on the fishing line. The jig-and-weight are cast out and allowed to sink. When the jig and slip-sinker are on bottom the angler pays out line, which causes the jig to rise, while the slip-sinker remains stationary on the river or lake bottom. Next, the angler jerks his rod, making the "jig" dive toward the slip-sinker—then he pays out line once more which causes the jig to rise again—and so on. "Jig-fishing" such as this is very similar to the floating plastic worm and slip-sinker technique used by some southern bass fishermen.

This "floating jig" method is great for walleye fishermen because it enables an angler to make just one cast and to fish one spot or "hole" thoroughly. And he can impart many different actions to the lure—all on *one cast!* To my knowledge no tackle company is manufacturing these "floating jigs." However, some types of ordinary fly rod popping bugs can be fished this way, and the Jack Crawford Tackle Co., P.O. Box 5634, Milwaukee, Wis. 53211, markets a somewhat similar jig-rig, which they call the "Pop-R-Jig."

Spoonplugs, made by Buck's Baits, Hickory, North Carolina, are excellent walleye lures. These strange looking spoons can be cast or trolled, but are especially well suited to trolling.

Briefly, "Spoonplugging" is an entire "system" of fishing based on fish migrations, lake and river "structure," and the proper methods of presenting Spoonplug lures to gamefish. (See Spoonplugging feature elsewhere in this book.)

The great advantage of "Spoonplugging" for walleyes is that it enables an angler to fish his lures at a known, prescribed depth. This is easily accomplished because Spoonplugs are available in a variety of different sizes, and each size is designed to travel at just one depth. Also, each size Spoonplug will dive to, and then "work" at, a certain depth—no matter how fast the lure is retrieved.

This is valuable for walleye fishing because occasionally walleyes will be very deep—sometimes 25 feet or more—and although it's easy to get some lures down that deep, it's often impossible to retrieve the lures fast enough to produce strikes. Spoonplugs eliminate that problem because this lure will travel at the depth it's designed for, and will stay at that depth whether the lure is cast and retrieved slowly or even if it is trolled fast.

No serious walleye angler should fish without a good assortment of Spoonplugs in his tackle box.

"Floating-diving" plugs, made of plastic or balsa wood, take walleyes too. Most fishermen employ these lures when fishing shallow, "flowage" type walleye lakes or rivers where it's impossible to work lures or baits deep due to snags, fallen trees, weeds, etc. on the bottom.

Floating-diving plugs also are productive when fishing shallow reefs, points, or underwater "bars," or during night fishing when walleye sometimes move into shallow shoreline areas to feed.

Two of the best floating-diving plugs for walleyes are the "Big-O," made by Cotton Cordell, Hot Springs, Ark., and the "Rebel Floater," manufactured by Plastics Research & Development Corp., Fort Smith, Ark.

Both plugs are excellent for trolling shallow, snag-filled water because they don't run too deep. Usually 100 to 150 feet of line is used when trolling these lures. This is necessary because a boat trolling through a shallow school of walleyes usually will make the fish jittery, but by the time the lure is brought through the school they'll hopefully have settled down enough to strike the plug.

These two floating-diving plugs also are deadly walleye lures when fished over shallow areas at night. Once, while fishing Wisconsin's Nelson Lake with Greg Moats, of Elgin, Ill., and Harry Leasure, owner-operator of Leasure's Resort on Nelson Lake, we had exceptional fishing with "Rebel Floaters." We fished all afternoon and tried every walleye lure and fishing method we knew. But we didn't take fish until after dark, and we worked those "Rebels" right up against the shoreline. We'd just barely twitch the lures along—right on the surface—which is a method very similar to the "knodding technique" employed by some bass fishermen. Fishing "Rebels" that way on top at night we filled our limits of walleyes in a short time. And although the best fish weighed only 3 pounds, I'm sure we wouldn't have done anything unless we fished those lures at night, on the surface, in very shallow water.

Spinning lures at times can "work up" walleyes. When the fish are shallow, a Mepps Spinner (put out by Sheldon's Inc., Antigo, Wis.) fished with a slow, erratic retrieve can be great. When walleyes are deep some fishermen take fish on spinners by pinching on several BB split-shots to the fishing line, about 2 feet above the lure, which helps get the spinner down.

A Mepps Spinner also is a fine lure when working rivers for walleyes, particularly in fast, turbulent water, or rocky "runs." The best technique is to cast the spinner upstream and then work the lure along the bottom—allowing the current to carry it downstream in a wide, slow arc. The trick is to not fish the lure too quickly, and to keep it bouncing right on the bottom.

Some of the new "tail-spinners," such as the "Little George," made by the Mann Bait Co., Eufaula, Ala., that have proved so effective for bass, also are good for walleyes. These lures are about 1½-inches long, are made of solid lead, and have a spinner attachment at one end. The lures aren't much to look at. However, they're easy to cast, sink like an anvil, and in addition to having a fish-attracting spinner, they also have an enticing, "wiggling," side-to-side action when retrieved. Few lures imitate a fast swimming minnow better than these new "tail-spinners."

Comparatively few walleye fishermen use plastic worms, but they're well worth using, and the "floating" variety are particularly good. Most expert walleye anglers prefer to use 4-inch worms, rigged weedless with a small, ¼-ounce slip-sinker. Some fishermen troll this rig slowly in snag-filled "flowage" waters and they do remarkably well when other techniques fail. Plastic worms also can be used effectively with jigs.

A floating plastic worm, rigged weedless, can be danced down rocky drop-offs, "slithered" over submerged islands, or "jigged" in deep holes—and it will rarely hang-up. Too, a "floating worm" wiggling and twitching above a slip-sinker or "jig-head" can usually make the biggest, smartest walleye in the school sit-up and take notice.

Porkrind "eels," chunks, and strips are often overlooked by walleye fishermen. They can be used in conjunction with most artificial lures, plain spinners, or even rigged alone on a bare, weighted, or weedless hook. Porkrind has fabulous fish-attracting action when retrieved in the water. Some 'rind even gives off "scent" that walleyes relish. Best of all, few lures or natural baits are as versatile or can be fished in as many different ways as porkrind.

Although this may surprise some anglers, walleyes can be taken on dry flies! At certain times of the year (usually in spring) huge hatches of Mayflies occur on some lakes and rivers. And when conditions are right (normally in the evening or at night) walleyes will come to the surface and "slurp" in Mayflies that float on the water. When walleyes are taking Mayflies on top most fishermen employ floating-diving plugs to catch fish. However, the most effective way (and the most fun) of taking walleyes then is with dry fly patterns that imitate Mayflies.

If there's one general rule that can be made about walleye fishing, it's that *most of the time* lures and baits should be fished on or near the bottom. And there are many different, specialized, and very successful methods of probing deep for walleyes.

On large rivers, such as the Mississippi and Wisconsin Rivers, drift-fishing with the current often is effective, as is drifting on lakes before a strong wind, across the lake's rocky points and over its reefs. Either natural baits or artificials can be used. Simply cast, then drift. Moving with the current or wind gives plenty of slow, bottom-bouncing action to a bait or lure, and also, the angler is able to cover a lot of water.

When you catch a walleye while drifting you may have found a school of fish, so anchor the boat and try to take more fish by casting. If you fail to hook more walleyes while casting, motor upwind and make another drift over the exact area where the first fish was caught. Occasionally the bait or lure must be retrieved from a certain direction and at a specific speed to make walleyes hit, and the "drifting method" at times on certain "structures" is the only way to take them.

Motor trolling (in Wisconsin it's allowed only on certain waters; check the Wisconsin Conservation Department's fishing regulations booklet) is probably the most popular method of fishing for walleyes. Trolling is very effective because great expanses of water can be covered, and lures and baits can be fished easily at various speeds and depths. Slow trolling is usually the rule for walleye fishing, however, if the fish aren't cooperating try different trolling speeds until the right one is found.

Sometimes, very fast trolling will take walleyes that otherwise refuse lures or baits fished any other way. Fast trolling is especially good for walleyes during summer when water temperatures are warm and fish metabolism is higher than at any other time. A lure moving very fast through a school of walleyes will often trigger a competitive urge among the fish, and cause them to chase and then strike the lure even though they are not "actively feeding."

Most experienced fishermen know that the most important aspects of trolling for walleyes is controlling the speed and depth that the lure or bait is fished. Usually it's easy to get proper lure control simply by varying the boat's speed. But occasionally it's difficult to present a fast-trolled lure deep enough to reach the fish. For example, if a school of walleyes is on bottom in 35 feet of water and won't strike anything except a very fast moving lure, presenting a lure to them properly would be almost impossible. This is because a lure that is fast-trolled will "plane" and not "run" on bottom. Therefore, the only way the lure can be trolled properly under such circumstances is with a down-rigger.

Down-riggers are trolling aids used extensively by salmon and trout fishermen on the West Coast and throughout the Great Lakes. Essentially, a down-rigger consists of a metal arm with a large reel connected to it. The reel is loaded with strong wire and a heavy "cannon-ball" weight, that may weigh 5 pounds or more, is attached. Rigged to the wire, about 2 feet above the "cannon-ball," is a "release mechanism" to which the fishing line is affixed.

When fishing, the angler fastens his line to the "release mechanism" and then lowers the "cannon-ball" over the side of the boat by unwinding the heavy wire from the reel device. The "cannon-ball" is lowered to whatever depth the angler wants to fish—and of course the fishing line and lure are taken down to that depth also. When the boat is moving the "cannon-ball" will not "plane" but will stay at the depth it was lowered to.

Consequently, the lure can be easily fished at any depth. When a fish strikes the lure the fishing line is pulled from the "release mechanism" and the angler plays just the fish with no interference from the heavy "cannon-ball."

With the help of a down-rigger a walleye fisherman can troll his lures at any depth and speed that he wants.

Back-trolling is often a sure-fire technique for catching walleyes. By putting the boat in reverse and trolling backwards it's possible to troll much slower than if the motor was in a forward gear; the boat can be maneuvered much more easily when trolling along a specific, detailed course—such as along an irregular weed-line or around an underwater island; and fishing lines will not become tangled or cut by the motor's propeller when back-trolling. Even bass boats (which so many anglers say can't be "idled-down" enough for slow trolling because of their big motors) can be back-trolled at a snail's pace when necessary.

Stillfishing, whether casting and using artificials or just fishing natural baits, is a good system for taking walleyes provided you are familiar with the specific bottom structure of the lake or river you're working. However, "blind" casting and stillfishing for walleyes is a great way to take fish anywhere if you use the new electronic "depth-finders." Electronic gear lets you "see" the kind of bottom or structure you're fishing over, thus helping you find walleye "holding areas." Electronic "finders" are especially valuable when fishing unfamiliar waters.

Hydrographic maps, which detail the bottom contours and terrain of lakes and rivers, also are priceless when trying to locate good walleye structure. Hydrographic maps usually can be purchased at local sporting goods stores, county court houses, or from state conservation departments. However, if it's impossible to find a good hydro' map of your favorite lake, maps of most lakes west of the Mississippi River can be ordered from the Distribution Section, Geological Survey, Federal Center, Denver, Colo. 80225. For waters east of the Mississippi, order from the Distribution Center, Geological Survey, 1200 South Eads St., Arlington, Va. 22202. Maps of most Wisconsin walleye lakes are available from either the Star Map Service, P.O. Box 3007, Milwaukee, Wis. 53218 or the Clarkson Map Co., 725 Desnoyer St., Kaukauna, Wis. 54130.

Walleyes are school fish, so it's often possible that when you take one you can catch more, provided you "stay" with the school. So most anglers use small, brightly colored buoys to mark the spot where they have taken a walleye, and then fish the area thoroughly until the fish either wise up or move on. But one good way to "follow" a walleye school is to take the first walleye caught and tie one end of about 50 feet of monofilament fishing line to the corner of his mouth and the other end of the line to a small, lightweight balloon. Then release the walleye. The fish usually will return to the school and the balloon he trails on the surface will normally reveal the location of the school. When the action is over, you can retrieve the balloon and "hand-line" the first walleye back to the boat.

For most fishermen the best time to take walleyes is during the spring, when they are in shallow water spawning. In the Midwest this usually occurs in April or May soon after the ice goes out. The fish are often in shallower water than they would be ordinarily, because the water is still cold. Since spawning walleyes usually don't migrate far from the spawning areas, and since they are in shallow water, they often are easy targets for fishermen.

Different walleye angling methods are needed during mid-summer's "dog-days." When the surface water warms to 80 degrees or more, walleyes drop to depths of 15 to 50 feet, avoiding the summer sun's rays and seeking water temperatures between 55 and 70 degrees. Deep trolling during the day, or night fishing in the shallows, is usually the rule because walleyes normally stay deep during the day and move into weedy bays and reefs to feed at night.

In fall, once again walleyes frequently feed in shallow, cool water. But if the water is very clear, and the sun is bright, they'll ordinarily feed after dark.

Although some Wisconsin waters have no closed season on walleyes, most do. The walleye fishing season generally opens on the first Saturday in May, and closes about the end of February. The daily creel limits vary according to the area fished. Incidentally, a seasonal, non-resident Wisconsin fishing license costs $12.50.

More information on Wisconsin walleye waters, and the state's fishing regulations can be had by writing: Wisconsin Department of Natural Resources, Box 450, Madison, Wis. 53701.

CHAPTER 39

Exploded Drawings: Shakespeare's 2091A Spinning Reel

CLEANING AND MAINTENANCE OF *Shakespeare* SPINNING REEL

---

(1) Unscrew drag adjusting nut assembly (28) from main shaft and remove spool.

(2) Remove cover screws (1) and cover assembly (2). Level wind lever pin (54) can now be pulled, releasing level wind lever (3) from main shaft. The main shaft assembly can then be taken out through front end of reel.

Further disassembly is unnecessary for general cleaning, lubrication and maintenance. However, for complete cleaning follow procedure outlined in paragraphs 3, 4 and 5.

(3) To remove crank assembly (18), put non-reverse lever into "on" (forward) position and turn crank backward.

(4) Take out drive gear assembly as shown in illustration. Slide helical pinion and ball bearing through front of frame assembly. (NOTE: Ball bearing is sealed and waterproof.)

(5) Using a cleaning solvent and brush, scrub exposed parts thoroughly. When all parts have been cleaned, wipe with a soft cloth. Make certain all parts are well dried. For proper lubrication use a good waterproof grease and light machine oil. Oil your reel frequently.

NON-REVERSE LEVER

The non-reverse lever is located below the crank. When lever is forward (straight up) crank is locked for forward turning only. When lever is pushed back, crank is free to turn forward or backward. The click tells you lever is in "on" position. Use non-reverse when playing fish, carrying rigged outfit, or trolling.

295

know your fishing reel

PICK UP LINE **COCK BAIL** **CAST** **RETRIEVE**

THE MAKE READY...
The line is held with index finger and bail cocked into "cast" position. Let lure hang about a foot from rod tip. The left hand is moved to the rear of the rod handle. Aim at target area... (See Fig. No. 1.)

THEN FORWARD...
While the weight of the lure is still pulling rod tip back, start the forward cast. Pull left hand back smartly toward body, at the same time, pushing forward with your right hand in one smooth motion. (See Fig. No. 3.)

BRING ROD BACK...
Bring rod tip back smartly by pulling right hand back, and at same time, pushing forward with your left hand. (See Fig. No. 2.)

RELEASE LINE...
When the rod tip is forward. The precise instant to release line will come with practice. The line is released by opening index finger. When lure hits water, simply turn crank forward to retrieve line. (See Fig. No. 4.)

TO INSTALL LINE ON SPOOL

After mounting reel on rod, turn crank until spool is completely exposed.

Pass end of line through lead guide (guide nearest handle of rod), cock bail into cast position and tie line to spool. As crank is turned forward bail will automatically pick up line and level-wind it onto spool.

For better spooling, have someone hold dispenser by the lip, applying light tension to line with thumb and forefinger (see illustration).

NOTE: To eliminate twist, be sure line comes off dispenser in same direction pickup rotates when crank is turned forward.

Fill spool to about 1/8" below edge of front flange.

REEL CAPACITY CHART
Approximate Yards

Lb. Rating Mono	10	12	15	20	30
Approx. Yds.	560	450	375	250	160

TIPS and SUGGESTIONS

1. **TO SET THE DRAG**— Mount reel on rod and pass line through guides. Move the non-reverse lever into "on" position and with rod tip held high, have someone strip off line as a running fish would do. Set drag tension just below breaking point of line by adjusting drag knob on front of the spool.

2. **WHEN FIGHTING A LARGE FISH**— Do not crank against the drag any more than necessary. PUMP THE ROD. With tip in lowered position, raise rod smoothly. Then retrieve line rapidly as you again lower rod and repeat the procedure.

3. **TO AVOID LINE TWIST**— Use a swivel at lure tie-on point.

4. **TIGHT LINE SPOOLING IS IMPORTANT**— Avoid loops or loose line on spool. When using small spinners or lure, it may be necessary to retrieve line under tension between thumb and forefinger of right hand.

5. **WHEN TROLLING**— Be sure the non-reverse lever is in the "on" position and that the drag is set as lightly as possible.

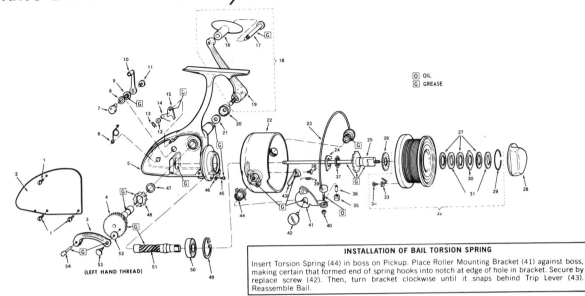

O OIL
G GREASE

INSTALLATION OF BAIL TORSION SPRING

Insert Torsion Spring (44) in boss on Pickup. Place Roller Mounting Bracket (41) against boss, making certain that formed end of spring hooks into notch at edge of hole in bracket. Secure by replace screw (42). Then, turn bracket clockwise until it snaps behind Trip Lever (43). Reassemble Bail.

(LEFT HAND THREAD)

PART NUMBERS AND PART NAMES

KEY	PART NUMBER	PART NAME	KEY	PART NUMBER	PART NAME
1	74-58-0055-01	Cover Screw	28(a)	75-40-0016-01	Drag Nut Assembly
2(a)	75-47-0044-01	Cover Assembly	29	74-67-4775-01	Retaining Ring
3	74-37-6420-01	Level Wind Lever	30	74-72-2154-01	Drag Eared Washer
4(a)	75-28-7934-01	Drive Gear Assembly	31	74-72-3952-01	Drag Keyed Washer
5(a)	75-27-8341-01	Frame Assembly			(2 Req'd.)
6	74-67-4814-01	Throwout Tension Spring	32(a)	75-66-0038-01	Spool Assembly (Includes
7	74-43-4717-01	Non-Reverse Pawl			Clutch Washers)
		Throwout	33	74-67-6885-01	Click Spring
8	74-72-4817-01	Throwout Washer	34	74-58-7025-01	Click Spring Screw
9	74-09-4823-01	Throwout Bushing	35	74-57-8550-01	Line Roller
			36	74-63-7712-01	Line Roller Sleeve
10(a)	75-37-4798-01	Throwout Lever	37	74-40-8355-01	Pickup Housing Nut
		Assembly	38	74-58-8343-01	Bail Trip Lever Screw
11	74-58-1493-01	Throwout Lever Screw	39	74-67-5831-01	Bail Trip Lever Spring
12	74-72-4891-01	Non-Reverse Spring	40	74-40-6645-01	Roller Lock Nut
		Washer	41(a)	75-07-8352-01	Roller Mounting Bracket
13	74-67-4475-01	Retainer Spring			Assembly
14	74-67-4716-01	Non-Reverse Pawl	42	74-58-5346-01	Roller Mounting Bracket
		Spring			Screw
15	74-43-4796-01	Non-Reverse Pawl	43	74-37-8344-01	Bail Trip Lever
16	74-32-4802-01	Crank Handle	44	74-67-5345-02	Bail Tortion Spring
17	74-71-4731-01	Handle Stud	45	74-58-8339-01	Bail Trip Screw
18(a)	75-20-8365-02	Crank Assembly	46	74-08-8338-02	Trip Lever Brake
19(a)	75-20-8089-02	Crank Shaft Assembly	47	74-72-6427-01	Washer (As Required)
20	74-17-8379-01	Thrust Collar	48	74-50-6441-01	Non-Reverse Ratchet
21	74-72-4736-01	Thrust Washer	49	74-53-5813-01	Bearing Retainer
22	74-34-8345-01	Pickup Housing	50	74-04-0016-01	Pinion Ball Bearing
23(a)	75-03-8348-01	Bail Wire Assembly	51	74-46-8335-03	Helical Pinion
24	74-72-8354-02	Lock Washer	52	74-72-6422-01	Level Wind Washer
25(a)	75-60-8357-02	Main Shaft Assembly	53	74-58-6428-01	Level Wind Screw
26	74-72-4824-01	Drag Washer	54	74-45-6369-01	Level Wind Pin
27	74-72-2155-01	Drag Washer (3 Req'd.)			

CHAPTER 40

Angler's Showcase

1. Mildrum Manufacturing Co., East Berlin, Conn. now offers their snake guides to fishermen for do-it-yourself repairs and replacement.

Called "Tough Snakes," these guides have a stainless steel base with a hard-chrome coating. They can be bought in a variety of sizes in bulk or boxed assortments and used on either fresh or salt water rods.

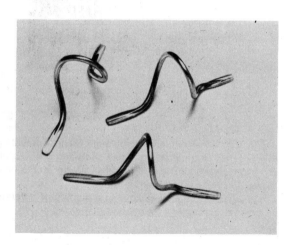

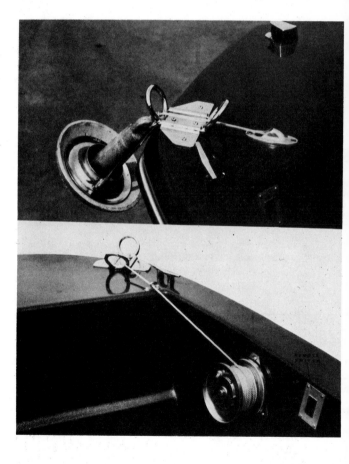

The manufacturer claims "the design is capable of withstanding the extreme stresses applied to modern synthetic fly rods by many fishermen and provides almost friction-free line travel." "Tough Snakes" can ward off destructive power of natural hazards such as salt water to give years of ordinary use, because of the combination of two corrosion materials.

2. Dutton-Lainson Company, Hastings, Neb. has a new electric anchor winch designed especially for bass boats. The anchor can be raised or lowered with fingertip control from one or more remote stations in the boat. Because of a 2 speed permanent magnet motor, a fast 75 ft. per-minute anchor release, as well as a rapid 45 ft. per-minute retrieve, are possible.

The anchor winch has been designed for easy mounting and can be placed anywhere on the boat for convenience. The reel capacity is up to 100 ft. of 3/6 inch braided nylon rope.

Small boat anchors are handled with ease and the winch offers extra power if the anchor is buried in mud or tangled in vegetation or other debris.

The anchor winch is constructed of high carbon steel gears, precision ball bearings on the reel shaft, heavy base, and a gear reduction drive system to prevent the motor shaft from bending. An electrical system circuit breaker provides added protection from motor overload. Suggested retail price is $99.95. For an added $8.45 you can buy an anchor bracket with deck mounting plate.

3. The Garcia Sporting Arms Corporation, Teaneck, New Jersey offers a quality survival knife. The knife has a broad, heavy blade of stainless steel and is 12 inches in length. The seven inch blade has a saw-blade back and the hefty handle is hollow, with a knurled, removable cap at the butt which can be used as a hammer. A neoprene ring makes the handle a waterproof container for storage of such survival items as a snare wire, matches, and first-aid items. With the cap removed, the hollow handle can accept a pole for emergency use as a spear.

The leather sheath has the standard belt loop as well as a detachable GI belt hook. There is a survival box in the pocket on the sheath containing a whetstone, integral compass, signalling whistle, hook sharpener, and fire starter. The whetstone has a sliding lid over a compartment that can contain fish hooks and line.

4. Berkley and Company, Inc., Spirit Lake, Iowa is introducing custom designed tapered leaders for the fly fisherman. These tapered nylon leaders have a butt section .022 of an inch in diameter. According to the company "the leaders start flat, taper, and then become round, graduating to a fine tip, permitting a smaller nail knot, and reduced air resistance for a tighter loop during fly casting. Knots hold better and casts are more precise."

Berkley fly leaders are available in a number of different lengths.

5. Lowrance Electronics, Tulsa, Okla. offers to the fresh and saltwater fisherman who trolls the new LTG 200 Fish-N-Temp Rig.

You can monitor the water temperature you're fishing to depths of 200 feet. The LTG 200 is self-contained with a permanent mount deep trolling system and temperature monitoring capabilities. The Rig finds the fish's comfort zone and puts the lure or bait at the proper depth.

LTG 200 Fish-N-Temp Rig includes: the trolling unit, 200 ft. of coaxial cable with thermister and temperature readout meter, snap release clip and trolling weight, and a three digit resettable mechanical counter that tells you the exact amount of cable in the water.

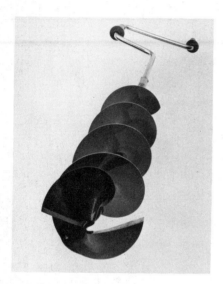

6. Normark Corporation, Minneapolis, Minn. introduces new equipment for the ice fisherman. Finbore II makes cutting through the ice much easier. The spiral-type auger has a crank handle and blades that have been improved for faster cutting. The handle is offset and provides leverage at all positions.

7. Ray Jefferson, Division of Jetronic Industries, Inc., Philadelphia, Pa. has a new Model "6006" Fish Flasher on the market. Model "6006" has a built-in battery meter that constantly shows the condition of the batteries. It also features a "high impact transducer housing for more positive soundings." This model will "scientifically" pinpoint the best fishing spots. It can be used on any type boat and accurately locates fish to 120 ft. and can, under favorable conditions, read down to 240 ft.

The Model "6006" comes with Indicator Unit, Transducer with 15 ft. of cable, and fully adjustable 36″ transducer mounting bracket that permits the beam to be aimed in almost any direction. The master arm of the bracket rotates in the mount to a full 360 degrees for easy scanning.

The unit comes with its own carrying case and when properly closed will float if dropped overboard. It weighs less than 5 lbs., and operates on two, six-volt lantern batteries. Model "6006" is completely transistorized and features solid state circuitry. Less batteries, it lists for $149.95.

8. Three new fish-finders are available from the Waller Corporation, Crystal Lake, Illinois. The "Fish Hawk 204" has interference-free solid state electronic circuits, a high-speed transducer, and a "Brite-Lite" signal bulb, plus high impact case on a gimbal mount. For the "structure" fisher-

Fish Hawk 204 for Coho & Bassboats
(Release WLC-189-C)

men, a combination of wide-cone signal projection and fine line read out insure accurate readings of bottom structure. Non-glare dial face is another feature.

The "304 Bassboat Special" among other features offers an exclusive "depth range indicator." Fishermen can tell if signals are coming from the range of 0–60 ft. or if the bottom is as deep as 240 ft. It has most of the standard features on the "Fish Hawk 204."

"Fish Hawk 102" is the new economy model. Anglers can locate schools and individual fish, and define bottom con-

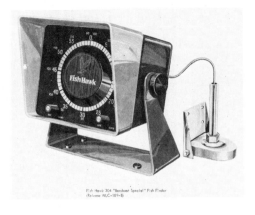

Fish Hawk 304 "Bassboat Special" Fish Finder
(Release WLC-189-B)

Fish Hawk 102 "Economy" Flasher
(Release WLC-189-D)

tours to depths of 100 ft. The owner can change the bulb that provides fish and bottom signals. Another feature is the triple-life/double-size "utility" batteries.

9. Motor-Guide Division, Starkville, Miss. has come up with The Weightlifter. This is an all electric anchor hoist that can lift up to 190 lbs. Designed primarily for bass boats, it will fit other craft and can be placed wherever convenient. It is powered by a 12-volt battery.

10. Normark Corporation, Minneapolis, Minn. adds to their famous four- and six-inch Rapala fillet knives a new nine-inch blade knife. It has the same basic Rapala lines and Laplander sheath. Made of stainless steel it was designed for cleaning "lunker" salt and fresh water fish.

11. Gladding-South Bend, South Otselic, N. Y. offers hip boots, boot-foot waders, chest high waders and All-Pro fishing vests. The boots have steel-belted soles and good traction to secure you on slippery rocks. Rayon lines the rubber boots, and the manufacturer says they are "puncture proof."

The hip boots have a "rugged" nylon upper shell with a heavy rubberized lining. Adjustable front and side straps at the top of the boots, snap and lace adjustments inside, above the knee, for stay-in-place convenience and comfort.

The chest highs have the addition of a drawstring at the top, heavy-duty suspender buttons, and an inside pocket.

All-Pro fishing vest has all the pockets you might need. It comes with fishermen's scissors and six hinged-lid English-style fly boxes, each in an elastic-top pocket. Each box has six compartments for flies.

12. Zebco Division, Brunswick Corporation, Tulsa, Okla. has a variety of new lures for the angler.

The Super Secret is a floater-diver and features a hardened aluminum diving lip in three sizes. It comes in one standard size, ½ ounce, and 12 different colors. Exact depth depends on the retrieve speed and size of line used.

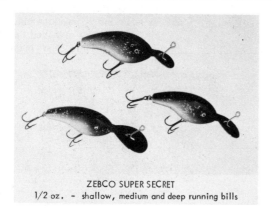

ZEBCO SUPER SECRET
1/2 oz. – shallow, medium and deep running bills

"Z-Plug" also is a floating/diving bait. Available in 12 colors and is ⅜ oz. It has three different size diving lips and its main feature is an internal sound chamber that emits "fish-attracting" vibrations as the lure is retrieved.

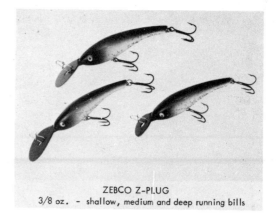

ZEBCO Z-PLUG
3/8 oz. – shallow, medium and deep running bills

"Doll-E-Pop" was designed for saltwater fishing. The 1½-oz. lure has its weight in the tail, making for good castability. It sinks tail first. It also has an internal rattler and a "scoop" mouth that causes it to rise and break the surface like a baitfish when retrieved. It should be fished very fast—skipped across the surface with a rapid pumping or twitching of the rod tip. The ½-oz. and ¾-oz. sizes are good for some freshwater fish.

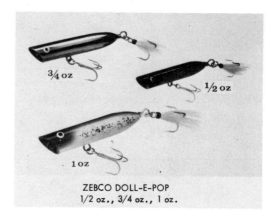

ZEBCO DOLL-E-POP
1/2 oz., 3/4 oz., 1 oz.

13. Tempo Products Company, Cleveland, Ohio introduces the Boat Loader. It permits one person to take any boat for car top transport and "wheelbarrow" it up the telescoping channel rail in a few minutes. Included are four sections of telescoping aluminum track, ground stand support, bow roller with mounting bracket, and bolts for mounting on any regular car top carrier.

Made of rust-free aluminum it weighs only 16 lbs. Suggested retail price is $59.95.

14. Umco Corporation, Watertown, Minn. has brought out Model 1104 Spinner-Bait box, and Umco SC-4 bait caddy units. Acording to the company, there are four separate spinner-bait caddies that lock together for rigidity, yet are individually removable for use outside the case. If using all four caddies, you can store 48 spinner-baits up to 5½-inch spread. Caddies also can be used with plugs and small spoons, and one or more can be removed to make room for reels and other gear.

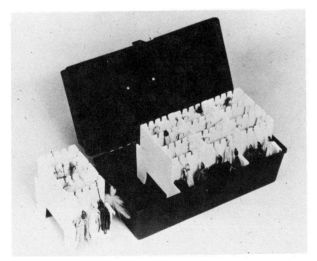

Caddies can be purchased separately and fit other Umco tackle box models. The spinner-bait box weighs two lbs. and is red with white caddy units.

15. New from Shakespeare Company, Columbia, S. C. is the "WonderTroll 505." This electric fishing motor uses transistorized variable speed control. The heat producing electronics have been removed and thus the upper housing of the "505" remains cool. The solid state control draws little current, and with speed settings from two to 20 the motor can produce a thrust from 1½ to 6 lbs. There is a special high speed setting on the variable speed control that permits the operator to by-pass the variable speed control. This results in all the current being directed to the motors lower unit and producing a thrust of 7½ lbs. The "WonderTroll 505" weighs almost 8 lbs., and has a 30-inch long motor shaft and forward/off/reverse toggle switch. The 12-volt motor has an adjustable tilt bracket with copilot feature.

16. Woodstream Corporation/Old Pal, Lititz, Pa. has a new Spinner-Bait box. PF-1036 is green and has a 55 lure capacity. The lift out racks have upright sections placed at an angle for easy selection of lures. The recessed handled spinner-bait box is molded of plastic lure proof materials.

17. Valley Tow-Rite, Inc., Lodi, Calif. has a new item called "Wheel-Block." It is made of heavy steel and can be used with almost any highway vehicle. According to the company, "it works on the principle of the wedge—increased pressure against the block produces increased resistance to movement due to the fact that part of it extends under the wheel." It is compact and has many uses. "Wheel-Block's" suggested retail price is $3.95.

18. Big Jon, Inc., Traverse City, Michigan offers two new downriggers. The "D-400-Deluxe" has an 18-inch fiberglass rod and comes complete with 200 ft. of stainless steel wire, a quick release, mounting plate, 7¼-lb. plastic coated cannonball and footage counter for accurate depth measurement. It is available with either right- or left-hand crank.

The "Siderigger Electric" has basically the same features, but also includes 360-degree Lexan swivel tip and is adaptable for use with the optional Big Jon electric drive unit that can be added. This downrigger includes 300-ft. of stainless steel wire and is available with 2, 3, or 4-ft. rods that permit additional downriggers on the gunwales as well as transom mounting where extra reach is necessary. It pivots upright and locks in a vertical position for storage or cannonball attaching.

19. Evinrude Motors, Milwaukee, Wisconsin is producing new 9.9 and 15-h.p. outboards, made with manual or electric start. Steering and speed control are more convenient, because the steering handle on both motors has been extended three inches. Other features include low tension ignition for easier starting, full gearshift, water shielded exhaust for additional silencing, and shallow water drive for fishing in hard to get at places.

20. From Boone Bait Co., Winter Park, Florida comes the "Shrimp Tout." This plastic bodied jig was originally designed for taking spotted seatrout. However, it has proved to be a deadly lure for many other species of both saltwater and freshwater gamefish, and is particularly effective for largemouth bass.

The "Shrimp Tout" is available in six different hook sizes and weights, and can be had in many different colors.

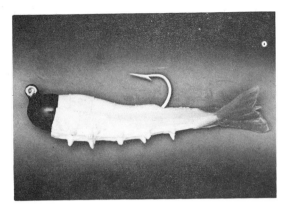

21. Following is what The Orvis Company, Inc., Manchester, Vt., has to say about their "Orvis Leader Tie Kit":

"This kit includes an Instruction Book with Diagrams and Dimensions for tying properly balanced, tapered leaders that will turn over and lie out straight. . . . Each length for each section of leader is clearly diagrammed. . . . Illustrated instructions for tying the barrel knot (to connect the tapering leader sections) also are included in the kit.

"And 20 spools of special imported Orvis leader monofilament are provided. . . . from butt size .021" down to .004" tippet, 4 spools .021, 3 spools .019, 2 spools .017 and 1 each of other sizes. Orvis Leader Monofilament (quite different from limp spinning line) carries the fly on out instead of collapsing. It has superior knot strength and good shock resistance to absorb a fish's strike."

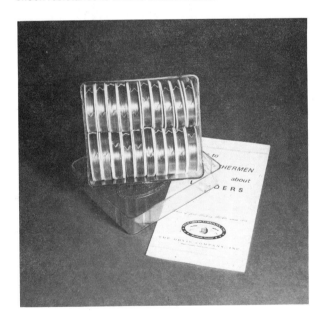

22. The "Orvis Fly Threader," from the Orvis Company, Inc., Manchester, Vt., will help put a fly on your leader quickly. This Threader isn't much larger than a ballpoint pen and even has a "pen's pocket clip." Put any size fly into the top slot and simply poke your leader end into the wide cone and the cone guides it through the hookeye. You lift up from the slot and the fly is on.

The bottom of the Threader covers a stainless steel needle that's used for poking glaze from a hookeye and also for tying the needle knot. The illustrated folder that comes with this Fly Threader has diagrams for five valuable fishermen's knots. Retails for $4.50.

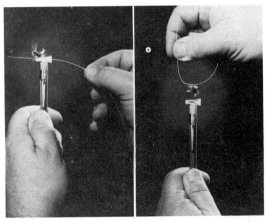

23. "Stud-Sole Waders" and "Hippers" are available from The Orvis Company, Inc., Manchester, Vt. The soles are of woven nylon core felt and with eleven nonskid hexagonal shaped studs embedded in the heel and sole; the wader is sure to feel more secure. The studs are of soft aluminum and protrude 1/8 inch outward. The uppers are of waterproof nylon and they have drawstring top, belt loops, and suspender buttons.

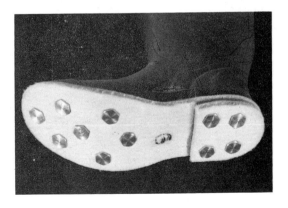

CHAPTER 41

Reviewing New Tackle

RODS

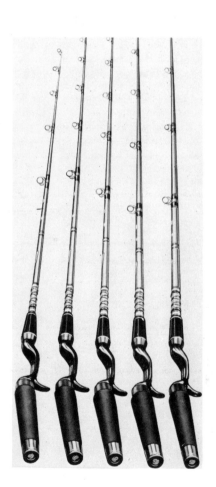

1. The Garcia Corporation has introduced new bait-casting rods, called the "Ambassadeur Worm Rods." Nine rods are in the series, ranging from 4½ to 6½-feet long. All are designed for heavy-duty plastic worm fishing. They have one-piece tubular fiberglass shafts, and the guides and tip-tops are made of tungsten carbide. "Ambassadeur Worm Rods" have red shafts with black wrappings and silver trim. The grips are black closed-cell neoprene.

2. Garcia also is making four new "Ultra-Light Pak Rods." They include a 6½-foot spinning rod, a 7½-foot fly rod, a 7-foot combination fly-and-spinning rod, and a 6-foot bait-casting rod. All come in 5-piece units, except the combination fly-spinning rod which is 4 pieces. The rods have internal fiberglass ferrules, which the manufacturer says gives them "action" superior to most other multi-piece rods.

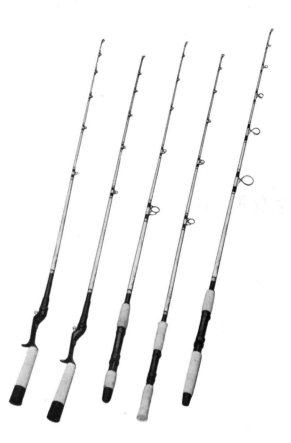

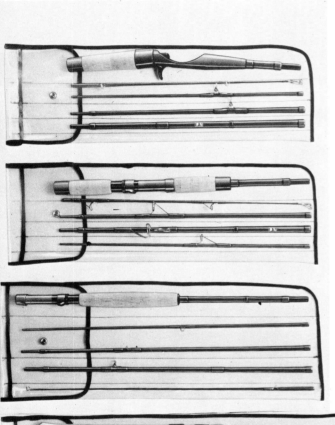

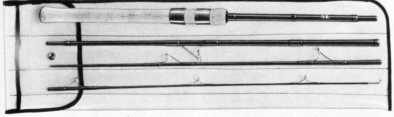

3. The "Eye-Crosser Wonderods," designed by Shakespeare of Columbia, South Carolina, are sturdily built to sink hooks in tough-mouthed fish and also to give an angler enough "rod-power" to move fish out of snag-filled areas. The new, white "Eye-Crosser Wonderods" have detachable handles with black anodized reel seats, and cork grips. There are four bait-casting models and three spinning models. All are one piece.

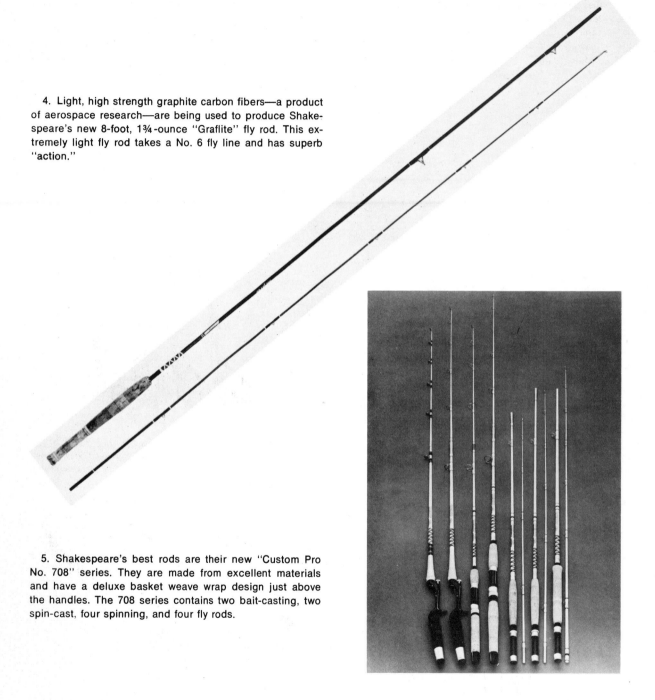

4. Light, high strength graphite carbon fibers—a product of aerospace research—are being used to produce Shakespeare's new 8-foot, 1¾-ounce "Graflite" fly rod. This extremely light fly rod takes a No. 6 fly line and has superb "action."

5. Shakespeare's best rods are their new "Custom Pro No. 708" series. They are made from excellent materials and have a deluxe basket weave wrap design just above the handles. The 708 series contains two bait-casting, two spin-cast, four spinning, and four fly rods.

6. Gladding-South Bend's "Classic III" rods offer an angler just about any type rod he needs for fresh or light salt water fishing. The series includes bait-casting, spin-cast, spinning, fly, and specialized salt water spinning rods. They are available in a variety of lengths and "actions," all have carbide guides and tip-tops, and they are well designed.

7. The "Millionaire" bait-casting rods, by Daiwa, have molded pistol grips on extended handles for added casting ease. These medium-heavy to heavy action rods have friction-free Dialoy guides and tip-tops, stainless steel reel seats with double-locking reel nuts, and they are available in either natural caramel brown or translucent epoxy.

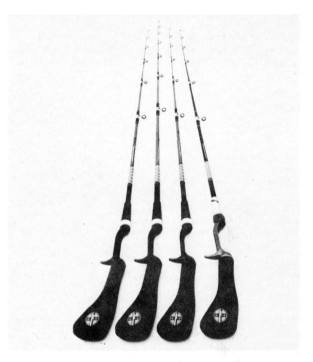

8. "Transa-Coil" tubular glass, permanent ABS butt caps, and plated stainless steel guides are featured on Zebco's new "Sundowner" rods. The "Sundowner" series includes six spin-cast rods, and six spinning rods.

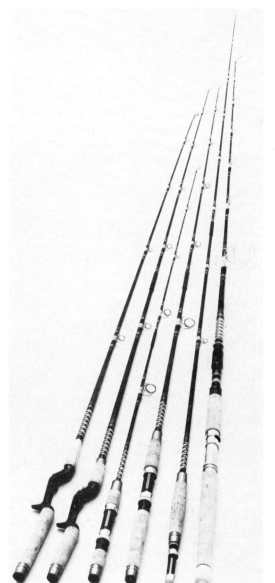

9. Three spinning and six spin-cast rods make up Zebco's new line of "Centennial Rods." The rods are modestly priced, yet are quality made, and include such features as hard chrome-plated steel guides, lightweight and strong aluminum handles, buttgrips and foregrips of select specie cork, and flared ABS butt caps on most models.

10. Zebco's "Pro Staff" rods are the best that company makes. Four spin-cast, five spinning and two fly rods are in the series. According to the company one of the advantages of "Pro Staff" rods is that they are equipped with "aluminum oxide Slip-stream Guides," which are lighter than carbide guides and dissipate the heat created by line friction. The result is that line casts and wears better because of less friction.

11. Twenty-two new "telescoping" rods are being marketed by the Trimarc Corp., Hillside, Ill. The models include fly, spinning, spin-cast, fly/spin combinations, ice fishing, and boat rods. New design features are tubular fiberglass shafts, double wrappings around carboloy guides, specie cork handles, and aluminum spiral-lock reel seats. All rods are life-time guaranteed.

12. True Temper Tackle Corporation is marketing three spinning rods and one spin-cast rod in their 5700 series. The rods have stainless steel guides, anodized aluminum reel seats with double locking rings, and specie cork grips.

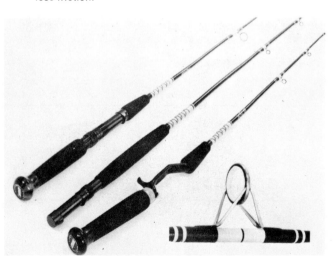

SPINNING REELS

13. Garcia's new economically priced ultralight "Mitchell 204" spinning reel has an adjustable Teflon drag, a 3.8-to-1 gear retrieve ratio, it holds 194 yards of 4-pound test monofilament line, and weighs only 6¼ ounces.

14. The new "XBL77" Zebco spinning reel has stainless steel ball bearings, 4.3-to-1 retrieve ratio, interchangeable spool, a handle that can be changed easily to either side, and a multiple disc drag.

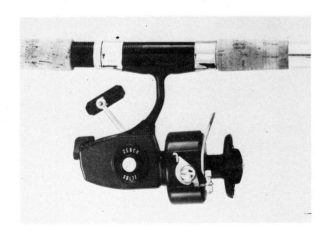

15. Zebco's new "Ambidextrous XBL39" was designed for fishermen who want the option of either right- or left-hand retrieve. The "XBL39" features a self-contained disc drag system, selective anti-reverse, aluminum alloy folding handle, 3.4-to-1 gear ratio, and holds 280 yards of 8-pound test line.

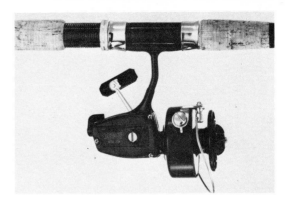

16. The Zebco "Cardinal 3" spinning reel is excellent for ultralight fishing. It has all the fine features found in the other members of Zebco's "Cardinal Reel" series, including stern-mounted drag control, multi-disc drag, 5-to-1 retrieve ratio, and it's corrosion proof.

17. Shakespeare has introduced a new "Model 2400" skirted spool spinning reel. It's designed for light spinning and has a fast 5.2-to-1 gear ratio.

18. The newest addition to St. Croix Corporation's "SL" line of spinning reels is the "SL-111QR." It's a well-balanced reel designed for fresh water fishing. The 12-ounce reel holds 200 yards of 10-pound test line and it's corrosion resistant.

19. The "Spinfisher Model 716" is the smallest, lightest reel the Penn Fishing Tackle Company has ever produced. The reel's ball-bearing design and high gear ratio of 5.1-to-1 insures smooth performance. The "716" is designed for fishing with 4- and 6-pound test mono line, and for casting lures as light as ⅛ ounce.

20. Daiwa's new, improved "8100" spinning reel features a snap-off spun aluminum reel spool that retards corrosion, a high speed gear ratio of 4.6-to-1, and a Teflon adjustable drag.

21. Shakespeare's "2081A Sea Wonder" spinning reel is made for heavy fresh and light salt water fishing. It weighs 20 ounces, has a 3.2-to-1 gear ratio, and holds 300 yards of 12-pound test mono. Also, Shakespeare offers a money-back guarantee if the buyer is not pleased with the "2081A" and returns it within 30 days.

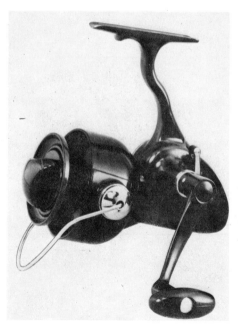

SPIN-CAST REELS

22. Garcia's new "Abu-Matic 290" spin-cast reel features double pick-up pins, a redesigned nose-cone, ball bearing drag, and is pre-wound with 20-pound test mono.

23. The "SC-3 Mustang" spin-cast reel by St. Croix is designed especially for heavy duty fishing where a reel with plenty of line capacity is needed. It holds 400 feet of 10-pound test line, and the handle converts to either left- or right-hand retrieve.

25. The Martin Reel Co., Mohawk, New York, one of the oldest manufacturers of fly reels, just introduced their "Model 500" spin-cast reel. It has a special "Monocon" spool for improved casting performance, a multiple disc star drag, and comes equipped with 100 yards of 8-pound test line. It weighs 9 ounces.

26. An adjustable star drag, push-button control, all metal gears, and permanent anti-reverse are just some of the features of the Famous Keystone Corporation's new "X8A" spin-cast reel.

24. St. Croix also offers another new spin-cast reel called the "RF-76 Range-Finder." The reel features a "Memory Lok," and when it's set it automatically stops all casts at the same distance. St. Croix says the "Memory Lok" makes consistent casting easy.

27. Zebco Tackle Company's "Model 700 Hoss" spin-cast reel is specially made for fighting large fresh water fish. The reel has precision metal gears, a tempered aluminum cover, silent anti-reverse, counterbalanced stainless steel handle, and weighs only 8 ounces.

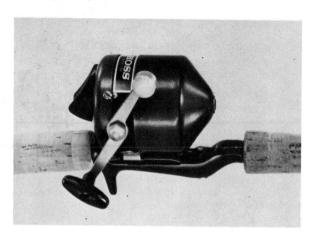

30. Stainless steel ball bearings, "over-sized" handle, quality star drag, centrifugal anti-backlash control, and a calibrated spool braking system are only some of the qualities of Daiwa's "Millionaire V" bait-casting reel.

28. The "Zebco One" probably is the best spin-cast reel manufactured today. It is equipped with stainless steel cover, ball bearings and gears. Also, it has a fast 4-to-1 gear ratio, contoured thumb control, and a quality star drag.

31. "Mark 3200" is the name for Heddon's new bait-casting reel. According to the firm, the "Mark 3200" is the easiest, smoothest casting reel on the market, and will give long, smooth casts with light lures. It comes with star drag control, handles monofilament or braided line—8 to 25 pounds, and weighs 10 ounces.

BAIT-CASTING REELS

29. Shakespeare is producing a bait-casting reel called the "No. 1975." This free spool reel has a carbide line guide, a 5-to-1 retrieve ratio, extra large crank handle, star drag, and helical metal gears.

32. Many black bass fishermen have been waiting for a bait-casting reel like Garcia's new "Ambassadeur 5000D." This reel utilizes a small knurled-knob drag, rather than the standard star drag used on other "Ambassadeur" reels, and it has "direct drive retrieve."

made of non-corrosive materials, and it has heavy-duty gears and stainless steel pinions.

33. The "5500C" and "6500C" are two brand new, fast-retrieve Garcia bait-casting reels. They have a 5-to-1 retrieve ratio and ball bearing spools.

35. Garcia's "Ambassadeur 10,000C" is a fine salt water reel. It features stainless steel ball bearings, centrifugal brake, and holds 300 yards of 30-pound test mono.

SALT WATER REELS

34. A superb salt water "service reel," the "Model 1960," made by Shakespeare, is built for heavy duty fishing. This lever controlled free-spool reel has a one-piece frame and head cap made of high-impact ABS plastic. All parts are

FLY REELS

36. The Martin Reel Co. is manufacturing a new, "Model 72," single-action fly reel. It's a fast, 3-to-1 retrieve model, and has a special disc drag, brass and steel gears, and an interchangeable reel spool system.

37. Martin also produces a quality automatic fly reel. Their "Sovereign 23 AXL" features steel gears, an all metal brake which never needs adjusting, a trigger that can be set to any desired angle, and it weighs only 10 ounces.

TACKLE BOXES

38. Vlchek Plastics Co., maker of AdVenturer Tackle Boxes, is producing a unique line of tackle boxes called "Tuff Tainers." They're available in five sizes and 11 different compartment arrangements. "Tuff Tainers" are made of high strength yellow polypropylene, are impervious to gasoline, oil, salt water, and plastic lures.

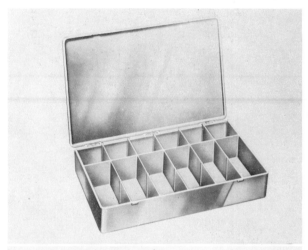

39. Designed especially for spinner-baits, the AdVenturer "Model 1203" tackle box is rustproof, crushproof, has a "lift-out" interior, a safety latch, and can accommodate 69 lures.

40. A "combination" tackle box that's specially designed to conveniently hold spinner-baits, plastic worms, and plugs are features of AdVenturer's "Model 1726."

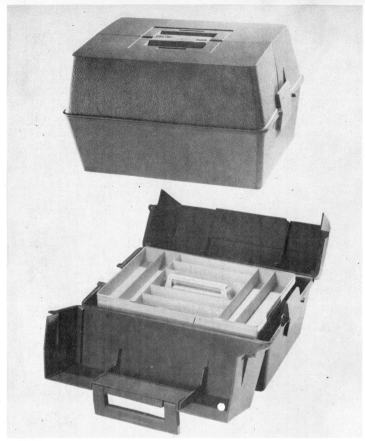

42. Old Pal/Woodstream's Model 1050" tackle box has 15 compartments, a strong "draw-bolt latch," luggage style handle, and it's lockable and watertight.

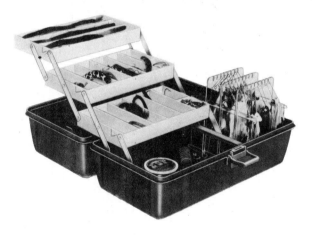

41. The Old Pal/Woodstream Corp., Lititz, Pa., has created an excellent tackle box for the angler who does various types of fishing, in many areas, with a lot of different gear. Called the "1580 Library Box" it holds up to six large removable trays. Therefore an angler can purchase extra trays and literally build his own tackle "library." Different trays can hold equipment for varied types of fishing, such as fresh water, salt water, stream, lake, fly, plug, jig, trolling, etc. This way, tackle that will not be used for a specific type of fishing doesn't have to be carried along.

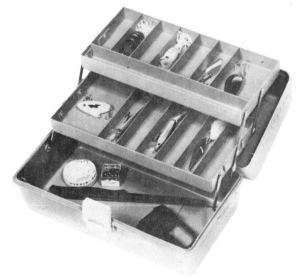

43. A lift-out tray, impervious to plastic lures, recessed handle, rustproof and a lockable latch are only some of the features of Old Pal/Woodstream's "Model 1035" economy tackle box.

44. UMCO Corp., Watertown, Minn., is marketing a new line of all-purpose tackle boxes which maximize space in a compact size. There are eight boxes in the line, ranging in size from one to three-tray models with 7 to 25 compartments. All boxes are plastic lure proof, and have quality locks and recessed handles.

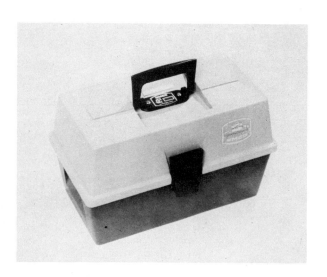

LURES

45. Fred Arbogast Co., Arkon, Ohio, has introduced a new lure called the "Mud-Bug." It's a deep-diving "rattling" plug and is available in ⅛, ¼, and ¾-ounce sizes.

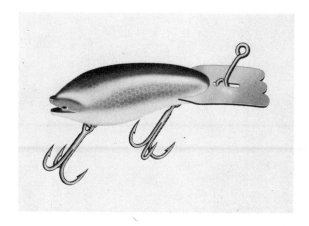

46. Also new from Arbogast is the "Tournament Hawaiian Wiggler." This spinner-bait has tandem blades, a flat "lead-head" which the manufacturer says helps the lure avoid snags, a rubber "skirt." and it can be had in ¼- and ⅝-ounce sizes.

47. The Prescott Spinner Co., Hamilton, Ohio, is producing a novel lure called the "Leadbelly." The lure is made entirely of lead so it casts like a bullet and sinks like an anvil. The company says the "Leadbelly" should be used as a "jigging-spoon." It's available in three sizes and several different colors.

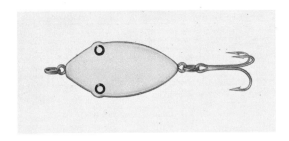

48. Three new models of "spinner-baits"—single spin, tandem spin, and twin spin—are being put out by Zebco. The company calls the lures "Z-Spins." They come in 10 colors and two sizes.

49. Zebco's "Skirted Top Secret" is a floating-diving lure that comes equipped with a built-in rattle and a 48-tail plastic skirt. The firm says that the "Skirted Top Secret" is very effective when fished with a "stop-and-go" retrieve near brush piles, "stick-ups," and other similar snags.

50. The "Gyro Hee-Haw," introduced by Featherweight Products, Glendale, Calif., is a floating-diving lure. It's a fast-diving, rattle-type plug and is available in two sizes and several colors.

51. The "Brush Popper" was just developed by Heddon for fishing snag-filled water without "hanging-up." It has a V-shaped keel which makes the lure land upright and plane over and through weeds and brush. The ½-ounce lure comes in eight different color combinations.

52. Garcia has added a new spinning lure to its famous line of fishing tackle. The manufacturer says that its "Alta Minnow" combines the appeal of a natural looking plastic

minnow with the added flash of a spinner blade for greater fish-attracting action. The "Alta Minnow" comes in ⅛-, ¼-, and ⅓-ounce sizes.

54. A new "Jointed Rapala" lure has been introduced by the Normark Corp., Minneapolis, Minn. It's a floating-diving plug and can be had in two sizes.

53. Lazy Ike Corp., Fort Dodge, Iowa, has recently introduced a lure called the "Lil Wigly." It's a combination spoon and plastic grub, and the company says it's excellent for most gamefish. The ¼-ounce "Lil Wigly" is available in six colors.

CHAPTER 42

World Fishing Records

Field & Stream Magazine
FRESH WATER RECORDS

Field & Stream annual fishing contest entry blanks may be obtained by writing Mike Ball, Fishing Contest Editor, *Field & Stream,* 383 Madison Ave., New York, N.Y. 10017.

SPECIES					CAUGHT BY ROD AND REEL		
Common Name	Scientific Name	Lb.-Oz.	Length	Girth	Where	When	Angler
BASS, Largemouth	Micropterus salmoides	*22-4	32½″	28½″	Montgomery Lake, Georgia	June 2 1932	George W. Perry
BASS, Redeye	Micropterus coosae	6-½	20½″	15⅘″	Hallawakee Creek, Alabama	Mar. 25 1967	Thomas L. Sharpe
BASS, Rock	Ambloplites rupestris	2-2	13″	14″	Mille Coquin Lake, Michigan	Aug. 13 1971	Richard M. Barta
BASS, Smallmouth	Micropterus dolomieui	*11-15	27″	21⅔″	Dale Hollow Lake, Kentucky	July 9 1955	David L. Hayes
BASS, Spotted	Micropterus punctulatus spp	8-10½	23½″	19⅞″	Smith Lake, Alabama	Feb. 25 1972	Billy Henderson
BASS, White	Roccus chrysops	*5-5	19½″	17″	Ferguson Lake, California	Mar. 8 1972	Norman W. Mize
BASS, Yellow	Roccus mississippiensis	2-2	14″	13″	Lake Monona, Wisconsin	Jan. 18 1972	James Thrun
BLUEGILL	Lepomis macrochirus	*4-12	15″	18¼″	Ketona Lake, Alabama	Apr. 9 1950	T. S. Hudson
BOWFIN	Amia calva	19-12	39″		Lake Marion, South Carolina	Nov. 5 1972	M. R. Webster
BUFFALO, Bigmouth	Ictiobus cyprinellus	36-8	41½″	27″	Cedar River, Iowa	Sept. 19 1973	Ella Mae Pidima
BUFFALO, Smallmouth	Ictiobus bubalus	22-½	33½″	22½″	Barbwell Creek, Wisconsin	May 25 1973	Greg Hougelin

SPECIES					CAUGHT BY ROD AND REEL		
Common Name	Scientific Name	Lb.-Oz.	Length	Girth	Where	When	Angler
BULLHEAD, Black	Ictalurus melas	8	24"	17¾"	Lake Waccabuc, New York	Aug. 1 1951	Kani Evans
CARP	Cyprinus carpio	55-5	42"	31"	Clearwater Lake, Minnesota	July 10 1952	Frank J. Ledwein
CATFISH, Blue	Ictalurus furcatus	97	57"	37"	Missouri River, South Dakota	Sept. 16 1959	Edward B. Elliott
CATFISH, Channel	Ictalurus punctatus	*58	47¼"	29⅛"	Santee-Cooper Res., South Carolina	July 7 1964	W. B. Whaley
CATFISH, Flathead	Pylodictis olivaris	76	53"	32"	Piedmont Lake, Ohio	July 12 1972	Dale C. Yoho
CHAR, Arctic	Salvelinus alpinus			Record being reviewed.			
CRAPPIE, Black	Pomoxis nigromaculatus	5	19¼"	18⅝"	Santee-Cooper Res., South Carolina	Mar. 15 1957	Paul E. Foust
CRAPPIE, White	Pomoxis annularis	*5-3	21"	19"	Enid Dam, Mississippi	July 31 1957	Fred L. Bright
DOLLY VARDEN	Salvelinus malma	32	40½"	29¾"	L. Pend Oreille, Idaho	Oct. 27 1949	N. L. Higgins
DRUM, Freshwater	Aplodinotus grunniens	54-8	31½"	29"	Nickajack Lake, Tennessee	Apr. 20 1972	Benny E. Hull
GAR, Alligator	Lepisosteus spatula	279	93"		Rio Grande River, Texas	Dec. 2 1951	Bill Valverde
GAR, Longnose	Lepisosteus osseus	50-5	72¼"	22¼"	Trinity River, Texas	July 30 1954	Townsend Miller
GRAYLING, Arctic	Thymallus arcticus			Record being reviewed.			
MUSKELLUNGE	Esox masquinongy	*69-15	64½"	31¾"	St. Lawrence River New York	Sept. 22 1957	Arthur Lawton
PERCH, White	Roccus americanus	4-12	19½"	13"	Messalonskee Lake, Maine	June 4 1949	Mrs. Earl Small
PERCH, Yellow	Perca flavescens	4-3½			Bordentown, New Jersey	May 1865	Dr. C. C. Abbot
PICKEREL, Chain	Esox niger	*9-6	31"	14"	Homerville, Georgia	Feb. 17 1961	Baxley McQuaig, Jr.
PIKE, Northern	Esox lucius	*46-2	52½"	25"	Sacandaga Res., New York	Sept. 15 1940	Peter Dubuc
SALMON, Atlantic	Salmo salar	79-2			Tana River, Norway	1928	Henrik Henriksen
SALMON, Chinook	Oncorhynchus tshawytscha	*92	58½"	36"	Skeena River, British Columbia	July 19 1959	Heinz Wichman
SALMON, Landlocked	Salmo salar	22-8	36"		Sebago Lake, Maine	Aug. 1 1907	Edward Blakely
SALMON, Coho or Silver	Oncorhynchus kisutch	31			Cowichan Bay, British Columbia	Oct. 11 1947	Mrs. Lee Hallberg
SAUGER	Stizostedion canadense	8-12	28"	15"	Lake Sakakawea, North Dakota	Oct. 6 1971	Mike Fischer
SHAD, American	Alosa sapidissima	*9-2	25"	17½"	Enfield, Connecticut	Apr. 28 1973	Edward P. Nelson
STURGEON, White	Acipenser transmontanus	360	111"	86"	Snake River, Idaho	Apr. 24 1956	Willard Cravens

SPECIES					CAUGHT BY ROD AND REEL		
Common Name	Scientific Name	Lb.-Oz.	Length	Girth	Where	When	Angler
SUNFISH, Green	Lepomis cyanellus	2	11¼"	12½"	Salem, Illinois	May 15 1972	Kenneth Collier, Sr.
SUNFISH, Redear	Lepomis microlophus	4-8	16¼"	17¾"	Chase City, Virginia	June 19 1970	Maurice E. Ball
TROUT, Brook	Salvelinus fontinalis	14-8	31½"	11½"	Nipigon River, Ontario	July 1916	Dr. W. J. Cook
TROUT, Brown	Salmo trutta	39-8			Loch Awe, Scotland	1866	W. Muir
TROUT, Cutthroat	Salmo clarki	41	39"		Pyramid Lake, Nevada	Dec. 1925	John Skimmerhorn
TROUT, Golden	Salmo aguabonita	11	28"	16"	Cook's Lake, Wyoming	Aug. 5 1948	Chas. S. Reed
TROUT, Lake	Salvelinus namaycush			Record being reviewed.			
TROUT, Rainbow, Stlhd. or Kamloops	Salmo gairdneri	*42-2	43"	23½"	Bell Island, Alaska	June 22 1970	David Robert White
TROUT, Sunapee	Salvelinus alpinus	11-8	33"	17¼"	Lake Sunapee, New Hampshire	Aug. 1 1954	Ernest Theoharis
WALLEYE	Stizostedion vitreum	*25	41"	29"	Old Hickory Lake, Tennessee	Aug. 1 1960	Mabry Harper
WARMOUTH	Chaenobryttus gulosus	1-13	10¾"	12¼"	Cumberland County, Illinois	May 22 1971	Wesley Mills
WHITEFISH, Lake	Coregonus clupeaformis	12-9	32"	18⅛"	Great Slave L., N.W.T.	July 28 1972	Eddie Drygeese
WHITEFISH, Mountain	Prosopium williamsoni	5	19"	14"	Athabasca R., Alberta	June 3 1963	Orville Welch

INTERNATIONAL GAME FISH ASSOCIATION RECORDS

International Game Fish Association world record entry forms may be obtained by writing: I.G.F.A., 2190 S.E. 17th St., Ft. Lauderdale, Fla., 33316.

Other common name: longfin tuna
Scientific name: Thunnus alalunga

ALBACORE

Line Class	Weight lbs. oz.	Length inches	Girth inches	Place	Date	Angler
M-6 lb.	27-8	37½	25	San Diego California	Oct. 4 1972	Joe Bahan
W-6 lb.	Vacant—No Minimum Weight					
M-12 lb.	39-8	43½	32½	Balboa California	July 23 1958	Dr. R. S. Rubaum

Line Class	Weight lbs. oz.	Length inches	Girth inches	Place	Date	Angler
*W–12 lb.	29–8	37	24½	San Diego California	Oct. 5 1963	Jane Holland
M–20 lb.	40–12	41½	29	San Diego California	Oct. 4 1972	Glenn R. Bracken
W–20 lb.	50	45½	29	Ocean City Maryland	Sept. 3 1970	Mrs. Carol R. Moss
M–30 lb.	63–13	48	33	Arguineguin Canary Islands	Oct. 28 1973	Ants Peeker
W–30 lb.	59–8	45½	29½	Montauck New York	Aug. 14 1971	Eileen B. Merten
M–50 lb.	71–1	45¼	33¾	Sao Miguel Azores	Nov. 17 1973	Eduardo Manuel do R Melo
W–50 lb.	41	42	27	Morro Bay California	Sept. 17 1967	Theresa Bullard
M–80 lb.	69–2	46	32	Montauck New York	Aug. 21 1964	Larry R. Kranz
W–80 lb.	29	37	23	Morro Bay California	Sept. 24 1967	Theresa Bullard
All–Tackle M–130 lb.	74–13	50	34¾	Arguineguin Canary Islands	Oct. 28 1973	Olof Idegren
W–130 lb.	Vacant—Minimum Acceptance Weight—55 lbs.					
*TIE W–12 lb.	29–8	37¼	24½	Morro Bay California	Sept. 3 1973	Barbara Louise McKinney

AMBERJACK (greater)

Scientific name: Seriola dumerili

Line Class	Weight lbs. oz.	Length inches	Girth inches	Place	Date	Angler
M–6 lb.	18–4	36	20¼	Hatteras N. Carolina	Oct. 14 1973	Michael E. Hayes
W–6 lb.	13	33½	17¾	Key West Florida	Mar. 6 1973	Charlyne Terrell
M–12 lb.	80	66	35½	Miami Beach Florida	May 19 1973	Jeffery F. Trotta
W–12 lb.	78–4	60¼	34½	Key Largo Florida	Mar. 23 1969	Pamela J. Habicht
M–20 lb.	101–8	61	39	Palm Beach Florida	Feb. 26 1964	Robert R. Boomhower
W–20 lb.	83–14	57¼	36	Challenger Bank Bermuda	July 28 1966	L. Edna Perinchief
All–Tackle M–30 lb.	149	71	41¾	Bermuda	June 21 1964	Peter Simons
W–30 lb.	101	67	45	Palm Beach Florida	Mar. 31 1970	Mrs. Cynthia Boomhower
M–50 lb.	132	63	39¼	La Paz Mexico	July 21 1964	Howard H. Hahn
W–50 lb.	108	69	36	Palm Beach Florida	Dec. 30 1967	Peggy Kester Mumford

Line Class	Weight lbs. oz.	Length inches	Girth inches	Place	Date	Angler
M–80 lb.	142–14	71¾	24¼	Bermuda	Aug. 7 1969	Nelson Chesterfield Simons
W–80 lb.	106–8	65	39	Pinas Bay Panama	July 9 1960	Helen Robinson
M–130 lb.	133	66	37	Islamorada Florida	Apr. 6 1968	Louis E. Woster
W–130 lb.	85	61	36	Palm Beach Florida	Apr. 29 1971	Mrs. Cynthia Boomhower

BARRACUDA (great)

Scientific name: Sphyraena barracuda

Line Class	Weight lbs. oz.	Length inches	Girth inches	Place	Date	Angler
M–6 lb.	26	51½	19¾	Key West Florida	July 8 1973	Martin R. Walker
W–6 lb.	17–12¼	46½	16	Sugarloaf Florida	Mar. 6 1974	Charlyne Terrell
M–12 lb.	49–4	56	21½	Margarita Venezuela SA	Jan. 9 1960	Gerardo Sanson
W–12 lb.	41	59	21	Jupiter Florida	Nov. 20 1967	Mrs. Cynthia Boomhower
M–20 lb.	60–10	64½	26½	Cairns Australia	Nov. 5 1968	Desmond R Schumann
W–20 lb.	48	64½	26	Heron Island Australia	Aug. 21 1970	Mrs. Glen Mactaggart
M–30 lb.	70–12	64	29	Malindi Kenya, Africa	Oct. 26 1973	Major D. C. Bagworth
W–30 lb.	43	60	26	Koy Largo Florida	Dec. 9 1956	Mrs. Robert M. Scully
All–Tackle M-50 lb.	83	72¼	29	Lagos Nigeria, Africa	Jan. 13 1952	K.J.W. Hackett
W–50 lb.	47–4	63	21	Pemba Channel Kenya, Africa	July 27 1973	Mrs. Ingrid Papworth
M–80 lb.	67	65	29¾	Islamorada Florida	Jan. 29 1949	Harold K. Goodstone
W–80 lb.	66–4	70	25⅕	Cape Lopez Gabon, Africa	July 17 1955	Mme. M. Halley
M-130 lb.	Vacant—Minimum Acceptance Weight—67 lbs.					
W-130 lb.	Vacant—Minimum Acceptance Weight—66 lbs.					

BASS (black sea)

Scientific name: Centropristis striata

Line Class	Weight lbs. oz.	Length inches	Girth inches	Place	Date	Angler
M–6 lb.	4–14½	23	15¾	Virginia Beach Virginia	Mar. 8 1974	Michael E. Hayes
W–6 lb.	4–3	20	13¼	Virginia Beach Virginia	Apr. 7 1974	Mrs. Charlotte J. Wright

Line Class	Weight lbs. oz.	Length inches	Girth inches	Place	Date	Angler
M–12 lb.	5–6	21½	16	Virginia Beach Virginia	May 16 1970	J. David Wright
W–12 lb.	4–4	20½	15¼	Virginia Beach Virginia	May 21 1972	Mrs. Michael E. Hayes
M–20 lb.	6–1	24⅛	17	Seabright New Jersey	July 13 1958	William Young
W–20 lb.	5–2	23	15	Virginia Beach Virginia	May 17 1971	Mrs. Charlotte J. Wright
*M–30 lb.	5–5	21	19	Virginia Beach Virginia	May 29 Hayes	Michael E. Hayes
W–30 lb.	5–14	25	14	Cape Henry Virginia	Oct. 2 1972	Mary Lou Penny Durney
All–Tackle M–50 lb.	8	22	19	Nantucket Sound Massachusetts	May 13 1951	H. R. Rider
W–50 lb.	5–1	20½	16	Panama City Beach Florida	July 21 1956	Mrs. R. H. Martin
M–80 lb.	Vacant—Minimum Acceptance Weight—8 lbs.					
W–80 lb.	Vacant—Minimum Acceptance Weight—5 lbs.					
M–130 lb.	Vacant—Minimum Acceptance Weight—8 lbs.					
W–130 lb.	Vacant—Minimum Acceptance Weight—5 lbs.					
*TIE M–30 lb.	5–8	24	15	Oregon Inlet N. Carolina	Sept. 1 1973	George F. Moore

BASS (giant sea)

Scientific name: Stereolepis gigas

Line Class	Weight lbs. oz.	Length inches	Girth inches	Place	Date	Angler
M–6 lb.	Vacant—No Minimum Weight					
.V–6 lbs.	Vacant—No Minimum Weight					
M–12 lb.	112–8	57	44	San Francisco Island Mexico	June 12 1957	D. B. Rosenthal
W–12 lb.	Vacant—Minimum Acceptance Weight—90 lbs.					
M–20 lb.	425	85	76	Point Mugu California	Oct. 1 1960	C. C. Joiner
W–20 lb.	120	55	40	Malibu California	Jan. 6 1957	Jane D. Hill
M–30 lb.	388–8	78	72	Catalina Island California	Sept. 29 1962	John W. Scott, Jr.
W–30 lb.	108–8	55	42½	San Pablo Mexico	Dec. 29 1963	Frances Enfinger
M–50 lb.	557–3	88¼	78	Catalina Island California	July 1 1962	Richard M. Lane

Line Class	Weight lbs. oz.	Length inches	Girth inches	Place	Date	Angler
W–50 lb.	419	87¾	63½	Coronado Island California	Oct. 8 1960	Bettie Sears
All–Tackle M–80 lb.	563–8	89	72	Anacapa Island California	Aug. 20 1968	James D. McAdam, Jr.
W–80 lb.	452	86¼	64¼	Coronado Island California	Oct. 8 1960	Lorene Wheeler
*M–130 lb.	514	86	82	San Clemente California	Aug. 29 1955	J. Patterson
*W–130 lb.	Vacant—Minimum Acceptance Weight—452 lbs.					
*TIE M–130 lb.	514	90	80	Box Canyon California	Nov. 15 1961	Joe M. Arve

BASS (striped)

Other common name: rockfish
Scientific name: Morone saxatilis

Line Class	Weight lbs. oz.	Length inches	Girth inches	Place	Date	Angler
M–6 lb.	38	48½	28	Atlantic City New Jersey	Nov. 5 1973	Charles P. Bliss
W–6 lb.	11–4½	29	15	San Pablo Bay California	Mar. 24 1974	Judith L. Souza
M–12 lb.	61–10	53	30	Block Island Rhode Island	July 5 1956	L. A. Garceau
W–12 lb.	47	49½	—	Umpqua R. Oregon	Aug. 21 1958	Mrs. Margaret Hulen
*M–20 lb.	67	55	29½	Block Island Rhode Island	May 31 1963	Jack Ryan
W–20 lb.	57–8	50	30	Block Island Sound New York	Aug. 28 1959	Mary R. Aubry
M–30 lb.	63–8	52½	29	Jones Beach Inlet New York	Aug. 17 1973	William E. King, Jr.
W–30 lb.	64–8	54	30	North Truro Massachusetts	Aug. 14 1960	Rosa O. Webb
All–Tackle M–50 lb.	72	54½	31	Cuttyhunk Massachusetts	Oct. 10 1969	Edward J. Kirker
W–50 lb.	64	50	31	Sea Bright New Jersey	June 27 1971	Mrs. Asie Espenak
M–80 lb.	Vacant—Minimum Acceptance Weight—64 lbs.					
W–80 lb.	56	53½	33½	Sandy Hook New Jersey	June 7 1955	Mrs. H. J. Sarnoski
M–130 lb.	Vacant—Minimum Acceptance Weight—64 lbs.					
W–130 lb.	Vacant—Minimum Acceptance Weight—64 lbs.					
*TIE M–20 lb.	67	54⅛	32½	Greenhill Rhode Island	Oct. 3 1955	Wilfred Fontaine

BLUEFISH   *Scientific name:* Pomatomus saltatrix

Line Class	Weight lbs. oz.	Length inches	Girth inches	Place	Date	Angler
M–6 lb.	18–11	40	20	Atlantic Beach North Carolina	Nov. 19	Daniel W. Able
W–6 lb.	14–15	36	19	Nantucket Massachusetts	Sept. 1 1972	Suzanne Cowan
M–12 lb.	24–3	41	22	San Miguel Azores	Aug. 27 1953	M. A. da Silva Veloso
W–12 lb.	16–10	36	19	Montauk New York	June 24 1961	Gloria Better
M–20 lb.	23–12	40	28	Cape May New Jersey	Oct. 9 1971	William Di Santo
W–20 lb.	24–8	40	23½	Nags Head North Carolina	Nov. 12 1971	Mrs. Rita Mazelle
M–30 lb.	22	39	22	Avon North Carolina	Nov. 27 1969	Michael E. Hayes
W–30 lb.	21–8	37	23	Truro Massachusetts	Oct. 10 1970	Ruth M. Anderson
All-Tackle M–50 lb.	31–12	47	23	Hatteras Inlet North Carolina	Jan. 30 1972	James M. Hussey
W–50 lb.	23–15	40½	23½	Nags Head North Carolina	Nov. 19 1970	Mrs. Joyce Payne Bell
M–80 lb.	22–12	38	21⅞	Arguineguin Gran Canaria	July 19 1971	Kenneth V. Oulton
W–80 lb.	21–8	39¾	21½	Virginia Beach Virginia	Aug. 8 1971	Katherine K. Ayers
M–130 lb.	Vacant—Minimum Acceptance Weight—24 lbs.					
W–130 lb.	Vacant—Minimum Acceptance Weight—19 lbs.					

BONEFISH   *Scientific name:* Albula vulpes

Line Class	Weight lbs. oz.	Length inches	Girth inches	Place	Date	Angler
M–6 lb.	12–3	32	17½	Islamorada Florida	Mar. 7 1972	Arnold Sobel
W–6 lb.	13–2	29½	18	Islamorada Florida	Apr. 5 1973	Charlotte Rowland
M–12 lb.	16	33½	18½	Bimini Bahamas	Feb. 25 1971	Jerry Lavenstein
W–12 lb.	15	32½	18½	Bimini Bahamas	Mar. 20 1961	Andrea Tose
*M–20 lb.	14	34¼	17½	Bermuda	Dec. 29 1950	Dr. H. R. Becker
W–20 lb.	13–12	30¾	17½	Exuma Bahamas	Jan .3 1956	Mrs. B. A. Garson
All-Tackle M–30 lb.	19	39⅝	17	Zululand South Africa	May 26 1962	Brian W. Batchelor
W–30 lb.	Vacant—Minimum Acceptance Weight—14 lbs.					

Line Class	Weight lbs. oz.	Length inches	Girth inches	Place	Date	Angler
M-50 lb.	17-8	40	18	Oahu Hawaii	Aug. 23 1952	Jack Yoshida
W-50 lb.	Vacant—Minimum Acceptance Weight—15 lbs.					
M-80 lb.	18-2	41½	17¹⁵⁄₁₆	Kauai Hawaii	Oct. 11 1954	Wm. Badua
W-80 lb.	Vacant—Minimum Acceptance Weight—15 lbs.					
M-130 lb.	Vacant—Minimum Acceptance Weight—19 lbs.					
W-130 lb.	Vacant—Minimum Acceptance Weight—15 lbs.					
*TIE M-20 lb.	14-4	31½	19	Islamorada Florida	Jan. 5 1972	Mike Hyman

COBIA

Other common name: ling
Scientific name: Rachycentron canadum

Line Class	Weight lbs. oz.	Length inches	Girth inches	Place	Date	Angler
M-6 lb.	45-8	54½	19½	Flamingo Florida	Nov. 28 1973	Ray Cantarrana, Jr.
W-6 lb.	Vacant—No Minimum Weight					
*M-12 lb.	70	60	31½	Gulf of Mexico Texas	May 13 1955	H. A. Norris, Jr.
W-12 lb.	55	60⅝₁₆	29⅜	Islamorada Florida	Feb. 14 1971	Mrs. Marcia Maizler
M-20 lb.	91	56	30	Crystal Beach Florida	Apr. 25 1962	Roy English
W-20 lb.	67	60	29	Cape Charles Virginia	July 5 1968	Judith Anne Gingell
M-30 lb.	100	71½	36	Point Lookout Queensland, Australia	Oct. 4 1962	Peter R. Bristow
W-30 lb.	68-8	60	28½	Onancock Virginia	June 6 1968	Mrs. Frances M. Roberts
All-Tackle M-50 lb.	110-5	63	34	Mombasa Kenya, Africa	Sept. 8 1964	Eric Tinworth
W-50 lb.	85	67	30½	Queensland Australia	Aug. 15 1964	Margaret Keid
M-80 lb.	90	65½	31	Ocean City Maryland	Aug. 31 1949	Charles J. Stine
W-80 lb.	97	66½	33	Oregon Inlet N. Carolina	June 4 1952	Mary W. Black
M-130 lb.	Vacant—Minimum Acceptance Weight—97 lbs.					
W-130 lb.	Vacant—Minimum Acceptance Weight—97 lbs.					
*TIE M-12 lb.	70-2	62	28	Key West Florida	Jan. 27 1973	Alan H. Walton

COD

Scientific name: Gadus morhua

Line Class	Weight lbs. oz.	Length inches	Girth inches	Place	Date	Angler
M-6 lb.	19-1½	38	22	Folkestone England	Jan. 10 1973	Christopher O'Hara
W-6 lb.	Vacant—No Minimum Weight					
M-12 lb.	55	66	38	Plum Island Massachusetts	July 6 1958	W. C. Dunn
W-12 lb.	17-7	36⅜	21¼	Plymouth England	Sept. 19 1971	Mrs. Rita Barrett
All-Tackle M-20 lb.	98-12	63	41	Isle of Shoals Massachusetts	June 8 1969	Alphonse J. Bielevich
W-20 lb.	71-8	58	31	Cape Cod Massachusetts	Aug. 2 1964	Muriel Betts
M-30 lb.	81	54⅞	35½	Brielle New Jersey	Mar. 15 1967	Joseph Chesla
W-30 lb.	26	41	25	Wedgeport Nova Scotia, Canada	July 19 1964	Catherine Bauer
M-50 lb.	80-9	58	38	Boston Massachusetts	May 14 1972	William Bright
W-50 lb.	54-2	55¼	33	Nantucket Island Massachusetts	Sept. 28 1970	Gail A. Mosher
M-80 lb.	Vacant—Minimum Acceptance Weight—81 lbs.					
W-80 lb.	81-12	59¾	39	Middlebank Massachusetts	Sept. 24 1970	Mrs. Sophie Karwa
M-130 lb.	Vacant—Minimum Acceptance Weight—81 lbs.					
W-130 lb.	Vacant—Minimum Acceptance Weight—81 lbs.					

DOLPHIN

Other common name: dorado
Scientific name: Coryphaena hippurus

Line Class	Weight lbs. oz.	Length inches	Girth inches	Place	Date	Angler
M-6 lb.	46-5	61¾	30	Point Venus Tahiti, Fr. Polynesia	Feb. 10 1973	Alban Ellacott
W-6 lb.	30	52½	22½	West Palm Beach Florida	Mar. 27 1974	Mrs. Herbert L. Allison
M-12 lb.	59-8	64	33	Pinas Bay Panama	Jan. 28 1971	Russell M. Anderson
W-12 lb.	55-2	59¾	32½	Mazatlan Mexico	Oct. 18 1964	Marguerite H. Barry
M-20 lb.	64-12	69	32¾	Islamorada Florida	June 7 1970	Donald H. Jackson
W-20 lb.	83-6	57½	37½	Mazatlan Mexico	Apr. 24 1972	Mrs. Eugene W. Wooten
M-30 lb.	65-4	69	35	Boca Chica Dominican Republic	Mar. 18 1973	Manuel Alfonso Garcia Dubus

Line Class	Weight lbs. oz.	Length inches	Girth inches	Place	Date	Angler
W–30 lb.	73-11	59½	43½	Baja California Mexico	July 12 1962	Barbara Kibbee Jayne
All-Tackle M–50 lb.	95	69	37½	Spanish Wells Bahamas	May 29 1968	Richard Seymour
W–50 lb.	67	68	31¾	Miami Beach Florida	Jan. 2 1968	Janet Shepro
M–80 lb.	77	74½	35	Nags Head N. Carolina	July 3 1973	Louis Van Miller
W–80 lb.	67	65	32	Chub Cay Bahamas	Mar. 13 1966	Ruth Stanley
M–130 lb.	72-8	58½	35¼	Honolulu Hawaii	Mar. 13 1956	G. Perry
W–130 lb.	Vacant—Minimum Acceptance Weight—73 lbs.					

DRUM (black) *Scientific name:* Pogonias cromis

Line Class	Weight lbs. oz.	Length inches	Girth inches	Place	Date	Angler
M–6 lb.	52	44	31½	Cape Charles Virginia	May 10 1973	Harry L. Gerwin
W–6 lb.	Vacant—No Minimum Weight					
M–12 lb.	89	51	40½	Delaware Bay New Jersey	May 14 1971	John K. Osborne, Jr.
W–12 lb.	58-12	45⅜	36	Atlantic Beach N. Carolina	May 8 1959	Juel W. Duke
M–20 lb.	88-4	58½	40	Delaware Bay New Jersey	June 8 1972	Josle A. Trolli, Jr.
W–20 lb.	80-8	52	39	Cape Charles Virginia	Apr. 27 1974	Louise M. Gaskill
M–30 lb.	107	53½	43	Cape Charles Virginia	Apr. 29 1974	Everett M. Masten, Jr.
W–30 lb.	78	49½	41	Cape Charles Virginia	April 29 1974	Lindley G. Webb
M–50 lb.	109	57	48	Cape Charles Virginia	May 25 1972	Steve Dennis
W–50 lb.	93	50½	42	Fernandina Beach Florida	Mar. 28 1957	Mrs. Stella Moore
M–80 lb.	Vacant—Minimum Acceptance Weight—98 lbs.					
All-Tackle W–80 lb.	111	53½	45¾	Cape Charles Virginia	May 20 1973	Betty D. Hall
M–130 lb.	Vacant—Minimum Acceptance Weight—98 lbs.					
W–130 lb.	Vacant—Minimum Acceptance Weight—93 lbs.					

DRUM (red)

Other common names: redfish/channel bass
Scientific name: Sciaenops ocellata

Line Class	Weight lbs. oz.	Length inches	Girth inches	Place	Date	Angler
M–6 lb.	25–4	41⅞	25	Empire Louisiana	Apr. 15 1973	Maumus F. Claverie
W–6 lb.	30–4	43	25	Empire Louisiana	Apr. 5 1973	Priscilla Jordan
M–12 lb.	60–8	50¾	29¾	Kill Devil Hills N. Carolina	Oct. 24 1954	A. Clark, Jr.
W–12 lb.	51–8	50¼	29	Cape Hatteras N. Carolina	Nov. 19 1958	Joan S. Dull
M–20 lb.	72–7	55¼	31¾	Cape Hatteras N. Carolina	Nov. 27 1973	Wayne Piageman
W–20 lb.	53–8	50¾	29	Cape Hatteras N. Carolina	Apr. 16 1972	Mrs. Lucille Herbig
All-Tackle M–30 lb.	90	55½	38¼	Rodanthe N. Carolina	Nov. 7 1973	Elvin Hooper
W–30 lb.	69–8	51½	33¼	Cape Hatteras N. Carolina	Nov. 16 1958	Jean Browning
M–50 lb.	83	52	29	Cape Charles Virginia	Aug. 5 1949	Zack Waters, Jr.
W–50 lb.	55	50	29	Smith Island Virginia	Oct. 9 1966	Margaret M. Hutson
M-80 lb.	Vacant—Minimum Acceptance Weight—83 lbs.					
W-80 lb.	Vacant—Minimum Acceptance Weight—69 lbs.					
M-130 lb.	Vacant—Minimum Acceptance Weight—83 lbs.					
W-130 lb.	Vacant—Minimum Acceptance Weight—69 lbs.					

FLOUNDER

Scientific name: Paralichthys

Line Class	Weight lbs. oz.	Length inches	Girth inches	Place	Date	Angler
M–6 lb.	7	26¼	22	Montauk New York	Sept. 13 1973	William Kuhle
W–6 lb.	2–10	20½	16	Wachapreague Virginia	May 11 1974	Mrs. Charlotte J. Wright
M–12 lb.	20	33	33	Topsail Island N. Carolina	Oct. 26 1972	Chris A. Bowen
W–12 lb.	12–2	31¼	25¼	Avalon New Jersey	Sept. 8 1957	Mrs. Alfred Bernstein
All-Tackle M–20 lb.	30–12	38½	30½	Vina del Mar Chile, SA	Nov. 1 1971	Agusto Nunez Moreno
W–20 lb.	16–15½	34½	28½	Captree New York	July 4 1971	Florence Eidman
M–30 lb.	22–1	37	35	Caleta Horcon Chile, SA	Dec. 8 1965	F. I. Aguirrezabal

Line Class	Weight lbs. oz.	Length inches	Girth inches	Place	Date	Angler
W–30 lb.	13–11	33	27½	Long Branch New Jersey	Aug. 20 1953	Mrs. Leslie H. Taylor
M–50 lb.	21–4	36½	35	Maitencillo Chile, SA	Dec. 8 1959	Daniel Varas Serrano
W–50 lb.	20–7	37	29½	Long Island New York	July 8 1957	Mrs. M. Fredriksen
M–80 lb.	Vacant—Minimum Acceptance Weight—22 lbs.					
W–80 lb.	Vacant—Minimum Acceptance Weight—20 lbs.					
M–130 lb.	Vacant—Minimum Acceptance Weight—22 lbs.					
W–130 lb.	Vacant—Minimum Acceptance Weight—20 lbs.					

JEWFISH

Scientific name: Epinephelus itajara

Line Class	Weight lbs. oz.	Length inches	Girth inches	Place	Date	Angler
M–6 lb.	Vacant—No Minimum Weight					
W–6 lb.	Vacant—No Minimum Weight					
M–12 lb.	349	82	62	Florida Bay Florida	May 25 1969	Ralph Delph
W–12 lb.	110	58½	39½	Islamorada Florida	Aug. 2 1961	Mrs. Gar Wood, Jr.
M–20 lb.	343	82	61	Flamingo Florida	Jan. 6 1968	Ralph Delph
W–20 lb.	42–8	43	29	Florida Bay Florida	Nov. 7 1969	Helen Robinson
M–30 lb.	430	96	67	Ft. Lauderdale Florida	Apr. 25 1967	Curt Johnson
W–30 lb.	318	87	65	Dry Tortugas Florida	Mar. 14 1966	Dottie Hall
M–50 lb.	369	77	65	Marathon Florida	Apr. 25 1956	C. F. Mann
W–50 lb.	290	79½	60	Marathon Florida	May 5 1967	Mrs. Leslie Lear
All-Tackle M–80 lb.	680	85½	66	Fernandina Beach Florida	May 20 1961	Lynn Joyner
W–80 lb.	366	88½	68	Guayabo Panama	Feb. 8 1965	Betsy B. Walker
M–130 lb.	396	94	67	Islamorada Florida	Mar. 22 1968	Frank J. Posluszny
W–130 lb.	327	80¾	54½	Flamingo Florida	June 24 1969	Helen Robinson

MACKEREL (king)

Line Class	Weight lbs. oz.	Length inches	Girth inches	Place	Date	Angler
M–6 lb.	44–5	53¼	23½	Empire Louisiana	Feb. 10 1974	John R. Peters, Jr.
W–6 lb.	30–12	51¾	19	Empire Louisiana	Apr. 12 1973	Pamela D. Levert
M–12 lb.	56	61	27½	Key West Florida	Jan. 19 1974	Ralph Parlato
W–12 lb.	44–2	52	24½	St. Thomas U.S. Virgin Islands	May 7 1969	Gloria J. Applegate
M–20 lb.	77	65	29	Bimini Bahamas	May 12 1957	Clinton Olney Potts
W–20 lb.	65–8	64	25½	Palm Beach Florida	Feb. 14 1965	Patricia E. Church
M–30 lb.	75	57	32	Walker Cay Bahamas	May 22 1966	Thomas J. Sims, Jr.
W–30 lb.	64	64	25	Palm Beach Florida	Dec. 23 1973	Barbara Hinkle
All-Tackle M-50 lb.	78–12	65½	30	La Romana Dominican Rep.	Nov. 26 1971	Fernando Viyella
W–50 lb.	78	66½	28½	Guayanilla Puerto Rico	May 25 1963	Ruth M. Coon
M–80 lb.	Vacant—Minimum Acceptance Weight—70 lbs.					
W–80 lb.	67	60	29	Pompano Beach Florida	Apr. 14 1972	Fran S. Colyer
M–130 lb.	76–8	63	31	Bimini Bahamas	May 22 1952	R. E. Maytag
W–130 lb.	71	60	31	Cat Cay Bahamas	June 19 1969	Ann C. Kunkel

MARLIN (Atlantic blue)

Line Class	Weight lbs. oz.	Length inches	Girth inches	Place	Date	Angler
M–6 lb.	Vacant—No Minimum Weight					
W–6 lb.	Vacant—No Minimum Weight					
M–12 lb.	448	138½	55	St. Thomas U. S. Virgin Islands	Sept. 6 1971	Frank L. Miller
W–12 lb.	223–1	122½	42	Bimini Bahamas	Apr. 9 1960	Suzanne H. Higgs
M–20 lb.	430	138	54	St. Thomas U.S. Virgin Islands	Aug. 31 1970	Charles R. Senf
W–20 lb.	392	134¾	52	St. Thomas U.S. Virgin Islands	Aug. 14 1973	Elsie Senf

Line Class	Weight lbs. oz.	Length inches	Girth inches	Place	Date	Angler
M–30 lb.	484–8	144	57	Near Hatteras N. Carolina	June 3 1973	Charles Wade Bailey
W–30 lb.	542–8	162	56	Walker's Cay Abaco, Bahamas	May 2 1974	Mrs. Almeta Schafer
M–50 lb.	666	142	71	Hillsboro Florida	May 24 1973	E. C. Brookshire
W–50 lb.	633–8	156	50	Bimini Bahamas	Mar. 27 1970	Mrs. Audrey Grady
All-Tackle M–80 lb.	845	157	71	St. Thomas U.S. Virgin Islands	July 4 1968	Elliot J. Fishman
W–80 lb.	705	167	64	St. Thomas U.S. Virgin Islands	July 8 1972	Gloria J. Applegate
M–130 lb.	810	157	68	Hatteras N. Carolina	June 11 1962	Gary Stukes
W–130 lb.	723	158	68	Bimini Bahamas	Aug. 10 1967	Mrs. J. M. Hollobaugh, Jr.

MARLIN (black)

Scientific name: Makaira indica

Line Class	Weight lbs. oz.	Length inches	Girth inches	Place	Date	Angler
M–6 lb.	Vacant—No Minimum Weight					
W–6 lb.	Vacant—No Minimum Weight					
M–12 lb.	309	124	49	Pinas Bay Panama	Jan. 24 1971	Russell M. Anderson
W–12 lb.	353	126½	55	Pinas Bay Panama	Mar. 6 1968	Evelyn M. Anderson
M–20 lb.	381	124	56¼	Pinas Bay Panama	Mar. 6 1970	Russell M. Anderson
W–20 lb.	418	130	59	Pinas Bay Panama	Jan. 11 1968	Mrs. Carl Dann III
M–30 lb.	816	152	69	Cairns Australia	Sept. 19 1971	Patrick Gay
W–30 lb.	552	147	62	La Plata Island Ecuador, SA	July 3 1953	Mrs. W. G. Krieger
M–50 lb.	1124	168	75	Cairns Australia	Oct. 31 1969	Edward Seay
W–50 lb	584	150	68	Pinas Bay Panama	Jan. 14 1962	Helen Robinson
M–80 lb.	1218	176	81	Cooktown Australia	Sept. 24 1973	D. Mead Johnson
W–80 lb.	1028–8	157	75½	Cairns Australia	Oct. 29 1970	Mrs. Colleen Seay
All-Tackle M–130 lb.	1560	174	81	Cabo Blanco Peru, SA	Aug. 4 1953	Alfred C. Glassell, Jr.
W–130 lb.	1525	172	80	Cabo Blanco Peru, SA	Apr. 22 1954	Kimberley Wiss

MARLIN (Pacific blue)   *Scientific name:* Makaira nigricans

Line Class	Weight lbs. oz.	Length inches	Girth inches	Place	Date	Angler
M–6 lb.	Vacant—No Minimum Weight					
W–6 lb.	Vacant—No Minimum Weight					
M–12 lb.	Vacant—Minimum Acceptance Weight—75 lbs.					
W–12 lb.	Vacant—Minimum Acceptance Weight—75 lbs.					
M–20 lb.	220	114	42	Baja California Mexico	Nov. 25 1967	W. Matt Parr
W–20 lb.	406	135	52½	Mazatlan Mexico	May 18 1972	Marguerite H. Barry
M–30 lb.	438	159	53	Bay of Islands New Zealand	Dec. 2 1972	William W. Hall
W–30 lb.	264	120½	45	Kailua–Kona Hawaii	Nov. 9 1965	Jeannette Alford
M–50 lb.	663	157	69	Kailua–Kona Hawaii	Aug. 27 1973	M. Welby Taylor
W–50 lb.	428	134	52½	Kailua–Kona Hawaii	Nov. 2 1965	Jeannette Alford
M–80 lb.	916	163½	72	Kailua–Kona Hawaii	Aug. 28 1973	Eric Tixier
W–80 lb.	607–8	152	60	Keahole Hawaii	Sept. 12 1973	Mrs. Lee Marvin
M–130 lb.	1100	165½	79½	Le Morne Mauritius	Feb. 20 1966	Andre D'Hotman de Villiers
W–130 lb.	669	156	66	Kailua–Kona Hawaii	Aug. 27 1973	Mrs. Doris H. Jones
All-Tackle M-180 lb.	1153	176	73	Ritidian Point Guam	Aug. 21 1969	Greg D. Perez

MARLIN (striped)

Other common name: barred marlin
Scientific name: Tetrapturus audax

Line Class	Weight lbs. oz.	Length inches	Girth inches	Place	Date	Angler
M–6 lb.	205	114	40	Cabo San Lucas Mexico	Apr. 3 1972	W. Matt Parr
W–6 lb.	Vacant—No Minimum Weight					
M–12 lb.	250	121	46	Palmilla Mexico	Apr. 16 1965	R. M. Anderson
W–12 lb.	210	114	40	Las Cruces Mexico	June 20 1959	Lynn F. Lee
M–20 lb.	338	125	47½	Sydney Australia	Oct. 20 1968	H. John McIntyre
W–20 lb.	321	127¼	47	Iquique Chile, SA	June 8 1954	Mrs. L. Marron

Line Class	Weight lbs. oz.	Length inches	Girth inches	Place	Date	Angler
M–30 lb.	261–8	129½	41	Tutakaka Australia	May 3 1972	G. Pierce
W–30 lb.	289	121	45	Iquique Chile, SA	May 18 1954	Mrs. L. Marron
M–50 lb.	365	134½	50	Whakatane New Zealand	Feb. 26 1972	A. T. Haultain
W–50 lb.	401	110	50½	Cavalli Islands New Zealand	Feb. 24 1970	Mrs. Margaret Williams
All-Tackle M–80 lb.	415	132	52	Cape Brett New Zealand	Mar. 31 1964	B. C. Bain
W–80 lb.	333	122	48	Ruahine Reef New Zealand	Apr. 20 1971	Jennifer Amos
M–130 lb.	394	134	54	Whangaroa New Zealand	Mar. 10 1972	E. H. Cox
W–130 lb.	Vacant—Minimum Acceptance Weight—332 lb.					

MARLIN (white)

Scientific name: Tetrapturus albidus

Line Class	Weight lbs. oz.	Length inches	Girth inches	Place	Date	Angler
M–6 lb.	Vacant—No Minimum Weight					
W–6 lb.	67	86½	26½	La Guaira Venezuela, SA	Sept. 20 1972	Kathryn McGinnis
M–12 lb.	103–8	96½	31½	Bimini Bahamas	Apr. 8 1952	G. A. Bass
W–12 lb.	122	99	44	Bimini Bahamas	Mar. 30 1953	Dorothy A. Curtice
M–20 lb.	128–8	102	36	Bimini Bahamas	Mar. 9 1960	James F. Baldwin
W–20 lb.	129–4	103	33½	Bimini Bahamas	Apr. 11 1963	Mrs. J. M. Watters
M–30 lb.	130–4	99	33	Bimini Bahamas	Apr. 18 1959	Leonard Hendrix
W–30 lb.	120–10	89¾	32¼	Bimini Bahamas	Mar. 29 1956	Mrs. M. Meyer, Jr.
All-Tackle M–50 lb.	159–8	108	36	Pompano Beach Florida	Apr. 25 1953	W. E. Johnson
W–50 lb.	130	95	34	Montauk New York	Aug. 13 1951	Mrs. P. Dater
M–80 lb.	Vacant—Minimum Acceptance Weight—130 lbs.					
W–80 lb.	142	98	34	Ft. Lauderdale Florida	Mar. 14 1959	Marie Beneventi
M–130 lb.	Vacant—Minimum Acceptance Weight—142 lbs.					
W–130 lb.	Vacant—Minimum Acceptance Weight—142 lbs.					

PERMIT

Scientific name: Trachinotus falcatus

Line Class	Weight lbs. oz.	Length inches	Girth inches	Place	Date	Angler
M–6 lb.	38	41½	33	Key West Florida	Mar. 19 1972	Stuart C. Apte
W–6 lb.	30–8	39	28¼	Loggerhead Key Florida	June 27 1973	Kathy Marvin
M–12 lb.	50	43	34½	Miami Florida	Mar. 27 1965	Robert F. Miller
W–12 lb.	37	41	30½	Islamorada Florida	Nov. 1 1972	Mrs. Kathrine Magee
All-Tackle M-20 lb.	50–8	44¾	33¾	Key West Florida	Mar. 15 1971	Marshall E. Earnest
*W-20 lb.	38	40	30½	Islamorada Florida	Mar. 21 1954	Mrs. W. K. Edmunds
M-30 lb.	43	44½	31½	Palm Beach Florida	Mar. 4 1974	Stephen Ray
W-30 lb.	38	43	31	Key West Florida	Apr. 9 1963	Helen Robinson
M-50 lb.	47–12	45	32	Boca Grande Pass Florida	May 5 1960	Frank G. Burke, Jr.
W-50 lb.	39	41	30	Islamorada Florida	Apr. 2 1966	Shelagh B. Richards
M-80 lb.	34–8	36¼	28	Naples Florida	Feb. 1 1951	R. R. Channel
W-80 lb.	Vacant—Minimum Acceptance Weight—39 lbs.					
M-130 lb.	38–8	40½	31¼	Boca Grande Florida	Sept. 9 1953	R. H. Martin
W-130 lb.	Vacant—Minimum Acceptance Weight—39 lbs.					
*TIE W-20 lb.	38	43	33	Islamorada Florida	June 11 1961	Louise Meulenberg

POLLOCK

Scientific name: Pollachius virens

Line Class	Weight lbs. oz.	Length inches	Girth inches	Place	Date	Angler
M-6 lb.	17–9½	35½	22½	Plymouth England	Jan. 1 1973	Roger William Palmer
W-6 lb.	15–2½	41½	22	Plymouth England	Mar. 10 1973	Mrs. Rita Barrett
M-12 lb.	36	47	32	Hunts Point Nova Scotia, Canada	Aug. 10 1965	Perry MacNeal
W-12 lb.	15–7	33¾	19	Nova Scotia Canada	July 9 1963	Janet D. Wallach
M-20 lb.	33	39	26	Wedgeport Nova Scotia, Canada	Aug. 30 1966	Dr. Duncan Sinclair
W-20 lb.	38	47	14	Westport Nova Scotia, Canada	Aug. 20 1971	Ruth G. Verber

Line Class	Weight lbs. oz.	Length inches	Girth inches	Place	Date	Angler
M–30 lb.	40	49½	27	Brielle New Jersey	Oct. 22 1973	Tom Wier
W–30 lb.	30–12	43	26	Brielle New Jersey	Apr. 17 1968	Ruth Gifford
All-Tackle M–50 lb.	43	48	29	Brielle New Jersey	Oct. 21 1964	Philip Barlow
W–50 lb.	29	42	24¼	Manasquan New Jersey	Nov. 3 1958	Ann Durik
M–80 lb.	Vacant—Minimum Acceptance Weight—43 lbs.					
W–80 lb.	Vacant—Minimum Acceptance Weight—30 lbs.					
M–130 lb.	Vacant—Minimum Acceptance Weight—43 lbs.					
W–130 lb.	Vacant—Minimum Acceptance Weight—30 lbs.					

RUNNER (rainbow)

Scientific name: Elagatis bipinnulata

Line Class	Weight lbs. oz.	Length inches	Girth inches	Place	Date	Angler
M–6 lb.	6–10	31½	11	Key Largo Florida	Aug. 16 1972	Dale Leverone
W–6 lb.	Vacant—No Minimum Weight					
M–12 lb.	18–12	38⅞	20½	Las Cruces Mexico	May 31 1961	Bing Crosby
W–12 lb.	10–14	38¼	15	Key Largo Florida	Aug. 10 1969	Pamela J. Habicht
M–20 lb.	25	48	23	Pinas Bay Panama	May 9 1965	Donald J. S. Merten
W–20 lb.	12–13	38¼	17	Challenger Bank Bermuda	Aug. 16 1969	Mrs. Harriet Madeiros
M–30 lb.	25–12	44¼	21	Oahu Hawaii	Nov. 26 1967	Richard Y. Sakimoto, MD
W–30 lb.	12–2	40	16¼	Guerro Mexico	Jan. 21 1963	Mrs. Joseph Krieger, Jr.
M–50 lb.	28	49	21½	Pinas Bay Panama	Jan. 15 1967	Thomas C. Dickinson
W–50 lb.	23	42	19½	Oahu Hawaii	May 9 1961	Lila M. Neuenfelt
M–80 lb.	28–6	49½	21½	Pulmo Reef Gulf of California	Nov. 11 1967	Joe C. Stuard
W–80 lb.	Vacant—Minimum Acceptance Weight—23 lbs.					
All-Tackle M–130 lb.	30–15	47	22	Kauai Hawaii	Apr. 27 1963	Holbrook Goodale
W–130 lb.	Vacant—Minimum Acceptance Weight—23 lbs.					

ROOSTERFISH

Scientific name: Nematistius pectoralis

Line Class	Weight lbs. oz.	Length inches	Girth inches	Place	Date	Angler
M–6 lb.	29-12	47½	25	Punta Colorado Mexico	June 24 1973	Bob Manos
W–6 lb.	34-3	48½	26½	Punta Colorado Mexico	July 5 1973	Pat Snyder
M–12 lb.	50-11	56	32	Guerro Mexico	Jan. 15 1961	Joseph Krieger, Jr.
W–12 lb.	45	52½	30	San Jose del Cabo Mexico	June 11 1951	Mrs. W. G. Krieger
M–20 lb.	85-13	58½	42¾	La Paz Mexico	June 15 1966	Willard E. Hanson
W–20 lb.	50-9	54½	30	Baja California Mexico	Nov. 20 1959	Lily Call
All-Tackle M–30 lb.	114	64	33	La Paz Mexico	June 1 1960	Abe Sackheim
W–30 lb.	99	59½	34½	La Paz Mexico	Nov. 30 1964	Lilly Call
M–50 lb.	80	46	27¼	Cabo Blanco Peru, SA	June 13 1954	Clyoce J. Tippett
W–50 lb.	85-2	54	36	La Paz Mexico	Nov. 24 1956	Mrs. Esther Carle
M–80 lb.	90	59½	32	Loreto Mexico	Dec. 22 1960	Clement Caditz
W–80 lb.	66	56	29½	La Paz Mexico	Dec. 1 1964	Lilly Call
M–130 lb.	100	54	32	Cabo Blanco Peru, SA	Jan. 12 1954	Miguel Barrenechea
W–130 lb.	Vacant—Minimum Acceptance Weight—99 lbs.					

SAILFISH (Atlantic)

Scientific·name: Istiophorus platypterus

Line Class	Weight lbs. oz.	Length inches	Girth inches	Place	Date	Angler
M–6 lb.	85–15	91½	31½	Luanda Angola Africa	Feb. 14 1974	Albino de Jesus Gaspar dos Santos
W–6 lb.	53	81½	24¼	Islamorada Florida	Jan. 25 1973	Jacqueline E. Knight
M–12 lb.	99–13	107	32	Luanda Angola, Africa	March 27 1974	Albino de Jesus Gaspar dos Santos
W–12 lb.	83	83¾	32¼	Key Largo Florida	Apr. 4 1965	Helen K. Grant
M–20 lb.	110–14	105⁹/₁₀	31½	Luanda Angola, Africa	Mar. 27 1974	Carlos Jose Picarra Alves Baptista
W–20 lb.	78–11	94½	28¾	Luanda Angola, Africa	Mar. 30 1974	Luisa Maria Baptista
M–30 lb.	116–5	103	32¼	Luanda Angola, Africa	Mar. 22 1972	Jose Eduardo Gaioso Vaz

Line Class	Weight lbs. oz.	Length inches	Girth inches	Place	Date	Angler
W–30 lb.	84	98	29	Jupiter Florida	May 3 1971	Jeanne C. Chatham
All–Tackle M–50 lb.	123	124	32¾	Walker Cay Bahamas	Apr. 25 1950	H. Teetor
W–50 lb.	108–4	105½	34	Luanda Angola, Africa	Mar. 30 1971	Mrs. Ellen Botha
M-80 lb.	Vacant—Minimum Acceptance Weight—104 lbs.					
W-80 lb.	Vacant—Minimum Acceptance Weight—97 lbs.					
M-130 lb.	Vacant—Minimum Acceptance Weight—104 lbs.					
W-130 lb.	Vacant—Minimum Acceptance Weight—104 lbs.					

SAILFISH (Pacific)   *Scientific name:* Istiophorus platypterus

Line Class	Weight lbs. oz.	Length inches	Girth inches	Place	Date	Angler
M–6 lb.	110	92	31	Bat's Island Costa Rica	Aug. 25 1973	Celso Surroca
W–6 lb.	96–8	113	31½	Pinas Bay, Republic of Panama	Mar. 15 1974	Mary Wallace Jose Pho
M–12 lb.	159	119	36	Pinas Bay Panama	July 23 1957	J. Frank Baxter
W–12 lb.	146–8	108½	35½	Palmilla Mexico	Nov. 14 1962	Evelyn M. Anderson
M–20 lb.	158	109	35½	Santa Cruz Island Galapagos	Mar. 4 1955	A. Hall
W–20 lb.	157	122	37	La Plata Island Ecuador, SA	Sept. 14 1961	Jeannette Alford
M–30 lb.	198	134	41	La Paz Mexico	Aug. 23 1957	Charles Kelly
W–30 lb.	178	119½	37	Santa Cruz Island Galapagos	Feb. 27 1955	Mrs. A. Hall
M–50 lb.	192–7	123	42	Acapulco Mexico	Oct. 4 1961	W. W. Rowland
W–50 lb.	192	125	40½	La Paz Mexico	Sept. 6 1950	Gay Thomas
M–80 lb.	198	126	33	Mazatlan Mexico	Nov. 10 1954	George N. Anglen
W–80 lb.	199	120	42	Pinas Bay Panama	Jan. 17 1968	Carolyn B. Brinkman
All–Tackle M–130 lb.	221	129	—	Santa Cruz Island Galapagos	Feb. 12 1947	C. W. Stewart
W–130 lb.	189	127	33	Yanuca Fiji	Dec. 7 1967	Mrs. C. L. Foster

SEABASS (white)

Other common name: white corvina
Scientific name: Cynoscion nobilis

Line Class	Weight lbs. oz.	Length inches	Girth inches	Place	Date	Angler
M-6 lb.	Vacant—No Minimum Weight					
W-6 lb.	Vacant—No Minimum Weight					
M-12 lb.	65	58	28	Ensenada Mexico	July 8 1955	C. J. Aronis
W-12 lb.	52-6	54	27¾	Newport Harbor California	June 3 1959	Ruth Jayred
M-20 lb.	72	59¾	30½	Catalina California	Aug. 13 1958	Dr. Charles Dorshkind
W-20 lb.	62	57	28	Malibu California	Dec. 6 1951	Mrs. D. W. Jackson
All-Tackle M-30 lb.	83-12	65½	34	San Felipe Mexico	Mar. 31 1953	L. C. Baumgardner
W-30 lb.	59-8	55¼	30	Catalina Island California	May 2 1968	Janice Jackson
M-50 lb.	77-4	61	33	San Diego California	Apr. 8 1950	H. P. Bledsoe
W-50 lb.	44-3	52	25	Catalina Island California	May 2 1968	Gail Cruz
M-80 lb.	74	63	33	Catalina Island California	May 11 1968	Allan D. Tromblay
W-80 lb.	Vacant—Minimum Acceptance Weight—62 lbs.					
M-130 lb.	Vacant—Minimum Acceptance Weight—77 lbs.					
W-130 lb.	Vacant—Minimum Acceptance Weight—62 lbs.					

SEATROUT (spotted)

Other common name: speckled trout/spotted weakfish
Scientific name: Cynoscion nebulosus

M-6 lb.	9-14	24½	15½	Jensen Beach Florida	June 16 1973	Ralph Boynton
W-6 lb.	8-1	29	15⅞	Pensacola Sound Florida	Apr. 24 1973	Rose Marie Travis
M-12 lb.	14-3	33	19	Jensen Beach Florida	Feb. 21 1974	Les Mowery
W-12 lb.	10-4	30½	16	Jupiter Florida	June 1 1958	Nancy Dukes
M-20 lb.	13-12	36	19	Vero Beach Florida	Mar. 11 1957	W. Miller Shaw, Jr.
W-20 lb.	10	30	18	Pellicer Creek Florida	Feb. 25 1950	Mrs. Bertram Lee

Line Class	Weight lbs. oz.	Length inches	Girth inches	Place	Date	Angler
All-Tackle Tie M-30 lb.	15-6	33	23¾	Jensen Beach Florida	May 4 1969	Michael J. Foremny
W-30 lb.	14	33	18	Stuart Florida	Apr. 25 1970	Marilyn C. Albright
All-Tackle Tie M-50 lb.	15-3	34½	20½	Fort Pierce Florida	Jan. 13 1949	C. W. Hubbard
W-50 lb.	Vacant—Minimum Acceptance Weight—10 lbs.					
M-80 lb.	Vacant—Minimum Acceptance Weight—15 lbs.					
W-80 lb.	Vacant—Minimum Acceptance Weight—10 lbs.					
M-130 lb.	Vacant—Minimum Acceptance Weight—15 lbs.					
W-130 lb.	Vacant—Minimum Acceptance Weight—10 lbs.					

SHARK (blue) *Scientific name:* Prionace glauca

Line Class	Weight lbs. oz.	Length inches	Girth inches	Place	Date	Angler
M-6 lb.	111-8	88	31	Sydney Australia	Oct. 22 1972	Graham Donaldson
W-6 lb.	55-9	65	24½	Sydney Australia	June 10 1973	Pamela Hudspeth
M-12 lb.	312	127	47	Montauk New York	Oct. 28 1963	John S. Walton
W-12 lb.	150	96	32	Montauk New York	July 22 1962	Dorothea L. Dean
M-20 lb.	218-2	117	42	Montauk New York	July 22 1955	M. B. Mittleman
W-20 lb.	293	126½	44	Montauk New York	July 21 1963	Lucette Rinfret
M-30 lb.	350	137	43	Sydney Heads Australia	Oct. 29 1961	John C. Kellion
W-30 lb.	284-8	128	42	Montauk New York	Aug. 11 1959	Jacqueline Mittleman
M-50 lb.	371-8	135	47	Montauk New York	Sept. 27 1969	Jack Bellock
W-50 lb.	298	138	40	Montauk New York	Oct. 5 1959	Valerie Wuestefeld
All-Tackle Tie M-80 lb.	410	138	52	Rockport Massachusetts	Sept. 1 1960	Richard C. Webster
All-Tackle Tie W-80 lb.	410	134	52½	Rockport Massachusetts	Aug. 17 1967	Martha C. Webster
M-130 lb.	341-8	121	45½	Las Palmas Canary Islands	Oct. 31 1966	John D. Nixon
W-130 lb.	334	128	47½	Rockport Massachusetts	Sept. 4 1964	Cassandra Webster

SHARK (hammerhead)   *Scientific name:* Sphyrnidae

Line Class	Weight lbs. oz.	Length inches	Girth inches	Place	Date	Angler
M-6 lb.	Vacant—No Minimum Weight					
W-6 lb.	Vacant—No Minimum Weight					
M-12 lb.	Vacant—No Minimum Weight					
W-12 lb.	Vacant—No Minimum Weight					
M-20 lb.	Vacant—No Minimum Weight					
W-20 lb.	46-15	60½	24¾	Laun da Angola, Africa	Mar. 17 1974	Luisa Maria Baptista
M-30 lb.	308	126	50	Sydney Australia	Feb. 17 1974	Eric Howarth
W-30 lb.	Vacant—No Minimum Weight					
M-50 lb.	Vacant—No Minimum Weight					
W-50 lb.	Vacant—No Minimum Weight					
M-80 lb.	264	97	42	Bay of Islands New Zealand	Mar. 18 1974	Raymond Floyd
W-80 lb.	253	96	47	Moko Hinau Islands New Zealand	Feb. 25 1974	Mrs. Elizabeth N. Graydon
M-130 lb.	273	106	42	Bay of Islands New Zealand	Apr. 9 1974	Robert Turvey
W-130 lb.	Vacant—No Minimum Weight					

SHARK (porbeagle)   *Scientific name:* Lamna nasus

Line Class	Weight lbs. oz.	Length inches	Girth inches	Place	Date	Angler
M-6 lb.	Vacant—No Minimum Weight					
W-6 lb.	Vacant—No Minimum Weight					
M-12 lb.	66	58	30	Montauk New York	June 8 1958	M. H. Merrill
W-12 lb.	Vacant—Minimum Acceptance Weight—66 lbs.					
M-20 lb.	180	103½	37	Block Island Rhode Island	Aug. 9 1960	Frank K. Smith
W-20 lb.	Vacant—Minimum Acceptance Weight—100 lbs.					
M-30 lb.	191-8	76	42	Montauk New York	May 28 1964	Carl Monaco

Line Class	Weight lbs. oz.	Length inches	Girth inches	Place	Date	Angler
W–30 lb.	222-8	75	44	Isle of Wight England	Aug. 14 1969	Mrs. Paula Everington
M–50 lb.	388	101½	62	Montauk Point New York	Oct. 28 1961	John S. Walton
W–50 lb.	238-8	92	41	Montauk New York	May 17 1966	Bea Harry
All-Tackle M–80 lb.	430	96	63	Channel Islands England	June 29 1969	Desmond Bougourd
W–80 lb.	230	78½	43	Montauk New York	May 17 1965	Bea Harry
M–130 lb.	300	120	55	Falmouth England	Sept. 5 1973	Keith Stokes
W–130 lb.	369	102	48	Looe, Cornwall England	July 20 1970	Mrs. Patricia Winifred Smith

SHARK (shortfin mako)   *Scientific name:* Isurus oxyrinchus

Line Class	Weight lbs. oz.	Length inches	Girth inches	Place	Date	Angler
M–6 lb.	91-8	71	31	Sydney Australia	Sept. 24 1972	Paul Edward Caughlan
W–6 lb.	56-8	58½	27½	Sydney Australia	July 29 1973	Pamela Hudspeth
M–12 lb.	261-11	88	44½	Montauk New York	Oct. 1 1953	C. R. Meyer
W–12 lb.	183	86	39	Sydney Australia	Aug. 1 1971	Mrs. Pamela Hudspeth
M–20 lb.	347	102	49	Mercury Bay New Zealand	Jan. 3 1973	Donald Keith Butters
W–20 lb.	316	98½	48½	Bimini Bahamas	May 25 1961	Dorothea L. Dean
M–30 lb.	854	140½	73½	Port Stephens NSW, Australia	May 9 1971	John Howard Barclay
W–30 lb.	376	120	46	Sydney Australia	Sept. 7 1969	Helen Gillis
M–50 lb.	690	126	61	Cavalli Island New Zealand	Nov. 7 1970	Noel R. Brady
W–50 lb.	478	132	46	Broughton Island Australia	May 17 1957	Mrs. Ron Duncan
M–80 lb.	820	125	68	Cavalli Island New Zealand	Mar. 28 1964	T. Culshaw
W–80 lb.	880	131	75¾	Bimini Bahamas	Aug. 3 1964	Florence Lotierzo
All-Tack.e M–130 lb.	1061	146	79½	Mayor Island New Zealand	Feb. 17 1970	James B. Penwarden
W–130 lb.	911-12	134	70	Palm Beach Florida	Apr. 9 1962	Audrey Cohen

SHARK (thresher)

Scientific name: Alopias vulpinus

Line Class	Weight lbs. oz.	Length inches	Girth inches	Place	Date	Angler
M-6 lb.	Vacant—No Minimum Weight					
W-6 lb.	Vacant—No Minimum Weight					
M-12 lb.	92-8	57	31	Long Beach California	Dec. 12 1959	D. F. Marsh
W-12 lb.	Vacant—Minimum Acceptance Weight—92 lbs.					
M-20 lb.	113-8	99½	32	Salinas Ecuador, SA	June 10 1972	Victor J. Maspons
W-20 lb.	Vacant—Minimum Acceptance Weight—92 lbs.					
M-30 lb.	227	141	40	Cavalli Islands New Zealand	July 6 1971	Douglas Rooke
W-30 lb.	300	152	45½	Bay of Islands New Zealand	June 23 1972	Mrs. Anne Clark
M-50 lb.	421	154½	51½	Bay of Islands New Zealand	May 27 1972	Barry McKenzie Hill
W-50 lb.	366	156	48½	Bay of Islands New Zealand	May 6 1972	Mrs. Avril Semmens
M-80 lb.	501	163	58	Port Stephens Australia	Mar. 27 1967	Barry Caldwell
W-80 lb.	413	180	49½	Bay of Islands New Zealand	June 28 1960	Mrs. E. R. Simons
M-130 lb.	600	170	61	Mayor Island New Zealand	Mar. 2 1972	Don Cowan
All-Tackle W-130 lb.	729	101	61	Mayor Island New Zealand	June 3 1959	Mrs. V. Brown

SHARK (tiger)

Scientific name: Galeocerdo cuvieri

Line Class	Weight lbs. oz.	Length inches	Girth inches	Place	Date	Angler
M-6 lb.	Vacant—No Minimum Weight					
W-6 lb.	Vacant—No Minimum Weight					
M-12 lb.	Vacant—Minimum Acceptance Weight—150 lbs.					
W-12 lb.	Vacant—Minimum Acceptance Weight—150 lbs.					
M-20 lb.	341	120	55½	Cape Moreton Australia	July 6 1957	Bob Dyer
W-20 lb.	294-8	110½	53	Sydney Australia	Feb. 24 1973	Pamela Hudspeth
M-30 lb.	494-8	119	62	Newport N.S.W., Australia	Jan. 29 1973	Peter Douglas Swavley

Line Class	Weight lbs. oz.	Length inches	Girth inches	Place	Date	Angler
W-30 lb.	Vacant—Minimum Acceptance Weight—250 lbs.					
M-50 lb.	1018	159	68	Cape Moreton Australia	June 12 1957	Bob Dyer
W-50 lb.	458	127	57	Cape Moreton Australia	July 3 1957	Mrs. Bob Dyer
M-80 lb.	1305	163½	86	Coogee Wide, Sydney, Australia	May 17 1959	Samuel Jamieson
W-80 lb.	1173	148	84	Cronulla NSW, Australia	Mar. 24 1963	June Irene Butcher
All-Tackle M-130 lb.	1780	166½	103	Cherry Grove S. Carolina	June 14 1964	Walter Maxwell
W-130 lb.	1314	165	89	Cape Moreton Australia	July 27 1953	Mrs. Bob Dyer

SHARK (white)

Other common name: man-eater shark
Scientific name: Carcharodon carcharias

Line Class	Weight lbs. oz.	Length inches	Girth inches	Place	Date	Angler
M-6 lb.	Vacant—No Minimum Weight					
W-6 lb.	Vacant—No Minimum Weight					
M-12 lb.	96-10	67	27½	Mazatlan Mexico	Apr. 30 1964	Ray O. Acord
W-12 lb.	Vacant—Minimum Acceptance Weight—96 lbs.					
M-20 lb.	1068	150	77	Cape Moreton Australia	June 18 1957	Bob Dyer
W-20 lb.	369	111	57	Cape Moreton Australia	July 6 1957	Mrs. Bob Dyer
M-30 lb.	1053	152	68	Cape Moreton Australia	June 13 1957	Bob Dyer
W-30 lb.	803	149	70	Cape Moreton Australia	July 5 1957	Mrs. Bob Dyer
M-50 lb.	1876	186	101½	Cape Moreton Australia	Aug. 6 1955	Bob Dyer
W-50 lb.	801	135	75	Cape Moreton Australia	June 11 1957	Mrs. Bob Dyer
M-80 lb.	2344	181	108	Streaky Bay Australia	Nov. 6 1960	Alfred Dean
W-80 lb.	912	143	71½	Cape Moreton Australia	Aug. 29 1954	Mrs. Bob Dyer
All-Tackle M-130 lb.	2664	202	114	Ceduna Australia	Apr. 21 1959	Alfred Dean
W-130 lb.	1052	166	72½	Cape Moreton Australia	June 27 1954	Mrs. Bob Dyer

Line Class	Weight lbs. oz.	Length inches	Girth inches	Place	Date	Angler
M-6 lb.	17	35½	18	Bay of Florida Florida	Mar. 15 1972	Edward F. Campion
W-6 lb.	20-2	39	19½	Captiva Florida	Aug. 2 1972	Wilma Bell Brantner
M-12 lb.	37	47	24½	Boynton Beach Florida	June 18 1959	Durling Drake
*W-12 lb.	32-8	45	24	Jupiter Florida	Aug. 2 1957	Mrs. Nancy Neville
M-20 lb.	41-8	42	29	Palm Beach Florida	June 30 1968	H. Wilder Clapp
W-20 lb.	35	43	25½	Fort Myers Florida	Feb. 16 1962	Mrs. Wade Miller
M-30 lb.	43	47	26½	Lake Worth Florida	May 18 1952	Lee K. Spencer
All-Tackle W-30 lb.	52-6	49½	26	La Paz Mexico	Jan 9. 1963	Jane Haywood
M-50 lb.	40	44½	27¼	West Palm Beach Florida	Apr. 8 1972	Ralph R. Boynton
W-50 lb.	31-8	41½	23	Stuart Florida	July 17 1951	Mrs. B. N. Fox
M-80 lb.	37	45	26	Lake Worth Florida	July 28 1959	James P. Nora
W-80 lb.	Vacant—Minimum Acceptance Weight—52 lbs.					
M-130 lb.	Vacant—Minimum Acceptance Weight—52 lbs.					
W-130 lb.	Vacant—Minimum Acceptance Weight—52 lbs.					
*TIE W-12 lb.	32-8	46	23¼	Ft. Lauderdale Florida	July 24 1966	Rosemary Schafer

Line Class	Weight lbs. oz.	Length inches	Girth inches	Place	Date	Angler
M-6 lb.	106-8	105½	32½	Cabo San Lucas Mexico	June 11 1972	James Perry
W-6 lb.	Vacant—No Minimum Weight					
M-12 lb.	120	103	33	Palmilla Mexico	June 1 1968	Russell M. Anderson
W-12 lb.	Vacant—Minimum Acceptance Weight—75 lbs.					
M-20 lb.	183-8	120	41	Cabo San Lucas Mexico	May 4 1971	Charles C. Yamamoto
W-20 lb.	157	108½	39	Baja California Mexico	Feb. 11 1972	Mrs. Susan Etzen

Line Class	Weight lbs. oz.	Length inches	Girth inches	Place	Date	Angler
M-30 lb.	208	116	43	Salinas Ecuador	Mar. 1 1974	Barry M. Fitzpatrick
W-30 lb.	Vacant—Minimum Acceptance Weight—180 lbs.					
M-50 lb.	444	145	57	Pompano Beach Florida	Apr. 27 1951	Fred J. Fleming
W-50 lb.	492-4	141	54	Montauk Point New York	July 4 1959	Dorothea Cassullo
M-80 lb.	530	149	59	Shinnecock New York	Aug. 26 1960	Walter P. Margulies
W-80 lb.	772	154	70	Iquique Chile, SA	June 7 1954	Mrs. L. Marron
All-Tackle M-130 lb.	1182	179¼	78	Iquique Chile, SA	May 7 1953	L. Marron
W-130 lb.	759	167	73	Iquique Chile, SA	June 30 1952	Mrs. D. A. Allison

TANGUIGUE

Other common name: narrow-barred mackerel
Scientific name: Scomberomorus commerson

Line Class	Weight lbs. oz.	Length inches	Girth inches	Place	Date	Angler
M-6 lb.	43	54½	22½	Grose Island Australia	Aug. 6 1972	Hilton Morrish Selvey
W-6 lb.	20-8	47	17¾	Cairns Australia	Aug. 25 1972	Dolly Dyer
M-12 lb.	53	60½	26	Shark Bay Australia	July 25 1972	Ross Albert Warman
W-12 lb.	Vacant—Minimum Acceptance Weight—40 lbs.					
M-20 lb.	78	67½	33½	Queensland Australia	May 16 1970	Edward J. French
W-20 lb.	Vacant—Minimum Acceptance Weight—50 lbs.					
M-30 lb.	73-8	65	28	Queensland Australia	May 9 1971	Edward J. French
W-30 lb.	68	68	26	Hayman Island Australia	May 14 1969	Lady Joan Ansett
M-50 lb.	78	66	29	Cape Moreton Australia	Apr. 8 1967	Ronald G. Jenyns
W-50 lb.	63	67	25½	Hayman Island Australia	Apr. 26 1970	Marie Gloria Maestracci
All-Tackle M-80 lb.	81	71½	29¼	Karachi Pakistan	Aug. 27 1960	George E. Rusinak
W-80 lb.	64	67	26	Mozambique East Africa	Sept. 12 1959	Mrs. A. C. Lee
M-130 lb.	Vacant—Minimum Acceptance Weight—64 lbs.					
W-130 lb.	Vacant—Minimum Acceptance Weight—64 lbs.					

TARPON   *Scientific name:* Megalops atlantica

Line Class	Weight lbs. oz.	Length inches	Girth inches	Place	Date	Angler
M-6 lb.	71-8	64½	30	Big Pine Key Florida	Mar. 13 1973	Stuart C. Apte
W-6 lb.	35-7	53½	23½	Islamorada Florida	June 23 1973	Mrs. Albert H. Ehlert
M-12	170-8	84	40	Big Pine Key Florida	Mar. 10 1963	Russell C. Ball
W-12	115	70	34½	Duck Key Florida	May 4 1972	Shirley A. Hyman
M-20 lb.	188	86	41	Islamorada Florida	Apr. 12 1973	Bill Hancock
W-20 lb.	150	80½	39½	Islamorada Florida	May 24 1973	Shirley A. Hyman
All-Tackle M-30 lb.	283	86⅗	—	Lake Maracaibo Venezuela, SA	Mar. 19 1956	M. Salazar
W-30 lb.	171	83	42¾	Marathon Florida	May 21 1968	Mrs. Henry Sage
M-50 lb.	242-4	88⅖	43⅖	Cienaga Ayapel Colombia, SA	Jan. 7 1955	A. Salazar
W-50 lb.	190-8	84	45	Boca Grande Pass Florida	May 27 1970	Patricia J. Mang
M-80 lb.	218	85	45	Tampa Bay Florida	May 6 1973	Rick Wotring
W-80 lb.	203	95	44	Marathon Florida	May 19 1961	June Jordan
M-130 lb.	210	86¼	45¼	Port Isabel Texas	Nov. 13 1973	Thomas F. Gibson
W-130 lb.	Vacant—Minimum Acceptance Weight—203 lbs.					

Other common name: blackfish
Scientific name: Tautoga onitis

TAUTOG

Line Class	Weight lbs. oz.	Length inches	Girth inches	Place	Date	Angler
M-6 lb.	14-6	25½	22½	Virginia Beach Virginia	May 17 1972	Linwood A. Martens
W-6 lb.	Vacant—No Minimum Weight					
M-12 lb.	12	25½	20½	Block Island Rhode Island	Oct. 18 1952	D. V. Marshall
W-12 lb.	10-8	23	18	Montauk New York	June 2 1973	Mrs. Joseph M. Rinaldi
M-20 lb.	21	30	—	Jamestown Island Rhode Island	Nov. 6 1954	C. W. Sundquist
W-20 lb.	10-12	24⅝	18¾	Asharoken Beach New York	May 7 1962	Trudy H. King
All-Tackle M-30 lb.	21-6	31½	23½	Cape May New Jersey	June 12 1954	R. N. Sheafer

Line Class	Weight lbs. oz.	Length inches	Girth inches	Place	Date	Angler
W–30 lb.	11-3	26	19½	Virginia Beach Virginia	May 17 1971	Mrs. Charlotte J. Wright
M–50 lb.	20-14	32	30	Newport Rhode Island	Oct. 20 1955	W. R. Peckham
W–50 lb.	17-6	27½	23¼	Virginia Beach Virginia	May 5 1971	L. Trula Becker
M–80 lb.	Vacant—Minimum Acceptance Weight—21 lbs.					
W–80 lb.	Vacant—Minimum Acceptance Weight—16 lbs.					
M–130 lb.	Vacant—Minimum Acceptance Weight—21 lbs.					
W–130 lb.	Vacant—Minimum Acceptance Weight—16 lbs.					

TUNA (Atlantic bigeye)

Scientific name: Thunnus obesus

Line Class	Weight lbs. oz.	Length inches	Girth inches	Place	Date	Angler
M-6 lb.	Vacant—No Minimum Weight					
W-6 lb.	Vacant—No Minimum Weigh					
M-12 lb.	Vacant—Minimum Acceptance Weight—35 lbs.					
W-12 lb.	Vacant—Minimum Acceptance Weight—35 lbs.					
M-20 lb.	Vacant—Minimum Acceptance Weight—35 lbs.					
W-20 lb.	46	43	31	N. Key Largo Florida	Jan. 17 1959	Dorothea L. Dean
M-30 lb.	Vacant—Minimum Acceptance Weight—60 lbs.					
W-30 lb.	Vacant—Minimum Acceptance Weight—60 lbs.					
All-Tackle M-50 lb.	321-12	88¼	58¼	Hudson Canyon New York	Aug. 19 1972	Vito Lo Caputo
W-50 lb.	Vacant—Minimum Acceptance Weight—60 lbs.					
M-80 lb.	198	67	51	St. Helena Atlantic Ocean	Apr. 13 1960	Donald J. Taylor
W-80 lb.	62	43	31	St. Helena Atlantic Ocean	Oct. 30 1957	Mrs. Brenda Dunlop
M-130 lb.	295	78½	40	San Miguel Azores	July 8 1960	Dr. Arsenio Cordeiro
W-130 lb.	182	68	56	Cat Cay Bahamas	June 2 1958	Mrs. Matilde Catta

TUNA (blackfin) *Scientific name:* Thunnus atlanticus

Line Class	Weight lbs. oz.	Length inches	Girth inches	Place	Date	Angler
M-6 lb.	29	35½	26¼	Challenger Bank Bermuda	Aug. 6 1972	Keith R. Winter
W-6 lb.	18-4	29½	21½	Southwest Bermuda	May 24 1973	Rosalind E. D. Dunmore
*M-12 lb.	29-12	36¼	27	Bermuda	Aug. 24 1968	Jay William Rewalt
W-12 lb.	26-12	35	23½	Bermuda	Oct. 18 1957	Mrs. L. Edna Perinchief
M-20 lb.	31-2	39	26	Bermuda	Oct. 17 1968	Vincent F. Schiumo
W-20 lb.	32-2	38	26¾	Bermuda	Oct. 23 1968	Mrs. Herbert N. Arnold
All-Tackle TIE M-30 lb.	38	39¼	28¾	Bermuda	June 26 1970	Archie L. Dickens
All-Tackle TIE W-30 lb.	38	41	28	Islamorada Florida	May 22 1973	Elizabeth Jean Wade
M-50 lb.	36	36¼	28⅞	Bermuda	July 14 1973	Joseph E. Baptiste, Jr.
W-50 lb.	31	36	26 5/16	Bermuda	Aug. 30 1967	Mrs. Glenn Sipe
M-80 lb.	Vacant—Minimum Acceptance Weight—29 lbs.					
W-80 lb.	29-4	36½	25½	Bermuda	Nov. 13 1965	Theresa Mary Phillips
M-130 lb.	Vacant—Minimum Acceptance Weight—36 lbs.					
W-130 lb.	Vacant—Minimum Acceptance Weight—31 lbs.					
*TIE M-12 lb.	29-12	36	25¾	Bermuda	July 13 1972	Norman Cove

TUNA (bluefin) *Scientific name:* Thunnus thynnus

M-6 lb.	Vacant—No Minimum Weight					
W-6 lb.	Vacant—No Minimum Weight					
M-12 lb.	56	47½	32	S. Neptune Island Australia	April 12 1965	Eldred H. V. Riggs
W-12 lb.	39-8	44½	28	Tasmania Australia	May 27 1963	Mrs. Bob Dyer
M-20 lb.	114-8	61	42	Montauk New York	July 25 1969	Mundy I. Peale
W-20 lb.	93	53⅛	37½	Provincetown Massachusetts	Sept. 14 1958	Willia H. Mather

Line Class	Weight lbs. oz.	Length inches	Girth inches	Place	Date	Angler
M-30 lb.	172	65	45	Cape Pillar, Tasmania Australia	May 8 1959	C. I. Cutler
W-30 lb.	117-8	61¾₁₆	42	San Diego California	Sept. 10 1968	Gladys A. Chambers
M-50 lb.	640	110	72	Massachusetts Bay Massachusetts	Sept. 5 1971	Joseph M. Di Carlo
W-50 lb.	518	109	69	Bimini Bahamas	May 13 1950	Mrs. G. A. Bass
M-80 lb.	881	119½	80¾	Newburyport Massachusetts	Sept. 20 1970	Wilbur E. Tobey
W-80 lb.	717	108	74	Prince Edward Island Canada	Sept. 1 1969	Doris R. Watts
All-Tackle M-130 lb.	1120	122	85½	North Lake Canada	Oct. 19 1973	Lee coffin
W-130 lb.	1000	124	84	P.E.I. Gloucester Massachusetts	Aug. 31 1973	Anna Cardinale

TUNA (dog-tooth)

Other common name: scaleless tuna/white tuna
Scientific name: Gymnosarda nuda

Line Class	
M-6 lb.	Vacant—No Minimum Weight
W-6 lb.	Vacant—No Minimum Weight
M-12 lb.	Vacant—No Minimum Weight
W-12 lb.	Vacant—No Minimum Weight
M-20 lb.	Vacant—No Minimum Weight
W-20 lb.	Vacant—No Minimum Weight
M-30 lb.	Vacant—No Minimum Weight
W-30 lb.	Vacant—No Minimum Weight
M-50 lb.	Vacant—No Minimum Weight
W-50 lb.	Vacant—No Minimum Weight
M-80 lb.	Vacant—No Minimum Weight
W-80 lb.	Vacant—No Minimum Weight
M-130 lb.	Vacant—No Minimum Weight
W-130 lb.	Vacant—No Minimum Weight

TUNA (Pacific bigeye)   *Scientific name:* Thunnus obesus

Line Class	Weight lbs. oz.	Length inches	Girth inches	Place	Date	Angler
M–6 lb.	Vacant—No Minimum Weight					
W–6 lb.	Vacant—No Minimum Weight					
M–12 lb.	32	38½	25	Salinas Ecuador, SA	May 18 1968	Cesar Baquerizo A.
W–12 lb.	27–1	36¼	24	Salinas Ecuador, SA	Jan. 29 1970	Mrs. Marilyn Schamroth
M–20 lb.	108	51½	37½	San Diego California	Aug. 10 1968	John E. Muckenthaler
W–20 lb.	27	34	24	Cabo Blanco Peru, SA	Aug. 13 1955	Mrs. O. Owinas
M–30 lb.	163	61	50½	San Diego California	Aug. 15 1970	Forrest N. Shumway
W–30 lb.	133	62½	41¾	Coronado Island California	Oct. 7 1970	Mrs. Sally Johnson
M–50 lb.	280	83	52½	Salinas Ecuador, SA	Jan. 21 1967	Luis Alberto Flores A.
W–50 lb.	240	75¼	52¾	Salinas Ecuador, SA	Jan. 11 1969	Helen C. King
M–80 lb.	332	87½	58	Cabo Blanco Peru, SA	Jan. 26 1953	Emil Wm. Steffens
W–80 lb.	335	85	59½	Cabo Blanco Peru, SA	Mar. 25 1953	Mrs. Wendell Anderson, Jr.
All–Tackle M–130 lb.	435	93	63½	Cabo Blanco Peru, SA	Apr. 17 1957	Dr. Russel V. A. Lee
W–130 lb.	336	87	56½	Cabo Blanco Peru, SA	Jan. 16 1957	Mrs. Seymour Knox III

TUNA (skipjack)

Other common name: oceanic bonito/striped tuna
Scientific name: Euthynnus pelamis

Line Class	Weight lbs. oz.	Length inches	Girth inches	Place	Date	Angler
M–6 lb.	21	31	22	Keahole Hawaii	July 19 1972	Rufus Spalding, Jr.
W–6 lb.	1–9	16½	8	Corona del Mar California	Nov. 24 1972	Kris Wilson
M–12 lb.	23–7	33	23	Oahu Hawaii	Aug. 10 1958	Raymond Y. Kagihara
W–12 lb.	24–6	30½	21	Walker Cay Bahamas	Mar. 26 1965	Patricia E. Church
M–20 lb.	32–8	36	26	San Juan Puerto Rico	May 23 1959	Juan Casellas, Jr.
W–20 lb.	25	33	22½	San Juan Puerto Rico	Oct. 1966	Carmen Perez Agudo
M–30 lb.	33–4	37	27	San Juan Puerto Rico	July 14 1966	Jose L. Campos

Line Class	Weight lbs. oz.	Length inches	Girth inches	Place	Date	Angler
W–30 lb.	28–8	32¼	23	Waianae Hawaii	June 8 1954	Mrs. C. T. Nottage
All Tackle TIE *M–50 lb.	39–15	39	28	Walker Cay Bahamas	Jan. 21 1952	F. Drowley
W–50 lb.	31	34½	24½	San Juan Puerto Rico	Dec. 26 1954	Gloria G. de Marques
M–80 lb.	38–8	34½	29	Waianae Hawaii	June 13 1964	Sueo Okimoto
W–80 lb.	31	35	24¾	Nassau Bahamas	Jan. 25 1956	Mrs. Barbara Wallach
M–130 lb.	38	—	—	Black River Mauritius	Mar. 15 1961	Frank Masson
W–130 lb.	31	35	24	Kona Hawaii	June 16 1963	Anne H. Bosworth
All-Tackle TIE *M–50 lb.	40	38¾	27½	Baie du Tambeau Mauritius	Apr. 19 1971	Joseph R. P. Caboche, Jr.

Other common name: allison tuna
Scientific name: Thunnus albacares

TUNA (yellowfin)

Line Class	Weight lbs. oz.	Length inches	Girth inches	Place	Date	Angler
M-6 lb.	33-8	41¼	25½	Bernier Island Australia	May 28 1973	Ivan Harold Quartermaine
W-6 lb.	Vacant—No Minimum Weight					
M-12 lb.	145	65½	40½	Port Stephens NSW, Australia	Aug. 23 1970	Don McElwaine
W-12 lb.	76	59	33	St. Thomas U.S. Virgin Islands	May 10 1969	Gloria J. Applegate
M-20 lb.	153	73	42½	Montague Island Australia	Feb. 15 1973	Thomas O. Mitchell
W-20 lb.	100	63	36	Sydney Australia	Nov. 20 1971	Mrs. Pamela Hudspeth
M-30 lb.	187-12	74½	47	Sydney Australia	July 15 1965	Frank Pfeiffer
W-30 lb.	137	63½	41¾	Challenger Bank Bermuda	Sept. 12 1965	Jan T. Helsel
M-50 lb.	240	73¾	51	Kona Hawaii	July 20 1966	Rufus P. Spalding, Jr.
W-50 lb.	211	76	47½	Islamorada Florida	Jan. 31 1972	Dorothea Hazelton
M-80 lb.	298	88½	56	Socorro Island Mexico	Jan. 10 1974	John Lighty
W-80 lb.	193-12	70	48	Pompano Beach Florida	Nov. 7 1957	Mrs. D. W. Miller
All-Tackle M-130 lb.	308	84	57	San Benedicto Island Mexico	Jan. 18 1973	Harold J. Tolson
W-130 lb.	254	75	52	Kona Hawaii	Aug. 19 1954	Jean Carlisle

TUNNY (little)

Other common name: bonito/false albacore
Scientific name: Euthynnus alletteratus

Line Class	Weight lbs. oz.	Length inches	Girth inches	Place	Date	Angler
M-6 lb.	Vacant—No Minimum Weight					
W-6 lb.	Vacant—No Minimum Weight					
M-12 lb.	Vacant—No Minimum Weight					
W-12 lb.	Vacant—No Minimum Weight					
M-20 lb.	Vacant—No Minimum Weight					
W-20 lb.	Vacant—No Minimum Weight					
M-30 lb.	Vacant—No Minimum Weight					
W-30 lb.	Vacant—No Minimum Weight					
M-50 lb.	15-10	33½	19½	Cape Hatteras N. Carolina	Mar. 28 1974	Howard Waller
W-50 lb.	Vacant—No Minimum Weight					
M-80 lb.	Vacant—No Minimum Weight					
W-80 lb.	Vacant—No Minimum Weight					
M-130 lb.	Vacant—No Minimum Weight					
W-130 lb.	Vacant—No Minimum Weight					

WAHOO

Scientific name: Acanthocybium solanderi

Line Class	Weight lbs. oz.	Length inches	Girth inches	Place	Date	Angler
M–6 lb.	28	53	19½	Coiba Island Panama	June 28 1973	George A. Bernstein
W–6 lb.	22–8	49¼	17¼	Nassau Bahamas	Oct. 27 1973	Patricia Sands
M–12 lb.	74	69½	28	Coiba Island Panama	June 26 1973	George A. Bernstein
W–12 lb.	66	68	25	St. Thomas U.S. Virgin Islands	Feb. 27 1969	Gloria J. Applegate
M–20 lb.	115	75½	32	Bermuda	July 2 1961	Leo Barboza
W–20 lb.	83	71	30	St. Thomas U.S. Virgin Islands	Mar. 5 1968	Gloria J. Applegate
M–30 lb.	98–10	73½	33	Bermuda	Sept. 5 1963	William P. Imhauser

Line Class	Weight lbs. oz.	Length inches	Girth inches	Place	Date	Angler
W–30 lb.	107–4	72½	33	Eleuthera Bahamas	Apr. 4 1965	Mrs. S. F. Briggs II
M–50 lb.	124	76	36	St. Thomas U.S. Virgin Islands	Mar. 29 1967	Joseph H. C. Wenk
W–50 lb.	113	74	33¼	Yanuca Fiji	June 30 1967	Jan K. Bates
M–80 lb.	139	81	33¾	Marathon Florida	May 18 1960	George Von Hoffman
W–80 lb.	104–8	78	30¼	Walker Cay Bahamas	May 2 1965	Mrs. Lloyd Dalzell
All–Tackle M–130 lb.	149	79¾	37½	Cat Cay Bahamas	June 15 1962	John Pirovano
W–130 lb.	110	73½	36½	Port Eades Louisiana	June 22 1964	Mrs. Homer J. Moore, Jr.

WEAKFISH   *Scientific name: Cynoscion regalis*

Line Class	Weight lbs. oz.	Length inches	Girth inches	Place	Date	Angler
M–6 lb.	10–2	31½	18	East Islip New York	May 10 1973	Fred Golofaro, Jr.
W–6 lb.	8–5	29⅜	15¾	Fire Island New York	May 13 1973	Mrs. Veronica Grebe
M–12 lb.	11–3	31¼	19½	Virginia Beach Virginia	May 9 1974	Buddy Marson
W–12 lb.	8–14	32	15	Fire Island New York	June 19 1954	Mrs. M. S. Hirsch
M–20 lb.	11	36	19	Virginia Beach Virginia	May 26 1973	Antonio M. Chantre, Jr.
W–20 lb.	Vacant—Minimum Acceptance Weight—8 lbs.					
M–30 lb.	10–10	36	—	Fire Island Light New York	Sept. 20 1951	J. E. Bailey
W–30 lb.	Vacant—Minimum Acceptance Weight—8 lbs.					
M–50 lb.	Vacant—Minimum Acceptance Weight—10 lbs.					
W–50 lb.	11–12	31¾	18	Morehead City N. Carolina	Oct. 29 1950	Mrs. L. A. Denning
All–Tackle M–80 lb.	19–8	37	25¾	Trinidad West Indies	Apr. 13 1962	Dennis B. Hall
W–80 lb.	Vacant—Minimum Acceptance Weight—11 lbs.					
M–130 lb.	Vacant—Minimum Acceptance Weight—19 lbs.					
W–130 lb.	Vacant—Minimum Acceptance Weight—11 lbs.					

Scientific name: Seriola dorsalis

Line Class	Weight lbs. oz.	Length inches	Girth inches	Place	Date	Angler
M–6 lb.	38	50½	25½	Bangitoto Channel New Zealand	Dec. 17 1972	Dr. Gabriel D. Tetro
W–6 lb.	16	37	19	Sydney Australia	Sept. 24 1972	Pamela Hudspeth
M–12 lb.	65–8	54	30¼	Cavalli Islands New Zealand	July 13 1972	J. Farrell
W–12 lb.	52–8	51	27½	Cavalli Islands New Zealand	July 5 1969	Mrs. Avril Semmens
M–20 lb.	74	59	31¼	Cavalli Islands New Zealand	May 29 1969	William Pocklington
W–20 lb.	66–8	53	32½	Cape Brett New Zealand	July 12 1970	Margaret Niven
M–30 lb.	88	55½	33	Cape Brett New Zealand	June 25 1963	J. R. Chibnall
W–30 lb.	68	54½	32	Mayor Island New Zealand	Apr. 17 1969	Mrs. Marjorie West
All–Tackle M–50 lb.	111	62	38	Bay of Islands New Zealand	June 11 1961	A. F. Plim
W–50 lb.	76	63½	31	White Island New Zealand	Feb. 28 1972	Mrs. Clare Bowler
M–80 lb.	108	—	—	Cape Brett New Zealand	Jan. 15 1962	Robin O'Connor
W–80 lb.	81	57½	32½	Cape Brett New Zealand	May 18 1960	Kura Beale
M–130 lb.	89	57	34	Mayor Island New Zealand	Jan. 29 1968	L. R. Hooper
W–130 lb.	81	59½	32½	Mayor Island New Zealand	Apr. 8 1966	Patricia E. Jack

International Spin-Fishing Association

Following are the spin-fishing world records certified by the International Spin-Fishing Association through 1972. Included are the 1974 updates.

FRESH WATER RECORDS

International Spin-Fishing Association, world record entry forms may be obtained by writing: ISFA, P.O. Box 81, Downey, California, 90241.

Line Test	Weight	Date Caught	Angler	Waters Caught
BASS (Largemouth)				
2 lb.	9 lbs., 13 oz.	Oct. 28, 1973	Phil Jay, Texas	California
4 lb.	18 lbs., 2 oz.	June 25, 1974	Phil Jay, Texas	Florida
6 lb.	15 lbs., 15 oz.	Apr. 4, 1972	Layton Gillette, California	Lake Wohlford California
8 lb.	19 lbs., 4½ oz.	June 30, 1974	Phil Jay, Texas	Florida
10 lb.	14 lbs., 13 oz.	Nov. 27, 1960	Mrs. W. Wall, Florida	Lake Tsala Apopka, Florida
12 lb.	10 lbs., 6 oz.	Oct. 8, 1969	Ken Asper, Pennsylvania	Letterkerry Res., Pennsylvania
BASS (Smallmouth)				
2 lb.	5 lbs., 11 oz.	June 20, 1966	Art Micklei, New York	Honeoye Lake, New York
4 lb.	6 lbs., 1 oz.	Sept. 31, 1955	Gene Schwietering, Wisconsin	Lac Du Flambeau, Wisconsin
6 lb.	6 lbs., 11 oz.	Apr. 5, 1970	H. L. Miller, Tennessee	So. Holiston Lake, Tennessee
8 lb.	5 lbs., 10 oz.	Apr. 29, 1973	Scott Buell	New Jersey
10 lb.	6 lbs., 4 oz.	Feb. 5, 1968	Wm. Kinch, Tennessee	Wautauga Lake, Tennessee
12 lb.	6 lbs., 1 oz.	Sept. 10, 1970	Clyde Rickard	Lake Manitou, Michigan
CATFISH				
2 lb.	4 lbs., 8 oz.	Aug. 18, 1973	Danny Hilburn, Florida	Florida
4 lb.	13 lbs., 0 oz.	July 22, 1973	Danny Hilburn, Florida	Florida
6 lb.	25 lbs., 8 oz.	Nov. 1, 1973	C. Wilkerson	California
8 lb.	28 lbs., 0 oz.	Sept. 19, 1971	Dayle Johnson, California	Lake Jennings, California
10 lb.	17 lbs., 2 oz.	July 26, 1971	Danny Hilburn, Florida	St. Johns River, Florida
12 lb.	17 lbs., 3 oz.	Mar. 24, 1973	Danny Hilburn, Florida	Florida
CRAPPIE				
2 lb.	2 lbs., 9 oz.	Aug. 3, 1963	Gene Newman, California	Lake Mead, Arizona
4 lb.	4 lb., 1½ oz.	Apr. 28, 1974	W. Wilson, California	California
6 lb.	2 lbs., 11 oz.	Apr. 17, 1972	Roger Bullock, California	Lake Naciemento, Califronia
8 lb.	2 lbs., 15 oz.	Apr. 20, 1972	Fred Haag, Missouri	Lake Enid, Mississippi
TIE				
8 lb.	2 lbs., 15 oz.	Mar. 9, 1972	Roger Bullock, California	Lake Naciemento, California
10 lb.	3 lbs., 0 oz.	Apr. 4, 1970	Dick Graves, California	Lake Mead, Arizona
12 lb.	Open			

Line Test	Weight	Date Caught	Angler	Waters Caught
GRAYLING (Arctic)				
2 lb.	4 lbs., 9 oz.	June 28, 1968	John Case, Illinois	Great Slave Lake, Canada
4 lb.	3 lbs., 8 oz.	July 10, 1968	Craig Nelsen, Kansas	Great Slave Lake, Canada
6 lb.	4 lbs., 6 oz.	July 28, 1972	Bob Hamilton, California	Great Bear Lake, Canada
8 lb.	3 lbs., 6 oz.	July 31, 1973	M. A. Coulombe, California	Canada
10 lb.	2 lbs., 15 oz.	Aug. 8, 1969	Herbert Prentice, California	Great Bear Lake, Canada
12 lb.	2 lbs., 12 oz.	Aug. 1, 1973	M. A. Coulombe, California	Canada
MUSKELLUNGE				
2 lb.	18 lbs., 7 oz.	July 15, 1959	Leonard Hartman, New York	St. Lawrence River, New York
4 lb.	42 lbs., 3 oz.	Sept. 7, 1963	Leonard Hartman, New York	St. Lawrence River, New York
6 lb.	47 lbs., 1 oz.	Sept. 2, 1962	Leonard Hartman, New York	St. Lawrence River, New York
8 lb.	59 lbs., 13 oz.	Aug. 6, 1960	Leonard Hartman, New York	St. Lawrence River, New York
10 lb.	67 lbs., 15 oz.	Aug. 10, 1961	Leonard Hartman, New York	St. Lawrence River, New York
12 lb.	61 lbs., 0 oz.	Nov. 8, 1964	Leonard Hartman, New York	St. Lawrence River, New York
PICKEREL (Chain)				
2 lb.	7 lbs., 1 oz.	July 18, 1968	Wm. Spaulding, Sr., Mass.	Assawamsett Pond, Mass.
4 lb.	6 lbs., 14 oz.	May 1, 1968	Wm. Spaulding, Sr., Mass.	Pocksha Pond, Massachusetts
6 lb.	6 lbs., 15 oz.	July 15, 1968	Wm. Spaulding, Sr., Mass.	Pocksha Pond, Massachusetts
8 lb.	6 lbs., 0 oz.	Apr. 19, 1965	Ralph Campitiello, New Jersey	Upper Erskin Lake, New Jersey
10 lb.	7 lbs., 4 oz.	July 28, 1968	Wm. Spaulding, Sr., Mass.	Pocksha Pond, Massacuhsetts
12 lb.	7 lbs., 1 oz.	July 18, 1968	Wm. Spaulding, Sr. Mass.	Assawampsett Pond, Mass.
PIKE (Northern)				
2 lb.	17 lbs., 5 oz.	May 8, 1961	Leonard Hartman, New York	St. Lawrence River, New York
4 lb.	32 lbs., 4 oz.	June 19, 1973	J. Thompson, New Jersey	Quebec
6 lb.	30 lbs., 9 oz.	Aug. 15, 1963	Ed Zaleski, Canada	Lake Abitibi, Canada
8 lb.	31 lbs., 0 oz.	Nov. 12, 1955	Capt. R. J. Oostdyke, USAF	Nortdeich, Wolfersheim, Germany
10 lb.	40 lbs., 0 oz.	June 11, 1969	Ken Asper, Pennsylvania	Delay Lake, Canada
12 lb.	26 lbs., 0 oz.	July 4, 1974	James Thompson, New Jersey	Lake Camachigama
TROUT (Brook)				
2 lb.	4 lbs., 2 oz.	July 4, 1965	Edwin Kennedy, New Jersey	Kepimits River, Canada
4 lb.	4 lbs., 2 oz.	June 13, 1970	David Bonser, Pennsylvania	Aquashicolia Creek, Pennsylvania
6 lb.	8 lbs., 8 oz.	June 25, 1954	Donnell Culpepper, California	Canada
8 lb.	2 lbs., 4 oz.	June 22, 1974	Michael Baz, Vermont	Lake Porteuef, Quebec
10 lb.	3 lbs., 9 oz.	Aug. 17, 1969	Ivan Grimshaw, Indiana	So. Knife River, Manitoba
12 lb.	Open			
TROUT (Brown)				
2 lb.	9 lbs., 0 oz.	Oct. 16, 1959	Ralph Munsen, Oregon	Wickiup Reservoir, Oregon
4 lb.	21 lbs., 1 oz.	June 5, 1970	James Hatcher, California	Robinson Creek, Calofirnia
6 lb.	19 lbs., 15 oz.	Dec. 14, 1971	John Lanza, Arkansas	White River, Arkansas
8 lb.	28 lbs., 3 oz.	Sept. 11, 1970	Lewis MacFarland, M. D.	White River, Arkansas
10 lb.	31 lbs., 8 oz.	May 24, 1972	Troy Lackey, Arkansas	Bull Shoals, Arkansas
12 lb.	16 lbs., 4 oz.	Nov. 7, 1970	Andy Lipjanec, California	Rush Creek, California

Line Test	Weight	Date Caught	Angler	Waters Caught
TROUT (Cutthroat)				
2 lb.	6 lbs., 15 oz.	Nov. 11, 1972	Frank Tabbert, Nevada	Pyramid Lake, Nevada
4 lb.	8 lbs., 15 oz.	Apr. 27, 1955	Lee Baun, California	Walker Lake, Nevada
6 lb.	12 lbs., 0 oz.	Mar. 4, 1957	Clem De Rocco, California	Walker Lake, Nevada
8 lb.	14 lbs., 7 oz.	Mar. 18, 1956	Leonard Hyduke, California	Walker Lake, Nevada
10 lb.	8 lbs., 5 oz.	Apr. 6, 1956	Alan Zeller, California	Walker Lake, Nevada
12 lb.	7 lbs., 7 oz.	Mar. 14, 1958	Ed Baun, California	Walker Lake, Nevada
TROUT (Dolly Varden)				
2 lb.	5 lbs., 0 oz.	July 30, 1960	Art Hamill, Oregon	Metolius River, Oregon
4 lb.	17 lbs., 0 oz.	Nov. 27, 1961	Yvonne Donaldson, Nevada	Lake Pend Oreille, Idaho
6 lb.	18 lbs., 8 oz.	June 8, 1962	Yvonne Donaldson, Nevada	Lake Pend Oreille, Idaho
8 lb.	20 lbs., 0 oz.	May 8, 1963	Yvonne Donaldson, Nevada	Lake Pend Oreille, Idaho
10 lb.	Open			
12 lb.	Open			
TROUT (Golden)				
2 lb.	4 lbs., 4 oz.	Oct. 14, 1961	Michael Mansfield, California	Horton Lake 3, California
4 lb.	3 lbs., 5 oz.	July 12, 1960	Dick More, Colorado	Valentine Lake, Wyoming
6 lb.	2 lbs., 2 oz.	July 22, 1959	E. L. Sharp, California	Cook Lake, Wyoming
8 lb.	1 lb., 5 oz.	Aug. 2, 1970	Gene Newman, California	Skyblue Lake, California
10 lb.	1 lb., 6 oz.	July 5, 1972	Gene Newman, California	Skyblue Lake, California
12 lb.	1 lb., 4 oz.	July 6, 1972	Gene Newman, California	Skyblue Lake, California
TROUT (Kamloops)				
2 lb.	24 lbs., 14 oz.	Oct. 17, 1962	Ralph Munsen, Oregon	Lake Pend Oreille, Idaho
4 lb.	25 lbs., 13 oz.	May 19, 1962	Yvonne Donaldson, Nevada	Lake Pend Oreille, Idaho
6 lb.	29 lbs., 12 oz.	Nov. 24, 1961	Jim Parsons, Idaho	Lake Pend Oreille, Idaho
8 lb.	25 lbs., 4 oz.	Nov. 17, 1960	Lester Lundblad, Oregon	Lake Pend Oreille, Idaho
10 lb.	23 lbs., 0 oz.	Oct. 27, 1953	Frank Natta, Washington	Lake Pend Oreille, Idaho
12 lb.	Open			
TROUT (Lake or Mackinaw)				
2 lb.	19 lbs., 0 oz.	July 27, 1965	Edwin Kennedy, New Jersey	Greak Slave Lake, Canada
4 lb.	37 lbs., 12 oz.	July 26, 1966	James Thurston, Canada	Tazin Lake, Canada
6 lb.	32 lbs., 9 oz.	Aug. 6, 1969	Herbert Prentice, California	Great Bear Lake, Canada
8 lb.	41 lbs., 6 oz.	Aug. 14, 1971	Ronald Schmieder, California	Great Bear Lake, Canada
10 lb.	36 lbs., 0 oz.	July 5, 1968	Bob Aurand, California	Great Bear Lake, Canada
12 lb.	46 lbs., 4 oz.	July 16, 1968	Dale Slocum, Arizona	Great Bear Lake, Canada
TROUT (Rainbow)				
2 lb.	11 lbs., 0 oz.	May 28, 1967	A. C. Anderson, N. Z.	Lake Tarawera, N. Z.
4 lb.	8 lbs., 7 oz.	May 8, 1964	John Miner, Florida	Antisana, Ecuador, S.A.
6 lb.	17 lbs., 2 oz.	June 29, 1958	Keith Davidson, Washington	Pend Oreille River, Washington
8 lb.	25 lbs., 1 oz.	Nov. 5, 1954	Jim Parsons, Idaho	Lake Pend Oreille, Idaho
10 lb.	7 lbs., 0 oz.	May 29, 1972	Gene Newman, California	Pleasant Valley Res., California
12 lb.	8 lbs., 8 oz.	July 11, 1970	B. A. Bixler, California	Upper Lake Klamath, Oregon

Line Test	Weight	Date Caught	Angler	Waters Caught
TROUT (Steelhead)				
2 lb.	12 lbs., 1 oz.	May 2, 1954	Frank Natta, Washington	Washougal River, Washington
4 lb.	22 lbs., 0 oz.	Feb. 22, 1959	Carlyle Brown, Washington	East Lewis River, Washington
6 lb.	24 lbs., 6 oz.	Nov. 21, 1972	Jerry Mahony, Washington	Thompson River, B..C.
8 lb.	24 lbs., 6 oz.	Feb. 21, 1959	Walter Winseman, Jr., Wash.	Skyomish River, Washington
10 lb.	28 lbs., 11 oz.	July 5, 1952	Rex York, California	Klamath River, California
12 lb.	25 lbs., 0 oz.	Oct. 1, 1971	Bob Aurand, California	Kispiox River, B. C.
WALLEYE				
2 lb.	8 lbs., 11 oz.	Aug. 31, 1960	Leonard Hartman, New York	St. Lawrence River, New York
4 lb.	13 lbs., 3 oz.	June 5, 1962	Leonard Hartman, New York	St. Lawrence River, New York
6 lb.	13 lbs., 2 oz.	July 5, 1963	Floyd Randolph, California	Curren River, Missouri
8 lb.	14 lbs., 8 oz.	Oct. 19, 1966	Fred Golden, Michigan	Otter Lake, Michigan
10 lb.	12 lbs., 2 oz.	June 1, 1961	Leonard Hartman, New York	St. Lawrence River, New York
12 lb.	9 lbs., 2 oz.	Oct. 19, 1962	Leonard Hartman, New York	St. Lawrence River, New York

International Spin-Fishing Association

SALT WATER RECORDS

Line Test	Weight	Date Caught	Angler	Waters Caught
ALBACORE				
2 lb.	Open			
4 lb.	25 lb., 10 oz.	Aug. 10, 1960	Wm. Hill, Jr., California	San Diego, California
6 lb.	25 lbs., 2 oz.	Aug. 25, 1960	H. S. Bonner, California	San Diego, California
8 lb.	25 lb., 11 oz.	July 31, 1957	Dr. E. A. Hershman, California	Coronados Isl., California
10 lb.	28 lbs., 8 oz.	Aug. 11, 1954	Harold Levitt, California	San Clemente Isl., California
12 lb.	39 lbs., 8 oz.	July 23, 1958	Dr. R. Rubaum, California	San Clemente Isl., California
AMBERJACK				
2 lb.	6 lbs., 2 oz.	May 29, 1961	Roy Martin, Florida	Gulf of Mexico, Florida
4 lb.	9 lbs., 6 oz.	May 19, 1963	Louis Tesar, Florida	Gulf of Mexico, Florida
6 lb.	20 lbs., 5 oz.	Sept. 5, 1971	Dale Leverone, Florida	Miami, Florida
8 lb.	56 lbs., 0 oz.	June 12, 1966	Mrs. Carl Dann III, Florida	Vero Beach, Florida
10 lb.	45 lbs., 0 oz.	Aug. 12, 1972	Lee Martines	Port Canaveral, Florida
12 lb.	78 lbs., 4 oz.	Mar. 23, 1969	Pamela Habicht	Key Largo, Florida
BARRACUDA (Great)				
2 lb.	16 lbs., 9 oz.	Apr. 26, 1971	Bertram Tepper	Bahia Honda, Key
4 lb.	30 lbs., 0 oz.	Mar. 6, 1969	Ray Acord, California	Palau Islands
6 lb.	30 lbs., 0 oz.	Feb. 26, 1972	Kenny Bittner, Florida	Key West, Florida
8 lb.	37 lbs., 4 oz.	June 7, 1960	Al Zapanta, California	St. George Cay, British Honduras
10 lb.	48 lbs., 0 oz.	May 8, 1971	Donald Aaron, Florida	Key West, Florida
12 lb.	42 lbs., 10 oz.	Oct. 19, 1959	Bill Moeser, Florida	Key Largo, Florida

Line Test	Weight	Date Caught	Angler	Waters Caught
BARRACUDA (Pacific)				
2 lb.	10 lbs., 9 oz.	Aug. 13, 1958	Dr. E. A. Hershman, California	San Diego, California
4 lb.	10 lbs., 9 oz.	Apr. 17, 1960	Bob Dragoo, California	Paradise Cove, California
6 lb.	12 lbs., 4 oz.	May 18, 1953	H. W. Craine, California	Catalina Isl., California
8 lb.	16 lbs., 0 oz.	Dec. 14 ,1971	Stu Apte, Florida	Cobia Isle, Panama
10 lb.	13 lbs., 8 oz.	Nov. 9, 1969	Alfredo Bequillard, Jr., Nicaragua	San Juan del Sor, Nic.
12 lb.	12 lbs., 7 oz.	May 20, 1960	Ernest Blumenthal, California	Redondo Beach, California
BASS (California Black Sea)				
2 lb.	Open			
4 lb.	Open			
6 lb.	8 lbs., 1 oz.	Feb. 24, 1963	James Haun, California	Seal Beach, California
8 lb.	23 lbs., 4 oz.	Aug. 24, 1958	Al Teachout, California	Dana Point, California
10 lb.	112 lbs. 8 oz.	June 12, 1957	D. B. Rosenthal, California	San Francisco Isl. Baja Calif., Mex.
12 lb.	83 lbs., 4 oz.	Feb. 23, 1958	J. N. Bertolino, California	Box Canyon, California
BASS (Channel)				
2 lb.	9 lbs., 0 oz.	Jan. 18, 1961	James Mastry, Florida	St. Petersburg, Florida
4 lb.	37 lbs., 4 oz.	July 6, 1961	W. H. Watters, N. C.	North Inlet, S. C.
6 lb.	53 lbs., 8 oz.	July 24, 1960	C. M. Vellines, N. C.	Portsmouth Isl., N. C.
8 lb.	44 lbs., 4 oz.	Apr. 18, 1968	Dave Elliott, Maryland	Cape Hatteras
10 lb.	44 lbs., 4 oz.	Jan. 22, 1961	R. E. Robinson, Texas	Galveston, Texas
12 lb.	60 lbs., 8 oz.	Oct. 24, 1954	Arhtur Clark, Jr., Pennsylvania	Kill Devil Hills, N. C.
BASS (Kelp)				
2 lb.	8 lbs., 3 oz.	May 17, 1961	Wm. R. Hill, Jr., California	San Diego, California
4 lb.	10 lbs., 7 oz.	July 17, 1954	Art Parra, California	Long Beach, California
6 lb.	8 lbs., 12 oz.	June 2, 1955	Jack Rous, California	San Clemente Isl., California
8 lb.	9 lbs., 12 oz.	Oct. 7, 1955	Fred Anderson, California	Santa Barbara, California
10 lb.	9 lbs., 8 oz.	June 12, 1967	Jack Hinshaw, California	Oceanside, California
12 lb.	10 lbs., 2 oz.	June 29, 1959	Bob Dragoo, California	Malibu, California
BASS (Sand)				
2 lb.	5 lbs., 2 oz.	June 27, 1960	Willis Carr, California	Long Beach, California
4 lb.	5 lbs., 0 oz.	June 9, 1963	Bob Dragoo, California	Newport Bay, California
6 lb.	8 lbs., 4 oz.	Jan. 26, 1965	Bob Bennett, California	Newport Bay, California
8 lb.	8 lbs., 14 oz.	Aug. 10, 1958	Maj. E. T. Nobles, USMC	Box Canyon, California
10 lb.	8 lbs., 8 oz.	July 8, 1972	Frederick Blesser, California	Oceanside, California
12 lb.	4 lbs., 15 oz.	June 30, 1962	Carlton Bishop, California	San Onofre, California
BASS (Striped)				
2 lb.	14 lbs., 13 oz.	July 18, 1969	Mrs. Frances Pasche, Mass.	Plum Isle, Massachusetts
4 lb.	40 lbs., 8 oz.	May 28, 1969	Doug Crawford, Oregon	No. Fork Coos River, Oregon
6 lb.	48 lbs., 0 oz.	Apr. 20, 1961	John Froehlich, Maryland	Susquehanna River, Maryland
8 lb.	52 lbs., 8 oz.	Aug. 18, 1969	John O'Neil, Massachusetts	Merrimac River
10 lb.	57 lbs., 1 oz.	July 8, 1963	Jon Kodwyck, New Hampshire	Plum Isl., Massachusetts
12 lb.	53 lbs., 8 oz.	May 2, 1962	Jack Stewart, Oregon	Coos River, Oregon

Line Test	Weight	Date Caught	Angler	Waters Caught
BLUEFISH				
2 lb.	11 lbs., 3 oz.	Mar. 21, 1970	Wm. Leffingwell, Florida	Port Canaveral, Florida
4 lb.	12 lbs., 2 oz.	Mar. 27, 1972	Donald Seib, Florida	Port Canaveral, Florida
6 lb.	17 lbs., 4 oz.	Mar. 27, 1970	Skip Mackey, Florida	Port Canaveral, Florida
8 lb.	19 lbs., 8 oz.	Nov. 19, 1970	D. M. Tatem, Jr.	Nags Head, N. C.
10 lb.	19 lbs., 6 oz.	Oct. 6, 1971	Daniel Catalano, New York	Long Isl. Sound, Rye, New York
TIE				
10 lb.	19 lbs., 6 oz.	Dec. 11, 1972	J. Marshell Crews, N. C.	Wilmington, N. L., Connecticut
12 lb.	17 lbs., 1 oz.	Sept. 29, 1971	Walter Mathews	Long Island Sound
BONEFISH				
2 lb.	7 lbs., 10 oz.	Mar. 17, 1968	Fred Johnson, Alabama	Bahia Honda Key, Florida
4 lb.	11 lbs., 0 oz.	Mar. 29, 1968	J. Hilton Parsons, Jr., S. C.	Islamorada, Florida
6 lb.	16 lbs., 0 oz.	Feb. 25, 1971	G. Lavenstein, Virginia	Bimini, Bahama Island
8 lb.	14 lbs., 8 oz.	Mar. 31, 1974	T. T. Sinclair, Massachusetts	Florida
10 lb.	13 lbs., 14 oz.	Apr. 15, 1969	N. J. Brown, Jr., Illinois	Islamorada, Florida
12 lb.	15 lbs., 0 oz.	Feb. 28, 1961	Nal Carlin, New York	Islamorada, Florida
BONITO (Atlantic)				
2 lb.	2 lbs., 15 oz.	Aug. 5, 1971	Crawford Adams, M.D., Tennessee	Marathon, Florida
4 lb.	11 lbs., 8 oz.	June 29, 1973	Dick Fleming, Florida	Florida
6 lb.	12 lbs., 8 oz.	July 7, 1973	W. Russell, Jr.	Florida
8 lb.	18 lbs., 0 oz.	July 6, 1970	Bill Kieldsen, Florida	Key Biscayne, Florida
10 lb.	17 lbs., 2 oz.	May 29, 1971	Mike Leverone, Florida	Key West, Florida
12 lb.	22 lbs., 8 oz.	Mar. 29, 1973	Leslie Turner	Florida
BONITO (Oceanic)				
2 lb.	Open			
4 lb.	7 lbs., 8 oz.	Dec. 14, 1970	Crawford Adams, M.D., Tennessee	Duck Key, Florida
6 lb.	12 lbs., 8 oz.	June 15, 1966	John Irvin, Florida	Vero Beach, Florida
8 lb.	15 lbs., 2 oz.	July 4, 1973	Bill Gleason	Florida
10 lb.	23 lbs., 7 oz.	Aug. 10, 1958	Raymond Kagihara, Hawaii	Oahu, Hawaii
12 lb.	17 lbs., 8 oz.	May 24, 1963	Alton Rowland, Florida	Boynton Beach, Florida
BONITO (Pacific)				
2 lb.	8 lbs., 10 oz.	Jan. 12, 1961	Wm. R. Hill, Jr., California	San Diego, California
4 lb.	11 lbs., 2 oz.	Aug. 24, 1959	Bob Dragoo, California	Ensenada, Baja California, Mex.
TIE				
4 lb.	11 lbs., 2 oz.	Nov. 4, 1970	Gordon Prentice, California	Loreto, Baja California, Mex.
6 lb.	13 lbs., 8 oz.	Aug. 8, 1963	John Miner III, Florida	Antogagasta, Chile
8 lb.	14 lbs., 6 oz.	June 24, 1959	George Ramsey, California	Bahia de Palmas, Baja, Cal., Mex.
10 lb.	12 lbs., 2 oz.	June 26, 1959	Clifford Getz, California	Bahia de Palmas, Baja, Cal., Mex.
12 lb.	17 lbs., 1 oz.	Apr. 3, 1953	Dan Alan Felger, California	Coronadoa Isls., California
CABRILLA				
2 lb.	6 lbs., 9 oz.	Jan. 22, 1971	Gordon Prentice, California	Loreta, Baja California, Mex.
4 lb.	4 lbs., 4 oz.	Jan. 11, 1970	Gordon Prentice, California	Loreta, Baja California, Mex.

Line Test	Weight	Date Caught	Angler	Waters Caught
6 lb.	16 lbs., 0 oz.	Jan. 14, 1966	Bernard Zwilling, California	Rancho Bueno Vista, Mexico
8 lb.	28 lbs., 0 oz.	Nov. 8, 1960	Russell Anderson, California	San Jose del Cabo, Baja, California, Mex.
10 lb.	13 lbs., 0 oz.	Feb. 27, 1959	Paul Braslow, California	Loreta, Baja California, Mex.
12 lb.	22 lbs., 0 oz.	May 8, 1970	Denton Hill, California	Rancho Bueno Vista, Baja, California, Mex.

COBIA

Line Test	Weight	Date Caught	Angler	Waters Caught
2 lb.	8 lbs., 2 oz.	Jan. 27, 1974	Mike Leverone	Florida
4 lb.	34 lbs., 8 oz.	Mar. 27, 1974	Mike Lindquist	Florida
6 lb.	47 lbs., 0 oz.	June 18, 1966	Mrs. Carl Dann III, Florida	Vero Beach, Florida
8 lb.	52 lbs., 8 oz.	Apr. 17, 1968	James Masters	St. Petersburg, Florida
10 lb.	50 lbs., 0 oz.	Sept. 28, 1961	Richard Delvalle, Florida	Tampa Bay, Florida
12 lb.	64 lbs., 8 oz.	Apr. 3, 1965	Tommy Norred, Florida	Destin, Florida

TIE

Line Test	Weight	Date Caught	Angler	Waters Caught
12 lb.	64 lbs., 8 oz.	July 1, 1972	Ralph Hypes, Jr., Florida	Port Canaveral, Florida

CORBINA

Line Test	Weight	Date Caught	Angler	Waters Caught
2 lb.	5 lbs., 12 oz.	Jan. 16, 1972	J. W. Holmes, California	Laguna Beach, California
4 lb.	7 lbs., 4 oz.	June 18, 1967	Tom Miller, California	Ventura, California
6 lb.	7 lbs., 6 oz.	July 10, 1966	Butch McCullough, California	Newport Bay, California
8 lb.	6 lbs., 6 oz.	Oct. 3, 1971	Michael Muravez, California	Mission Bay, California
10 lb.	12 lbs., 0 oz.	July 12, 1963	Jack Smith, Florida	Club de Pesca, Panama, C. Z.
12 lb.	5 lbs., 8 oz.	Dec. 12, 1959	Arthur Baca, California	Newport Bay, California

CORVINA

Line Test	Weight	Date Caught	Angler	Waters Caught
2 lb.	11 lbs., 4 oz.	Oct. 5, 1961	Willis Carr, California	Salton Sea, California
4 lb.	11 lbs., 1 oz.	May 23, 1970	Ken Hadden, California	Salton Sea, California
6 lb.	12 lbs., 4 oz.	May 2, 1962	Ira Shoemaker, California	Salton Sea, California

TIE

Line Test	Weight	Date Caught	Angler	Waters Caught
6 lb.	12 lbs., 4 oz.	May 16, 1964	H. J. Ray, California	Salton Sea, California
8 lb.	34 lbs., 0 oz.	May 25, 1961	Maurine Cloe, California	San Felipe, Baja, California, Mex.
10 lb.	25 lbs., 8 oz.	May 15, 1962	Willis Carr, California	Salton Sea, California
12 lb.	24 lbs., 12 oz.	Sept. 20, 1972	James McKibben, California	Salton Sea, California

CROAKER (Spotfin)

Line Test	Weight	Date Caught	Angler	Waters Caught
2 lb.	8 lbs., 2 oz.	Feb. 3, 1963	Milton Miller, California	Newport Bay, California
4 lb.	9 lbs., 12 oz.	Apr. 18, 1971	Lawrence Appleby, California	Newport Bay, California
6 lb.	11 lbs., 13 oz.	July 9, 1963	Robert Austin, California	Agua Hedionda Lagoon, California
8 lb.	10 lbs., 11 oz.	Apr. 18, 1970	H. J. Ray, California	Newport Bay, California
10 lb.	9 lbs., 9 oz.	May 16, 1971	Lawrence Appleby, California	Newport Bay, California
12 lb.	9 lbs., 8 oz.	Apr. 24, 1962	R. M. Harrison, California	Newport Bay, California

DOLPHIN

Line Test	Weight	Date Caught	Angler	Waters Caught
2 lb.	14 lbs., 8 oz.	July 25, 1971	Crawford Adams, M.D., Tennessee	Key Colony, Florida
4 lb.	33 lbs., 12 oz.	May 9, 1973	Gordon Prentice, California	Baja, California
6 lb.	32 lbs., 0 oz.	Apr. 27, 1971	J. Barton Carver, Florida	W. Palm Beach, Florida
8 lb.	36 lbs., 4 oz.	July 17, 1965	Mrs. Carl Dann III, Florida	Pinos Bay, Panama, C. Z.

Line Test	Weight	Date Caught	Angler	Waters Caught
10 lb.	52 lbs., 8 oz.	Feb. 12, 1972	Edward Slane, Jr., Florida	Key Largo, Florida
12 lb.	33 lbs., 0 oz.	Apr. 5, 1953	Myron Glauber, California	Mazatlan, Mexico

DRUM (Black)

Line Test	Weight	Date Caught	Angler	Waters Caught
2 lb.	4 lbs., 3 oz.	Dec. 29, 1972	R. McCollum, Jr., Florida	Sykes Creek, Florida
4 lb.	30 lbs., 8 oz.	Jan. 25, 1969	James Masters, Florida	St. Petersburg, Florida
6 lb.	45 lbs., 0 oz.	Jan. 14, 1958	Gus Getner, Texas	So. Padre Island, Texas
8 lb.	64 lbs., 0 oz.	July 20, 1960	Joseph Bucciarelli, New Jersey	Beach Haven, New Jersey
10 lb.	66 lbs., 0 oz.	May 13, 1973	Chas. Biashke	Virginia
12 lb.	89 lbs., 4 oz.	May 15, 1971	John Osborne, Jr., New Jersey	Delaware Bay, Delaware

HALIBUT

Line Test	Weight	Date Caught	Angler	Waters Caught
2 lb.	15 lbs., 8 oz.	Aug. 13, 1969	John Smart, Washington	Fort Casey, Washington
4 lb.	35 lbs., 11 oz.	Aug. 10, 1969	John Smart, Washington	Fort Casey, Washington
6 lb.	38 lbs., 8 oz.	July 4, 1965	Eugene Duke, California	Newport Bay, California
8 lb.	57 lbs., 2 oz.	June 1, 1958	Merlin Wilson, Oregon	Coos Nay, Oregon
10 lb.	74 lbs., 1 oz.	June 3, 1957	Paul McDonald, Oregon	Coos Bay, Oregon
12 lb.	35 lbs., 8 oz.	Sept. 6, 1964	Al Binder, California	Santa Barbara Isl., California

JACK CREVALLE

Line Test	Weight	Date Caught	Angler	Waters Caught
2 lb.	7 lbs., 4 oz.	Dec. 6, 1966	Ted Eggers, Florida	Lake Worth, Florida
4 lb.	17 lbs., 8 oz.	Jan. 3, 1966	G. S. Braden, Florida	Dry Tortugas, Gulf of Mexico
6 lb.	26 lbs., 4 oz.	Apr. 13, 1973	D. Chermanski, Florida	Florida
8 lb.	25 lbs., 8 oz.	Apr. 19, 1957	Harry Okamura, Hawaii	Oahu, Hawaii
10 lb.	39 lbs., 8 oz.	May 16, 1961	P. A. Lund, Florida	Hobe Sound, Florida
12 lb.	32 lbs., 2 oz.	Aug. 1, 1965	Mrs. Carl Dann III, Florida	Vero Beach, Florida

LADYFISH

Line Test	Weight	Date Caught	Angler	Waters Caught
2 lb.	3 lbs., 7 oz.	July 29, 1972	Wm. Spaulding, Sr., Florida	Tarpon Springs, Florida
4 lb.	6 lbs., 0 oz.	June 28, 1959	Jackson Morisawa, Hawaii	Pearl Harbor, Hawaii
6 lb.	5 lbs., 9 oz.	Mar. 26, 1954	Dr. Alexis Burso, Hawaii	Oahu, Hawaii
8 lb.	12 lbs., 5 oz.	Jan. 26, 1956	Dr. Alexis Burso, Hawaii	Pearl Harbor, Hawaii
10 lb.	8 lbs., 0 oz.	Mar. 3, 1957	Ralph Ohtani, Hawaii	Oahu, Hawaii
12 lb.	4 lbs., 1 oz.	Oct. 6, 1960	William Smith, Florida	Panama City Beach, Florida

MACKEREL (King)

Line Test	Weight	Date Caught	Angler	Waters Caught
2 lb.	12 lbs., 0 oz.	June 17, 1962	Douglas Carl, Florida	Panama City Beach, Florida
4 lb.	12 lbs., 12 oz.	Apr. 29, 1962	Nancy Tobias, Florida	St. Petersburg, Florida
6 lb.	40 lbs., 0 oz.	Apr. 19, 1964	James Gerling, Florida	Anna Maria Isl., Florida
8 lb.	36 lbs., 6 oz.	May 30, 1966	John Irvin, Florida	Vero Beach, Florida
10 lb.	43 lbs., 1 oz.	Apr. 28, 1959	Eugene Wilhite, Florida	St. Petersburg, Florida
12 lb.	44 lbs., 0 oz.	May 20, 1963	Clyde Fore, Florida	Anna Maria Isl., Florida

MACKEREL (Spanish)

Line Test	Weight	Date Caught	Angler	Waters Caught
2 lb.	8 lbs., 0 oz.	Feb. 15, 1964	Dr. R. B. Hehenberger, Florida	Miami Beach, Florida
4 lb.	11 lbs., 1 oz.	Dec. 20, 1970	Gordon Prentice, California	Loreto, Baja California, Mex.
6 lb.	9 lbs., 1 oz.	Nov. 6, 1970	Gordon Prentice, California	Loreto, Baja California, Mex.
8 lb.	10 lbs., 4 oz.	Dec. 29, 1969	Ed Macaulay, New York	Islamorada, Florida

Line Test	Weight	Date Caught	Angler	Waters Caught
10 lb.	10 lbs., 0 oz.	Feb. 14, 1973	Barry Ross	Florida
12 lb.	13 lbs., 0 oz.	Mar. 8, 1958	Lily Call, California	Loreto, Baja California, Mex.

MARLIN (Black)

Line Test	Weight	Date Caught	Angler	Waters Caught
2 lb.	Open			
4 lb.	Open			
6 lb.	Open			
8 lb.	176 lbs., 6 oz.	Aug. 2, 1962	Bernard Zwilling, California	Rancho Buena Vista, Baja, California, Mex.
10 lb.	247 lbs., 0 oz.	Jan. 2, 1967	Dr. Carl Dann III, Florida	Pinas Bay, Panama
12 lb.	312 lbs., 3 oz.	July 17, 1958	Robert Gaxiola, California	Guaymas, Mexico

MARLIN (Striped)

Line Test	Weight	Date Caught	Angler	Waters Caught
2 lb.	Open			
4 lb.	129 lbs., 0 oz.	June 8, 1962	Dr. Reuben Rubaum, California	Pamilla, Baja California, Mex.
6 lb.	128 lbs., 0 oz.	Feb. 21, 1974	Ed Kennedy	Panama
8 lb.	126 lbs., 7 oz.	Mar. 14, 1958	Albert Zapanta, California	Mazatlan, Mexico
10 lb.	183 lbs., 7 oz.	July 15, 1958	Robert Gaxiola, California	Guaymas, Mexico
12 lb.	165 lbs., 0 oz.	Mar. 15, 1955	Harry Goza, Jr., California	Mazatlan, Mexico

MARLIN (White)

Line Test	Weight	Date Caught	Angler	Waters Caught
2 lb.	Open			
4 lb.	Open			
6 lb.	64 lbs., 0 oz.	Mar. 16, 1972	Jacqueline Knight, Pennsylvania	Walkers Cay, Bahama Isl.
8 lb.	Open			
10 lb.	Open			
12 lb.	92 lbs., 0 oz.	Feb. 18, 1973	Ruth Stoky	Florida

MILK FISH

Line Test	Weight	Date Caught	Angler	Waters Caught
2 lb.	Open			
4 lb.	12 lbs., 13 oz.	Dec. 9, 1956	Thomas Shintani, Hawaii	Pearl Harbor, Hawaii
6 lb.	11 lbs., 6 oz.	Aug. 20, 1955	James Nakai, Hawaii,	Hilo, Hawaii
8 lb.	17 lbs., 9 oz.	Aug. 30, 1964	Curtis Ohama, Hawaii	Honolulu, Hawaii
10 lb.	18 lbs., 2 oz.	Aug. 20, 1958	Hank Uechi, Hawaii	Oahu, Hawaii
12 lb.	21 lbs., 3 oz.	Dec. 4, 1957	Robert Becht, Hawaii	Honolulu, Hawaii

OPALEYE

Line Test	Weight	Date Caught	Angler	Waters Caught
2 lb.	4 lbs., 3 oz.	Mar. 17, 1962	Jim Phelan, California	Laguna Beach, California
4 lb.	6 lbs., 4 oz.	Oct. 27, 1968	Roger Lawrence, California	Long Beach, California
6 lb.	5 lbs., 8 oz.	June 4, 1967	Roger Lawrence, California	Long Beach, California
8 lb.	4 lbs., 15 oz.	Oct. 16, 1971	Joe Wilson, California	Laguna Beach, California
10 lb.	4 lbs., 10 oz.	Mar. 6, 1966	Jessie Harmon, California	Laguna Beach, California
12 lb.	4 lbs., 8 oz.	June 1, 1972	Thomas Bette, California	Laguna Beach, California

PERCH (Saltwater)

Line Test	Weight	Date Caught	Angler	Waters Caught
2 lb.	4 lbs., 4 oz.	May 24, 1969	John Smart, Washington	Dungeness, Washington
4 lb.	4 lbs., 12 oz.	June 18, 1971	Thomas Bette, California	Laguna Beach, California
6 lb.	5 lbs., 3 oz.	June 4, 1967	Roger Lawrence, California	Long Beach, California
8 lb.	3 lbs., 10 oz.	Mar. 31, 1956	Tom Payne, California	Baja California, Mexico

Line Test	Weight	Date Caught	Angler	Waters Caught
10 lb.	4 lbs., 1 oz.	Apr. 12, 1957	P. T. Peterson, California	Santa Monica, California
12 lb.	3 lbs., 12 oz.	Apr. 7, 1956	James Johnson, California	Hermosa Beach, California

PERMIT

Line Test	Weight	Date Caught	Angler	Waters Caught
2 lb.	18 lbs., 12 oz.	Oct. 11, 1962	B. A. Knauth, Florida	Big Pine Key, Florida
4 lb.	24 lbs., 0 oz.	Sept. 9, 1968	Stanley Fried, Florida	Biscayne Bay, Florida
6 lb.	30 lbs., 4 oz.	Aug. 22, 1971	Hugh Anderson, Florida	Keywest, Florida
8 lb.	47 lbs., 0 oz.	June 15, 1971	Stu Apte, Florida	Marathon, Florida
10 lb.	41 lbs., 4 oz.	Mar. 19, 1968	Walt Reed, New York	Marathon, Florida
12 lb.	40 lbs., 8 oz.	May 18, 1967	A. Martin Mondl, Florida	Bahia Honda Key, Florida

POMPANO

Line Test	Weight	Date Caught	Angler	Waters Caught
2 lb.	2 lbs., 13 oz.	May 28, 1961	G. O. Thorne, Florida	Panama City Beach, Florida
4 lb.	5 lbs., 3 oz.	June 4, 1963	Roy Martin, Florida	Panama City Beach, Florida
6 lb.	6 lbs., 0 oz.	Nov. 9, 1970	Chip Laudone, Florida	Lakeworth, Florida
8 lb.	6 lbs., 3 oz.	Feb. 15, 1959	Myrtis Shrives, Florida	Vero Beach, Florida
10 lb.	12 lbs., 8 oz.	June 14, 1960	Harry Gearhart, Jr.	Guantanamo Bay, Cuba
12 lb.	5 lbs., 12 oz.	Dec. 13, 1958	Myrtis Shrives, Florida	Vero Beach, Florida

POMPANO (African)

Line Test	Weight	Date Caught	Angler	Waters Caught
2 lb.	Open			
4 lb.	23 lbs., 4 oz.	May 26, 1974	F. Oblak	Florida
6 lb.	17 lbs., 5 oz.	May 19, 1973	Gordon Prentice, California	Baja, California
8 lb.	24 lbs., 8 oz.	Feb. 1, 1969	Bob Kilgore, Florida	Triumph Reef, Florida
10 lb.	11 lbs., 0 oz.	June 15, 1964	Joyce Perkins, California	Rancho Buena Vista, Baja, California, Mex.
12 lb.	.42 lbs., 8 oz.	Mar. 6, 1973	Mrs. Bobbie McReynolds	Pennsylvania

ROOSTERFISH

Line Test	Weight	Date Caught	Angler	Waters Caught
2 lb.	10 lbs., 2 oz.	Apr. 4, 1960	Dr. E. A. Hershman, California	Bahia de Palmas, Baja Cal., Mex.
4 lb.	18 lbs., 4 oz.	July 18, 1972	Gordon Prentice, California	Punta Colorado, Mexico
6 lb.	27 lbs., 8 oz.	July 15, 1967	Bernard Zwilling, California	Rancho Bueno Vista, Baja California, Mex.
8 lb.	27 lbs., 10 oz.	June 30, 1973	Bob Aurand, California	Baja, California
10 lb.	50 lbs., 0 oz.	Sept. 6, 1954	Maurice Levy, Jr., California	Loreto Baja, California, Mex.
12 lb.	50 lbs., 11 oz.	July 15, 1967	Ron Zollinger, California	Rancho Bueno Vista, Baja California, Mex.

SAILFISH (Atlantic)

Line Test	Weight	Date Caught	Angler	Waters Caught
2 lb.	Open			
4 lb.	Open			
6 lb.	54 lbs., 0 oz.	Jan. 25, 1974	Jacqueline Knight, Pennsylvania	Florida
8 lb.	57 lbs., 8 oz.	Nov. 24, 1968	Stu Apte, Florida	Marathon, Florida
10 lb.	73 lbs., 0 oz.	June 25, 1970	Jeffery Cicero, Florida	Miami, Florida
12 lb.	81 lbs., 8 oz.	Jan. 5, 1973	Seth Sizer, Tennessee	Florida

SAILFISH (Pacific)

Line Test	Weight	Date Caught	Angler	Waters Caught
2 lb.	Open			
4 lb.	95 lbs., 0 oz.	Apr. 10, 1968	Stu Apte, Florida	Pinas Bay, Panama

Line Test	Weight	Date Caught	Angler	Waters Caught
6 lb.	123 lbs., 1 oz.	Apr. 24, 1959	Ben Rodkin, California	Mazatlan, Mexico
8 lb.	128 lbs., 0 oz.	May 24, 1960	Evelyn Fuller, California	Mazatlan, Mexico
10 lb.	132 lbs., 0 oz.	Dec. 11, 1958	George Ramsey, California	Mazatlan, Mexico
12 lb.	145 lbs., 0 oz.	Mar. 14, 1955	Dr. E. A. Hershman, California	Mazatlan, Mexico

SALMON (Chinook)

Line Test	Weight	Date Caught	Angler	Waters Caught
2 lb.	25 lbs., 8 oz.	Sept. 2, 1966	John Smart, Washington	Double Bluff, Washington
4 lb.	45 lbs., 0 oz.	Sept. 22, 1969	John Smart, Washington	Marrowstone Island, Washington
6 lb.	54 lbs., 2 oz.	May 24, 1972	John Smart, Washington	Whidby Isle, Washington
8 lb.	55 lbs., 4 oz.	Sept. 21, 1963	J. A. Bell, Sr., Canada	Alberni Inlet, B. C., Canada
10 lb.	42 lbs., 8 oz.	July 10, 1955	Herman Hudson, Oregon	Coos Bay, Oregon
12 lb.	56 lbs., 0 oz.	Oct. 16, 1955	Al Weismeyer, California	Smith River, Oregon

SALMON (Silver)

Line Test	Weight	Date Caught	Angler	Waters Caught
2 lb.	18 lbs., 5 oz.	Oct. 29, 1966	John Smart, Washington	Whidby Isle, Washington
4 lb.	22 lbs., 12 oz.	Oct. 27, 1968	John Smart, Washington	Whidby Isle, Washington
6 lb.	23 lbs., 10 oz.	Sept. 25, 1966	John Smart, Washington	Quillayuter, Washington
8 lb.	26 lbs., 14 oz.	Oct. 18, 1971	John Smart, Washington	Hoods Canal, Washington
10 lb.	20 lbs., 0 oz.	July 25, 1967	Oscar Hagen, California	Shelter Cove, California
12 lb.	22 lbs., 8 oz.	July 27, 1953	Henry Helmuth, California	Trinidad, California

SHAD (American)

Line Test	Weight	Date Caught	Angler	Waters Caught
2 lb.	4 lbs., 4 oz.	Mar. 1, 1972	Robert McCollum, Jr., Florida	St. Johns River, Florida
4 lb.	7 lbs., 12 oz.	May 11, 1974	C. H. Knerr, Pennsylvania	Pennsylvania
6 lb.	5 lbs., 10 oz.	May 31, 1968	R. N. Schiesmayer	Feather River, California
8 lb.	6 lbs., 4 oz.	May 27, 1971	David Bonser, Pennsylvania	Delaware River, Delaware

TIE

Line Test	Weight	Date Caught	Angler	Waters Caught
8 lb.	6 lbs., 4 oz.	May 9, 1968	Wm. Spaulding, Sr., Massachusetts	Indian River, Massachusetts
10 lb.	5 lbs., 3 oz.	June 6, 1967	Henry Drew, Massachusetts	Connecticut River, Massachusetts
12 lb.	7 lbs., 10 oz.	May 17, 1968	Wm. Spaulding, Sr., Massachusetts	Indian River, Massachusetts

SHARK (Mako)

Line Test	Weight	Date Caught	Angler	Waters Caught
2 lb.	21 lbs., 12 oz.	Feb. 7, 1967	A. C. Andreson, N. Z.	Ti Point N. I., N. Z.
4 lb.	Open			
6 lb.	31 lbs., 4 oz.	Aug. 29, 1960	Bob Dragoo, California	Paradise Cove, California
8 lb.	Open			
10 lb.	23 lbs., 12 oz.	Sept. 25, 1971	Richard McIver, Florida	Steward, Florida
12 lb.	261 lbs., 11 oz.	Oct. 1, 1953	Chuck Meyer, New York	Montauk Point, L. I., New York

SHARK (Thresher)

Line Test	Weight	Date Caught	Angler	Waters Caught
2 lb.	Open			
4 lb.	20 lbs., 1 oz.	June 19, 1960	Clifford Garver, California	San Pedro, California
6 lb.	89 lbs., 0 oz.	June 4, 1969	Tom Miller, California	Hermosa Beach, California
8 lb.	40 lbs., 0 oz.	May 29, 1969	Henry Galle, California	Hermosa Beach, California
10 lb.	Open			
12 lb.	Open			

Line Test	Weight	Date Caught	Angler	Waters Caught
SNAPPER (Mutton)				
2 lb.	Open			
4 lb.	11 lbs., 8 oz.	Aug. 24, 1971	Hugh Anderson, Florida	Key West, Florida
6 lb.	13 lbs., 12 oz.	July 16, 1972	Marcia Maizler, Florida	Key West, Florida
8 lb.	14 lbs., 9 oz.	Apr. 30, 1968	Dave Chambers, Jr., Florida	Biscayne Bay, Florida
10 lb.	20 lbs., 0 oz.	Nov. 18, 1970	Bill Kieldsen, Florida	Key Biscayne, Florida
12 lb.	26 lbs., 0 oz.	Mar. 10, 1973	J. Stewart	Florida
SNAPPER (Yellowtail)				
2 lb.	1 lb., 6 oz.	May 5, 1970	C. W. Adams, M.D., Tennessee	Big Pine Key, Florida
4 lb.	2 lbs., 8 oz.	Sept. 20, 1969	Dr. James Robertson, Florida	Bimini, Bahamas
6 lb.	2 lbs., 8 oz.	Dec. 15, 1973	Leslie Turner	Florida
8 lb.	5 lbs., 8 oz.	Apr. 21, 1974	Crawford Adams, Tennessee	Florida
10 lb.	4 lbs., 9 oz.	Apr. 21, 1974	C. W. Adams, M.D., Tennessee	Florida
12 lb.	5 lbs., 3 oz.	Dec. 15, 1973	J. R. Cooper, Michigan	
SNOOK				
2 lb.	11 lbs., 9 oz.	Feb. 11, 1961	Leonard Hartman, Florida	Caloosahatchee River, Florida
4 lb.	39 lbs., 8 oz.	July 16, 1973	D. Chermanski, Florida	Florida
6 lb.	26 lbs., 12 oz.	June 6, 1964	Theodore Eggers, Florida	Lake Worth, Florida
8 lb.	33 lbs., 12 oz.	May 7, 1972	Lewis Newkirk, Florida	S. Fork, St. Lucia R.
10 lb.	30 lbs., 0 oz.	July 29, 1959	Chas. Warwick, III, Florida	Lake Worth, Florida
12 lb.	36 lbs., 0 oz.	Sept. 26, 1969	Donald Dobbins, Florida	Costa Rica
TARPON				
2 lb.	17 lbs., 5 oz.	Mar. 14, 1966	Fred Johnson, Alabama	Bahia Honda Key, Florida
4 lb.	20 lbs., 11 oz.	Aug. 2, 1972	Henry Ogden, Georgia	Marathon, Florida
6 lb.	88 lbs., 0 oz.	May 17, 1955	Chuck Meyer, New York	Summerland Key, Florida
8 lb.	91 lbs., 0 oz.	Mar. 7, 1971	Alfredo Bequillard, Jr.	Tarpon Camp, Nicaragua
10 lb.	115 lbs., 0 oz.	Aug. 18, 1958	Gus Getner, Texas	Port Isabel, Texas
12 lb.	103 lbs., 4 oz.	Apr. 4, 1970	Franz Johansen, Utah	Marathon, Florida
TOTUAVA				
2 lb.	Open			
4 lb.	Open			
6 lb.	Open			
8 lb.	16 lbs., 2 oz.	May 27, 1969	Chuck Berto, California	Puertecitos, Baja California, Mex.
10 lb.	20 lbs., 6 oz.	Mar. 11, 1958	Harold Lane, California	San Felipe, Baja California, Mex.
12 lb.	28 lbs., 14 oz.	Feb. 24, 1962	Bob Dragoo, California	Puertecitos, Baja California, Mex.
TRIPLETAIL				
2 lb.	7 lbs., 2 oz.	June 25, 1966	Gerald Braden, Florida	St. James, Florida
4 lb.	14 lbs., 0 oz.	Oct. 1, 1965	Gerald Braden, Florida	San Carlos Bay, Florida
6 lb.	24 lbs., 4 oz.	May 20, 1965	Gerald Braden, Florida	Caloosahatchee River, Florida
8 lb.	20 lbs., 14 oz.	Aug. 9, 1967	Brownie Hayes, Florida	Pine Isle, Florida
10 lb.	18 lbs., 8 oz.	July 28, 1968	Loretta Rollins, Florida	Pine Isle, Florida
12 lb.	32 lbs., 0 oz.	Sept. 28, 1960	Clarence Wiederecht, La.	Venice, Louisiana

Line Test	Weight	Date Caught	Angler	Waters Caught
TUNA (Blackfin)				
2 lb.	Open			
4 lb.	13 lbs., 2 oz.	Aug. 6, 1972	Robert Metz, Florida	Bimini Isl.
6 lb.	7 lbs., 14 oz.	Jan. 31, 1971	Dale Leverone, Florida	Homestead, Florida
8 lb.	14 lbs., 3 oz.	May 1, 1974	Jay Wright, Jr.	Florida
10 lb.	15 lbs., 2 oz.	Nov. 22, 1968	Stu Apte, Florida	Marathon, Florida
12 lb.	19 lbs., 4 oz.	Mar. 16, 1974	Mike Leverone	Florida
TUNA (Bluefin)				
2 lb.	Open			
4 lb.	16 lbs., 0 oz.	Sept. 20, 1953	A. E. Moore, California	Guadalupe Isl., Mexico
6 lb.	15 lbs., 6 oz.	Aug. 26, 1962	Harry Vickers, California	San Diego, California
8 lb.	22 lbs., 3 oz.	July 15, 1970	Dan Bartfield, California	Coronado Isle, Mexico
10 lb.	28 lbs., 0 oz.	July 17, 1957	Ralph Chevalier, California	Long Beach, California
12 lb.	30 lbs., 4 oz.	Oct. 7, 1956	Glenn Bracken, California	Catalina Isl., Valifornia
12 lb.	30 lbs., 4 oz.	Oct. 7, 1956	Glenn Bracken, California	Catalina Isl., California
TUNA (Little)				
2 lb.	5 lbs., 7 oz.	Nov. 5, 1960	G. O. Thorne, Florida	Panama City Beach, Florida
4 lb.	14 lbs., 4 oz.	Nov. 20, 1971	Ray Cantarrana, Jr., Florida	Clear Water, Florida
6 lb.	15 lbs., 2 oz.	Sept. 18, 1965	Wm. Rosenthal, Pennsylvania	Barnegat, New Jersey
8 lb.	19 lbs., 0 oz.	May 27, 1960	Dick Craik, Florida	Panama City Beach, Florida
10 lb.	18 lbs., 9 oz.	July 18, 1959	Robert Ryder, Florida	Palm Beach, Florida
12 lb.	19 lbs., 0 oz.	Feb. 8, 1959	William Yamashita, Hawaii	Waianae, Oahu, Hawaii
TUNA (Yellowfin)				
2 lb.	Open			
4 lb.	5 lbs., 6 oz.	Sept. 7, 1970	Ray Acord, California	Koror, Palau, Trust Terr.
6 lb.	23 lbs., 11 oz.	July 16, 1967	Bernard Zwilling, California	Bancho Rueno Vista, Baja California, Mex.
8 lb.	18 lbs., 3 oz.	Sept. 25, 1960	Chet Umberham, California	Newport Beach, California
10 lb.	26 lbs., 6 oz.	Dec. 21, 1960	N. R. Rehm, California	Cabo San Lucas, Baja Cal., Mex.
12 lb.	27 lbs., 3 oz.	July 16, 1967	Ron Zollinger, California	Rancho Bueno Vista, Baja California, Mex.
WAHOO				
2 lb.	Open			
4 lb.	13 lbs., 9 oz.	July 15, 1974	Robert Griffin, Sr.	Panama
6 lb.	15 lbs., 8 oz.	July 15, 1973	Stu Apte, Florida	Panama
8 lb.	22 lbs., 2 oz.	Sept. 23, 1972	Gordon Prentice, California	Punta Colorado, Mexico
10 lb.	38 lbs., 8 oz.	Mar. 18, 1970	R. O. Acord, California	Koror, Palau
12 lb.	51 lbs., 0 oz.	Apr. 17, 1971	Lewis Carroll, M.D., Florida	Cay Sal, Bahamas
WEAKFISH				
2 lb.	8 lbs., 5 oz.	Apr. 30, 1959	S. F. Still, Florida	Banana River, Florida
4 lb.	10 lbs., 7 oz.	Apr. 6, 1969	John Yockel, Florida	Port Canaveral, Florida
6 lb.	12 lbs., 3 oz.	May 18, 1974	Ed Hansen, New Jersey	Delaware Bay, Delaware
8 lb.	14 lbs., 3 oz.	Feb. 21, 1974	Les Mowry	Florida
10 lb.	12 lbs., 12 oz.	Dec. 17, 1973	R. J. Dwyer	Florida
12 lb.	12 lbs., 9 oz.	May 11, 1957	Gus Getner, Texas	Arroyo Colorado, Texas

Line Test	Weight	Date Caught	Angler	Waters Caught
WHITE SEABASS				
2 lb.	3 lbs., 12 oz.	Apr. 14, 1957	R. C. Salamon, California	Dana Point, California
4 lb.	12 lbs., 5 oz.	Aug. 20, 1958	Dr. E. A. Hershman, California	San Onofre, California
6 lb.	38 lbs., 14 oz.	May 20, 1952	Rex York, California	Coronados Isl., California
8 lb.	35 lbs., 8 oz.	July 19, 1953	Wilfred Sargent, California	San Clemente, California
10 lb.	45 lbs., 8 oz.	July 15, 1959	John Mullen, California	Point Mugu, California
12 lb.	65 lbs., 0 oz.	July 8, 1955	Costa Aronis, California	Ensenada, Baja California, Mexico
YELLOWTAIL				
2 lb.	12 lbs., 6 oz.	Aug. 23, 1959	Bob Dragoo, California	Ensenada, Baja California, Mexico
4 lb.	26 lbs., 4 oz.	Apr. 27, 1957	Floyd Randolph, California	Torrey Pines, California
6 lb.	26 lbs., 6 oz.	Oct. 11, 1962	Willis Carr, California	La Jolla, California
8 lb.	22 lbs., 8 oz.	Feb. 25, 1958	Dr. E. A. Hershman, California	Rancho Buena Vista, Baja, California, Mexico
10 lb.	42 lbs., 0 oz.	Apr. 7, 1955	Albert Zapanta, California	Rancho Buena Vista, Baja, California, Mexico
12 lb.	36 lbs., 15 oz.	Mar. 20, 1974	Hugh Robertson, North Dakota	Baja, California

CHAPTER 43
State Fishing Records

ALABAMA

Species	Weight	Where	When	Angler
BASS, Largemouth	13 lbs., 14 ozs.	Private Pond	Jan. 31, 1974	Johnny Duncan
BASS, Redeye	6 lbs., ½ oz.	Hallawakee Creek	Mar. 24, 1967	Thomas Sharpe
BASS, Smallmouth	10 lbs., 8 ozs.	Wheeler Dam	Oct. 8, 1950	Owen Smith
BASS, Spotted	8 lbs., 10½ ozs.	Lewis Smith Lake	Feb. 25, 1972	Billy Henderson
BASS, Striped (Rockfish)	55 lbs.	Tallassee		Charles Totty
BASS, White	4 lbs., 4 ozs.	Lake Jordan	Apr. 7, 1972	Donald Connell
BLUEGILL	4 lbs., 12 ozs.	Ketona Lake	Apr. 9, 1950	T. S. Hudson
BOWFIN	16 lbs., 2 ozs.	Lake Eufaula	Sept. 2, 1970	Bill Bergloff
BUFFALO	16 lbs., 15 ozs.	Lake Jordan	July 23, 1974	Craig Kelley
CARP	24 lbs., 8 ozs.	Lake Eufaula	May 14, 1973	Robert Purswell
CATFISH, Channel	40 lbs.	Inland Lake	June 17, 1967	Donald Cox
CATFISH, Flathead	40 lbs.	Tallapoosa River	Oct. 4, 1973	S. C. Butler
CATFISH, Spoonbill	35 lbs.	Warrior River	June 24, 1973	William Burleson
CRAPPIE	3 lbs., 13 ozs.	Rock Mountain Lake	June 1, 1974	Toni Dahlrot
DRUM, Freshwater	26 lbs.	Lake Jordan	Feb. 22, 1970	Larry Roberts
GAR, Alligator	120 lbs.	Mobile Bay	July 18, 1974	Archie Denton
GAR, Longnose	25 lbs., 8 ozs.	Lake Eufaula	Aug. 26, 1973	Paul Shirley
MUSKELLUNGE	19 lbs., 8 ozs.	Below Wilson Dam, Tenn. River	Dec. 31, 1972	Steve Leatherwood
PICKEREL, Chain	5 lbs., 8 ozs.	Lake Eufaula	Feb. 7, 1971	Benny Meadows
SAUGER	5 lbs., 2 ozs.	Wilson Dam	Mar. 5, 1972	William Huntley
SUNFISH, Redear	4 lbs., 4 ozs.	Chattahoochee State Park	May 5, 1962	Jeff Lashley
TROUT, Rainbow	5 lbs., 13½ ozs.	Below Lewis Smith Res.	Aug. 16, 1973	Jimmy Phillips
WALLEYE	8 lbs., 4 ozs.	Tallapoosa River	May 17, 1970	Curtis Fannin
WARMOUTH	1 lb., 5 ozs.	Private Pond	June 12, 1972	R. W. Phillippi

ALASKA

Freshwater Species	Weight	Where	When	Angler
BURBOT	22 lbs., 8 ozs.	Lake Louise	1968	Robert Bronson
CHAR, Arctic	17 lbs., 8 ozs.	Wulik River	1968	Peter Winslow
GRAYLING, Arctic	4 lbs., 3 ozs.	Ugashik Lake	1973	John McLay
PIKE, Northern	28 lbs., 2 ozs.	Wilson Lake	1971	Elmer Kurrus, Jr.
SHEEFISH	52 lbs., ½ oz.	Kobuk River	1968	Jim Keeline
TROUT, Cutthroat	6 lbs., 12 ozs.	Orchard Lake	1973	Muriel Ulmer
TROUT, Lake	47 lbs.	Clarence Lake	1970	Daniel Thorsness
TROUT, Rainbow	42 lbs., 2 ozs.	Bell Island	1970	David White
WHITEFISH	5 lbs., 8 ozs.	Naknek River	1973	Merland Clark

Saltwater Species	Weight	Where	When	Angler
HALIBUT	340 lbs.	Thomas Bay	1971	George Rice
SALMON, Chum	24 lbs., 4 ozs.	Margarita Bay	1974	Dick Coleman
SALMON, King	87 lbs.	Favorite Bay	1971	Orville Carter
SALMON, Pink	11 lbs., 9 ozs.	Montana Creek	1973	John Nielson
SALMON, Red	14 lbs., 8 ozs.	Kenai River	1973	Alwin Krause
SALMON, Silver	23 lbs., 10 ozs.	Behm Narrows	1973	John Lincoln

ARIZONA

Species	Weight	Where	When	Angler
BASS, Largemouth	14 lbs., 2 ozs.	Roosevelt Lake	1956	Ed Smith
BASS, Smallmouth	4 lbs., 12 ozs.	Bartlett Lake	July, 1973	Bill Rood
BASS, Striped	47 lbs., 0.5 oz.	Colorado River	May, 1972	Ed Higgins
BASS, White (World Record)	5 lbs., 5 ozs.	Imperial Reservoir	March, 1972	Norman Mize
BASS, Yellow	1 lb., 6 ozs.	Saguaro Lake	May, 1972	Joe Stone
BLUEGILL	3 lbs., 5 ozs.	San Carlos Reservation	1965	Ernest Garcia
CATFISH, Blue	31 lbs.	Randolph Park	July 1970	Richard Lujan
CATFISH, Channel	35 lbs., 4 ozs.	Topock Swamp	1952	Wando Tull
CATFISH, Flathead	65 lbs.	San Carlos Lake	1951	Pat Coleman
CRAPPIE, Black	4 lbs., 10 ozs.	San Carlos Lake	1959	John Shadrick
CRAPPIE, White	2 lbs., 0.4 oz.	Bartlett Lake	Nov., 1973	Gary Bees
PIKE, Northern	21 lbs., 4 ozs.	Lake Mary	June, 1974	Norman Nicklin
TROUT, Brown	17 lbs.	Lake Powell	May, 1971	Chuck Holland
TROUT, Rainbow	21 lbs., 5.5 ozs.	River, Willow Beach	Sept., 1966	John Reid
WALLEYE	7 lbs., 0.7 oz.	Saguaro Lake	June, 1972	W. F. Lindsey

ARKANSAS

Species	Weight	Where	When	Angler
BASS, Largemouth	13 lbs., 2 ozs.	Lake Bull Shoals	May 29, 1973	Robert Brenkman
BASS, Rock	1 lb., 6½ ozs.	Lake Norfork	May 5, 1963	Randy Screws

Species	Weight	Where	When	Angler
BASS, Smallmouth	7 lbs., 5 ozs.	Lake Bull Shoals	Apr. 1, 1969	Acie Dickerson
BASS, Spotted (Ky.)	6 lbs., 9 ozs.	Lake Bull Shoals	Apr. 1, 1971	Joe Huff
BASS, Striped	40 lbs.	Lake Ouachita	Apr. 25, 1971	Bill Bars
BASS, Warmouth	1 lb., 7 ozs.	Spring River	Sept. 25, 1965	Jay Kaffka
BASS, White	4 lbs., 15 ozs.	White River	May 8, 1969	Bud Stopple
BLUEGILL	2 lbs., 1 oz.	Farm Pond	May 2, 1974	Danny Sexton
CATFISH, Blue	47 lbs., 8 ozs.	Arkansas River	May 28, 1970	Richard Been
CATFISH, Channel	18 lbs.	Lake Fayetteville	Mar. 27, 1963	Elmer Powers
CATFISH, Flathead	48 lbs.	Arkansas River	May 2, 1974	Leon Burke
CRAPPIE, Black	3 lbs., 14 ozs.	Scroggins Lake	Mar. 16, 1966	Junior Berryman
CRAPPIE, White	4 lbs.	Okolona Stock Pond	Mar. 21, 1969	Charlie Jones
GAR, Alligator	215 lbs.	Arkansas River	July 31, 1964	Alvin Bonds
PICKEREL, Chain	5 lbs.	Little Red River	May 23, 1971	Harvey Darnell
PIKE, Northern	16 lbs., 1 oz.	Degray Reservoir	Dec. 27, 1973	Dick Cooley
SAUGER	3 lbs., 15 ozs.	Lake Norfork	Mar. 23, 1967	Lucille Cantwell
SUNFISH, Green	1 lb., 7½ ozs.	Batesville Stock Pond	Aug. 10, 1973	John Hunt
SUNFISH, Longear	7 ozs.	Melwood Old River Lake	May 15, 1971	Bill McCaughan
SUNFISH, Redear	2 lbs., 8 ozs.	Lake Boswell	Oct. 30, 1961	Charlie Henderson
TROUT, Brown	31 lbs., 8 ozs.	White River	May 24, 1972	Troy Lackey
TROUT, Rainbow	16 lbs., 12 ozs.	North Fork River	July 1, 1972	Raymond Sullivan
WALLEYE	19 lbs., 12 ozs.	White River	Feb. 12, 1963	Mrs. L. E. Garrison

CALIFORNIA

Freshwater Species	Weight	Where	When	Angler
BASS, Largemouth	20 lbs., 15 ozs.	Lake Miramar	June 23, 1973	Dave Zimmerlee
BASS, Smallmouth	7 lbs., 11 ozs.	Trapper Slough	Nov. 16, 1951	C. H. Richey
BASS, Striped	65 lbs.	San Joaquin River	May 16, 1951	Wendell Olson
BASS, White	5 lbs., 5 ozs.	Ferguson Lake	Mar. 8, 1972	Milton Mize
BLUEGILL	2 lbs., 9 ozs.	Middle Legg Lake	July 4, 1971	Willi Mae McKinney
CARP	52 lbs.	Nacimento Lake	Apr., 1968	Lee Bryant
CATFISH, Channel	41 lbs.	Lake Casitas	Aug. 24, 1972	Joe Creek
CATFISH, Flathead	51 lbs., 8 ozs.	Colorado River	Mar. 18, 1973	Robert Adams
CATFISH, White	15 lbs., 1 oz.	Snodgrass Slough	June 1, 1951	O. J. McArdle
CORVINA, Orangemouth	32 lbs., 8 ozs.	Salton Sea	May 11, 1960	Dick Paul
CRAPPIE, Black	4 lbs.	Mendota Pool	Mar. 16, 1956	Alex Berg
CRAPPIE, White	4 lbs., 8 ozs.	Clear Lake	Apr. 26, 1971	Carol Carlton
SALMON, King	85 lbs.	Feather River	Oct., 1935	Manford Cochran
SALMON, Kokanee	4 lbs., 13 ozs.	Lake Tahoe	Aug. 1, 1973	Dick Bournique
SALMON, Silver	22 lbs.	Paper Mill Creek	Jan. 3, 1959	Milton Hain
SHAD, American	6 lbs., 15 ozs.	Yuba River	June 7, 1970	Hal Janssen
STURGEON, White	420 lbs.	Sacramento River	Apr. 30, 1973	Armond Baggett
TROUT, Brook, Eastern	9 lbs., 12 ozs.	Silver Lake	Sept. 9, 1932	Texas Haynes
TROUT, Brown	25 lbs., 11 ozs.	Crowley Lake	July 1, 1971	Richard Reinwald
TROUT, Cutthroat	31 lbs., 8 ozs.	Lake Tahoe	1911	William Pomin

Freshwater Species	Weight	Where	When	Angler
TROUT, Dolly Varden	9 lbs., 1 oz.	McCloud Reservoir	May, 1968	James Scott
TROUT, Golden	9 lbs., 8 ozs.	Virginia Lake	Aug. 18, 1952	O. A. Benefield
TROUT, Lake	37 lbs., 6 ozs.	Lake Tahoe	June 21, 1974	Robert Aronsen
TROUT, Rainbow	25 lbs., 8 ozs.	Smith River	Jan. 20, 1973	Raymond Robinson

Saltwater Species	Weight	Where	When	Angler
BARRACUDA, California	15 lbs., 15 ozs.	San Onofre	Aug. 24, 1957	C. O. Taylor
BASS, Giant Sea	503 lbs.	Anacapa Island	July 23, 1956	M. C. Peters
BASS, Kelp	14 lbs., 7 ozs.	San Clemente Island	July 30, 1958	C. O. Taylor
BASS, Sand	9 lbs., 2 ozs.	Dana Point	June 23, 1973	Brian Nantais
BASS, White Sea	77 lbs., 4 ozs.	San Diego	Apr. 8, 1950	H. P. Bledsoe
BONITO	16 lbs., 15 ozs.	Coronado Island	July 25, 1953	Herbert Juenke
CABEZON	23 lbs., 4 ozs.	Los Angeles	Apr. 20, 1958	Bruce Kuhn
CROAKER, Spotfin	14 lbs.	Playa Del Rey	Sept. 24, 1951	Charles Dusart
HALIBUT	40 lbs.	Catalina Island	Apr. 23 1972	C. F. Breslin
LINGCOD	53 lbs.	Trinidad	1969	Steve Hedglin
MARLIN, Blue	672 lbs.	Balboa	Aug. 18, 1931	A. Hamann
OPALEYE	6 lbs., 1¼ ozs.	Los Flores Creek	May 13, 1956	Leonard Itkoff
RAY, Bat	158 lbs.	Elkhorn Slough	Mar. 15, 1972	Robert Goulart
SALMON, Silver	33 lbs., 8 ozs.	Newport Beach	Sept. 9, 1970	Harry Bouchard
SHARK, Bonito	298 lbs., 8 ozs.	Anacapa Island	July 20, 1970	Jack Cleric
SHARK, Thresher	380 lbs.	Los Angeles	Apr. 28, 1970	Henry Galle
SHARK, Blue	195 lbs.	Catalina Island	1969	Gerald Borges
SHEEPHEAD	26 lbs., 5 ozs.	Paradise Cove	Nov. 30, 1958	Tom Reynolds
SWORDFISH, Broadbill	337 lbs., 12 ozs.	San Clemente	July 6, 1958	Keith Grover
TUNA, Albacore	42 lbs., 8 ozs.	San Diego	Aug. 15, 1971	Tom Forbes
TUNA, Bluefin	71 lbs., 4 ozs.	San Diego	Sept. 13, 1972	Lee Bays
TUNA, Pacific Bigeye	194 lbs., 8 ozs.	Laguna Beach	Sept. 13, 1971	Ray Prothro, Jr.
TUNA, Yellowfin	218 lbs.	San Diego	Sept. 13, 1970	Charles Bales
TUNA, Skipjack	26 lbs.	San Diego	Aug. 28, 1970	William Hall
YELLOWTAIL	62 lbs.	La Jolla	June 6, 1953	George Willett

COLORADO

Species	Weight	Where	When	Angler
BASS, Largemouth	9 lbs., 6 ozs.	Cherry Creek Reservoir	1970	Richard Gassaway
BASS, Smallmouth	3 lbs., 14 ozs.	Kluver Reservoir	1971	Steven Schroeder
BASS, Striped	6 lbs., 12 ozs.	N. Sterling Reservoir	1974	Harley Nosler
BASS, White	4 lbs., 7 ozs.	Blue Lake	1963	Pedro Martinez
BLUEGILL	1 lb., 5 ozs.	Farm Pond	1972	Melvin Hanners
BULLHEAD, Black	2 lbs., 6.4 ozs.	Alexander Pond	1972	Tom Powell
CARP	22 lbs.	Cherry Creek Reservoir	1973	August Raisch
CATFISH, Blue	16 lbs., 8 ozs.	Upper Queen's Lake	1974	Pete Driskil
CATFISH, Channel	33 lbs., 4 ozs.	Nee Noshe Reservoir	1973	Russell Good

Species	Weight	Where	When	Angler
CRAPPIE	3 lbs.	Kendrick Reservoir	1971	Dave Wood
DRUM	11 lbs., 10.3 ozs.	Two Buttes Reservoir	1972	Doug Thompson
PIKE, Northern	30 lbs., 1 oz.	Vallecito Reservoir	1971	Earl Walden
SALMON, Kokanee	3 lbs., 15.5 ozs.	11 Mile Reservoir	1972	H. A. Freeman
TROUT, Brook	7 lbs., 10 ozs.		1940's	George Knorr
TROUT, Brown	24 lbs., 10 ozs.	Vallecito Reservoir	1972	William Young
TROUT, Golden	1 lb., 4 ozs.	Upper Crystal Lake	1974	Thomas Walker
TROUT, Grayling	1 lb., 7 ozs.	Zimmerman Lake	1974	Darrell Siekman
TROUT, Mackinaw	36 lbs.	Deep Lake	1949	R. H. Wisley
TROUT, Native	16 lbs.	Twin Lakes	1964	George Hranchek
TROUT, Rainbow	18 lbs., 5.25 ozs.	S. Platte River	1972	Richard Brandl
TROUT, Splake	16 lbs., 12 ozs.	Island Lake	1973	Del Canty
WALLEYE	16 lbs., 8 ozs.	Cherry Creek Reservoir	1973	Julius Steuer
WHITEFISH	3 lbs., 11.75 ozs.	Roaring Fork River	1973	Del Cesko

CONNECTICUT

Species	Weight	Where	When	Angler
BASS, Calico	4 lbs.	Pataganset Lake	1974	James Boos
BASS, Largemouth	12 lbs., 14 ozs.	Mashapaug Lake	1961	Frank Domurat
BASS, Rock	1 lb., 1 oz.	Highland Lake	1973	Albert Beck
BASS, Smallmouth	7 lbs., 10 ozs.	Mashapaug Lake	1954	Frank Domurat
BLUEGILL	2 lbs.	Waskewicz Pond	1974	Scott Rich
BULLHEAD, Brown	2 lbs., 14 ozs.	Pritchard Pond	1968	Albert E. Podzunes, Jr.
CATFISH, White	9 lbs., 13 ozs.	Shaker Pines Lake	1973	Diane Wadsworth
PERCH, White	2 lbs., 8 ozs.	Connecticut River	1961	Barney Walden
PERCH, Yellow	2 lbs., 13 ozs.	Black Pond	1973	Miller Bassett
PICKEREL, Chain	7 lbs., 14 ozs.	Wauregan Reservoir	1969	Charles Loman
PIKE, Northern	17 lbs., 5 ozs.	Bantam Lake	1974	Cindy Gubitose
SHAD	9 lbs., 2 ozs.	Connecticut River	1973	Edward Nelson
TROUT, Brook	4 lbs., 6 ozs.	Housatonic River	1950	Fred Mazzafemo
TROUT, Brown	16 lbs., 4 ozs.	Mashapaug Lake	1968	Albert Jarish
TROUT, Lake	29 lbs., 13 ozs.	Wononscopomuc Lake	1918	Dr. Thompson
TROUT, Rainbow	9 lbs., 7 ozs.	Saugatuck Reservoir	1962	Ed Mayo
TROUT, Sea	9 lbs., 10 ozs.	Golden Spur	1968	Albert DeLoge
TROUT, Tiger	4 lbs., 15 ozs.	Farmington River	1972	Stephen Chirico
WALLEYE	14 lbs., 8 ozs.	Candlewood Lake	1941	George Britto

DELAWARE

Freshwater Species	Weight	Where	When	Angler
BASS, Largemouth	9 lbs., 8 ozs.	Noxontown Pond	Apr. 25, 1969	John Moore
BASS, Smallmouth	5 lbs., 5 ozs.	Red Mill Pond	July 25, 1968	Ronald Holmes
BLUEGILL	1 lb., 8 ozs.	Courseys Pond	Apr. 25, 1972	Robert Robarge

Freshwater Species	Weight	Where	When	Angler
CRAPPIE	3 lbs., 3 ozs.	Noxontown Pond	May 13, 1967	Harry Nicholson III
PERCH, White	1 lb., 13 ozs.	Reynolds Pond	Oct. 17, 1970	Helma Ranka
PERCH, Yellow	1 lb., 12 ozs.	Nanticoke River	Mar. 23, 1969	Alexander Rybicki
TIES				
	1 lb., 12 ozs.	Millsboro	Dec. 4, 1971	Robert Widerman
	1 lb., 12 ozs.	Silver Lake	Mar. 14, 1972	John Haug
PICKEREL, Chain	7 lbs., 3 ozs.	Horseys Pond	Apr. 22, 1972	Earl Messick
SHAD, White	6 lbs., 12 ozs.	Brandywine	May 2, 1972	Bayard Conaway
TROUT, Freshwater	5 lbs., 3 ozs.	Mill Creek	Apr. 9, 1973	Harold Fisher

Saltwater Species	Weight	Where	When	Angler
ALBACORE, False	17 lbs.	Atlantic Ocean	Oct. 9, 1971	John Mentzer
BASS, Channel	68¾ lbs.	Slaughter Beach	May 21, 1971	William Sollars
BASS, Sea	3 lbs., 12 ozs.		Aug. 7, 1971	Peter Smulski
BASS, Striped	47 lbs.	Hawks Nest	Apr. 14, 1972	Bobby Parker
BLUEFISH	20 lbs., 4 ozs.	Indian River Inlet	Aug. 16, 1973	Stephen Dunn
COD	43 lbs.	S. of "B" Buoy	Jan. 17, 1971	Linford Palmer
DOLPHIN	34 lbs.	S.E. Indian River	Sept. 6, 1971	Tim Good
DRUM, Black	76 lbs.	Mispillion	June 1, 1968	Carson Stoneman
FLOUNDER	17 lbs., 1 oz.	Masseys Landing	July 7, 1968	Albert Leager
KINGFISH	4 lbs.	Bethany Beach	Oct. 13, 1973	Billy Hastings
MACKEREL, Atlantic	2 lbs., 3 ozs.	Indian River Inlet	Apr. 16, 1972	Russell Ash
TIE				
	2 lbs., 3 ozs.	Indian River Inlet	Apr. 16, 1972	William Wenger
MACKEREL, King	22 lbs., 8 ozs.	Dewey Beach	Oct. 7, 1973	Marvel McWilliams
MARLIN, White	120 lbs.	Balt. Canyon	Sept. 25, 1972	William J. Garner, Jr.
PORGY	3 lbs., 7 ozs.	Brandywine Light	1973	Charles Fitzwater
SHARK	390 lbs.	Bowers Beach	July 29, 1967	Richard Muschamp
TAUTOG	14 lbs., 6½ ozs.	East End Light	Oct. 29, 1971	Don Daisey, Sr.
TROUT, Sea	12 lbs., 10 ozs.	Fowlers Beach	May 19, 1973	Anthony Karpinski
TUNA	153 lbs.	Balt. Canyon	July 3, 1972	Henry Berliner

FLORIDA

(No Records Maintained)

GEORGIA

Species	Weight	Where	When	Angler
BASS, Flint River Smallmouth	6 lbs., 15 ozs.	Flint River	Feb. 20, 1967	James Lewis
BASS, Largemouth (World Record)	22 lbs., 4 ozs.	Montgomery Lake	June 2, 1932	George Perry
BASS, Redeye	2 lbs., 10 ozs.	Jacks River	July 4, 1967	John R. Cockburn, Jr.
BASS, Smallmouth	7 lbs., 2 ozs.	Lake Chatuge	Mar. 28, 1973	Jack Hall

Species	Weight	Where	When	Angler
BASS, Spotted	7 lbs., 8 ozs.	Little Tesnatee River	May 20, 1969	Donald Palmer
BASS, Striped	63 lbs.	Oconee River	May 30, 1967	Kelley Ward
BASS, White	5 lbs., 1 oz.	Lake Lanier	June 16, 1971	J. M. Hobbins
BLUEGILL	3 lbs., 5 ozs.	Shamrock Lake	July 19, 1972	P. F. Gumm
BOWFIN	15 lbs., 12 ozs.		June 4, 1971	W. F. George
TIE				
	15 lbs., 12 ozs.	Tchukolako Lake	Sept. 29, 1973	R. H. Melton
CARP	35 lbs., 12 ozs.	Lake Jackson	1972	Rev. Donald Clark
CATFISH, Channel	44 lbs., 12 ozs.	Altamaha River	May 18, 1972	Bobby Smithwick
CATFISH, Flathead	51 lbs., 15 ozs.	Lake Nottely	June 2, 1969	Hoyt McDaniel
CRAPPIE, Black	4 lbs., 4 ozs.	Acree's Lake	June 1, 1971	Shirley Lavender
CRAPPIE, White	4 lbs., 11 ozs.	Brickyard Lake	May 31, 1972	Lewis Little
MUSKELLUNGE	38 lbs.	Blue Ridge Lake	June, 1957	Rube Golden
PICKEREL, Chain	9 lbs., 6 ozs.		Feb., 1961	Baxley McQuaig, Jr.
SUNFISH, Redear	3 lbs., 1 oz.	McKenzie's Lake	Aug. 8, 1971	John Reid
TROUT, Brook	5 lbs., 5 ozs.	Waters Creek	Sept. 3, 1973	James Harper
TROUT, Brown	18 lbs., 3 ozs.	Rock Creek	May 6, 1967	William Lowery
TROUT, Rainbow	12 lbs., 4 ozs.	Coosawattee River	May 31, 1966	John Whitaker
WALLEYE	11 lbs.	Lake Burton	Apr. 13, 1963	Steven Kenny
WARMOUTH	1 lb., 11 ozs.	Private Pond	1972	Bruce Soles

HAWAII

(No Records Maintained)

IDAHO

Species	Weight	Where	When	Angler
BASS, Largemouth	10 lbs., 15 ozs.	Anderson Lake		Mrs. M. W. Taylor
BASS, Smallmouth	5 lbs., 14 ozs.	Snake River	May, 1962	B. B. Bacharach
BLUEGILL	3 lbs., 8 ozs.	C. J. Strike Reservoir	May, 1966	Darrell Grim
BULLHEAD	2 lbs., 9 ozs.	Farm Pond	May 13, 1967	Charles Carpenter
CATFISH, Channel	21 lbs., 8 ozs.	Snake River	Mar. 27, 1970	Gary Kluksdal
CATFISH, Flathead	28 lbs., 11 ozs.	Snake River	July 31, 1974	Larry Walker
CRAPPIE	2 lbs., 8 ozs.	Shepherd Lake	1954	Mrs. Carl Tifft
LING	14 lbs.	Kootenai River	1954	P. A. Dayton
PERCH	2 lbs., 8 ozs.	Murtaugh Reservoir		Dewey Julian
SALMON, Chinook	45 lbs.	Salmon River	Sept. 5, 1964	Hurbert Staggie
SALMON, Kokanee	5 lbs.	Priest Lake	June 9, 1974	Melissa Stevens
SALMON, Sockeye	5 lbs.	Redfish Lake	Aug. 8, 1970	Mrs. June McCray
STURGEON	394 lbs.	Snake River	1956	Glen Howard
TROUT, Brook	6 lbs., 12¾ ozs.	Henrys Lake	June 24, 1972	Mrs. Denver Littleton
TROUT, Brown	25 lbs., 12 ozs.	Palisades Reservoir	Mar. 23, 1969	Jim McMurtrey
TROUT, Cutthroat	18 lbs., 15 ozs.	Bear Lake	Apr. 30, 1970	Roger Grunig
TROUT, Cutthroat-Rainbow (hybrid)	23 lbs., 4 ozs.	Blackfoot Reservoir	1957	Phil Adderly

Species	Weight	Where	When	Angler
TROUT, Dolly Varden	32 lbs.	Pend Oreille Lake	1959	Nelson Higgins
TROUT, Golden	5 lbs., 2 ozs.	White Sands Lake	1958	George Wolverton
TROUT, Kamloops	37 lbs.	Pend Oreille Lake	1947	Wes Hamlet
TROUT, Lake	57½ lbs.	Priest Lake	Nov. 14, 1971	Lyle McClure
TROUT, Rainbow	19 lbs.	Hayden Lake	1947	R. M. Williams
TROUT, Steelhead	30 lbs., 2 ozs.	Clearwater River	Nov. 23, 1973	Keith Powel
WHITEFISH, Mountain	5 lbs., 4 ozs.	South Fork Payette River	1941	

ILLINOIS

Species	Weight	Where	When	Angler
BASS, Largemouth	12 lbs., 8 ozs.	Carlinville Lake	1969	James Crandall
BASS, Rock	1 lb., 9 ozs.	Strip Mine Lake	May 22, 1968	Eugene Matsko
BASS, Smallmouth	5 lbs., 15½ ozs.	Kankakee River	June 9, 1974	John Bochler
BASS, Spotted	6 lbs., 10 ozs.	Charleston Stone Co. Lake	July 9, 1972	Ron DeHollander
BASS, Striped	16 lbs., 10 ozs.	Olmsted Landing Bayou	Mar. 9, 1974	Rose Marie Blanchard
BASS, White	3 lbs., 13½ ozs.	Baldwin Lake	Mar. 17, 1974	Arthur Webster
BLUEGILL	2 lbs., 10 ozs.	Strip Mine Lake	1963	Rip Sullivan
BUFFALO	48 lbs.	Mississippi River	1936	C. B. Merritt
BULLHEAD, Black	3 lbs., 7 ozs.	Sutton Lake	Mar. 1, 1970	John Cearlock
BULLHEAD, Yellow	5 lbs., 4 ozs.	Fox River	1955	Bill Snow
CARP	42 lbs.	Kankakee River	1928	Clarence Heinze
CATFISH, Blue	65 lbs.	Alton Lake	1956	Ernest Webb
TIE				
	65 lbs.	Alton Lake	1956	Andrew Coats, Jr.
CATFISH, Channel	28 lbs.	Strip Mine Lake	1963	Tom Giles
CATFISH, Flathead	51 lbs.	Hennepin Canal	1950	Les Beyer
CRAPPIE, Black	4 lbs., 4 ozs.	Craig Lake	Apr. 20, 1967	Gilbert Parker
CRAPPIE, White	4 lbs., 7 ozs.	Farm Pond	Apr. 8, 1973	Kevin Dennis
DRUM, Freshwater	35 lbs.	DuQuoin City Lake	1960	Joe Rinella
GAR, Alligator	157 lbs.	Mississippi River	1944	Clarence Cousins & Nudge Collins
GAR, Spotted	7 lbs., 8 ozs.	Lake Chautauqua	Feb. 26, 1973	Edward Kelly
MUSKELLUNGE	22 lbs.	Spring Lake	May 6, 1973	Richard L. Emmons, Jr.
PADDLEFISH	46 lbs., 8 ozs.	Mississippi River	1968	Dick Vant
PERCH, Yellow	2 lbs., 5 ozs.	Atkinson Strip Mine Lake	1951	William Hodgson
PIKE, Northern	20 lbs., 5 ozs.	Near Coal City	Nov. 3, 1974	James Tomsheck
SALMON, Atlantic	6 lbs., 3 ozs.	Lake Michigan	Aug. 7, 1974	Ron Nelson
SALMON, Chinook	32 lbs., 3 ozs.	Lake Michigan	Nov. 11, 1972	Ronald Hagen
SALMON, Coho	20 lbs., 9 ozs.	Lake Michigan	May 24, 1972	Garry VandeVusse
SAUGER	5 lbs., 12½ ozs.	Mississippi River	July 30, 1967	Bill Rolando
STURGEON, Lake	57 lbs., 2 ozs.	Mississippi River	May 23, 1971	John Hicks
SUNFISH, Green (World Record)	2 lbs.	Farm Pond	May 15, 1972	Kenneth Collier, Sr.
SUNFISH, hybrid	2 lbs., 4 ozs.	Farm Pond	May 11, 1974	Charles Robinson

Species	Weight	Where	When	Angler
SUNFISH, Redear	2 lbs., 6½ ozs.	Strip Mine Lake	Sept. 24, 1972	Michael Stairwalt
TROUT, Brook	4 lbs., 1 oz.	Lake Michigan	Nov. 29, 1970	August Bulleri
TROUT, Brown	19 lbs., 6 ozs.	Lake Michigan	June 6, 1973	Curtis Creech
TROUT, Lake	17 lbs., 5 ozs.	Lake Michigan	Sept. 4, 1973	Roger Laird
TROUT, Rainbow	20 lbs., 4 ozs.	Lake Michigan	July 16, 1974	William Ball
WALLEYE	14 lbs.	Kankakee River	1961	Fred Goselin
WARMOUTH (World Record)	1 lb., 13 ozs.	Farm Pond	May 22, 1971	Wesley Mills

INDIANA

Species	Weight	Where	When	Angler
BASS, Largemouth	11 lbs., 11 ozs.	Ferdinand Reservoir	1968	Curt Reynolds
BASS, Rock	3 lbs.	Sugar Creek	1969	David Thomas
BASS, Smallmouth	6 lbs., 8 ozs.	Stream	1970	Jim Connerly
BASS, Spotted	4 lbs., 9 ozs.	Marriott Lake	1970	Charles Underhill
BASS, White	4 lbs., 3 ozs.	Lake Freeman	1965	James Wagner
BLUEGILL	3 lbs., 4 ozs.	Pond	1972	Harold Catey
BOWFIN	13 lbs., 8 ozs.	Stream	1971	Jim Spice & J. Holtsclaw
BULLHEAD	3 lbs., 13 ozs.	Pond	1970	Fred Stewart
CARP	38 lbs., 1 oz.	Lake	1967	Frank Drost
CATFISH, Blue	50 lbs.	White River	1970	Dick Teising
CATFISH, Channel	27 lbs.	Tippecanoe River	1970	Chester Keith
CATFISH, Flathead	79 lbs., 8 ozs.	White River	1966	Glen Simpson
CRAPPIE	4 lbs., 7 ozs.	Pond	1965	Mary Ann Leigh
DRUM, Freshwater	30 lbs.	White River	1963	Garland Fellers
MUSKELLUNGE	12 lbs.	Little Blue River	1965	Jim Vinyard
PERCH, Yellow	1 lb., 11 ozs.	Pond	1966	Jim Harper
PIKE, Northern	26 lbs., 8 ozs.	Lake	1972	Wayne Lewis
SALMON, Chinook	35 lbs.	Lake Michigan	1973	Richard Slamkowski
SALMON, Coho	20 lbs., 12 ozs.	Lake Michigan	1972	John Beutner
SAUGER	5 lbs.	Wabash River	1964	N. L. Merrifeld
SUNFISH, Redear	2 lbs., 11 ozs.	Pond	1964	Joan Janeway
TROUT, Brook	3 lbs., 15 ozs.	Lake Gage	1973	Sonny Bashore
TROUT, Brown	12 lbs., 13 ozs.	Lake Michigan	1972	Ronald Blanton
TROUT, Lake	15 lbs., 12 ozs.	Lake Michigan	1973	Don Halus
TROUT, Rainbow	10 lbs., 2½ ozs.	Lake Gage	1973	Sonny Bashore
TROUT, Steelhead	20 lbs., 11 ozs.	Lake Michigan	1972	Dan Bowen
WALLEYE	13 lbs.	Kankee River	1969	John McEwan

IOWA

Species	Weight	Where	When	Angler
BASS, Largemouth	10 lbs., 5 ozs.	Farm Pond	Aug., 1970	Paul Burgund
BASS, Rock	1 lb., 8 ozs.	Mississippi River	June, 1973	Jim Driscoll
BASS, Smallmouth	6 lbs., 4 ozs.	Upper Iowa River	May, 1973	Duane Duneman

Species	Weight	Where	When	Angler
BASS, White	3 lbs., 14 ozs.	West Okoboji	May, 1972	Bill Born
BLUEGILL	2 lbs., 3 ozs.	Farm Pond	Apr., 1971	Bob Adam
BULLHEAD	4 lbs., 8 ozs.	Farm Pond	Apr., 1966	Dennie Karas
TIE				
	4 lbs., 8 ozs.	Boyer River	Aug., 1971	Ralph Cooney
BUFFALO	43 lbs., 8 ozs.	West Okoboji	Apr., 1974	James Grim
CARP	50 lbs.	Glenwood Lake	May, 1969	Fred Hougland
CATFISH, Channel	30 lbs., 4 ozs.	Viking Lake	Aug., 1974	Glenn Harms
CATFISH, Flathead	62 lbs.	Iowa River	July, 1965	Roger Fairchild
CRAPPIE	4 lbs., 1 oz.	Farm Pond	May, 1969	John Lenhart
MUSKELLUNGE	29 lbs., 8 ozs.	Clear Lake	June, 1974	Cecil Carberry
PADDLEFISH	83 lbs.	DeSoto Bend	May, 1973	Lawrence Bonham
PERCH, Yellow	1 lb., 13 ozs.	Mississippi River	Sept., 1963	Neal Palmer
PIKE, Northern	24 lbs., 15¾ ozs.	Cedar River	Mar., 1974	Kenneth Eastman
SAUGER	5 lbs., 2 ozs.	Mississippi River	Nov., 1963	Art Hurlburt
SHEEPSHEAD	46 lbs.	Spirit Lake	Oct., 1962	R. F. Farran
STURGEON, Shovelnose	12 lbs.	Des Moines River	Apr., 1974	Randy Hemm
TROUT, Brown	12 lbs., 14½ ozs.	Elk Creek	Nov., 1966	Billy Lee
TROUT, Rainbow	13 lbs., 8 ozs.	Richmond Spring	Nov., 1968	C. Melvin Vaughn
WALLEYE	14 lbs., 2 ozs.	Spirit Lake	Oct., 1968	Herbert Aldridge

KANSAS

Species	Weight	Where	When	Angler
BASS, Largemouth	11 lbs., 3 ozs.	Private Lake	Jan. 6, 1965	Charles Prewett
BASS, Smallmouth	2 lbs., 9½ ozs.	Norton Reservoir	May 15, 1972	Mrs. Max Ball
BASS, Spotted (Ky.)	4 lbs., 2 ozs.	Council Grove City Lake	Sept. 9, 1973	Newell Julian
BASS, Striped	16 lbs.	Glen Elder Reservoir	May 19, 1974	Joe Patterson
BASS, White	5 lbs., 4 ozs.	Toronto Reservoir	May 4, 1966	Henry Baker
BLUEGILL	2 lbs., 5 ozs.	Farm Pond	May 26, 1962	Robert Jefferies
BUFFALO	54 lbs., 4 ozs.	Farm Pond	May 24, 1971	Randy Lee
BULLHEAD	5 lbs.	Strip Pit	June 2, 1974	Mary Louise Sachetta
CARP	35 lbs., 4 ozs.	Sand Pit	May 2, 1970	W. Amos Henry
CATFISH, Blue	33 lbs., 12 ozs.	Kansas River	June 21, 1974	Harold Hunsinger & G. D. Chappell, Jr.
CATFISH, Channel	32 lbs.	Gardner City Lake	Aug. 14, 1962	Edward Daily
CATFISH, Flathead	86 lbs., 3 ozs.	Neosho River	Aug. 24, 1966	Ray Wiechert
CRAPPIE, Black	4 lbs., 10 ozs.	Woodson Cty. State Lake	Oct. 21, 1957	Hazel Fey
CRAPPIE, White	4 lbs., ¼ oz.	Farm Pond	Mar. 30, 1964	Frank Miller
DRUM	28 lbs., 2 ozs.	KOP Dam Neosho River	Aug. 12, 1974	Tony Fornelli
GAR	31 lbs., 8 ozs.	Perry Reservoir	May 21, 1974	Ray Schroeder
GOLDEYE	1 lb., 14½ ozs.	Milford Lake	May 20, 1973	Kris Eenhuis
PADDLEFISH	73 lbs.	Neosho River	Apr. 10, 1973	John Krider
PIKE, Northern	24 lbs., 12 ozs.	Council Grove Reservoir	Aug. 28, 1971	Mr. & Mrs. H.A. Bowman
STURGEON	4 lbs.	Kaw River	Nov. 17, 1962	J. W. Keeton
SUNFISH, Green	2 lbs., 2 ozs.	Strip Pit	May 28, 1961	Louis Ferlo
WALLEYE	13 lbs., 1 oz.	Rocky Ford Fishing Area	Mar. 29, 1972	David Watson

KENTUCKY

Species	Weight	Where	When	Angler
BASS, Largemouth	13 lbs., 8 ozs.	Greenbo Lake	Aug. 3, 1966	Delbert Grizzle
BASS, Rock	1 lb., 7 ozs.	Brashears Creek	July 6, 1972	Rondell Pitcock
BASS, Smallmouth (World Record)	11 lbs., 15 ozs.	Dale Hollow Lake	July 11, 1955	David Hayes
BASS, Striped	44 lbs., 4 ozs.	Herrington Lake	July 19, 1970	James Fugate & Ronald Warner
BASS, White	5 lbs.	Kentucky Lake	July 11, 1943	Lorne Eli
TIE				
	5 lbs.	Herrington Lake	June 3, 1957	B. B. Hardin
BLUEGILL	3 lbs., 6 ozs.	Buchanon Pond	May 30, 1955	William Wolley
BOWFIN	3 lbs., 4 ozs.	Kentucky River	June 15, 1971	Gladys Horton
BUFFALO	32 lbs.	Kentucky River	July, 1969	P. Childers
CARP	54 lbs., 14 ozs.	South Fork, Licking River	Mar. 13, 1971	Ricky Vance
CATFISH, Blue	100 lbs.	Tennessee River	Aug. 21, 1970	J. E. Copeland
CATFISH, Channel	15 lbs., 6 ozs.	Beaver Lake	Apr. 7, 1973	Fred Cornett
CATFISH, Flathead	97 lbs.	Green River	June, 1956	
CRAPPIE	4 lbs., 3 ozs.	Lake Pewee	Apr. 16, 1969	David Crowe
DRUM, Freshwater	31 lbs.	Kentucky Lake	June 2, 1956	Jack Rowe
GAR	40 lbs.	Ohio River	Aug. 8, 1956	Kelsie Travis, Jr.
MUSKELLUNGE	42 lbs.	Licking River	Feb. 23, 1973	Glen Terrell
SAUGER	6 lbs., 1 oz.	Kentucky Lake	July 26, 1972	William Price
SPOONBILL	72 lbs.	Lake Cumberland	Mar. 6, 1957	Ralph Pierce
STURGEON	36 lbs., 8 ozs.	Lake Cumberland	Oct. 3, 1954	Barney Frazier
SUNFISH	2 lbs., 5 ozs.	Caulk's Lake	May 30, 1964	R. C. Masters
TROUT, Rainbow	14 lbs., 6 ozs.	Cumberland River	Sept. 10, 1972	Jim Mattingly
WALLEYE	21 lbs., 8 ozs.	Lake Cumberland	Oct. 1, 1958	Abe Black

LOUISIANA

Freshwater Species	Weight	Where	When	Angler
BASS, Largemouth	11 lbs., 13 ozs.		Apr., 1972	Jack O'Connor
BASS, Spotted (Kentucky)	4 lbs., 3 ozs.			Carroll Perkins
BASS, White	3 lbs., 14 ozs.		Feb., 1969	Sam Parrish
BOWFIN	17 lbs., 8 ozs.		Feb., 1973	Julius Aaron
BREAM	2 lbs., 8 ozs.		1959	Grant Kelly
TIE				
	2 lbs., 8 ozs.		June, 1961	J. W. Parker, Jr.
BUFFALO	24 lbs.		Aug., 1973	Robert Prator
CATFISH	62 lbs.		Mar., 1970	James Hibben
CRAPPIE	6 lbs.		Nov., 1969	Lettie Robertson
WARMOUTH	1 lb., 8¾ ozs.		Sept., 1973	Allen Polk

Saltwater Species	Weight	Where	When	Angler
AMBERJACK	86 lbs., 8 ozs.		July, 1974	Sonny Ourso
BARRACUDA	50 lbs.		Aug., 1970	A. C. Mills
BLUEFISH	16 lbs., 8 ozs.		Sept., 1971	Leon Kolmaister
BONITO	29 lbs., 12 ozs.		July, 1974	Sidney Gonsouin
COBIA	149 lbs., 12 ozs.		May, 1965	Garnett Caudell
CROAKER, Atlantic	8 lbs.		Aug., 1972	Douglas Bernard
DOLPHIN	62 lbs., 8 ozs.		June, 1973	Mike Pratt
DRUM	56 lbs., 9 ozs.		July, 1974	Davis Doucet
FLOUNDER	12 lbs., 2 ozs.		Feb., 1969	Clarence Craig
JACK CREVALLE	41 lbs., 14 ozs.		Oct., 1973	Elmo Robichaux, Sr.
MACKEREL, King	68 lbs., 8 ozs.		Mar., 1974	Edward C. Beshoner, Sr.
MACKEREL, Spanish	10 lbs., 9 ozs.		Aug., 1972	Mike LeBlanc
MARLIN, Blue	686 lbs.		Aug., 1969	Alvin E. DuVernay, Jr.
MARLIN, White	134 lbs.		July, 1967	Dennis Good
POMPANO	8 lbs., 8 ozs.		Dec., 1969	Buddy Pons
POMPANO, African	13 lbs.		Jan., 1973	Jesse Lane
REDFISH	56 lbs., 8 ozs.		Sept., 1963	O. L. Comish
SAILFISH	96 lbs.		Oct., 1953	John Lauricella
SHARK, Mako	400 lbs.		July, 1972	Jules E. Guglielmo, Sr.
SHEEPHEAD	14 lbs., 12 ozs.		May, 1970	John Bourg
SPADEFISH	9 lbs., 4 ozs.		Dec., 1969	Benny Avera
SPEARFISH	78 lbs.		July, 1964	Larry Bulot
SNAPPER	74 lbs.		Oct., 1963	Jim Meriwether
SWORDFISH, Broadbill	112 lbs., 8 ozs.		July, 1969	Geo. M. Sneelings III
TARPON	206 lbs.		July, 1973	Johnny Guidry
TRIPLETAIL	39 lbs., 8 ozs.		July, 1959	Mrs. Jimmy Toups
TROUT, Speckled	12 lbs., 6 ozs.		May, 1950	Leon Mattes
TROUT, White	11 lbs.		Sept., 1973	Donald Marion
TUNA, Blackfin	24 lbs., 12 ozs.		Nov., 1971	Mrs. Adelea Robichaux
TUNA, Bluefin	859 lbs.		June, 1971	Jack Brown
TUNA, Yellowfin	201 lbs., 8 ozs.		June, 1971	Alvin DuVernay
WAHOO	124 lbs., 8 ozs.		May, 1974	Salvadore Perino, Jr.

MAINE

Species	Weight	Where	When	Angler
BASS, Largemouth	11 lbs., 10 ozs.	Moose Pond	1968	Robert Kamp
BASS, Smallmouth	8 lbs.	Thompson Lake	1970	George Dyer
CUSK	14 lbs., 1 oz.	St. Froid Lake	1972	Gordon Saucier
PERCH, White	4 lbs., 10 ozs.	Messalonskee Lake	1949	Mrs. Earl Small
PICKEREL, Chain	6 lbs., 8 ozs.	Sebago Lake	1969	Eugene Laughlin
SALMON, Atlantic	26 lbs., 2 ozs.	Narraguagus River	1959	Harry Smith
SALMON, Landlocked	22 lbs., 8 ozs.	Sebago Lake	1907	Edward Blakeley
TROUT, Blueback	4 lbs., 4 ozs.	Basin Pond	1973	Merton Wyman
TROUT, Brook	8 lbs., 5 ozs.	Pierce Pond	1958	Dixon Griffin
TROUT, Brown	19 lbs., 7 ozs.	Sebago Lake	1958	Norman Stacy

Species	Weight	Where	When	Angler
TROUT, Lake	31 lbs., 8 ozs.	Beech Hill Pond	1958	Hollis Grindle
WHITEFISH	7 lbs., 8 ozs.	Sebago Lake	1958	Neil Sullivan

MARYLAND

Freshwater Species	Weight	Where	When	Angler
BASS, Largemouth	10 lbs., 1 oz.	Loch Raven Reservoir	May, 1966	Jerry Sauter
BASS, Smallmouth	8 lbs.	Loch Raven Reservoir	May, 1968	Gene Carter
BLUEGILL	1 lb., 14 ozs.	Wicomico River	Feb., 1970	Pete Tippett
CARP	44 lbs.	Patuxent River	May, 1970	Jean Ward
CATFISH	24 lbs.	Potomac River	Oct., 1964	James Turner
CRAPPIE	3 lbs., 4 ozs.	Rocky Gorge	Apr., 1968	Tyrone Fennell
GAR	16 lbs., 8 ozs.	Pocomoke River	Aug., 1970	Thad Feetham
MUSKELLUNGE	31 lbs., 8 ozs.	Susquehanna River	June, 1966	Don Wise
PERCH, Yellow	2 lbs., 5 ozs.	Allens Fresh	Mar., 1971	Anthony Aloi
PICKEREL, Chain	7 lbs., 9 ozs.	Choptank River	Feb., 1970	Frank Shoemaker
PIKE, Northern	19 lbs., 4 ozs.	Loch Raven Reservoir	Apr., 1970	Roger Bowen
TROUT, Brown	13 lbs., 8 ozs.	Deep Creek Lake	Aug., 1968	Simon Cogley
TROUT, Rainbow	8 lbs., 2 ozs.	Beaver Creek	Apr., 1971	Jack Willy
WALLEYE	8 lbs., 12 ozs.	Deep Creek Lake	June, 1970	Fred McGee

Saltwater Species	Weight	Where	When	Angler
ALBACORE	18 lbs., 8 ozs.	Ocean City	July, 1971	Richard Roberts, Jr.
BASS, Channel	65 lbs.	Tangier Sound	May, 1970	Lake Scott
BASS, Sea	7 lbs.	Ocean City	Nov., 1970	Ralph Walsh
BASS, Striped	50 lbs., 1 oz.	Dumping Grounds	July 22, 1965	Carol Rothwell
BLUEFISH	20 lbs., 1 oz.	Ocean City	Oct., 1970	Joe Clarkson, Jr.
COBIA	99 lbs.	Chesapeake Bay	July, 1948	R. B. Frost, Jr.
CROAKER	5 lbs., 11 ozs.	Sharps Island	Aug., 1962	Jim Shupe
DOLPHIN	40 lbs.	Ocean City	Sept., 1965	Joseph Rogers
DRUM, Black	92 lbs.	Choptank River	Aug., 1955	James Aaron
FLOUNDER	16 lbs.	Sinepuxent Bay	July, 1970	Jacob Fry
MACKERAL, King	21 lbs.	Ocean City	July, 1970	Walter Pike
MARLIN, Blue	554 lbs.	Ocean City	July, 1969	Francis Day
MARLIN, White	130 lbs., 8 ozs.	Ocean City	Aug., 1956	H. Howard
PERCH, White	1 lb., 12 ozs.	Susquehanna River	Apr., 1970	Philip Rizzo, Sr.
PORGY	6 lbs., 3 ozs.	Ocean City	July, 1966	Pearl Hopple
SHAD, Hickory	4 lbs., 4 ozs.	Susquehanna River	May, 1968	Pietro Matastasio
SHAD, White	8 lbs., 1 oz.	Wicomico River	Apr., 1971	Jim Revelle
SHARK	284 lbs., 8 ozs.	Ocean City	Sept., 1970	Margaret Coleman
SPOT	1 lb., 4 ozs.	Chesapeake Bay	June, 1969	David Miles
TAUTOG	15 lbs., 8 ozs.	Ocean City	May, 1970	Robert Miller
TUNA	253 lbs.	Ocean City	Aug., 1970	Francis Day
WAHOO	90 lbs.	Ocean City	Sept., 1970	Harper Smith

Saltwaer Species	Weight	Where	When	Angler
WEAKFISH	9 lbs.	Sharps Island	Sept., 1971	Gayle Mitchell
WHITING	2 lbs., 12 ozs.	Ocean City	Oct., 1970	Gary Beckner

MASSACHUSETTS

Species	Weight	Where	When	Angler
BASS, Largemouth	12 lbs., 1 oz.	Palmer River	May 9, 1963	George Pastick
BASS, Smallmouth	7 lbs.	Lovells Pond	Aug. 20, 1972	Marshall Hunter
BULLHEAD	5 lbs., 9 ozs.	Connecticut River	June 8, 1963	Mrs. Erna Storie
CALICO	3 lbs.	Ames Pond	Jan. 23, 1973	William Twiraga
CATFISH, Channel	13 lbs., 14 ozs.	Metacomet Pond	Sept. 15, 1971	Wayne Briggs
PERCH, White	2 lbs., 12 ozs.	Herring Pond	May 21, 1971	Manual Souza
PERCH, Yellow	2 lbs., 5 ozs.	Wachusett Reservoir	Apr. 23, 1970	Arnold Korenblum
PICKEREL	9 lbs., 5 ozs.	Pontoosuc Lake	1954	Mrs. James Martin
PIKE, Northern	25 lbs.	Onota Pond	Feb. 5, 1973	Ralph Fiegel
SALMON	9 lbs., 5 ozs.	Quabbin Reservoir	Sept. 5, 1971	John Courtney
SHAD	8 lbs., 12 ozs.	South River	May 9, 1974	Richard Kie-Wyekhan
TROUT, Brook	6 lbs., 4 ozs.	Otis Reservoir	June 24, 1968	Thomas Laptew
TROUT, Brown	19 lbs., 10 ozs.	Wachusett Reservoir	May 19, 1966	Dana DeBlois
TROUT, Lake	17 lbs., 3 ozs.	Quabbin Reservoir	May 20, 1973	Paul Drenzek
TROUT, Rainbow	8 lbs., 4 ozs.	Deep Pond	Oct. 15, 1966	Roger Walker
WALLEYE	11 lbs.	Quabbin Reservoir	June 11, 1973	Bob Methot

MICHIGAN

Species	Weight	Where	When	Angler
BASS, Largemouth	11 lbs., 15 ozs.	Big Pine Island Lake	1934	William Maloney
TIE				
	11 lbs., 15 ozs.	Bamfield Dam, Backwaters	1959	Jack Rorex
BASS, Rock	3 lbs., 10 ozs.	Lenawee County	1965	Edward Arnold
BASS, Smallmouth	9 lbs., 4 ozs.	Long Lake	1906	W. F. Shoemaker
BASS, White	2 lbs., 5 ozs.	Little Bay de Noc	1972	Edward Platt
BLUEGILL	2 lbs., 10 ozs.	Silver Lake	1945	F. M. Broock
CARP	61 lbs., 8 ozs.	Big Wolf Lake	1974	Dale France
CATFISH, Channel	47 lbs., 8 ozs.	Maple River	1937	Elmer Rayner
CATFISH, Flathead	38 lbs., 2 ozs.	Grand River	1974	John Kamyszek
CISCO	3 lbs., 7 ozs.	Big Traverse Harbor	1973	Ronald MacGregor
CRAPPIE, Black	4 lbs., 2 ozs.	Lincoln Lake	1947	E. Frank Lee
MUSKELLUNG, Great Lakes	62 lbs., 8 ozs.	Lake St. Clair	1940	Percy Haver
MUSKELLUNGE, Northern Wisconsin	36 lbs., 8 ozs.	Thornapple Lake	1973	Dale Ossenheimer
MUSKELLUNGE, Tiger (hybrid)	31 lbs.	Lake George	1974	Vernell King
PERCH, Yellow	3 lbs., 12 ozs.	Lake Independence	1947	Eugene Jezinski
PIKE, Northern	39 lbs.	Dodge Lake	1961	Larry Clough
SALMON, Atlantic	16 lbs., 3 ozs.	Lake Charlevoix	1974	David Baxter

Species	Weight	Where	When	Angler
SALMON, Chinook	43 lbs., 3 ozs.	Muskegon Lake	1972	Brad Owens
SALMON, Coho	30 lbs., 8 ozs.	E. Arm Grand Traverse Bay	1971	George Adema
SALMON, Kokanee	1 lb. 10 ozs.	Cass Lake	1974	Greg Gerling
SAUGER	6 lbs., 6 ozs.	Torch Lake	1973	Jack Neuman
SHEEPSHEAD	26 lbs.	Muskegon Lake	1973	James Black
STRUGEON, Lake	193 lbs.	Mullet Lake	1974	Joe Maka
TROUT, Brook	6 lbs., 2 ozs.	Big Bay De Noc	1974	Wiebert Sorenson
TROUT, Brown	27 lbs., 12 ozs.	Lake Huron	1974	Claude Nensewitz
TROUT, Lake	53 lbs.	Lake Superior	1944	Kenyon Boyer & E. C. Watson
TROUT, Splake	10 lbs., 13 ozs.	Bellaire Lake	1974	James Howey
TROUT, Steelhead	22 lbs., 6 ozs.	Lake Michigan off Manistee	1971	Harvey Huttas
WALLEYE	17 lbs., 3 ozs.	Pine River	1951	Ray Fadely
WHITEFISH, Lake	8 lbs., 6 ozs.	Intermediate Lake	1974	George Kropp

MINNESOTA

Species	Weight	Where	When	Angler
BASS, Largemouth	10 lbs., 2 ozs.	Prairie Lake	1961	Harold Lehn
BASS, Rock	1 lb. 8 ozs.,	Mille Lacs Lake	June 3, 1973	Sigmond Schultz
BASS, Smallmouth	8 lbs.	W. Battle Lake	1948	John Creighton
BASS, White	4 lbs.	St. Croix	Feb. 12, 1972	Dan Dickhausen
BLUEGILL	2 lbs., 13 ozs.	Lake Alice	1948	Bob Parker
BULLHEAD, Brown	7 lbs., 1 oz.	Shallow Lake	May 21, 1974	William Meyer
CARP	86 lbs.	Minnesota River	1906	C. A. Cameron
CATFISH, Channel	37 lbs.	White Bear Lake	1962	Larry Peterson
CATFISH, Mud	157 lbs.	Minnesota River	1930	
CRAPPIE	5 lbs.	Vermillion River	1940	Tom Christenson
DOGFISH	10 lbs.	Priest's Bay	1941	Roger Lehman
MUSKELLUNGE	56 lbs., 8 ozs.	Lake of the Woods	July 24, 1931	J. W. Collins
PERCH, Yellow	3 lbs., 4 ozs.	Lake Plantaganette	1945	Merle Johnson
PIKE, Northern	45 lbs., 12 ozs.	Basswood Lake	May 16, 1929	J. V. Schanken
SALMON, Chinook	18 lbs., 8 ozs.	Sucker River	Oct. 9, 1973	Gary Pearson
SALMON, Coho	10 lbs., 6½ ozs.	Lake Superior	Nov. 7, 1970	Louis Rhode
SALMON, Kokanee	2 lbs., 15 ozs.	Caribou Lake	Aug. 6, 1971	Lars Kindem
SAUGER	6 lbs., 2½ ozs.	Mississippi River	1964	Mrs. Wylis Larson
SHEEPSHEAD	30 lbs.	Mississippi River	1960	Dick Campbell
STURGEON, Lake	236 lbs.	Lake of the Woods	1911	
SUCKER, White	8 lbs., 9 ozs.	Mississippi River	Apr. 24, 1971	Leonard Krueger
TROUT, Brook	9 lbs.	Ash River	1958	Frank Hause
TROUT, Brown	16 lbs., 8 ozs.	Grindstone Lake	1961	Mr. Lovgren
TROUT, Lake	43 lbs., 8 ozs.	Lake Superior	May 30, 1955	G. H. Nelson
TROUT, Ohrid	6 lbs., 6 ozs.	Tofte Lake	Jan. 9, 1973	Jim Crigler
TROUT, Rainbow	17 lbs., 37 ozs.	Knife River	Jan. 19, 1974	Ottway Stuberud
TROUT, Splake	9 lbs., 6 ozs.	Beaver Lake	May 23, 1971	Gerald Quade
WALLEYE	16 lbs., 11 ozs.	Basswood Lake	1955	

MISSISSIPPI

Species	Weight	Where	When	Angler
BASS, Largemouth	13 lbs., 2 ozs.	Theo Costas Lake	May 2, 1963	Noel Mills
BASS, Spotted	7 lbs., 14 ozs.	Sardis Reservoir	May, 1965	Ed Stone
BASS, Striped	20 lbs.	Ross Barnett Reservoir	Mar. 1, 1974	A. E. Miley
BASS, White	5 lbs., 2 ozs.	Grenada Spillway	July 9, 1960	Eddy Vaughn
BLUEGILL	2 lbs., 5 ozs.	Deemer	May 20, 1963	Leonard Busby III
BOWFIN	17 lbs., 8 ozs.	Ross Barnett Reservoir	May 17, 1969	David Braband
BULLHEAD, Black	2 lbs., 10 ozs.	Farm Pond	June 4, 1970	Bryan Stringer
CARP (World Record)	74 lbs.	Pelahatchie Lake	June 13, 1963	Curtis Wade
CATFISH, Blue	8 lbs.	Mossy Lake	July 20, 1969	Keith Elliott
CATFISH, Channel	21 lbs., 8 ozs.	Lake Lamar Bruce	Mar. 20, 1972	Johnny Dunnaway
CATFISH, Flathead	59 lbs.	Sardis Spillway	July 27, 1971	Roger Dilworth
CRAPPIE, White (World Record)	5 lbs., 3 ozs.	Enid Reservoir	July 31, 1957	Fred Bright
DRUM	10 lbs., 12 ozs.	Grenada Spillway	Nov. 25, 1973	Pete Marascalco
GAR, Longnose	24 lbs., 2 ozs.	Lake Piomingo	Apr. 27, 1974	Joe Franks
PADDLEFISH	65 lbs.	Ross Barnett Reservoir	June 23, 1974	Randy Pues
PICKEREL, Chain	4 lbs., 6 ozs.	Fort Bayou	Mar. 27, 1971	W. R. Groseclose
STURGEON, Atlantic	173 lbs.	Bogue Chitto River	Dec. 1, 1969	Alfred Wilkinson
SUNFISH, Redear	2 lbs., 2½ ozs.	Lake Tiak O'Khata	July 2, 1963	Ben Smythe

MISSOURI

Species	Weight	Where	When	Angler
BASS, Kentucky	7 lbs., 8 ozs.	Table Rock	Apr. 6, 1966	Gene Arnaud
BASS, Largemouth	13 lbs., 14 ozs.	Bull Shoals	Apr. 1961	Marvin Bushong
BASS, Rock	2 lbs., 12 ozs.	Big Piney River	June 15, 1968	William Rod
BASS, Smallmouth	6 lbs., 7 ozs.	Valley Dolomite Pond	1952	Burt Koester
BASS, Striped	22 lbs., 9 ozs.	Lake of the Ozarks	Aug. 27, 1974	Gary Dinwiddie
BASS, White	5 lbs., 2 ozs.	Table Rock	Apr. 25, 1973	Junior Horton
BLUEGILL	3 lbs.	Pond		Mike Giovanni
BOWFIN	19 lbs.	Duck Creek	Mar. 1963	Clois Coomer
BUFFALO	40 lbs.	Current River	Nov. 19, 1971	Lovel Hall
BULLHEAD, Black	3 lbs., 2 ozs.	Pond	Apr. 8, 1972	Mrs. Roger Horstman
TIE				
	3 lbs., 2 ozs.	Pond	May 14, 1974	Mark Long
CARP	47 lbs., 7 ozs.	Busch Wildlife Area	May 7, 1974	Elmer Henson
CATFISH, Blue	56 lbs.	Osage River	June 5, 1961	Melvin Smith
CATFISH, Channel	29 lbs., 12 ozs.	Lake Jacomo	May 5, 1969	Richy Rodenbaugh
CATFISH, Flathead	61 lbs.	New Madrid Co.	Apr., 1963	Don Hawkins
CRAPPIE, Black	4 lbs., 8 ozs.	Fish Pond	May 28, 1967	Ray Babcock
CRAPPIE, White	3 lbs., 12 ozs.	Sugar Creek Lake	May, 1964	Dee Embree

Species	Weight	Where	When	Angler
DRUM, Freshwater	34 lbs.	Warsaw	Apr. 19, 1959	Gene Davis
MUSKELLUNGE	26 lbs., 12 ozs.	Pomme de Terre	Apr. 1, 1974	Franklin Stackhouse
PICKEREL, Chain	4 lbs., 5 ozs.	Black River	Feb. 12, 1974	Chris Siegmund
PIKE, Northern	18 lbs., 3 ozs.	Stockton Lake	May 27, 1974	Mike Miller
STURGEON	53 lbs.	Missouri River	1950	Whitelan & Drohr
SUNFISH, Green	2 lbs., 2 ozs.	Stockton Lake	June 20, 1971	Paul Dilley
SUNFISH, Longear	1 lb., 5 ozs.	Kenney Pond	June 30, 1966	Tom Nelson
SUNFISH, Redear	2 lbs., 4 ozs.	Lake St. Louis	June 27, 1974	William Hargrove
TROUT, Brown	14 lbs., 10 ozs.	Current River	Aug. 15, 1970	Michael Whitaker
TROUT, Rainbow	14 lbs., 6 oz.	Bennett Spring	July 3, 1974	Bob Lamm
WALLEYE	20 lbs.	St. Francis River	1961	John Bacholke

MONTANA

Species	Weight	Where	When	Angler
BASS, Largemouth	7 lbs., 6 ozs.	Ninepipe Reservoir	1973	
BASS, Smallmouth	4 lbs., 4 ozs.	Loon Lake	1971	
BLUEGILL	2 lbs., 8 ozs.	Dengel Reservoir	1967	George Schlosser
BURBOT	11 lbs., 12 ozs.	Fort Peck Reservoir	1967	Jim Cooper
CATFISH, Channel	21 lbs., 5 ozs.	Missouri River	1964	Gary Eppers
CRAPPIE, Black	3 lbs., 3½ ozs.	Tongue River Reservoir	1973	
CRAPPIE, White	1.72 lbs.	Tongue River Reservoir	1972	
DRUM	13 lbs., 6 ozs.	Fort Peck Reservoir	1973	
PADDLEFISH	142 lbs., 8 ozs.	Missouri River	1973	
PERCH, Yellow	2 lbs.	Nelson Reservoir	1974	
PIKE, Northern	39 lbs., 8 ozs.	Tongue River Reservoir	1972	
SALMON, Chinook	4 lbs., 7 ozs.	Missouri River	1972	
SALMON, Coho	4 lbs., 14 ozs.	Fort Peck Reservoir	1973	
SALMON, Kokanee	5 lbs., 4 ozs.	Helena Valley Reservoir	1969	
SAUGER	5 lbs.	Tongue River	1974	
STURGEON, Pallid	38 lbs.	Mouth of Tongue River	1950	
STURGEON, Shovelnose	8 lbs., 12 ozs.	Missouri River	1974	
STURGEON, White	96 lbs.	Kootenai River	1968	
TROUT, Brook	9 lbs., 1 oz.	Lower Two Medicine Lake	1940	John Cook
TROUT, Brown	29 lbs.	Wade Lake	1966	E. H. Bacon
TROUT, Cutthroat	16 lbs.	Red Eagle Lake	1955	William Sands
TROUT, Dolly Varden	16 lbs., 12 ozs.	Blackfoot River	1974	
TROUT, Golden	1 lb., 6¼ ozs.	Island Lake	1973	
TROUT, Grayling	2 lbs., 9 ozs.		1971	
TROUT, Lake	27 lbs., 12 ozs.	Flathead Lake	1973	
TROUT, Rainbow	20 lbs.	Cliff Lake	1952	C. J. Brohaugh
TROUT, hybrid	17 lbs., 10 ozs.	Ashley Lake	1973	
WALLEYE	13 lbs.	Nelson Reservoir	1972	
WHITEFISH, Mountain	4 lbs., 2½ ozs.	Clark Fork River	1973	

NEBRASKA

Species	Weight	Where	When	Angler
BASS, Kentucky Spotted	3 lbs., 11 ozs.	Sandpit	Mar. 24, 1968	Tom Pappas
BASS, Largemouth	10 lbs., 11 ozs.	Sandpit	Oct. 2, 1965	Paul Abegglen
BASS, Rock	2 lbs., 4 ozs.	Farm Pond	May 6, 1972	Edna Zuege
BASS, Smallmouth	5 lbs., 14 ozs.	Red Willow Reservoir	May 4, 1974	Richard Bessey
BASS, Striped	14 lbs., 9 ozs.	Lake McConaughy	Sept. 20, 1973	Greg Shearer
BASS, White	4 lbs., 15 ozs.	Sandpit	1962	Frederick Baldwin
BLUEGILL	2 lbs., 8 ozs.	Farm Pond	Aug. 27, 1968	Charles Randolph
BUFFALO	33 lbs., 8 ozs.	Seirs Lake	Sept. 4, 1966	Mrs. Lyle Clemens
BULLHEAD	3 lbs., 14 ozs.	Farm Pond	July 22, 1974	Dick Dunn
BURBOT	3 lbs., 8 ozs.	Gavins Point Dam Tailwaters	Apr. 12, 1969	Gene Brown
CARP	28 lbs., 2 ozs.	Hall County Lake	May 18, 1967	Harry Lassen
CATFISH, Blue	100 lbs., 8 ozs.	Missouri River	Nov. 29, 1970	Raynold Promes
CATFISH, Channel	37 lbs.	Fremont State Recreation Area	June 10, 1972	James Millin
CATFISH, Flathead	76 lbs.	Missouri River	Mar. 10, 1971	Orville Sudbeck
CRAPPIE, Black	3 lbs., 15 ozs.	Lake McConaughy	Apr. 29, 1962	Delmer Butler
CRAPPIE, White	3 lbs., 13 ozs.	Red Willow Reservoir	May 15, 1973	Robert Berglund
DRUM, Freshwater	28 lbs., 4 ozs.	Missouri River	Oct. 1, 1971	Vincent Prazak
GAR, Longnose	19 lbs.	Lake in Cass County	June 29, 1974	Ronald Hardin
MUSKELLUNGE	18 lbs., 4 ozs.	Merritt Reservoir	Apr. 20, 1969	Kenneth Cook
PADDLEFISH	89 lbs.	Gavins Point Dam Tailwaters	Feb. 9, 1973	Kay Hill
PERCH, Sacramento	2 lbs., 8 ozs.	Clear Lake	June 20, 1971	John Bush
PERCH, White	1 lb., 6 ozs.	Wagon Train Lake	May 16, 1972	Curtis Kadlick
PERCH, Yellow	2 lbs., 1 oz.	Lake Minatare	Feb. 1, 1974	Larry Benzel
PIKE, Northern	27 lbs., 8 ozs.	Lake McConaughy	July 14, 1962	Cletus Jacobsen
QUILLBACK	8 lbs., 8 ozs.	Johnson Lake	May 12, 1974	Rhonda Desmond
SALMON, Coho	5 lbs., 12 ozs.	Lake McConaughy	July 3, 1971	Lyle Fry
SALMON, Kokanee	4 lbs., 2 ozs.	Lake McConaughy	July 11, 1971	Neal Dunbar
SAUGER	8 lbs., 5 ozs.	Missouri River	Oct. 22, 1961	Mrs. Betty Tepner
STURGEON	45 lbs., 4 ozs.	Niobrara River	Nov. 29, 1973	Ed Pearson
SUCKER	4 lbs.	Lake Minatare	Apr. 29, 1968	Jack Keller
SUNFISH, Green	1 lb., 1¼ ozs.	Farm Pond	May 23, 1968	William Fattig
SUNFISH, Redear	1 lb., 6 ozs.	Conestoga Lake	May 4, 1970	Gary Reagan
TROUT, Brook	5 lbs., 1 oz.	Pawnee Springs	Nov. 3, 1965	Joe Gray
TROUT, Brown	20 lbs., 1 oz.	Snake River	July 26, 1973	Denny Doolittle
TROUT, Rainbow	13 lbs., 2 ozs.	Tub Springs	Mar. 16, 1972	Kevin Vernon
WALLEYE	16 lbs., 2 ozs.	Lake McConaughy	July 5, 1971	Herbert Cutshall

NEVADA

Species	Weight	Where	When	Angler
BASS, Largemouth	11 lbs.	Lake Mohave	1972	H. P. Warner
BASS, Striped	31 lbs., 12 ozs.	Colorado River	1971	Chuck Grable

Species	Weight	Where	When	Angler
BASS, White	3 lbs., 3 ozs.	Lahontan Reservoir	1971	Wynn Schumacher
BLUEGILL	1 lb., 2 ozs.	Lake Mead	1972	Jim Nelson
BULLHEAD	2 lbs.	Ft. Churchill Pond	1973	Paul Bouteiller
CARP	29 lbs., 7 ozs.	Lake Mohave	1973	Donald Stevenson
CATFISH, Channel	25 lbs., 1 oz.	Lake Mohave	1971	Walter Zeman
CATFISH, White	11 lbs.	Lahontan Reservoir	1969	Stan Havens
CRAPPIE, Black	3 lbs.	Lake Mead	1972	Marguerite Kinney
CRAPPIE, White	2 lbs., 8 ozs.	Lahontan Reservoir	1968	Charles Grant
PERCH, Sacramento	4 lbs., 9 ozs.	Pyramid Lake	1971	John Battcher
PIKE, Northern	15 lbs., 12 ozs.	Bassett Lake	1973	Marvin Carrick
SALMON, Kokanee	4 lbs., 13 ozs.	Lake Tahoe	1973	Dick Bournique
SALMON, Silver	8 lbs., 4 ozs.	Lake Mead	1972	William Haggard
TROUT, Brook	5 lbs., 4 ozs.	Round Mtn. Reservoir	1972	Henry Forcier
TROUT, Brown	13 lbs., 8 ozs.	Comins Lake	1973	James Kaseman
TROUT, Cutthroat	19 lbs., 9 ozs.	Pyramid Lake	1972	Bob Carrol
TROUT, hybrid	18 lbs., 1 oz.	Pyramid Lake	1973	Tom Gjonovich
TROUT, Rainbow	16 lbs., 4 ozs.	Lake Mohave	1971	Mike Soskin
TROUT, Mackinaw	35 lbs., 8 ozs.	Lake Tahoe	1970	Sam Sigwart
WALLEYE	4 lbs., 15 ozs.	Ryepatch Reservoir	1973	Ron Geyer
WHITEFISH, Mountain	7 ozs.	Truckee River	1973	Kay Johnson

NEW HAMPSHIRE

Species	Weight	Where	When	Angler
BASS, Largemouth	10 lbs., 8 ozs.	Lake Potanipo	May, 1967	G. Bullpitt
BASS, Smallmouth	7 lbs., 14 ozs.	Goose Pond	Aug., 1970	F. H. Loud
CARP	21 lbs.	Mascoma River	June, 1969	B. Prior
COD	60 lbs.	Atlantic Ocean	July 22, 1971	M. Lenoard
CUSK	10 lbs., 8 ozs.	Diamond Pond	Mar., 1972	K. Strong
PERCH, White	3 lbs.	Winnipesaukee Lake	May, 1965	A. Santos
PERCH, Yellow	2 lbs., 6 ozs.	Heads Pond	Mar. 4, 1969	Roger Hebert
PICKEREL, Chain	8 lbs.	Plummer Pond	Apr. 26, 1966	C. R. Akerley
PIKE, Northern	17 lbs., 14 ozs.	Spofford Lake	May 21, 1972	A. Trudeau
SALMON, landlocked	18 lbs., 8 ozs.	Pleasant Lake	Aug. 31, 1942	Mrs. E. D. Clark
TROUT, Brook	9 lbs.	Pleasant Lake	1911	A. V. Woodruff
TROUT, Brown	15 lbs., 6 ozs.	Connecticut River	May 30, 1953	Calvin Hall
TROUT, Lake	28 lbs., 8 ozs.	Newfound Lake	Apr. 24, 1958	A. Staples
TROUT, Rainbow	13 lbs.	Dublin Lake	1953	
TROUT, Splake	8 lbs., 8 ozs.	White Lake	May 9, 1963	R. Walker
TROUT, Sunapee	11 lbs., 8 ozs.	Sunapee Lake	Aug. 1, 1954	E. Theoharris
WALLEYE	9 lbs.	Merrimack River	Apr. 12, 1971	Mrs. L. Hebert
WHITEFISH	2 lbs., 12 ozs.	Winnipesaukee Lake	Feb., 1973	J. Comali

NEW JERSEY

Freshwater Species	Weight	Where	When	Angler
BASS, Calico	3 lbs., 5½ ozs.	Alloway Lake	1961	William Hanna
BASS, Largemouth	10 lbs., 12 ozs.	Mt. Kimble Lake	1960	Logan Whitesell
BASS, Rock	1 lb. 2¼ ozs.	Lake Hopatcong	1968	Harold Webb
BASS, Smallmouth	6 lbs., 4 ozs.	Delaware River	1957	Earl Trumpore
BASS, Striped (landlocked)	23 lbs., 8 ozs.	Union Lake	1952	Mrs. Albert Beebe
BLUEGILL	2 lbs.	Farm Pond	1956	Silas Matthew, Jr.
BULLHEAD, Brown	22 lbs., 15 ozs.	Spring Lake	1966	Robert Dorf
CARP	41 lbs., 2 ozs.	Delaware River	1971	John Pisa
CATFISH, Channel	28 lbs.	Greenwood Lake	1968	William Otten
CATFISH, White	4 lbs., 8 ozs.	Cranberry Lake	1973	Tom Calandra
MUSKELLUNGE	19 lbs.	Delaware River	1970	John Fleming
PERCH, White	2 lbs., 8 ozs.	Lake Hopatcong	1950	Robert Huber
PERCH, Yellow	4 lbs., 3½ ozs.	Bordentown	1865	Dr. C. C. Abbot
PICKEREL, Chain	9 lbs., 3 ozs.	Lower Aetna Lake	1957	Frank McGovern
PIKE, Northern	21 lbs.	Lake Wawayanda	1971	Edward Kistner
SALMON, landlocked	8 lbs.	New Wawayanda Lake	1951	John Mount
SHAD, American	7 lbs., 13½ ozs.	Delaware River	1971	Richard Lepes
TROUT, Brook	6 lbs., 8 ozs.	Lake Hopatcong	1956	George Hornung
TROUT, Brown	16 lbs., 11 ozs.	Greenwood Lake	1964	Howard Devore
TROUT, Rainbow	8 lbs., 5½ ozs.	Round Valley Reservoir	1970	Richard Ruis, Sr.
WALLEYE	12 lbs., 12¾ ozs.	Delaware River	1934	Stanley Norman

Saltwater Species	Weight	Where	When	Angler
ALBACORE	69 lbs., 1 oz.	Hudson Canyon	1961	Walter Timm
BASS, Black Sea	6 lbs., 4 ozs.	Delaware Bay	1973	Clarence N. Davis III
BASS, Striped	68 lbs.	Off Sandy Hook	1970	Donald Zboyan
BLUEFISH	23 lbs., 14 ozs.	Off Cape May	1971	William DiSanto
BONITO, Atlantic	13 lbs., 8 ozs.	Sandy Hook	1945	Frank G. Lykes, Jr.
COBIA	45 lbs., 2 ozs.	Delaware Bay	1972	Eli Hitchner
COD, Atlantic	81 lbs.	Brielle	1967	Joseph Chesla
DOLPHIN	48 lbs., 15 ozs.	Cape May	1969	Yvonne DiSanto
DRUM, Black	92 lbs.	Delaware Bay	1944	Herschel Layton
DRUM, Red	46 lbs.	Sandy Hook	1953	Dr. R. D. Alexander
FLOUNDER, Summer	19 lbs., 12 ozs.	Cape May	1953	Walter Lubin
FLOUNDER, Winter	3 lbs., 2 ozs.	Great Egg Harbor	1968	Frank Coleman
MACKEREL, Atlantic	3 lbs.	Atlantic City	1969	Rosemary Sackawicz
MARLIN, Blue	620 lbs.	Atlantic City	1964	Joseph Teti, Jr.
MARLIN, White	123 lbs.	Ambrose Light	1968	Merrill Arden
POLLACK	43 lbs.	Brielle	1964	Philip Barlow
PORGY	4 lbs., 6 ozs.	Off Barnegat Light	1967	Ernest Ritchie
SEATROUT, Spotted	9 lbs., 8 ozs.	Near Stone Harbor	1973	Clay C. Sutton, Jr.
SHAD, American	7 lbs.	Great Bay	1967	Rodger West
SHARK, Shortfin Mako	322 lbs.	Elberon	1952	W. J. Mahan

Saltwater Species	Weight	Where	When	Angler
SWORDFISH, Broadbill	530 lbs.	Wilmington Canyon	1964	Edmund Levitt
TARPON	42 lbs., 8 ozs.	Shrewsbury Rocks	1972	Jack Hoagland
TAUTOG	21 lbs., 6 ozs.	Cape May	1954	R. N. Sheafer
TUNA, Bluefin	796 lbs.	Off Long Branch	1973	Joseph Casale
TUNA, Yellowfin	138 lbs., 2 ozs.	Hudson Canyon	1969	Tony Keeley
WAHOO	93 lbs., 10 ozs.	Cape May	1969	Dr. Wm. DiSanto
WEAKFISH	17 lbs., 8 ozs.	Mullica River	1952	A. Weisbecker, Jr.

NEW MEXICO

Species	Weight	Where	When	Angler
BASS, Largemouth	9 lbs., 8½ ozs.	McAllister Lake	Aug. 11, 1968	Rufus Hill
BASS, Smallmouth	4 lbs., 8 ozs.	Gila River Box	May 22, 1972	Bob Sattelmeyer
BASS, White	4 lbs.	Elephant Butte	June 23, 1974	O. A. Karstendeir
BLUEGILL	1 lb., 3 ozs.	Lake Carlsbad	Apr. 10, 1973	J. R. Mansfield
CATFISH, Channel	22 lbs., 9 ozs.	Ute Lake	Oct. 18, 1973	Harold Stoering
CATFISH, Flathead	73 lbs., 6 ozs.	Ash Canyon	June 4, 1974	Jim & Bobbi Wilson
CRAPPIE	2½ lbs.	Ute Lake	Feb. 24, 1973	Bill Stout
PIKE, Northern	15 lbs.	Miami Lake	Apr. 5, 1969	Delton Emmett
TROUT, Brown	14 lbs.	Navajo Lake	Dec. 30, 1973	Dorothy Roache
TROUT, Rainbow	11 lbs., 10 ozs.	San Juan River	June 16, 1973	Don Coswell
WALLEYE	10 lbs., 8 ozs.	Ute Lake	May 31, 1973	O. H. Jones

NEW YORK

Species	Weight	Where	When	Angler
BASS, Largemouth	10 lbs., 8 ozs.	Ballston Lake	1973	Woody Gibson
BASS, Smallmouth	9 lbs.	Friends Lake	1925	George Tennyson
MUSKELLUNGE	69 lbs., 15 ozs.	St. Lawrence River	1957	Arthur Lawton
PIKE, Northern	46 lbs., 2 ozs.	Sacandaga Reservoir	1940	Peter Dubuc
SALMON	16 lbs., 14 ozs.	Lake George	1958	Neil Hughes
TROUT, Brook	8 lbs., 8 ozs.	Punchbowl Pond	1908	William Keener
TROUT, Brown	21 lbs., 5 ozs.	Owasco Lake	1954	Thomas Klink
TROUT, Lake	31 lbs.	Follensby Pond	1922	Malcolm Hain
TROUT, Rainbow	21 lbs.	Keuka Lake	1946	Earl Crane
WALLEYE	15 lbs., 3 ozs.	Chemung River	1952	Blanche Baker

NORTH CAROLINA

Freshwater Species	Weight	Where	When	Angler
BASS, Largemouth	14 lbs., 15 ozs.	Santeetlah Reservoir	Apr. 26, 1963	Leonard Williams
BASS, Roanoke	1 lb., 16 ozs.	Fishing Co.	Apr. 28, 1974	Harrel Lee Warren
BASS, Smallmouth	10 lbs., 2 ozs.	Hiwassee Reservoir	June, 1953	Archie Lampkin

Freshwater Species	Weight	Where	When	Angler
BASS, Striped (landlocked)	39 lbs., 4 ozs.	Lake Hickory	May 10, 1969	Bill Dula
BASS, White	4 lbs., 15 ozs.	Fontana Reservoir	July 27, 1966	Leonard Williams
BLUEGILL	4 lbs., 5 ozs.	Edneyville Pond	July 27, 1967	Danny Case
BOWFIN	13 lbs., 8 ozs.	Tar River	May 6, 1973	Douglas Bonds
CARP	45 lbs., 2 ozs.	Badin Lake	June 8, 1974	Max Lowder
CATFISH, Channel	40 lbs., 8 ozs.	Fontana Reservoir	Apr. 15, 1971	P. P. Paine
CRAPPIE	4 lbs., 13 ozs.	Jordan's Lake	Apr. 4, 1961	W. T. Roberson
PICKEREL, Chain	8 lbs.	Gaston Reservoir	Feb. 13, 1968	John Leonard
SAUGER	5 lbs., 15 ozs.	Lake Norman	July 25, 1971	David Shook
SHAD, American	7 lbs., 15½ ozs.	Tar River	Apr. 10, 1974	R. S. Proctor
SHAD, Hickory	2 lbs., 13 ozs.	Pitchkettle Creek	Feb. 17, 1974	John Moore
SHELLCRACKER	4 lbs., 4 ozs.	Lee County Pond	Feb. 3, 1968	Bill Arnold
TROUT, Brook	3 lbs., 9 ozs.	Oconaluftee River	Sept. 18, 1971	Steve Clevinger
TROUT, Brown	12 lbs., 8 ozs.	South Toe River	July 6, 1974	Kirk Murphy
TROUT, Rainbow	14 lbs., 1 oz.	Glenville Reservoir	Mar. 6, 1949	Max Rogers
WALLEYE	13 lbs., 4 ozs.	Santeetlah Reservoir	May, 1966	Leonard Williams
WARMOUTH	1 lb., 8 ozs.	Ellis Creek	Aug. 10, 1971	William Butler

Saltwater Species	Weight	Where	When	Angler
ALBACORE	57 lbs.	Off Oregon Inlet	Oct. 9, 1971	Harry Lee Wray, Jr.
AMBERJACK	125 lbs.	Off Cape Lookout	1973	Paul Spencer Bailey, Jr.
BARRACUDA	47 lbs.	Off Cape Lookout	Sept. 4, 1969	David Meyers
BASS, Black Sea	9 lbs., 12 ozs.	Off Wrightsville Beach	1926	J. E. Bland
BASS, Channel (IGFA all-tackle)	90 lbs.	Rodanthe	Nov. 7, 1973	Elvin Hooper
BASS, Striped	60 lbs.	Cape Point	Feb. 26, 1972	Catherine Willis
BLUEFISH (IGFA all-tackle)	31 lbs., 12 ozs.	Hatteras Inlet	Jan. 30, 1972	James Hussey
COBIA	97 lbs.	Off Oregon Inlet	June 4, 1952	Mary Black
CROAKER, Atlantic	3 lbs., 12 ozs.	Gloucester Straits	Oct. 11, 1969	James Murphy
DOLPHIN	77 lbs.	Off Hatteras	July 31, 1973	Van Miller
DRUM, Black	83 lbs., 8 ozs.	Topsail Island	Oct. 27, 1959	George Sherrell
FLOUNDER, Summer	20 lbs.	Topsail Beach	Oct. 26, 1972	Chris Bowen
GROUPER, Strawberry	28 lbs., 8 ozs.	Off Topsail Beach	June 26, 1972	Jackie Blanchard
GROUPER, Warsaw	245 lbs.	Off Wrightsville Beach	Aug. 19, 1967	Cora Keen
GRUNT, White	4 lbs., 8 ozs.	Off Cape Lookout	June 28, 1969	Vernon Councilman
CREVALLE, Jack	34 lbs.	New Topsail Ocean Pier	Sept. 25, 1972	Gerald Wagoner
KINGFISH, Northern	3 lbs., 8 ozs.	Morehead City	Mar. 26, 1971	Ted Drinnon
MACKEREL, King	57½ lbs.	Cape Lookout	Oct. 10, 1966	Russell DeMent
MACKEREL, Spanish	11 lbs., 4 ozs.	Morehead City	Oct. 6, 1971	James Jenkins
MARLIN, Blue	1143 lbs.	Off Oregon Inlet	July 26, 1974	Jack Herrington
MARLIN, White	108 lbs., 8 ozs.	Off Oregon Inlet	Oct. 12, 1968	Robert Luckwitz
PERCH, White	1 lb., 11½ ozs.	Pamlico River	Mar. 18, 1972	Richard Avery
PIGFISH	1 lb., 1 oz.	Wrightsville Beach	Aug. 18, 1959	Wayne Sutton
POMPANO	6 lbs., 8 ozs.	Wrightsville Beach	Oct. 19, 1970	John Cain

Saltwater Species	Weight	Where	When	Angler
PORGY, Jolthead	9 lbs., 3 ozs.	Off Hatteras	July 29, 1970	Andrew Decker
SAILFISH, Atlantic	76 lbs.	Off Hatteras	Aug. 6, 1970	Judith Huff
SHARK, Blue	478 lbs.	Wrightsville Beach	July 1, 1961	Bobby Kentrolis
SHARK, Dusky	610 lbs.	Nags Head	Aug. 12, 1963	Robert Keller
SHARK, Hammerhead	710 lbs.	Nags Head	Aug. 20, 1960	Robert Keller
SHARK, Lemon	368 lbs.	Nags Head	Oct. 24, 1971	Lawrence Dunston
SHARK, Mako	250 lbs.	Off Wrightsville Beach	May 3, 1970	Dorothy Horton
SHARK, Tiger	1150 lbs.	Yaupon Beach	Aug. 28, 1966	Walter Maxwell
SHEEPSHEAD	16 lbs., 8 ozs.	Cape Fear River	Aug. 23, 1969	Pete Hart
SNAPPER, Red	40 lbs.	Off Cape Lookout	Apr. 27, 1970	Ben Grant
SPOT	1 lb. 10 ozs.	Topsail Island	Oct. 22, 1973	Becky Owen
SEATROUT, Spotted	12 lbs., 4 ozs.	Wrightsville Beach	Dec. 29, 1961	John R. Kenyon, Jr.
STURGEON, Atlantic	9 lbs., 8 ozs.	Cape Point	Jan. 22, 1972	Garland Williams
SWORDFISH	271 lbs.	Off Oregon Inlet	June 24, 1959	E. H. Haley
TARPON	152 lbs.	Wrightsville Beach	June 1, 1961	Bobby Kentrolis
TRIGGERFISH, Gray	8 lbs., 9 ozs.	Off Cape Hatteras	June 28, 1974	Joe Cheek
TUNA, Bigeye	253 lbs.	Off Oregon Inlet	Oct. 6, 1971	Jack McIntyre
TUNA, Blackfin	32 lbs.	Off Morehead City	May 20, 1972	L. David Veasey
TUNA, Bluefin	491 lbs.	Off Cape Hatteras	May 29, 1963	Dick Derbyshire
TUNA, Skipjack	22 lbs., 3 ozs.	Off Wrightsville Beach	July 6, 1968	J. W. Johnson, Jr.
TUNA, Yellowfin	203 lbs.	Off Oregon Inlet	July 30, 1960	John Asburn
TUNNY, Little	25 lbs.	Off Cape Lookout	Oct. 13, 1970	John Sides
TIES				
	25 lbs.	Topsail Beach	May 10, 1971	Lorenzo Godwin
	25 lbs.	Off Cape Lookout	June 19, 1971	Richard Beam
WAHOO	127 lbs.	Off Oregon Inlet	Aug. 8, 1973	Richard Harris
WEAKFISH	12 lbs., 3½ ozs.	Masonboro Inlet	Apr. 6, 1972	Bert Barnes

NORTH DAKOTA

Species	Weight	Where	When	Angler
BASS, Largemouth	7 lbs., 12 ozs.	Welk Dam	1951	George Marquardt
BASS, Smallmouth	3 lbs., 10 ozs.	Sheyenne River	1971	R. Hansen
BASS, White	4 lbs., 4 ozs.	Sakakawea Lake	1969	T. Porter
BLUEGILL	2 lbs., 12 ozs.	Strawberry Lake	1963	Bud Hystad
BUFFALO	18 lbs., 8 ozs.	Garrison	1971	A. Abbey
CARP	21 lbs., 12 ozs.	Red River	1958	Don Pasco
CATFISH, Channel	26 lbs., 8 ozs.	Sakakawea Lake	1968	Clyde Coe
CRAPPIE	3 lbs.	James River	1958	John Kinney
DRUM	8 lbs., 8 ozs.	Sheyenne River	1964	E. Kuchera
LING	16 lbs., 8 ozs.	Missouri River	1970	W. Wolf
MUSKELLUNGE	24 lbs., 9 ozs.	Gravel Lake	1972	L. Leonard
PADDLEFISH	60 lbs.	Sakakawea River	1971	T. Kokkeler
PERCH, Yellow	2 lbs., 4½ ozs.	Coldwater Lake	1972	L. Krueger

Species	Weight	Where	When	Angler
PIKE, Northern	37 lbs., 8 ozs.	Sakakawea Lake	1968	Melvin Slind
SAUGER	8 lbs., 12 ozs.	Sakakawea Lake	1971	Mike Fischer
STURGEON	37 lbs.	Oahe Reservoir	1970	D. Schramm
TROUT, Brown	5 lbs., 15½ ozs.	N. Lemmon Lake	1969	L. Shortridge
TROUT, Rainbow	9 lbs., 11 oxs.	Garrison Tailrace	1960	Michael Stoick
WALLEYE	15 lbs., 12 ozs.	Wood Lake	1959	Blair Chapman

OHIO

Species	Weight	Where	When	Angler
BASS, Largemouth	10 lbs., 2 ozs.	Locus Grove	Oct. 11, 1972	Thomas Buck
BASS, Rock	1 lb., 15½ ozs.	Deer Creek	Sept. 3, 1962	George Keller
BASS, Smallmouth	7½ lbs.	Mad River	June 17, 1941	James Bayless
BASS, Spotted	5 lbs., 4 ozs.	Lake White	May 2, 1967	Roger Trainer
BASS, Striped	15 lbs.	Grand Lake St. Marys	June 15, 1973	Roy Schaefer
BASS, White	4 lbs., 2 ozs.	Lake Erie	May 13, 1972	A. F. Root
BOWFIN	6 lbs.	Dillion Dam	May 28, 1973	Joe Geiger
BULLHEAD	3 lbs., 14¾ ozs.	Glandof Lake	May 9, 1966	Roy Kuhlman
CARP	50 lbs.	Paint Creek	May 24, 1967	Judson Holton
CATFISH, Channel	25 lbs.	Piedmont Lake	May 10, 1964	Charles McGrath
CATFISH, Flathead	76 lbs.	Piedmont Lake	July 17, 1972	Dale Yoho
CRAPPIE, Black	3½ lbs.	Scioto Lakes	Apr. 10, 1968	M. W. Grover
CRAPPIE, White	3 lbs., 3 ozs.	Muzzy Lake	July 27, 1968	Christy Buckeye
DRUM, Freshwater	20¾ lbs.	Muskingum River	Apr. 16, 1969	Brennie Lynch
GAR	25 lbs.	Ohio River	Aug. 31, 1966	Flora Irvin
MUSKELLUNGE	55 lbs., 2 ozs.	Piedmont Lake	Apr. 12, 1972	Joe Lykins
PADDLEFISH	16 lbs., 5 ozs.	Brush Creek	June 4, 1969	Buford Ricks
PERCH, Yellow	2 lbs., 8 ozs.	Lake Erie	Nov. 14, 1954	J. H. Olasky
PICKEREL, Chain	6 lbs., 4 ozs.	Long Lake	Mar. 25, 1961	Ronald Kotch
PIKE, Northern	16 lbs., 4 ozs.	Aquilla Lake	May 6, 1972	Robert Root
SALMON, Chinook	26½ lbs.	Daniels Park	Oct. 23, 1972	Jim Siggers
SALMON, Coho	7¾ lbs.	Huron River	Oct. 13, 1971	Alan Kalfus
SUCKER	9 lbs., 10¾ ozs.	Rocky River	Apr. 10, 1954	Milan Kutner
SUNFISH	2 lbs., 4 ozs.	Chagrin River	June 15, 1970	Michael Moritz
TROUT, Brook	2 lbs., 11 ozs.	East Branch Chagrin River	June 30, 1955	S. Graboshek
TROUT, Brown	13 lbs., 8 ozs.	Cold Creek	Sept. 10, 1942	J. S. Harris
TROUT, Rainbow	11 lbs., 11 ozs.	Chagrin River	May 2, 1972	Dean Ballek
WALLEYE	15 lbs.	Pymatuning Reservoir	Nov. 13, 1951	William Heathman

OKLAHOMA

Species	Weight	Where	When	Angler
BASS, Largemouth	11 lbs., 15 ozs.	Kiamichi River	June 5, 1941	Herbert Rodgers
BASS, Smallmouth	4 lbs., 12 ozs.	Mountain Fork River	Mar. 30, 1968	Dan Moseley
BASS, Spotted	8 lbs., 2 ozs.	Pittsburg Co. Pond	June 27, 1958	O. J. Stone

Species	Weight	Where	When	Angler
BASS, Striped	32 lbs.	Lake Eufaula	Nov. 22, 1972	Jim Burns
BASS, White	4 lbs., 14 ozs.	Lake Eucha	Apr. 9, 1969	Danny Feemster
BLUEGILL	1 lb., 7 ozs.	Osage Co. Pond	Sept. 8, 1968	David Noss
BUFFALO, Bigmouth	43 lbs., 8 ozs.	Washita River	Mar. 3, 1973	Bill Wingate
CARP	32 lbs., 12 ozs.	Lake Rush	May 13, 1968	Bob Penick
CATFISH, Blue	50 lbs., 4 ozs.	Red River	May 23, 1973	Charles McGee
CATFISH, Channel	30 lbs.	Washita River	June 30, 1974	Richard Sirmons
CATFISH, Flathead	66 lbs.	Lake Spavinaw	May 25, 1970	Nick Freling
CRAPPIE, Black	4 lbs., 2 ozs.	U.S. Field Station	June 28, 1972	Kirby Lillard
CRAPPIE, White	4 lbs., 13 ozs.	Tillman Co. Pond	Mar. 4, 1967	Buddy Mealor
DRUM, Freshwater	35 lbs., 4 ozs.	Lake Texoma	Nov. 5, 1967	R. J. Loilar
PICKEREL, Chain	2 lbs., 8 ozs.	Farm Pond	Feb. 25, 1973	Thomas Brown
PIKE, Northern	15 lbs., 12 ozs.	Lake Carl Etling	Apr. 3, 1971	Leroy Bass
SUNFISH, Green	2 lbs., 7 ozs.	Pontotoc Co. Pond	Oct. 16, 1972	Eddie Schulanberger
SUNFISH, Redear	2 lbs., 1¼ ozs.	Logan Co. Pond	Nov. 15, 1973	Ruby Lee Farmer
TROUT, Rainbow	10 lbs., 4 ozs.	Illinois River	July 3, 1966	Billy Payne
WALLEYE	11 lbs., 4 ozs.	Lake Hefner	Mar. 31, 1967	Garret Knol

OREGON

Species	Weight	Where	When	Angler
BASS, Largemouth	10 lbs., 8 ozs.	Columbia Slough	1915	Harvey Fisher
BASS, Smallmouth	5 lbs., 2 ozs.	Columbia River Potholes	May 18, 1970	Dan Harmon
BASS, Striped	61 lbs.	Umpqua River	May, 1970	Don Carnfarth
BLUEGILL	1 lb., 14 ozs.	Tahkenitch Lake	May 29, 1938	H. T. Schofield
BULLHEAD, Yellow	3 lbs., 2 ozs.	Willamette River	Mar. 15, 1961	Ted Schneider
CATFISH, Channel	29 lbs.	Devils Lake	Aug. 20, 1971	Jim Overguard
CATFISH, Flathead	33 lbs., 8 ozs.	Brownlee Reservoir	Sept. 28, 1973	Ray Gardner
CRAPPIE, Black	2 lbs., 6 ozs.	Sauvie Island	May 26, 1964	Virgil Briggans
CRAPPIE, White	4 lbs., 12 ozs.	Gerber Reservoir	May 22, 1967	Jim Duckett
PERCH, Yellow	2 lbs., 2 ozs.	Brownsmead	June 5, 1971	Ernie Affolter III
SALMON, Chinnok	83 lbs.	Umpqua River	1910	Ernie St. Claire
SALMON, Coho	25 lbs., 5¼ ozs.	Siltcoos Lake	Nov. 5, 1966	Ed Martin
TROUT, Brown	24 lbs., 14 ozs.	Wickiup Reservoir	1959	Donald LaDuke
TROUT, Rainbow	24 lbs., 24 ozs.	Lake Simtustus	June, 1974	Jerry Fifield
TROUT, Steelhead	31 lbs., 4 ozs.	Cascade Locks	Sept., 1963	Gus Hesgard

PENNSYLVANIA

Species	Weight	Where	When	Angler
BASS, Largemouth	8 lbs., 8 ozs.	Stillwater Lake	1936	Stanley Pastula
BASS, Rock	3 lbs., 2 ozs.	Elk Creek Lake	1971	David Weber
BASS, Smallmouth	6 lbs., 2 ozs.	Conodoguinet Creek	1937	Ed Meadows
CARP	52 lbs.	Juniata River	1962	George Brown

Species	Weight	Where	When	Angler
CATFISH, Channel	35 lbs.	Allegheny River	1970	Jim Rogers
CATFISH, Flathead	36 lbs., 8 ozs.	Allegheny River	1973	William Quick
CRAPPIE	3 lbs., 4 ozs.	Pinchot State Park Lake	1971	Stephen Sauve
MUSKELLUNGE	54 lbs., 3 ozs.	Conneaut Lake	1924	Lewis Walker, Jr.
PICKEREL, Chain	8 lbs.	Shohola Falls	1937	Frank Strenznetcky
PIKE, Northern	21 lbs., 4 ozs.	Lake Erie	1971	David Strait, Jr.
SHAD, American White	7 lbs., 4 ozs.	Delaware River	1965	Vincent Graziano
SHEEPSHEAD	14 lbs.	Virgin Run Lake	1964	Gregory Parella
SUCKER	9 lbs., 12 ozs.	French Creek	1938	George Kemper
SALMON, Chinook	16 lbs., 2 ozs.	Lake Erie	1973	William Merz
TROUT, Brook	4 lbs., 5 ozs.	Penns Creek	1972	Edward Ritz
TROUT, Brown	24 lbs.	Lake Wallenpaupack	1967	Frank Kociolek
TROUT, Lake	24 lbs.	Crystal Lake	1952	Mrs. Arthur Cramer
TROUT, Rainbow	9 lbs., 8 ozs.	Logan Branch	1961	Paul Roberts
TROUT, Steelhead	10¼ lbs.	Twelve Mile Creek	1973	Roy Tenney
WALLEYE	12 lbs.	Allegheny River	1951	Firman Shoff

RHODE ISLAND

Freshwater Species	Weight	Where	When	Angler
BASS, Largemouth	9 lbs., 12 ozs.	Barber Pond	Apr., 1963	Edward Ahern
TIE				
	9 lbs., 12 ozs.	Johnson Pond	June, 1963	Daniel Hill
PICKEREL, Chain	6 lbs., 8 ozs.	Black Rock	Jan. 24, 1969	Joseph Golomb
PIKE, Northern	15 lbs., 3 ozs.		Feb., 1972	Mark Edwards

Saltwater Species	Weight	Where	When	Angler
BASS, Striped	67 lbs.	Block Island	June, 1963	Jack Ryan
TIE				
	67 lbs.	Green Hill	Sept., 1965	Wilfred Fontaine
FLOUNDER	17 lbs., 8 ozs.	Narrow River	1962	Gary Farmer

SOUTH CAROLINA

Freshwater Species	Weight	Where	When	Angler
BASS, Largemouth	16 lbs., 2 ozs.	Lake Marion	Dec., 1949	P. H. Flanagan
BASS, Smallmouth	5 lbs., 4 ozs.	Toxaway River	July, 1971	C. Hoot, Jr.
BASS, Spotted	1 lb., 2 ozs.	Lake Hartwell	Mar., 1972	D. Knight
BASS, Striped	55 lbs.	Lake Moultrie	Jan., 1963	Tiny Lund
BASS, White	1 lb., 14 ozs.	Lake Murray	Jan., 1974	W. D. Richardson
BLUEGILL	3 lbs.	York Co. Pond	May, 1972	J. Strickland
BOWFIN	19 lbs., 12 ozs.	Lake Marion	Nov., 1971	M. R. Webster

Freshwater Species	Weight	Where	When	Angler
BULLHEAD	6 lbs., 3 ozs.	Edisto River	May, 1973	D. R. Dewitt
CATFISH, Blue	11 lbs., 3 ozs.	Lake Moultrie	Apr., 1974	W. D. Fretland
CATFISH, Channel	58 lbs.	Lake Moultrie	July, 1964	W. Whaley
CATFISH, Flathead	34 lbs., 8 ozs.	Wateree River	Apr., 1974	Mrs. J. Willard
CATFISH, White	9 lbs., 1 oz.	Keowee River	Apr., 1971	G. Keasler
CRAPPIE, Black	5 lbs.	Lake Moultrie	1957	P. Foust
CRAPPIE, White	5 lbs., 1 oz.	Lake Murray	Mar., 1949	Mrs. H. Owen
PERCH, Yellow	1 lb., 10 ozs.	Richland Co. Pond	Oct., 1972	J. C. Priester
PICKEREL, Jack	6 lbs.	Lake Marion	Jan., 1962	H. Avinger
SAUGER	3 lbs., 4 ozs.	Clark Hill	Feb., 1974	S. Duncan
TROUT, Brook	1 lb., 6 ozs.	Oconee Co.	Jan., 1973	E. G. Nutz
TIE				
	1 lb., 6 ozs.	Pickens Co.	Apr., 1974	D. Knight
TROUT, Brown	13 lbs., 4 ozs.	Chauga River	July, 1961	J. Addis
TROUT, Rainbow	5 lbs., 8 ozs.	Hartwell Tailrace	Apr., 1971	D. Knight
WALLEYE	9 lbs.	Lake Hartwell	Mar., 1974	T. O. Sheriff
WARMOUTH	2 lbs., 3 ozs.	Clarendon Co.	May, 1973	W. Singletary

Saltwater Species	Weight	Where	When	Angler
AMBERJACK	93 lbs.	Little River	Sept., 1957	J. N. Canup
BARRACUDA	65 lbs.	Georgetown	July, 1948	H. Shelor
BASS, Black Sea	6 lbs., 4 ozs.	Beaufort	July, 1968	R. Cooler
BASS, Channel	75 lbs.	Murrells Inlet	1965	A. J. Taylor
BLUEFISH	17 lbs., 1 oz.	Charleston	Apr., 1974	J. G. Thornhill
BONITO, Atlantic	6 lbs., 3 ozs.	Little River	May, 1973	G. McLaughlin
COBIA	78 lbs., 4 ozs.	Beaufort	June, 1973	H. G. Brown
CROAKER	4 lbs., 1 oz.	Georgetown Jetties	Nov., 1974	F. Wheeler
DOLPHIN	64 lbs., 8 ozs.	Charleston	June, 1971	B. C. Tuttle
TIE				
	64 lbs., 8 ozs.	Murrells Inlet	June, 1974	R. T. Swatzel
DRUM, Black	74 lbs., 8 ozs.	Beaufort	Apr., 1974	W. J. Warner
FLOUNDER	17 lbs., 6 ozs.	South Santee	Sept., 1974	L. C. Floyd
GROUPER, Scamp	23 lbs., 10 ozs.	Charleston	Aug., 1972	R. E. Tobin
GROUPER, Speckled Hind	45 lbs.	Little River	July, 1973	H. R. Murray
GROUPER, Warsaw	303 lbs.	Charleston	July, 1969	O. C. Polk, Jr.
GRUNT	18 lbs., 8 ozs.	Murrells Inlet	Sept., 1971	J. L. Flowers
HOGFISH	14 lbs., 7 ozs.	Charleston	Aug., 1973	J. E. Reeder
HOUNDFISH	9 lbs., 4 ozs.	Murrells Inlet	Aug., 1974	W. Kirby
JACK CREVALLE	33 lbs., 8 ozs.	Georgetown	July, 1972	W. L. Cromer, Jr.
LADYFISH	4 lbs., 8 ozs.	Bull Island	Aug., 1968	W. A. Silcox
MARLIN, Blue	481 lbs., 8 ozs.	Hilton Head	May, 1973	R. W. Gaskill
MARLIN, White	84 lbs., 8 ozs.	Charleston	May, 1969	B. Smith
MACKEREL, King	55 lbs., 8 ozs.	Beaufort	May, 1973	J. B. Franklin
MACKEREL, Spanish	10 lbs., 4 ozs.	Charleston	June, 1970	H. L. Timmerman
POMPANO	6 lbs., 11 ozs.	Murrells Inlet	1960	H. Taylor

Saltwater Species	Weight	Where	When	Angler
PORGY	16 lbs.	Charleston	July, 1968	F. A. Bailey
RUNNER, Rainbow	12 lbs.	Georgetown	Sept., 1968	J. S. Johnston
SAILFISH	75 lbs.	Georgetown	July, 1968	G. A. Reid
SHARK, Blacktip	133 lbs.	Port Royal Sound	June, 1968	B. Weldon
SHARK, Mako	75 lbs.	Charleston	Aug., 1971	B. R. Jenkins
SHARK, Tiger	1780 lbs.	Cherry Grove	June, 1964	W. Maxwell
SHEEPSHEAD	15 lbs., 4 ozs.	Charleston Jetties	June, 1969	J. Percival
SNAPPER, Red	37 lbs., 8 ozs.	Little River	Aug., 1964	K. Henry
SNAPPER, Vermilion	5 lbs., 6 ozs.	Charleston	Apr., 1974	S. W. Cox
SPADEFISH	9 lbs., 1 oz.	Murrells Inlet	July, 1965	Mrs. J. Brooks
SPOT	1 lb., 1 oz.	Crescent Lake	Aug., 1967	J. Stehmeyer
TARPON	137 lbs., 8 ozs.	Morris Island	July, 1954	W. M. Ball
TUNA, Blackfin	25 lbs., 8 ozs.	Georgetown	May, 1973	J. Nahrgang
TUNA, Little	23 lbs.	Charleston	June, 1967	J. Cain
TUNA, Skipjack	9 lbs., 8 ozs.	Charleston	Sept., 1974	M. Berg
TUNA, Yellowfin	217 lbs., 4 ozs.	Georgetown	July, 1974	B. H. Peace III
TRIPLE Tail	25 lbs., 8 ozs.	Mt. Pleasant	Oct., 1971	R. Hanckel, Jr.
TROUT, Summer	8 lbs., 8 ozs.	Myrtle Beach	Apr., 1974	J. Vance
TROUT, Winter	8 lbs., 15 ozs.	Breach Inlet	June, 1968	G. Joyner
WAHOO	88 lbs., 12 ozs.	Hilton Head	May, 1972	W. Roller
WHITING	2 lbs., 10 ozs.	Pawleys Island	Nov., 1968	C. Michau

SOUTH DAKOTA

Species	Weight	Where	When	Angler
BASS, Largemouth	8 lbs., 12 ozs.	Hayes Lake	1957	Verne Page
TIE				
	8 lbs., 12 ozs.	Fraiser Lake	1974	Roger Kowell
BASS, Rock	1 lb., 8 ozs.	Enemy Swim Lake	1974	Norene Loraff
BASS, Smallmouth	3 lbs., 2 ozs.	Ft. Randall Tailwaters	1972	Harry Rice
BASS, White	4 lbs., 2 ozs.	Enemy Swim Lake	1972	Gerald Perry
BLUEGILL	2 lbs., 4¼ ozs.	Leola Lake	1971	William Lapka
BUFFALO, Bigmouth	37 lbs., 8 ozs.	Lake Mitchell	1970	Harry Durst
BUFFALO, Smallmouth	8 lbs., 2 ozs.	Oahe Tailwaters	1969	Marvin Stratton
BULLHEAD, Black	3 lbs., 5 ozs.	Waubay Lake	1972	Donavan Dean
BULLHEAD, Brown	2 lbs., 7 ozs.	Crystal Lake	1963	Norman Clark
BULLHEAD, Yellow	2 lbs., 6 ozs.	Big Stone Lake	1973	Dale Thorson
BURBOT	12 lbs., 3 ozs.	Lake Sharpe	1974	Norman Sheldon
CARP	20 lbs., 12 ozs.	Sioux River	1974	Todd Schaefer
CATFISH, Blue (World Record)	97 lbs.	Missouri River	1959	Edward Elliott
CATFISH, Channel	55 lbs.	James River	1949	Roy Groves
CATFISH, Flathead	35 lbs., 4 ozs.	James River	1966	Daniel Leair
CRAPPIE, Black	3 lbs., 2 ozs.	Ft. Randall Reservoir	1964	Richard Hermanek
CRAPPIE, White	3 lbs., 9 ozs.	Farm Pond	1974	Gary Ernst

Species	Weight	Where	When	Angler
DRUM, Freshwater	36 lbs., 8 ozs.	Missouri River	1971	Alvin Williams
GAR, Longnose	13 lbs., 9½ ozs.	Missouri River	1965	Terry Coulson
GAR, Shortnose	2 lbs., 3 ozs.	Oahe Tailwaters	1970	Raymond Merchant
GOLDEYE	2 lbs., 2½ ozs.	Bad River	1970	Marvin Stratton
PADDLEFISH	114 lbs.	Big Bend Dam	1974	Leonard Potter
PERCH, Yellow	2 lbs., 4 ozs.	Cottonwood Lake	1972	Martin Hartze
PIKE, Northern	25 lbs.	Lake Sharpe	1972	Donald Matson
SALMON, Coho	3 lbs., 5 ozs.	Oahe Dam Tailwaters	1974	Barbara Poaches
SALMON, Kokanee	2 lbs., 6 ozs.	Pactola Reservoir	1973	Lloyd Foster
SAUGER	7 lbs., 7 ozs.	Oahe Tailwaters	1960	Harvey Holzworth
STURGEON, Lake	25 lbs.	Missouri River	1968	Delbert Henn
STURGEON, Pallid	28 lbs., 8 ozs.	Lake Sharpe	1971	Donald Chambers
STURGEON, Shovelnose	2 lbs., 6½ ozs.	Lake Mitchell	1973	Howard Frederick
SUCKER, Blue	11 lbs., 11 ozs.	James River	1967	Vernon Sarha
SUNFISH, Green	1 lb., 2 ozs.	Hayes Lake	1971	Mike Pellerzi
TROUT, Brook	5 lbs., 6 ozs.	Deerfield Reservoir	1966	Tom Sawyer
TROUT, Brown	22 lbs., 8 ozs.	Pactola Reservoir	1973	Jerry Romanowski
TROUT, Rainbow	12 lbs., 8 ozs.	Oahe Dam Tailwaters	1974	Marian Lenoch
WALLEYE	15 lbs.	Lake Kampeska	1960	Carl Wiese

TENNESSEE

Species	Weight	Where	When	Angler
BASS, Largemouth	14 lbs., 8 ozs.	Sugar Creek	Oct. 17, 1954	Louge Barnett
BASS, Rock	2 lbs., 8 ozs.	Stones River	1958	Bill Sanford
BASS, Rockfish (hybrid)	18 lbs.	Norris Lake	Apr. 2, 1974	Evan Bowers
BASS, Smallmouth	11 lbs., 15 ozs.	Dale Hollow Reservoir	July 13, 1955	D. L. Hayes
BASS, Spotted	5 lbs., 2 ozs.	Kentucky Lake	Mar. 21, 1971	Ted Carpenter
BASS, Striped	33 lbs.	Norris Reservoir	Apr. 26, 1974	Lynville Harvey
BASS, White	4 lbs., 10 ozs.	Pickwick Tailwaters	1949	Jack Allen
BLUEGILL	2 lbs., 8 ozs.	Linger Lake	Sept. 13, 1956	Forest Kidwell
TIE				
	2 lbs., 8 ozs.	Cheatham Lake	Feb. 22, 1961	Walter McFarland
BOWFIN	14 lbs., 11 ozs.	Reelfoot Lake	May 11, 1974	Jim Stevens
BUFFALO, Black	52 lbs.	Kentucky Lake	Mar. 29, 1973	James Smith
CARP	42 lbs., 8 ozs.	Boone Lake	Aug. 12, 1956	Al Moore
CATFISH, Blue	115 lbs.	Kentucky Lake	Oct. 9, 1971	Joe Potts
CATFISH, Channel	24 lbs., 3-1/5 ozs.	Laurel Hill Lake	Aug. 26, 1967	Carl Spencer
CATFISH, Flathead	40 lbs., 1 oz.	Kentucky Lake	Mar. 18, 1973	Charles Collins
CRAPPIE, Black	2 lbs., 12 ozs.	Center Hill	Apr. 4, 1969	Tom Graham
CRAPPIE, White	5 lbs., 1 oz.	Pond	Apr. 20, 1968	Bill Allen
DRUM	54 lbs., 8 ozs.	Nickajack Dam	Apr. 20, 1972	Benny Hull
GAR	23 lbs.	Pickwick Tailwaters	1963	Jimmy Gauvitts
MUSKELLUNGE	37 lbs., 8 ozs.	Norris Reservoir	Feb. 17, 1972	Ray Jones
PADDLEFISH	65 lbs.	Center Hill Lake	June 24, 1969	David Buttram
PICKEREL, Chain	6 lbs., 9 ozs.	Kentucky Lake	Feb. 24, 1951	Roy Stone

Species	Weight	Where	When	Angler
PIKE, Northern	6 lbs., 15½ ozs.	South Holston Reservoir	Oct. 10, 1973	John Lindamood
SAUGER	7 lbs., 6 ozs.	Chambers Creek	Feb. 19, 1973	Rayford Voss
TROUT, Brook	3 lbs., 14 ozs.	Hiwassee River	Aug. 15, 1973	Jerry Wills
TROUT, Brown	26 lbs., 2 ozs.	Dale Hollow Tailwaters	May, 1968	George Langston
TROUT, Rainbow	14 lbs., 8 ozs.	Obey River	Dec. 18, 1971	Jack Rigney
WALLEYE (World Record)	25 lbs.	Old Hickory Lake	Aug. 3, 1960	Mabry Harper

TEXAS

Freshwater Species	Weight	Where	When	Angler
BASS, Largemouth	13 lbs., 8 ozs.	Medina Lake	Jan., 1943	H. R. Magee
BASS, Spotted	5 lbs., 9 ozs.	Lake O'Pines	Mar. 13, 1966	Turner Keith
BASS, Striped	22 lbs., 4 ozs.	Toledo Bend Reservoir	Feb. 10, 1973	Charles Dickerson
BASS, White	5 lbs., 4¼ ozs.	Colorado River	Mar., 1968	Raymond Rivers
BLUEGILL	3 lbs., 4 ozs.	Farm Pond	Apr. 25, 1966	Winfred Hoke
BOWFIN	17 lbs., 3 ozs.	Toledo Bend	Aug. 15, 1972	R. M. Spier
BUFFALO	58 lbs.	Stock Tank	Apr. 6, 1969	Bobby Thompson
CARP	41 lbs.	Pure Oil Lake	May 14, 1972	Scott Helsley
CATFISH, Channel	36 lbs., 8 ozs.	Pedernales River	Mar. 7, 1965	Mrs. Joe Cockrell
CATFISH, Flathead	67 lbs.	Lake Tyler	Feb. 19, 1972	J. H. Beardin
CRAPPIE, White	4 lbs., 9 ozs.	Navarro Mills Lake	Feb. 14, 1968	G. G. Wooderson
DRUM, Freshwater	22½ lbs.	Eagle Mountain Lake	June 22, 1974	Joe Chaloupka
GAR, Alligator	279 lbs.	Rio Grande	1951	Bill Valverde
GAR, Longnosed	50 lbs., 5 ozs.	Trinity River	1954	Townsend Miller
PADDLEFISH	7 lbs., 1.6 ozs.	Pat Mayse Lake	Apr. 7, 1973	Gene Rader
PICKEREL	4 lbs., 6½ ozs.	Caddo Lake	Apr. 10, 1971	Perry Morris
PIKE, Northern	13 lbs., 4 ozs.	Greenbelt Lake	Jan. 23, 1973	Clarence Hamilton
REDFISH	26 lbs.	Chub Lake	May 11, 1971	Jack Kimbrough
SUNFISH, Green	2 lbs., 3¼ ozs.	Farm Pond	May 18, 1969	Alex Short
SUNFISH, Redear	2 lbs., 8½ ozs.	Farm Pond	June, 1974	Kenneth Wortham
TROUT, Rainbow	4 lbs., 12 ozs.	Guadalupe River	1968	Ron Sharp
WALLEYE	8 lbs., 14 ozs.	Lake Meredith	May 27, 1972	Mrs. Alice Peters

Saltwater Species	Weight	Where	When	Angler
AMBERJACK	66 lbs.	Port Arkansas	Sept. 3, 1972	Gentry Barnes
BARRACUDA	41½ lbs.	Port Arkansas	Aug. 19, 1973	Mrs. Hunter Barrett
BONITO	27 lbs.	Freeport	July, 1969	Eddie Groth
COBIA	90 lbs.	Freeport	June 7, 1969	John Walker
CROAKER	5 lbs., 2 ozs.	East Galveston Bay	July 10, 1971	Earl Merendino
DORADO	54½ lbs.	Off Port Aransas Jetties	June, 1974	Barbara Evans
DRUM, Black	78 lbs.	Sabine	June 25, 1964	Marvin McEachern
FLOUNDER	11 lbs., 2 ozs.	Galveston West Bay	May 9, 1972	Jefferson D. Huddleston, Jr.
GAFFTOP	9 lbs.	Matagorda Bay	1965	Fabian Koronczok

Saltwater Species	Weight	Where	When	Angler
JACK CREVALLE	49½ lbs.	Galveston Surf	June 14, 1972	Dave Huddleston, Sr.
JEWFISH	551 lbs.	Galveston	1937	Gus Pangarakis
LADYFISH	3 lbs., 6¼ ozs.	Espirtu Santo Bay	Sept. 29, 1973	John Thomas Parker III
MACKEREL, King	68 lbs.	Port O'Connor	July 31, 1971	Clay Hammonds
MACKEREL, Spanish	6 lbs., 13 ozs.	Freeport	July, 1969	Jerry Calvert
MARLIN, Blue	547 lbs.	Port Aransas	1963	Dean Hawn
MARLIN, White	106 lbs.	Port Aransas	May 23, 1970	Dale Dorn
POMPANO	6 lbs., 1 oz.		Apr. 23, 1971	Mrs. Jerald Feldman
POMPANO, African	19 lbs.	Port Aransas	Dec. 9, 1972	Dr. B. L. Payne
REDFISH	51½ lbs.	Padre Island Surf	Jan., 1967	Johnny Cizmar
SAILFISH	95 lbs.	East Breaks	July 12, 1972	Martin Cohn
SAWFISH	736 lbs.	Galveston	1939	Gus Pangarakis
SHARK, Blacktip	136 lbs.	Port Isabel	Aug. 25, 1973	Robert Cline
SHARK, Bull	496 lbs.	Off Port Aransas	July 21, 1974	Dan Countiss
SHARK, Hammerhead	870 lbs.	Port Aransas	July 14, 1973	Ross Havard
SHARK, Lemon	322 lbs.	Port Isabel Jetty	May 12, 1972	Michael Gibbs
SHARK, Mako	325 lbs.	Port Aransas	Aug. 11, 1973	Pat Hawn
SHARK, Sand	380 lbs.	Padre Island Surf	Mar. 18, 1972	Morris Kocurek
SHARK, Sandbar	139 lbs.	Bob Hall Pier	Mar. 18, 1973	Robert Gulley
SHARK, Spinner	165 lbs.	Port Aransas	Sept. 3, 1973	O. E. Ballard
SHARK, Tiger	760 lbs.	Galveston Jetties	July 3, 1971	Ken Higginbotham
SNAPPER, Dog	128 lbs.	Port Aransas	1962	Chris Page
SNOOK	57½ lbs.	Padre Island	1937	Louis Rawalt
SPADEFISH	7 lbs., 12 ozs.	Port O'Connor	July 7, 1971	Durrell Hyatt
TARPON	210 lbs.	South Padre Island	Nov. 13, 1973	Thomas Gibson
TRIPLETAIL	28 lbs., 8 ozs.	Port O'Connor	July 3, 1971	Theodore Flick
TROUT, Sand	6 lbs., 4 ozs.	Texas City	Feb. 26, 1972	Dennis Herrick
TROUT, Speckled	13 lbs., 2 ozs.	Arroyo Colorado	Mar. 17, 1957	Walter Hentz
TIE				
	13 lbs., 2 ozs.	Galveston	May 25, 1969	Lanny Myers
TUNA, Blackfin	36 lbs.	Port Isabel	Aug., 1968	John Walker
TUNA, Yellowfin	146 lbs., 4 ozs.	Port O'Connor	June 9, 1973	Stewart Campbell
WAHOO	87 lbs., 10 ozs.	Port Aransas	July 10, 1960	Mrs. Arnold Morgan
WHITING	2 lbs., 12 ozs.	Galveston	Mar. 11, 1972	Mike Walker

UTAH

Species	Weight	Where	When	Angler
BASS, Black	8 lbs., 3 ozs.	Lake Powell	1969	Afton Hansen
BASS, White	4 lbs., 1 oz.	Utah Lake	1970	John Welcker
CARP	30 lbs.	Great Salt Lake Marshes	1960	Ralph Merrill
CATFISH, Channel	23 lbs.	Utah Lake	1970	LeRoy Martinsen
CRAPPIE, Black	2 lbs., 5 ozs.	Lake Powell	1974	E. J. Smith
SALMON, Kokanee	4 lbs.	Utah Lake	1967	Park Leo
SQUAWFISH	14¾ lbs.	Green River	1961	Phil Dotson

Species	Weight	Where	When	Angler
TROUT, Brook	7 lbs., 8 ozs.	Boulder Mountain	1971	Milton Taft
TROUT, Brown	29 lbs., 8 ozs.	Flaming Gorge Reservoir	1974	Verl Hanchett
TROUT, Cutthroat	26¾ lbs.	Strawberry Reservoir	1930	Mrs. E. Smith
TROUT, Lake	36 lbs.	Fish Lake	1960	Katherine White
TROUT, Rainbow	21½ lbs.	Mill Creek Reservoir	1947	La Mar Westra
WALLEYE	10 lbs.	Provo River	1967	P. J. Keller

VERMONT

Species	Weight	Where	When	Angler
BASS, Largemouth	7 lbs., 6 ozs.	Lake St. Catherine	1971	Cecil Brown
BASS, Smallmouth	6 lbs., 7 ozs.	Harriman Reservoir	1969	Chester Burgess
BOWFIN	9 lbs., 15 ozs.	Winooski River	1971	John Shaw
BULLHEAD	1 lb., 8 ozs.	Lake Hortonia	1969	John Finnessy
CARP	19 lbs., 12 ozs.	Winooski River	1973	Quentin Potter
CATFISH, Channel	32 lbs., 4 ozs.	Lake Champlain	1974	Dr. S. Warren Kluger
CRAPPIE, Black	1 lb., 2 ozs.	Lake Bomoseen	1971	Julian Sbardella
GAR	2 lbs., 12 ozs.	Lake Champlain	1972	Robert Horton
MUSKELLUNGE	23 lbs., 8 ozs.	Missisquoi River	1970	Richard Gross
PERCH, Yellow	1 lb., 3 ozs.	Lake Memphremagog		Shawn Blais
PICKEREL, Chain	6 lbs., 4 ozs.	Harriman Reservoir	1974	Robert Purdy
PIKE, Northern	26 lbs.	Lake Champlain	1970	Robert Bearor
SALMON	5 lbs., 8 ozs.	Lake Seymour	1969	Edward Ashman
SHEEPSHEAD	13 lbs., 2 ozs.	Lake Champlain	1971	Ray LaValley
TROUT, Brook	4 lbs., 12 ozs.	Jail Branch	1973	Frederick Lapan
TROUT, Brown	11 lbs., 12 ozs.	Little River	1974	Lawrence Kingsbury
TROUT, Lake	27 lbs., 8 ozs.	Little Averill	1971	Percy Mason
TROUT, Rainbow	10 lbs., 1 oz.	Lake Bomoseen	1969	Thomas Beauregard
WALLEYE	12 lbs., 6 ozs.	Lake Memphremagog	1972	Charles Butterfield

VIRGINIA

Species	Weight	Where	When	Angler
BASS, Largemouth	14 lbs.	Gaston Lake	Apr. 17, 1972	Paul Creggar
BASS, Kentucky	5 lbs., 12 ozs.	Claytor Lake	May 25, 1973	Samuel Turner
BASS, Rock	2 lbs., 2 ozs.	Pigg River	Mar. 29, 1964	J. Monaghan
BASS, Smallmouth	8 lbs.	Claytor Lake	May 22, 1964	C. A. Garay
BASS, Striped	34 lbs.	Buggs Island	May 22, 1973	Billy Crutchfield
BASS, White	4 lbs.	Claytor Lake	May 17, 1974	E. V. Clark
BLUEGILL	4 lbs., 8 ozs.	Private Pond	Feb. 7, 1970	Thomas Jones
BOWFIN	17 lbs., 8 ozs.	Chickahominy Lake	Nov. 14, 1964	E. C. Cutright
CATFISH, Channel	30 lbs.	Smith Mt. Reservoir	June 2, 1973	Robert Underwood
CATFISH, Flathead	57 lbs.	South Holston	July 29, 1972	Allan Robinette
CRAPPIE	4 lbs., 14 ozs.	Lake Conner	Apr. 8, 1967	E. L. Blackstock
GAR	20 lbs., 8 ozs.	Northwest River	Aug. 20, 1973	R. H. Marshall

Species	Weight	Where	When	Angler
MUSKELLUNGE	31 lbs.	Smith Mt. Lake	May 26, 1973	Pete Fuqua
PERCH, White	2 lbs., 4 ozs.	Lake Smith	Nov. 21, 1973	Rick Shoemaker
PERCH, White	2 lbs., 4 ozs.	New River	Mar. 25, 1972	Richard Irvin
PICKEREL, Chain	8 lbs., 4 ozs.	Gaston River	Oct. 7, 1973	Howard Evans
PIKE, Northern	18 lbs., 5 ozs.	Occoquan	May 3, 1974	Ollie Richardson
SALMON, Coho	8 lbs., 12 ozs.	Philpott	Dec. 27, 1971	Melvin Chilton
SAUGER	5 lbs., 8 ozs.	S. Holston Lake	July 2, 1972	R. Stallard
SUNFISH, Redear	4 lbs., 8 ozs.	Private Pond	June 19, 1970	Gene Ball
TROUT, Brook	4 lbs., 2 ozs.	Back Creek	Nov. 13, 1973	O. G. Burkholder
TROUT, Brown	14 lbs., 6 ozs.	Smith River	Aug. 8, 1974	Al Teachout
TROUT, Lake	5 lbs., 6 ozs.	Philpott Dam	July 6, 1966	Arthur Conner
TROUT, Rainbow	9 lbs., 14 ozs.	Pond	May 5, 1967	D. L. Talbott
WALLEYE	22 lbs., 8 ozs.	New River	Aug. 20, 1973	Roy Barrett

WASHINGTON

Species	Weight	Where	When	Angler
BASS, Largemouth	11 lbs., 8 ozs.	Newman Lake	July, 1966	Don Milleton
BASS, Smallmouth	8 lbs., 12 ozs.	Columbia River	Apr., 1967	Ray Wanacutt
BLUEGILL	1 lb., 4 ozs.		1973	Thomas Price
BURBOT	13 lbs.	Roosevelt Reservoir	Apr., 1955	
CATFISH, Blue	14 lbs., 10 ozs.	Mouth of Yakima River	June 14, 1970	DeVerne Dunnum
CATFISH, Channel	15 lbs.	Snake River	June, 1971	John Leat
CRAPPIE	4 lbs., 8 ozs.	Lake Washington	May, 1956	John Smart
PERCH, Yellow	2 lbs.	Spanaway Lake	May 4, 1972	Robert Turnmire
TROUT, Brook	6 lbs., 12 ozs.	Lake Cavanaugh		Gregory Anderson
TROUT, Brown	22 lbs.	Sullivan Lake	May, 1965	R. L. Henry
TROUT, Cutthroat Resident	12 lbs.	Lake Crescent	July, 1961	W. Welsh
TROUT, Cutthroat Sea-Run	6 lbs.	Carr Inlet	May, 1943	Bud Johnson
TROUT, Dolly Varden	22 lbs., 8 ozs.	Tieton River		Louis Schott
TROUT, Lake	30 lbs., 4 ozs.	Loon Lake	June, 1966	Ken Janke
TROUT, Rainbow Resident	22 lbs., 8 ozs.	Waitts Lake	1957	Bill Dittner
TROUT, Steelhead Summer-Run	35 lbs., 1 oz.	Snake River	1973	Gilbert Pierson
TROUT, Steelhead Winter-Run	32 lbs., 10 ozs.	Cowlitz River	Mar. 9, 1971	Clifford Aynes
WALLEYE	15 lbs., 9 ozs.	Billy Clapp Lake	1973	Gary Holzhaner

WEST VIRGINIA

Species	Weight	Where	When	Angler
BASS, Largemouth	10 lbs.	Coal River	1968	Arlen Ash
BASS, Rock	1 lb.	Big Sandy Creek	1964	Warren Ryan

Species	Weight	Where	When	Angler
BASS, Smallmouth	9 lbs., 12 ozs.	South Branch	1971	David Lindsay
BASS, Spotted	3 lbs.	So. Fork Hughes River	1966	Henry Fenney
BASS, Striped	3 lbs.	Kanawha Falls	1974	Robert Kirk
BASS, White	4 lbs.	Kanawha River	1964	Robert Peyton
BLUEGILL	2 lbs., 2 ozs.	Farm Pond	1973	Arlie Thompson
BOWFIN	5 lbs.	South Branch	1973	Howard White
BUFFALO	30 lbs.	Tygart Creek	1970	Kenneth Casto
BULLHEAD	3¼ lbs.	Ohio River	1972	Gale Murray
CARP	40 lbs.	New River	1970	Jerry Spicer
CATFISH, Channel	19 lbs.	Coal River	1963	Donald Foreman
CATFISH, Shovelhead	/0 lbs.	Little Kanawha R.	1956	L. L. McClung
CRAPPIE	4 lbs.	Meathouse Fork	1971	Leonard Edgell
DRUM, Freshwater	25 lbs.	Little Kanawha R.	1954	Bill Dawkins
GAR, Longnose	17 lbs.	Little Kanawha R.	1952	A. J. Keith
MUSKELLUNGE	43 lbs.	Elk River	1955	Lester Hayes
PICKEREL, Chain	4 lbs.	Back Creek	1968	Kenny Noll
PIKE, Northern	11 lbs., 4 ozs.	Elk River	1973	Buster Sizemore
STURGEON	12 lbs.	Ohio River	1949	Emmett Wheeler
TROUT, Brook	3 lbs., 12 ozs.	Rich Creek	1969	Stephen Meadows
TROUT, Brown	16 lbs.	South Branch	1968	Paul Parker
TROUT, Golden Rainbow	3 lbs., 12 ozs.	Back Fork of Elk River	1973	Granville Davis
TROUT, Rainbow	10 lbs.	Spruce Knob Lake	1956	John Manley
WALLEYE	16 lbs.	New River	1967	E. C. Cox

WISCONSIN

Species	Weight	Where	When	Angler
BASS, Largemouth	11 lbs., 3 ozs.	Lake Ripley	Oct. 12, 1940	Robert Miklowski
BASS, Rock	1 lb., 12 ozs.	Big Green Lake	Feb. 14, 1971	Mrs. Celia Walker
BASS, Smallmouth	9 lbs., 1 oz.	Indian Lake	June 21, 1950	Leon Stefoneck
BASS, White	3 lbs., 9 ozs.	Wisconsin River	1962	J. L. Griffith
BASS, Yellow (World Record)	2 lbs., 2 ozs.	Lake Monona	Jan. 18, 1972	Jim Thrun
BLUEGILL	2 lbs., 4 ozs.	Squash Lake	June 25, 1971	L & L Ferries
BULLHEAD, Black	2 lbs., 9 ozs.	Trappe Lake	May 24, 1967	Richard Kincaid
BULLHEAD, Brown	3 lbs., 12 ozs.	Nelson Lake	July 31, 1972	Mrs. Eugene Mable
BULLHEAD, Yellow	3 lbs., 3 ozs.	Nelson Lake	July 5, 1972	Ocelee Reppond
CARP	57 lbs., 2 ozs.	Lake Wisconsin	Aug. 28, 1966	Mike Prorok
CATFISH, Channel	44 lbs.	Wisconsin River	1962	Larry Volenec
CATFISH, Flathead	61 lbs.	Fox River	June 28, 1966	Mike Tanner
CISCO	4 lbs., 10½ ozs.	Big Green Lake	June 12, 1969	Joe Miller
CRAPPIE, White	4 lbs., 8 ozs.	Gile Flowage	Aug. 12, 1967	Allen Dollar
MUSKELLUNGE	69 lbs., 11 ozs.	Lake Chippewa Flowage	Oct. 20, 1949	Louis Spray
PERCH, Yellow	3 lbs., 4 ozs.	Lake Winnebago	1954	Mike Lamont
PIKE, Northern	38 lbs.	Lake Puckaway	Aug. 6, 1952	J. A. Rahn
SALMON, Atlantic	9 lbs., 15 ozs.	Lake Michigan	July 13, 1974	Howard Kinn

Species	Weight	Where	When	Angler
SALMON, Chinook	40 lbs., 4 ozs.	Menominee River	Sept. 15, 1973	Myron Graaf
SALMON, Coho	22 lbs., 2 ozs.	Lake Michigan	July 16, 1972	Donald Warzyn
SAUGER	4 lbs., 5 ozs.	Mississippi River	Apr. 10, 1970	Mrs. James Carlson
TIE				
	4 lbs., 5 ozs.	Mississippi River	June 4, 1971	Lee Paul
SHEEPSHEAD	26 lbs.	Fox River	May 12, 1971	Nolan Rothenback
STURGEON, Rock	94 lbs., 3 ozs.	Menominee River	Sept. 20, 1968	Thomas Winter
SUNFISH, Green	1 lb., 9 ozs.	Wind Lake	Aug. 23, 1967	Thomas Tart
TROUT, Brook	9 lbs., 15 ozs.	Prairie River	Sept. 2, 1944	John Mixis
TROUT, Brown	29 lbs., 9 ozs.	Lake Superior	May 24, 1971	Michael Brasic
TROUT, Lake	47 lbs.	Lake Superior	Sept. 9, 1946	Waino Roose
TROUT, Rainbow	24 lbs., 4 ozs.	Lake Michigan	Aug. 19, 1973	James Schuh
TROUT, Splake-hybrid	14 lbs., 4 ozs.	Ada Lake	June 7, 1967	Bill Keeler
TROUT, Tiger	10 lbs.	Deerskin River	May 23, 1974	Charles Matlek
WALLEYE	18 lbs.	High Lake	Sept. 26, 1933	Tony Brothers

WYOMING

Species	Weight	Where	When	Angler
BASS, Largemouth	7 lbs., 2 ozs.	Stove Lake	1942	John Teeters
CRAPPIE, Black	1 lb., 7 ozs.	Boysen Reservoir	1968	Jim Jacobsen
LING	19 lbs., 4 ozs.	Pilot Butte Reservoir	1965	K. E. Moreland
PIKE, Northern	9 lbs., 15 o s.	Keyhole Reservoir	1974	S. T. McWhirter
SAUGER	6 lbs., 8 ozs.	Wind River	1942	
TROUT, Brook	10 lbs.	Torrey Lake	1933	
TROUT, Brown	21 lbs., 2 ozs.	North Platte	1972	Deryl Beckel
TROUT, Cutthroat	15 lbs.	Native Lake	1959	Alan Dow
TROUT, Golden	11 lbs., 4 ozs.	Cook's Lake	1948	C. S. Read
TROUT, Lake	44 lbs.	Jackson Lake	1967	Pat Christensen
TROUT, Rainbow	23 lbs.	Burnt Lake	1969	Frank Favazzo
WALLEYE	14 lbs., 4 ozs.	Keyhole Reservoir	1973	Wilmer Swindler
WHITEFISH	4 lbs.	Wind River		

CHAPTER 44

State Conservation Departments

ALABAMA
Department of Conservation and Natural Resources, Game and Fish Division, 64 N. Union Street, Montgomery, AL 36104

ALASKA
Department of Fish & Game, Sport Fish Division, Subport Building, Juneau, AK 99801

ARIZONA
State Game and Fish Commission, Arizona State Building, Phoenix, AZ 85001

AKANSAS
Game and Fish Commission, Game and Fish Building, State Capitol Grounds, Little Rock, AR 72201

CALIFORNIA
Department of Fish and Game, Marine Resources Branch, 1416 Ninth Street, Sacramento, CA 95814

COLORADO
Department of Natural Resources, Information Services, 6060 Broadway, Denver, CO 80216

CONNECTICUT
Department of Environmental Protection, Fish and Water Life, State Office Building, Hartford, CT 06115

DELAWARE
Department of Natural Resources and Environmental Control, Division of Fish & Wildlife, Dover, DE 19901

FLORIDA
Game and Fresh Water Fish Commission, Farris Bryant Building, 620 S. Meridian Street, Tallahassee, FL 32304

GEORGIA
Department of Natural Resources, 270 Washington Street, S.W., Atlanta, GA 30334

HAWAII
Department of Land and Natural Resources, Division of Fish and Game, 1179 Punchbowl Street, Honolulu, HI 96813

IDAHO
Fish and Game Department, Information Division, 600 S. Walnut Street, Boise, ID 83707

ILLINOIS
Department of Conservation, Division of Fisheries, 605 State Office Building, 400 S. Spring Street, Springfield, IL 62706

INDIANA
Department of Conservation, Division of Fish and Wildlife, 607 State Office Building, Indianapolis, IN 46204

IOWA
State Conservation Commission, Valley National Bank Building, 4th & Walnut Streets, Des Moines, IA 50308

KANSAS
Forestry, Fish and Game Commission, Box 591, Pratt, KS 67124

KENTUCKY
Department of Fish & Wildlife, State Office Building Annex, Frankfort, KY 40601

LOUISIANA
Louisiana Outdoor Writers, c/o Wild Life and Fisheries Commission, Wild Life and Fisheries Building, 400 Royal Street, New Orleans, LA 70130

MAINE

Department of Inland Fisheries and Game, State House, Augusta, ME 04330

MARYLAND

Fish and Wildlife Administration, State Office Building, Annapolis, MD 21401

MASSACHUSETTS

Division of Fisheries and Game, Field Headquarters, Westboro, MA 01581

MICHIGAN

Department of Natural Resources, Stevens T. Mason Building, Lansing, MI 48926

MINNESOTA

Department of Conservation, Section of Fisheries, Division of Game and Fish, St. Paul, MN 55101

MISSISSIPPI

State Game and Fish Commission, Woolfolk State Office Building, Jackson, MS 39201

MISSOURI

Department of Conservation, 2901 N. Ten Mile Drive, Jefferson City, MO 65101

MONTANA

Department of Fish and Game, Fisheries Division, Helena, MT 59601

NEBRASKA

Game and Parks Commission, P.O. Box 30370, Lincoln, NB 68503

NEVADA

Department of Fish and Game, P.O. Box 10678, Reno, NV 89510

NEW HAMPSHIRE

Fish and Game Department, 34 Bridge Street, Concord, NH 03301

NEW JERSEY

Information and Education Section, Division of Fish, Game and Shell Fisheries, Box 1809, Trenton, NJ 08625

NEW MEXICO

Department of Game and Fish, State Capitol, Santa Fe, NM 87501

NEW YORK

New York State Department of Environmental Conservation, 50 Wolf Road, Albany, NY 12201

NORTH CAROLINA

Department of Natural and Economic Resources, Travel and Promotion Division, Box 27687, Raleigh, NC 27611 and/or Sports Fisheries Studies, P.O. Box 769, Morehead City, NC 28557

NORTH DAKOTA

State Game and Fish Department, Bismarck, ND 58501

OHIO

Outdoor Writers of Ohio, Inc., Record Fish Committee, c/o The Fremont News-Messenger, 107 S. Arch Street, Fremont, OH 43420

OKLAHOMA

Department of Wildlife Conservation, 1801 N. Lincoln Blvd., P.O. Box 53465, Oklahoma City, OK 73105

OREGON

State Wildlife Commission, 1634 S.W. Alder Street, P.O. Box 3503, Portland, OR 97208

PENNSYLVANIA

Fish Commission, Box 1673, Harrisburg, PA 17120

RHODE ISLAND

Department of Natural Resoruces, Division of Fish & Wildlife, Veterans' Memorial Building, Providence, RI 02903

SOUTH CAROLINA

Wildlife and Marine Resources Department, P.O. Box 167, Columbia, SC 29202

SOUTH DAKOTA

Department of Game, Fish and Parks, Communications Division, Pierre, SD 57501

TENNESSEE

Wildlife Resources Agency, Fish Management Division, Ellington Agricultural Center, P.O. Box 40747, Nashville, TN 37204

TEXAS

Parks and Wildlife Department, Information and Education, John H. Reagan Building, Austin, TX 78701

UTAH

Department of Fish and Game, 1596 W. North Temple, Salt Lake City, UT 84116

VERMONT

Department of Fish and Game, Montpelier, VT 05602

VIRGINIA

Commission of Game and Inland Fisheries, 4010 W. Broad Street, Richmond, VA 23230

WASHINGTON
Department of Game Fishery Management Division, 600 N. Capitol Way, Olympia, WA 98501

WEST VIRGINIA
Division of Wildlife Resources, Department of Natural Resources, Charleston, WV 25305

WISCONSIN
Department of Natural Resources, Box 450, Madison, WI 53701

WYOMING
Game and Fish Commission, Information and Education Division, Cheyenne, WY 82001

CHAPTER 45

Canada and the Bahamas
Fishing Information Department

ALBERTA
Department of Lands and Forests, Edmonton, Alta.

BRITISH COLUMBIA
Fish and Game Branch, Department of Recreation and Conservation, 567 Burrard St., Vancouver 1, B.C.

MANITOBA
Department of Mines and Natural Resources, Winnipeg, Man.

NEWFOUNDLAND
Department of Mines and Resources, St. John's, Newfoundland

NORTHWEST TERRITORIES
Northern Administration Branch, Department of Northern Affairs and National Resources, Ottawa, Ontario, Canada

NOVA SCOTIA
Department of Lands and Forests, Halifax, N.S.

ONTARIO
Department of Lands and Forests, Parliament Bldgs., Toronto, Ontario

PRINCE EDWARD ISLAND
Department of Industry and Natural Resources, Charlottetown, P.E.I.

QUEBEC
Department of Game and Fisheries, Quebec, Que.

SASKATCHEWAN
Department of Natural Resources, Government Administration Bldg., Regina, Sask.

YUKON TERRITORY
Game Department, Yukon Territorial Government, Box 2029, Whitehorse, Y.T., Canada

Bahamas Fishing Information Bureau
The Development Board, Nassau, The Bahamas

CHAPTER 46

Conservation, Professional and Sportsmen's Organization

AMERICAN CASTING ASSOCIATION: P.O. Box 51, Nashville, Tenn.

AMERICAN FISHING TACKLE MANUFACTURER'S ASSOCIATION: 20 North Wacker Drive, Chicago, Illinois 60606

AMERICAN INSTITUTE OF BIOLOGICAL SCIENCES: Box 9173, Roslyn Station, Arlington, Virginia

AMERICAN FISHERIES SOCIETY: 1404 New York Ave., N.W., Washington, D.C.

AMERICAN LITTORAL SOCIETY: Sandy Hook Marine Laboratory, Box 117, Highlands, New Jersey

ATLANTIC SEA RUN SALMON COMMISSION: University of Maine, Orono, Maine

ATLANTIC STATES MARINE FISHERIES COMMISSION: 336 E. College Ave., Tallahassee, Florida

FRIENDS OF THE WILDERNESS: 3515 E. 4th Street, Duluth, Minnesota

GULF AND CARIBBEAN FISHERIES INSTITUTE: Institute of Marine Science, University of Miami, 1 Rickenbacker Causeway, Virginia Key, Miami, Florida

GULF STATES MARINE FISHERIES COMMISSION: 312 Audubon Bldg., New Orleans, Louisiana

GREAT LAKES FISHERY COMMISSION: 106 Natural Resources Bldg., University of Michigan, Ann Arbor, Michigan

INTERNATIONAL ASSOCIATION OF GAME, FISH AND CONSERVATION COMM.: 16413 Canterbury Drive, Hopkins, Minnesota

INTERNATIONAL CASTING FEDERATION: 1400 South Peters Street, New Orleans, Louisiana

INTERNATIONAL COMM. FOR THE NORTHWEST ATLANTIC FISHERIES: Education Bldg., Dalhousie University, Halifax, North Carolina

INTERNATIONAL GAME FISH ASSOCIATION: Alfred 1, DuPont Bldg., Miami, Florida

INTERNATIONAL OCEANOGRAPHIC FOUNDATION: 1 Rickenbacker Causeway, Virginia Key, Miami, Florida

INTERNATIONAL PACIFIC SALMON FISHERIES COMM.: Box 30, New Westminster, B.C., Canada

INTERNATIONAL SPIN FISHING ASSOCIATION: P.O. Box 81, Downey, California

IZAAK WALTON LEAGUE OF AMERICA: Arlington, Virginia

NATIONAL ASSOCIATION OF MARINE ANGLER'S CLUBS: Box 117, Highlands, New Jersey

NATIONAL FISHERIES INSTITUTE, INC.: 1614 20th St., N.W., Washington, D.C.

NATIONAL PARTY BOAT OWNER'S ASSOCIATION: Box 117, Highlands, New Jersey

NATIONAL WILDLIFE FEDERATION: 1412 16th St., N.W., Washington, D.C.

NEW ENGLAND ADVISORY BOARD FOR FISH & GAME PROBLEMS: 319 Linwood St., West Lynn, Mass.

NEW ENGLAND OUTDOOR WRITER'S ASSOCIATION: 1003 N. Westfield St., Feeding Hills, Mass.

OUTBOARD BOATING CLUB OF AMERICA: 401 N. Michigan Ave., Chicago, Ill. 60611

OUTDOOR RECREATION INSTITUTE: 5003 Wapakoneta, Washington, D.C.

OUTDOOR WRITER'S ASSOCIATION OF AMERICA: 105 Guitar Bldg., Columbia, Missouri

PACIFIC MARINE FISHERIES COMM.: 741 State Office Bldg., 1400 S.W. Fifth Ave., Portland, Oregon

SPORT FISHERY RESEARCH FOUNDATION: 1404 New York Avenue, Washington, D.C.

SPORT FISHING INSTITUTE: Bond Bldg., Washington, D.C.

THE BROTHERHOOD OF THE JUNGLE COCK: 10 E. Fayette St., Baltimore, Md.

THE CAMP FIRE CLUB OF AMERICA: 19 Rector Street, New York, New York

TROUT, UNLIMITED: 900 Lapeer Avenue, Saginaw, Michigan

U.S. FOREST SERVICE, U.S. SOIL CONSERVATION SERVICE, U.S. BUREAU OF OUTDOOR RECREATION, U.S. FISH AND WILDLIFE SERVICE, U.S. NATIONAL PARK SERVICE: Washington, D.C.

U.S. TROUT FARMERS ASSOCIATION: 110 Social Hall Avenue, Salt Lake City, Utah

WILDLIFE MANAGEMENT INSTITUTE: 709 Wire Bldg., Washington, D.C.

CHAPTER 47

Directory of Fishing Manufacturers and Importers

Able 2 Products Co., 504 E. 19th St., P.O. Box 543, Cassville, Mo. 65625 (Bass Lite, reel covers, ice cleats, etc.)

Academy Broadway Corp., 5 Plant Ave., Vanderbilt Industrial Park, Smithtown, N.Y. 11787 (waders, creels)

Acme Tackle Co., 69 Bucklin St., Providence, R.I. 02907 (lures)

Actionrod, Inc., 912 W. State St., Hastings, Mich. (rods)

AFTCO, 1559 Placentia Ave., Newport Beach, Ca. 92660 (guides and tops)

Airlite Plastics Co., 2915 N. 16th St., Omaha, Neb. (bobbers, decoys, minnow buckets)

Aladdin Laboratories, Inc., 620 S. 8th St., Minneapolis, Minn. (Perrine fly reels)

Al's Goldfish Lure Co., 516 Main St., Indian Orchard, Mass. 01051 (lures)

Allan Manufacturing Co. Inc., 325 Duffy Ave., Hicksville, NY 11802 (fishing rod hardware)

Alliance Manufacturing, 3121 Milwaukee Ave., Chicago, Ill. 60618 (landing nets, fish bags, tackle)

Allied Sports Co., One Humminbird Lane, Eufaula, Ala. 36027 (depth sounders)

American Foreign Ind., 640 Sacramento St., San Francisco, Ca. (Importers)

The American Import Co., 1167 Mission St., San Francisco, Ca. 94103 (rods, reels)

The American Pad and Textile Co., 6230 Bienvenue St., New Orleans, La. (fishing clothing, life vests, cushions)

Anglers' Mfg. Corp., 1345 W. Thorndale Ave., Chicago, Ill. (fishing tool)

Angler Products, Inc., 210 Spring St., Butler, Pa. 16001 (worm bedding)

Fred Arbogast Co., 313 W. North St., Akron, Ohio 44303 (lures)

Arndt & Sons, Inc., 1000 Fairview Ave., Hamilton, Ohio (baits)

The Arnold Tackle Corp., Box 87, Paw Paw, Mich. (ice fishing tackle)

Art Wire and Stamping Co., 227 High St., Newark, NJ (tackle)

Atlantic Lures, Inc., 85 South St., Providence, R.I. (lures, terminal tackle)

Axelson Fishing Tackle Co., P.O. Box 231, West Point, Miss. 39773 (bamboo poles)

Jim Bagley Bait Co. Inc., P.O. Box 110, Recker at Spring Lake Rd., Winter Haven, Fla. 33880 (lures)

Bait Boy Products, 708 60th St. NW, Bradenton, Fla. (bait bucket aerator)

Bass Busters Inc., Div. of Johnson Diversified Inc., 301 Main, Amsterdam, Mo. 64723 (lures)

Bay de Noc Lure Co., 14 Central Ave., Gladstone, Mich. 49837 (lures)

The Bead Chain Mfg. Co., 110 Mountain Grove St., Bridgeport, Conn.

Berkley & Co., Highways 9 & 71, Spirit Lake, Ia. 51360 (Trilene line, leaders)

Big Jon Inc., 14393 Peninsula Dr., Traverse City, Mich. 49684 (downriggers)

Bomber Bait Co., Gainesville, Texas

Boone Bait Co., Inc., Forsyth Road, Winter Park, Fla. 32789 (lures)

Bornemann Products Co., 2117 Rockwell Rd., Aurora, Ill. (depth 0 plug)

Bradlow, Inc., 3923 W. Jefferson, Los Angeles, Ca. (Quick Finessa reel)

Brainerd Bait Co., 1564 Englewood Ave., St. Paul, Minn. (Dr. Spoon)

Bronson Reel Co., Bronson, Mich. (fishing reels, rods)

Browning-Silaflex Co., 1706 Washington Ave., St. Louis, Mo. (rods)

Buckeye Bait Corp., 120 Liberty St., Council Grove, Kan. (fishing floats)

Paul Bunyan Co., 1030 Marshall St. NE, Minneapolis, Minn. (lures)

Burke Fishing Lures, 1969 S. Airport Rd., Traverse City, Mich. 49684 (lures)

Tony Burmek, 4173 N. 17th St., Milwaukee, Wis. (Burmek's secret bait)

Byrd Industries Inc., 201 Rock Industrial Park Drive, Bridgeton, Mo. 63044 (electric motors)

Carron Net Company, 1623 17th St., Two Rivers, Wis.

Central Molding & Mfg. Co., 1509 Central Ave., Kansas City, Mo. (Tackle boxes)

John Chatillon & Sons, 85 Cliff St., New York, NY (fish scalers)

Lew Childre & Sons Inc., 110 Azalea Ave., Foley, Ala. 36535 (Lew's speed sticks)

Cisco Kid Tackle Co., Boca Raton, Fla. (Cisco Kid lures & rods)

Conolon Corp., (Garcia), 636 W. 17th St., Costa Mesa, Ca. (rods)

Continental Arms Corp., 697 Fifth Ave., New York, NY (Micron and Alcedo reels)

Converse Rubber Co., 55 Fordham Rd., Wilmington, Mass. 01887 (waders, boots)

Cordell Tackle Inc., P.O. Box 2020, Hot Springs, Ark. 71901 (lures)

Cortland Line Co., 67 E. Court St., Cortland, NY 13045 (lines)

Cover Guard Mfg. Co., 1414 S. Michigan Ave., Chicago, Ill. 60605 (rods & reel cases)

Creek Chub Bait Co., 113 E. Keyser St., Garrett, Ind. 46738 (lures)

Creme Lure Co., P.O. Box 87, Chandler Highway, Tyler, Tex. 75701 (plastic lures)

J. Lee Cuddy Associates Inc., 450 N.E. 79th St., Miami, Fla. 33138 (rod components, etc.)

Daiwa Corporation, 14011 S. Normandie Ave., Gardena, Ca. 90247 (tackle)

Davis Mills, Inc., Lake City, Tenn. (nets)

Day Bait Co., 1824 Howard St., Pt. Huron, Mich. (preserved baits)

Dayton Bait & Marine Prod., Inc., 2701 S. Dixie Dr., Dayton, O. (floats, rod holders)

DeLong Lures Inc., 85 Compark Rd., Centerville, O. 45459 (plastic lures)

Detty's Fish Gripper, 132 Atkins Ave., Lancaster, Pa. (fish gripper)

De Witt Plastics, 26 Aurelius Ave., Auburn, NY (boxes, stringers, buckets)

E. I. DuPont de Nemours & Co., Wilmington, Del. 19898 (fishing line)

Dura Pak Corp., Box 1173, Sioux City, Ia. 51102 (terminal tackle)

Dynamic Sales, Inc., (Roddy Recreation Products, Inc.), 1526 W. 166th St., P.O. Box 431, Gardena, Ca. (rods, reels, line)

Earlybird Co., P.O. Box 1485, Boise, Id. 83701 (worm bedding)

Enterprise Mfg. Co., (Pflueger), 110 N. Union St., Akron, O (reels, rods)

Lou J. Eppinger Mfg. Co., 6340 Schaefer Highway, Dearborn, Mich. 48126 (Dardevle lures)

Glen L. Evans, Inc., Caldwell, Tex. (lures)

Ever-Wear Seal Co., 850 Main St., Lake Geneva, Wis. (worm lure)

Fabrico Mfg. Corp., 1300 W. Exchange Ave., Chicago, Ill. 60609 (stocking foot wader, parkas)

Falls Bait Co., Chippewa Falls, Wis. (lures)

Famous Keystone Corp., 1344 W. 37th St., Chicago, Ill. 60609 (rods, reels)

Fenwick, Box 723, Westminster, Ca. 92683 (rods)

Feurer Bros. Inc., 77 Lafayette Ave., No. White Plains, NY (reels)

The Fish Net and Twine Co., Menominee, Mich.

Flambeau Products, 801 Lynn Ave., Baraboo, Wis. 53913 (rod cases)

Florida Fish Tackle Mfg. Co., 2100 First Ave. S, St. Petersburg, Fla. (lures)

Frabill Manufacturing Co., 2018 S. First St., Milwaukee, Wis. 53207 (minnow buckets, boat seats)

Isaac Franklin Co. Inc., 630 N. Pulaski St., Baltimore, Md. 21217 (net, crab traps)

Fury Imports Inc., 264 Columbus Ave., Roselle, NJ 07203 (rods)

Gapen Fly Co., Onoka, Minn.

The Garcia Corp., 329 Alfred Ave., Teaneck, NJ 07666 (complete tackle)

Gladding Corp., 441 Stuart St., Boston, Mass. 02116 (line, tackle boxes)

Gliebe Co., 1154 Myrtle Ave., Brooklyn, NY (terminal tackle)

B. F. Goodrich Footwear Co., 36 Nichols Ave., Watertown, Mass. (fishing footwear)

Great Lakes Products Inc., 312 Huron Blvd., Marysville, Mich. 48040 (rods, reels)

Gudebrod Bros. Silk Co., 12 S. 12th St., Philadelphia, Pa. 19107 (line)

The Hamilton-Skotch Corp., 295 Fifth Ave., New York, NY 10016 (tackle boxes)

Harnell, Inc., 4094 Glencoe Ave., Venice, Ca. (fishing rods)

Harrington & Richardson Inc., Industrial Rowe, Gardner, Ma. 01440 (Hardy Bros. rods, reels)

Harrison Industries, Inc., 250 Passaic St., Newark, NJ (lures)

James Heddon's Sons, 414 West St., Dowagiac, Mich. 49047 (rods, reels)

Helin Tackle Co., 4099 Beaufait, Detroit, Mich. (flatfish lures)

Hettrick Mfg. Co., Taylorsville Rd., Statesville, N.C. (fishing clothing)

John J. Hildebrandt Corp., P.O. Box 50, Logansport, Ind. 46947 (spinners)

Hodgman Rubber Co., Tripp St., Framington, Mass. (waders, fishing clothing)

The Hoffschneider Corp., 848 Jay Street, Rochester, NY 14611 ("Red Eye" lures)

Hopkins Lures Co. Inc., 1130 Boissevain Ave., Norfolk, Va. 23507 (stainless steel lures)

Hurricane Import Co., 70 Tenth St., San Francisco, Ca.

Ideal Fishing Float Co. Inc., 20th and Franklin Sts., Richmond, Va. 23203 (terminal tackle)

International Seaway Tranding Corp., 1387 W. 9th St., Cleveland, Ohio

Irving Raincoat Co., 657 Broadway, New York, NY 10012

Jamison Tackle Co., 3654 Montrose, Chicago, Ill. 60608 (lures)

Ray Jefferson, Main & Cotton Sts., Philadelphia, Pa. 19127 (fish finders)

Jet-Aer Corp., 100 Sixth Ave., Paterson, NJ 07524 (insect repellent)

Jetco Inc., 1133 Barranca Dr., El Paso, Tex. 79935 (fish locators)

Albert J. John Mfg. Co., 118 W. 69th St., Chicago, Ill. (lead sinkers)

Louis Johnson Co., 1547 Old Deerfield Rd., Highland Park, Ill. 60035 (Johnson lures)

Johnson Reels Co., 1531 Madison Ave., Mankato, Minn. 56001

Kar-Gard Co., 2201 Grand Ave., Kansas City, Mo. (lure retriever)

Kennedy Mfg. Co., P.O. Box 151, Van Wert, Ohio (tackle boxes)

Klamerus & Co., 4557 W. 59th St., Chicago, Ill. 60629 (rod holders)

Kodiak Corp., Van Buskirk Rd., Ironwood, Mich. 49938 (rods)

Kolpin Bros. Inc., 119 S. Pearl, Berlin, Wis. (fishing accessories)

L & S Bait Co. Inc., 148 S. Kennedy, Bradley, Ill. 60915 (lures)

Land-O-Tackle Inc., 4650 N. Ronald St., Harwood Heights, Ill. 60656 (lure bodies, components)

Lazy Ike Corp., P.O. Box 1177, Fort Dodge, Ia. 50501 (lures)

Lectromatic Sports, Inc., 11405 E. 7th Ave., Aurora, Colo. (battery powered reel, rods)

Leisure Lures, 7315 Atoll Ave., (Box 353 Station 1) North Hollywood, Ca. (plastic lures)

Le Trappeur, Inc., Southwest Industrial Park, Westwood, Mass. (Luxor reels)

Liberty Mfg. Co., 4026 N. 20th St., St. Louis, Mo. (terminal tackle)

Liberty Steel Chest Corp., 16 Dowling Place, Rochester, NY

Lindy/Little Joe, Box 488, Brainerd, Minn. 56401 (spinner baits, plastic worms, etc.)

Lisk Fly Mfg. Co., 659 S. Spring St., Greensboro, NC (lures, rods)

Little Atom Lures, 1415 N. California, Chicago, Ill. (orig. Pinkie lures)

Longfellow Corp., 31795 Groesbeck Highway, Fraser, Mich. (rods)

Lutz Pork Bait Co., 1234 Jefferson, Kansas City, Mo. (pork baits)

Magic Snell Tackle Co., Inc., 45 Niagara St., Canandaigua, NY

Major Rod Manufacturing Co. (U.S.) LTD, Demars Blvd., Tupper Lake, NY 12986 (rods)

Mann's Bait Mfg. Co., State Dock Road, P.O. Box 604, Eufaula, Ala. 36027 (lures)

Manufacturers Import Co., 1323–27 E. Cary St., Richmond, Va. 23201 (rods, reels)

Marathon Bait Co., Box 298, Wausau, Wis.

Martin Reel Co., 30 E. Main St., Mohawk, NY 13407 (rods, reels)

Mason Tackie Co., G 11273 N. State Rd., Otisville, Mich. 48463 (line)

Maybrun Manufacturing Co., 2250 Clybourn Ave., Chicago, Ill. 60614 (rod holders)

Meinzinger & Rade Co., 19000 Doris, Livonia, Mich. (hooks, scalers)

Mildrum Manufacturing Co., 230 Berlin St., East Berlin, Conn. 06023 (rod tops, guides)

Mile Hi Tackle Co., P.O. Box 7022, Capitol Hill Station, Denver, Colo. (snelled hooks, swivels)

Mill Run Products Co., 1360 W. Ninth St., Cleveland, Ohio (lures, stringers)

Mills Products Co., Mills Industrial Park, Safety Harbor, Fla. (lures)

Millsite Tackle Co., Howell, Mich. (box/stringers)

Minneapolis-Honeywell Co., 2753 4th Ave. S, Minneapolis, Minn. (Fish-o-therm)

Bruce B. Mises Inc., P.O. Box 35284, Los Angeles, Ca. 90035 (Maxima lines)

Mister Twister Inc., P.O. Box 598, Minden, La. 71055 (lures)

Mit-Shel Co., 640 S. 5th, Quincy, Ill. 62301 (minnow buckets)

Molded Carry-Lite Products, 3000 W. Clarke St., Milwaukee, Wis. (bait buckets)

O. Mustad & Son (USA) Inc., 185 Clark St., Auburn, NY 13021 (hooks)

National Expert Inc., 2928 Stevens Ave S, Minneapolis, Minn. 55402 (lures)

National Fiber Glass Products Inc., 52 St. Casimir Ave., Yonkers, NY 10701 (rods, reels)

Nature Faker Lures Inc., Windsor, Mo. 65360 (bait boxes)

Newland Lure Co., Box 266, Bull Shoals, Ark. 72619 (lures)

Newton Line Co., Inc., S. Main St., Homer, NY (line)

O. A. Norlund Co., Div. of Mann Edge Tool Co., Lewiston, Pa. (gaffs)

Normark Corp., 1710 E. 78th St., Minneapolis, Minn. 55423 (lures, fillet knives)

Norton Mfg. Corp., 2700 N. Pulaski Rd., Chicago, Ill. (bamboo fishing poles)

Oberlin Canteen Co., 212 Summer St., P.O. Box 208, Oberlin, O 44074

Old Pal, Inc., Lititz, Pa. (minnow buckets, tackle boxes)

Lee E. Olsen Knife Co., 7–11 Joy St., Howard City, Mich. (filet knives)

Charles F. Orvis Co., Manchester, Vt. 05254 (Orvis rods, reels, etc.)

Padre Island Co. (PICO lures), 2617 N. Zarsamora St., P.O. Box 5310, San Antonio, Tex. 78201

Palsa Sales, Box 55, Hales Corners, Wis. (Palsa lure)

Paw Paw Bait Co., 400 S. Kalamazoo St., Paw Paw, Mich. (lures)

Penn Fishing Tackle Mfg. Co., 3028 W. Hunting Ave., Philadelphia, Pa. 19132 (reels)

Perfection Tip Co., 3020 E. 43rd Ave., Denver, Colo.

Pflueger Sporting Goods Division, 301 Ansin Blvd., Hallandale, Fla. 33009 (reels, rods, etc.)

Phantom Products, Inc., 1800 Central, Kansas City, Mo. (rods, reels)

Plano Molding Co., 113 S. Center Ave., Plano, Ill. 60545 (tackle boxes)

Plas/Steel Products Inc., Industrial Park, Walkerton, Ind. 46574 (rods)

J. R. Plasters Co., 111 N. Denver Ave., Kansas City, Mo. (trot lines, floats, leaders)

Plastics Research Corp., 3601 Jenny Lind, Fort Smith, Ark. (lures)

Plastilite Corp., 9409 N. 45th St., P.O. Box 12235, Omaha, Neb. 68112 (floats, rods)

Powerscopic Corp., P.O. Box 278, Westwood, NJ 07675 (telescopic rods)

Prescott Spinner Co., P.O. Box 239, Mankato, Minn.

Quick Corp. of America, 620 Terminal Way, Costa Mesa, Ca. 92627 (reels and rods)

Rapala, P.O. Box 5027, Minneapolis, Minn.

Rectack of America, 7528 Buell St., Downey, Ca. 90241 (spinning reels)

Rettinger Importing Co., 70 Caven Point Ave., Jersey City, NY 07305 (boots, vests)

C. C. Roberts Bait Co., Mosinee, Wis. (mud puppy lures)

Rod Caddy Corp., 920 W. Cullerton St., Chicago, Ill. 60608 (rod cases)

St. Croix Corp., 9909 S. Shore Dr., Minneapolis, Minn. 55441 (rods, reels)

Sampo Inc., North St., Barneveld, NY 13304 (swivels)

Scientific Anglers, Inc., 1012 Jefferson, Midland, Mich. 48640 (rods, reels, etc.)

Seneca Tackle Co. Inc., 1834 Westminster St., Providence, R.I. 02909 (lures)

The Servus Rubber Co., 1100 Block Second St., Rock Island, Ill. (fishing footwear)

Sevenstrand Tackle Mfg. Co., 1207 Euclid Ave., Long Beach, Ca. (leaders, rods)

Shakespeare Company, Sporting Goods Division, 241 E. Kalamazoo Ave., Kalamazoo, Mich. 49001 (rods, reels, line)

Sheldon's Inc., P.O. Box 508, West Center St., Antigo, Wis. 54409 (spinners)

Shurkatch Fishing Tackle Co., Inc., S. Elm St., Richfield Springs, NY (gaffs, floats, terminal tackle)

Simonsen Industries, Inc., 1414 S. Michigan Ave., Chicago, Ill. 60605 (tackle boxes)

Skirt Minnow Seine Mfg. Co., P.O. Box 144, East Liverpool, Ohio

Snagproof Mfg. Co., 4153 E. Galbraith, Cincinnati, Ohio (lures)

Sportsmen Inc., 131 Saw Mill River Rd., Yonkers, NY (rods)

Stearns Manufacturing Co., P.O. Box 1498, St. Cloud, Minn. 56301 (buoyant boatwear)

Stratton & Terstegge Co., P.O. Box 1859, Louisville, Ky. 40201 (tackle boxes)

Style-Cast Tackle Corp., 29866 John R., Madison Hts., Mich. (rods)

Suick Lure Mfg. Co., Antigo, Wis. (lures)

Sunset Line & Twine Co., Jefferson & Erwin Sts., Petaluma, Ca. 94952 (lines)

Sutton Co., Naples, NY (lures)

Tack-L-Tyers, 939 Chicago Ave., Evanston, Ill. (fly tying kits)

Taylor Instrument Co., Rochester, NY (fisherman's barometer)

Thompson Fishing Tackle Co., P.O. Box 275, Knoxville, Tenn. (lures)

Townsend Engineering Co., P.O. Box 1433, Des Moines, Ia. (fish skinners)

Trimarc Corp., High Point Plaza, Hillside, Ill. 60162 (rods)

True Life Minnow Harness, 29251 Grandview, Mount Clements, Mich.

True Temper Corp., 1623 Euclid Ave., Cleveland, Ohio 44115 (rods, reels)

Tycoon/Fin-Nor Corp., 7447 N.W. 12th St., Miami, Fla. 33126

Umco Corp., Highway 25, P.O. Box 608, Watertown, Minn. 55388 (tackle boxes)

Uncle Josh Bait Co., 524 Clarence St., Fort Atkinson, Wis. 53538 (Pork Rind)

Union Steel Chest Corp., 54 Church St., LeRoy, NY

U.S. Rubber Co., 1230 Avenue of Americas, New York, NY (fishing footwear)

Vlchek Plastics Co., Middlefield, Ohio 44062 (tackle boxes)

Walker International, 1901 W. Lafayette Blvd., Detroit, Mich. 48216 (rods, reels)

Water Gremlin Co., 4370 Otter Lake Rd., White Bear Lake, Minn. 55110 (lures)

Water King Sales, P.O. Box 10, Pearl Beach, Mich. (rods)

Weber Dot Ling Mfg. Co., 4601 W. 47th St., Chicago, Ill. 60632 (nets, fish bags, rod cases)

Weber Tackle, Co., 133 W. Ellis St., Stevens Point, Wis.

H. A. Whittemore & Co., Inc., 32 Kearney Rd., Needham Hts., Mass. (lures)

Whopper Stopper Inc., Highway 36 West, P.O. Box 1111, Sherman, Tex. 75090 (lures)

Williams Gold Refining Co., Inc., 2978 Main St., Buffalo, NY (lures)

Woodstock Line Co., 83 Canal St., Putnam, Conn. (line)

World Famous Sales, Inc., 1601 S. Michigan Ave., Chicago, Ill. 60616 (rain suits, tackle)

The Worth Co., P.O. Box 88, Stevens Point, Wis. 54481 (lures)

Wright & McGill Co., 4245 E. 46th Ave., Denver, Colo. 80216 (rods, reels, etc.)

York-Eger Mfg. Co., Inc., P.O. Box 1210, Sanford, Fla. (nets, lures)

Zebco Div. Brunswick Corp., 6101 E. Apache, Tulsa, Okla. 74101 (rods, reels)

CHAPTER 48

Professional Fly Tiers

DAN BAILEY, Dan's Fly & Tackle Shop, Livingston, Mont.

PAT BARNES, Barnes' Fly Shop, West Yellowstone, Mont.

WAYNE BUSZEK, Visalia, Ca.

GEORGE CORNISH, Driftwood Marina, Box 296, Avalon, NJ 98202

RUBE CROSS, 606 Public St., Providence, R.I.

HARRY DARBEE, Livingston Manor, N.Y.

JIM DEREN, Angler's Roost, Chrysler Bldg., N.Y. 10017

ART FLICK, Westkill, N.Y.

BILL GALLASCH, 8705 Weldon Drive, Richmond, Va. 23229

DAN GAPEN, Gapen Fly Co., Anoka, Minn.

H. J. GREB, 2188 N.W. 24th Ave., Miami, Fla.

BILL KEANE, Box 371, Bronxville, NY 10708

ED KOCH, Koch's Tackle Shop, 936 Franklin St., Carlisle, Pa.

EDDIE LACHMANN, Amherst, Wis.

MERTON PARKS, Parks' Fly Shop, Gardiner, Mont.

PHIL PATTERSON, Phillip's Fly & Tackle Co., Alexandria, Pa.

JIM POULOS, 411 Stone Place, Wheeling, Ill.

HANK ROBERTS, 1033 Walnut St., Boulder, Colo.

HELEN SHAW, 246 E. 46th St., NY 10017

NORM THOMPSON, Angler's Guide, 1805 N.W. Thurman, Portland, Ore.

DICK RIDEOUT, 78 Katahdin Ave., Millinocket, Me.

GLEN WEST, c/o Ed's Tackle Shop, Ennis, Mont. 59729

Professional fly tiers not named here and wishing to be included in the fly tiers listing, 1976 Tom McNally's Fishermen's Bible, are urged to write Tom McNally, c/o J. Philip O'Hara Inc., Publishers, 20 E. Huron, Chicago, Ill. 60611

CHAPTER 49

Fly Tying Materials Supply Houses

Each firm listed does not carry complete lines of fly tying materials. Write for catalogs or merchandise sheets.

ALL-LURE TACKLE CO., 47–10 48th St., Woodside, N.Y.

ANDY'S QUALITY FLY TYING MATERIALS, P.O. Box 269, Peabody, Mass.

R. S. CHASE CO., P.O. Box 208, South Duxbury, Mass.

DANIELSON FLY MFG. CO., P.O. Box 94, Mercer Island, Wash.

DERSH FEATHER AND TRADING CORP., 494 Broadway, N.Y.

F & S PRODUCTS CO., R–250, Sixth St., Mansfield, Ohio

FINNY SPORTS (DD), Toledo, Ohio

GENE'S TACKLE SHOP, Box 162, Newark, N.Y.

HACKLE HOUSE, P.O. Box 1001, San Mateo, Ca.

D. E. HECHT, 80 University Place, N.Y. 10003

HERTER'S CO., Waseca, Minn.

E. HILLE ANGLER'S SUPPLY HOUSE, P.O. Box 269, Williamsport, Pa.

M. J. HOFFMAN CO., 989 Gates Ave., Brooklyn, N.Y.

J. J. KLEIN, LTD, 2077 E. Gouin Blvd., Montreal 12, Quebec, Can.

MANGROVE FEATHER CO., 42 West 38th St., N.Y. 10018

MARTIN TACKLE & MFG. CO., 431 Eastlake Ave. E., Seattle, Wash.

NETCRAFT CO., Box 5510, Toledo, Ohio

PASSLOFF, INC., 19 West 36th St., N.Y. 10018

PRIEST RIVER TACKLE CO., Landfall, Coolin, Id.

REED TACKLE CO., Box 390, Caldwell, N.J.

HANK ROBERTS, INC., 1033–37 Walnut, Boulder, Colo.

M. SCHWARTZ & SONS, INC., 321 E. 3rd St., N.Y. 10009

SHOFF FISHING TACKLE CO., 407 W. Gowe St., Kent, Wash.

SONNIES, P.O. Box 126, Wilmot, Wis.

TACK-L-TYERS, 939 Chicago Ave., Evanston, Ill.

D. H. THOMPSON, 335 Walnut Ave., Elgin, Ill.

THOMPSON FISHING TACKLE CO., 2308 N. Broadway, Knoxville, Tenn.

UNIVERSAL VISE CO., P.O. Box 335, Holyoke, Mass.

E. VENIARD, LTD, 138 Northwood Road, Thorton Heath, Surrey, England

WOODSLORE PRODUCTS, Box 821, Costa Mesa, Ca.

WORTH CO., P.O. Box 88, Stevens Point, Wis.

PAUL H. YOUNG CO., 23800 W. Eight Mile Road, Southfield, Mich.

CHAPTER 50

Rod Building Kits and Supplies

DUNTON & SON, INC., 4 Fiske Ave., Greenfield, Mass.

FINNY SPORTS, 462 Sports Bldg., Toledo, Ohio

GLIEBE CO., 1154 Myrtle Ave., Brooklyn, N.Y.

HERTER'S CO., Waseca, Minn.

E. HILLE ANGLER'S SUPPLY HOUSE, P.O. Box 269, Williamsport, Pa.

IOWA ROYAL RODS, Perry, Iowa

MAKIT FISHING ROD MFG. CO., 113 Adolph St., Fort Worth, Tex.

E. MILTENBERG, INC., 43 Great Jones St., N.Y. 10012

NETCRAFT CO., Toledo, Ohio

CHARLES F. ORVIS CO., INC., Manchester, VT 05254

PASTOR & CO., 11423 Vanowen St., North Hollywood, Ca.

PRIEST RIVER TACKLE CO., Landfall, Coolin, Id.

REED TACKLE CO., Box 390, Caldwell, N.J.

REEDER MFG. CO., Box 346, Vancouver, Wash.

SHOFF FISHING TACKLE CO., 407 W. Gowe St., Kent, Wash.

PAUL H. YOUNG CO., 23800 W. Eight Mile Road, Southfield, Mich.

CHAPTER 51

Roster of American Casting Association

as of July 15, 1974

CALIFORNIA

GOLDEN GATE ANGLING & CASTING CLUB
A. Cameron Ball, Sec.
227 Cervantes
San Francisco, Calif. 94123

LONG BEACH CASTING CLUB
Howard Isley, Sec.
440 Fowler St.
Costa Mesa, Calif. 94501

OAKLAND CASTING CLUB
Mrs. Yoshi Miller, Sec.
2417 Francis St.
Oakland, Calif. 94601

PASADENA CASTING CLUB
Wayne Stron, Sec.
P.O. Box 6M
Pasadena, Calif. 91102

ILLINOIS

CATERPILLAR ROD CLUB
Lillian Nicholson, Sec.
2513 N. Peoria
Peoria, Illinois 61603

LINCOLN PARK CASTING CLUB
Fred Molzahn, Sec.
611 N. Home St.
Park Ridge, Illinois 60068

ROXANA FLY & BAIT CASTING CLUB
Gary G. Kirby, Sec.
884 E. Airline
East Alton, Illinois 62024

INDIANA

GARY ANGLERS CLUB
Bill Chadwick, Sec.
1221 Garfield
Hobart, Indiana 46342

INDIANAPOLIS FLY CASTERS
Wayne Mendell, Casting Chmn
5028 Bonnie Brae
Indianapolis, Indiana 46208

KENTUCKY

BLUE GRASS CASTING CLUB
Bobby Brinegar, Sec.
602 Freeman Dr.
Lexington, Kentucky 40505

LOUISVILLE CASTING CLUB
Robert Budd, Sec.
1216 Akers Ave.
Jeffersonville, Indiana 47130

MARYLAND

NATIONAL CAPITOL CASTING CLUB
Lloyd C. Bowers, Sec.
2805 Jutland Rd.
Kensington, Maryland 20795

MICHIGAN

DETROIT BAIT & FLY CASTING CLUB
Bernie Merkl, Sec.
20215 Coachwood Rd.
Riverview, Michigan 48192

MISSOURI

CARDONDELET FLY & BAIT CASTING CLUB
Victor C. Wiedeman, Sec.
18 Smoke Tree Drive
Fenton, Missouri 63026

NORTHEAST CASTING CLUB
F. W. Desenberger, Sec.
107 N. Lawndale
Kansas City, Mo. 64123

ST. LOUIS FLY & BAIT CASTING CLUB
Robert L. Coe, Sec.
6648 Oakland Ave.
St. Louis, Mo. 63139

NEW YORK STATE

BUFFALO CASTING CLUB
Mrs. Jeanne R. Null, Sec.
12 Sidway
Buffalo, New York 14210

CAMP FIRE CLUB OF AMERICA
Dumont Rush, Sec.
59 Kipp St.
Chappaqua, New York 10514

FRESHWATER ANGLERS OF LONG ISLAND
Dr. John H. Murray,
22 Hillside Ave.
Blue Point, New York 11715

OHIO

BARBERTON CASTING CLUB
Joseph Masa, Sec.
7200 Cleve. Mass. Rd.
Clinton, Ohio 44216

BEREA CASTING CLUB
Ken Dudley, Sec.
219 Franklin Drive
Berea, Ohio 44017

CINCINNATI CASTING CLUB
Bill Biltz, Sec.
2674 Montana, Apt. #7
Cincinnati, Ohio 45211

COLUMBUS CASTING CLUB
Eltha E. Dixon, Sec.
2452 N. High St., Apt. 11
Columbus, Ohio 43202

TOLEDO CASTING CLUB
Mrs. Esther Hansen, Sec.
7116 Kipling Dr.
Holland, Ohio 43528

TEXAS

HILL COUNTRY CASTING CLUB
Mrs. Pat McTee, Sec.
137 Scott Ave.
Universal City, Texas

HOUSTON ANGLERS CLUB
F. L. Gilbert, Sec.
3123 Plumb St.
Houston, Texas 77005

VIRGINIA

TIDEWATER ANGLERS CLUB
Box 5566, Parcel Post Annex
Norfolk, Virginia 23516

WISCONSIN

WAUKESHA CASTING CLUB
Clarence Anthes, Sec.
707 N. Moreland Blvd.
Waukesha, Wisconsin 53186

CANADA

CANADIAN NATIONAL SPORTSMENS CLUB
Joe Phillips, Sec.
149 Leighland Ave.
Oakville, Ontario

CONSERVATION CLUB OF WEST LINCOLN
Ken Lounsbury
465 Hixon St.
Beamsville, Ontario LOR 180

St. CATHARINES FISH & GAME PROT. ASSN.
Ross MacSporran, Corr.
82 Cecil St.
St. Catharines, Ontario L2N 4B2

TORONTO ANGLERS & HUNTERS' ASSN.
Pete Edwards, Sec.
61 Edgehill Rd., James Gardens
Islington, Ontario M9A 4N1

LADIES CLUBS

CARONDELET WOMEN'S CASTING CLUB
Mrs. Kalma S. Boyle, Sec.
6942 Winona
St. Louis, Mo. 63109

HEART OF AMERICA ROD & REEL CLUB
Mrs. Ronnie Miller, Sec.
1308 So. Ash Ave.
Independence, Missouri 64052

LONG BEACH WOMEN'S CASTING CLUB
Mrs. Mary Marks, Sec.
4106 Vermont St.
Long Beach, Calif. 90814

ASSOCIATIONS

ILLINOIS CASTING ASSN.
Mr. Fred Molzahn, Sec.
611 N. Home
Park Ridge, Illinois 60068

MISSOURI VALLEY AM. CASTING ASSN.
Mrs. Kalma Doyle
6942 Winona Ave.
St. Louis, Mo. 63109

OHIO STATE CASTING ASSN.
Mrs. Eltha E. Dixon, Sec.
2452 N. High St., Apt. 11
Columbus, Ohio 43202

WESTERN TOURNAMENT CASTING ASSN.
Earle H. Thomas, Sec.
530 Margo Ave.,
Long Beach, Calif. 90814

CHAPTER 52

Federation of Fly Fishermen, Member Clubs

Membership Service Office
15513 Haas Ave., Gardena, Calif. 90249

MEMBER CLUBS

ALASKA FLY FISHERS, Anchorage, AK
ALPINE FLY FISHERS, Federal Way, WA
AMERICAN MEDICAL FLY-FISHING ASSOC., Loomis, CA
ANDOVER FLY FISHERS, Andover, MA
ANGLERS' CLUB OF CHICAGO, Norhbrook, IL
ANGLERS CLUB OF PORTLAND, Portland, OR
ARIZONA FLYCASTERS CLUB, Phoenix, AZ
ARKANSAS FLY FISHERS, Little Rock, AR
BEAVERKILL FLYFISHERS, INC., L.I. City, NY
BEAVERKILL-WILLOWEMOC, Roscoe, NY
THE DAME JULIANA BERNERS FLY FYSSHYNGE ASSOC., Anchorage, AK
BLUE DUN ANGLING & GUNNING CLUB, Medford, MA
BOISE VALLEY FLY FISHERMEN, INC., Boise, ID
BOULDER FLYCASTERS, Boulder, CO
BRODHEADS FOREST & STREAM ASSOC., East Stroudsburg, PA
CALIFORNIA FLY FISHERMEN, UNLIMITED, Sacramento, CA
CAMAS VALLEY FLY FISHERS, Camas Valley, OR
CASCADE FLY FISHING CLUB, Sumner, WA
CASTLE CREEK FISHING CLUB, Corning, NY
CHICO FLY FISHING CLUB, Chico, CA
CLEARWATER FLY CASTERS, Pullman, WA

CONNECTICUT FLY FISHERMEN'S ASSOC., INC., Windsor Locks, CT
CONNECTICUT SALT WATER FLYRODDERS ASSOC., Norwalk, CT
CORVALLIS CHAPTER OF T. U., Corvallis, OR
CRONTON WATERSHED CHAPTER T. U., Yorktown Heights, NY
DALLAS FLYFISHERS, Dallas, TX
DESERT FLY CASTERS, Mesa, AZ
DIABLO VALLEY FLY FISHERMEN, Walnut Creek, CA
EAST JERSEY CHAPTER T. U., Fort Lee, NJ
EVERGREEN FLY FISHING CLUB, Everett, WA
FLAT ROCK CLUB, Salt Lake City, UT
FLYCASTRS, INC., Campbell, CA
FLY FISHERS CLUB OF CHILE, Santiago, Chile
FLY FISHERMEN FOR CONSERVATION, INC., Fresno, CA
FLY FISHERS OF DAVIS, Davis, CA
FLY FISHERS CLUB OF ORANGE COUNTY, INC., Fullerton, CA
FONTINALIS FLY FISHERMEN, Port Jervis, NY
FOURTH CORNER FLY FISHERS, Bellingham, WA
FREESTONE FLY FISHERS, Saginaw, MI
FRESH & SALTY FLYFISHERS OF GARDENA, CA
FRONT RANGE FLY FISHERS, Denver, CO
GOLDEN GATE ANGLING & CASTING CLUB, San Francisco, CA

GOLDEN SPREAD FLYFISHERS, Amarillo, TX
GRANTS KENNABAGO CAMPS, INC., Oquossoc, ME
GREEN COUNTRY FLYFISHERS, Bartlesville, OK
HENRYVILLE CONSERVATION CLUB, INC., New York, NY
HOOK & HACKLE CLUB, Calgary, Alberta, Can.
HUDSON RIVER FISHERMEN'S ASSOC., Demarest, NJ
INDIANAPOLIS FLY CASTERS, IN
INGLEWOOD FLY FISHERMEN, CA
INLAND EMPIRE FLY FISHING CLUB, Spokane, WA
INTERNATIONAL FARIO CLUB, Paris, France
IZAAK WALTON LEAGUE OF AMERICA, INC., Feeding Hills, MA
JOE JEFFERSON CLUB, INC., Saddle River, NJ
KAMLOOPS FLYFISHERS, Kamloops, BC
KLAMATH COUNTRY FLY CASTERS, Klamath Falls, OR
LAS VEGAS FLY FISHING CLUB, NV
LIVERMORE FLY FISHERMEN, Livermore, CA
LONG BEACH CASTING CLUB, CA
LONG BEACH WOMEN'S CASTING CLUB, CA
LOWER COLUMBIA FLY FISHERS, Longview, WA
MAGIC VALLEY FLY FISHERMEN, Murtaugh, ID
MANITOBA FLY FISHERS ASSOC., Winnipeg, Manitoba, Can.
MARYLAND FLY ANGLERS, INC., Baltimore, MD
McKENZIE FLYFISHERS, Eugene, OR
MICHIGAN FLY FISHING CLUB, Dearborn, MI
MONTREAL ANGLERS & HUNTERS, INC., Montreal, Quebec, Can.
MOUNTAIN HOME FLY FISHING CLUB, Mountain Home AFB, ID
NAPA VALLEY FLY FISHERMEN, Napa, CA
NORTHERN CALIFORNIA JAPANESE AMERICAN FLY-CASTERS, Sunnyvale, CA
NORTHERN ILLINOIS FLY TYERS, Arlington Hgts., IL
NORTHWEST FLY ANGLERS, Seattle, WA
NORTHWEST FLY FISHERMEN, Seattle, WA
NORTHWEST FLY TYING CLUB, Chicago, IL
OAKLAND CASTING CLUB, CA
OLYMPIC FLY FISHERS, Edmonds, WA
OLYMPIC PENINSULA FLYFISHERS, Port Angeles, WA
OSPREY FLYFISHERS OF BC, Burnaby, BC, Can.
OZARK FLYFISHERS, St. Louis, MO
PALM SPRINGS ROD & GUN CLUB, INC., CA
PALO ALTO FLY FISHERS, CA

PASADENA CASTING CLUB, CA
PIKES PEAK FLYFISHERS, Colorado Springs, CO
PLATTE VALLEY FLY CASTERS, Saratoga, WY
POTOMAC VALLEY FLY FISHERMEN, Frederick, MD
PRAIRIE FLY FISHERS, Oklahoma City, OK
PUGET SOUND FLYFISHERS, Tacoma, WA
PUTNAM TROUT ASSOCIATION, Brewster, NY
RHODY FLY RODDERS, Warwich, RI
ROCKWELL SPRINGS TROUT CLUB, Castalia, OH
ROGUE FLYFISHERS, Central Point, OR
SALINAS VALLEY FLY FISHERMEN, Salinas, CA
SALTWATER FLYRODDERS OF AMERICA INT., Altadena, CA
"SALTY" FLYRODDERS OF NEW YORK, INC., Astoria, NY
SAN DIEGO FLY FISHERMAN'S CLUB, San Diego, CA
SIERRA PACIFIC FLY FISHERS, Van Nuys, CA
SOUTH SOUND FLY FISHING CLUB, Olympia, WA
SOUTHWESTERN MONTANA FLY FISHERS, W. Yellowstone, MT
STANISLAUS FLY FISHERMEN, Modesto, CA
SUN VALLEY FLY FISHERS, INC., ID
SUSQUEHANNOCK FLY FISHERS, Lebanon, PA
THE STEAMBOATERS, Salem, OR
THE FEDERATION OF LAKE TAUPO ANGLING, SHOOTING & BOATING CLUBS, Taupe, NZ
THEODORE GORDON FLYFISHERS, INC., New York, NY
TOTEM FLYFISHERS OF BC, Burnaby, BC, Can.
TRI-CITY FLYFISHERS, Riverside, CA
TUCSON FLY FISHING CLUB, AZ
TWIN HARBORS FLYFISHERS, Aberdeen, WA
UNITED FLY TYERS, INC., Boston, MA
UPPER FISHING CREEK FLY FISHERS, Berwick, PA
UPPER SNAKE RIVER FLY-FISHERMEN, St. Anthony, ID
VENTURA FLYFISHERS, CA
WADERS OF THE WOLF, Wauwatosa, WI
WASATCH FLY CASTERS, Salt Lake City, UT
WASHINGTON FLY FISHING CLUB, Seattle, WA
WEST KOOTENAY FLYFISHERS' CLUB, Trail, BC, Can.
WHITE CLAY FLY FISHERMEN, Landenberg, PA
WILDERNESS FLY FISHERS, Santa Monica, CA
WYNDHAM ANGLERS CLUB, New Zealand
YAKIMA FLY FISHERS ASSOCIATION, WA
ZANEFIELD ROD & GUN CLUB, INC., Columbus, OH

CHAPTER 53

State Tourist Office Listing

ALABAMA—Bureau of Publicity and Information, State Hwy. Bldg., Montgomery, Ala. 36104

ALASKA—Alaska Travel Division, Pouch E, Juneau, Alaska 99801

ARIZONA—Department of Economic Planning and Development, 3003 N. Central Ave., Phoenix, Ariz. 85012

ARKANSAS—Arkansas Dept. of Parks and Tourism, 149 State Capitol, Little Rock, Ark. 72201

CALIFORNIA—State Office of Tourism, 1400 Tenth Street, Sacramento, Cal. 95814

COLORADO—Colorado Division of Commerce & Development, 602 State Capitol Annex, Denver, Colo. 80203

CONNECTICUT—Development Commission, State Office Building, Hartford, Conn. 06115

DELAWARE—Bureau of Travel Development, State of Delaware, 45 The Green, Dover, Del. 19901

DISTRICT OF COLUMBIA—Washington Area Convention and Visitors Bureau, 1129 20th St., N.W., Washington, D.C. 20036

FLORIDA—Florida Development Commission, Collins Building, Tallahassee, Fla. 32304

GEORGIA—Department of Community Development, P.O. Box 38097, Atlanta, Ga. 30334

HAWAII—Hawaii Visitors Bureau, 2270 Kalakaus Ave., Honolulu, Hawaii 96815 or 400 N. Michigan Ave., Chicago, Ill. 60611

IDAHO—Department of Commerce and Development, Room 108, Capitol Building, Boise, Idaho 83707

ILLINOIS—Department of Business and Economic Development, Division of Tourism, 222 S. College, Springfield, Ill. 62706. Also: The Illinois Adventure Centure, Division of Tourism and Conservation, 160 N. LaSalle St., Chicago, Ill.

INDIANA—Department of Commerce, Tourist Division, 336 State House, Indianapolis, Ind. 46204

IOWA—Iowa Development Commission, Tourism and Travel Division, 250 Jewett Building, Des Moines, Ia. 50309

KANSAS—Department of Economic Development, State Office Building, Topeka, Kansas 66612

KENTUCKY—Department of Public Information, Capitol Annex, Frankfort, Ky. 40601

LOUISIANA—Louisiana Tourist Development Commission, Box 44291, Baton Rogue, La. 70804

MAINE—Department of Economic Development, State Office Building, Augusta, Maine 04330

MARYLAND—Division of Tourism, 2525 Riva Road, Annapolis, Md. 21401

MASSACHUSETTS—Department of Commerce and Development, 100 Cambridge St., Boston, Mass. 02202

MICHIGAN—Michigan Tourist Council, 300 St. Capitol Ave., Suite 102, Lansing, Mich. 48926. Also: Southeast Michigan Tourist Association, Executive Plaza, 1200 6th St., Detroit, 48226; Upper Michigan Tourist Association, Box 400, Iron Mountain, 49801; East Michigan Tourist Association, The Log Office, Box 5, Bay City, 48706; West Michigan Tourist Association, 136 Fulton East, Grand Rapids, 49502; Michigan Tourist Information Center, 52 E. Monroe St., Chicago 60603

MINNESOTA—Minnesota Department of Economic Development, 51 E. 8th St., St. Paul, Minn. 55101

MISSISSIPPI—Travel Department, Mississippi Agricultural and Industrial Board, 1504 State Office Building, Jackson, Miss. 39205

MISSOURI—Missouri Tourism Commission, 308 E. High St., Jefferson City, Mo. 65101

MONTANA—Advertising Unit, Montana Department of Highways, Helena, Mont. 59601

NEBRASKA—Department of Economic Development, 1342 M St., Box 94666, Lincoln, Neb. 68509

NEVADA—Nevada Department of Economic Development, State Capitol, Carson City, Nev. 19701

NEW HAMPSHIRE—New Hampshire Division of Economic Development, Box 856, Concord, N.H. 03301

NEW JERSEY—New Jersey Department of Labor & Industry, P.O. Box 2766, Trenton, N.J. 08625

NEW MEXICO—Tourist Division, Department of Development, 113 Washington Ave., Santa Fe, N.M. 87501

NEW YORK—New York State Department of Commerce, 99 Washington Ave., Albany, N.Y. 12210. Also: New York (City) Convention and Visitors Bureau, 90 E. 42d St., New York, N.Y. 10017

NORTH CAROLINA—Department of Natural and Economic Resources, P.O. Box 27685, Raleigh, N.C. 27611

NORTH DAKOTA—State Travel Department, Capitol Grounds, Bismarck, N.D. 58501

OHIO—Ohio Development, 65 S. Front St., Columbus, Ohio 43216

OKLAHOMA—Oklahoma Tourism and Recreation Division, 500 Will Rogers Building, Oklahoma City, Okla. 73105

OREGON—Travel Information Division, Oregon State Highway Department, 101 State Highway Building, Salem, Ore. 97310

PENNSYLVANIA—Travel Development Bureau, Department of Commerce, South Office Building, Room 402, Harrisburg, Pa. 17120

RHODE ISLAND—Rhode Island Development Council, Roger Williams Building, Providence, R.I. 02908

SOUTH CAROLINA—Travel Division, Department of Parks, Recreation and Tourism, Box 1358, Columbia, S.C. 29202

SOUTH DAKOTA—Publicity Division, Department of Highways, Pierre, S.D. 57501

TENNESSEE—Division of Tourist Promotion, 2611 West End Ave., Nashville, Tenn. 27203

TEXAS—Tourist Development Agency, Box 12008, Capitol Station, Austin, Tex. 78711. Also: Texas Highway Department, Travel and Information Division, Austin, Tex. 78701

UTAH—Tourist and Publicity Council, Council Hall, State Capitol, Salt Lake City, Utah 84114

VERMONT—Publicity Division, Vermont Development Department, 61 Elm St., Montpelier, Vt. 05602

VIRGINIA—Virginia State Travel Service, 199 E. Broad St., Richmond, Va. 23219

WASHINGTON—Tourist Division, Department of Commerce and Economic Development, General Administration Building, Olympia, Wash. 98504

WEST VIRGINIA—Department of Commerce Travel Division, State Capitol, Charleston, W.Va. 25305

WISCONSIN—Wisconsin Conservation Department, Vacation and Travel Service, Box 450, Madison, Wis. 53701. Also: State of Wisconsin Vacation and Travel Service, 205 N. Michigan Ave., Chicago, Ill. 60601

WYOMING—Wyoming Travel Commission, 2320 Capitol Ave., Cheyenne, Wyo. 82001

Tourist Offices in Chicago

ANDORRA Bureau for Tourism and Information
    1923 W. Irving Park Rd. 60613 (312)472-7660
AUSTRIAN National Tourist Office
    200 E. Randolph Dr. (R 5130) 60601 (312)861-0102
BAHAMAS Tourist Office
    875 N. Michigan Ave. (R 1816) 60611 (312)787-8203
BRITISH Tourist Authority
    875 N. Michigan Ave. (R 2450) 60611 (312)787-0490
CANADIAN Government Office of Tourism
    332 S. Michigan Ave. (R 410) 60604 (312)782-3760
CAYMAN ISLANDS Department of Tourism
    6 N. Michigan Ave. (R 1401) 60602 (312)368-1787
GERMAN National Tourist Office
    11 S. LaSalle St. (R 930) 60603 (312)AN 3-2958
HAITI Government Tourist & Trade Office
    11 S. LaSalle St. (R 901) 60603 (312)332-0746
HAWAII Visitors Bureau
    410 N. Michigan Ave. (R 1060) 60611 (312)944-6694
HONG KONG Tourist Association
    333 N. Michigan Ave. (R 218) 60601 (312)782-3872
Government of INDIA Tourist Office
    201 N. Michigan Ave. 60601 (312)236-7869
ILLINOIS Division of Tourism
    160 N. LaSalle St. (R 100) 60601 (312)793-2094
IRISH Tourist Board
    224 N. Michigan Ave. 60601 (312)726-9356
ISRAEL Government Tourist Office
    5 S. Wabash Ave. (R 1402) 60603 (312)ST 2-4306
ITALIAN Government Travel Office (E.N.I.T.)
    500 N. Michigan Ave. (R 314) 60611 (312)644-0990
JAMAICA Tourist Board
    36 S. Wabash Ave. (R 1210) 60603 (312)346-1546
JAPAN National Tourist Organization
    333 N. Michigan Ave. 60601 (312)332-3975
MALAYSIA Department of Tourism
    11 E. Adams St. (R 903) 60603 (312)922-1677
MEXICAN Government Tourism Department
    625 N. Michigan Ave. (R 1220) 60611 (312)664-5779
MEXICAN National Tourist Council
    875 N. Michigan Ave. (R 3615) 60611 (312)649-0090
MICHIGAN Tourist Council
    52 E. Monroe St. 60603 (312)372-0080

POLISH Travel Office (ORBIS)
333 N. Michigan Ave. 60601 (312)236-3388
Commonwealth of PUERTO RICO
11 E. Adams St. (R 1600) 60603 (312)922-9701
QUEBEC Tourist Office
72 W. Adams St. 60603 (312)726-0681
SPANISH National Tourist Office
180 N. Michigan Ave. 60601 (312)641-1842
SWISS National Tourist Office
104 S. Michigan Ave. (R 630) 60603 (312)641-0050
TURKS and CAICOS Tourist Board
650 N. Wabash Ave. 60611 (312)787-8557
U.S. VIRGIN ISLANDS Government Information Center
535 N. Michigan Ave. (1st fl.) 60611 (312)329-1814
WISCONSIN Official Information Center
205 N. Michigan Ave. 60601 (312)DE 2-7274

Tourist Offices Elsewhere

ALPINE Tourist Commission, P.O. Box 91, New York, N.Y. 10010
AUSTRALIAN Tourist Commission, 1270 Avenue of the Americas, New York, N.Y. 10020
BELGIUM National Tourist Office, 720 Fifth Ave., New York, N.Y. 10019
BERMUDA Department of Tourism, 610 Fifth Ave., New York, N.Y. 10020
CARIBBEAN Travel Association, 20 E. 46th St., New York, N.Y. 10017
CEDOK (Czechoslovakia Travel Bureau), 10 E. 40th St., New York, N.Y. 10016
CEYLON Tourist Board, 609 Fifth Ave., New York, N.Y. 10017
COLOMBIAN Government Tourist Office, 140 E. 57th St., New York, N.Y. 10022
DANISH National Tourist Office, 505 5th Ave., New York, N.Y. 10017
FINNISH National Tourist Office, 505 Fifth Ave., New York, N.Y. 10017
FRENCH Government Tourist Office, 610 Fifth Ave., New York, N.Y. 10017

GREEK National Tourist Organization, 601 Fifth Ave., New York, N.Y. 10017
ICELANDIC National Tourist Office, 505 Fifth Ave., New York, N.Y. 10017
KENYA Tourist Office, 15 E. 51st St., New York, N.Y. 10022
KOREA Tourist Association, 331 Madison Ave., New York, N.Y. 10019
LEBANON Tourist and Information Office, 527 Madison Ave., New York, N.Y. 10022
MOROCCAN National Tourist Office, 597 Fifth Ave., New York, N.Y. 10017
NETHERLANDS National Travel Office, 576 Fifth Ave., New York, N.Y. 10036
NEW ZEALAND Government Tourist Office, 630 Fifth Ave., New York, N.Y. 10020
NORWEGIAN National Travel Office, 505 Fifth Ave., New York, N.Y. 10017
PACIFIC Area Travel Association, 228 Grant St., San Francisco, Calif. 94108
PORTUGUESE Information & Tourist Trade Office, 570 Fifth Ave., New York, N.Y. 10036
REPUBLIC OF CHINA Tourism Bureau (TAIWAN), 210 Post St., San Francisco, Calif. 94108
RHODESIA National Tourist Board, 535 Fifth Ave., New York, N.Y. 10017
SCANDINAVIAN National Tourist Office, Scandinavia House, 505 Fifth Ave., New York, N.Y. 10017
SINGAPORE Tourist Promotion Board, 251 Post St., San Francisco, Calif. 94108
SOUTH AFRICAN Tourist Corporation, 610 Fifth Ave., New York, N.Y. 10020
SOUTH AMERICAN Travel Organization, 1699 Coral Way, Suite 308, Miami, Fla. 33145
SWEDISH National Travel Office, 505 Fifth Ave., New York, N.Y. 10017
TAHITI Tourist Board, P.O. Box 3720, Hollywood, Calif. 90028
THAILAND Tourist Organization, 510 W. 6th St., Los Angeles, Calif. 90014
TURKISH Tourism and Information Center, 500 Fifth Ave., New York, N.Y. 10036
U.S.S.R. (Intourist), 45 E. 49th St., New York, N.Y. 10017
YUGOSLAV State Tourist Office, 509 Madison Ave., New York, N.Y. 10022

CHAPTER 54

National Canoe Rental Directory

ALASKA

Alaska Pioneer Canoers Assoc.
Box 16
Sterling, Alaska 99672

ARIZONA

W. C. "Bob" Trowbridge Canoe Trips
Roy Reynolds, Mgr.
Box 1882
Green Meadow Lane
Havasu City, Arizona 86403

ARKANSAS

Many Islands Camp on Spring River
Route 2
Mammoth Spring, Arkansas 72554

Hedges' Canoes
On the Buffalo River
Ponca, Arkansas 72670

Buffalo River State Park
Yellville, Arkansas 72687

CALIFORNIA

California Canoe Company
960 E. Gaillard
Azusa, California 91702

Gerald F. Smith
Rt. #1, Box 4
Jamul, California 92035

Harold E. Henry
7718 Marie Avenue
LaMesa, California 92041

Sacramento River Canoe Trips
547 N. 99E
Los Molinos, California 96055

Lane's Marine Sales, Inc.
11120 Atlantic Avenue
Lynwood, California 90262

W. C. "Bob" Trowbridge Canoe Trips
Dick Bergtsen & Al Riola, Mgrs.
Box 5488
Sacramento, California 95817

W. C. "Bob" Trowbridge Canoe Trips
625 B Street
Santa Rosa, California 95401

CONNECTICUT

Boat Bay
Candlewood Lake Road
Brookfield, Connecticut 06804

Boyce Town & Country Marine
126 Main Street, Rt. #25
Monroe, Connecticut 06468

The INN on Lake Waramaug
Lake Shore Road
New Preston, Connecticut 06777

Ole M. Amundsen
350 Riverside Avenue
Riverside, Connecticut 06878

Gessay's Outboard Shop
Cor. East Main & Prospect
Rockville, Connecticut 06066

Alan R. Mead
52 Skinner Road
Rockville, Connecticut 06066

Olsen Marine Co., Inc.
76 Ferry Blvd.
Stratford, Connecticut 06497

DELAWARE

Wick's Ski Shops, Inc.
1201 Philadelphia Pike
Wilmington, Delaware 19809

Wilderness Canoe Trips, Inc.
1002 Parkside Drive, Oak Lane Manor
Wilmington, Delaware 19803

FLORIDA

Canoe Outpost
Tex Stout, Outfitter
R. #2, Box 745-H
Arcadia, Florida 33821

Alexander Springs
Astor, Florida 32002

Vacation Boat Rentals, Inc.
5131—14th Street West
Bradenton, Florida 33505

Canoe Outpost
Tex Stout, Outfitter
P.O. Box 473
Branford, Florida 32008

Manatee Springs State Park
Chiefland, Florida 32626

Camp Bell Ridge
Redwater Lake
Hawthorne, Florida 32640

Barrett's Marine
4503 North Orange Blossom Trail
Orlando, Florida 32804

Fisheating Creek Campground and Wilderness Area
P.O. Box 100
Palmdale, Florida 33944

Col. Jack & Betty Carpenter's Campers' World
Hwy 44 Withlacoochee River
(Rutland), Panasoffkee, Florida 33538

Juniper Springs Recreational Services
R. 1, Box 650
Silver Springs, Florida 32688

Bill Jackson, Inc.
1100 4th Street South
St. Petersburg, Florida 33701

Otter Springs Campground
Trenton, Florida 32693

GEORGIA

Amplay Canoe Rentals
Ross Newall, Manager
P.O. Box 805
Folkston, Georgia 31537

Suwannee Canal Recreation Area
Harry Johnson, Concessionaire
Okefenokee National Wildlife Refuge
Folkston, Georgia 31537

Riverboat—Stone Mountain Park
P.O. Box 778
Stone Mountain, Georgia 30083

ILLINOIS

Pirate's Cove Marina
H'way 13—East
Carbondale, Illinois 62901

Mid-West Boating & Camping
Robert L. Hardin
1804 Bellamy Drive
Champaign, Illinois 61820

The Chicagoland Canoe Base
Ralph C. Frese
4019 N. Narragansett
Chicago, Illinois 60634

H₂O Sports
716½ W. Lincoln Hwy.
DeKalb, Illinois 60115

Campertown, Inc.
1337 Dundee Avenue
Elgin, Illinois 60120

Shoppers Center
301 E. Harris Avenue
Greenville, Illinois 62246

Wooster Lake Camping Resort
999-E Rt. 134
Ingleside, Illinois 60041

A-1 Rental
1010 Kennedy Drive
Kankakee, Illinois 60901

Reed's Rent All
907 N. Indiana Avenue
Kankakee, Illinois 60901

Congdon Canoe Company
828 N. Western Avenue
Lake Forest, Illinois 60045

Camper's Center
7215 W. Ogden Avenue
Lyons, Illinois 60534

Camper's Center
8900 No. Waukegan Road
Morton Grove, Illinois 60053

Two Rivers Sports Center
U.S. 36 & 54
Pittsfield, Illinois 62363

Zimmerman Canoes
503 Lockport
Plainfield, Illinois 60544

Merkels Marine & Camping Center
1720 Broadway
Quincy, Illinois 62301

The Ski Shop, Inc.
4871 E. State Street
Rockford, Illinois 61105

The Ski Shop, Inc.
215 W. Ogden Avenue
Westmont, Illinois 60559

Wheaton Rental Center
908 E. Roosevelt Road
Wheaton, Illinois 60187

Canoe Trails, Inc.
Skokie Lagoons
Tower Rd. & Edens Hwy.
Winnetka, Illinois 60093

INDIANA

Elmer's Marine Sales
Route #5, Crooked Lake
Angola, Indiana 46703

Lantz's Canoe Rental
c/o Brookville Marine
10 W. 4th Street
Brookville, Indiana 47012

Whitewater Valley Canoe Rental
Ron Ritz, Director
Rt. 52, Brookville, Indiana
(Mail: R.R. #1,
Metamora, Indiana 47030)

Clements Canoes Rental & Sales
Robert J. Clements
911 Wayne Avenue
Crawfordsville, Indiana 47933

Canoes from Kendall's Inc.
1919 North "B" Street
Elwood, Indiana 46036

Root's Camp 'n Ski Haus
6844 Clinton Street
Fort Wayne, Indiana 46805

Water Meister Sports
Canoe and Kayak Center
6137 Lincoln Highway E.
Fort Wayne, Indiana 46803

Oldfather Canoe Center
State Road 15 North
Goshen, Indiana 46526

The Kajak Haus
7501 Westfield Blvd. E.
Indianapolis, Indiana 46240

A to Z Rental Center
2370 Lafayette Road
Indianapolis, Indiana 46222

Myers Bait & Tackle
Don J. Myers
Mongo, Indiana 46771

J & J Marine & Sales
1728 South 9th Street
Richmond, Indiana 47374

Burnham's
1060 West By Pass 52
West Lafayette, Indiana 47906

IOWA

Reynoldson's Service
3rd and Division
Boone, Iowa 50036

Olsen Boat House
117 N. Franklin
Cedar Falls, Iowa 50613

Ahrens & Johnson, Inc.
621–25 Des Moines Street
Des Moines, Iowa 50316

Marina 218, Inc.
North Liberty, Iowa 52317

KANSAS

Fairfax Boats
148 S. 7th
Salina, Kansas 67401

Fairfax Boats
926 S. Santa Fe
Salina, Kansas 67401

Kansas Sailing Center
3216 Turnpike Drive
Wichita, Kansas 67210

KENTUCKY

Camping World
Beech Bend Park
Bowling Green, Kentucky 42101

LOUISIANA

Ricky's Guide Service
Rt. 1, Box 375
Bogalusa, Louisiana 70427

New Orleans Canoe Shop
624 Moss Street
New Orleans, Louisiana 70119

MAINE

McBreairty's Service
Allagash, Maine 04774

Twin City Marine, Inc.
99 S. Main Street
Brewer, Maine 04412

Capt. Carl Selin
Maine Wilderness Canoe Basin
Carroll, Maine 04420

Pierre Z. Freeman
47 W. Main Street
Fort Kent, Maine 04743

Folsom's Air Service
Greenville, Maine 04441

Robert K. Somes
Somes Used Cars
11 Water Street
Hallowell, Maine 04347

Smith Hardware, Inc.
Jackman, Maine 04945

Tip-A-Canoe Camp Grounds
Route 25
Kezar Falls, Maine 04047

Al's Sport Center
1822 Lisbon Street
Lewiston, Maine 04240

Allagash Wilderness Outfitters
P.O. Box 73
On Sourdnahunk Lake in Baxter State Park
Millinocket, Maine 04462

Moose Horn Trading Post
Route 4
North Jay, Maine 04262

Hall's Trading Post
Pleasant Avenue
Sangerville, Maine 04479

Norcross Boat & Motor Service
Winthrop, Maine 04364

York Harbor Marine Service, Inc.
P.O. Box 178
Route 103 "On the Harbor"
York, Maine 03909

MARYLAND

Glen Cove Marina, Inc.
Rt. #2
Darlington, Maryland 21034

Pier 7—South River
Rt. 2
Edgewater (Annapolis),
Maryland 21037

Appalachian Outfitters
Box 44, 8000 Main Street
Ellicott City, Maryland 21043

WEF Canoe Sales
1717 Burnside Avenue
Halfway—Greenberry Hills
Hagerstown, Maryland 21740

River & Trail Outfitters
Box 246, Valley Road
Knoxville, Maryland 21758

Fort Washington Marina
Oxon Hill, Maryland 20022

Hill's Boat Rental
Harry L. Hill
Seneca, Box 139
Poolesville, Maryland 20837

MASSACHUSETTS

Canoe Camp Outfits
8 Cherry Street
Belmont, Massachusetts 02178

South Bridge Boat House, Inc.
Main Street, (Rt. #62)
Concord, Massachusetts 01742

Taylor Rental Center
626 Main Street
Falmouth, Massachusetts 02540

Goodhue Enterprises
Rt. 28 & 39
Harwich Port, Massachusetts 02646

Goose Hummock Shop
Route 6A
Orleans, Massachusetts 02653

MICHIGAN

Fox Sporting Goods
624 South Main Street
Ann Arbor, Michigan 48104

G & L Canoe Livery
Box 92
Atlanta, Michigan 49709

Baldwin Boat & Canoe Livery
Edward H. Andersen
P.O. Box 265
Baldwin, Michigan 49304

Ivan's Canoe Livery
RR #1, Box 1013
Baldwin, Michigan 49304

Gardner's Favorite Sports & Marine
741 River View Drive
Benton Harbor, Michigan 49022

Poser's Park Company
6465 Kensington Road
Brighton, Michigan 48116

Chippewa Landing
On Manistee River & Pine River
P.O. Box 245
Cadillac, Michigan 49601

Chief Shavehead Recreation Park
Rt. 3—Union Rd.
Cassopolis, Michigan 49031

Nichols Sports & Marine
7048 Greenfield Road
Dearborn, Michigan 48126

Teddy Kotowich Boats & Canoes
109 Main Street
East Jordan, Michigan 49727

White Birch Canoe Livery
R. #1
Falmouth, Michigan 49632

Grand River Boat Sales
28928 Grand River
Farmington, Michigan 48024

Olson Bros. Sports Center
705 28th Street, S.W.
Grand Rapids, Michigan 49509

Borchers Ausable Canoe Livery
101 Maple Street
Grayling, Michigan 49738

Carlisle Canoes
110 State Street
Grayling, Michigan 49738

Carr's Pioneer Canoe Livery
217 Alger Street
Grayling, Michigan 49738

Jim's Canoe Livery
Star Route 1, Box 165
Grayling, Michigan 49738

Jolly Redskin Canoe Livery
400 Ingham, Box 396
Grayling, Michigan 49738

Long's Canoe Livery
Manistee River
507 Peninsular Street
Grayling, Michigan 49738

Penrod's Cabins & Canoe Livery
100 Maple Street
Grayling, Michigan 49738

Ray's Canoe Livery
200 Ingham Street
Grayling, Michigan 49738

Ray Haywood
R. #1
Hastings, Michigan 49058

Kellogg's Canoe Livery
White River
Hesperia, Michigan
(Mail: Twin Lake, Michigan 49457)

Miller's Marine
M-22 Platte River
Honor, Michigan 49640

Charles Packer's Water Wheel Resort
M-22, Scenic Drive
Honor, Michigan 49640

Riverside Canoes
M-22 at the Platte River
Honor, Michigan 49640

Ashley's Canoe Livery
Howard City, Michigan 49329

Sail Shop, Inc.
Kewadin, Michigan 49648

Smithville Landing, Inc.
Box 341
Lake City, Michigan 49651

Carl's Canoe Livery
State Road
Luther, Michigan
(Mail: S. 15 Mile Road
Hoxeyville, Michigan 49641)

Camp Bear Paw
Box 52
Luzerne, Michigan 48636

Manistee Canoe Cruises
354 Third Street (or)
267 Arthur Street
Manistee, Michigan 49660

W. D. Campbell
7690 Irving Road, RFD 2
Middleville, Michigan 49333

Heavner Canoe Rental
2775 Garden Road
Milford, Michigan 48042

Mio Sport Shop
406 Morenci
Mio, Michigan 48647

Hinchman Acres Canoe Rental
Box 146
Mio, Michigan 48647

Happy Mohawk Canoe Livery
351 Fruitvale Road
Montague, Michigan 49437

Skippers Landing
4464 Dowling
Montague, Michigan 49437

Chippewa Canoe Livery
933 S. Mission Road
Mt. Pleasant, Michigan 48858

Derks Marine Sales
1672 Croton Drive
Newaygo, Michigan 49337

Dukes Sport Shop
205 Handy
Newberry, Michigan 49868

Dollarville Canoe & Boat Rentals
Robert L. Schneider
Box 209
Newberry, Michigan 49868

Lovell's Canoe Rental & Resort
718 W. River Road
Oscoda, Michigan 48750

Fix's Vagabond Resort
Located on Little Bay De Noc
In Upper Peninsula, County Rd. 513
Rt. 11, Box 125
Rapid River, Michigan 49878

Campbell's Canoe Livery
At the M-144 Bridge
Roscommon, Michigan 48653

Hiawatha Canoe Livery
South Branch of the Au Sable
Box 667
Roscommon, Michigan 48653

Chuck & Linda Mires
Paddle Brave Canoe Livery-Camp
Box 998, Route 1
Roscommon, Michigan 48653

Watters Edge Canoe Livery
RR #1, Box 990
Roscommon, Michigan 48653

Wolf's Enterprises
205 Wayne Street
St. Joseph, Michigan 49085

Richard Hoffman
424 Water Street
Saugatuck, Michigan 49453

D-R-D Canoe Livery
R-1, 10 mi. east of Mt. Pleasant
Shepherd, Michigan 48883

The Golden Anvil
251 Broadway
South Haven, Michigan 49090

The River
M-70
Sterling, Michigan 48659

Dudd, Harmon Marina
Klinger Lake
Sturgis, Michigan 49091

Murray's Boats & Motors
447 East Front Street
Traverse City, Michigan 49684

The Horina Canoe Rental
on Highway M-37
20 Miles west of Cadillac
Wellston, Michigan 49689

Chippewa Pine River Cabins
Wellston, Michigan 49689

Skippers Landing
Whitehall, Michigan 49461

MINNESOTA

Rum River Canoe Trails
Anoka Count Fairgrounds Park
Route 6, Box 105
Anoka, Minnesota 55303

Bob Anderson's
Crane Lake Outfitters
Crane Lake, Minnesota 55725

Campbell's Trading Post
Crane Lake, Minnesota 55725

Taylor Rental Center
1710 London Road
Duluth, Minnesota 55812

Bill Rom's Canoe Country Outfitters
629 East Sheridan Street
Ely, Minnesota 55731

B.P.Z. Outfitters
611 East Harvey Street
Ely, Minnesota 55731

Border Lakes Outfitters
P.O. Box 569
Ely, Minnesota 55731

Boundary Waters Canoe Outfitters
Box 447
Ely, Minnesota 55731

Bob Cary's Canadian Border Outfitters
Box 117
Ely, Minnesota 55731

Canadian Waters, Inc.
111 East Sheridan Street
Ely, Minnesota 55731

Don Beland's Wilderness Canoe Trips
Box 358
Ely, Minnesota 55731

Fishermen's Headquarters & Canoe Outfitting
209–223 East Sheridan Street
Ely, Minnesota 55731

Kawishiwi Lodge (on Lake One)
Box 480
Ely, Minnesota 55731

Pipestone Outfitting Company
P.O. Box 780
Ely, Minnesota 55731

Quetico Superior Canoe Outfitters
Box 89
Ely, Minnesota 55731

Wilderness Outfitters
Box 358
Ely, Minnesota 55731

Cliff World's Canoe Trip Outfitting
Box 72, 1731 East Sheridan Street
Ely, Minnesota 55731

Blankenburg's Saganaga Outfitters
Grand Marais, Minnesota 55604

Northpoint Outfitters
Gunflint Trail
Grand Marais, Minnesota 55604

Janet's Outfitters
Box 119
Grand Marais, Minnesota 55604

Jocko's Clearwater Outfitters
Grand Marais, Minnesota 55604

Trail Center
Gunflint Trail, Box 50
Grand Marais, Minnesota 55604

Tuscarora Outfitters
Grand Marais, Minnesota 55604

Adentures Unlimited
Hibbing, Minnesota 55746

Point of Pines Marina, Inc.
Island View Route
International Falls, Minn. 56649

Mr. Outdoors Sporting Goods
8565 Central Ave. N.E.
Minneapolis, Minnesota 55431

Northern Wilderness Outfitters
Box 98
Ranier, Minnesota 56668

Earl's Sales & Service, Inc.
Hwy. 43 South
Rushford, Minnesota 55971

Irv Funk Nimrod Outfitters
Route 2, Box 51
Sebeka, Minnesota 56477

Bill and Dave's Texaco Service Center
I694 and Lexington Ave. North
St. Paul, Minnesota 55112

Taylors Falls Canoe Co.
Taylors Falls, Minnesota 55084

Marlin Marine, Inc.
1034 South Robert Street
West St. Paul, Minnesota 55118

MISSOURI

Harvey's Alley Spring Canoe Rental
Hwy. 106
Alley Spring, Missouri 65431

Hufstedler Canoe Rental
Riverton Rural Branch
Alton, Missouri 65606

Blue Springs Resort
Eldridge, Missouri 65463

Bales Boating
Eminence, Missouri 65466

Current River Canoe Rental
Eminence, Missouri 65466

Two Rivers Canoe Rental
Ozark Boating Co.
Eminence, Missouri 65466

Windy's Canoe Rental
Box 151
Eminence, Missouri 65466

Silver Arrow Canoe Rental
George Purcell
Gladden, Missouri 65478

Jadwin Canoe Rental
Jadwin, Missouri 65501

Sand Spring Resort
Bennett Spring—Brice Route
Lebanon, Missouri 65536

Vogels Resort
Brice Route (Bennett Spring)
Lebanon, Missouri 65536

Big M Resort
Success Route
Licking, Missouri 65542

Midwest Big Piney Floats
Route 7—Box 138
Licking, Missouri 65542

Ozark Equipment Co.
Black & Bishop Streets
Rolla, Missouri 65401

Carr's Grocery & Canoe Rental, Inc.
North End of Current River Bridge
Highway 19
Round Spring, Missouri 65467

Sullivan Canoe Rental
Round Spring, Missouri 65467

Crestwood Boats & Motors, Inc.
9979 Highway 66
St. Louis, Missouri 63126

Midwest Floats & Camp Grounds, Inc.
4109 Malcolm Drive
St. Louis, Missouri 63125

Marlin's Sports Shop
5408 Hampton Avenue
St. Louis, Missouri 63109

Eureka Valley Floats
6347 N. Rosebury Avenue
St. Louis, Missouri 63105

Rock Hill Boat & Motor
9225 Manchester
St. Louis, Missouri 63144

Akers Ferry Resort
On Current River
Cedar Grove Rt.
Salem, Missouri 65560

Wild River Canoe Rental
Arnold Smith & Jim Purcell
Cedargrove
Salem, Missouri 65560

Payne's Boat Co.
R.R. 1, Box 10
Steelville, Missouri 65565

Stroud & Sons, Inc.
Rt. 2, Box 107A
Sullivan, Missouri 63080

House's Grocery and Canoe Rentals
Norfork River and U.S. Hwy. 160
Tecumseh, Missouri 65760

Ozark Canoe Rental Service
614 Tuxedo Blvd.
Webster Groves, Missouri 63119

MONTANA

Lee Craft Marine, Inc.
On Flathead Lake
Somers, Montana 59932

NEBRASKA

Holmes Lake Marina
3150 South 58th Street
Lincoln, Nebraska 68506

Holmes Lake Marina
70th Normal
Lincoln, Nebraska 68502

NEW HAMPSHIRE

Alexandria Boat Shop
R.D. #1
Bristol, New Hampshire 03222

Norman B. Wright
Box 105
Dublin, New Hampshire 03444

Harry F. Ashley
c/o Brown Owl Camps
Errol, New Hampshire 03579

John A. or John W. Sargent
Box 417
George's Mills, N.H. 03751

Squam Boats, Inc.
Squam Lake
Holderness, New Hampshire 03245

Goodhue Enterprises
Rt. 3, Weirs Blvd.
Laconia, New Hampshire 03246

Shir-Roy Camping Area
Roy B. Heise
R.F.D. #3—Richmond—on Rt. 32
Winchester, New Hampshire 03470

Northeast Marina Corp.
36 N. Main Street
Wolfeboro, New Hampshire 03894

NEW JERSEY

Sunset Landing
1215 Sunset Avenue (Deal Lake)
Asbury Park, New Jersey 07712

Morgan's Wharf
589 24th Street
Avalon, New Jersey 08202

Stanley's Marine & Sport Shop
Route 46
Belvidere, New Jersey 07823

Cranford Boat & Canoe Co., Inc.
Springfield & Orange Ave.
Cranford, New Jersey 07016

Denville Boat & Sport Center
Route #46
Denville, New Jersey 07834

Canal Canoe Rental & Studio
Box 21, Amwell Road
East Millstone, New Jersey 08849

Lentine Marine Div.
Rt. 31
Flemington, New Jersey 08822

Bel Haven Lake
Egg Harbor, R.D. #2
Green Bank, New Jersey 08215

Rutgers Gun & Boat Center
127 Raritan Avenue
Highland Park, New Jersey 08904

Bernard's Boat Rental
Route 27—on the Canal
Kingston, New Jersey 08528

Elmer K. Bright
Bright's Boat Basin
Box 34, R.D. #2
Lake Hopatcong, New Jersey 07849

Zephyr Products Co.
Park Road
Mays Landing, New Jersey 08330

Winding River Campground
R.D. #2, Box 246—Weymouth Road
Mays Landing, New Jersey 08330

The Outdoor Trader
Stokes Road, Rt. 451
Medford, New Jersey 08055

C. F. Dicks
320 N. High Street, Box 67
Millville, New Jersey 08332

Hack's Canoe Retreat
100 Mill Street
Mount Holly, New Jersey 08060

Oscar Jenkins Co.
Rt. 45, P.O. Box 98
Mullica Hill, New Jersey 08062

Hanover Equipment & Marine
444 Rt. 23
Pompton Plains, New Jersey 07444

Recreation Unlimited, Inc.
926 Route 17
Ramsey, New Jersey 07446

Bowcraft Sport Shop
Route 22
Scotch Plains, New Jersey 07076

Abbott's Marine Center
Rt. 29
Titusville, New Jersey 08560

Zephyr Products Co.
305 N. Dorset Avenue
Veatnor, New Jersey 08406

Yacht Shops International
Route 22
Whitehouse Station, New Jersey 08889

NEW YORK

Bob Lander's
Minisink Ford Canoe Base
Barryville, New York 12719
   (See Bob Lander's,
   Narrowsburg, New York)

Kittatinny Campgrounds
Box 95—Rt. 97
Barryville, New York 12719

Blue Mountain Lake Boat Livery
Rt. 28
Blue Mountain Lake, New York 12812

Griffin's Livery
Blue Mountain Lake, New York 12812

Lamb Bros., Inc.
Main Street
Bolton Landing, New York 12814

Van Cortlandt Park Boat House
Bronx, New York

Upper Delaware Outdoor Recreation, Inc.
Box 188
Creamery Road
Callicoon, New York 12723

Loon Lake Marina
Rt. 9
Chestertown, New York 12817

Packs & Paddles Outfitters
c/o Donald Kenyon
R.D. 1, Box 166
Cleveland, New York 13042

Cooperstown Marine & Service
10 Fair Street
Cooperstown, New York 13326

Moutain View Marina
P.O. Box Y
Cranberry Lake, New York 12927

Murray's Copake Lake Marina
Copake Lake Road
Craryville, New York 12521

Pepacton Sport Center
Downsville, New York 13755

Buzz-Arina, Inc.
140 Williamson Street
East Rockaway, New York 11518

A. W. Rollins
Edmeston, New York 13335

Benson, Jessup & Knapp, Inc.
809 Pennsylvania Avenue
Elmira, New York 14904

Buzz-Arina, Inc.
Route 28
Fleischmans, New York 12430

Roy's Marina, Inc.
R.D. #1
Geneva, New York 14456

Hankins House
Edward C. Sykes
Hankins, New York 12741

Inlet Park Marine, Inc.
435 Taughannock Blvd.
Ithaca, New York 14850

Liverpool Sport Center, Inc.
125 First Street
Liverpool, New York 13088

Adventure Outfitters, Inc.
Box 332
Lyons, New York 14489

Scandaga Marine, Inc.
School St. (at the Bridge)
Mayfield, New York 12117

Taconic Sports & Camping Center
RD #2, Rudd Pond Road
Millerton, New York 12546

West River Marine, Inc.
Rt. 245, R.D. #1
Naples, New York 14512

Bob Lander's
Ten Mile River Lodge
Narrowsburg, New York 12764
    (See Barryville, N.Y.)

Bob Lander's
Narrowsburg Campground
Narrowsburg, New York 12764
    (See Barryville, N.Y.)

Hillside Inn
Route 97
Narrowsburg, New York 12764

Skip Feagles—Canoe Rentals
Box 128
Narrowsburg, New York 12764

72nd Street Boathouse
Central Park
New York, New York

Old Forge Sports Center, Inc.
Route 28
Old Forge, New York 13420

Rivett's Boat Livery
Lake Trail
Old Forge, New York 13420

Pilot Knob Boat Shop, Inc.
Pilot Knob, New York 12844

Janco's Northern Sports
R.D. #3, Box 90, Lake Shore Road,
Plattsburgh, New York 12901

Jerry's Canoe Rentals
Pond Eddy, New York 12770

Kelly's Canoe Rentals
Route 97
Pond Eddy, New York 12770

White Water Rentals, Inc.
R.D. #1, Berme Road
Port Jervis, New York 12771

Arlington Sporting Goods, Inc.
794 Main Street
Poughkeepsie, New York 12603

Flushing Meadow Park Boathouse
Flushing Meadow Park
Queens, New York 11380

Bird's Marine, Inc.
Raquette Lake, New York 13436

Raquette Lake Marina, Inc.
Raquette Lake, New York 13436

Black Creek Marina
20 Black Creek Road
Rochester, New York 14623

John Monthony
Sabael, New York 12864

Hickok Boat Livery
c/o Stockade Trading Post
Rt. 30 at Fish Creek Ponds Camp Site
Saranac Inn, New York 12982

Skaneateles East Shore Marine, Inc.
2745 East Lake Road
Skaneateles, New York 13152

Kittatinny Canoes
Skinners Falls Base
  (See Kittatinny Campgrounds
  Barryville, N.Y.)

Curt's Canoe Livery
Rt. 97
Sparrow Bush, New York 12780

Clove Lakes Boat House
Clove Lakes Park
Staten Island, New York 10301

Wolf's Boat House
327 South Endicott Creek Road
Tonawanda, New York 14150

Taylor Rental Center
150 Orchard Street
Webster, New York 14580

NORTH CAROLINA

Appalachian Outfitters
Highway 321 South
Boone, North Carolina 28607

Silver Creek Canoe Livery
Silver Creek Road
Rt. 2, Box 37
Mill Spring, N. C. 28756

Rent-a-Canoe
Tommy McNabb
Corner of Pinebrook Lane & Tern Court
Route #7
Winston-Salem, North Carolina 27105

OHIO

Molly's Cheese House
Kenneth Hyatt, Rt. 603
Box 531, R.D. #4
Ashland, Ohio 44805

Richard G. Dailey
Brinkhaven Canoe Livery
Brinkhaven, Ohio 43006

River Bend Recreational Park
1092 Whetstone River Road So.
Caledonia, Ohio 43314

River Run Canoe Livery
Rt. 93
Canal Fulton, Ohio 44319

Ronald Vaughn
Vaughn's
Hurd Road
Carey, Ohio 43316

Northmoor Marina, Inc.
R.D. #4, Box 222D, (Rt. 29 East)
Celina, Ohio 45822

Zucker Marine, Inc.
860 East Washington Street
Chagrin Falls, Ohio 44022

Flerlage Marine, Inc.
2233 Eastern Avenue
Cincinnati, Ohio 45202

Western Hills Honda
3110 Harrison Avenue
Cincinnati, Ohio 45211

All Ohio Canoe
320 S. Ardmore Road
Columbus, Ohio 43209

Alcawi Canoe Base
Rt. 1
Coshocton, Ohio 43812

Beaver Creek Recreation Co.
PO Box 931, Fredricktown Road
East Liverpool, Ohio 43920

Ehrhart Sport Center, Inc.
308 West Main Street
Fairborn, Ohio 45324

Portage Trail Park Canoe Livery
1773 South River Road
Fremont, Ohio 43420

Camp Hi Canoe Livery
Box 275, Abbott Road
Hiram, Ohio 44234

Helmick's Haven Marina
Box 89, Rt. 1
Little Hocking, Ohio 45742

Mohican Wilderness
Wally Road—9 miles south of Loudonville, Ohio
(Mail: Rt. 1
Glenmont, Ohio 44628)

Loudonville Canoe Livery
424 West Main Street
Loudonville, Ohio 44842

Mohican Canoe Livery
Routes 3 & 97
Loudonville, Ohio 44842

Masek Marine & Woodcraft
131 Union Street
Madison, Ohio 44057

Miami Canoe Livery
202 Wooster Pike
Milford, Ohio 45150

Bob & June Morgan's Canoe Liveries
Box 159, R.R. #2
Morrow, Ohio 45152

Licking Valley Canoe Livery
Rt. 16, east of Newark
(Mail: Robert Minot, Rt. 1
Newark, Ohio 43055)

Lake County Canoes
81 Elevator Avenue
Painesville, Ohio 44077

Honda of Piqua
6100 N. Cty. Rd. 25A, (S. Main St.)
Piqua, Ohio 45356

Ohio Canoe Adventures, Inc.
5128 Colorado Avenue
Sheffield Lake, Ohio 44054

Romp's Water Port, Inc.
5055 Liberty Street
Vermilion, Ohio 44089

Trigg's Marine Supply Co.
4174 Market Street
Youngstown, Ohio 44512

PENNSYLVANIA

Yough Lake Marina
Youghiogheny Reservoir
Addison, Pennsylvania 15411

Ideal Park
R.D. #1
Catawissa, Pennsylvania 17820

Allegheny Outfitters
19 S. Main St.
Clarendon, Pennsylvania 16313

Cook Riverside Cabins, Inc.
Cook Forest State Park
Cooksburg, Pennsylvania 16217

Kittatinny Canoes
Silver Lake Road
Dingmans Ferry, Pennsylvania 18328

Pasch Marine
Route 611 North
R.D. #1
Easton, Pennsylvania 18042

Presque Isle Sports
3214 West Lake Road
Erie, Pennsylvania 16505

Baker's Marine Co.
Lake Wallenpaupack
Hawley, Pennsylvania 18428

Hulmeville Park Association, Inc.
Beaver Street
Hulmeville, Pennsylvania 19047

Woodrow W. Behney
R.D. #4, Box 320
Hummelstown, Pennsylvania 17036

Algonquin Wilderness College
307 South 13th Street
Indiana, Pennsylvania 15701

S. Bryan & Son
2032 Second Street Pike
Ivyland, Pennsylvania 18974

Central Service Station
10 South Second Street
Jeannette, Pennsylvania 15644

Conestoga Marine & Cyclery
1361 Manheim Pike
Lancaster, Pennsylvania 17601

Louis P. Stefan
Linesville Boat Livery
R.D. #2, Whispering Trails Campground
Linesville, Pennsylvania 16424

Hileman's Boat Service
On the Allegheny
Manorville, Pennsylvania 16238

Bob's Beach
Milford, Pennsylvania 18337

Laurel Highlands River Tours
Mill Run, Pennsylvania 15464

Oil City Canoe Sales
Rt. 62 N., R.D. #2
Oil City, Pennsylvania 16301

John Wright, Jr.
328 W. Queen Lane
Philadelphia, Pennsylvania 19144

Uniservice, Inc.
Moraine State Park
R.D., Portersville, Pa.
(Mail: 132 Adele Avenue
Pittsburgh, Pennsylvania 15237)

The Pocono Boathouse
Rt. 423
Pocono Pines, Pennsylvania 18350

Point Pleasant Canoe Rentals
Box 6
Point Pleasant, Pennsylvania 18950

Wolfe's Equip. & Rental Co.
208 Revere Blvd.
Reading, Pennsylvania 19609

Wick's Ski Shop
321 West Woodland Avenue
Springfield, (Delaware County)
Pennsylvania 19064

Valley Buick, Inc.
629 Brown Ave. Exit
(Beulah Road—1 mi.
S. Parkway Exit 13)
Turtle Creek, Pennsylvania 15145

Wolf Run Marina
Box 465
Warren, Pennsylvania 16365

Harrisburg Seaplane Base
333 South Front Street
Wormleysburg, Pennsylvania 17043

RHODE ISLAND

Fin & Feather Lodge
95 Frenchtown Road
East Greenwich, Rhode Island 02818

SOUTH CAROLINA

Harris Sporting Goods, Inc.
123 By Pass
Seneca, South Carolina 29678

TENNESSEE

B & B Sports Center
235 Buffalo Valley Road
Cookeville, Tennessee 38501

Buffalo Canoe Rental Co.
Flatwoods, Tennessee 38458

Concord Dock
c/o Athletic House Marine
Alcoa Highway
Knoxville, Tennessee 37920

Chad's Apache Camping Center
336 Welch Road
Nashville, Tennessee 37211

TEXAS

Arlington Canoe Rental
3103 W. Pioneer Parkway
Arlington, Texas 76015

Teffy's Hobby House
6179 39th Street
Groves, Texas 77619

Houston Canoe Sales & Rentals
3930 Broadway
Houston, Texas 77017

Comanche Outfitters
c/o Charles Keyser
Horseshoe Bay, Drawer 4
Marble Falls, Texas 78654

Comanche Outfitters
2008 Bedford
Midland, Texas 79701

Stephen Snow
415 Oakleaf
San Antonio, Texas 78209

Rod Rylander Realty and Boat Sales
2213 Hwy. 75 North
Sherman, Texas 75090

UTAH

Tex's Colorado River Cruises
PO Box 67, Colorado River Bridge
Moab, Utah 84532

VERMONT

Canoe Imports, Inc.
74 South Willard Street
Burlington, Vermont 05401

Tudhope Marine Company
Rt. 2, on Lake Champlain
North Hero, Vermont 05474

Woodstock Sports
30 Central Street
Woodstock, Vermont 05091

VIRGINIA

John Shaffer
Spring Valley Canoe Base
Rt. 2, Box 175
Berryville, Virginia 22611

Blue Ridge Mountain Sports
1417 Emmet Street
Charlottesville, Virginia 22901

Sport Center Marine
3425 Jefferson Davis Blvd.
Fredericksburg, Virginia 22401

Three Springs Campground
P.O. Box 274
Front Royal, Virginia 22630

Shenandoah River Outfitters
RFD #3
Luray, Virginia 22835

Canoe Center
2930 Chain Bridge Road
Oakton, Virginia 22124

Matacia Outfitters
Box 32
Oakton, Virginia 22124

Ralph Good
Riverton, Virginia 22651

Louis J. Matacia
2700 Gallows Road
Vienna, Virginia 22180

Camping Servicenter
4975 Holland Road
Virginia Beach, Virginia 23462

WASHINGTON

The Lodge
P.O. Box 86
Ashford, Washington 98304

Cascade Canoe & Kayak
2610 Sunset Drive
Bellingham, Washington 98225

Mt. St. Helens Lodge
Spirit Lake
P.O. Box 96
Castle Rock, Washington 98611

Lake Ozette Lodge
Lake Ozette, Washington

Merle's Boat Rentals
Ocean Shores Marina
Ocean Shores, Washington 98551

WEST VIRGINIA

Don Wolford
Capon Bridge, West Virginia 26711

WISCONSIN

Spangler Sales
134 S. Spring Street
Beaver Dam, Wisconsin 53916

Brule River Canoe Rental
Twin Gables Restaurant & Motel
Brule, Wisconsin 54820

Brule River Tackle Supply, Inc.
P.O. Box 200
Brule, Wisconsin 54820

McCann's Barbershop
Canoe Sales & Rental
200 Main Street
Cornell, Wisconsin 54732

Camp One
Rt. 1, Box 606
Danbury, Wisconsin 54830

Deywer Boat Works
Eagle River, Wisconsin 54521

Tomlinson Auto & Marine Co.
Box 579 (1½ Bl. west of Downtown on the Eagle River)
Eagle River, Wisconsin 54521

Heileman Marine
10549 West Forest Home Ave.
Hales Corners, Wisconsin 53130

Historyland
Hayward, Wisconsin 54843

Flambeau Lodge
Rt. 1
Ladysmith, Wisconsin 54848

Smith's Landing & Canoe Rentals
Route 2 on the Kickapoo River
LaFarge, Wisconsin 54639

Outing Center
Wisconsin Union
University of Wisconsin
800 Langdon Street
Madison, Wisconsin 53706

Liske Marine
Medford, Wisconsin 54451

Middleton Paint & Hardware Co.
6319 University Avenue
Middleton, Wisconsin 53562

Jim's Canoe Rental
Box 323
Minong, Wisconsin 54859

Wa Du Shuda Canoe Rental
Bridge Street
New Lisbon, Wisconsin 53950

Kinn Motors Marine
650 East Wisconsin Avenue
Oconomowoc, Wisconsin 53066

Beauti-View Drive-In
R. 1, Ontario, Wisc.

(Mail: R. 1, Box 138
LaFarge, Wisc. 54639)

Fox River Marina
South Main at Bridge
Oshkosh, Wisconsin 54901

Morgan's Sportsland
Park Falls, Wisconsin 54552

Big Bear Lodge
Phillips, Wisconsin 54555

Martwick Bait & Sport Shop
286 N. Lake Avenue
Phillips, Wisconsin 54555

Riverside Marine
Rhinelander, Wisconsin 54501

Blackhawk Ridge
P.O. Box 92
Sauk City, Wisconsin 53583

Northwest Outlet, Inc.
1815 Belknap
Superior, Wisconsin 54880

Tomahawk Trailer & Boat Sales
Hwy. 51 North
Tomahawk, Wisconsin 54489

Wild River Canoe Rentals
Rtt. 1, Box 33
Trego, Wisconsin 54888

Russell's Marina
Route #2, off 113
Waunakee, Wisconsin 53597

Ding's Dock, Inc.
Route 1
Waupaca, Wisconsin 54981

Lake of the Woods
Tent and Trailer Park
Route 1, Box 207
Wautoma, Wisconsin 54982

Marineland, Inc.
7105 W. North Avenue
Wauwatosa, Wisconsin 53212

Indian Shores
P.O. Box 12
Woodruff, Wisconsin 54568

WYOMING

Wapiti Canoe Rental
P.O. Box 351
Jackson, Wyoming 83001

CANADA

The Happy Outdoorsman, Ltd.
433 St. Mary's Road
Winnipeg, Manitoba, Canada R2M 3K7

Algonquin Outfitters
R.R. #1, (Algonquin Park Area)
Dwight, Ontario, Canada

Voyageurs North Canoe Outfitters
Box 507, (Mile 9—Highway 72)
Sioux Lookout, Ontario, Canada
(June 10–Sept. 1)

Churchill River Canoe Outfitters
(Summer)—P.O. Box 26
LaRonge, Saskatchewan, Canada

(winter)—509 Douglas Park Crescent
Regina, Saskatchewan, Canada

SHOOTING THE MUZZLE LOADERS

Edited By R.A. Steindler

The revived sport of black powder shooting sorely needs a textbook of this caliber; a one-volume reference source that contains complete loading information for rifle, shotgun and pistol with special emphasis on the popular caplock revolver. Includes complete loading tables and ballistical data. Also covers competitive formats with full coverage of the last international matches in a special 16-page section in brilliant color. Undoubtedly the most comprehensive black powder text yet published; edited by the noted firearms authority, R.A. Steindler. Contains 256-pages, size 8'' by 10'', profusely illustrated, paperback **6.95**

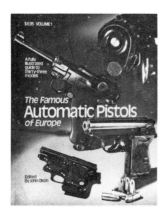

THE FAMOUS AUTOMATIC PISTOLS OF EUROPE

Compiled by John Olson

This is the book handgun enthusiasts have been clamoring for—the inside story on 33 famous European automatic pistols; handguns that have carved an important niche in firearms history. Researchers spent almost two years gathering the material that is presented, information that had to be pried out of military archives or manufacturer's vaults, data that is now available for the first time. This volume is a "must" for the collector, gunsmith, firearms dealer, and serious student of handguns.

8 x 10, 256 pages

Paper **6.95**

THE STANDARD DIRECTORY OF PROOF-MARKS!

Edited by R. A. Steindler

Finally, a comprehensive illustrated directory to the proof-marks of the world—the marks and symbols of virtually every country operating under the national proof house system. Each make is illustrated and defined and every step of proofing is covered. Also, black powder proofs have been included. A table of German manufacturer's codes—3-letter combinations that serve to identify producers—is a highly valuable section. A must for the gunsmith, collector, firearms dealer, and serious student of firearms.

5¼ x 8, 144 pages

Paper **5.95**

TOM McNALLY'S COMPLETE BOOK OF FISHERMEN'S KNOTS

406X

By Tom McNally
Compiled by Bob McNally

Ever lost a fish because your knot pulled loose or didn't hold? This book is the first and only guide presenting all known knots of practical value to aid all anglers. The copy and illustrations explain knot typing from A to Z. Knot-tying problems are solved and special tips make knot tying easy. Tom McNally, the outdoor editor for *The Chicago Tribune,* has written and edited many books and articles on conservation, fishing, hunting, and camping.

5¾ x 8½, 272 pages, LC 73-20850 $4.95

BACKPACK FISHING

By Charles J. Farmer

Be a self-contained fisherman and enjoy freedom and self-reliance in the back country. Take individualized trips, a day or a month, a half mile from the main road or ten miles away. Catch more and bigger fish in every state in the country. This book gives all the essentials and techniques necesary for backpack fishing.

Charles J. Farmer is a frequent and successful contributor to such major outdoor magazines as *Field & Stream, Outdoor Life* and *Sports Afield.* He is a member of the Outdoor Writers Association of America.

8 x 10, 224 pages, LC 73-20839

Paper $6.95

A Tom McNally Outdoors Series Selection

BOWHUNTING
For Whitetail and Mule Deer

By M. R. James

The bowhunting and archery book that will appeal to newcomer and veteran alike. Includes hunting secrets of the experts and their opinion on the best ways to hunt deer and other game. Primarily a how-to deer hunting guide, the book fulfills a long-felt need among bowhunters. Everything from bowhunting basics to advanced hunting techniques. Illustrated with black and white photographs.

M. R. James is Editor-Publisher of *Bowhunter* magazine and also does free-lance writing specializing in bowhunting and archery. His stories have appeared in *Outdoor Life, Bow and Arrow, Archery,* and *Archery World.*

8 x 10, 224 pages, LC 73-20851

Paper $6.95
A Tom McNally Outdoors Series Selection